NORTHERN CALIFORNIA BEST PLACES

NORTHERN CALIFORNIA BEST PLACES

Restaurants, Lodgings, and Touring

Edited by Laura Hagar and Stephanie Irving

SASQUATCH BOOKS
Seattle

Library of Congress Cataloging-in-Publication Data
Hagar, Laura, 1960–
    Northern California best places : restaurants, lodgings, and
    touring/ Laura Hagar, Stephanie Irving.
        p. cm.
    Includes index.
    ISBN 0-912365-63-3 (pbk.) : $16.95
    1. Restaurants, lunch rooms, etc.—California, Northern—
Guidebooks. 2. Hotels, taverns, etc.—California, Northern—
Guidebooks. I. Irving, Stephanie, 1962– . II. Title.
TX907.3.C22H34 1992
647.95794—dc20   92-21851
                                                            CIP

Design: Lynne Faulk
Regional maps: Karen Schober
City maps: Greeneye Design
Composition: *Seattle Weekly* Typesetting

The Best Places guidebooks have been published continuously since 1975. Evaluations are based on numerous reports from locals and traveling inspectors. Final judgments are made by the editors. Our inspectors never identify themselves (except over the phone) and never take free meals or other favors. Readers are advised that places listed in previous editions may have closed or changed management or may no longer be recommended by this series. The editors welcome information conveyed by users of this book, as long as they have no financial connection with the establishment concerned. A report form is provided at the end of the book. Contact us at the address below for a catalog of our regional books.

Published by Sasquatch Books
1931 Second Avenue
Seattle, Washington 98101
(206)441-5555

CONTENTS

Preface

Northern California is no secret. Numerous guidebooks extol the best San Francisco restaurants, the finest Napa Valley establishments, the wealth of activities in the Sierra. What's been missing, however, is a guide that dares to push the limits of the Golden Gate–Wine Country sensibility. One that explores the far corners of the state, that candidly evaluates the best establishments in the *entire* region, from Napa to the Trinity Alps, Lake Tahoe to Half Moon Bay. *Northern California Best Places* does just that.

This is not a book for tourists; it is a book written by—and for—the people who live in California, those who like out-of-the-way places of high character and individualism, and who take the time to seek such places out. Paradoxically, those very characteristics make *Northern California Best Places* ideal for tourists, too. The best places in the region are the ones that local denizens favor: independently owned places of good value, touched with local history, run by lively individualists, and graced with natural beauty. Here is a guide that will lead you not only to duck foie gras in San Jose but also to olallieberry buttermilk pancakes in Grass Valley. To a glorious spa in the North Mountains and to a quiet, 60-year-old log lodge in South Lake Tahoe.

What makes our guidebook different? Our knowledgeable reviewers both re-evaluate the old favorites and seek out new discoveries. All visits are anonymous; we accept no free meals, accommodations, or other complimentary services. This allows us to be tough and candid about places that have rested too long on their laurels and frees us to delight in new places whose efforts have paid off. Our forthright reviews rate establishments on a scale of zero to four and describe the true strengths, foibles, and unique characteristics of each.

So, here it is: *Northern California Best Places*, a thoroughly researched guide to all corners of the region. This wealth of honest reviews and frank reports will arm travelers with the information they need: where to go and when, what to order, which rooms to request (and which to avoid). If you think Northern California has become too crowded, too trendy, too *done*, then try *Northern California Best Places*. It will change your mind.

The Editors

Acknowledgments

Sasquatch Books, publisher of the Best Places guidebooks, has spent the past year working in cooperation with the *East Bay Express* in Berkeley and Oakland to create a guide to Northern California. Thanks to the wholehearted support of the *Express* staff—especially publisher Nancy Banks, editor John Raeside, and staff writer Laura Hagar—*Northern California Best Places* is a comprehensive and authoritative travel guide you'll want to keep in your glove compartment at all times.

Of course, we could not have produced this book without an army of nearly 50 expert reviewers, who sharpened their pencils, loosened their belts, and went on the road to discover and report on the region's outstanding establishments. Our inspectors remain anonymous during visits and do not accept free meals or services, but now that their words are in print, we can publicly acknowledge their invaluable contribution. Thanks to Deborah Belgum, Michael Bowker, Barbara Braasch, Laura Christman, Rosemary Cleese, Melanie Curry, David Darlington, Janice Dice, Gus Di Zerega, Linnea Due, Elaine Fink, David Fullerton, Lorraine Gengo, Michael Goodwin, Joann Gutin, Kris Haedrich, Roy Hagar, Matt Herman, Laurel Hilde, Robert Hurwitt, Kat Keigharn, Kristan Lawson, Catherine McEver, Pat McNally, Pam Mendelson, Harriet Moss, Chris Newbound, Bill O'Brien, John Raeside, Paul Rauber, Kate Raymond, Daphne Reimer, Gary Rivlin, David Roth, Anneli Rufus, Debra Salonen, Kent Simmons, Dashka Slater, Anne Stanley, Rick Steinberg, Debra Stuller, Eric Taller, Ginie Thorp, Cleve Twitchell, Kim Weir, Walt Williams, and Naomi Wise.

Thanks are also due to ever-diligent editorial assistants Dmitri Cavander, Sam Hurwitt, Deborah Stenger, and Mary van Clay, who verified that every fact in the book was true at press time. And kudos to the keen eyes of copy editor Holly Wunder and proofreaders Barry Foy, Marina Gordon, and Edie Neeson for putting the finishing touches on this enormous undertaking.

How to Use This Book

★ **Star Rating System** Every place listed in this book is recommended. We rate restaurants and lodgings on a scale of zero to four stars, based on uniqueness, enjoyability, value, loyalty of local clientele, excellence of cooking, performance measured against goals, cleanliness, and professionalism of service.

(no stars)   Worth knowing about, if nearby

★   A good place

★★   Some wonderful qualities

★★★   Distinguished, many outstanding features

★★★★   The very best in the region

Price Range When prices range between two categories (for instance, moderate to expensive), the lower one is given. Call ahead to verify.

$$$ (expensive) Indicates a tab of more than $70 for dinner for two, including wine (but not tip), and more than $120 for one night's lodging for two.

$$*   (moderate) Falls between *$$$* (expensive) and *$ (inexpensive).

$ (inexpensive) Indicates a tab of less than $30 for dinner, and less than $70 for lodgings for two.

Checks and Credit Cards Most establishments that accept checks also require a major credit card for identification. American Express is abbreviated as AE, Diners Club as DC, Discover as DIS, MasterCard as MC, Visa as V.

Maps and Directions Each section in this book begins with a map that shows the geographic region and towns being covered. Throughout the book are town maps, and directions are provided with each entry. Whenever possible, call ahead to confirm hours and location. Many B&Bs are private homes and discourage drop-in visits.

Reader Reports At the end of the book is a report form. We receive hundreds of these reports from readers, suggesting new finds or agreeing or disagreeing with our assessments. They greatly help in our evaluations. We encourage you to respond.

SAN FRANCISCO BAY AREA

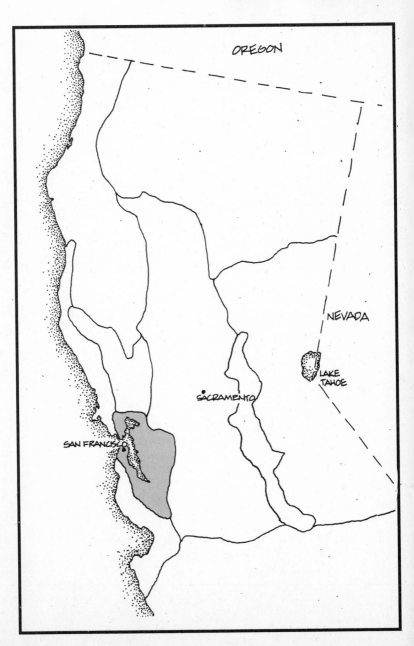

OREGON

NEVADA

LAKE
TAHOE

SACRAMENTO

SAN FRANCISCO

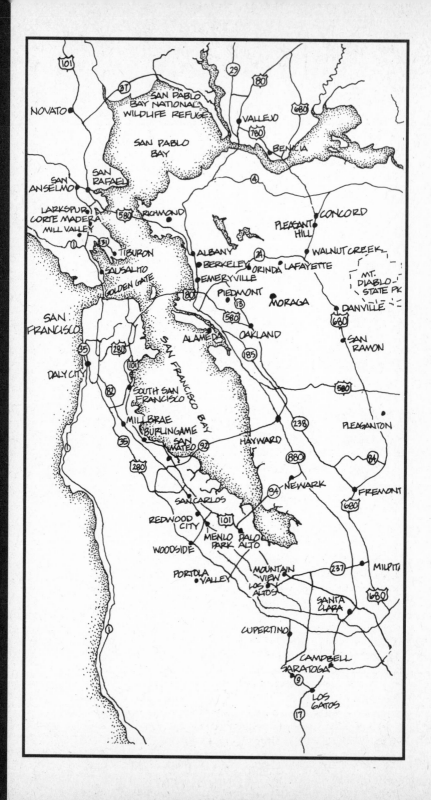

San Francisco Bay Area

San Francisco then clockwise around the bay. North to Marin, east to Berkeley, south to San Jose, and continuing up the peninsula to Daly City.

SAN FRANCISCO

San Franciscans know they are uniquely blessed. Nowhere, they tell themselves, is the meeting of land and sea so spectacular. The vistas that appear without warning, at any moment, in any neighborhood, are still heart-stopping. Poised on the edge of the continent, San Franciscans seem on the cutting edge of the new global culture, and nowhere, they tell themselves, is the mix of cultures—in food, music, and art—so graceful and beneficent—especially for those with the money to take advantage of the bounty. The late afternoon sun flashes off the water of the bay and lights up the red towers of the Golden Gate Bridge. Almost every evening, the fog pours in from the Pacific, spilling over the towers of downtown like a white wave. Lovers of all persuasions kiss on street corners. Poets still scribble in coffee shops. No wonder it's everyone's favorite city.

Of late, however, San Fran has begun to view this magnetism as something of a liability. Drawn by the city's fabled beauty and tolerance, newcomers from around the country (and the world) have poured into this hilly, 8-square-mile oasis. Housing prices have soared, driving most middle-class families out to distant suburbs. On a bad day, it seems like the entire city is populated with frazzled workaholic singles, grumpy long-distance commuters, and the ever-present legions of homeless people—but even on those days most people are smiling.

THE ARTS

Music The world-class San Francisco Opera, exuberantly directed by Lotfi Mansouri, alternates warhorses with rarities from September through December (301 Van Ness, (415) 864-3330). Subscribers grab up most seats, but fanatics can line up at 6am on performance-mornings to buy standing room tickets. The San Francisco Symphony, under Herbert Blomstedt, performs at acoustically-impaired Davies Hall at the corner of Grove and Van Ness from September through May (201 Van Ness, (415) 431-5400). Other classical groups include the

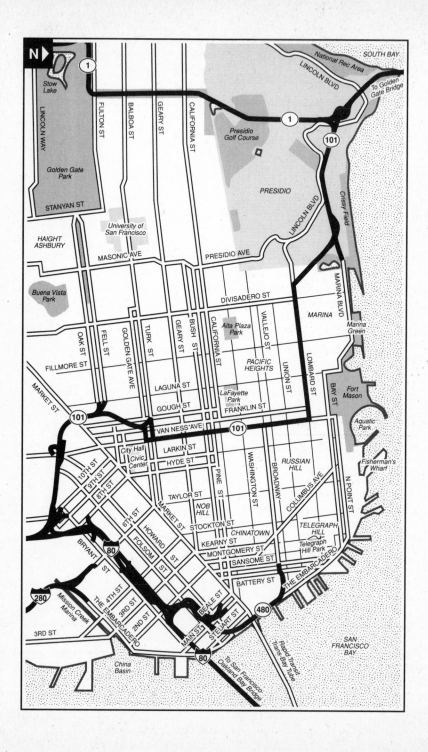

Lamplighters (Gilbert and Sullivan) (2350 Turk, (415) 752-7755); the Women's Philharmonic (330 Townsend Street for box office, (415) 543-2297); and the San Francisco Early Music Society,(510) 528-1725. On summer Sundays, free outdoor performances at Stern Grove (Sloat and 19th Avenue, (415) 391-2000) draw crowds.

Theater ACT (American Conservatory Theater), the city's best-known company, presents solid productions of new works and classics (mostly at the Stage Door Theatre, 420 Mason; the ACT theater building was destroyed by the 1989 quake, (415) 749-2228). Current Broadway touring shows can be found at the Golden Gate, Curran, and Orpheum theaters (info for all three: (415) 474-3800). Off-Broadway fare can be caught at the Theater on the Square (450 Post, between Powell and Mason, (415) 433-9500) and Marine's Memorial Theater (609 Sutter, (415) 771-6900). Generally, the small local companies are more exciting: for new, ethnic, or imported plays, try the Asian-American Theater Company (403 Arguello, (415) 751-2600), Eureka (415) 558-9898), the Lorraine Hansberry (620 Sutter Street, (415) 474-8800), or the Magic Theater (Fort Mason Center, Bldg D, 3rd floor, on Marina Boulevard, (415) 441-8822); Theatre Rhinoceros (2926 16th Street, (415) 861-5079) specializes in gay drama. Cutting edge, experimental work (including the annual Solo Mio monologue festival in September) can be found at Life-on-the-Water Theatre (Fort Mason, Bldg B, (415) 252-5967) and the Climate Theater (252 9th Street, (415) 626-9196). Summer and early autumn bring free outdoor performances by the hilarious, political San Francisco Mime Troupe (for info on performance locations, (415) 285-1720), and the San Francisco Shakespeare Festival (Golden Gate Park, (415) 666-2222). San Francisco has launched many comic headliners (Robin Williams, Whoopi Goldberg, et al); top comedy venues are the Improv (401 Mason, at Geary, (415) 441-7787), the Punchline (444 Battery, 2nd floor, (415) 397-7573), and Cobb's Comedy Club (2801 Leavenworth at Beach, (415) 928-4320).

Dance The San Francisco Ballet (301 Van Ness, at War Memorial Opera House, (415) 621-3838), directed by Helgi Tomasson, kicks off around Thanksgiving with the *Nutcracker*, before embarking on more interesting compositions after Christmas. Ethnic dance troupes abound, coming together at a springtime Ethnic Dance Festival (performances at Fort Mason, (415) 441-5705). Theatre Artaud (450 Florida Street, (415) 621-7797) regularly presents modern dance recitals.

Visual Arts Don't miss the great Brundage collection of Asian art at the de Young Museum (415) 863-3330) in Golden Gate Park. The de Young also displays American art, and traveling international exhibits. The dynamic Museum of Modern Art downtown (401 Van Ness, (415) 863-8800), and several small folk-art museums (especially the Mexican Folk Art Museum) at Fort Mason (Buchanan and Marina Boulevard, (415) 441-5706 or (415) 441-5705) are well worth visiting. Galleries for established artists are concentrated on lower Grant Avenue and near Union Square; upcoming artists exhibit south of Market. Vibrant murals decorate public spaces in the Mission District (especially 24th Street from Folsom to York). For more current art and entertainment listings, check the *Chronicle-Examiner's* "pink section."

Film The San Francisco International Film Festival plays to movie-mad San Francisco for a fortnight in spring; (415) 931-3456 or (415) 567-4641. For rare revivals and premieres, check the palatial Castro Theatre (429 Castro Street, (415) 621-6120), the funky (but finely programmed) Roxie (3117 16th Street, (415) 863-1087), and the homey Red Vic (1727 Haight Street, (415) 668-3994).

OTHER THINGS TO DO

Science The Exploratorium (next to the Palace of Fine Arts, (415) 561-0360) is a unique, interactive museum that brings scientific concepts to vivid life; it's a blast at any age. Its marvelous Tactile Dome requires reservations; (415) 561-0362. The California Academy of Sciences (Golden Gate Park, (415) 750-7145) offers a superb aquarium, herpetarium, planetarium, and Laserium. The San Francisco Zoo (45th Avenue and Sloat Boulevard, (415) 753-7061), vastly improved over the last decade, has apes-in-condos at its famed glass-walled Primate Center.

Nightlife Although fabled dance halls like the Fillmore are long gone, great clubs abound. Many of the hippest, like blues and jazz of Slim's (333 11th Street; (415) 621-3330) and hip-hop and reggae of DNA (375 11th Street; (415) 626-1409), are in SOMA (the neighborhood south of Market Street); loud new bands play several Haight Street venues. The ornate Great American Music Hall (859 O'Farrell Street, (415) 885-0750) and the minimalist Kennel Club (628 Divisadero Street, (415) 931-1914) specialize in world music. Jazz happens at Kimball's (300 Grove Street, (415) 861-5555) and Rasselas (2801 California Street, (415) 567-5010).

Bars San Franciscans have to have something to cut the chill of those long foggy nights. Edinburgh Castle (950 Geary, off Hyde, (415) 885-4074) specializes in Scottish quaffs; sometimes a bagpiper even comes blasting through. Little City (673 Union, just off Washington Square, (415) 434-2900) is a great spot for flirting over terrific tapas. Gino and Carlo's (548 Green, near Columbus, (415) 421-0896), a rough and ready Italian saloon, mixes super-cool literary types with street-wise locals. Another pleasant (and semi-secret) North Beach bar is Spec's, (415) 421-4112, an old beat generation hangout on tiny Saroyan Alley off Columbus downhill from Broadway. In warm weather, sip chilled white wine or lattes on the patio of Cafe Flore (2298 Market at 16th, (415) 621-8579).

Festivals Winter's week-long Chinese New Year culminates explosively with a crowded, exciting parade through Chinatown (415) 391-9680. Dry weather (April through October) brings street fairs that typify their neighborhoods (from upscale Union Street to the still hairy Haight). Labor Day weekend, the San Francisco Urban Fair (Events Hotline, (415) 391-2000) features "fog-calling" instead of hog-calling.

Parks Running 2½ miles from Stanyan Street to the Ocean, Golden Gate Park is a masterpiece of park design, with hundreds of distinct environments and interesting things to do: the Arboretum (9th and Lincoln) is especially splendid—check out the California Native Plants area abloom in spring and early summer. Right next door is the lovely, but crowded Japanese Tea Garden. (Our secret: Go when it's raining.) Nearby is the Conservatory of Flowers (Kennedy Drive, just past Stanyan), a Victorian fairyland hothouse full of tropical flora. The Children's Playground (off Kezar Drive) includes a Golden Age carousel that runs on weekends.

The city's entire northwest corner is part of the **Golden Gate National Recreation Area** (GGNRA), (415) 556-0560, and includes a ravishing hiking trail along the headlands overlooking the Golden Gate. The Presidio, a military base that's about to become part of the GGNRA, also offers superb views to hikers (and drivers). Sundays, Golden Gate Park's Kennedy Drive is given over to roller skaters and bicyclers; it's easy to rent whatever wheels you want. Crissy Field is a fabulous windsurfing spot, and the nearby Marina Green is prime kite-flying territory. Riptide-ridden Ocean Beach affords no water-sports, but on warm days swimmers splash at Baker Beach (25th Avenue North, off Sea Cliff Drive). Other scenic walking spots include Glen Park, Stern Grove, and Lake Merced.

Sports San Francisco sports fans are justly proud of the champion 49ers football team, but less enthusiastic about their windswept, bone-chilling home stadium, Candlestick Park. The Giants take over "the Stick" during baseball season (Giants info: (415) 467-8000; 49ers info:(415) 468-2249). The San Jose Sharks play pro hockey at the Cow Palace—where a world-class rodeo, now bedevilled by animal rights activists, is also held annually during Halloween-week. The top-rated Volvo Tennis Tournament fills Brooks Hall, (415) 267-6400 every February. The San Francisco Marathon, (415) 391-2123, usually runs in June, but if you'd rather race against two-legged Brillo boxes, centipedes, and Snow White and the Seven Dwarves, there's the antic, 8-mile Bay to Breakers race in May; (415) 391-2000.

Shopping The Union Square area and the nearby San Francisco Centre at Market and 5th streets, house a cluster of six department stores and countless specialty shops. The vast Embarcadero Center, (415) 772-0500, is a sophisticated neo-mall. Many famed fashion firms (including Jeanne-Marc, Gunne Sax and Esprit) have factory outlets south of Market. Sacramento Street (from Lyon to Locust) offers elegant clothing and furnishings; for vintage, cutting-edge, and folksy fashions and crafts, stroll 24th Street (Castro to Church), Fillmore (Bush to Clay) and Haight (Masonic to Schrader). Little remains of pre-World War II "Japantown," but the Japanese Cultural and Trade Center (Post Street from Laguna to Fillmore) houses good restaurants and shops selling Japanese crafts, housewares, and books.

Cosmopolitan cooks can stock up on Asian foodstuffs in Chinatown along Stockton Street (California to Broadway) or in "New Chinatown" (Clement from Arguello to 10th Avenue, and 18th to 25th). North Beach holds Italian treats along Columbus (Broadway to Bay); the Mission (24th Street, Mission to Potrero) offers Latin specialties. **Good bookstores** include City Lights (261 Columbus, at Stockton, (415) 362-8193), still Beat after all these years; A Clean Well-Lighted Place for Books (601 Van Ness Avenue, Opera Plaza, (415) 441-6670); Stacey's (581 Market and 2nd Street, (415) 421-4687), and Green Apple (506 Clement at 6th Avenue, (415) 387-2272).

Sightseeing San Francisco, like Paris, is a great walking town, and many great views are accessible only to pedestrians such as Fort Point, at the base of the Golden Gate Bridge—and as long as you're there walk across the Bridge. Another scenic stroll follows the Embarcadero north from Market to the handsome new pier opposite Washington Street, affording amplified views of the Bay and the Bay Bridge. Fisherman's Wharf and Pier 39 are locally scorned as venal Disneyworlds (with awful food!). Alcatraz, Chinatown's Grant Avenue, and even those adorable malls, Ghirardelli Square and the Cannery, can be disappointing; however, a visit to the Cliff House (1090 Point Lobos Road, (415) 386-3330) for a view of the ocean is well worth the time, as are Coit Tower's Depression-era WPA murals. An alternative to the tour-boats might be a ferry to Sausalito, Larkspur, or Oakland from the Ferry Building at the base of Market. An outside perch on a Powell Street cable car is always a kick.

Transportation Parking in town can be an ordeal; many neighborhoods limit non-residents to only two hours. Major hotels have taxi-stands; otherwise, phone for cabs since they rarely cruise. Public transportation reaches every neighborhood but grows sparse after midnight. San Francisco Municipal Railway (MUNI, which includes buses and overground/underground streetcars) requires exact change; free transfers grant two more rides within the allotted time period, (415) 673-6864. Cable cars cost extra. Short-term MUNI passes are available at City Hall during weekday business hours. Transfers between MUNI and BART's underground commuter trains are mutually accepted within city limits (BART; (415) 788-2278). For transportation to or from the airport, try one of the fast, reliable shuttle services, charging about $10 each way.

Weather San Francisco's climate can come as a shock to novice visitors. Years of propaganda about sunny California (Southern California) have fooled millions of tourists into freezing miserably. San Francisco is rarely warm enough to go without a coat or sweater. Spring and fall are the best seasons to visit. Summer is usually foggy except for midday. Locals beat summer morning chills by dressing in layers.

RESTAURANTS

Ernie's ★★★★ If you haven't been to Ernie's in years, try it again. Ernie's has been through many redecorations and culinary reinventions since 1958 when Kim Novak and Jimmy Stewart called it "our restaurant" in Alfred Hitchcock's *Vertigo*, but its latest incarnation is probably the best of all. Chef Alain Rondelli, a veteran of some of France's greatest kitchens, turns out cuisine of exquisite subtlety that blends California ingredients with Gallic technique: tournedos come with an intense black bean and chocolate sauce; meltingly tender roast duck thighs sit on a buttery, sherry-touched corn custard; and the desserts—like the ethereal phyllo chrysanthemum with a soft apple mousse center—dazzle. The prix-fixe menu for dinner includes a pricey seven-course feast and a more sparse three-course economy meal available Sunday through Thursday. Lunches are more affordable. The wine list is long but costly, with too many young reds. The service is ultraprofessional, and reservations are strongly advised. ■ *Montgomery between Pacific and Jackson; (415) 397-5969; 847 Montgomery St, San Francisco; $$$; full bar; AE, DC, DIS, MC, V; no checks; lunch Mon–Fri, dinner every day.*

La Folie ★★★★ After a stingy San Francisco restaurateur fired him for spending too much on ingredients and serving overly generous portions, French-born chef Roland Passot decided to open his own place where he could spend as much as he liked to make the food perfect. The paradisiacal result is La Folie. This may be the best new restaurant in San Francisco—or maybe the best restaurant, period. You simply can't err when you order from Passot's creative, exuberant, but disciplined cuisine. Our favorite starters include any of the foie gras appetizers, pressed lobster salad, rabbit loin stuffed with vegetables, corn and oyster soup, and lobster consommé. For an entrée, choose whatever meat or fish suits your fancy, and it will be exquisitely prepared and consistently inspired. In winter, La Folie serves caribou (rare, with cranberry sauce). Also be on the lookout for entrées that include Passot's celestial garlic or marrow flans. The pear strudel with chocolate sorbet and ginger sauce Anglaise is, alone, four stars. Mondays through Thursdays there's a relatively inexpensive three-course prix-fixe dinner. The wine list is fine (but costly); parking is horrible, so take a taxi. Reservations very strongly recommended, especially on weekends. ■ *Polk between Union and Green; (415) 776-5577; 2316 Polk St, San Francisco; $$$; beer and wine; AE, DC, DIS, MC, V; no checks; dinner Mon–Sat.*

Masa's ★★★★ No one just drops in for dinner at Masa's. Not only do you need to reserve three weeks in advance, but it may take that long to arrange financing: this is probably San Francisco's most expensive restaurant. That said, the prices accurately reflect the precious ingredients, generous portions, stunning presentation, and labor-intensive nature of the elegant French-California cuisine invented by the late Masa Kobayashi and carried on flawlessly by chef Julian Serrano. At the same time, Masa's atmosphere is neither glitzy nor snobbish; nor is the ultra-professional service overly intimidating.

Among the highlights of the mutable menu are the first courses of seafood sausages stuffed with lobster, scallops, and shrimp and served with beurre blanc, and the splendid truffle-spattered block of fresh sautéed foie gras on spinach. Entrées may include a delectable Maine lobster served with shrimp quenelles and beurre blanc, a filet of beef served with marrow and sauce périgueux, fine grilled fish dishes, tenderly treated game birds, or a richly sauced and tender venison steak. Dessert is aesthetically necessary: even if you've already had enough to eat, it will elevate your spirits just to admire the moiré sunbursts of the sauces.

The wine list is even more exorbitantly priced than the food; moreover, if you want to bring a special bottle of your own, you should know that the corkage fee is equal to the retail value of a top-flight chardonnay. ■ *Bush between Stockton and Powell; (415) 989-7154; 648 Bush St, San Francisco; $$$; full bar; AE, DC, DIS, MC, V; checks OK; dinner Tues–Sat.*

Zola's ★★★★ With its absolutely unpretentious service and post-modern decor of peach and shadow, Zola's is emblematic of San Francisco at its best: impeccably serious yet friendly and informal. Chef-owner Catherine Pantsios changes her menu every week, but you can count on a European slant that features very fresh local produce. A typical selection might include chicken liver crostini with arugula and melted onions, gratin of squash gnocchi with fried sage, polenta with roasted vegetables and wild mushrooms, or roast guinea hen with sausage and polenta. The cooking is fabulous and extremely consistent; we've rarely encountered a failed dish here. The wine collection is also one of the best in town, with a multitude of excellent choices at moderate prices and many selections available by the glass or the quarter-bottle. (Be sure to ask host/co-owner Larry Bain if there's anything special that hasn't made it onto the list yet.)

Situated around the corner from the opera, Zola's gets *very* crowded with people in *very* expensive clothes from 6 to 8pm. If you plan to join them, you'll definitely need to reserve a table in advance; if you don't mind dining on the late side, however, you can usually drop in after 8 and sit right down. ■ *Hayes and Gough streets, (415) 864-4824; 395 Hayes St, San Francisco; $$$; full bar; AE, M, V; checks OK; dinner Tues-Sun.*

Aqua ★★★ Aqua fulfills a long-standing hunger. In a city rich with both seafood houses and haute cuisine, this is the first restaurant to unite the two currents. Chef George Morrone's best dishes are as brilliantly conceived and gorgeously composed as you'll find at Fleur de Lys, La Folie, or Masa's. And just as impeccably prepared. Seared scallops and duck foie gras, for instance, make a startlingly successful marriage in one appetizer, while an entrée of walnut-crusted freshwater pike served with plump morels, smokey bacon, and a subtly sweetened julienne of Belgian endive is another fine connubial concoction. Pungent, fresh snipped oregano graces a luscious Mexican grouper steak, and rock shrimp and fresh mild chiles make a tender filling in the deep-fried calamari. Dinner begins with an appetizer (pray for the heavenly lobster bisque) and ends with a complimentary assortment of sensual sweets. Service is a bit too attentive. The neo-deco façade and handsome dining room attract a well-dressed financial district crowd—so reservations are advised. ■ *California St near Battery, (415) 956-9662; 252 California St, San Francisco; $$$; full bar; AE, MC, V; no checks; lunch Mon-Fri, dinner Mon-Sat.*

Bentley's Seafood Grill ★★★ Master chef Amy Shaw (who revitalized Berkeley's Fourth Street Grill) has found a marvelous new venue for her fiery, venturesome fare: a stylish fish house in the financial district where the brass rails and etched glass evoke the feeling of being in a Parisian railway station bistro. Bentley's oysters have always been fresh and varied, but Shaw has invigorated the rest of the menu with inspirations drawn largely from parts of the globe that prize hot peppers (Louisiana, Mexico, Asia). The fiery, thyme-infused seafood gumbo would do a New Orleans nouvelle-Creole restaurant proud; the honest (flour-free) New England clam chowder is voluptuously creamy; and crisp, greaseless shellfish cakes—crab, shrimp, and scallops—come perched beside a coral pool of incendiary rémoulade. Shaw's signature entrée is out-and-out spectacular: spicy homemade salmon sausages—neo-quenelles, really—accompanied by a ginger-flavored cabbage.

The cooking is always good, but it's best on weekday evenings when Shaw herself is on duty at the sauté station.

Weekdays find execs in three-piece suits powering through lunch; dinners are more relaxed (except on weekend evenings, when the bar pulls its slickest trick and turns into a live jazz joint with a hip, heterogeneous San Francisco crowd). The oyster bar is open all day. The mainly-California wine list won't shred your wallet unless you ask it to. Reservations advised. ■ *Sutter near Kearny (at the Galleria); (415) 989-6895; 185 Sutter, San Francisco; $$$; full bar; AE, DC, MC, V; no checks; lunch Mon–Sat, dinner every day, brunch Sun.*

Casa Aguila ★★★ This merry neighborhood cafe in the foggy Sunset district serves the kind of authentic, imaginative, beautifully presented dishes you'd find in Acapulco or Cozumel. Casa Aguila draws diners from all over the city, so you'd better come early or be prepared to wait. By the time you sit down, you may be so hungry that you'll be tempted to order one or two of the terrific appetizers; but be warned that it's a rare fellow who can finish both an appetizer and an entrée. Chef/owner Luis Angeles Hoffman produces an amazingly broad range of dishes—putting to shame the unambitious variations on the stuffed tortilla that characterize most Mexican restaurants. While the clever menu includes many classics, even the most familiar are newly imagined: Hoffman's mole poblano sauce, for instance, includes raisins and dates, while crisp spears of jicama sweeten the lime-marinated, very fresh ceviche. ■ *Noriega between 19th and 20th; (415) 661-5593; 1240 Noriega, San Francisco; $$; beer and wine; AE, MC, V; no checks; brunch, lunch, dinner every day.*

Fleur de Lys ★★★ Fleur de Lys is definitely a Grand Occasion restaurant, with fine food, formal service, breathtaking decor, a supernal wine list—and fiendishly expensive food. Wunderkind chef Hubert Keller (formerly of Alsace's renowned Auberge de l'Ill) is currently giving Masa's Julian Serrano a serious fight for top chef status in San Francisco. Some of his more peculiar flights of fancy don't always work out, however, and now and then he indulges in a trendy cliché, but his formidable technique—beautifully prepared ingredients accompanied by surprising garnishes and subtle sauces—is legendary and many of his dishes are near-miracles. His sea-bass fillet, for example—crunchy without and tender within, served on spinach-wrapped lobster meat and sauced with beets and onions—is bafflingly brilliant. The restaurant's decor matches the splendor of the food step for step: the dining area is draped with rich red floral fabric cascading over half the room, peaking around a giant floral arrangement in the center; mirrored walls double this visual spectacle while simultaneously allowing you to admire yourself and your glitteringly attired fellow diners. Fleur de Lys isn't always crowded, but reservations are required; this is the sort of establishment that wants to know who's coming to dinner. ■ *Sutter between Taylor and Jones; (415) 673-7779; 777 Sutter, San Francisco; $$$; full bar; AE, DC, MC, V; no checks; dinner Mon–Sat.*

Flying Saucer ★★★ A few weeks after landing in the outer Mission district, Flying Saucer owner/chef Albert Trodjman tossed a well-known restaurant critic out onto the sidewalk. The reviewer wrote a rave anyway, and the legend of Flying Saucer (named after the wacky amusement-park spaceship hanging over the door) was launched. This small, plain, very hip bistro specializes in attitude as well as excellent food. To get a taste of the latter, you'll have to put up with hard little chairs, bare floors, a fuzzy menu projected on the wall from a funky overhead projector, and a two-week wait for an undersized table. The credentials Trodjman brings to his enterprise are top-flight: an apprenticeship in his native Lyon, followed by jobs at such high-profile eateries as London's Dorchester, New Orleans' Commander's Palace, and Napa Valley's Auberge du Soleil. Trodjman's menu can be a bit formulaic, but most of it works rambunctiously well. Entrées are huge, complicated, intense in flavor, and baroque in presentation: duck confit with black chanterelles or coconut-curry lentils, scallion-smothered chicken breast, and the crisp-skin salmon with tangerine-basil sauce. Precious ingredients are used abundantly (the fresh duck foie gras appetizer is twice the size and half the price of similar dishes at Masa's). Co-owner and pastry chef Donna Meadows offers only one dessert each night; white chocolate and passion fruit mousse cake, coconut-lemongrass-ginger flan, or brandied cherry tart with pecan ice cream. The Saucer's bad attitude doesn't extend to the service, which is smart, energetic, and friendly. ■ *Guerrero and 22nd St; (415) 641-9955; 1000 Guerrero, San Francisco; $$; beer and wine; no credit cards; local checks only; dinner Wed–Sun.*

Harris's ★★★ Not just another steak house, Harris's is a living monument to the not-quite-bygone joys of guiltless beef-eating. The hushed, club-formal setting boasts deep carpets, roomy booths, well-spaced white-draped tables, and plush chairs roomy enough to accommodate the most bullish build. Jackets are appreciated (though no longer required). Harris's prime Midwestern beef, impeccably aged for three weeks on the premises, bears the same relation to supermarket beef as foie gras bears to chicken liver; the tender steaks, grilled to order, can be chosen by cut and by size. The larger bone-in cuts (such as the Harris steak and the T-bone) have the finest flavor, but we're also partial to the pepper steak and the rare prime rib. Those who prefer calf brains to these sanguine beauties will find a flawless version here. You might want to skip the usual steak house appetizers in favor of Harris's excellent spinach salad. For true-blue traditionalists, the exemplary

▼

martini—served in a carafe placed in a bucket of shaved ice—makes an excellent starter course. ■ *Van Ness and Pacific; (415) 673-1888; 2100 Van Ness Ave, San Francisco; $$$; full bar; AE, DC, DIS, M, V; no checks; dinner every day, lunch Wed.*

The Hayes Street Bar & Grill ★★★

If you're looking for one of the best fish dinners in San Francisco, visit Hayes Street Grill, a serene and elegant ichthyological oasis near Davies Symphony Hall. With its gleaming white dining rooms lined with photos of stars from the nearby opera and symphony, Patricia Unterman's highly focused restaurant does only a few things, but it does those things extremely well. The open kitchen emphasizes perfectly fresh Pacific seafood, mesquite-grilled or delicately sautéed. The culinary talent here shines well beyond the entrées: succulent raw oysters, surprising subtle soups, sparkling fresh salads, and a few elaborate options such as grilled quail salad or a superb calamari fritto misto. French fries are a house specialty; and the deep-dish pies and crisps are always delicious. The polite, efficient staff will move mountains (and kitchen priorities) to get you out the door in time for opera and symphony curtains. Reservations are strongly recommended, especially for pre-opera dining. ■ *Hayes near Franklin; (415) 863-5545; 320 Hayes St, San Francisco; $$$; full bar; AE, DC, DIS, MC, V; no checks; lunch Mon–Fri, dinner Mon–Sat.*

Helmand ★★★

An oasis of good taste on Broadway's topless strip, Helmand serves delicious renditions of Afghanistan cuisine. The restaurant's light and variously spiced house-made yogurts (a staple of Afghani cooking) dress several of our favorite appetizers: mantwo (a pastry shell filled with onions and beef) is topped with a vegetable-and-meat sauce and served on yogurt; the sweetness of kaddo borawni (tender baby pumpkin) is tempered by a piquant yogurt-garlic sauce. For a main course, try the chopan—a tender rack of lamb marinated like fine Armenian-style shish kabob, then grilled pink and served with sauteed rice pallow; other fine choices include sabzi challow (beautifully seasoned mixtures of spinach and meat), mourgh challow (chicken and split peas), and koufta challow (light, moderately spicy meatballs with tomatoes and peas), each served with a ramekin of flavorful fresh cilantro sauce and aromatic white rice. Service is personable (if sometimes slightly scattered); the wine list well-chosen and well-priced. Also—importantly in this very crowded neighborhood—there's validated parking at a lot down the block. ■ *Broadway between Kearny and Montgomery; (415) 362-0641; 430 Broadway, San Francisco; $$; full bar; AE, MC, V; no checks; lunch Mon–Fri, dinner every day.*

House of Nanking ★★★

The dinnertime waiting line outside this tiny, popular hole-in-the-wall starts at 5:30pm; by 6pm, you may face a 90-minute wait for a cramped, crowded table with a plastic menu on which half the best dishes are unlisted and half the listed dishes are dull, tourist-pleasing clichés. Lunchtime crowds make midday dining just as problematic.

Here's a solution: arrive for a late lunch or a very early dinner (between 2:30 and 5:15pm) and walk right in. When owner/chef/headwaiter Peter Fang can give you his full attention, he'll be glad to apprise you of the day's unlisted specials: succulent duck dumplings, an exotic shrimp-and-green-onion pancake with peanut sauce, or tempuralike sesame-battered Nanking scallops in a spicy garlic sauce. Nanking, Fang's hometown, is at the inland end of the Shanghai railroad, making it an exchange point for foods from Sichuan, Peking, Guangdong, and the local coast. Like the true chef he is, Fang concocts wily revisions of many traditional dishes, mingling the different regional cuisines with his own inventions. ■ *Kearny between Jackson and Pacific; (415) 421-1429; 919 Kearny, San Francisco; $; beer and wine; no credit cards; no checks; lunch Mon–Sat, dinner Mon–Sun.*

Kabuto Sushi ★★★ Kabuto is probably the finest sushi bar in Northern California—and some would find even that statement too modest. Many of the area's best chefs find inspiration here for the Pacific Rim innovations that are changing the face of California cuisine. It's perfectly possible to eat a competent Japanese dinner (tempura, sashimi, yakitori, what-have-you) in Kabuto's drab dining room—but why? Kabuto's raison d'être lies behind the semicircular, black-lacquered sushi bar where the celebrated Sachio performs swift staccato magic in a blur of bamboo rollers and blades, shouts hello to new arrivals, and proves definitively that fresh raw fish is the world's most perfect food. Don't be surprised if you find yourself treated to some wonderful unlisted (and unordered) tidbit. The kitchen also prepares grilled shellfish, soups, and tofu dishes that are listed on little blackboards along the bar. Kabuto doesn't take reservations, so go early to avoid the peak-hour wait. ■ *Geary at 15th Ave; (415) 752-5652; 5116 Geary, San Francisco; $$; beer, wine, and sake; AE, MC, V; no checks; dinner Tues–Sun.*

L'Avenue ★★★ An unassuming but handsome little bistro out in the avenues, L'Avenue is *le venue* for Nancy Oakes' original yet comforting California-French cooking, in which great ingredients are prepared with consistent excellence: fish are gleamingly fresh; vegetables come from nearby organic farms; sausages are made by award-winning local charcutier Bruce Aidell (Oakes' husband). Most of the meats and poultry are free-range as well as organic—even those who scorn pallid formula-fed veal delight in L'Avenue's large, juicy, grilled chops. Whatever you order is likely to combine flavors in a way that's fresh without being shocking. Grilled items are accompanied by a mound of smartly dressed vegetables, along with savory buttermilk mashed potatoes or wild mushroom polenta. Most evenings, Oakes offers a hearty stew or casserole; starter courses tend to be more light and flashy: very fresh salads, clever vegetable creations, richly topped tartlets on the thinnest of crusts. The wine list is well-chosen and affordable. ■ *Geary at 3rd Ave; (415) 386-1555; 3854 Geary Blvd, San Francisco; $$$; full bar; AE, MC, V; checks OK; dinner every day.*

McCormick & Kuleto's Seafood Restaurant ★★★

If great seafood with a fabulous view of the bay sounds like your kettle of fish, welcome to McCormick & Kuleto's in Ghirardelli Square. Partitially owned by famed local restaurant designer Pat Kuleto, the restaurant's appearance is suitably spectacular. The informal Crabcake Lounge has an ice table heaped high with lovely fish, oysters, and clams. The serious glitz starts in the restaurant proper—a tri-level room with lots of wood and copper grillwork, a deco bar (with an impressive collection of single-malt Scotches), an oak-paneled smoking section at the very top, and gigantic windows overlooking Alcatraz, the Golden Gate, and the Marin headlands. The cooking may be a little gimmicky; but factor in the scenery and you end up with a stupendous mix of local color and gourmet seafood: perfectly grilled alder-smoked salmon (served with saffron-chive butter), a splendid white bass with Jamaican spice (basted with a fiery sauce). The simplest appetizers—fried calamari and rock-shrimp popcorn—are best. Service is attentive without being obsequious. There's a large wine list with a broad selection of glasses as well as bottles. ■ *Ghirardelli Square, on North Point near Larkin; (415) 929-1730; 900 North Point St, San Francisco; $$$; full bar; AE, DC, DIS, MC, V; no checks; lunch, dinner every day.*

North India Restaurant ★★★

Considering San Francisco's reputation as a center of international cuisine, it's odd how hard it is to find good Indian food here. The Pakistani-owned North India Restaurant is one of a few West Coast restaurants where the depth and complexity of seasonings, distinctly varied sauces, and pepper heat on the palate actually resemble India's best food offerings. Each vegetable dish has its own distinct flavor, while the rice, dal (legumes), and raita (seasoned yogurt, vital for fire eaters) are splendid. Rogan josh is a deeply spiced, sautéed lamb in a dark savory sauce. Tandoori seafood delicacies emerge from the kitchen tender enough to please the most demanding Keralese. The menu is long enough to be intimidating, but the indecisive or inexperienced can choose one of several prix-fixe dinners. Desserts include mango ice cream and a saffron-laden version of the dense spiced-nut ice cream called kulfi. Service is genial, although some recently arrived staffers have a little trouble with English. ■ *Webster just S of*

Lombard; (415) 931-1556; 3131 Webster, San Francisco; $$; beer and wine; AE, DC, MC, V; no checks; lunch Mon–Fri, dinner every day.

Stars ★★★ With Stars, chef Jeremiah Tower (who helped put Chez Panisse on the map) has created a major power scene in which to see and be seen, if not heard. Stars is vast and noisy—by design, with tons of gleaming wood, brass, and mirrors to redouble the din. The place attracts an international set of luminaries from social, political, artistic, and culinary spheres, and the walls are covered with celebrity photos, French liquor posters, old menus, awards, and framed copies of (apparently) every article in which Tower—the true star—has ever been mentioned. In light of all this—and notwithstanding its creator's culinary talent—Stars' status has superseded its food as the main draw. Not that the food is bad—even if Tower rarely cooks nowadays, executive chef Mark Franz faithfully follows his Mediterranean-American prescriptions. Many dishes—including anything involving sweetbreads—are splendidly imagined and executed. But the quality is inconsistent. No such problem with Emily Luchetti's desserts: late in the evening, lower-key locals sneak in for her exquisite soufflés and sublime fresh-fruit pastries. The wine list is large, splendid, and costly; dinnertime reservations are advised. The service is friendly and adept—even if you're not a star.

Reservations are not accepted at **Stars Cafe** next door; (415) 861-4344. Here twenty-somethings are as noisy as their deep-pocketed forty-something brethren at Stars piano bar. Appetizers involve such calculated culinary risks as an avocado salad dressed with smoked trout cream or the crisp roast potatoes and garlic cloves with squab-liver butter. The flawless fish and chips is most popular. Desserts echo Stars' fine offerings. Service here can get downright frazzled when the cafe suddenly (and invariably) fills up at 8pm sharp. ■ *150 Redwood Alley (between McAllister and Golden Gate) off Van Ness; (415) 861-7827; 150 Redwood Alley, San Francisco; $$$; full bar; AE, DC, MC, V; no checks; lunch Mon–Fri, dinner every day.*

Thep Phanom ■ Thepin ★★★ Thailand's complex, spicy, cosmopolitan cuisine has always been adaptive, incorporating flavors from India, China, Burma, Malaysia, and more recently the West. San Francisco boasts dozens of Thai restaurants; virtually all of them are good, and many (including Dusit, Khan Toke, and Menora's) are excellent. Why, then, does Thep Phanom alone have a permanent line out its front door even though it takes reservations? At Thep Phanom, a creative touch of California enters the above cultural mix, resulting in dishes of special sparkle and sophistication. The signature dish here, ped sawn, is a boneless duck in a light honey sauce served on a bed of spinach—and it ranks with the city's greatest dishes. Tart, minty, spicy yum plamuk (calamari salad) and larb ped (minced duck salad) are superb choices, too. The velvety basil-spiked seafood curry served on banana leaves is wonderful. Service is charming and efficient; the tasteful decor, informal atmosphere, eclectic crowd, and discerning wine list are all very San Francisco.

At press time, Thep Phanom's owners opened Thepin near the Opera; early reports indicate a slightly different menu from Thep Phanom, but comparable quality and a longer wine list. Reservations are advised at either establishment. ▪ *Fillmore and Waller (near Haight); (415) 431-2526; 400 Waller, San Francisco; $$; beer and wine; AE, DIS, MC, V; no checks; dinner every day.* ▪ *Gough at Fell; (415) 863-9335; 298 Gough, San Francisco; $$; beer and wine; AE, DIS, MC, V; no checks; lunch Mon–Fri, dinner every day.*

Bix ★★ Bix is one of Cyndi Pawlcyn's (Fog City Diner, Rio Grill, Mustards, et al) newest postmodern dining places. Designed to simulate a sophisticated '30s supper club, it's dark and noisy with deco decor, live dinner jazz, and a high-spirited thirty-something crowd playing Nick and Nora over retro-chic cocktails. Pawlcyn originated the concept of dining by nibbles, and Bix's appetizers (corn custard or a crisp, ethereal potato-leek pancake with sour cream, lox, and ink-free lumpfish caviar) are generally good. More substantial is the clever chicken hash. Unlike the appetizers, not all the main dishes work. The textures and flavors of the crisp fried chicken—served with mashed potatoes and a spicy stir of blackeyed peas, corn, okra, and smoked bacon—are delightful, whereas a rich duck breast dressed with light and rather ingenuous berry sauce is ill-conceived. The long, venturesome wine list concentrates on California boutique wineries, with some modestly priced bottles (from Silverado Vineyards) offered under the Bix label. Desserts such as crème brulée are competently executed, if a bit faddish. But fads are what this place is all about. ▪ *Gold St (alley just N of Jackson) between Sansome and Montgomery; (415) 433-6300; 56 Gold St, San Francisco; $$$; full bar; AE, DC, DIS, MC, V; no checks; lunch Mon–Fri, dinner every day.*

Cafe Jacqueline ★★ There are evenings—say, after a vacation of gluttony—when the only conceivable dinner is an airy soufflé. When such an evening comes your way, Cafe Jacqueline is waiting. French-born Jacqueline Margulis (her last name comes from her Argentine husband) opened this charming cafe in the heart of North Beach in 1979, offering just the soufflé. As you'd expect from so serious a specialist, Jacqueline's creations are light and luscious as can be. Some mingle Gruyère cheese with a choice of vegetables—or garlic—or seafood—or prosciutto and mushrooms—or whatever other ingredients Margulis has chosen for the evening's special. Those with garlic are *so* garlicky that you and your date better plan on sharing it—but then, people often share the soufflés anyway. The dessert soufflés are truly ethereal (particularly the fresh peach). Service is very sweet, though you may have to pry the prices (which verge on exorbitant) out of the waiters. Parking in North Beach is always horrible, but cabs do cruise nearby. ■ *Grant near Union; (415) 981-5565; 1454 Grant Ave, San Francisco; $$$; beer and wine; AE, DC, DIS, MC, V; no checks; dinner Wed–Sun.*

Cafe Macaroni ★★ This may be one of the smallest restaurants in San Francisco (we're talking 28 cramped, comfortless seats—14 downstairs, 14 upstairs), and it could also be one of the noisiest, with a maddening subsonic rumble coming from some piece of kitchen equipment or other. However, word of Macaroni's Neopolitan cooking spread quickly from the canyons of the financial district to the heights of Telegraph Hill—and lawyers, literati, and homesick Romans packed in, enabling this spartan deli-bistro (where mindlessly bouncy Italian canzonettas mingle with the roar of the buses outside) to become an instant success. Except for the close quarters it's hard to find another fault. Diners are particularly fond of the mixed antipasto plate. Many regulars start with a combination platter of three savory pastas (including an aromatic ravioli with wild mushrooms, perhaps). The generous, soulful main courses stress tender, long-simmered items like oxtails and Italian sausage or braised lamb shank, each with flavors stolen from the recipe of somebody's mama. For dessert there are rich cakes with copious whipped cream; and the wine list, muscular espresso, and affable servers are as genuinely Italian as everything else. ■ *Columbus near Jackson; (415) 956-9737; 59 Columbus, San Francisco; $$; beer and wine; no credit cards; no checks; lunch Mon–Fri, dinner Mon–Sat.*

Crustacean ★★ Out near the ocean where the fog is thick and the prices are low, a family-owned Vietnamese nook named Thanh Long has been packed since the '70s on the strength of its giant roasted Dungeness crabs. Early in 1991, the family's younger generation opened Crustacean—an extremely elegant seafood paradise floating two stories above earthy Polk Street. This vast modern mermaid fantasyland boasts three dining levels, a giant glass wave sculpture, gentle lighting from hand-blown fixtures, and colorful maritime murals. Appetizers include well-marinated satay sticks and shrimp crisps sprinkled with flying-fish roe. The grilled tiger prawns are juicy giants bedded on garlic noodles; the pork-stuffed calamari are tenderly braised and subtly scented with Vietnamese fish sauce. But almost everyone comes for the biggest crustacean of all—roasted crab, a salty finger-licking feast meant to be shared with a good friend. The dessert list—including a creamy lemon sorbet served in an actual lemon-rind cup—is brief, while the intelligent wine list includes several California whites in half-bottles. The top-flight service is quite knowledgeable and genuinely warm. ▪ *Third floor of mini-mall at Polk and Pine; (415) 776-2722; 1475 Polk St, San Francisco; $$; full bar; AE, MC, V; no checks; lunch Mon–Fri; dinner every day.*

The Garden Court ★★ For almost a century, afternoon tea and Sunday brunch at the Garden Court have been among San Francisco's most beloved traditions; today they offer time-travel escapes to a voluptuous age of luxury and calm. The building itself—an architectural masterpiece and now an official city landmark—has been recently restored with fin-de-siècle accoutrements including marble columns, giant chandeliers, mirrored doorways, and potted palms set beneath a soaring dome of amber-stained glass. Cherubic strains of harp and chamber music waft down from a balcony above.

Teatime brings an awesome selection of teas, tasty light sandwiches, scones with lemon curd, and rose-petal marmalade, all served on bone china. The Sunday buffet is an utter cornucopia. Service is extravagantly helpful. Reserve well in advance unless you're a hotel guest. ▪ *Sheraton-Palace Hotel, Market between 2nd and 3rd streets; (415) 392-8600; 2 New Montgomery, San Francisco; $$$; full bar; AE, DC, DIS, MC, V; no checks; breakfast, lunch, tea, dinner every day; brunch Sun.*

Greens ★★ As Le Tour D'Argent in Paris is to the dedicated duck fancier, and as the Savoy Grill in London is to the roast-beef connoisseur, so is Greens at Fort Mason to vegetarian aesthetes. Not only is the food politically correct here, it's so good that even omnivores find it irresistible. Part of the treat is visual: located in a converted barracks in historic Fort Mason Center, the enormous, airy dining room is surrounded by huge windows with a spectacular view of the Golden Gate; tables are free-form wooden sculptures; and a gigantic petrified tree serves as a Buddhist-flavored centerpiece. Yes, Greens is owned and operated by the San Francisco Zen Center—but this is a restaurant, not a monastery. Expect to see such dishes as mesquite-grilled polenta; phyllo turnovers stuffed with mushrooms, spinach, and Parmesan; pizza with onion confit and roasted garlic; and fettuccine with mushrooms, peas, goat cheese, and crème frâiche. Baked goods come from the Zen Center's popular Tassajara Bakery. By picking your night, you can elect to order à la carte (Tues–Thurs) or enjoy a prix-fixe dinner (Fri–Sat). If you were expecting to be deprived for your own good here, think again. ▪ *Marina Blvd and Buchanan St; (415) 771-6222; Building A, Fort Mason Center, San Francisco; $$$; beer and wine; MC, V; local checks only; lunch, dinner Tues–Sat; brunch Sun.*

Harbor Village ★★ A favorite of prosperous Pacific Rim businessmen, middle-class Chinese-American families, and downtown office workers out for a lunchtime treat, this giant Hong Kong–style Gold Cup restaurant has great food—but it misses top honors because of minor inconsistencies in cooking and major flaws in service. Some of the standard Chinese dishes suffer from perfunctory preparation—Yang Chow fried rice is ordinary at best—and all too often, entire orders are piled on the undersized tables all at once, whether or not there's room. Miraculously, the food is worth it. Lunch is a state-of-the-art dim sum extravaganza, with master chefs from Hong Kong turning out plate after plate of sublime morsels in vast, interesting variety; if you drop in for dinner, you get to choose from an enormous Cantonese menu that includes dishes rarely found on this edge of the Rim—among them prized varieties of China Sea shellfish, kept alive in tanks until the moment of cooking and served with exquisite simplicity (albeit at exorbitant cost). Many of the more affordable seafood dishes are just as marvelous. So be adventurous: go with a gang and get a large table, or try ordering only a few dishes and then re-ordering when those are nearly gone. Reservations are strongly recommended. ■ *Drumm and Clay; (415) 982-7777; 4 Embarcadero, San Francisco; $$$; full bar; AE, DC, MC, V; no checks; lunch, dinner every day.*

Maykadeh ★★ For many centuries, Persia (now Iran) was the culinary capital of the civilized world; its enduring influence penetrated court cuisines from the Middle East to Southeast Asia, from India to Iberia. At Maykadeh, one can sample the fare of medieval princes for a less than princely price. A meal at this cheerful, comfortable restaurant begins with complimentary sabzee—a refreshing snack of feta cheese, onions, fresh basil, and mint tucked into warm pita bread. Most venturesome among the appetizers is the tender lamb tongue in a creamy sauce seasoned like rice pudding, or perhaps the succulent mesquite-grilled calf brains with saffrony lemon butter. Main-course choices are mainly stews and kabobs, but culinary explorers may enjoy the exotic ghorme sabzee (lamb shank braised in an assertive charred sauce of onions, red beans, dried lime, and mysterious Persian herbs). Kabobs are well-marinated and tender. Entrées come with buttery basmati rice pilaf and a ramekin of tart crimson sumac powder (from a Middle Eastern berry) to sprinkle on it. A sexy rose-perfumed ice cream is a fine finale. ■ *Green between Kearny and Grant; (415) 362-8286; 470 Green St, San Francisco; $$; beer and wine; MC, V; no checks; lunch, dinner every day.*

Narai ★★ A reliable charmer in the westernmost stretch of the Richmond district's New Chinatown, Narai serves a spicy but delicate version of Chou Chow cuisine, reflecting the travels of

the owners' family. Half a century ago, Kietisak Komindr's parents moved from Swatow, on the South China coast, to Bangkok and opened a restaurant. Later the family came to the Bay Area, where Komindr opened Narai in 1981. Narai's cuisine, accordingly, is a delicious mingling of Thai and southern Chinese elements in dishes that are simultaneously refined, homey, and explosively flavorful. Start with tofu skins stuffed with crab sausage; finely balanced sweet-sour-spicy mee krob (puffed rice noodle salad); warm silver noodle salad with shrimp and pork; and any of the intensely flavorful soups. Next try the Swatow-style duck simmered in seasoning sauce, stir-fried spicy lamb over puffed rice noodles, and the seafood hot pots (especially with catfish or succulent New Zealand mussels). Wade into new waters with a taro-root sticky pudding (a house dessert special). The wine list is inadequate to its task.
■ *Clement and 24th Ave; (415) 751-6363; 2229 Clement, San Francisco; $$; beer and wine; MC, V; no checks; lunch, dinner Tues–Sun.*

Phnom Penh ★★ The spicy complexity of Cambodia's cuisine is a slightly gentler, subtler version of that from neighboring Thailand. San Francisco is blessed with several fine Cambodian restaurants (each with its fanatical partisans). Phnom Penh is one standout among them. The cooking here is distinguished by clarity and freshness: you can taste every element in every dish, even if you can't name them all. The superlative green papaya salad is a perfect balance of tart, spicy, salty, and herbal; chicken-pineapple-curry soup sounds shocking, but turns out splendidly. Complex curries are smooth and sublime. The marinated beef with peanuts and five-spice sauce is aromatic with star anise, while the humble pan-fried catfish is heavenly enough to be a slumming angelfish in disguise. The short wine list is smart and affordable. ■ *Larkin and Eddy; (415) 775-5979; 631 Larkin, San Francisco; $$; beer and wine; AE, MC, V; no checks; lunch Mon–Fri, dinner every day.*

Postrio ★★ Postrio—co-owned by Southern California superstar chef Wolfgang Puck—is a madly insistent slice of Hollywood, with superglitz decor by the ubiquitous Pat Kuleto, slightly weird flavor combinations by chefs/co-owners Anne and David Gingrass, and the perpetual hope of catching sight of some celeb at the next booth. One enters through a spiffy street-level bar that serves tapas and little Puckish pizzas to the unreserving; from there a grand staircase—on which everybody can at least *play* a star—descends into a crowded, pink-lighted dining room with expensive-looking paintings. As for the food, some of it works for all of the people, but most of it only works for some of the people—and all of it costs a fortune. Dishes adopt fashionable Asian postures or a chic California formula of fish or fowl bedded on strong greens and dressed with a sweet fruit sauce, vinaigrette, or salsa: Chinese-style roast duck with mango sauce on arugula, roasted salmon with almond-black-pepper crust on warm spinach salad, scallops and potato chips with soy vinaigrette on baby greens. Those who like this sort of thing (and there are a lot of them) adore Postrio.

Desserts—the likes of vanilla crème brulée with fresh berries or caramel pear tart with Grand Marnier crème fraîche—are lavish. Execution is usually competent (although when crowds are thickest, slip-ups are not unknown). The wine list is excellent, the service professional, and the reservations essential, except for breakfast. ■ *Post between Mason and Taylor; (415) 776-7825; 545 Post St, San Francisco; $$$; full bar; AE, DC, DIS, MC, V; no checks; breakfast Mon–Fri; lunch Mon–Sat, dinner every day, brunch Sat–Sun.*

Rasselas ★★ San Francisco has three or four Ethiopian restaurants; Rasselas (named after the Samuel Johnson hero) is the only one without a ton of atmosphere—there's nary a mask, fan, nor woven wall hanging. It's also the only one with authentic home-style cooking and a live jazz club every night. The cook blends seasonings sent by her Ethiopian kinfolk into her incendiery nitr kibbeh—the spiced, clarified butter upon which Ethiopian cuisine is based. Her doro wat—a dark, savory chicken stew—and the fierce and fiery kitfo (Ethiopian steak tartare) are among the best selections. There's a tempting vegetarian platter, and a citrusy lettuce, tomato, sweet onion, and mild lentil salad and tongue-searing split-pea purées. Most importantly, Rasselas' injera—the spongy pancake that serves as a spoon for the food—is remarkably light and succulent. A glass of tej—a thick Ethiopian honey wine—suits the food and should be tried, at least once. ■ *California at Divisadero; (415) 567-5010; 2801 California St, San Francisco; $$; full bar; AE, DC, DIS, MC, V; no checks; dinner every day.*

Ristorante Ecco ★★ Despite its elusive location in an alley whose name nobody knows (pssst, it's Jack London Street), Ristorante Ecco has been a hit since opening day in early 1992. Part of its instant success lies with the hungry hordes of magazine editors who work nearby and can't all squeeze into nearby South Park Cafe. An even greater attraction, though, is the sensuous Italian fare of chef Steven Lucas, whose dishes are simultaneously fresh and earthy, rustic and urbane—and always intelligent. Lunchtime brings sparkling salads, including a clever antipasto plate with grilled eggplant, roasted peppers, marinated mozzarella bocconcini and prosciutto wrapped in greens; thin-crusted New Yorkish pizzas; tasty panini (baguette sandwiches) filled with elaborate textures such as chicken with goat cheese spread, and grilled eggplant, roasted red peppers, and provolone. Heartier choices include the justly popular stracotto al vino rosse (fork-tender, wine braised short ribs, topped with a sassy parsley pesto, set on a toothsome stew of white beans, onion, and tomato). Dinner offers more venturesome options such as a light, fresh linguine with pears, pecans, and Gorgonzola, a rich array of desserts, and a marginally better chance of getting a table without a reservation. The decor is airy, simple, and chic-free, but the tall windows in the main dining room afford a marvelous view of the action in the park. The wine list is mainly Italian. ■ *South Park near 3rd St, (415) 495-3291; 101 South Park St, San Francisco; $$; beer and wine; MC, V; no checks; lunch Mon–Fri, dinner Mon–Sat.*

Ristorante Milano ★★ This popular Northern Italian pasta spot has recently changed ownership, but the newcomers were smart not to fix something that wasn't broken. There have been no alterations in the elements that have made this cheerful little bistro a terrific success—the service is as exuberant as ever, the food just as sensual. Starter courses are pleasant and fresh (among the best are the garlicky eggplant appetizer and the grilled chicken livers), but house-made pasta is Milano's greatest glory. When lasagne is on the menu, order it: Milano's version is a revelation—(one version employs porcini mushrooms). Risotto and polenta are no less exemplary. Save room for the creamy-dreamy tiramisu, widely considered the best pick-me-up in San Francisco. ■ *Pacific at Hyde; (415) 673-2961; 1448 Pacific Ave, San Francisco; $$$; beer and wine; MC, V; no checks; dinner Tues–Sun.*

San Francisco Bar-B-Que ★★ While the East Bay holds the winning hand on Tennessee-style BBQ joints, San Franciscans have an ace in the hole with the San Francisco Bar-B-Que—a fabulous Thai grill where you can get not only the familiar but also the unusual. For instance, try the barbecued squid (in a light, luscious sauce that's delicately sweet and very slightly hot), chicken, meatballs, lamb, oysters, salmon, and frogs' legs. Lord have mercy! Nor is that all: the barbecued duck noodles are moist, aromatic, and totally habit-forming, as are some of the vegetarian barbies. Instead of the standard accompaniments of white bread and potato salad, marinated carrot salad and a ball of sweet, sticky rice come with each dish. Eat in or order to-go; either way, this Potrero Hill anomaly is an institution. There are two other branches called Thai Bar-B-Que: one on Van Ness at Turk, (415) 441-1640, and another in Berkeley; (510) 549-1958. SF Bar-B-Que is the original. ■ *18th St between Missouri and Texas; (415) 431-8956; 1328 18th St, San Francisco; $; beer and wine; no credit cards; no checks; lunch Tues–Sat, dinner Tues–Sun.*

South Park Cafe ★★ Whatever *je ne sais quoi* gives Parisian bistros their delightful character can be found in Gallic profusion at the South Park Cafe. Maybe it's the rack of newspapers

near the door that always includes *Le Figaro* and the *International Herald Tribune*. Perhaps it's the chalkboard listing 50 reasonably priced wines. It might be the impeccably prepared croque-monsieur (grilled ham and cheese) or the sinfully rich boudin noir (blood sausage) served with sautéed apples and perfect french fries. Across the street, South Park itself—one of the nicest, smallest, least known commons in the city—beckons with green grass, picnic tables, and swings; if the weather's nice, you can take your order and *déjeuner sur l'herbe*. It's a great spot for a quiet breakfast if you like baked goods and strong coffee. At lunch, the staffs of several nearby magazines adopt the place. The place quiets down again after 5pm.
■ *South Park near 3rd St; (415) 495-7275; 108 South Park, San Francisco; $$$; beer and wine; MC, V; checks OK; breakfast, lunch, Mon–Fri; dinner Mon–Sat.*

Taqueria San Jose ★★ Similarly to the history of the pizza—which pretends to be Italian but achieved its apotheosis in America—the taqueria is more a Mexican-American phenomenon than it is puro Mexicano. Sure, you can get delicious tacos and burritos in Mexico, but they're generally quite simple: stewed or roasted meat doused with salsa and wrapped in a soft tortilla—nothing like the deluxe varieties obtainable in the US. The San Jose is the best of the multitude of San Francisco's taquerias. It's also the prettiest: gorgeous paintings grace every surface, including the huge glass windows that flood the airy dining room with light. At the San Jose you can range beyond standard charcoal-grilled steak and stewed pork fillings to sample beef tongue, head, and brains. Bored with burritos? Try quesadillas Suizas, pollo adobado, a carne asada plate, or any one of the outstanding tostadas. Five incendiary salsas inhabit every table. ■ *Mission St off 24th St; (415) 282-0203; 2830 Mission St, San Francisco; $; beer only; no credit cards; no checks; breakfast, lunch, dinner every day.*

Tommaso's ★★ For more than 50 years, this small, noisy, jam-packed pizzeria (which until 1971 was called Lupo's) has served the only pie in San Francisco good enough to earn the approval of know-it-all New York pizza fascists. Sure: if you want *California* pizza, you can go to Pauline's in the Mission District and snack on home-grown designer greens while waiting for a pie topped with pancetta and goat cheese, or you can get pizza with a cornmeal crust at Vicolo near the Civic Center. But for classicists, Tommaso's is the end of the line. And that line starts forming at 6:30pm and doesn't thin out until well past 9pm. The pizzas are baked in a wood-burning oven, so they have smokey, crisp, medium-thick crusts that don't soak through and fresh toppings. Pizza's not the only thing. The delicate marinated vegetable plates (peppers and string beans are tops) make great starters, and superb calzones or gently steamed fresh clams work well for those not interested in a piece of the pie. ■ *Kearny at Broadway; (415) 398-9696; 1042 Kearny St, San Francisco; $$; beer and wine; MC, V; no checks; dinner Tues–Sun.*

Yank Sing ★★ Living on the edge of the Pacific Rim has its advantages. For example, Bay Area dim sum is probably the best in the United States. Harbor Village offers some of the best dim sum that money can buy—trouble is, you need a *lot* of money to get it. Yank Sing's fare, on the other hand, is as good as any dim sum you'll get in Hong Kong and reasonably priced to boot. Servers wander past your table with carts bearing steamer-baskets, bowls, and tureens. If you want some, nod. Yank Sing serves all the basic types (pot stickers, spring rolls, har gow, siu mai, bao with fillings of aromatically seasoned minced meat or shellfish wrapped in thin skins made of flour dough, as well as vegetables like bean curd or green peppers). Barbecued chicken—wrapped in tinfoil, moist and aromatic— is a house specialty, not to be missed; the adventurous should nibble on the likes of braised chicken feet, duck webs, jellyfish, and sea cucumber. ■ *Stevenson St off 1st St; (415) 541-4949; 49 Stevenson St, San Francisco; $$; beer and wine; MC, V; no checks; lunch Mon–Fri.* ■ *427 Battery St, San Francisco; (415) 781-1111; $$; full bar; AE, MC, V; no checks; lunch every day.*

Yuet Lee Seafood Restaurant ★★ When savvy San Franciscans want ultrafresh seafood in sensitive preparations that emphasize flavors—and don't want to pay the world—they school to the new Yuet Lee's on Valencia Street. It's less crowded than the too busy, too bright, too ugly branch on Stockton Street in Chinatown. Among the most acclaimed Hong Kong–style dishes are clams or crabs in black bean sauce, salt-and-pepper fried squid or prawns, catfish clay pot with pork and tofu, and anything with geoduck. Vegetable dishes—stir-fried tender greens, asparagus with preserved bean curd, eggplant with pork—are splendid too, and (for a genuine Hong Kong late-night or late-breakfast restorative) the soothing, habit-forming rice porridge called jook. (Skip the batter-fried stuff that comes with mayonnaise.) The Stockton Street branch is particularly notorious for surly service—so go early or late and order just a few dishes at a time, lest your whole dinner get slapped onto your table at once. ■ *26th St and Valencia; (415) 550-8998, 3601 26th St, San Francisco;* ■ *Stockton and Broadway; (415) 982-6020; 1300 Stockton, San Francisco; $$; beer and wine; no credit cards; no checks; lunch, dinner Wed–Mon.*

Ya Ya Cuisine ★★ Just a few steps from Golden Gate Park, Ya Ya is a handsome little cafe with a Babylonian mural on one wall. The Iraqi chef/owner Yahya Salih creates an aromatic cuisine, mingling California attitudes with the exuberant pantry of his homeland—an altogether terrific mix. Meals begin with flatbread and a dipping sauce of olive oil, sesame seeds, and fresh herbs; Salih's rich, brilliant signature dish is an appetizer of mini-raviolis stuffed with dates and topped with Parmesan cheese, walnuts, olive oil, and roasted red peppers. Bourek (stuffed phyllo) is filled with a cheese-spinach combo or with seasoned ground beef napped in a date and sesame sauce. The mustardy herb salad and oniony fatoosh may be too fierce for most palates. The most successful entrées are roast chicken stuffed with cashews, raisins, and rice; a gorgeous vegetarian dolma; and an aromatic lamb biriani with lemony cream sauce. Portions are large and service is terrific. ■ *9th Ave at Lincoln Way; (415) 566-6966; 1220 9th Ave, San Francisco; $$; beer and wine; MC, V; local checks only; lunch, dinner Tues–Sun.* ■ *397½ 8th St, San Francisco; (415) 255-0909.*

Zuni Cafe ★★ Before it got famous, Zuni was a tiny Southwestern-style lunch place in a low-class neighborhood. When Chez Panisse alumna Judy Rodgers came on board as chef and co-owner, the cafe became so popular that it had to move down the block to larger quarters. Today, with its roaring bar and exposed-brick dining room, it's nearly as quintessential a San Francisco institution as Herb Caen and sourdough bread. It wouldn't be stretching the truth to claim that one reason the neighborhood started improving was Zuni's Mediterranean-influenced upscale food—as divinely simple as only the supremely sophisticated can be: a plate of mild, house-cured anchovies sprinkled with olives, peppers, and Parmesan; the gone-to-heaven polenta with delicate mascarpone cheese, a small roasted chicken on a delicious bed of Tuscan bread salad, a grilled rib-eye steak accompanied by sweet white corn piqued with fresh basil. If it's after 10pm, you can get one of the best burgers in town. Service is first-rate for regulars and those who resemble them. Reservations are essential. ■ *Market at Gough; (415) 552-2522; 1658 Market St, San Francisco; $$$; full bar; AE, MC, V; checks OK; breakfast, lunch, dinner, late supper Tues–Sun.*

Bohemian Cigar Store ★ The real San Francisco treat isn't Rice-a-Roni but a leisurely cappuccino in North Beach with street dramas unfolding outside the coffeehouse window. When residents of the city's liveliest neighborhood want sustenance along with caffeine, they head for the historic Bohemian Cigar Store (aka Mario's). This well-windowed, threadbare cafe—erstwhile haunt of aged Sicilians and beat poets—now finds women in biker gear elbow-to-elbow with aerobics outfits and long graying male ponytails swinging alongside shiny short ones. Mario's main dishes are huge, hot, delicious sandwiches (the meatballs and the eggplant are especially popular) dressed with grilled onions and luscious melted cheese on triangles of crisp, puffy, scallion-laced focaccia from the nearby Gloria Bakery (home of the world's best sacripantina, incidentally). Numerous Italian and California wines are served by the glass at refreshingly affordable prices; and the cappuccino (the best outside of Italy) has won numerous awards. ■ *Columbus at intersection of Union and Powell; (415) 362-0536; 566 Columbus Ave, San Francisco; $; beer and wine; no credit cards, no checks; breakfast, dinner Mon–Sat; lunch every day.*

Campo Santo ■ Pozole ★ These twin fantasy tacquerias started by talented chef Jesse Acevedo turn traditional Mexican fare into fabulous concoctions. Newer and larger Campo Santo (holy ground) has a Dias de los Meurtes dining room decorated with costumed papier-mâché skeletons and pastel tombstones inscribed with messages of desperate love and the brevity of life. The food is cheerfully inauthentic interpretations of Yucatan cuisine—fresher, lighter, less spicy, and a lot sweeter than you'd get in Merida. Try the quesadilla San Juan with smoked chicken, chorizo sausage, and diced potatoes, or the pseudo burrito that pairs rock shrimp with nopal cactus pads. Equally colorful Pozole offers more recognizable (though lighter and larger) antojitos including a chicken tamale with the airiest of masa (Mexican polenta). ■ *Columbus south of Broadway; (415) 433-9623; 240 Columbus, San Francisco; $; beer and wine; local checks only; lunch, dinner every day.* ■ *Market between Noe and Castro; (415) 626-2666; 2337 Market, San Francisco; $; beer and wine; no credit cards; no checks; lunch Fri–Sun, dinner every day.*

Campton Place Restaurant ★ This elegant but unexciting hotel dining room is a longstanding favorite of many local and national food critics—whether because or in spite of its exorbitant prices, we can't say. It's remained a critics' pet even though the original chef—the celebrated Bradley Ogden—has departed; his replacement, Jan Birnbaum, has maintained the idea of an upscale version of American hotel dining-room food in a highly stylish setting. Somewhat emblematically, a breadbasket filled with measured portions of divine cornbread sticks, miniature biscuits, and whole-wheat nutbread starts your meal in promising fashion (and indicates why this is a favorite breakfast site for the local power elite), but once the basket is empty, it stays that way. On the whole, appetizers are more amusing than entrées; for main dishes, individual elements are usually quite pleasant—for instance, the barbecued shrimp comes in a very nice buttery sauce—but most plates carry an assortment of elements that seem to have just met and aren't at all sure they want to be friends. Execution can be problematic, too: a small heap of potatoes may contain some undercooked slices as well as some oversalted ones. Service is cool and sometimes neglectful, but—to give credit where due—the wine list is well-chosen and fairly priced. ■ *Stockton between Post and Sutter;*

(415) 781-5155; 340 Stockton St, San Francisco; $$$; full bar; AE, DC, DIS, MC, V; no checks; breakfast, lunch Mon–Sat; dinner every day; brunch Sun.

Cha Cha Cha ★ This tiny, wildly colorful, Caribbean-looking cafe serves spicy, whimsical food to a diverse and hip clientele (expect to see any type of hair from crew cuts to long and graying to Day-Glo chartreuse with spikes). The eclectic and constantly changing menu has its deepest roots in the Spanish Caribbean—with touches of Africa, Spain, Louisiana, and Brazil. The finest offerings are found among the vibrantly seasoned tapas: don't miss the cold mussels, the garlicky chicken wings, or the occasional dish of stewed or roasted meat. Friendly (and frequently gorgeous) servers responsibly tell you which dishes turned out best on any given night. To wash them down, try one of the several available sangrias. Cha cha cha! ■ *Haight at Schrader; (415) 386-5758; 1805 Haight, San Francisco; $$; beer and wine; no credit cards; no checks; lunch Mon–Sat, dinner every day.*

Clown Alley ★ This local burger landmark—a block from North Beach in the shadow of the TransAmerica Pyramid—is really three restaurants in one. From noon to 2:30pm, its outdoor patio is a favorite spot for lunchtime workers and neighborhood businesspeople to sit in the sun and dawdle over a burger. Evenings, the inside dining room becomes a lively teen hangout. From midnight to 3am...well, if you've always wanted to visit Mars but can't wait for NASA to sell you a ticket, try Clown Alley in the wee hours. Many a North Beach bar-crawl makes a midnight pit stop here for a life-saving snack. No matter what time you go, the eats are great. The burgers are charcoal-grilled over an open fire; the fries are low on grease and high on flavor; the shakes, floats, and malts are thick but not too thick. The jukebox is loaded with oldies, and this close to North Beach, good strong espresso and cappuccino are staples. ■ *Columbus at Jackson; (415) 421-2540; 42 Columbus, San Francisco; $; beer only; no credit cards; no checks; breakfast, lunch, dinner every day.*

Fina Estampa ★ At Fina Estampa, Japanese-Peruvian chef/co-owner Gus Shinzato produces sensitive, reasonably authentic renditions of the food of his coastal hometown, Lima. His anticuchos (marinated beef-heart kabobs) would pass muster anywhere in Peru. Rigorously trimmed, absolutely tender, and highly aromatic, they're accompanied by a fiery, cilantro-laden dipping sauce. Fried calamari and ceviche are usually good maritime introductions, but on our last visit, the cold mussels with a zippy onion-tomato dressing had been overcooked and the papas huancaina (an Andean-style potato salad) were sauced with an overly salty local feta. Seafood predominates: the jalea de pescado offers wonderful deep-fried calamari, shrimp, squid, and fish in a light tempuralike batter; parihuela de mariscos is a tasty tomato-laden seafood stew; and the paella marinera is a giant portion of mixed seafood and tomato-drenched rice. Our only serious complaint with Fina Estampa is that the pepper level in the food—customarily intense in its native habitat—has been tuned down for norteamericano palates. Fina Estampa is located in one of the worst neighborhoods in the city. ▪ *Mission between 19th and 20th streets; (415) 824-4437; 2374 Mission, San Francisco; $$; beer and wine; MC, V; no checks; lunch, dinner Tues–Sun.*

Mandalay ★ Like most Burmese restaurants—even in Burma—Mandalay is Chinese owned. Nevertheless, the Chinese food here is at best mediocre; it's the Burmese specialties for which many return. Appetizers include samu sa (deep-fried dumplings filled with minced-meat curry) and satays (chewy, fish-sauce-marinated kabobs accompanied by ethereal peanut sauce). An intriguing salad is the lap pat dok (tangy fermented tea leaves with a complex host of accompaniments), while the fascinating Burmese soups are equally flavorful. Alluring entrées include the chin mong jaw (minty-sour Burmese greens—grown by the owner—served with prawns in hot-sour sauce) and the Mandalay squid (served on tender spinach with a similar sauce). Overall, alas, the execution can be uneven and the seasonings, traditionally very hot, are wildly inconsistent. Order one course at a time or the servers may bring all the dishes at breakneck speed and then try to make room at the table by whisking away the ones you haven't finished yet. ▪ *California St at 6th Ave; (415) 386-3895; 4348 California St, San Francisco; $; beer and wine; DIS, MC, V; no checks; lunch, dinner every day.*

LODGINGS

Campton Place Kempinski Hotel ★★★★ Almost as soon as Campton Place reopened after extensive (and expensive) restoration in 1983, its posh surroundings, stunning objets d'art, superlative service, and elegant accommodations began swaying the loyalties of the carriage trade away from traditional San Francisco hotels. The gallery-like lobby with its domed ceiling, miles of marble, crystal chandeliers, and striking Asian art work and contemporary paintings is worth the price of admission. Upstairs, while the guest rooms could be a bit bigger, they couldn't be more beautiful: Henredon armoires, custom chairs, handsome work desks, and remote-control lighting create a pervasive air of luxury. The Travertine marble bathrooms come with wall telephones, terrycloth robes, hair dryers, and bath scales. For the best views, ask for one of the larger double deluxe corner rooms on the upper floors ($270). No matter what room you choose, you'll get a daily newspaper of your choice, assistance with packing and unpacking, laundry, dry cleaning, immediate pressing, and an overnight shoeshine; a concierge will make any and all of your arrangements (a reservation for the hotel's downtown limousine?); and room service will deliver whatever you wish from the highly regarded Campton Place Restaurant (see review). There's also an alluring rooftop garden and a full line of business services. ■ *Between Sutter and Post near Union Square; (415) 781-5555, toll free (800) 647-4007; 340 Stockton St, San Francisco, CA 94108; $$$; AE, DC, DIS, MC, V; checks OK.*

Four Seasons Clift Hotel ★★★★ The individually designed rooms in this resplendent 17-story mansion sport beautiful hardwood furnishings, marbleized bathrooms, and robes, hair dryers, stocked bars, phones with computer jacks, and TVs (VCR on request). The higher the floor, the better the view. Downstairs, music from a grand piano floats through the Redwood Room (one of the most perfect bars in the city) with its carved redwood panels polished to a high gloss, art deco lamps, and gorgeous Gustav Klimt prints. The lobby glows with sparkling chandeliers and fine Oriental rugs. All the usual high-class perks are here: 24-hour room service, complimentary limo, and exemplary business aids encompassing everything from an interpreter to freshly typed manuscripts. Guests can exercise in the small gym or—for a fee—use the extensive fitness center nearby at the Nikko. The Clift's VIK (Very Important Kids) program offers younger guests (and their grateful parents) a staggering array of services, ranging from pacifiers, strollers, and diapers for babies to Disney movies, video and board games, and activities for older kids. With conditioning like this, another generation of enthusiastic Clift guests is virtually guaranteed. ■ *1½ blocks from Union Square at Taylor; (415) 775-4700; 495 Geary, San Francisco, CA 94102; $$$; AE, DC, MC, V; checks OK.*

The Mansions Hotel ★★★★ The Mansions is so entertaining, so mind-boggling, so only-in-San Francisco a place that you could spend your whole vacation just touring the ground floors. Housed in two Victorian mansions—a Queen Anne and a Greek Revival–style—the Mansions features the largest collection of Benny Bufano sculptures in the world, flamboyant murals (including a pig mural), stuffed life-size figures perched on chairs in various parlors, and a billiards room with a doll house stretching the length of one wall. Friday and Saturday evenings, guests are regaled with downright bizarre entertainment in the music room. The guest rooms live up to the grandeur and giddiness. Each is individually decorated with antiques and collectibles; most have fireplaces; many have private terraces; some have ceilings that slant all the way to the floor. All the rooms in the main house have fresco portraits of the historical figures for which they were named. (Check out the

Empress Josephine with its private sundeck, stocked fridge, and Louis XIV antiques.) Breakfast is a bountiful English-style feast, with crumpets, bangers, eggs to order, fresh-squeezed juice, fruit, and cereal. A fixed-price dinner is available most evenings in the spectacular stained-glass dining room. The staff is good humored. ■ *Between Laguna and Buchanan in Pacific Heights; (415) 929-9444; 2220 Sacramento St, San Francisco, CA 94115; $$$; AE, DC, DIS, MC, V; checks OK.*

The Sherman House ★★★★ Turn-of-the-century luminaries like Lillian Russell and Enrico Caruso used to sing in the private, three-story recital hall of this 1876 mansard-roofed Victorian mansion, home of musical instrument magnate Leander Sherman. Remodeled seven years ago, Sherman House is more splendid than ever, thanks to new owners Manou and Vesta Mobedshahi (also responsible for the refurbished and far more affordable Savoy). The stunning decor is based on a French Second Empire motif with fine antiques and choice custom replicas, richly upholstered sofas and chairs, and gorgeous carpets covering polished hardwood floors. The huge, sky-lit recital hall still has a grand piano, but now serves as a sumptuous lobby with a chateau bird cage that houses a bevy of musically minded finches. The 14 guest rooms feature bronze Dore chandeliers, brocaded bed hangings, rich tapestries and fabrics, and beautifully crafted wainscoting. Most of the rooms have wood-burning marbleized fireplaces. Ask for one of the upstairs rooms with their broad bay windows, cushy window seats, and fine views of the bay. For the utmost privacy, take the cobblestone path through the English-style garden out back (complete with gazebo, fountains, and greenhouse) to the carriage house.

Concierge and valet services are as superb as you'd expect them to be at these prices, and 24-hour room service commands gourmet fare from the house restaurant (recently the focus of favorable attention for chef Donia Bijan's French-California cuisine). Dinner is served in a handsome dining room with a hearth and view of the bay, while a leaded-glass solarium offers a delightful setting for breakfast. Afternoon tea occurs in an upstairs gallery decked out like a Second Empire salon. ■ *Between Fillmore and Webster, 1 block above Union St; (415)563-3600; 2160 Green St, San Francisco, CA 94123; $$$; AE, DC, MC, V; checks OK.*

The Archbishops Mansion ★★★ This stately Belle Epoque mansion, built in 1904 for San Francisco's Archbishop, is an exercise in Victorian splendor and excess: a three-story staircase winds beneath a gorgeous stained-glass dome while redwood Corinthian columns, crystal chandeliers, Oriental carpets, and gorgeous antiques create an aura of almost papal splendor. The 15 rooms and suites, each named after a famous opera, are richly decorated with lush fabrics and embroidered linens. All have canopied beds and private baths with stacks of plush towels and French-milled soap. Most rooms have fireplaces; some have parlors and sitting areas; many have fine views. The cabbage-rose-colored Carmen Suite has a claw-footed tub in front of the fireplace *in the bathroom* and a fine sitting room—with *another* fireplace— and view of Alamo Park across the way. You can breakfast in bed on scones and croissants, then trip downstairs in the afternoon for wine in the French parlor (the grand piano once belonged to Noel Coward). The concierge can arrange limo service to the nearby Opera House or Symphony Hall (the neighborhood is unsavory enough to make foot touring unwise). ■ *Corner of Fulton and Steiner across from Alamo Park; (415) 563-7872, toll free (800) 543-5820; 1000 Fulton St, San Francisco, CA 94117; $$$; AE, MC, V; checks OK.*

Hotel Nikko San Francisco ★★★ George Bush probably gets a kick out of the Hotel Nikko: the executive services include a document shredder, and room locks use computer-coded cards that are reprogrammed after each visit. The irreverent can easily get the giggles in this state-of-the-art, 25-story Japanese tower, but the fact of the matter is that its amenities and services are unbeatable, particularly for business people. The executive center has everything a corporate traveler could conceivably require: personal computers, translation services, VCRs, shipping services to the Pacific Rim, and conference rooms. Suites range in price from $375 all the way up to $1,500 (for a setting fit for a shogun). Savvy travelers often negotiate attractive bargains when occupancy is down. The best rooms in the house are located on the uppermost stories with special computer-coded elevator access (George probably likes that, too) and a private lounge with spectacular views. The guest spa is a knockout, with a swimming pool, fitness center, sauna, Jacuzzi, soaking tubs, and massage services available (for a fee) on-site or in your room.

San Francisco

Lodgings

The penthouse-level Benkay Restaurant has private tatami dining rooms and serves noteworthy Japanese cuisine. (The kaiseki dinner—delectable small dishes originally designed to accompany the tea ceremony—is a delight.) Japanese chefs from the Benkay also pitch in at Cafe 222 on the second floor during breakfast and lunch, so the California cuisine offered there is now counterbalanced by Asian specialties (including a Japanese-style breakfast). ■ *Corner of Mason and O'Farrell near Union Square; (415) 394-1111, toll free (800) 645-5687; 222 Mason St, San Francisco, CA 94102; $$$; AE, DC, MC, V; checks OK.*

Huntington Hotel ★★★ The doorman always seems delighted to see you, the staff treats you like a favored guest, and the small lobby is a refined retreat with antique bookcases, leafy palms, comfortable wine-colored sofas, and choice objets d'art (no conventioneers or confused tourists here). Perhaps that's why both Old World and New Wave aristocracy are drawn to this intimate luxury hotel. Security, as you might expect, is superb—and accommodations are spacious and lavish, with imported silks, 17th-century paintings, and stunning views of the city and bay. The individual rooms and suites are sufficiently distinctive to have appeared in *Architectural Digest*. Each one has its own decor—some feature traditional antiques, while others have modern leather sofas and marble bars. Guests are treated to formal tea or complimentary sherry and a morning paper. Valet parking and room service is available, along with a full range of business services. The hotel's restaurant, The Big Four (named after a quartet of railroad tycoons), offers seasonal continental cuisine in a dining room harking back to the age of robber barons. ■ *Top of Nob Hill across from Grace Cathedral; (415) 474-5400, toll free (800) 227-4683 in California, (800) 652-1539 outside California; 1075 California St, San Francisco, CA 94108; $$$; AE, DC, DIS, MC, V; checks OK.*

Inn at the Opera ★★★ This splendid small hotel is ideally situated for art, opera, ballet, and symphony lovers. Built in 1927 as a haven for visiting opera stars, it's furnished with antiques, art work, and lush bouquets. The 48 rooms range from small-but-stylish to grand. All are individually decorated with pastel colors and antiques (the armoires have sheet music lining the drawers) and stocked with the usual glut of amenities. Valet service—packing and unpacking on request, overnight shoe-shine, complimentary light pressing on arrival—is included, and an attentive concierge can wangle last-minute opera or symphony tickets and arrange for a limo. There's a complete line of business and secretarial services, with 24-hour room service available from the Act IV Restaurant downstairs. Just as lovely as the hotel, with a fireplace and live piano, the Act IV offers outstanding continental fare and is open late for symphony goers who want to unwind with a late-night meal or linger over Cognac and luscious desserts. ■ *Between Gough and Franklin near Opera House, Davies Hall; (415) 863-8400, toll free (800) 423-9610 inside California, (800) 325-2708 outside California; 333 Fulton St, San Francisco, CA 94102; $$$; full bar; AE, MC, V; checks OK; breakfast every day, lunch Mon-Fri, dinner every day, brunch Sun.*

Mandarin Oriental ★★★ There's a Chinese good-luck symbol inlaid on the marble lobby floor of this alluring hotel, and guests are offered jasmine tea and Thai silk slippers upon arrival. Owned by a hotel group with elegant hostelries in Hong Kong, Bangkok, and Singapore, this Mandarin occupies the top 11 stories of the First Interstate building. Its padded, embroidered elevators with painted silk scrolls whisk you above the city to a pair of towers linked by a glass-walled skyway. Decorated with fine Asian art, the spacious rooms have handsome blond-wood furniture, astonishing views, and marble bathrooms with telephones and deliciously deep tubs. The Mandarin rooms have floor-to-ceiling windows above the tubs. (The room rates don't vary according to scenery, so request a bay view.) Amenities include full business services, same-day laundry, valet, and complimentary shoeshine. Silks—a critically acclaimed restaurant with whimsical watery murals and a menu that's shifted from California-French to California-Asian with good results. ■ *Financial district between Pine and California; (415) 885-0999, toll free (800) 622-0404; 222 Sansome St, San Francisco, CA 94104-2792; $$$; AE, DC, MC, V; checks OK.*

The Ritz-Carlton, San Francisco ★★★ This ritzy, white-columned newcomer is already beginning to rival the city's top establishments. Valets in top hats rush to park your car as a gaggle of natty, nimble young men leap to usher you through the entryway. (We find this a bit annoying, but some folks are wild about the Ritz for just this type of display.) The lobby is spectacular—a series of enormous, high-ceilinged lounges with huge floral bouquets, lots of art and antiques, and crystal chandeliers. The Lobby Lounge offers afternoon tea to live piano accompaniment. The upscale-generic guest rooms could use a bit more personality, but they're loaded with amenities from spiffy marble bathrooms to honor bars and plush terrycloth robes. Some (though not many) have wonderful views of the city and the bay. Business services abound, with a range of conference and meetings rooms and a limo to whisk you off to the financial district or Union Square. The fitness center—open to all guests—has an indoor pool, whirlpool, and sauna. With luck, the irritating staff attitudes—we've experienced everything from snippy to abrupt to indifferent—will improve with time; otherwise, things looks promising for the birth of what could be a new grand SF hotel. ■ *At California St on Nob Hill; (415) 296-7465, toll free (800) 241-3333; 600 Stockton, San Francisco, CA 94108-2305; $$$; AE, DC, DIS, MC, V; checks OK.*

Sheraton Palace Hotel ★★★ Redolent with memories of more romantic times, this grand old hotel built in 1875 (and, like most everything else in town rebuilt after 1906) has housed such luminaries as Thomas Edison, D.H. Lawrence, Amelia Earhart, and Enrico Caruso, as well as the usual array of presidents and aristocrats. Hoping to attract a similarly high-class clientele in the future, the management has poured $150 million into restoring the Palace to its original robber baron

splendor. Unfortunately, after all the breathtaking decor downstairs, the 552 spiffed-up rooms are a tad generic. The hotel provides the full range of amenities: concierge, 24-hour room service, overnight valet, fully equipped business center, plus a new, palm-embellished health club with an exercise room and a stunning white-tiled lap pool. The Palace has an embarrassment of riches when it come to restaurants: The fabulous Garden Court is famed for its Sunday brunch and elegant afternoon teas; the Pied Piper Bar sports a fine Maxfield Parrish mural; Kyo-Ya offers an authentic Japanese restaurant with an eight-seat sushi bar; and the masculine Maxfield's, with its stained-glass ceiling, serves traditional San Francisco grill fare. ■ *On Market St at Montgomery BART stop; (415) 392-8600, toll free (800) 325-3535; 2 New Montgomery St, San Francisco, CA 94105; $$$; AE, DC, DIS, MC, V; checks OK.*

The Bed-and-Breakfast Inn ★★ San Francisco's first bed and breakfast maintains the convincing illusion that it's a charming old English inn in a picturesque mews somewhere in Cornwall. Two adjoining Victorians—graced with twining ivy, bright red geraniums in window boxes, and a birdhouse bobbing from a tree out front—offer 10 enchanting guest rooms, each individually decorated with antiques, floral prints, and appealing personal touches. The sunny penthouse has a living room, kitchen, latticed balcony, and spiral staircase leading to a bedroom loft. (Ask for a room that opens directly onto the alluring back garden.) You can take your simple breakfast in your room, in the garden, or in the diminutive English tea room. ■ *In a cul-de-sac off Union St between Buchanan and Laguna; (415) 921-9784; 4 Charlton Court, San Francisco, CA 94123; $$$; no credit cards; checks OK.*

The Inn at Union Square ★★ Tucked discreetly amid posh shops on busy Post Street, the small street-level foyer of this elegant, European-style bed and breakfast doesn't do justice to the lovely accommodations upstairs. Each floor has its own little lobby, complete with fireplace, where guests are treated to a light breakfast of croissants and fruit, an afternoon tea with cakes and crisp cucumber sandwiches, and evening pleasures of wine and hors d'oeuvres. The 30 rooms—individually decorated by San Francisco interior designer Nan Rosenblatt—have Georgian furniture, canopy beds, huge vases of fresh-cut flowers, and a profusion of floral-print fabrics; some have fireplaces and sitting rooms. The penthouse suite has a whirlpool bath, sauna, fireplace, fridge, powder room, and wet bar. The one drawback here is that you trade tranquility for a view. The quietest rooms, facing away from Post Street, have a fine view of the neighbors' brick wall. Amenities include room service, 24-hour concierge, valet parking, overnight shoeshine, morning paper, one-day laundry, and such nice options as a baby-sitter or specially packed picnic lunches. ■ *Between Mason and Powell, half a block from Union Square; (415) 397-3510, toll free (800) AT-THE-INN; 440 Post St, San Francisco, CA 94102; $$$; AE, DC, MC, V; checks OK.*

The Hotel Majestic ★★ An orgy of Victorian grandeur, this five-story Edwardian, close to Japantown, was one of San Francisco's earliest grand hotels. Marble steps and beautiful beveled glass doors lead to a magnificent lobby. Upstairs, the guest rooms are individually decorated with a mixture of French Empire and English antiques. For maximum charm, request a Deluxe "03"—these have fireplaces, full canopy beds, and wonderfully spacious, semicircular bay windows. Concierge services, business facilities, valet service (same-day laundry), limo, and valet parking (for a fee) are all available. Check out the tiny lounge with a 19th-century French mahogany bar and a fascinating framed butterfly collection displayed on deep, turquoise-blue walls. ■ *Corner of Sutter and Gough; (415) 441-1100, toll free (800) 869-8966; 1500 Sutter St, San Francisco, CA 94109; $$$; full bar; AE, DC, MC, V; no checks; breakfast, lunch Tues–Fri, dinner every day, brunch Sat–Sun.*

Jackson Court ★★ Tucked away behind a brick archway and a white-trellised garden courtyard, this three-story brownstone is located right in the heart of the exclusive Pacific Heights neighborhood. The living room of this sedate manse is comfortably grand, with Oriental carpeting, gilt-framed mirrors, and a striking, oversized fireplace adorned with figures of wind sprites and storm gods. The blissfully quiet guest rooms have handsome architectural details, pleasantly spare high-quality antiques, telephones, and private baths; some have fireplaces. We particularly like the luxurious Garden Court Suite with its hand-crafted wood paneling and cabinets, period furnishings, and colorful garden. After a light breakfast downstairs, hit the shops of Union Street. ■ *Corner of Jackson and Buchanan in Pacific Heights; (415) 929-7670; 2198 Jackson St, San Francisco, CA 94115; $$$; AE, MC, V; checks OK.*

Petite Auberge ★★ Petit Auberge is a romantic, quasi-French country inn with terra-cotta tile floors, Pierre Deux fabrics, oak furniture, lace curtains, and dried floral wreaths decking the walls. You'll also see lots of teddy bears on parade, vintage children's toys on shelves and mantels, and a carousel horse cantering in the lobby—not everyone's taste, for sure. In truth, the rooms here are sweet, decorated in the same vein as the lobby with inviting window seats. Nightly turndown includes a chocolate and a rose on your pillow. Guests are supplied with terrycloth robes; shoes are shined overnight and delivered with the morning paper. A generous buffet breakfast is served downstairs in a cutesy breakfast room with French doors opening onto a small garden. In the afternoon, you can drink tea in a lounge where a horde of teddy bears on gingham-checked couches face off with a row of rabbits arranged in front of the fireplace. Guests who have the urge to work can avail themselves of the business services at the White Swan two doors down. ■ *Between Taylor and Mason near Union Square and Nob Hill; (415) 928-6000; 863 Bush St, San Francisco, CA 94108; $$$; AE, MC, V; checks OK.*

Savoy Hotel ★★ Originally built in 1913 for the Panama-Pacific Exposition, this seven-story relic had degenerated into a shabby budget hotel before Manou and Vesta Mobedshahi worked their magic on this remnant from San Francisco's past. Now it's a posh little French country inn with a gorgeous facade of richly veined black marble, beveled glass, mahogany, and polished brass, situated in the heart of the theater district, just 2½ blocks from Union Square. The 83 guest rooms are beautifully appointed with Toile de Jouy fabrics, cotton Matelasse bedspreads, imported Provence-style furnishings, feather beds, goose down pillows, and fresh-cut flowers. The most tranquil rooms are on the northeast corner, farthest from the traffic noise and facing a rear courtyard. Guests are nurtured with a simple breakfast of granola, fresh fruit, and bagels with lox and cream cheese—and afternoon tea and sherry.

Downstairs, sample an array of fresh shellfish from the handsome marble seafood bar at the Brasserie Savoy. Chef Mark Meyer works wonders with seafood dishes (Pacific sole on a bed of apples and celery root; succulent squid salad) and traditional grill fare. ■ *Between Taylor and Jones; (415) 441-2700, toll free (800) 227-4223; 580 Geary St, San Francisco, CA 94102; $$$; full bar; AE, DC, DIS, MC, V; checks OK; dinner, late supper every day.*

Victorian Inn on the Park ★★ Serendipitous architecture and an extraordinarily friendly and helpful staff make this 1897, three-story Victorian one of the most entertaining bed and breakfasts in town. (The staff actually scrawls "Good Morning" in colored chalk on the pavement at the bottom of the steps.) Interesting architectural details such as alcoves under the eaves, a bay window with seating nook, and a deck overlooking the park make each of the rooms unique. All rooms have private baths (from claw-footed tubs to tiled, sunken baths), plus telephones and TVs available on request. Traffic along the Panhandle (a narrow extension of Golden Gate Park) can be pretty noisy, so the third-floor rear rooms are best). All rooms have decanters of sherry and honor baskets full of goodies for casual snacks or late-night nibbling. ■ *Corner of Lyon and Fell opposite the Panhandle; (415) 931-1830; 301 Lyon St, San Francisco, CA 94117; $$$; AE, DC, MC, V; checks OK.*

The Washington Square Inn ★★ Located in the midst of lively North Beach opposite Washington Park, this architecturally nondescript building conceals a truly delightful European-style bed and breakfast. San Francisco designer Nan Rosenblatt created the attractive interior, filling the rooms with English and French antiques, whimsical art work, and bright flower-print drapes and down comforters. Ask for one of the large corner rooms with their sitting areas, bay windows with window seats, and views of Washington Square. Every morning you'll find a local newspaper (and the *Wall Street Journal*) and your freshly polished shoes placed discreetly outside your door. The lobby has inviting seating around the fireplace. You can nosh your way through the day here: croissants and wonderful Graffeo coffee in the morning; a bountiful afternoon tea of crisp cucumber sandwiches, cheese and pâté with crackers and cornichons, cookies, and cakes; and wine and hors d'oeuvres at night. ■ *Stockton and Filbert in North Beach; (415) 981-4220, toll free (800) 388-0220; 1660 Stockton St, San Francisco, CA 94133; $$$; DC, MC, V; checks OK.*

The White Swan Inn ★★ It doesn't get any more adorable than this—unless you opt for the sister inn, Petite Auberge, a few doors away. The theme here harkens back to a cozy English garden B&B, embellished with teddy bears piled on steps, shelves, and couches, as well as a carousel horse that cavorts in the small lobby. The 1903 building with curved bay windows has 27 spacious rooms charmingly decorated with art prints, comfy armchairs, antiques, and floral print wallpaper. Some have inviting window seats tucked into the bays under folding white shutters; each has a fireplace, fridge, TV, phone, and wet bar. For peace and quiet, ask for a room in back overlooking the sunny, tree-lined courtyard. Guests are treated to a big breakfast, morning paper, afternoon tea, and home-baked cookies. The adjacent library has antique furnishings, a roaring fire, and yet more teddy bears. ■ *Between Taylor and Mason near Union Square and Nob Hill; (415) 775-1755; 845 Bush St, San Francisco, CA 94108; $$$; AE, MC, V; checks OK.*

The Albion House Inn ★ This elegant European-style pensione, owned by the same folks who operate the popular Inn on Castro, caters to a mostly gay clientele. With its cheery red facade and white window boxes full of flowers, this turn-of-the-century rooming house is one of the best deals in San Francisco. Nine lovely guest rooms are decked out with fresh flowers, intriguing framed prints, brass beds with a variety of whimsical canopies, an eclectic mix of bamboo and wicker, and some handsome antiques. TV is available on request (though clearly considered déclassé). Unlike most B&Bs, people actually do socialize in the roomy living room with its exposed redwood beams and massive marble fireplace (kept ablaze all night). A grand piano awaits the touch of a talented guest. Breakfast downstairs at the long dining table, then quiz omniscient host Jan de Gier about nearby restaurants and points of interest. Albion House is within walking distance of fashionable Hayes Street and Civic Center restaurants and a short MUNI trip to the Castro. ■ *Between Oak and Page, 1½ blocks above Market and Van Ness MUNI station; (415) 621-0896; 135 Gough St, San Francisco, CA 94102; $$; AE, MC, V; checks OK.*

Edward II Bed & Breakfast Inn ★ This three-story English country–style B&B located in the fashionable Marina District has flying banners, window boxes, and white shutters that are surprisingly effective at muffling traffic noise—though you're still better off with a room away from Scott and Lombard streets. A central staircase with a high stained-glass window ascends to second- and third-story rooms with floral-print wallpaper, nice antiques, and a wonderful assortment of painted wicker furniture. The charm of the decor succeeds in making even the smallest room seem cozy rather than cramped. The accommodations range from classic pensione (pedestal sink in the room, bath down the hall) to larger, lovelier rooms with queen-size beds and private baths. The lovely Brambles Suite has a four-poster canopy bed, wicker armchairs, a wet bar in an oak cabinet, a TV in an antique armoire, and a deliciously deep bathtub. A light breakfast is included. ■ *Corner of Scott and Lombard in Marina District; (415) 922-3000, toll free (800) 473-2846; 3155 Scott St, San Francisco, CA 94123; $$; AE, MC, V; checks OK for advance reservations.*

Inn on Castro ★ This convivial bed and breakfast, catering to the gay and lesbian community, has developed an ardent following—hence the entertaining collection of hearts on the sideboard in the hallway, left behind by a legion of wistful patrons. Housed in a restored Edwardian, the hostelry is run by the same folks who operate the Albion House Inn. The exterior is painted in a pleasing medley of blue, rose, and green, with gilded details and dentils; the interior has contemporary furnishings with lots of art work and elaborate flower arrangements. There are eight guest rooms ranging from a small single to two suites. Avoid the sunny but noisy rooms facing Castro Street. Some rooms have decks and fireplaces; TVs are available but noses wrinkle if you ask for one. Breakfast includes fresh fruit salad, homemade muffins, fruit juice, and the likes of scrambled eggs, French toast, or pancakes. ■ *½ block above Market and Castro St MUNI station; (415) 861-0321; 321 Castro St, San Francisco, CA 94114; $$; AE, MC, V; checks OK.*

The Inn San Francisco ★ If you like San Francisco but can't stand the fog, take a trip out to Inn San Francisco in the Mission District, center of San Francisco's Mexican-American

community and the sunniest neighborhood in town. There's
nothing very Spanish about this Italianate Victorian: the decor
in the huge double parlors downstairs is resolutely turn-of-the-
century Anglo. The 16 rooms in the main house continue the
period theme with antique furniture and lots of elaborately
beautiful details from marble sinks to polished brass fixtures.
Ask for one of the larger featherbed rooms in the main house.
Some rooms have private spas, fireplaces, and redwood hot
tubs—though we prefered to soak in the hot tub in the white-
lattice gazebo in the garden or to relax on the rooftop sundeck.
After breakfast, explore the neighbor botanicas and Mexican
bakeries. ■ *Mission District between 20th and 21st; (415) 641-
0188, toll free (800) 359-0913; 943 S Van Ness Ave, San
Francisco, CA 94110; $$$; AE, DC, MC, V; checks OK.*

Moffatt House Bed and Breakfast ★ Thanks to Ruth Mof-
fatt's warm hospitality, good humor, and wealth of tips about
local attractions, this unpretentious B&B at the edge of Golden
Gate Park is indeed warm and friendly. What Moffatt House of-
fers is simple, comfortable rooms with shared baths. There are
four guest rooms in the original two-story blue stucco Edwar-
dian house and four more rooms in a flat across the street.
Most of the rooms have TVs; some have outdoor balconies
(though this isn't the sunniest part of town). A full breakfast is
included with the bargain room price. Parking is a breeze com-
pared to the rest of the city and the Haight-Ashbury district is
just around the corner. Ruth also rents a four-room guest house
at 6th Avenue and Kirkham for $125 per night, three night min-
imum. ■ *Between 5th and 6th avenues, 1 block from Golden
Gate Park; (415) 661-6210; 431 Hugo St, San Francisco, CA
94122; $; MC, V; checks OK.*

The Monte Cristo ★ The Monte Cristo was once just another
in a long list of floral Victorian B&Bs, but new owner George
Yuan has put his own creative (and a bit wacko) stamp on the
decor. It's hard to say just what appealing—albeit odd—com-
bination of Victoriana and quirky decor you'll find behind the
velvet-curtained doorways in this 1875 hotel. The rooms in this
former bordello and speakeasy are cluttered with an assort-
ment of porcelain figurines and random kitsch. TV is available
on request—but you'll find enough magazines (like 20 years of
National Geographics) to keep you entertained for months.
The Laurel Campus of UCSF is right across the street and the
shops and restaurants on Sacramento Street are just two blocks
away. ■ *Corner of Presidio and Pine, 1 block from California
St; (415) 931-1875; 600 Presidio Ave, San Francisco, CA
94115; $$; AE, DC, DIS, MC, V; no checks.*

Nob Hill Inn ★ Any well-appointed bed and breakfast ought to
have a resident ghost or two. This elegant establishment—
housed in a four-story Edwardian built in 1907—has three: a

wispy woman who likes to linger in room 12, a well-bred gentleman in room 21, and a winsome lass who wanders about this Louis XIV- and XV-styled inn at whim. Take the etched-glass English elevator upstairs to the rose and pink, antique-filled guest rooms with color TVs tucked discreetly inside the wardrobes and armoires. Some of the bathrooms are real museum pieces. The low-end rooms are a bit close for comfort, so splurge on a suite. Downstairs, ceiling fans turn slowly in the wicker-styled parlor and dining nook. You can sip wine among the racks in the atmospheric wine cellar or lounge on the sundeck and in the hot tub on the roof. What with Nob Hill's afternoon tea and nightly turndown service, it's little wonder that even the ghosts don't want to leave. ■ *At Pine and Taylor one block below Nob Hill; (415) 673-6080; 1000 Pine St, San Francisco, CA 94109; $$$; MC, V; no checks.*

The Queen Anne Hotel ★ This appealing four-story Queen Anne mansion is pleasantly spare and masculine for a Victorian bed and breakfast. A mahogany staircase with a stained-glass skylight leads upstairs to the simple, high-ceilinged rooms. All the rooms have remote-control TVs, modern baths with hair dryers, and private telephones with bathroom extensions; as prices go up, features like wood-burning fireplaces, bay windows, sitting areas, and marble-top wet bars do too. The enormous drawing room—a bit stark despite the large fireplace—has some appealingly bizarre furniture, including an ornately carved throne, pulpit, and pew. The small library-bar in the rear contains neither books nor booze but does offer a nice seating nook with comfy armchairs in front of the fireplace. A breakfast of pastries (and a morning paper) can be taken downstairs or in bed, and there's the usual tea and sherry routine in the afternoon. Concierge, valet, and laundry services are available and the friendly staff is helpful and good humored. ■ *Corner of Sutter and Octavia near Japan Center; (415) 441-2828, toll free (800) 227-3970; 1590 Sutter St, San Francisco, CA 94109; $$$; AE, DC, MC, V; checks OK.*

The Red Victorian Bed & Breakfast Inn ★ To say that this isn't a typical tourist hotel is putting it a tad lightly. Fifteen years ago, owner Sami Sunchild (her real name) sort-of-accidentally acquired this sprawling 1904 Victorian hotel in the heart of the Haight-Ashbury district, world capital of '60s hippiedom. The 18 upstairs guest rooms have sinks and telephones but most share New Age bathrooms: one is mirrored with strips of twinkling lights and another has a fish tank suspended over the toilet and a sunken tub. The guest rooms themselves are equally as intriguing: one includes feline-inspired art work, an elaborate scratching post the length of the room and—should you wish—a real live cat; another has a horde of dolls and mannequins peering through a side window

San Francisco

Lodgings

(not recommended for the nervous or those who've watched too many "Twilight Zone" reruns). All we can say about the deluxe Peacock Suite is that it carries the concept of exoticism to previously uncharted levels. In an attempt to create her own little global village, Sami has also added an eco-bazaar, a coffeehouse, a computer network center, a meditative art gallery, and a seminar space. In the morning, guests are encouraged to hang loose and get in touch with fellow guests at the breakfast table. ■ *2 blocks from Golden Gate Park; (415) 864-1978; 1665 Haight St, San Francisco, CA 94117; $$; AE, MC, V; no checks.*

Union Street Inn ★ Owner Helen Stewart has lent such a personal touch to the period decor, and the staff here is so convivial, that this comfortable bed and breakfast wins the prize for overall ambience. While this two-story Edwardian is situated amid the bustle of trendy Union Street, it's high above the traffic up a steep set of stairs. The five guest rooms and a deluxe carriage house have private baths (ranging from Jacuzzis to claw-footed tubs), telephones, and TVs on request (for those who can't survive the Edwardian era without a media fix). Each room has its own theme and color scheme, enhanced by bay windows, patterned wallpaper, Oriental carpets, antiques, and comforters. Rooms facing the back garden are the best. The parlor downstairs is furnished with a fireplace and a beguiling range of period finds; Charlie—the resident golden retriever—adds to the relaxed atmosphere by lolling about on lazy afternoons. Start your day with a breakfast in the beautiful English garden. ■ *Between Steiner and Fillmore; (415) 346-0424; 2229 Union St, San Francisco, CA 94123; $$$; AE, MC, V; checks OK.*

SAUSALITO

RESTAURANTS

Sushi Ran ★★★ Far enough from the main drag to keep the tourists at bay, this small but very charming sushi bar is where the crème de la crème of Sausalito go for their raw-fish fix. The clientele is strictly local (you may even rub elbows with one of Marin's many rock stars) and everyone seems to know everyone else. The sushi is sublime: the kamikaze roll reveals glisteningly fresh yellowtail tuna, bright flying fish roe, and crunchy green onions. The portions are huge, and the preparation exquisite. Sample some of the more unusual creations like spider rolls (a tempura soft-shell crab in a hoso-maki roll). Rice-wine lovers will delight in the long list of sakes. ■ *Next door to the Marin Theater; (415) 332-3620; 107 Caledonia St, Sausalito; $$$; beer, wine, and sake; AE, DIS, MC, V; no checks; lunch Mon–Fri, dinner every day.*

Casa Madrona Hotel and Restaurant ★★★★ Casa Madrona is something very special. From its small lobby, you take an elevator up a steep, gorgeously landscaped hillside studded with cottages, open decks, and two main buildings—a 120-year-old Victorian at the top of the property and a 10-year-old white stucco affair below—connected by meandering brick pathways. The best room in the Victorian is number 308, the Fireside Room, a nostalgia fest with a fireplace, original mahogany mantle piece, and a private verandah, but in general the rooms in the newer buildings are more posh. With its pretty pine furniture and rose-colored walls, Rose Chalet (#204) has a great view of the yacht harbor from bed, plus a fireplace and private deck. Right below is the slightly less expensive Lord Ashley's Lookout with its understated English nautical motif and another fine view of the water. Artists check into the Artist's Loft complete with easel, paints, and brushes, as well as a fireplace, large deck, and bay view. For the ultimate in privacy, look to the cottages: Upper and Lower Casitas (rooms 403 and 404) have gigantic decks.

The food is as stratospheric as the view. Chef Kirke Byers' innovative California cuisine takes advantage of seasonal produce and fish (salmon with crisp soba noodles and orange-tamari wasabi; Byers' succulent Australian lamb loin cooked with artichokes, new potatoes, olives, and fresh herbs). For the ultimate view, make a reservation for the glassed-in dining room. ■ *Downtown Sausalito; (415) 332-0502; 801 Bridgeway, Sausalito, CA 94965; $$$; full bar; AE, MC, V; no checks; breakfast, dinner every day, lunch Mon–Fri.*

Sausalito

Lodgings

Alta Mira Hotel ★★ With its singular view of Sausalito harbor, Angel Island, and San Francisco, this beautiful Spanish colonial hotel with red tile roofs has the feel of a stately, old-fashioned seaside inn. There are 14 rooms in the main building and 15 spaces in cottages scattered throughout the grounds. In general, rooms in the main building are more elegant than those in the cottages (room 8 has the best view of the harbor), but we still prefer the rustic cottages amidst the grove of redwood trees because of their funky sense of history and casual approach to decor—a nice change from the relentless poshness of many Marin inns. The two-story Honeymoon Cottage has its own fireplace in the living room and a great deck with the bay beyond. The food at the Alta Mira is basic continental but decent enough. At sunset, head for cocktails on the deck. ■ *125 Bulkley Ave, just up the hill off Princess; (415) 332-1350; Mail: PO Box 706, Sausalito, CA 94966; $$$; full bar; AE, DC, MC, V; checks OK; breakfast, lunch, dinner every day.*

TIBURON

RESTAURANTS

Guaymas ★★★ This lively, anything-but-run-of-the-mill Mexican restaurant turns out specialties rarely found north of the border. From one direction in the dining room (decorated with Mexican art and playful arrangements of produce) you can watch the goings-on in the huge open kitchen. From the other you can scan the San Francisco skyline. For salad, try the tender, marinated slices of cactus with onion and Mexican cheese or the pico de gallo, a large plate of fresh fruit served with wedges of lime and a dish of hot red pepper (mix the lime and pepper to make a dip). Once your palate's warmed up, move onto don cacahuate (grilled chicken breast served with a mild, chunky peanut-serrano chile sauce). Great margaritas. ¡Ole! ■ *Tiburon Harbor at the ferry landing; (415) 435-6300; 5 Main St, Tiburon; $$; full bar; AE, DC, MC, V; no checks; lunch, dinner every day.*

MILL VALLEY

RESTAURANTS

Buckeye Roadhouse ★★ If a restaurant on a road is a roadhouse, then the Buckeye is a roadhouse—but really it seems that this place can't decide whether it wants to be a diner, a 1930s hunting lodge, or just a '90s yup joint. The noisy dining room has lofty ceilings, mahogany beams, deco drinking horn chandeliers, a massive stone fireplace covered with brass, and animal candlestick holders. (We advise you to take in the scene from the quieter balcony dining room upstairs.) The Buckeye's eclectic American cuisine is whimsical and first-rate: oysters broiled with spinach and aioli; a memorable caesar; and the tangled mound of thin, sweet onion rings in a feathery batter with homemade ketchup. The marinated grilled pork chop with pickled watermelon is always sweet and tender. The outstanding seafood hash, with big chunks of pink shrimp, comes with a side of hot, velvety corn bread pudding. Finish up with one of the nostalgia-fest desserts, including pineapple upside-down cake, butterscotch brulée, or s'more pie, an astoundingly realistic rendition of the campfire classic. ■ *At the Stinson Beach–Mill Valley exit off Hwy 101; (415) 331-2600; 15 Shoreline Hwy, Mill Valley; $$; full bar; DC, DIS, MC, V; no checks; lunch Mon–Sat, dinner every day, brunch Sun.*

Jennie Low's Chinese Cuisine ★★ Jennie Low, author of *Chop Stick, Cleaver and Wok*, that '70s-era bible of Chinese cooking, opened this fine Chinese restaurant in pastoral Mill Valley in 1987. Inspired by Cantonese, Mandarin, Hunan, and Sichuan cooking styles, Low's very personal cuisine features simple, home-style dishes with velvety textures and sweet, subtle sauces. Start out with the rich rainbow chowder, a colorful mix of shrimp, crab, baby corn, green onions, carrots, and cellophane noodles. For entrées, anything preceded by the word Jennie is a guaranteed treat: Jennie's crisp Sichuan green beans are lightly sautéed in a spicy garlic sauce; Jennie's scallops and asparagus matches crisp, glistening vegetables with scalding, barely cooked scallops in a sweet black bean sauce. This place is always jammed, but Low and her family do a fine job managing the chaos. ■ *Mill Creek Plaza, downtown Mill Valley; (415) 388-8868; 38 Miller Ave, Mill Valley; $; beer and wine; AE, MC, V; local checks only; lunch Mon–Sat, dinner every day.*

LODGINGS

Mountain Home Inn ★★ On top of the world and not too many miles from town, the Mountain Home Inn has one of the best views in the Bay Area, encompassing the Pacific Ocean, San Francisco Bay, the East Bay hills, and—on a clear day—Mount Diablo at the edge of the Central Valley. The inn has 10 guest rooms decorated in what might best be described as Marin modern, furnished with plush carpeting and wood-paneled walls. All the rooms have private baths. The standard rooms have pleasing decks, but opt for a deluxe with a fireplace, deck, and oversize tub with Jacuzzi jets. The food at the Mountain Home restaurant is light and appealing; breakfast is included with your stay. The place becomes a madhouse on weekends when hikers descend for après-trek snacks after a long day on nearby Mount Tamalpais or in Muir Woods. ■ *Call for directions; (415) 381-9000; 810 Panoramic Hwy, Mill Valley; $$$; beer and wine; MC, V; local checks only; lunch, dinner Tues–Sun.*

CORTE MADERA

RESTAURANTS

Il Fornaio ★★ Il Fornaio is a classy Bay Area chain of bakeries and cafes well known for its brick-oven breads and pizzas. The Corte Madera branch is a full-blown restaurant with muted lighting, terra-cotta and marble floors, a garden patio, and the requisite fleet of brick ovens turning out impeccable nouveau pizza and calzone with thin, crisp, wood-smoke-flavored crusts. (Try the sausage and roasted red pepper, or the duck sausage, broccoli, and ricotta.) Equally irrestible is the juicy, spit-roasted chicken rubbed with sage, rosemary, and garlic. A basket of warm Il Fornaio breads comes with every meal. For dessert, opt for one of the fresh Italian cakes, like the creamy tiramisu with zabaglione and mascarpone, or get a sampler tray of Italian cookies to go. ■ *Paradise Dr exit W off Hwy 101;*

(415) 927-4400; 223 Corte Madera Town Center, Corte Madera; $$; full bar; AE, MC, V; no checks; breakfast, lunch Mon–Fri, dinner every day, brunch Sat–Sun.

Island Cafe ★★ When the Island Cafe first opened next door to a tanning salon in the mid-'80s, healthy food was considered boring and a tan was considered healthy. Times do change. Island Cafe's subtly tropical dining room has bright white walls decorated with soothing pastel paintings, a huge fish tank, and an open prep area with counter seating. Its health-conscious California cuisine includes an array of vegetarian entrées (firm, flavorful tofu brochettes marinated in tamari, white wine, and herbs) plus meat dishes such as rich, savory Moroccan lamb stew; a pleasantly sagey breast of chicken with mushrooms; and grilled flank-steak fajitas made from naturally raised local beef. The outstanding caesar salad features bite-size bits of romaine in a light anchovy dressing topped with crunchy, homemade, garlic herb croutons. The pies and bread pudding are homemade and the cinammon iced tea sparkles. ■ *In Market Place shopping center; (415) 924-6666; 59 Tamal Vista Blvd, Corte Madera; $$; beer and wine; MC, V; no checks; lunch Tues–Fri, dinner Tues–Sun, brunch Sat–Sun.*

LARKSPUR

RESTAURANTS

Lark Creek Inn ★★★★ When famed Bay Area chef Bradley Ogden took over the Lark Creek Inn in 1989, he was faced with the unique task of creating a restaurant around a well-established local landmark. This beautiful century-old Victorian, nestled in a stately redwood grove along Lark Creek, demanded a strong presence—and Ogden, fresh from worldwide acclaim at San Francisco's Campton Place, was equal to the challenge. He soon opened what many believe to be the best restaurant in Marin County. There's a strong sense of familiarity with the American food here and at the same time you'll be wildly surprised. There is no doubt that many of Ogden's creations give a nod to the roots of American cooking, with a healthy dash of California ingenuity. For instance, Ogden marries a tender Yankee pot roast with roasted vegetables and onion-chive dumplings; he roasts a free range chicken with a tang of lemon and herbs; and he grills the thickest, most perfect pork chop and enhances it with sweet braised red cabbage. Instead of potatos au gratin, you might find root vegetable au gratin. And if shoestring potatoes are on the menu beside succulent grilled rabbit, they will probably be made from sweet potatoes. For dessert, a feather-light angel food cake is blessed with blood orange sherbet and strawberry compote. The turnover might be strawberry-rhubarb but Ogden adds a scoop of lemon ice for a kick.

The glass ceiling creates a wonderfully airy atmosphere and the extensive windows give the restaurant a chance to show off the gardens outside (a great treat for a summer Sunday brunch which features fresh corned beef hash, banana-sour cream pancakes, and home-fried doughnuts). This is a world class dining destination in a classic Marin County setting. Reservations highly recommended; walk-in seating is available at the bar and on the garden patio. ■ *On the northern edge of downtown Larkspur; (415) 924-7766; 234 Magnolia Ave, Larkspur; $$$; full bar; AE, DC, MC, V; no checks; lunch Mon–Fri, dinner every day, brunch Sun.*

Coyote Grill ★★★ It's standing room only at this festive Southwestern cafe. With its large open kitchen and miniscule dining room filled with colorful original paintings and howling papier-mâché coyotes, there's often a crush of hungry patrons in the entryway. Dinner starts with a basket of puffy, triangular sopaipilla with honey butter. Move on to a spate of mouthwatering appetizers such as papitas (deep-fried potato thins), a wonderfully creamy guacamole, and a thin but flavorful chipotle-chile-infused gazpacho. Dinners run the gamut from the world's most perfect burrito to tender grilled snapper in Veracruzano sauce or Yucateca fresca (grilled chicken strips, onions, and tomatoes in a homemade flour tortilla with cilantro pesto and a sweet, thin Mexican sour cream). The three handmade corn pinch-pots (called gorditas) are filled with black beans, queso fresco (Mexican cheese), and a choice of meats. There's a good selection of beers—both Mexican and boutique—and a short but well-chosen wine list. ■ *In the center of Larkspur's downtown shopping district; (415) 924-7232; 531 Magnolia Ave, Larkspur; $$; beer and wine; MC, V; no checks; dinner Tues–Sun.*

Remillard's ★★ Remillard's cavelike dining room (literally the inside of a giant kiln of the former Greenbrae Brick Company) occupies a long, horseshoe-shaped brick passageway lit by torchlike lamps on the wall and dotted with linen-draped tables with fresh white roses. It would be nice if the food was as dramatic and experimental as the setting. Instead, it's simply run-of-the-mill French, tempered by a California concern for fat content. There are standouts: the roast chicken marinated in olive oil and bay leaves and served with Parisian potatoes and julienne of roast duck; and the fabulous half salmon—layered and rolled with scallop mousse and thin fillet of halibut, cooked in parchment, and served with a cream and Pernod sauce. Dinners come with string beans and a delightful little phyllo satchel stuffed with crab, sautéed spinach, and shiitake mushrooms. Service is attentive but peculiar. We strongly recommend the exceedingly rich, nonrubber, chocolate soufflé. ■ *½ mile E of Hwy 101 on Sir Francis Drake; (415) 461-3700; 125 E Sir*

Francis Drake Blvd, Larkspur; $$$; full bar; AE, MC, V; no checks; lunch Mon–Fri, dinner every day, brunch Sun.

Marin Brewing Company ★ This popular spot—located in the pleasant Larkspur Landing shopping center across from the ferry terminal—has been booming ever since it opened a few years ago. The main event is beer—fresh, delicious micro-brewed ales and stouts such as the light, golden Mount Tam Pale Ale or the hoppier Albion Amber Ale. The kitchen turns out crisp, pleasantly smokey, one-person pizzas and enormous cal-zones from a wood-burning Italian oven, as well as a delicious Oriental salad (lots of grilled chicken, rice noodles, and fresh red bell peppers on a bed of organic lettuces). The scrumptious grilled sausage and chicken sandwiches on crunchy French rolls are sloppy but good. Avoid the overcooked fish 'n' chips. There's usually a rowdy dart game going on and live music on weekends; even in the restaurant section, the din from the bar can make conversation with your dinner partner difficult. ■ *W side of Larkspur Landing center; (415) 461-4677; 1809 Larkspur Landing Circle, Larkspur; $; beer and wine; DIS, MC, V; no checks; lunch, dinner every day.*

SAN ANSELMO

RESTAURANTS

Bubba's Diner ★★ Bubba's actually looks like the real thing—red Naugahyde booths and a classic black and white tile floor. Sisters Cathy Allinger and Laura Allinger-Leavitt's diner fare is, however, healthier than the real thing. For breakfast, try the heavy, whole grain, orange juice pancakes or the crisp potato pancakes with green onions and garlic, served with sour cream and applesauce. The crisp turkey hash combines fresh roasted turkey, scallions, and potatoes. For lunch and dinner, choose from a healthy selection of salads (go for the crunchy, orange-tinged, almond chicken salad), roast turkey and pastrami sand-wiches, or a burger with blue cheese and jalapeños. Finish up with a tart slice of blackberry or strawberry-rhubarb pie, or a real ice cream milk shake or malt. ■ *Downtown San Anselmo; (415) 459-6862; 566 San Anselmo Ave, San Anselmo; $; beer and wine; MC, V; no checks; breakfast, lunch, dinner every day.*

Caffe Alberto ★★ Located along San Anselmo's antique row (one of Marin's best window-shopping neighborhoods), su-premely tasteful Caffe Alberto serves some of the best Italian cuisine around. White enamel fans spin slowly above a dining room decorated with tasteful pencil drawings, ceramic masks, and Swedish ivy. Begin with a toothsome grilled radicchio salad in a gutsy vinaigrette, some prosciutto and melon, or a simple bowl of stracciatella with delicate egg ribbons and bright spinach. For dinner, try the capellini with slices of salmon in a meatless marinara or the smooth, cheesy, chicken-mushroom risotto. Lighten up afterwards with a delicious fruit ice in a hollowed-out orange cup. Nice Italian wine list, too. ■ *On Sir Francis Drake, 2 blocks E of Miracle Mile; (415) 453-3025; 208 Sir Francis Drake Blvd, San Anselmo; $$; beer and wine; MC, V; no checks; dinner Mon–Sat.*

Easy Street Cafe ★ With its high beamed ceilings, green plants, and wacky urban archeological artifacts, this open-front cafe in the Red Hill Shopping Center is one of Marin's favorite breakfast stops, especially among weary parents (a second branch is in Larkspur). Easy Street has a toy-filled play area where you can drop the kids while you savor your morning latte. (If you actually want to feed the little monsters, the waitress will bring a big box of toys to your table.) The morning repast here is anything but juvenile. You can get eggs Benedict in its classic form—or topped with bacon and tomato; sautéed vegetables, or snow crab, green onions, and creamed spinach. The delicious egg scramble with feta and dill or the special dried apricot and mixed nut waffle perk up the morning. Good espressos and fresh-squeezed juices, too. ■ *Red Hill Shopping Center; (415) 453-1984; 882 Sir Francis Drake Blvd, San Anselmo.* ■ *Corner of Dougherty and Magnolia; (415) 924-9334; 574 Magnolia, Larkspur; $; beer and wine; AE, MC, V; local checks only; breakfast, lunch every day, dinner Mon–Sat.*

KENTFIELD

RESTAURANTS

Half Day Cafe ★★ It's hard to believe that this beautiful, soothing cafe was once a mechanic's garage. There's not a trace of grime left in the light, barnlike dining room with its flourishing greenery, big open kitchen, and sunny patio. The Half Day started out as just that—breakfast and lunch. Breakfast opens with fluffy omelets, vast, currant-studded scones, and fine, dark espresso; lunch offers fresh salads and sandwiches to the ravenous hordes from the College of Marin across the street. As with most good businesses, half days never stay that way. Dinner is where chef Donna Eichhorn really shines: prawn rolls (large, fresh shrimp with oriental herbs rolled in big sheets of rice paper and served cold with a spicy sauce); grilled mahi-mahi in a soy-cilantro marinade; slow-baked, country-style meat loaf. It'll make you wish all days were half days. ■ *Across from College of Marin; (415) 459-0291; 848 College Ave, Kentfield; $; beer and wine; MC, V; checks OK; breakfast, lunch Mon–Fri, dinner every day, brunch Sat–Sun.*

▮

50

Reviewers for the Best Places series accept no free meals or accommodations; the books have no sponsors or advertisers.

RESTAURANTS

Ma'Shauns ★★★ T-shirts and suits are equally acceptable at this French-California cafe. Ma'Shauns' simple but classy dining room features mauve linen tablecloths, tiny white lamps, and cut-crystal wine glasses. Start with the barbecued prawn and grilled duck salad with a mango vinaigrette. The heavenly baked Saint André cheese appetizer comes in a phyllo shell with lemon-thyme sauce and roasted garlic. The menu changes seasonally, but you'll usually find succulent meat and seafood dishes with light, slightly sweet sauces. Look for the spicy-as-you-want-it half chicken in a tequila-orange-red-chile zing, or the butter-tender filet mignon in a demiglace of truffles, shallots, and brandy. From the limited but divine dessert menu, choose the black and white chocolate mousse in a swirl of berry purée and white chocolate sauce. The wine list is overpriced, so try the house wines by the glass or bring your own and pay a corkage. ■ *Downtown San Rafael, 1 block W of Lincoln on 4th; (415) 453-9481; 857 4th St, San Rafael; $$$; beer and wine; AE, DIS, MC, V; local checks only; lunch Mon, Wed–Fri, dinner Wed–Fri.*

San Rafael

Restaurants

Royal Thai ★★★ Royal Thai is a requisite for Thai aficionados weary of the commonweal of Thai classics now available in almost every neighborhood in the Bay Area. All of Pat and Jimie Disyamonthon's dishes are expertly prepared and beautifully presented, but what really distinguishes this restaurant is its range. In addition to thick coconut-milk curries and perfect phad Thai, it also turns out a kaleidoscope of beef, chicken, and seafood sautés sparkling with ginger paste, chile oil, fresh mint and basil, garlic, and nuts. Roll up the miang kham appetizer—dried shrimp, peanuts, small chunks of fresh lime, red onion, baked coconut, ginger, and chile—in butter-lettuce leaves and dip in a sweet tamarind sauce. Or explore the som-tum salad, a wonderfully textured combination of shredded green papaya mixed with carrots, green beans, and ground peanuts. ■ *3rd and Irwin; (415) 485-1074; 610 3rd St, San Rafael; $$; beer and wine; AE, DC, MC, V; no checks; lunch Mon–Fri, dinner every day.*

Carlo's ★★ Remember what Italian restaurants looked like before the invention of faux-marble tables and textured stucco? Carlo's does. Dark enough to make you squint and covered with plastic flowers, colored lights, and mementos of the old country, this festive eatery owned by Carlo and Marie Avola still draws enthusiastic crowds. Mama Marie will tell you what and what not to eat—and not everyone in your party will get the same advice! The pot roast marinated in red wine and vegetables with a heavy dose of cloves gets the most returnees. Other good bets include Carlo's chicken (topped with finely chopped carrots, celery, onions, and lemon rind and served with a lemon-wine sauce) or the porcini agnolotti (bite-sized raviolo filled with savory chopped porcini mushrooms in a creamy tomato sauce with slivered wild mushrooms). All portions are huge and the bread very tempting, but do save room for Carlo's version of frozen zabaglione with crushed chocolate cookies and a splash of Marsala. ■ *Corner of 4th and G streets; (415) 457-6252; 1700 4th St, San Rafael; $$; beer and wine; AE, MC, V; no checks; dinner Tues–Sun.*

Las Camelias ★★ The sprightly, authentic Mexican cuisine dished up at this adobe-walled cafe comes straight from the recipe file of owner/chef Gabriel Fregoso's mother in Jalisco. Grab a chair at one of the wooden tables, and start in with the ceviche. The caesar-like ensalada casa features a mound of romaine topped with tomatoes, tiny flecks of anejo cheese, avocado, and corn chips. For dinner, try the arroz Mexicana (a giant plate of rice stir-fried with shrimp, scallops, chicken, and fresh salsa) or the delicious pollo en mole—a clean, unmuddied version of the chocolate-based classic. The unadventurous will find well-prepared versions of familiar Mexican favorites on the back of the menu. ■ *Lincoln between 3rd and 4th; (415) 453-5850; 912 Lincoln Ave, San Rafael; $; beer and wine; AE, MC, V; no checks; lunch Mon–Sat, dinner every day.*

Anita's Kitchen ★ This is the Thai version of soul food. Although this was Marin's first Thai restaurant, there are now dozens—including many more subtle and refined. But no one else offers owner Anita Chantrapai's vast portions and rich, knock-your-socks-off flavors. Start with the creamy tom kah kai soup with chicken, coconut milk, lemon grass, and red curry paste, or a refreshingly biting seafood salad with large fresh shrimp, delicate squid, chiles, and basil. Curries are the mainstay of the menu: the bold massamun chicken curry comes in a thick, rich red sauce with wafts of coconut and cinnamon; tamer palates should select the milder yellow curries. The best noncurry choice is the tender but searing fresh prawns and squid in roasted chile paste. ■ *Central San Rafael exit, 1 block E of Hwy 101 on 4th St; (415) 454-2626; 534 4th St, San Rafael; $$; beer and wine; MC, V; no checks; lunch, dinner Mon–Sat.*

Chrysanthemum ★ Housed in an appealing Spanish-style building on San Anselmo's Miracle Mile, Chrysanthemum offers an array of impressively prepared Chinese favorites (crisp greaseless onion cakes studded with scallions, and fat crunchy pot stickers filled with sweet pork, Chinese cabbage, and ginger) in an elegant dining room. The seafood sizzling rice soup swarms with shrimp, squid, whitefish, and crunchy rice in a subtle chicken broth. Chrysanthemum's cooks specialize in delicate and distinctive sauces; their refreshingly light hand with vegetables enlivens even old standards like sizzling iron platter with beef, shrimp, or chicken. Anything here with spicy garlic sauce is sure to win our hearts. Homemade almond cookies are a nice addition to the traditional fortune cookies. ■ *On the San Anselmo/San Rafael border at 4th St; (415) 456-6926; 2214 4th St, San Rafael; $$; beer and wine; MC, V; no checks; lunch Mon–Fri, dinner every day.*

Taqueria La Fiesta ★ Taqueria la Fiesta is Marin's answer to San Francisco's Mission District: first-rate Mexican food served in a storefront cafe with bright lights, linoleum, and a loud jukebox. Tacos, burritos, and tostadas come with a choice of wonderful grilled marinated chicken or steak, carnitas, or chile verde, along with subtly flavored Mexican rice, refried or whole beans, and freshly made salsa. A taco will set you back a whopping $2.50; the deluxe lobster burrito tops the chart at $6. ■ *On Lincoln between 3rd and 4th; (415) 456-9730; 927 Lincoln Ave, San Rafael.* ■ *Corner of Alameda del Prado and Ignacio Blvd inside the Alameda Shopping Center; (415) 883-0340; 524 Alameda del Prado, Ignacio; $; beer and wine; no credit cards; no checks; lunch, dinner every day.*

LODGINGS

Panama Hotel ★★★ We can't figure out what to call this collage of Banana Republic, Casablanca, and upscale rummage sale. Suffice to say that it works, even though absolutely nothing matches: not the brightly colored napkins, chairs, or cushions on the tropical dining patio nor the wildly eclectic furniture in the individually decorated rooms. In spite of this (or maybe because of it), the Panama Hotel is attractive and comfortable enough to tempt you to settle in for a long while. (Film folk do just that on a fairly regular basis.) The small and medium-size economy rooms share kitchens and baths; suites, bungalows, and patio apartments have private kitchens and baths, plus claw footed tubs. Our favorites are Mimi's Bungalow (Room 20), with its sunny deck, and Rosie's Room (Room 18), with its large kitchen and sunny wraparound porch. There's no air conditioning here, so in summer, beat the heat by requesting a downstairs or east-facing room. In winter, ask for a lighter, west-facing room. Decorated with Panama hats, old photographs, and other knickknacks, the dining room features vaguely south-of-the-border fare (plus a garlicky caesar). Breakfast comes with the room. ■ *At the end of B St, 3 blocks W of 2nd St; (415) 457-3993; 4 Bayview St, San Rafael, CA 94901; $$; beer and wine; AE, MC, V; no checks; lunch Mon–Fri, dinner every day, brunch Sun.*

All places in this book are recommended; even those without stars are worth knowing about.

NOVATO

RESTAURANTS

North Bay Seafood Restaurant ★★ The large tanks of live crab and lobster at the front of this unassuming little strip mall eatery are a good omen of things to come. Here you'll find over 100 Cantonese and Mandarin specialties utilizing prawns, abalone, lobster, squid, oysters, scallops, catfish, and cod. The delightful coconut seafood soup is served in a coconut shell. Dip the fresh lobster in a light butter-ginger-scallion sauce. Particularly noteworthy are the enormous braised sea scallops in an edible nest of fried noodles, and the tender squid in a rich and spicy black bean sauce. Although the chefs have a tendency to include chopped red and green bell pepper in nearly every dish, we deem this to be a small quibble. Exuberant host Chico Wong gets our vote for the most Californian name in the book. ■ *In the Novato Fair Shopping Center; (415) 897-8498; 936 Diablo Ave, Novato; $$; beer and wine; AE, MC, V; no checks; lunch, dinner every day.*

Hilltop Cafe ★ The view might be paleo-suburban, but the dining room is large and open and the service is better than Nordstrom's. Avoid anything that smacks of California cuisine and stick to the well-prepared Italian and red meat dishes. The eggplant Parmesan, baked fresh with a side of pasta with pesto, is one of the best renditions around. All the meats are top quality: locally raised beef, Petaluma chicken, naturally fed veal. (If you're having trouble deciding, the incredibly friendly and helpful waitstaff might bring you a sample.) Don't miss the hearty garlic soup in a hollowed round of sourdough bread. For dessert, spoon the mud pie (espresso ice cream topped with chocolate fudge and toasted almonds on a crumbled Oreo cookie crust). ■ *Top of the hill between Redwood Blvd and Hwy 101; (415) 892-2222; 850 Lamont Ave, Novato; $$; full bar; AE, DC, DIS, MC, V; no checks; lunch Mon–Fri, dinner every day, brunch Sun.*

VALLEJO

RESTAURANTS

Princess Garden East ■ Princess Garden West ★ Set in a suburban strip mall close to the I-80 corridor, the Princess Garden Chinese restaurant has a surprisingly soothing, upscale interior with soft, indirect lighting, brocade rosewood chairs, and interesting objets d'art on tall rosewood stands. The crisp sizzling rice dishes and the wonderful Phoenix and Dragon—tender chicken and large, juicy shrimp in a peppery citrus sauce—is as fresh and surprising as the decor. The efficient and friendly waiters will stir-fry and prepare many dishes at your table (and the restaurant has a good ventilation system so you won't get smoked out). The same family runs the Mongolian barbecue in the next room, where you can create your own dinner by mixing an assortment of meats and vegetables with hot oils and sauces for the chef to quick-fry on the big round barbecue. Most Mongolian barbecues look like subway stations. This one is a spotless exception to the rule. The Princess Garden West does not offer the Mongolian options. ■ *In the Vallejo Corners shopping center across from Marine World Africa USA, (707) 643-0808; 960 Admiral Callaghan Lane, Vallejo; $; beer and wine; AE, MC, V; no checks; lunch, dinner every day.* ■ *(707) 648-0808; 3611 Sonoma Blvd, Vallejo.*

BENICIA

RESTAURANTS

The Union Hotel and Restaurant ★★ The Union's restaurant is indisputably the best in town. The lovely dining room glows with stained glass, ivory walls, and hand-sponged teal wainscoting. Israeli chef Lev Dagan uses fresh, local Sonoma ingredients in all his dishes. The homemade orange-and-dill gravlax was exceptionally sweet and subtle, served on a crisp bed of greens with a delicious drizzle of honey mustard. A recent dinner found a succulent flower of golden roast Petaluma duck with well-seasoned, crackling skin, topped by tart mango and strawberry chutney, and a competent baked salmon with red bell pepper aioli and a grilled Anaheim chile, served with crisp, bright, but unseasoned baby vegetables. Dagan is an ace dessert maker, too: his heavenly hazelnut parfait consistently wins raves from local critics.

Founded in 1882, this grand old hotel on Benicia's main street did time as a brothel. The best rooms in the house are the George III and the Ritz: big, elegant rooms with views of the water and Jacuzzis built for two. ■ *Corner of D and First St; (707) 746-0100; 401 First St, Benicia; $$; full bar; AE, DC, DIS, MC, V; checks OK; breakfast, lunch, dinner every day.*

Mabel's Cafe ★ This neat little diner on Benicia's main street has authentic chrome and vinyl tables, a tiled counter, and a fine collection of vintage martini shakers. But the blue neon sign on the back wall and the pink, grey and purple splattered walls are strictly nouveau and so is the menu: look for a dash of Tex-Mex and Cajun mixed in with the traditional California diner fare of hamburgers, pasta, fresh fish, and sausages like Bruce Aidell's whiskey fennel wonders. Chef Richard Whitfield, a graduate of the California Culinary Academy, is an ace at anything blackened. Desserts are terrific: try the rich, dense chocolate mousse cake topped with a thick, fresh raspberry purée. The flavorful bread pudding with rum-soaked golden raisins had nice mélange of creamy and cakey textures, but its purity was violated by the heresy of yet more raspberry purée. (One really can have too much of good thing!) Just ask for it straight. Service was friendly and casual, but the kitchen seemed numbingly slow. ■ *Downtown, between H and G streets, (707) 746-7068; 635 1st St, Benicia; $$; beer and wine; MC, V; checks OK; lunch Mon–Fri, dinner Mon–Sat, brunch Sat-Sun.*

LODGINGS

Captain Walsh House ★★★ This gorgeous pre-Victorian Carpenter Gothic bed and breakfast is worth going to even if you don't have any business in Benicia, a small-town-turned-sprawling-suburb on the bluffs above the Carquinez strait. Architect Reed Robbins and her husband Steve (an escapee from the computer industry) have done a masterful job restoring this exquisite home, originally built in Boston, dismantled, and shipped around the horn in 1849. Every room here is startlingly original. Downstairs in the living room and dining room, subtly painted hardwood floors, hand-sponged walls with elaborate hand-painted stripes, and interesting modern window treatments blend with unusual antique pieces such as square grand piano and a churchman's vestment rack. With a view of the strait through tall Gothic windows, the rose, gold, and ivory colored Epifina's Room has a soaring ceiling and a massive four-poster canopy bed in the middle of the room. Its princess-style bathtub with 24-carat dipped claw-feet and fixtures reclines behind an arched screen. The almost hidden Library Room has a real zebra carpet, a terrific reading loft (accessible by a ladder), floor-to-ceiling bookshelves filled with interesting books, a stuffed armadillo, and a Murphy bed behind a trompe l'oeil bookcase. In the morning, you'll find coffee or tea served in an antique silver tea service decorated with a twist of ivy outside your door, and breakfast of croissants, fresh fruit, yogurt, and fresh-squeezed juice downstairs. If you want something heartier, just ask. ■ *Hwy 780 to Central Benicia Exit, left on 2nd St, left on L St; (707) 747-5653; 235 East L St, Benicia, 94510; $$; AE, MC, V; checks OK.*

Benicia

Restaurants

ORINDA

RESTAURANTS

Casa Orinda ★ This Orinda cowboy institution has taken culinary eclecticism into the realm of the surreal. The decor combines wrangler chic—wagonwheel chandeliers and large Remingtonesque canvases—with splendid Italianate floral arrangements in the foyer and dining room. Chef Jairo Gomez, who's been driving the Casa Orinda cook wagon for 24 years, offers a range of hearty, if not always subtle, pastas, veal, and grilled steaks. The veal and prosciutto canneloni comes in a robust marinara. Stick to the Italian and frontier specials; don't bother with the kitchen's sporadic, ill-conceived forays into Californiana. The extensive wine list includes California and imported vintages, many available by the glass. While the place's origins may be rustic, there's nothing unpolished about the service: it's first-rate. ■ *Across from the Orinda Theater; (510) 254-2981; 20 Bryant Way, Orinda; $$; full bar; AE, MC, V; no checks; dinner every day.*

LAFAYETTE

RESTAURANTS

Tourelle Cafe and Bar ★★★ Tourelle Cafe and Bar is the reincarnation of a closely named predecessor, the staid and traditional Tourelle Restaurant and Cafe—which was generally considered the best restaurant in Contra Costa County. No longer quite so grand an occasion, dining at Tourelle Cafe and Bar is more fun—and the food is better than ever. Executive chef Stephen Silva's menu includes the requisite house-smoked meats, fresh mesquite-grilled seafood, and brick-oven pizza, but also reflects his fondness for Mediterranean country dishes such as polenta timbale with its crisp yellow shell and filling of hot creamy wild mushrooms and mascarpone. The lovely, moist, house-smoked pork chop—redolent of hardwoods and topped with a sweet relish of fresh tomatoes and sun-dried cranberries—is wonderful, while the grilled loin of lamb is beautifully presented with baby carrots and green beans in a sauce of roasted garlic and eggplant. Warm goat cheese salad (on baby greens with walnuts and crostini) is tangy and delicious. For dessert, cross your fingers and hope for the pear poached in wine (served on a slice of discreetly sweet white cake with a cinnamon glaze). The lively dining room with its glass-roofed atrium and open kitchen give the place an exciting, upbeat feel, enhanced by its young, top-notch staff. ■ *½ block W on Mt Diablo Blvd from the Central Lafayette exit off Hwy 24; (510) 284-3565; 3565 Mt Diablo Blvd, Lafayette; $$$; full bar; AE, DC, MC, V; local checks only; lunch Mon–Fri, dinner every day, brunch Sun.*

Tokyo Chicken Restaurant ★★ Tokyo Chicken has a loyal following and disarming warmth that makes you feel like one of the family. Diminutive owner Nariko Tanikawa greets her guests with handshakes, smiles, even embraces, while dinner is served at long family-style tables in a rustic wood dining room decorated with paper lanterns and shoji screens. The cuisine ranges from elegantly presented, sea-air fresh sashimi and sushi to ethereally light tempuras and tangy sweet teriyakis.

Lafayette

Restaurants

■ *Near Almanor Lane and Pleasant Valley Blvd; (510) 283-3890; 3406 Mt Diablo Blvd, Lafayette; $$; beer and wine; MC, V; local checks only; lunch Tues–Fri, dinner Tues–Sun.*

LODGINGS

Lafayette Park Hotel and Duck Club Restaurant ★★ Set at the end of a cobblestone drive on a hill at the east end of town, this newly built, 140-room ersatz French château is a briskly efficient operation catering to the booming Contra Costa corporate scene. In keeping with an upscale image, rates are steep ($135–$300), but the rooms—half of which are designated non-smoking—are suitably commodious, with attractive furnishings that include armoires, wet bars, refrigerators, and remote-control TVs. Wood-burning fireplaces and vaulted ceilings adorn the more luxurious rooms and suites; bathrooms have marble counters, hair dryers, and telephones. A morning newspaper is delivered to each room. There's also a 50-foot lap pool, Jacuzzi, redwood sauna, and fitness center. Duck Club Restaurant is overpriced and understaffed, and the entrées are poorly executed—skip it. ■ *Central Lafayette exit off Hwy 24, 1½ miles E on Mt Diablo Blvd; (510) 283-3700; 3287 Mt Diablo Blvd, Lafayette, CA 94549; $$$; full bar; AE, DC, MC, V; no checks; breakfast, lunch, dinner every day.*

MORAGA

RESTAURANTS

Chez Maurice ★ Everything about this 10-year-old restaurant—from the bartender in formal black tie to the stuffed pheasant and gilt mirror behind the bar to the subdued lighting and floral lithographs in the small dining room—speaks to upscale-suburban Moraga's need for respectability and tradition. The cooking is continental French in the old style: no effete herbed vinegars or precious fruit purées drizzled Jackson Pollock–like over your dessert—just buttery, caper-dotted veal piccata and rich medallions of beef in a velvet brown sauce. They've even found a way to make salmon ultra-fattening by encasing it in a rich buttery crust. All entrées are executed with a skillful hand and are elegantly presented. The dining room is a bit understaffed on busy Saturday evenings, but if you're seeking an escape from nouvelle, Chez Maurice can keep your cholesterol at an acceptably macho level. ■ *At Park and Rheem, near the historic Rheem Theater; (510) 376-1655; 360 Park St, Moraga; $$$; full bar; AE, MC, V; no checks; lunch Tues–Fri, dinner Tues–Sun.*

The facts in this book were correct at press time, but places close, chefs depart, hours change. It's best to call ahead.

RESTAURANTS

Prima Cafe and Wine Shop ★★ When Italophiles Michael and Janet Verlander first offered sidewalk dining outside their restaurant on Walnut Creek's tree-lined Main Street, the city had laws against it. The city politicos soon wised up, however, so now you can people-watch to your heart's content while savoring chef Doug Wendt's fresh repertoire of California-Tuscan specialties. Start off with a generous hunk of thick, rosemary focaccia dipped in olive oil; then move on to a perfectly al dente fettuccine with big chunks of salmon and sweet tomatoes topped with a fresh basil coulis. The grilled-chicken salad with walnuts, fresh Parmesan, and a delicate caesar-style dressing comes on a bed of crisp new romaine leaves. The wine list, naturally, is encyclopedic. The Verlanders offer a comparative tasting line-up that changes every week, with selections offered by the taste, glass, or bottle. The friendly and experienced staff (several are 10-year veterans) can always be counted on for good advice. ■ *1 block S of Civic Dr on N Main; (510) 935-7780; 1522 N Main, Walnut Creek; $$; full bar; MC, V; local checks only; lunch Mon–Sat, dinner Mon–Sun.*

La Cigale Restaurant Francais ★ Trained at L'Ecole Chevalier in the south of France, La Cigale's chef/owner Jacques Jakovleski has been turning out dependable, reasonably priced French fare for 19 years. All the classics are here—from veal Cordon Bleu to steak aux poivre verte. A bit more out of the ordinary are the brains, veal tongue, chicken livers, and tripe (on 24-hour advance notice). We'll vouch for the sweetbreads—prepared in a rich beef-Madeira reduction sauce with mushrooms—and the tender rabbit with a tangy hint of wild game in a Cognac glaze. Dinner comes with a lusciously creamy leek and potato soup and a simple salad of lightly dressed butter lettuce. The white linen, lace curtain decor is as traditional and predictable as the food. Service is amiable, but a tad slow. ■ *Broadway and Pine St, 1 block N of Ygnacio Valley Rd; (510) 937-8800; 2195 N Broadway, Walnut Creek; $$; full bar; AE, DC, MC, V; no checks; lunch Tues–Fri, dinner Tues–Sat.*

▼

Walnut Creek

Lodgings

▲

LODGINGS

The Mansion at Lakewood ★★★ It's hard to believe that this luxurious Victorian bed and breakfast is three minutes away from downtown Walnut Creek, the nerve center of Contra Contra's sprawling suburbolopolis. Nestled behind elegant white wrought-iron gates at the end of a quiet street, this 19th-century home has seven guest rooms. Juliet's Balcony room is a standout with its view of the garden, as is the Summerhouse with its flowered-canopy bed and sunny porch with private entrance. The most luxurious room is the romantic Estate Suite, with its private sitting room, terrace overlooking the gardens, extraordinary antique brass canopy bed, and spectacular black marble bath with a Jacuzzi tub for two, double vanity, and large shower. Nice touches abound in all the rooms: lace curtains, extraordinary antiques, stacks of soft towels and fluffy robes in the bathrooms, and fresh flowers everywhere. Downstairs there's a splendid library, and an exquisitely furnished formal dining room where guests enjoy a sumptuous continental breakfast. Three acres of landscaped gardens add to the aura of luxurious seclusion. ■ *Take Ygnacio Valley Rd North from Hwy 680, right on Homestead, left on Hacienda; (510) 946-9075; 1056 Hacienda Dr, Walnut Creek, CA 94590; $$$; AE, DIS, MC, V; checks OK.*

PLEASANT HILL

RESTAURANTS

India Restaurant ★ Slivered between the freeway, an old Greyhound bus station, and an ugly gravel parking lot, this unprepossessing little cafe is the place to go in Contra Costa for delicious Indian home-style cooking. Big chunks of lamb and chicken grace the thin but richly flavorful curries served with fine basmati rice. The special curries, including shahi (chicken with yogurt) and karahi gosht (lamb with fresh onions, tomatoes, and cilantro), are just hot enough to make the icy raita (yogurt with cucumbers and mustard seeds) taste like heaven. Well-done standbys like greaseless and steaming hot nan (flat bread) and honest dal with firm vegetables make this place just right for a quick, inexpensive meal. Service is cheerful and friendly. ■ *Corner of Boyd Rd and Contra Costa Blvd at Hwy 680 on-ramp; (510) 934-7740; 2371 Contra Costa Blvd, Pleasant Hill; $; beer and wine; AE, DIS, MC, V; checks OK; lunch, dinner every day.*

Mexican Burritos Restaurant ★ Hombre-size burritos bursting with authentic, fiery fillings like chile Colorado, pork chile verde, machaca, and lengua are what keep us coming back to this spartan little burrito-teria. These big juicy monsters aren't finger food; they demand a knife and fork. Service here is efficient and friendly, with each burrito custom-assembled while you watch (ask for whole beans if you don't like them refried). The utilitarian interior is impeccably clean, but you'll probably want to kick back at the tables outside. ■ *Corner of Trelany and Contra Costa Blvd; (510) 687-3870; 2101 Contra Costa Blvd, Pleasant Hill; ■ In the Monument Plaza shopping center, ½ mile E of Hwy 680; (510) 671-7745; 1500 Monument Blvd, Concord; $; beer only; no credit cards; no checks; lunch, dinner Mon–Sat.*

CONCORD

RESTAURANTS

TR's Bar & Grill ★ This local landmark's interior betrays its fiduciary origins—brass fixtures, stained glass, and dark wood wainscoting blend with the hip swankness of ceiling fans and wine posters. The regular menu offers a fine hamburger and a reassuring chicken potpie. They've also got more up-to-date daily specials like well-grilled fish and California pastas. Keep an eye out for the special fresh spinach salad topped with shredded chicken, cold pasta, diced fresh tomatoes, green onions, and an herbed vinaigrette. The wine list offers an astute selection of lesser-known but distinctive California wines, several available by the glass. Service is cheerful and prompt. ■ *Corner of Gallindo and Salvio streets, 1 block N of Willow Pass Rd; (510) 827-4660; 2001 Salvio St, Concord; $$; full bar; AE, MC, V; no checks; lunch, dinner every day, brunch Sunday.*

DANVILLE

RESTAURANTS

Blackhawk Grille ★★★ In the exclusive community of Blackhawk, this glamorous, offbeat eatery is a testament to California's adoration of the automobile. There's always a vintage beauty on display in the middle of the dining room (on loan from the Behring Auto Museum at the other end of the plaza), and the booths are covered in the gold-flecked vinyl coveted by '50s hot-rodders. The Grille's exotic interior shines with brushed steel, gleaming copper, and verdigris. Lighting fixtures are stylized hubcaps. In the midst of this glitz, chef Eliot King's eclectic, but down-to-earth menu offers wood-fired pizzas, satisfying pastas, and superb entrées like ribeye steak with sweet onions and rosemary. Better yet, compose a meal from the wide range of smaller dishes—buttery-tender carpaccio, sweet crab cakes, or—our favorite—grilled rabbit and wild mushrooms in phyllo with a sweet onion sauce. The wine list is vast. (Oenophiles can take a peek at the wine room through picture windows in the banquet hall.) Desserts, like everything else about this place, are excessive: try the double-layered chocolate-walnut brownie served warm in a pool of caramel sauce with a scoop of vanilla gelato. ■ *I-680 to Crow Canyon exit E, left on Crow Canyon 7 miles to Camino-Tassajara, right on Tassajara to Blackhawk Plaza Circle, (510) 736-4295; 3540 Blackhawk Plaza Circle; Danville; $$$; full bar; AE, DC, DIS, MC, V; no checks; lunch Mon–Sat, dinner every day, brunch Sun.*

Bridges ★★★ Japanese businessman Kazuo Sugitani was so happy with the education his son received at Danville's famed

Danville

Restaurants

Athenian prep school that he wanted to give something back to the town. Blending the best of East and West, Bridges is a pretty nifty gift. Beautifully landscaped grounds and an inviting outdoor terrace encircle a building that mingles the brown-shingle architecture of Morgan and Maybeck with soaring angles and interior spaces reminiscent of 17th-century Kyoto. Chef Alison Negrin (a talented veteran of the Bay Area food scene whose track record includes a stint at Chez Panisse) likes to embellish her ever-changing array of savory dishes: a superbly tender roast leg of lamb with a sweet pine nut and currant relish; crab cakes with a red pepper rémoulade; a mixed grill of quail and duck sausage with apricot chutney and a currant and pecan salad; black-pepper fettuccine studded with artichokes, wild mushrooms, goat cheese, and flavorful croutons. Strictly Asian dishes like soba noodles served in broth with shrimp and onion tempura are a tad boring, but cross-cultural dishes such as ahi tuna carpaccio with wasabe and cucumber salad dazzle. The wine list includes an extensive collection of dessert and after-dinner wines to match delights such as lemon tart with plump blueberries and sweet raspberry sherbet ■ *I-680 to Diablo Road W exit, right on Diablo Rd, left on Hartz to corner of Church and Hartz; (510) 820-7200; 44 Church St, Danville; $$; full bar; AE, MC, V; no checks; dinner every day.*

Marcello's ★★ Pierangelo Bigotti has come a long way from the humble storefront restaurant he ran for seven years in a working class section of Oakland while building his reputation for classic Northern Italian food. Bigotti's Milanese cuisine, focusing on freshly made pasta and exceptionally fine veal dishes, is lighter than most Italian food, more akin to French food in conception and approach. Bigotti's light touch is apparent in the delicate veal-chicken and vegetable canneloni with a fresh, herby marinara that comes with every dinner, and in the moist, well-balanced veal saltimbocca alla Romana with tender prosciutto and creamy fontina. The service, presided over by dapper and gracious co-owner and maitre d' Germano Foschi, is gracious and efficient. ■ *Right on San Ramon Valley Blvd off I-680 for ¼ mile; (510) 838-8144; 515 San Ramon Valley Blvd, Danville; $$$; full bar; AE, DC, MC, V; local checks only; lunch Tues–Fri, dinner Tues–Sun.*

La Ultima ★ From this old house in the heart of Danville, the Gaben family serves New Mexican specialties rarely available outside the Southwest. Using chiles roasted in their Taos, New Mexico, restaurant and trucked here by their son, the Gabens create Southwestern wonders that are milder and more complex than most California Mexican food. Among the specialties are New Mexico–style flat enchiladas (two moist tortillas layered with meat and cheese and topped with eggs) and the chunky chile Colorado in a pungent chile-kissed mahogany sauce. The balloonlike sopaipillas with butter and honey make a perfect dessert. Steer clear of the blasé Mexican standards. Other branches include one in Walnut Creek (1516 Bonanza St, (510) 937-0383) and another in Oakland (3912 MacArthur Blvd, (510) 482-1122). ■ *2 blocks S of Diablo Rd; (510) 838-9705; 455 Hartz Ave, Danville; $; beer and wine; AE, DC, MC, V; no checks; lunch, dinner every day.*

SAN RAMON

RESTAURANTS

Mudd's Restaurant ★★ During the height of the summer harvest, more than 90 percent of Mudd's fruits and vegetables are produced in the 10-acre municipal garden on view outside the dining-room windows—the bright idea of founder and former owner Virginia Mudd. Fresh herbs from the garden complement every aspect of the cooking, from the unique flavorings (basil-accented applesauce) to the delicate, edible herb and flower garnishes adorning every plate. Innovative chef Ron Ottobre (formerly of La Tourelle and Trader Vic's) turns out consistent winners like the thick, subtle zucchini lasagne with fresh herbed tomato sauce; a fat, zippy, Cajun-spiced pork chop with fresh fruit relish; and a homey grilled free-range chicken marinated in buttermilk and whole-grain mustard, served with tomatillo salsa and black beans. With an extremely low staff turnover, Mudd's runs smoothly and courteously. On nice days, eat in the garden-side patio—then stroll through the gardens to see where your repast originated. ■ *Just off Crow Canyon Rd and Park Pl; (510) 837-9387; 10 Boardwalk, San Ramon; $$$; full bar; AE, DC, MC, V; local checks only; lunch Mon–Fri, dinner Tues–Sat, brunch Sun.*

PLEASANTON

RESTAURANTS

Pleasanton Hotel ★★ An oasis in the surrounding fast-food desert, the graceful, turn-of-the-century Pleasanton Hotel is the sort of place that makes you want to linger over lunch. The good news is that chef Paul Wiggins's interesting and experimental dishes are well worth lingering over. Beyond the de rigueur slabs of beef or grilled fish, specials include a delightful quail stuffed with veal and enhanced by one of Wiggins' fine, light sauces. On the regular menu try the giant house-smoked marinated pork chops with a currant glaze and a zippy apple-horseradish sauce, or the grilled sea scallops with roasted potatoes and a fennel cole slaw. The interesting wine list includes many selections from local vineyards, and the staff's advice is dependable (perhaps because they've attended the restaurant's monthly winemaker dinner series.) The adjoining bar features live top-40 music for dancing away calories or, on Sunday, tea dancing with a big jazz band. ■ *Santa Rita exit off I-580, 2 miles S; (510) 846-8106; 855 Main St, Pleasanton; $$$; full bar; AE, DC, DIS, MC, V; local checks only; lunch, dinner every day, brunch Sun.*

LODGINGS

Plum Tree Inn ★ Speeding past all those shimmering, neo–Silicon Valley glass buildings along Interstate 580, it's hard to believe that Pleasanton has a charming turn-of-the-century core. Located smack in the middle of old town, Joan and Bob Cordtz's stylishly restored 1890s Victorian has six unique suites—each with its own private bath and a tasteful but not overbearing collection of antiques. Ask for one of the rooms overlooking the patio in back: we particularly like the Cherry Room with its vast, cherry-wood four-poster bed. Business travelers (perhaps seeking refuge from all that glass) will find hookups for faxes and computers in every room. Breakfast is served in the Cordtzes' home across the street. Plead for their Belgian waffles. ■ *Just W of Main St; (510) 426-9588; 262 W Angela, Pleasanton, CA 94566; $$; AE, MC, V; checks OK.*

LIVERMORE

RESTAURANTS

Wente Brothers Restaurant ★★★ The Wente brothers couldn't have devised a better way to showcase their wines than with this exquisite neo–Spanish Colonial restaurant set among the vineyards and rolling hills of the 1,200-acre Wente estate. The interior is all glass and glowing wood, and, for warm summer nights, there's a fine broad patio overlooking the vineyards. Chef Kimball Jones's seasonally changing menu is a pleasant blend of traditional and experimental: perfectly fresh Hog Island oysters on the half-shell in a sparkling wine mignonette, and corn chowder swimming with smoked chicken, potatoes, and jalapeño peppers topped with a dollop of basil butter. House-smoked meats and fresh fish are presented with intriguing, tangy sauces and exotic chutneys. Wente's trademark beef dishes, like the exquisite ribeye steak with fire-roasted onion and portabella mushroom relish, are all made from organic grain-fed cattle raised on the estate. While it's unfortunate that Wente Brothers wines don't usually measure up to the food, the good news is that the list is not limited to Wente Brothers wines. Reservations are strongly advised. (The winery is open for tours and tasting seven days a week.) ■ *Take L St 4½ miles S of town; (510) 447-3696; 5050 Arroyo Rd, Livermore; $$$; wine only; AE, DC, MC, V; no checks; lunch, dinner Mon–Sat, brunch Sun.*

Lemon Grass ★★ As the name of the place indicates, Chef Vichurasmee is enamored of authentic Thai herbs: galangal, lime leaves, sweet basil—and, yes, lemon grass, deployed in subtle and delightful ways. Don't miss the spring roll–like goong-hom-pa (marinated prawns and chopped chicken breast with garlic and Thai spices, deep-fried in rice paper, with sweet chile sauce for dipping). Seafood is always dependable, fresh, and expertly prepared, as is the special green curry of salmon and shrimp. You can sample the local Livermore Valley wines, or try their Thai iced tea or coffee—a perfect soothing counterpoint to the exhilarating mélange of spices. ■ *North Livermore exit off I-580, right on 1st St; (510) 606-6496; 2216 1st St, Livermore; $; beer and wine; MC, V, MC; local checks only; lunch Mon–Sat; dinner every day.*

RICHMOND

RESTAURANTS

Hawthorne's Restaurant at Marina Bay ★★ Cossetted away from the rough and tumble world of industrial Richmond in the prestigious development of Marina Bay is a genuine find; it's a gorgeous restaurant in an old sea captain's house at the water's edge, but no one outside of Richmond has ever heard of it, yet. That's a pity, since it offers one of the best combinations of interesting food and fine views in the entire East Bay. Ask to sit in front of the fireplace or in the sunny enclosed sun porch room with its white-washed pine and cane chairs and wall of windows topped with elegant pink floral flounces. Entrées are generally good (as in a delicious roasted chicken salad with red onions, toothsome white beans and thick, crisp triangles of fried polenta), but sometimes uninspired (as in a bed of undercooked French lentils under a perfectly grilled, smoky salmon), but such quirks shouldn't stop you from savoring the rest of the morsels on your plate. For dessert, try the exquisite Earthquake Cake, a fine dark chocolate cake with a texture somewhere between a mousse and a decadence. Service is efficient, if a bit snippy. ■ *Marina Bay exit of 580, right on Regatta Blvd, left on Schooner which turns into Esplanade; (510) 620-0400; 1900 Esplanade Drive, Richmond; $$$; full bar; AE, MC, V; no checks; lunch Mon–Fri, dinner Wed–Sun, brunch Sun.*

Richmond

Restaurants

▲

Taqueria La Bamba ★ This neat little spot looks a lot like every other nouveau diner, but a little closer and you'll notice that all the jukebox selections are Spanish and the menu on the wall is decidedly south of the border as well. Taqueria La Bamba offers usual Mexican fare plus Salvadoran specialties such as papusas (handmade tortilla pockets filled with meat and cheese) and the quesadilla Zuiza, a 15-inch tortilla topped with cheese and diced steak. Dishes like chile Colorado, al pastor (barbe-

cued pork), and costillos al horno (spicy country spareribs) are
available for the stout of heart. ■ *At Barrett Ave; (510) 235-
2288; 12345 San Pablo Ave, Richmond; $; beer and wine; no
credit cards; no checks; lunch, dinner Mon–Sat.*

Taj Kesri ★ Beyond the ugly strip mall exterior, beyond the
bright yellow neon sign is a highly regarded Indian cafe, where
a broad range of well-prepared specialities go well beyond
usual standards. Huge, crisp vegetable samosas filled with
spiced potatoes, green peas, and coriander come with a vibrant
tamarind sauce and refreshingly biting mint sauce. The tan-
door oven delivers exquisitely cooked yogurt-marinated
chicken, lamb kabobs, and trout (avoid the uninteresting
shrimp). Though the sauces were vibrant and fragrant, we
found the lamb in most curries a tad overcooked. The stellar
vegetarian entrées, however, have no such problems: mattar
paneer (farmers cheese and firm green peas in a spicy gravy),
aloo gobhi (cauliflower and potatoes in a rich spicy sauce), and
channa masala (a delightful mélange of garbanzo beans). Finish with a cooling, pleasantly sweet lassi yogurt drink which in
addition to satisfying your sweet tooth will also help cut the
heat of the your meal. Exotic mango lassi is close to heaven. ■
*In Mira Vista Plaza between Barrett and MacDonald,
(415) 233-3817; 12221 San Pablo Avenue; $; beer and wine;
MC, V; no checks; lunch Sun–Fri, dinner every day.*

POINT RICHMOND

RESTAURANTS

Hidden City Cafe ★ Like the pretty little enclave of Point Richmond itself, this neighborhood cafe is a hidden jewel right next
to the industrial sprawl of Richmond. The local artists and business execs who crowd in here for breakfast and lunch don't
come here for the decor, they come for food. For breakfast,
look for polenta scrapple with bacon, red onion and two eggs
or spiced French toast with cinnamon, ginger, and Quattre
Epices (French fourspice) served with real maple syrup. Try
some house-made fennel sausages on the side. The lunch
menu might include a good organic hamburger with homemade french fries or an uncommonly rich vegetarian sandwich
with grilled mushrooms, caramelized onions, Gruyère cheese,
and dijon on rye. A meal can be nicely finished when a tart
apricot and blackberry cobbler on a crumbly multigrain shortcake with vanilla ice cream appears on the table. The service
can be flakier than the shortcake. ■ *On Park Place just off
Washington St; (510) 232-9738; 109 Park Place, Point Richmond; $; beer and wine; no credit cards; no checks; breakfast,
lunch Tues–Sun.*

RESTAURANTS

Ristorante Enoteca Mastro ★★ At a time when faux marble Northern Italian cafes are multiplying like—well—faux marble, it's a pleasure to find a place as mellow and authentic as Enoteca Mastro, a wine store and restaurant owned by Mark Anthony and Diane Mastro. You enter through the wine shop, an unprepossessing room with a few tables stashed between wine racks (this is where you sit if you if don't have reservations) and a wine bar in back. The austere but comfortable main dining room has off-yellow walls, minimalist decor, and a short, richly seasonal menu offering an ever-changing selection of pastas, intense risottos (including the Siracusa, a creamy mélange with a tomato-anchovy-eggplant sauce studded with pine nuts, raisins, and mint), and grilled meats. The meal's introduced with a thick Tuscan white bean soup, redolent of onions and smoked pork and topped with a poached duck egg; and refreshing salad of mixed greens tossed with nectarines, loganberries, toasted pecans, and Gorgonzola in a balsamic vinaigrette. The seafood lasagne reveals firm layers of housemade pasta filled with fresh crab, ricotta, chard, and caramelized onions with a light, almost creamy marinara. The pot de crème tastes remarkably like Jell-O instant chocolate pudding, but the poached pear in a rhubarb purée with a swirl of creamy zabaglione is heavenly. The vast wine list is 99-percent Italian, and the by-the-glass selection is particularly choice. Reservations essential. ■ *San Pablo, just S of Solano; (510) 524-4822; 933 San Pablo Ave, Albany; $$$; beer and wine; MC, V; checks OK; dinner Tues–Sun.*

Albany

Restaurants

Yujean's Modern Cuisine of China ★★ Founder Yujean Kang's first name is hint enough that something very East-meets-West is up at this almost invisible, minimally decorated storefront restaurant on ugly San Pablo. Now run by his gregarious sister Mary Kang Perkins, Yujean's offers a very Chinese version of Pacific Rim cuisine, blending their mother's recipes with fresh California ingredients, careful presentation, miniscule portions, a vast French and California wine list, and steep prices. Start with a sweet, almost molassesy hot and sour soup dosed heavily with cilantro, and the mysterious-sounding Ants on a Tree—minced beef with chopped shiitake mushrooms and Sichuan pickled cabbage heart on a bed of crisp noodles served in an iceberg lettuce cup. Entrées include tea-smoked duck (delicious, mahogany-colored slices of duck with scallions in a delicate crêpe with plum sauce) and Chinese polenta (an appetizer-size portion of crisp-on-the-outside, velvet-on-the-inside corn-flour and egg triangles topped with spicy minced beef, diced shiitake mushrooms, and celery. Yujean's remarkable apple fritters are served astride two tart pools of kiwi and strawberry purée with a fan of fresh fruit. ■ *On San Pablo, just N of Solano; (510) 525-8557; 843 San Pablo Ave, Albany; $$; wine and beer; AE, MC, V; no checks; lunch, dinner Tues–Sun.*

BERKELEY

You can still buy tie-dyed "Berserkly" T-shirts from vendors on Telegraph Avenue, but the wild days of this now middle-aged, upper-middle-class burg are gone. There's nary a whiff of tear gas in the air; most Univeristy of California students seem more interested in cramming for exams than mass protest. Thanks to much-disputed People's Park (owned by Cal, occupied by the homeless), occasional street battles rattle Telegraph, though pillage, not protest, seems the order of the day. On the other hand, the city still has an official Peace and Social Justice Committee and sister cities in every politically correct corner of the globe.

ARTS AND CULTURE

Literature Most folks around here agree if you can't find a book at Cody's Books, Berkeley's best new-book store, it probably isn't worth reading; 2454 Telegraph, (510) 845-7852. Nationally known literary and political writers appear at Cody's and at Black Oak Books (new and used books) (1491 Shattuck, (510) 486-0698), almost every night. The four-story Moe's Books specializes in used books and remainders; 2476 Telegraph, (510) 849-2087.

Theater and Film The Berkeley Repertory Theatre has a national reputation for experimental productions of the classics and innovative new work; 2025 Addison, (510) 845-4700. The Black Repertory Group offers a whole range of plays, dance, and art by black artists; 3201 Adeline, (510) 652-2120. The California Shakespeare Festival offers Shakespeare at an outdoor theater (bundle up 'cause it's usually freezing) every summer in the hills near Orinda; 100 Gateway Blvd, (510) 548-3422. The UC Theater is a revivalist movie house where the movies change every night; 2036 University, (510) 843-6267. And the Pacific Film Archive shows underground avant-garde films as well as classics; 2625 Durant, (510) 642-1412. For up-to-date listings of cultural events, check out *The Express,* the East Bay's alternative press weekly.

Museums The University Art Museum, with its small permanent collection of modern art, attracts peculiar but riveting exhibitions, like the Robert Mapplethorpe exhibit and the Art of the Insane; 2626 Bancroft, (510) 642-1207). The Judah L. Magnes Museum, the largest Jewish museum in the West, has several collections of Jewish art and culture, including a Holocaust exhibit and a collection of modern Jewish painting. Their

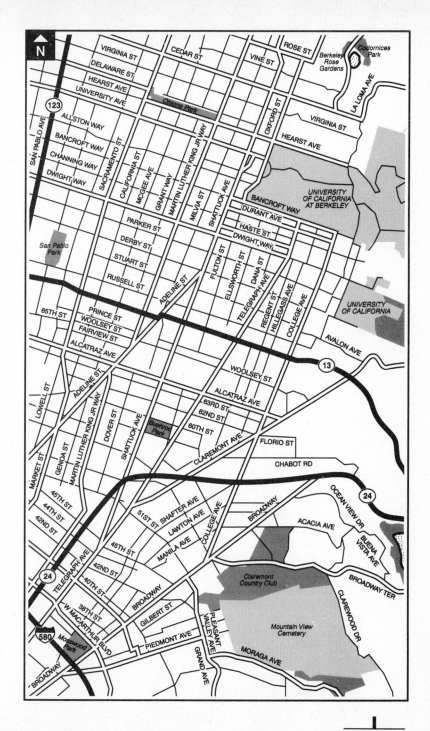

extensive library is open to the public; 2911 Russell Street, (510) 849-2710. Catch the interesting native American and other anthropological artifacts at the Phoebe Hearst Museum of Anthropology in Cal's Kroeber Hall; at the corner of College and Bancroft, (510) 643-7648. Hands-on exhibits about lasers, holograms, and cutting-edge computers can be found at the Lawrence Hall of Science. While you're there, duck outside to see (and hear) the giant, eerie wind chimes and check out the Stonehenge-like solar observatory; above UC on Centennial Drive, (510) 642-5133.

Music The Berkeley Symphony, under the direction of Kent Nagano, blends new and experimental music with the classics at Zellerbach Hall on the Berkeley campus (for tickets call (510) 841-2800). Blues and R&B can be found at Larry Blake's (2367 Telegraph, (510) 848-0888) or Pasand Lounge (2284 Shattuck, (510) 848-0260). You can rock out to world beat and other ethnic music at Ashkenaz (1317 San Pablo, near Gilman, (510) 525-5054) or mellow out at Freight and Salvage (1111 Addison Street, (510) 548-7603)—the prime Euro-folkie hangout. Rock, jazz, folk, reggae, and everything else show up at the University's open air Greek Theater; (510) 642-9988.

OTHER THINGS TO DO

Although PC politics still reign in Berkeley's city government, most of its well-heeled citizens seem more concerned about the plight of their palate than the plight of the poor. The best bread comes from Chez Panisse owner Alice Waters's Acme Bread Company (1601 San Pablo Avenue, (510) 524-1327), though the Cheeseboard, with its collectively owned bakery and vast gourmet cheese shop is a close runner-up (1504 Shattuck Avenue, (510) 549-3183). Noah's Bagels (3170 College, (510) 654-0944; 1883 Solano, (510) 524-3104) and Brothers' Bagels (1469 Shattuck, (510) 649-9422; 1281 Gilman, (510) 524-3104) rival Brooklyn's best.

Like many university towns, this one seems to run on coffee: Peet's Coffee, with its vast selection of beans and teas, is the local favorite (2124 Vine Street, (510) 841-0564; 2916 Domingo, (510) 843-1434; 1825 Solano, (510) 526-9607). Cool cafes, swarming with students, abound: try Cafe Strada (2300 College Ave, (510)843-5282) for an outdoor latte beneath the trees or the hip, crowded Cafe Milano (2522 Bancroft, (510)644-3100) down the street. Caffe Mediterraneum (2475 Telegraph, (510)841-5634), with its excellent cappuccino, captures the bohemian flavor of Telegraph Avenue, still a haunt of students, street people, runaways, hipsters, professors, tarot readers, and street vendors.

The best beer can be found at the frat-packed Triple Rock Brewery (1920 Shattuck Avenue, (510) 843-2739) and the hipper, more experimental Bison Brewery (2598 Telegraph,

(510) 841-7734) with unusual offerings such as sagebrush ale and licorice porter. Takara Sake USA offers tastings of sake and plum wine at their factory; 708 Addison, (510) 540-8250.

Gardens For more pastoral diversions, check out the Berkeley Rose Garden (on Euclid between Bay View and Eunice), a terraced park with hundreds of varieties of roses and a great view of San Francisco. Tilden Regional Park, in the hills above town, offers miles of hiking trails, plus a steam train, Golden Age merry-go-round, and farm and nature area for kids. Tilden also has an exquisite Botanical Garden specializing in California native plants; (510) 635-0135.

RESTAURANTS

Chez Panisse ★★★★ In the heart of Berkeley's gourmet ghetto, the most famous restaurant in Northern California is almost invisible—from the street, that is. Good-food lovers know where to find it, though. They look for the small, hand-carved sign in front of the ivy-covered fence. Chez Panisse doesn't need to advertise. Owner and ever-present inspiration Alice Waters has been at the forefront of the California Cuisine revolution since 1971, when she started cooking elaborate meals for selected groups of friends, then expanded into a restaurant. Waters has never specialized in the showier, sometimes downright bizarre flights of culinary imagination that characterize so much of modern California cuisine. Instead, Chez Panisse concentrates on simple, exquisitely orchestrated meals using the finest all-natural ingredients available. Chez Pannisse single-handedly supports dozens of small organic enterprises in Sonoma County.

Chez Panisse is divided into a more-expensive, prix-fixe dining room downstairs, and a light-hearted upstairs cafe. Upstairs, meals begin with a dish of olives and warm Acme bread and move on to aromatic, seasonal dishes. Perhaps an appetizer of thin-sliced salmon flash (cooked on the plate in a hot oven for 40 seconds) and served with an herbed edible flower butter or a smooth, aromatic corn and garlic soup with a subtle touch of leek. Boneless pigeon wrapped and grilled in edible vine leaves has a lovely smokey quality with a hint of mint and shallots. A simple mixed green salad cleanses the palate before the appearance of the kirsch-infused Bavarian, a smooth pudding topped with red currant sauce and fresh raspberries.

The warm upstairs cafe has a fine wine bar and a few hotly-contested tiny bar tables. Try the baked Sonoma goat cheese salad, or the antipasto of prosciutto, baked ricotta, and roasted red peppers. Pizza and calzone, baked in the wood-burning ovens, can be topped with interesting ingredients such as squid and roasted onion. We recommend the meat or fish dishes (for example, an exquisite salmon wrapped in fig leaves, bursting with the flavor of baby carrots and onions). Anything with duck and anything in a galette is an almost sure winner. The cafe's delightful desserts include homemade ice creams and sherberts, fruit cobblers, and pies.

At press time Chez Panisse's longtime chef Paul Bertolli is leaving and no one knows yet who will replace him. Local foodies aren't very worried about the shift. Chez Panisse has weathered changes in chefs before and has always come out better for it in the end. ■ *On Shattuck Ave between Cedar and Vine; (510) 548-5525; 1517 Shattuck Ave, Berkeley; $$$; beer and wine; AE, DIS, MV, V; no checks; restaurant: dinner Mon–Sat; cafe: lunch, dinner Mon–Sat.*

O Chamé ★★★ Even jaded Berkeley food fanatics are bewitched by the fare in this exotic realm of the senses. Chef David Vardy spent years studying Buddhist-Taoist cooking in Taiwan, as well as Kansei and Kaiseki cuisine in Japan. (Kansai is the regional cuisine of Osaka; Kaiseki, developed to complement the Japanese tea ceremony, consists of small dishes that can be consumed in a couple of bites.) Vardy developed an ardent local following when he opened the Daruma Teashop in North Berkeley in 1988, serving an intriguing assortment of teas, bento box lunches, and his popular Nambu teacakes—thin, sesame-based biscuits flavored with nuts or seeds. These and more elaborate works of culinary art can now be found at O Chamé, a soothing cafe crafted in the style of a rustic, wayside inn from Japan's Meiji period.

You can get anything on the menu cold, steamed, simmered, or grilled. A $25 prix-fixe menu provides a doll-size selection from each category. A meal might include an exquisitely fresh vinegared wakame seaweed, cucumber, and crab salad; steamed fish cakes with shrimp and scallions; tender, simmered sea scallops with garlic flowers and kiwi; grilled duck with vinegared carrot and daikon radish. O Chamé also offers a range of delicately flavored teas, sakes, and both Japanese and American microbrewery beers. O Chamé is casual enough for jeans and running shoes, and the waitstaff is composed of interesting artsy types. Vardy's gracious wife, Hiromi, clad in kimonos she designs, greets the guests. ■ *Fourth St near Hearst; (510) 841-8783; 1830 Fourth St, Berkeley; $$; beer and wine; MC, V; no checks; lunch, dinner Mon–Sat.*

Cambodiana's ★★★ There aren't many Cambodian restaurants in Cambodia, where wayfarers rely on teahouses and noodle shops, and traditional dishes can only be sampled in private homes. It took a forward-thinking Assyrian priest—Father Nazarin—to convince the local immigrant community that a Cambodian restaurant could be a hot property. Cambodiana is the best of the bunch. Owner Sidney Sok Ke and his wife Carol Bopha Ke, the restaurant's talented chef, have assembled a menu organized around six different regional sauces—based on tamarind, ginger, lemon grass, lamb juice, curry, and anchovy—each designed to complement delectable renditions of chicken, salmon, rabbit, lamb, prawns, quail, beef, and trout. Try the deboned quail, stuffed with ground pork, shrimp, and garlic, or the exquisite lamb chops grilled after being marinated in a mixture of garlic, lemon grass, galangal, paprika, and soy sauce. The country-style smokey eggplant, roasted and tossed with pork, shrimp, green onion, and garlic, also wins raves. The place is usually packed, so make reservations, especially on weekend evenings. ■ *Above Shattuck near UC campus; (510) 843-4630; 2156 University Ave, Berkeley; $$; beer and wine; AE, MC, V; checks OK; lunch Mon–Fri, dinner every day.*

Lalime's ★★★ It's hard to pass Lalime's at night without stopping to stare at the lush goings-on through its fishbowl front window: its radiant, pale pink dining room has high ceilings, big, brilliantly splattered collages on the walls, and a crush of sleek patrons leaning intimately over candle-lit, white-linen tables. The menu changes every night, but the starters, like the soup made with Finn potatoes, golden beets and ginger, and the roast garlic and shiitake mushroom ravioli, are universally exquisite. Desserts, like the creamy homemade anise ice cream, mango flan, and chocolate cake with brandied cherries, are equally splendid. The entrees, while very good, rarely measure up to the wonders surrounding them. One exception is the thick, sweet, juniper berry–cured pork chop, but be sure to ask for a substitute for the gluey roast garlic mashed potatoes that usually come with it. Lalime's prix-fixe dinners are usually a good bet: a June offering featured seared spearfish marinated in fresh lime and curry and served with a blood orange and fennel salad; grilled chicken breast served with crisp polenta triangles and a sweet onion, red pepper, and raisin relish; and a crisp, candied pecan tart with a buttery crust. The witty, efficient, and exceptionally knowledgeable staff can lead you to the gems on Lalime's extensive wine and beer list. ■ *Gilman between Neilson and Peralta; (510) 527-9838; 1329 Gilman St, Berkeley; $$$; beer and wine; MC, V; checks OK; dinner every day.*

New Delhi Junction ★★ This soothing, diminutive restaurant tucked away on the second level of a funky, hippie-era shopping center offers some of the finest Northern Indian cuisine in the Bay Area. The main problem here is deciding what to order: it's pretty tough to pass up a featured special like murg mumatz mahal (tender boneless chicken cooked in a saffron-perfumed sauce with ground cashew nuts, yogurt, and paneer cheese); it's even more difficult to turn away from the regular tandoori dishes—the best rendition you may experience in this incarnation. The full thali dinner is served on metal trays with

Berkeley

Restaurants

▲

heavenly basmati rice and an assortment of vegetables and condiments. Be sure to sample some of the delicious nan, in versions flavored with garlic, studded with cashew nuts, or stuffed with onions. Chef/owner Laxman Moorjani gleans his specials from rare old Kashmiri cookbooks, treats named after famous mogul rulers, and popular regional specialties you're unlikely to find anywhere else. ■ *At Blake, 2nd floor of The Village; (510) 486-0477; 2556 Telegraph Ave, Berkeley; $$; beer and wine; MC, V; local checks only; lunch, dinner every day.*

Panini ★★ A delicious, cost-effective way to savor the fruits of Berkeley's obsession with all things gourmet, Panini's lunch menu offers an ever-changing array of creative sandwiches: look for exotic collages like prosciutto, sliced pears, creamy blue-veined Brie, crisp greens, basil, and walnut vinaigrette, or a mix of melted mozzarella, coppa, tomatoes, chopped olives, greens, pesto, and sun-dried tomatoes, all served on anise- and sesame-seeded baguettes. Fresh soups and a variety of salads round out a menu blessed with fresh-squeezed juices, strong espresso, and luscious pastries. Panini's is operated with the efficiency of an assembly line, but the surroundings are sufficiently laid back. Dispense with the airy but utilitarian dining room and head for the courtyard where the walls are covered with ivy and flamboyant trumpet vines. ■ *In Trumpet Vine Court at Shattuck and Allston; (510) 849-0405; 2115 Allston Way, Berkeley; $; no alcohol; no credit cards; checks OK; lunch Mon–Sat.*

Plearn Thai Cuisine No. 2 ★★ To people who spend most of their time dreaming about a trip to Chiang Mai, Plearn's glitzy, modern interior may seem a bit sterile, but no one could argue with the quality of the food. Plearn offers an astounding range of faultlessly executed Thai specialities: the curries, whether red or green, offer a delightfully complicated medley of flavors (coconutty kang curry with chicken is our favorite), and the beef satay is a blue-ribbon winner with a sauce of ground peanuts, lemon grass, fish sauce, chiles, and cumin. Fans of fiery food will find more than enough combustible choices on the menu, including the delicious yum-nua—slices of barbecued beef on a bed of mint leaves, ground chiles, lettuce, lime juice, and onion. The chicken in thick coconut broth alone would make the lines form at the door. ■ *Between Shattuck and Milvia; (510) 841-2148; 2050 University Ave, Berkeley; $; beer and wine; no credit cards; local checks only; lunch, dinner every day.*

Bette's Oceanview Diner ★ The charm of Bette's Oceanview Diner doesn't have anything to do with the ocean (not even a view). What this nouveau '50s diner does have is red booths, chrome stools, a checkerboard tile floor, hip waitresses, and the best jukebox around. And damn good breakfasts, too. We quail at the usual 45-minute stomach-growling weekend wait, but understand the motivation: enormous, soufflélike pancakes stuffed with pecans and ripe berries; farm-fresh eggs scrambled with prosciutto and Parmesan; outstanding omelets; and anything with black beans, especially the quintessential huevos rancheros. If you can't bear the wait, pop into Bette's-to-Go (right next door). Later in the day, BTG offers superlative focaccia sandwiches and California pizzas. ■ *2 blocks N of University Ave; (510) 644-3230; 1807A Fourth St, Berkeley; $; beer and wine; no credit cards; local checks only; breakfast, lunch every day.*

Fatapple's ★ When Berkeley carnivores hear the call of the wild and nothing but a big, rare burger will do, they head for this comfortable, clubby spot lined with big, grainy photos of Jack London, and packed with wood tables laminated with vintage illustrations from his novels. A prime contender in the ongoing Berkeley burger wars, Fatappple's burgers feature exceptionally lean, high-quality ground beef on homemade wheat rolls with a variety of toppings, including five different, very good cheeses (ask for the creamy, crumbled blue cheese). The soups, like the rich beef barley or creamy corn chowder, are usually sure winners, as is the delicious spinach salad with feta cheese, walnuts, red onions, and marinated black beans in a tart vinaigrette. Standout desserts include flaky olallieberry or pecan pie, huge thick milk shakes (seven kinds from mocha to olallieberry) served in icy metal tins, or cheese puffs (ethereal pastry satchels stuffed with baker's cheese and dusted with powdered sugar). ■ *At MLK and Rose; (510) 526-2260; 1346 Martin Luther King Jr Way, Berkeley.* ■ *At Colusa and Fairmont; (510) 528-3433; 7525 Fairmont, El Cerrito; $; beer and wine; no credit cards; no checks; breakfast, lunch, dinner every day.*

Flint's ★ There's nothing like a sinful serving of juicy barbecued ribs in a sinus-blasting sauce around 1am to ruin the upholstery of your car and make you feel like you're probably going to hell. Of course, if hell hath ribs like Flint's, who cares? Owned by the Flintroy family, this nitty-gritty rib joint has red-eye hours ('til 4am on weekends) and the best barbecue in town: the lip-smacking pork ribs and the hot links retain their succulent juiciness after slow cooking in the massive black oven. (The dried-out, stringy chicken doesn't.) The sweet, thick, mahogany sauce comes mild, medium, or incendiary (back off if your taste buds are timid). Everything is piled onto a flimsy paper plate, covered with butcher paper, and shoved into a paper sack. The 14th Street location offers table service, but we prefer the culture clash of the Shattuck branch where students, yups, and neighborhood folks queue up late into the night. ■ *Berkeley-Oakland border N of Alcatraz; (510) 653-0593;*

6609 Shattuck Ave, Berkeley. ■ Between 73rd and Haven-scourt; (510) 569-1312; 6672 E 14th Street, Oakland; $; no alcohol; no credit cards; no checks; lunch, dinner every day.

Westside Bakery Cafe ★ Once Berkeley's blue collar base, most of the big factories and warehouses in West Berkeley have been broken up into live-work studios for artists, film-makers, and computeroids. You can catch up with these urban pioneers at the Westside Bakery Cafe, an airy, light-filled breakfast and lunch spot, glowing with natural wood and win-dows all around. The Westside specializes in heavy sustenance and brisk service: a plateful of their rich, chewy banana-blueberry or apple-cornmeal pancakes will hold you for the rest of the day. Ditto for the delicious chilaquiles—soft corn tortillas scrambled with eggs, onions, chiles, and Jack cheese, served with a side of smokey-flavored, spicy black beans and salsa. For lunch, opt for a sandwich of ham, Brie, and apples on thick slabs of whole wheat and potato bread. ■ *9th and Parker; (510) 845-4852; 2570 9th St, Berkeley; $; beer and wine; MC, V; no checks; breakfast, lunch every day.*

Zachary's Chicago Pizza ★ For years, Bay Area transplants from the East complained about the wretched local pizza. Then along came Zachary's with its tasty rendition of Chicago-style, deep-dish pie: a deep bottom crust packed with a choice of fill-ings, covered with a thin second crust, and topped with tomato sauce. (The bottom crust turns crisp in the oven, the top one melts into the filling.) Try the gooey spinach, cheese, and mushroom, or the chicken, spinach, and whole-wheat crust combos. (The sausage isn't anything you'd want to write to Chicago about, and their single crust pizza is just so-so.) Both Zachary's are permanently packed with screaming students, children, and others with high decibel tolerance—though the Solano branch is somewhat tamer. The wildly creative kids' drawings of pizzas on the walls offer a little visual entertain-ment as you wait—and wait . . . and wait. The wisest call ahead and pick up a whole pie to go, which works until the harried staff takes the phone off the hook. ■ *Top of Solano, near The Oaks Theatre; (510) 525-5950; 1853 Solano Ave, Berkeley. ■ Near Rockridge BART at Oak Grove; (510) 655-6385; 5801 College Ave, Oakland; $; beer and wine; no credit cards; no checks; lunch, dinner every day.*

LODGINGS

Gramma's Bed & Breakfast Inn ★★ Gramma seems to be in the process of building an empire—and a delightful realm it is. This comfortable B&B began in a restored Tudor-style man-sion furnished with wonderful old furniture and period an-tiques; then it swallowed the house next door, added a cottage, garden, and carriage house, and swathed the grounds with beautifully landscaped lawns and an inviting English country garden tucked away in back. The best rooms are in the Fay House with its glowing hardwood walls and stunning stained-glass windows. All of the rooms in the Garden and Carriage houses—in back overlooking the garden—have fireplaces (room 4 in the Carriage House is best). Of course, the rooms facing away from Telegraph are the most tranquil. Breakfast is uneventful, but each evening, guests are invited to partake of complimentary wine and cheese. Coffee is available all day; cookie jars are stocked; and every guest room is graced with a basket of crunchy apples. ■ *Between Ward and Stuart, 9 blocks from UC; (510) 549-2125; 2740 Telegraph Ave, Berkeley, CA 94705; $$; AE, DC, MC, V; checks OK.*

Hillegass House ★ The rustic but stately Berkeley brown shingle is the town's most influential contribution to American architecture—and Hillegass House is a classic of the genre. With its large, shaded side porch, lovely backyard, and well-manicured front lawn, this three-story affair on a quiet street close to campus has a spacious downstairs and four big, high-ceilinged guest rooms awash with light. Ask for one of the corner rooms with their high windows framing the trees outside. The proprietor, Richard Warren, occupies the third floor, but he keeps a low profile: guests are given a private code to the front door lock, and the house telephone has voice mail. Breakfast comes from the popular Nabalom Bakery nearby. ■ *2 blocks above Telegraph Ave between Russell and Stuart; (510) 548-5517; 2834 Hillegass Ave, Berkeley, CA 94705; $$; no credit cards; checks OK.*

Hotel Durant ★ Despite extensive renovations five years ago, proximity to the UC campus remains the key advantage of this modestly appointed hotel. The lobby—with comfortable armchairs, handsome wood paneling, and stained-glass windows—and the adjacent restaurant, Henry's Publick House and Grille, succeed in imparting an aura of ersatz Old World charm, but the halls and rooms still have the faintly generic, institutional ambience of an upscale YMCA. In a neighborhood known for nightmarish traffic, valet parking is a blessing and a bargain at $5 a day (reserve this when you reserve your room, since there aren't enough spaces to go around); transport services to both San Francisco and Oakland airports, moderately priced with frequent departures, are another plus. Henry's bar stays open till midnight—but it's a madhouse on football weekends (especially if the Cal Bears have prevailed). ■ *Corner of Durant and Bowditch, 1 block from UC; (510) 845-8981; 2600 Durant Ave, Berkeley, CA 94704; $$; AE, DC, DIS, MC, V; checks OK.*

French Hotel At ground zero of Berkeley's famed gourmet ghetto, with Chez Panisse across the street and a staggering

▼
▲

array of specialty food purveyors on all sides, your trip to the Bay Area could begin and end right here. Simply haul an unending stream of goodies up to your room and stagger downstairs every now and then to quaff an espresso at the hotel's cafe; there you can relax at a sidewalk table while wondering what twist of fate turned a town from a hotbed of radicalism into a world-renowned culinary center in just a few short years. Despite the friendly concierge and efficient room service, the 18 rooms at the French Hotel are suitable only for sleeping. Avoid the noisy first-floor rooms facing Shattuck. The back room on the third floor is the quietest. ■ *N Berkeley between Cedar and Vine; (510) 548-9930; 1538 Shattuck Ave, Berkeley, CA 94709; $$; AE, DC, MC, V; checks OK.*

EMERYVILLE

This wired, artsy live-work town slivered between Oakland, Berkeley, and the bay was once a dowdy, industrial area, but 10 years of manic redevelopment has turned it into one of the most intriguing urban centers in the Bay Area: computer jockeys, artists, biotechies abound. Emeryville's town center is a nouveau ultramall called the Emerybay Public Market (Powell Street exit off I-80), featuring great ethnic food stands, gourmet markets, stores, and **hot clubs,** like Kimball's East, a jazz and blues club with national headliners, (510) 658-2555; Politics dance club, (510) 601-4888; and the Other Cafe comedy nightclub, (510) 601-4888.

RESTAURANTS

Hong Kong East Ocean Seafood Restaurant ★★★ With its green pagoda-style tile roof topped with writhing gold dragons, and with white Imperial lions guarding the front door, Hong Kong East Ocean looks more like a temple than a restaurant. Indeed, its worshippers are legion, thanks to a rumor circulating in Chinatowns throughout the Bay Area that Hong Kong East Ocean offers superior dim sum. Set at the very tip of the Emeryville Marina, the sleek, modern dining room has a magnificent view of the Bay Bridge and San Francisco. For the full dim sum treatment, come on the weekend when the dining room swarms with dozens of carts pushed by Chinese waitresses with a limited grasp of English and when most of your fellow diners will be well-heeled Chinese. (During the week, you order your dim sum from a menu—an efficient but sterile departure from tradition.) Best are the crystal buns (delicate, steamed dumplings filled with plump shrimp, chopped water chestnuts, cilantro, and ginger); crisp, baked baos filled with sweet red pork and topped with crunchy sesame seeds; and shrimp embedded in a melting noodle dough crêpe in a savory sauce. Besides dim sum, Hong Kong East Ocean offers authentic and exquisitely prepared Cantonese-style lunches and dinners: try the whole black cod in a satiny soy, ginger, garlic sauce; the addictive, peppery deep-fried squid topped with chopped chiles and scallions; and anything with their feathery egg noodles. ■ *End of the Emeryville Marina; (510) 655-3388; 3199 Powell St, Emeryville; $$; beer and wine; AE, MC, V; no checks; lunch, dinner every day.*

Bucci's ★★ Located in a beautifully restored warehouse, Bucci's is all brick and glass, with soaring ceilings, an open kitchen, and a small patio garden. At lunch, biotech execs and multimedia artists nosh on rich focaccia sandwiches and crisp thin-crust pizzas topped with prosciutto, roasted peppers, provolone, mozzarella, and cherry tomatoes. Dinner offers more elaborate fare, including a tender roast duck served with a rich butternut squash risotto, and delicate cannelloni stuffed with spinach, walnuts, roasted red peppers, and cheese in a lemon cream sauce. Desserts and espressos are top flight. ■ *On Hollis, between 59th and 61st; (510) 547-4725; 6121 Hollis, Emeryville; $$; beer and wine; no credit cards; checks OK; lunch Mon–Fri, dinner Mon–Sat.*

Carrara's Cafe and Gallery ★ An airy Emeryville warehouse environment with rotating art shows and a bohemian clientele, Carrara's is the perfect spot for people-watching, long lingering conversations, late night rendezvous, and feeling utterly comfortable all alone at the counter. The tasty Italian sandwiches (mozzarella, sun-dried tomatoes, and pesto on toasted focaccia, *per esempio*) are terrific, as is the antipasto plate with a full selection of exotic meats and cheeses, crisp toast rounds, and a ramekin containing spicy mustard and delectable parsley pesto. The spicy, salsa-spiked black bean soup with a swirl of crème fraîche is so popular they often run out. Folks seem to have passionate feelings both for and against the general acoustics (loud and echoing), the sound system, and the offbeat alternative music playing in the background. ■ *Powell St exit off I-80, between Doyle and Beaudry; (510) 547-6763; 1290 Powell St, Emeryville; $; beer and wine; MC, V; local checks only; breakfast, lunch, dinner Mon–Sat.*

▼
Oakland
▲

OAKLAND

A few years ago, as part of his plan to improve Oakland's image, Oakland mayor Elihu Harris ordered the city to change all of the vaguely forboding "Entering Oakland" signs to read "Welcome to Oakland." Some thought improving the city's wretched schools or cutting its alarming murder rate might be more to the point, but others appreciated the gesture. Most folks who live here agree that Oakland has gotten a bad rap. While the media keeps close tabs on the body count, few seem to notice Oakland's peaceful, integrated neighborhoods and richly diverse cultural life.

ARTS AND CULTURE

Music Oakland Symphony offers classical and choral concerts, combining jazz, classical, and folk at the Calvin Simmons Theater (10 10th Street, (510) 446-1992). Catch the hottest jazz at Yoshi's (6030 Claremont Ave, (510) 652-9200) or the bluest blues at Eli's Mile High Club (3629 Martin Luther King Jr. Way, (510) 655-6661). The Fifth Amendment (3255 Lakeshore Ave, (510) 832-3242) also offers live jazz and blues every night. Gospel acts abound, but they're hard to find. For information and tickets, call Reid's Records in Berkeley; (510) 843-7282.

Dance The Oakland Ballet performs at the Paramount Theater, (510) 465-6400; but Oakland is also home to dozens of innovative contemporary and African dance troupes including the Nuba Dance Theater, (510) 532-6405; Dimensions, (510) 428-2466; and the Fuadia Congo Dance Company, (510) 562-0831.

Film and Theater The Oakland Ensemble Theater offers multicultural works from an African-American perspective at the Alice Arts Theater; (510) 763-7774. Downtown's Paramount Theatre is a restored Deco masterpiece offering pipe organ concerts, plays, and films from Hollywood's golden age; 2025 Broadway, (510) 465-6400. The Grand Lake Theatre, a

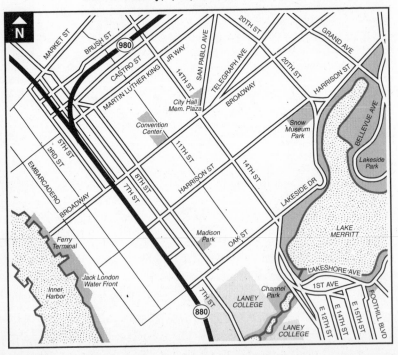

beautifully restored Egypto-Deco movie palace, shows new films and has a great live organist on weekends; 3200 Grand Ave, (510) 452-3556.

Museums The architecturally spectacular Oakland Museum offers innovative exhibits on the art, history, and ecology of California; Corner of Oak and 10th, (510) 834-2413. Exhibits on African-American culture and African art can be found at the Ebony Museum of Art; 30 Jack London Village, (510) 763-0141.

Sports Those hot-shot boys of summer, the Oakland A's, can be found knocking 'em dead at the Oakland Coliseum (take the Coliseum exit off I-80 or better yet, avoid the freeway crawl by taking BART, (510) 638-0500). Likewise for the tall guys of the Golden State Warriors who play at the Oakland Coliseum Arena; (510) 638-6300.

OTHER THINGS TO DO

In genteel North Oakland, the Rockridge neighborhood along College Avenue boasts dozens of bookstores, cafes, antique stores, expensive clothing stores, and a gourmet ghetto to rival North Berkeley's. Check out Rockridge Market Hall (5655 College Ave), a chic open air market offering fresh pasta, gourmet cheeses, breads from the awesome Grace Baking Company, exquisite produce, and wine. Grittier but just as interesting are downtown Oakland's Chinatown (more open and less touristy than San Francisco's Chinatown) and the Hispanic sprawl of tacquerias, bakeries, and botanicas along East 14th Street, between 2nd and 13th. The Pacific Coast Brewing Company offers a lively bar scene and good microbrewery suds; 906 Washington Street, (510) 836-2739. On the other side of Merritt Lake, you'll find Walden Pond Books (3316 Grand Avenue, (510) 832-4438) and the Coffee Mill (3363 Grand Avenue, (510) 465-4224)—your best bet for books and coffee near downtown.

You can stroll or jog around Lake Merritt, one of the largest saltwater tidal lakes in the world. It's also home of Festival at the Lake, an annual celebration of dance, arts, and music at the beginning of June; (510) 464-1061. Kids will like Lake Merritt's Children's Fairyland, a kid-sized amusement park where all adults must be accompanied by a child. They'll also approve of the Oakland Zoo; 9777 Golf Links Road, (510) 632-9523. But for the ultimate urban escape, head for the hills in Redwood Regional Park with its miles of trails through ferny redwood groves and oak woodland; (510) 531-9300.

RESTAURANTS

Bay Wolf Restaurant ★★ Located in an attractive Victorian house with dark wood wainscoting and pale yellow walls, the Bay Wolf first became a local favorite under the direction of co-owner and chef Michael Wild. Now new chef Nathan Peterson is continuing Wild's tradition of subdued Mediterranean Californiana. Don't look for bizarre flights of food fancy; fresh ingredients and careful preparation take the place of culinary acrobatics (a tender spiced scallop and endive salad, a rich, smokey asparagus and hazelnut soup with lemon cream). Dinner might consist of tender braised lamb shanks with white beans, artichokes, and rosemary, and a flavorful seafood stew, kissed with saffron and swarming with cracked Dungeness crab, prawns, rockfish, and mussels. For dessert, there's a sweetly spicy peach pie with a scoop of homemade cinammon ice cream and chocolate-topped profiteroles stuffed with white moons of homemade almond ice cream. The extensive, well-chosen wine list, includes a number of moderately priced vintages. Service is efficient, but a little stiff in the evenings; the help loosens up in the afternoons. ■ *On Piedmont Ave, just E of MacArthur, (510) 655-6004; 3853 Piedmont Ave, Oakland; $$$; beer and wine; MC, V; checks OK; lunch Mon–Fri, dinner every day.*

Chez Goldberg ★★ Located on a desolate stretch of Mac-Arthur Boulevard in East Oakland, Chez Goldberg is a stylish, neighborly bistro run by omnipresent chef, owner, and mâitre d' Bob Goldberg. With its long counter and booths, Chez Goldberg still looks a bit like the storefront diner it once was, but the white tablecloths, fresh flowers, soft pastels, and subtle art on the walls soften the effect. You can always count on finding interesting pastas (large, tender pumpkin and ricotta ravioli in sage-butter sauce) and Goldberg's homemade sausages (a mousselike seafood sausage; fiery chorizo, served with pink beans; or Yucatán chicken sausage with achiote, lime, cilantro, and jalapeño). There's always a fine fresh grilled fish on the menu, plus Goldberg's wonderful roast chicken seasoned to perfection with garlic, lemon, and rosemary. The well-chosen wine list won't strain your pocketbook. ■ *On MacArthur Blvd between 35th and High St; (510) 530-5332; 3719 MacArthur Blvd, Oakland; $$; beer and wine; V, MC; local checks only; dinner Tues–Sat.*

Lantern ★★ Dating back to 1947, this forbidding, concrete fortress is the biggest, oldest, most mind-boggling restaurant in Oakland's Chinatown. The ornate downstairs dining room offers up a tempting array of dinners, but the real reason to come here is the dim sum, served from early morning to midafternoon in an auditorium-size banquet room on the third floor that seats a neat 700. Sip a cup of aromatic tea as servers circulate through the room pushing carts laden with assorted delicacies. They'll pause by your table and lift the lids of tiered metal steamers to let you inspect the barbecued pork buns, stuffed dumplings, wedges of green pepper stuffed with shrimp, and more. You're charged by the plate. You can afford to experiment here—two people can bloat themselves for about 20 bucks. ■ *Chinatown at 8th and Webster; (510) 451-0627;*

814 Webster St, Oakland; $; full bar; MC, DIS, V; no checks; breakfast, lunch, dinner every day.

Nan Yang ▪ Nan Yang Rockridge ★★ When Nan Yang opened in 1983, restaurants offering a full spectrum of genuine Burmese delights were virtually nonexistent; even in Rangoon, hungry travelers had to trudge from festival to festival and stall to stall to gain any sense of the cuisine. Chef and owner Philip Chu assembled the menu for Nan Yang by tracking down recipes from monasteries, street vendors, festival food booths, and family homes to create the first Burmese restaurant in the Bay Area. His noble efforts have been rewarded with rave reviews and long lines of customers clamoring for his titillating ginger salad (a crunchy, textural delight with 16 ingredients including split peas, fava beans, shredded cabbage, coconut slices, sun-dried shrimp, garlic oil, roasted peanuts, and shredded ginger). The generous curries come with giant chunks of beef, chicken, and fish; there are also plenty of seductive vegetarian variations. One note of caution: the staff at the Chinatown branch occasionally urges you to order more than you can possibly consume. The recently opened Rockridge branch is a sleeker, slicker operation run by Chu's very hip, very American children. ▪ *Corner of Harrison and 8th, (510) 465-6924; 301 8th St, Oakland; $; beer and wine; MC, V; no checks; lunch, dinner Tues–Sun.* ▪ *On College, just S of Claremont; (510) 655-3298; 6048 College Ave, Oakland; $$; beer and wine; MC, V; no checks; lunch, dinner Tues–Sun.*

Oakland

Restaurants

▲

Pizza Rustica ★★ Located in a white, postmodern building with red Corinthian columns, this jazzy nouveau pizza joint has a cramped, noisy dining room with tiny, knee-bruising tables, bright pop art on the walls, and California pizzas on light, crunchy cornmeal crusts or traditional peasant bread crust. Their traditional Mediterranean-style pizzas are impeccable, but the pizza adventurers will want to try one of their more exotic offerings: the Thai pizza comes with roasted chicken in spicy ginger peanut sauce, mozzarella, julienne carrots, scallions, daikon, peppers, and sesame seeds; the Cuban comes with smoked ham, roasted chicken, chorizo, black beans, capers, mozzarella, and fresh tomatoes. The desserts aren't particularly inspiring, but the chocolate-dipped, rice crisp and marshmallow bars will remind you of mom. ▪ *College at Manila; (510) 654-1601; 5422 College Ave, Oakland; $; beer and wine; MC, V; checks OK; lunch Wed–Sat, dinner every day.*

Sangthong Thai Restaurant ★★ Key and Elli Keovyphone originally opened this charming eatery as a Thai restaurant, realizing only later that the cuisine of their native Laos might appeal just as much to the culinarily curious of the East Bay. Now the menu balances a repertoire of top-notch Thai selections with wondrous specialties that harken back to old Vientiane.

Key's grilled Laotian hot sausages are made with pork, chile, scallions, lemon grass, paprika, and cilantro and served with a bowl of clear, sweet, zingingly hot sauce and mounds of red and white cabbage. Laap pa—deep-fried fish tossed with fresh herbs, chile flakes, lemon grass, mint leaves, and lime juice—is another rare treat. Vegetarians will like the grilled eggplant with tofu and basil in a richly flavored sauce. Round up a few friends for the Laotian-style family dinner, a hands-on gastronomical fête of Northern Mekong cuisine, requiring a minimum of four diners and four hours' advance notice. ■ *Between 8th and 9th; (510) 839-4017; 850 Broadway, Oakland; $; beer and wine; DIS, MC, V; local checks only; lunch Mon–Fri, dinner Mon–Sat.*

Zza's Trattoria ★★ Bright, cramped, cheerful, and noisy, Zza's Trattoria has an intensely loyal following. There's always a long line winding out the door for dinner, and one wall is decorated with photos of Zza's regulars wearing the Trattoria's coveted T-shirt in front of the Eiffel Tower and other places around the world. The thin, crisp-crust pizzas come with interesting toppings like smoked bacon, eggplant, onion, red chile, tomatoes, smoked mozzarella, and basil. Other winners include the garlic-infused roast chicken in rosemary sauce or the fresh, delightfully spicy pasta puttanesca. Also be on the lookout for Zza's incredible osso bucco special: veal shanks braised in red wine and veal stock with thyme and bay, served on a creamy polenta. We've never minded the wildly extroverted staff and general din, but we know it grates on some people's nerves. ■ *Take the Grand Lake exit off Hwy 580, turn right; (510) 839-9124; 552 Grand Ave, Oakland; $; beer and wine; MC, V; no checks; lunch Wed–Fri, dinner every day, brunch Sat–Sun.*

Asmara Restaurant and Bar ★ Asmara has a split personality: the comfortable restaurant is full of East African kitsch, while the adjacent bar—stark white and brightly lit—is a sterile jolt to the senses. (Ethiopian expatriates seem to prefer the bar, while locals enjoy the restaurant's African decor.) Both groups get caught up in the communal spirit of the place, however, scooping their dinner from a common platter, using pieces of spongy injera bread to grab globs of tasty ziggni watt (beef marinated in a surprisingly mild berbere sauce made with jalapeño and chile peppers) and ye-gomen alicha (mustard greens simmered in spices). Make the most of this culinary adventure by getting one of the combination dinners. ■ *Corner of 51st; (510) 547-5100; 5020 Telegraph Ave, Oakland; $; full bar; MC, V; no checks; lunch, dinner Wed–Mon.*

Le Cheval ■ Le Cheval II ★ This family-owned restaurant is a local favorite and the occasional inconsistency of the fare doesn't seem to daunt loyal followers. Located in a transitional neighborhood that can make visitors nervous after dark, the original Cheval's dilapidated interior adds a touch of authenticity to the Franco-Viet postcolonial atmosphere. The strictly Asian fare here isn't very interesting, but dishes based on French techniques shine. Try the bo tai chanh (slices of marinated meat in sweet lemon juice topped with chopped peanuts, caramelized garlic, onion slices, and chiles) or the bun rieu (minced shrimp and crab with rice vermicelli in a flavorful stock prepared from the shells). They've also got an ambitious selection of beers from around the globe. Le Cheval II, in the heart of corporate Oakland, caters to the business crowd, closes early, and lacks the atmosphere that makes the original so evocative. ■ *W of Broadway just off 14th St; (510) 763-8495; 1414 Jefferson St, Oakland.* ■ *First floor of Kaiser Center; (510) 763-3610; 344 20th St, Oakland; lunch, early dinner Mon–Fri; $; beer and wine; AE, DC, MC, V; no checks; lunch, dinner Mon–Sat, dinner Sun.*

Morelia Taqueria ★ Oakland has been called the nation's most integrated city, and nowhere is this more evident than in this big, boisterous taqueria and bar deep in the heart of East Oakland. The food may be basic taqueria fare—burritos, tortas, and tacos—but the vast range of ingredients includes hard-to-find specialties, and everything is startlingly fresh. Try Morelia's savory carnitas with a dose of the fiery green house salsa. Avoid the neon-drenched bar; eat in the bright dining room lined with portraits of athletes. Better yet, get your food to go and chow down in the center field bleachers of the nearby Oakland Coliseum. ■ *E 14th St at 45th; (510) 535-6030; 4481 E 14th St, Oakland; $; full bar; no credit cards; no checks; lunch, dinner Mon–Sun.*

Oakland

Restaurants

Oakland Seafood Cuisine ★ Seafood at this restaurant, with a mostly Chinese clientele, is exceptionally fine and the service and decor are especially refined. Linen tablecloths, floral wallpaper, and wine-colored napkins share the dining room with a red Confucian shrine. The seafood ranges from sea cucumbers to scallops and rock cod (and lots of tasty creatures in between) prepared in a variety of delectable sauces. When crab is in season, go for a delicious, absorbingly messy whole critter, with black bean sauce or ginger and scallions. Exquisite treats are most often found on the special menu (sizzling eggplant stuffed with shrimp, or shrimp with candied walnuts). Kids and adults alike will love the shrimp Hong Kong chow mein—plump, pink shrimp and tender bok choy topping a nest of succulent noodles. Although it's only listed on the lunch menu, the kitchen will make it anytime. ■ *Chinatown between Harrison and Webster; (510) 893-3388; 307 10th St, Oakland; $; beer and wine; MC, V; no checks; lunch, dinner every day.*

Oliveto Cafe and Restaurant ★ Oliveto's is *so* popular with normally choosy North Oakland folks that we're always a little shocked by the quality of the food here. It's not bad, of course; but it's never as exciting as the apricot-sponged archways, terra-cotta tiles, and the well-dressed, well-heeled stockbroker-cum-filmmaker crowd lead you to expect. Upstairs in the dining room (chic-unto-death), the food is merely expensive and very standard Northern Italian–Californian. Opt instead to see and be seen in the downstairs cafe. You may have to knock someone over the head to get a table, but so be it: the tapas and the scene, especially at prime commuting hour, are worth the effort. Here tense-but-chic workaholic singles size each other up over small, crisp California pizzas and sophisticated salads like the panzanella, cherry tomato, and fresh mozzarella. Flirt with your neighbor over awe-inspiring desserts like brioche bread pudding with apricot sauce or dark chocolate torte with poached sour cherries and whipped cream. Expert espressos, plenty of good wines by the glass, and exotic beers add to the air of sophisticated debauchery. ■ *Across from Rockridge BART; (510) 547-5356; 5655 College Ave, Oakland; $$; beer and wine; DC, MC, V; checks OK in dining room, no checks in cafe; breakfast, lunch, dinner every day in the cafe; lunch Mon–Fri, dinner every day in the dining room.*

Phnom Penh House ■ New Phnom Penh ★ This family enterprise began in 1986 with wonderful food, intimate and infinitely gracious service, and a lot of do-it-yourself gumption—the tile renditions of Angkor Wat on the walls were made by a friend of the family in his garage. It wasn't long before lines started forming and the service became rather rushed. The food, however, is still terrific. Start out with the noum om beng (a hefty, crisp crêpe stuffed with pork, shrimp, bean curd, coconut, and bean sprouts, served with a bowl of spicy peanut sauce). We also like number 28—the moarn ann kreun (chicken wings deboned and stuffed with lemon grass, bean thread, and chicken, deep-fried and served with chile-peanut sauce)—and number 34 with the same name, different number—go figure—a finger-licking-good barbecued chicken, chopped up and piled on a plate with a side dish of pickled vegetables. Leave room for the best fried bananas around, with coconut and sesame seeds and served with a scoop of ice cream. ■ *Near Alice at the edge of Chinatown; (510) 893-3825; 251 8th Street, Oakland; lunch, dinner Mon–Sat.* ■ *Shattuck at Cedar; (510) 841-9405; 1600 Shattuck Ave, Berkeley; $; beer and wine; MC, V; no checks; lunch, dinner every day.*

Rockridge Cafe ★ Another heavy hitter in the contest for the title of best East Bay burger, this neighborhood hangout does diner food the old-fashioned way, only better: juicy, all-American hamburgers on nicely toasted whole-wheat or regular buns; fat, toothsome fries; and greasy-but-good onion rings. For dessert, try one of their tart fruit pies like olallieberry or apricot-rhubarb, or the orgasmic fudge-walnut pie. Fine breakfasts feature sweet ricotta pancakes, crisp cornmeal waffles, or zippy scrambled chorizo and eggs. Some folks like the diner-like ambience in the old section, but we prefer to hunker down in the polished wood booths in the new dining room next door. ■ *College between Lawton and Forest; (510) 653-1567; 5492 College Ave, Oakland; $; beer and wine; MC, V; no checks; breakfast, lunch, dinner every day.*

Sabina India Cuisine ★ The Desai family lucked out when they opened their gracious North Indian eatery in this fanciful former tile store: the restaurant's narrow, columned facade is covered with handsome ceramic work, and inside the dining room there's a tile fountain. Less elaborate than the decor, Sabina's specialties are mildly spiced, Indian comfort foods: tempting renditions of tandoori dishes, curries, and vegetarian features, all served up with wonderfully aromatic basmati rice. Try the chicken pasanda—chunks of tender roasted white chicken served in a cashew cream sauce. Start out with the crisp samosas and pakoras. The buffet lunch, where you can sample 11 different courses and refill your plate as often as you wish for under six bucks, is a bargain. ■ *2 blocks W of Broadway at 17th St; (510) 268-0170; 1628 Webster St, Oakland; $; beer and wine; AE, DC, DIS, MC, V; checks OK; lunch Mon–Sat, dinner every day.*

Saigon Deli ★ The 1989 quake totaled Saigon Deli's original building, and its new home, set on a deserted block of earthquake-damaged buildings, isn't much better. But the deli's apocalyptic surroundings haven't deterred the hordes of lunchtime business execs, Vietnamese families, hip Asian teenagers, and savvy world travelers come flocking here for the fabulous pho—a delicious, hard-to-find noodle dish. Pho tai—fresh beef noodle soup with tender slices of meat and soft rice noodles in a rich and pungent broth—comes with a large side of fresh basil, bean sprouts, hot peppers, and lemon, so you can season your pho just the way you like it. The barbecued shrimp roll with rice paper is another hands-on delight; the friendly young waitstaff will help you figure out how to soak the paper-thin rice pancakes and pack them with chopped scallions, rice noodles, romaine lettuce, mint, basil, tomatoes, cucumber, bean sprouts, and scrumptious barbecued shrimp. You can stuff yourself here for about a five spot. ■ *N of 14th St, diagonally opposite City Hall; (510) 465-4545; 1526 San Pablo Ave, Oakland; $; beer and wine; MC, V; local checks only; breakfast, lunch, dinner every day.*

Yoshi's ★ After a recent misguided detour into ill-conceived Pacific Rim cuisine, this combination Japanese restaurant and top-flight jazz club has returned to the kind of fresh, traditional Japanese food that made it famous in the first place. Dinner starts out with a refreshing appetizer of crisp diced cucumber and wakame seaweed in a rice wine vinaigrette, and a subtle bowl of miso soup with velvety button mushrooms and firm cubes of tofu. Avoid their tough gyoza. The best deal here is the Yoshi's dinner for two, with its huge rose made of fresh red tuna surrounded by generous portions of light tempura, not-too-sweet yakitori, grilled salmon, and a variety of brightly colored pickles. In addition to the traditional green tea ice cream, Yoshi's offers an array of very good Western cakes and pastries. If you're planning to catch the show in Yoshi's intimate jazz club, reserve your table before you go into dinner. ■ *1 block S of College; (510) 652-9200; 5030 Claremont Ave, Oakland; $$; full bar; DIS, MC, V; no checks; lunch Mon–Fri, dinner every day.*

LODGINGS

The Claremont Resort and Tennis Club ★★★ With its towers and cupolas gleaming white against the green Berkeley hills, this haughty prima donna of a hotel holds fast to its Edwardian roots. It's hard to hurry here: the posh lobby with its plush furniture, crystal chandeliers, and extensive art collection is made for loitering and gaping, while 22 acres of beautifully landscaped grounds (flower gardens, waving rows of exotic palms, and even a modern sculpture garden) invite leisurely strolling. The only rushing that gets done around here is by folks rushing the net on the Claremont's 10 courts. The guest rooms are spacious and attractively decorated, with views of either the eucalyptus-covered hills or San Francisco Bay. For an unobstructed view of the bay, be prepared to shell out for a junior or full suite ($295–$720).

Amenities include everything you'd expect from a grand hotel, including concierge and room service and a fully equipped business center; parking and transportation to airports and San Francisco are available for a fee. Besides the tennis courts, guests have access to two heated pools, saunas, a hot tub, and a jogging course. The staff—influenced, no doubt, by the aristocratic environs—has at times been known to act irritatingly haughty. The best views in the region can be enjoyed from the bar or restaurant. ■ *In the hills above Berkeley, at Ashby and Domingo; (510) 843-3000; Ashby and Domingo avenues, Oakland, CA 94623-0363; $$$; AE, DC, DIS, MC, V; checks OK.*

Lake Merritt Hotel ★★ This art deco masterpiece right next to downtown looks out on Lake Merritt—a large, landscaped lake that's mecca for joggers, walkers, and rowers. Built in 1927, the vintage white stucco hotel was recently restored to its original deco opulence with stunning light fixtures, richly patterned carpeting, plush furniture, and lush flower arrangements. Most of the rooms are standard suites appointed in the charming manner of studio apartments circa 1930 (except for the thoroughly modern microwaves and coffee-makers). The deluxe suites with separate living rooms are a bargain at $149. All of the rooms have cable TV, modern bath, stocked minibar, and phone with dataport. Ask for a room facing the lake. The hotel provides a complimentary limo to whisk you to the nearby Oakland financial district. They also have fax and copy services, a concierge, complimentary wine tasting, and a light continental breakfast served downstairs in the Mural Room—delightfully decorated with scenes of Lake Merritt during the mid-'50s. ■ *At 19th and Madison facing Lakeside Dr; (510) 832-2300, toll free (800) 933-HOTEL; 1800 Madison, Oakland, CA 94612; $$$; AE, DC, DIS, MC, V; checks OK.*

Washington Inn ★★ An intimate corporate hotel could sound like an oxymoron, but this inviting 1913 inn, recently restored to turn-of-the-century elegance, pulls it off with panache. It's the attentive service and special personal touches that make a stay here so pleasurable (the rates—from $89 to $129—are an added bonus). Nightly turndown service includes a chocolate on your pillow and a cordial on the nightstand. You'll also find a newspaper at your door each morning. The 47 rooms are decorated in soft rose tones with attractive period furniture. Rooms on the northwest corner of the building offer intriguing views of the Bay Bridge in the distance, while rooms on the central airshaft get ample sunlight and less street noise. The Washington Inn Bar & Restaurant downstairs serves creamy corn chowder and chicken potpie. Guests are invited to complimentary hors d'oeuvres every weekday evening. And then there *is* work: A small, fully equipped business center is open 24 hours a day, and the hotel's location couldn't be more convenient—BART is just two blocks away, with Oakland's City Center within a few minutes' walk. ■ *Between Washington and Broadway opposite Oakland Convention Center; (510) 452-1776, toll free (800) 464-1776 in California, (800) 477-1775 outside California; 495 10th Street, Oakland, CA 94607; $$; AE, DC, MC, V; checks OK with credit card ID; lunch, dinner Mon–Fri.*

Alameda

Restaurants

ALAMEDA

RESTAURANTS

Chevy's Mexican Restaurant ★ Scattered throughout Northern California, Chevy's is a chain Mexican restaurant with a difference: the food is terrific. Everything is made fresh, including the tortillas, made by the child-pleasing *el machino*. Add a great location on the Oakland estuary, a bevy of outside tables (warmed by efficient heat lamps for chilly evenings), a fine view of the Oakland skyline, and big, icy margaritas—and how can you resist? The house specialty here is fajitas: fresh, hot tortillas served with mesquite-grilled chicken, beef, shrimp, shark, or quail, marinated in beer, soy, garlic and onions, and served with grilled asparagus and squash on a sizzling iron platter. Nice light, hot tortilla chips, too. Three other East Bay locations are in El Cerrito, (510) 526-2551; Richmond, (510) 222-9802; and San Leandro, (510) 276-0962. ■ *On Mariner Square Dr (and branches); (510) 521-3768; 2400 Mariner Square Dr, Alameda; $$; full bar; AE, MC, V; no checks; lunch, dinner every day, brunch Sun.*

LODGINGS

Garratt Mansion ★★ Surrounded by lush gardens and just four blocks from the beach, this three-story, 1893 Colonial Revival manse is a picture-perfect example of Victoriana with gorgeous stained-glass windows, hand-carved interior woodwork, and a wealth of wonderful architectural details. All six spacious guest rooms have sitting areas; three have private baths; four have phones. On the second floor, we like Diana's Room, a large suite with a fireplace, separate sitting room, bamboo canopy bed, and private bath with claw-footed tub and stall shower. Kelly's Room next door, with its fluffy down pillows, has a vintage sewing machine. On the third floor, Martha's and Angela's rooms enchant with seating alcoves under the dormer windows looking out over the treetops and a sheltered lagoon. Innkeeper Betty Gladden puts fresh flowers in the sitting room every day and lays out platters of home-baked cookies in the late afternoon. ■ *Between Encinal and Clinton; (510) 521-4779; 900 Union St, Alameda, CA 94501; $$; AE, DC, MC, V; checks OK.*

Webster House Bed and Breakfast Inn ★ This intriguing example of Gothic Revival architecture was built in New York in the early 1850s, shipped around the Horn, and assembled in Alameda for a cousin of Daniel Webster. The spiked finials on the roof and around the perimeter of the property are supposed to prevent evil spirits from alighting, while the doll house on the front porch is placed to lure and trap curious spirits before they can enter the house proper. The problem with this otherwise intriguing place is it seems to have been built for midgets. Petite owner Susan McCormick, who lives with her husband Andrew in the cottage out back, explains that people were much tinier way back when, but unless you too are tiny—and nimble-footed to boot—you may feel like a bull in a china shop. The four small guest rooms share a single bathroom and small living room with a fireplace and a friendly cockatiel named Bogie. Crammed with small dining tables, the living room doubles as a coffeeshop Thursday through Sunday, offering brunch on weekends and high tea every Sunday. There's a little too much going on in this little house. At bedtime, guests are served hot chocolate, warm vanilla milk, or sherry by the fireside. ■ *Near the corner of Versailles and Encinal; (510) 523-9697; 1238 Versailles Ave, Alameda, CA 94501; $$; no credit cards; checks OK.*

HAYWARD

RESTAURANTS

Le Maconnais ★★ Housed in a small cottage off one of Hayward's busier streets, this romantic and tasteful restaurant looks from the inside like a secluded French country inn. Chef and expert saucier Guy Grenier does a fine job with the escalopes de veau in a fresh sorrel and mushroom sauce, as well as the tender salmon in beurre blanc spiked with Cognac and capers. Exquisite desserts include barely sweetened spoonfuls of meringue floating in a custard sea and drizzled with caramelized sugar. Host/owner Daniel Pont maintains an ample wine list from both California and France, including several from eponymous Mâcon. In November, an annual five-course dinner celebrates the release of Beaujolais Nouveau. ■ *Top of Foothill Blvd, 2 blocks from I-580; (510) 538-3522; 21181 Foothill Blvd, Hayward; $$; beer and wine; AE, DC, DIS, MC, V; checks OK; lunch Wed–Fri, dinner Tues–Sat.*

Buffalo Bill's Brewpub ★ Beer fanciers may already know about Buffalo Bill's through *American Brewer*, the magazine published by owner Bill Owens. You can sample the products of the house in the cafe or under the benevolent gaze of the large stuffed buffalo head above the bar. The three Buffalo brews on tap (Brew, Amber, and dark, sweet Bock) are all available in anything from a slender glass to a hulking jug 10 times as big (called the buffalo bladder). You can watch the brewing process through a window in the back. The food is simple pub grub: sandwiches, personal pizzas, buffalo wings (naturally)— even a British-style ploughman's board of cheese, salami, and French bread. ■ *Off Foothill Blvd in downtown Hayward; (510) 886-9823; 1082 B St, Hayward; $; beer and wine; MC, V; no checks; lunch, dinner every day.*

Val's ★ Home of the Ur-burger since 1958, Val's proves that the secret to success is excess. The juicy delicious Papa, for example, nudges the scales at a full pound. An order of enormous (and exquisitely cooked) fries can easily satisfy two. The old-fashioned milk shakes deliver two full glasses in a stainless steel container, and the malteds taste like malt. Should the prospect of a full-pound burger give you pause, there are many smaller-scale classics to choose from: BLTs, grilled cheese, even a fried-egg sandwich. Everything at Val's is as it should be, and then some. ■ *Take Center St exit from*

I-580, corner of B and Kelly; (510) 889-VALS; 2115 Kelly St, Hayward; $; no alcohol; no credit cards; no checks; breakfast, lunch, dinner Tues–Sat.

NEWARK

RESTAURANTS

Hungarian Huszar ★ Two guarantees of authenticity: the bilingual, Magyar-English menu, and the signed photo of Zsa Zsa by the door. No wonder this out-of-the-way place is a home away from home for every other homesick Hungarian in the East Bay. Where else can you get cold sour-cherry soup or Transylvanian goulash? The sour-cherry items are universally interesting, especially the succulent duck breast with sour-cherry sauce. There are also a number of enticing fish specialties: breaded catfish with mushroom sauce and dilled lobster casserole. The native theme extends to the wine list (Hungary's viticultural tradition is long and surprisingly honorable), and don't neglect a nice strudel or palacsinta (crêpe) for dessert. Service is rather slow, but you can use the time to help the charming waitress with her English. ■ *In the Old Town shopping center, between Cedar and Thornton; (510) 796-8061; 36601 Newark Blvd, Newark; $$; beer and wine; AE, DC, DIS, MC, V; checks OK; dinner Tues–Sun.*

FREMONT

LODGINGS

Lord Bradley's Inn ★★ Rebuilt after the devastating earthquake of 1868 that flattened large sections of the East Bay, this atmospheric frontier hotel offers a good sense of what it must have been like to live in the Bay Area during the 19th century (though it's considerably more comfortable). Separated from historic Mission San Jose by a row of ancient olive trees, the inn looks out over oak- and grass-covered hills that look much as they did in the time of the great ranchos. The eight guest rooms have antique bedsteads and private baths. Lord Keith's spacious attic room has a pitched ceiling and a window seat from which you can see Mission Peak. Breakfast includes fresh and dried fruit, croissants, and muffins with orange butter. While here, hike up Mission Peak (the highest prominence hereabouts, with panoramic views of the South Bay), or go winetasting at Weibel Winery half a mile away. Unless you have a Persian cat or Scottie (sentimental exceptions), leave your pet at home. ■ *Just past Mission San Jose; (510) 490-0520; 43344 Mission Blvd, Fremont; $; DC, MC, V; checks OK.*

MILPITAS

RESTAURANTS

Zahir's Cafe ★ Zahir's Cafe's sophisticated decor, open kitchen, and exuberant cuisine come as somewhat of a surprise given its nondescript locale. Everything is prepared fresh daily, and the byword here is profusion. (The menu is a tome—there's a page of chicken entrées, another of veal specials, another for seafood, one for pasta, and on and on.) A typical plate is dressed like a woman who can't decide what jewelry to wear—piled high with garnishes, including mounds of shredded red cabbage, orange slices, and parsley. Portions are huge. Star appetizers include the platter of skinned red potatoes slathered with melted cheddar, the perfectly cooked shrimp in a tomatillo sauce, and the mushrooms stuffed with crab and cheese and, naturally, lots of edible garnishes. Some entrées are uninspired, but chicken Zahir—a tender chicken breast wrapped in roasted red peppers and mushrooms inside a pastry shell and served on a pool of red-pepper coulis seasoned with tarragon and cayenne—is delightful. ■ *Corner of Landess and S Park Victoria Dr; (408) 946-4000; 1350 S Park Victoria Dr, Milpitas; $$$; beer and wine; AE, DIS, MC, V; no checks; lunch Mon–Fri, dinner Tues–Sun.*

San Jose

The Arts

SAN JOSE

All the boomers who grew up with Dionne Warwick's "Do You Know the Way to San Jose," a paean to the relaxed small-town San Jose of yesteryear, may be shocked to see the freeway-locked surburban sprawl spreading out from San Jose's gentrified chrome, glass, and pastel downtown. The new light rail system is your best bet for getting around this booming "edge city," though you'll probably need a car to reach the outer edges. Call (408) 287-4210 for rail system info.

THE ARTS

Culture San Jose has a community of theater, ballet, and opera groups called The Big Six, most of whom revolve around the San Jose Center for The Performing Arts; 255 Almaden Boulevard at Park Avenue, (408) 277-3900. The San Jose Civic Light Opera, (408) 971-1212, shows primarily musicals, while the Opera San Jose (12 S First Street, (408) 283-4880), the San Jose Cleveland Ballet, (408) 288-2800, and the San Jose Symphony Orchestra, (408) 288-2828, offer the more traditional cultural enrichments. Los Lupenos de San Jose dance company reflects the Spanish heritage of the city; 34 N First Street, (408) 292-0443. For drama, the San Jose Repertory Theatre does innovative productions of new works and classics; 1 N First Street, (408) 291-2255. The San Jose Stage Company

(490 S First Street, (408)283-7142) shows American contemporary drama and comedy, while City Lights Theatre goes the more experimental route; 529 S Second Street, (408)295-4200.

Museums The San Jose Museum of Art (110 S Market Street, (408) 294-2787) features contemporary European and American art; the Rosicrucian Museum (on the corner of Park and Naglee Avenue, (408) 287-2807), run by an obscure, mail-order mystical group, has a remarkable collection of Egyptian artifacts, mummies, and tombs. The Children's Discovery Museum, painted in shocking Easter egg purple, re-creates urban life for kids to explore and operate things like traffic lights and the water department; 180 Woz Way, (408) 298-5437. Adults might get more out of the Tech Museum of Innovation across from the convention center, a hands-on science museum where you can play with robots, get an insight into gene engineering, or design your own high-tech bicycle; 145 W San Carlos Avenue, (408) 279-7150. The Winchester Mystery House isn't really worth $12.50 a head, but it's got an intriguing history: after inheriting $20 million from her husband's Repeating Rifle company, Sarah Winchester became convinced that the ghosts of people killed with Winchester rifles were coming back to find her. Her paranoia led her to have additions built to her home 24 hours a day for 38 years to house their restless spirits, fearing that if she stopped building, the spirits would kill her. The house is a 160-room labyrinth of crooked corridors, doors opening into space, and dead-end stairways; 525 S Winchester Boulevard, (408) 247-2101.

OTHER THINGS TO DO

Night Spots At night, SoFA is the place where the hipsters go. Once the red light district, the area south of First Street (known comfortably as SoFA) has had a truly gradual development into a clean, hip home for many nightclubs and the slightly more alternative scene. For dancing, try the Cactus Club for hip hop and live rock (417 S First Street, (408) 986-0866) or F/X The Club for funk, house, and hip hop; 400 S First, (408) 298-9796. The Ajax Lounge (374 S First, (408) 298-2529) is a good neighborhood bar, and J.J.'s Blues Club has live blues or reggae every night of the week; 14 S Second, (408) 286-3066.

Parks Kelley Park (corner of Senter Road and Keyes Street, (408) 277-4193) is a good place for a picnic, and you can stop off in the Japanese Friendship Garden, complete with a koi fish pond and a tea house. Guadalupe River Park has recently been redone as well, though it's not really a river because of the drought. Public artworks celebrating river life and the Ohlone Indians' sacred animals appear around the park; corner of San Carlos and Almaden, (408) 295-9600.

Wineries They may lack the glamour and spectacular settings of their country cousins, but the wineries inside the

San Jose city limits are interesting and convenient. Both wineries feature tours and have a variety of vintages available for tasting. Housed in a former brewery in the middle of town, Lohr Winery produces a wide range of wines, mostly from grapes grown in Monterey County, plus the increasingly popular Ariel non-alcoholic wines; 1000 Lenzen Avenue, (408) 288-5057. Mirassou Vineyards was once a country winery, but it's now surrounded by several miles of newish, lookalike suburban-style housing developments. The tasting room is spacious and pleasant, and the staff friendly and well-informed; 3000 Aborn Road, (408) 274-4000. Mirassou also has a separate facility in Los Gatos where it produces sparkling wine. (300 College Ave, Los Gatos, (408) 395-3790).

RESTAURANTS

Emile's ★★★ At San Jose's best restaurant, chef/owner Emile Mooser offers a California version of the cuisine he learned in his homeland, the Gruyère region of Switzerland. The menu features classic French preparations such as foie gras frais (fresh duck foie gras sautéed with walnut oil and served on a bed of seasonal greens) and cuisine minceur (a leaner style of French cooking that's sparing with cream sauces). Using fine stocks and the best seasonal ingredients, the kitchen does a particularly good job with fish and game. Consider the splendid ahi tuna marinated in soy sauce and fresh ginger, coated with crushed black pepper in the manner of steak au poivre, seared, and served carpaccio-style with spicy radish sprouts and shaved carrots dressed in a sauce of rice vinegar, sesame oil, and soy. The tender, sliced roast venison loin served on a bed of fava beans, shallots, and venison sausage in a light game stock is refreshingly mild. Keep an eye out for regional specialties; roesti—a crunchy, Swiss version of hash browns— is out of this world. Everything is made on the premises, from the house-cured gravlax (served with a yogurt-dill sauce and onion compote) to flawless desserts like the Grand Marnier or cappuccino soufflés. Emile's wine cellar contains more than 300 selections, ranging from the very reasonable to the very, very expensive. Reservations are advised. ■ *Between Williams and Reed streets; (408) 289-1960; 545 S Second St, San Jose; $$$; full bar; AE, DC, DIS, MC, V; no checks; lunch Tues–Fri, dinner Tues–Sat.*

La Foret French Restaurant ★★★ Located in an old two-story hotel overlooking Los Alamedos Creek, this 13-year-old restaurant offers interesting and unusual wild game flown in daily. Chef Vazgen Davoudi, a natural cook who honed his craft through trial and error and the instincts of his own palate, can always be counted on to create superb sauces for the day's special, which might be something like tender medallions of wild boar marinated in shallots, balsamic vinegar, brandy, and cumin and topped with an outstanding pink-peppercorn sauce, paired with medallions of elk in an equally masterful tarragon cream sauce. Davoudi's prowess isn't limited to game; he works equally well with meltingly tender Maine lobster tail (in a balanced sauce of tarragon, balsamic vinegar, and herbed cream cheese) and black eastern mussels (in a saffron cream sauce with shallots). Desserts usually include a selection of cakes, cheesecakes, and exotic soufflés; wines are mostly Californian with some European exceptions. ■ *Almaden Rd exit off Almaden Expwy, S 2½ miles, left at Almaden Way, cross small bridge to Bertram Rd, (408) 997-3458; 21747 Bertram Rd; San Jose; $$$; full bar; AE, DC, DIS, MC, V; no checks; dinner Tues–Sun.*

California Sushi and Grill ★★

This chic sushi spot is very popular with the downtown crowd who wants something fast and delicious and doesn't mind parting with a chunk of change to get it. The venue is small and very attractive with the grill and sushi chef in full view of the small sushi bar. An upstairs loft provides a more intimate setting that will also accommodate larger groups. The creative, unerringly fresh sushi preparations range from classics like ebi and yellow-fin nori to provocative specials like spider rolls—half a deep-fried softshell crab with slices of buttery avocado and crisp cucumber rolled inside sticky rice and seaweed. They're fashioned so that the crab's spidery claws protrude menacingly from the roll. The miso soup here is a standout as is the delicious seaweed salad tossed with a few slices of sashimi, smoked salmon, or crab. The teriyaki entrées, particularly the rare beef and salmon, are expertly rendered and nothing short of delicious. ■ *On San Fernando between 1st and 2nd streets, (408) 297-1847; 1 E San Fernando St, San Jose; $$; beer and wine; AE, MC, V; no checks; lunch Mon–Fri, dinner Mon–Sat.*

Chez Sovan Restaurant ★★

Despite its name, Chez Sovan isn't going to win any prizes for ambience. Tucked between a filling station and a car-repair joint in San Jose's gritty warehouse district, it resembles your typical down-at-the-heels diner, right down to the faded posters and the plastic flowers. The authentic Cambodian cuisine here is anything but typical. The soul of the menu is the samlaws, a Cambodian stew. Samlaw korko is a brothy concoction that combines tender chicken with an exotic array of vegetables including Asian eggplant, green papaya, dark-green French string beans, roasted ground rice, and an Asian squash that resembles fresh pumpkin. Several fried catfish dishes include a dynamite version with black beans, green onions, vinegar, and loads of fresh ginger. Skip the house specialty, amok—an unappetizing blob of mystery meat wrapped inside a banana leaf (a little too authentic for untutored Western tongues). The fresh, room-temperature salads are packed with fresh cilantro, mint, shredded Napa cabbage, bell peppers, and carrots, plus your choice of chicken, pork, or beef. Everything on the menu is less than $10. ■ *At 13th St and Oakland Rd, 2 blocks S of Hwy 101; (408) 287-7619; 923 Old Oakland Rd, San Jose; $; beer and wine; AE, MC, V; no checks; breakfast, lunch, dinner every day.*

Gombei Restaurant ★★ Among the many worthy restaurants in San Jose's Japantown, Gombei stands out for its lively atmosphere and unparalleled noodle dishes. The food at this tiny, immaculately clean restaurant is no secret: Gombei rocks with the near-volcanic energy of its devoted patrons and legion of youthful staff (we've counted 11 buzzing around on a semibusy evening). If tables are scarce, head for the wide, gray Formica counter. Gombei's menu offers everything from teriyaki and donburi to Gombei's renowned udon—the Japanese equivalent of Jewish chicken soup that arrives in a huge ceramic bowl filled with fat wheat noodles, loads of tender strips of chicken, ribbons of egg, green onion, and a sheaf of dried seaweed. The rich, lovely broth is made even better by the red pepper and black sesame-seed mixture that accompanies the soup on your wooden tray. Before ordering anything else on the menu, check the specials board for irresistibles like deep-fried oysters or cold chicken salad on buckwheat noodles with fish cake. ■ *Corner of 5th and Jackson; (408) 279-4311; 193 E Jackson St, San Jose; $; wine, beer, and sake; no credit cards; no checks; lunch, dinner Mon–Sat.*

Le Papillon ★★ In a landscape of strip malls and bowl-o-ramas, it's almost disconcerting to find a place as elegant and classic as Le Papillon. While the lunch menu leans toward the lighter, eclectic stylings of California cuisine, the dinner menu is squarely continental, right down to the steak Diane, roasted rack of lamb, and baked Alaska. Chef Scott Cooper's marinated and grilled beef medallions come with two brilliant sauces: a dark cabernet glaze with thyme, and a white sherry cream sauce with grated fresh horseradish. Dinners come with the day's soup and a hearts of romaine salad—but pass these up if the chef is offering his special salad made of assorted baby greens, toasted hazelnuts, pears, and tomatoes, dressed in a raspberry vinaigrette and topped with a very mild French feta. For dessert, try the chocolate pâte—a dense chocolate paste laced with hazelnuts and Frangelico that is served in ultra-thin slices on a swirl of Grand Marnier crème Anglaise and raspberry coulis. ■ *S of Kiely Blvd on Saratoga Ave; (408) 296-3730; 410 Saratoga Ave, San Jose; $$$; full bar; AE, DC, DIS, MC, V; no checks; lunch Mon–Fri, dinner Mon–Sat.*

Palermo Ristorante Italiano ★★ Palermo native Renato Cusimano's small storefront eatery offers authentic Sicilian food to San Jose's power-dining crowd in a traditional white-linen dining room. Pasta is the specialty here—homemade and always perfectly al dente. Try the penne Palermo, delicate pencil-shaped pasta with fresh tomato sauce, ricotta, roasted eggplant, and grated Reggiano. Another winner is the fresh clams in the shell with garlic and olive oil or a blush of red sauce. For dessert, it's a cakey tiramisu—layers of rum and espresso-soaked ladyfingers and mascarpone topped with cocoa. ■ *Downtown between San Carlos and San Salvador; (408) 297-0607; 380 S 2nd St, San Jose; $$$; beer and wine; AE, MC, V; no checks; lunch Mon–Fri, dinner Mon–Sat.*

Thanh Hien Restaurant ★★ Tucked behind a McDonald's next to an Oriental supermarket in one of San Jose's ubiquitous strip malls, this inconspicuous yet attractive restaurant offers authentic Vietnamese food. The Tran family has a knack for steering customers to pleasing dishes that provide an interesting excursion into the cuisine: a tasty fire pot full of catfish or duck; the fried salted crab, an omeletlike dish with deep-fried crab meat mixed with scallions, garlic, black pepper, a touch of sugar, and an egg; or the salad of paper-thin raw beef slices marinated in lime juice, fish sauce, sugar, and rice-wine vinegar and garnished with translucent slices of raw onion, coarsely chopped peanuts, dried onion flakes, and basil. Good strong coffee, too. ■ *McKee Rd exit off I-680, go W and look for K-Mart on the right; (408) 926-1056; 2345 McKee Rd, San Jose; $$; beer and wine; MC, V; no checks; lunch, dinner every day.*

Bini's Bar and Grille ★ When was the last time you ate in a restaurant where the waitress called you honey and said "it was nice to meet you"? This San Jose institution offers the kind of working-class bonhomie that does your soul and pocketbook good. As soon as you step inside, you know you've come to the right place for a cheeseburger, fries, and large chocolate shake. The menu's a veritable relic, offering Spam-and-eggs (breakfast is served all day) and blue-plate specials like meat loaf and pork chops with real mashed potatoes. (The dirt-cheap prices are from another era, too.) For dessert, try the homemade pie à la mode from a list of apple, cherry, pumpkin, pecan, or lemon. Sit at the counter where your drink (coffee or soda) is replenished regularly, gratis, while you listen to the waitresses swap tips on hair-color products. Off the dining room is a working stiff's bar (oldest in San Jose, in fact) that serves a sublime ice-cold martini in a 24-ounce malt tin. ■ *By the railroad tracks at Taylor and 7th; (408) 279-9996; 337 E Taylor St, San Jose; $; full bar; no credit cards; checks OK; breakfast, lunch Mon–Sat.*

Henry's World Famous Hi-Life ★ Henry's Hi-Life is more than just a rib joint or roadside steak house—it's the only real McCoy San Jose has left after an era of redevelopment. The exterior has a Depression-era look while the inside is a cross between a bordello and the stage set for *Li'l Abner*. Formica tables are set with paper placemats and candles wrapped in plastic netting. None of this, however, has stopped office workers, college students, and laborers from queuing up each day for the best barbecued ribs, steaks, and chops in town. All the meats are cooked in a white-oak barbecue pit, but the ribs, accompanied by a tangy, sweet barbecue sauce served in a side bowl, get our vote. Dinners come with a basket of garlic bread, a huge baked potato heaped with cheese, butter, and chives, and an insignificant salad. The bar's jukebox offers vintage selections by the Ink Spots and Ella Fitzgerald—reason enough to join the ranks of Henry's devotees. ■ *Corner of W Saint John St and Almaden Blvd, near the I-280 overpass, (408) 295-5414; 301 W Saint John St, San Jose; $$; full bar; MC, V; no checks; lunch Tues–Fri, dinner every day.*

San Jose Tied House Cafe and Brewery ★ This better-than-average brewery restaurant draws crowds with its high-quality beers and something-for-everyone menu. Like the original Tied House in Mountain View, the San Jose place has a noisy, boisterous atmosphere that may prove a little wearing if you enjoy hearing yourself think. The bar pours eight beers—three original brews and five specialties. The menu features traditional pub fare (ribs, burgers, and fish and chips) but the best choices, oddly enough, are the seafood and vegetarian dishes. The generously portioned seafood appetizers include a house-smoked salmon with calamata olives, red onions, and raw vegetables on a bed of greens with lemon aioli, and blackened catfish strips on curly lettuce. Confront the peanut butter mud pie with a cookie crumb crust for dessert. ■ *Downtown between Santa Clara and Saint John, at 65 N San Pedro St, San Jose; (408) 295-2739; $$; beer and wine; DC, DIS, MC, V; no checks; lunch Mon–Sat; dinner every day.*

Teske's Germania Restaurant and Beer Garden ★ Renowned for its excellent selection of German beers, schnapps, and cordials (including a wonderful gold wasser—schnapps with flakes of 22-karat gold), Teske's is a kind of cult enclave for South Bay Germanophiles. Its Teutonic meat-and-potatoes menu is dominated by pork dishes and bratwursts. Try the schweinefilet, a pork filet in mushroom sauce served with hot and delicious tangy German potato salad with plenty of bacon and onions. The delicious rinderbraten—a beef roast served in a very light beef and vegetable roux—hails from chef/owner Hans Baumann's home burg of Crailsheim. Venison, antelope, and boar also put in exotic appearances. There's a lovely European-style beer garden out back. ■ *Downtown on corner of 1st St and Devine; (408) 292-0291; 255 N 1st St, San Jose; $$; full bar; AE, MC, V; no checks; lunch Mon–Fri, dinner Mon–Sat.*

Thepthai ★ The Darwinism of the restaurant industry has winnowed the number of Thai restaurants in this part of San Jose down to one resilient, pleasant little eatery. Anything with crisp, golden fried tofu is a delight: purists will want to get the fried tofu appetizer with a delicious peanut sauce. The exemplary phad Thai strikes a masterful balance between the soft rice noodles and crunchy red cabbage and sprouts, while the heat of the dried red chiles is nicely counterbalanced by lots of cilantro and lime. The zingy ginger chicken features good-quality, velvet textured chicken, stir-fried with green onions and plenty of fresh ginger. The pace of the service here can be glacial, so be prepared to linger. ■ *Market between Santa Clara and Saint John; (408) 292-7515; 23 N Market St, San Jose; $$; beer and wine; MC, V; no checks; lunch, dinner every day.*

LODGINGS

The Briar Rose Bed & Breakfast Inn ★★ This 1875 Victorian on a tree-lined street just north of downtown San Jose isn't just a quiet respite for travelers, it's a virtual Maxfield Parrish Museum. Innkeepers James and Cheryl Fuhring have been collecting Parrish's work for 15 years. The five guest rooms are filled with original prints and magazine covers from the '20s and 30s, while the sitting room on the main floor contains a small library on the artist (including the fascinating chronicle of his longtime affair with his principal model and maid, Sue Lewin). You'll even find the work of his protegés. The separate, two-story Pubhouse Cottage has a parlor, wraparound porch, and treehouse-like bedroom upstairs with dormer windows that look out into the leaves of a sheltering mulberry. On warm days, breakfast is served on the porch of the main house, with its view of the pond, gazebo, and half-acre of English gardens. Peruse the morning paper while mopping up forkfuls of French toast with slices of fresh kiwi, sausage links, and real maple syrup. ■ *N of downtown at the corner of E Jackson and N 19th; (408) 279-5999; 897 E Jackson St, San Jose, CA 95112; $$; AE, DIS, MC, V; checks OK.*

The Hensley House ★★ Close to museums, theaters, and restaurants, this stately Queen Anne Victorian is a haven for corporate visitors and child-weary couples in the South Bay. Innkeepers Sharon Layne and Bill Priest have restored this landmark's dark wood interiors and decorated it with crystal chandeliers, stately antiques, and crisp linens. Each of the five guest rooms has a queen-size bed, private bath, and telephone. If you're looking to splurge, try the Judge's Chambers, with its wet bar, whirlpool bath, and fireplace. Guests are treated to afternoon hors d'oeuvres and, of course, breakfast. The ghost of Superior Court Judge Perley F. Gosbey, one of the original owners of the house, sometimes turns up as a guest. ■ *N 3rd at Hensley; (408) 298-3537, toll free (800) 634-2567 in*

California; 456 N 3rd St, San Jose, CA 95112; $$; AE, DC, DIS, MC, V; checks OK.

Hotel De Anza ★★ Renovations that took 10 months and $10 million have brought this circa-1931 grande dame of San Jose back to life after years of decay. The richly colored Moorish ceilings in the De Anza Room and the Hedley Club are deco-jewels. The deluxe, neo-deco guest rooms offer televisions and telephones with hookups for fax machines and modems. All the rooms have large armoires with honor bars and VCRs (you can check out movies free from the video library downstairs). Ask for one of the south-facing rooms with their sweeping views of downtown. The hotel's restaurant La Pastaia offers top-notch Italian cuisine as well as breakfast, which is not, alas, in-cluded with the price of a room. The stately Palm Court Terrace is a favorite place to meet for drinks in the warmer months, and the Hedley Club has a live jazz trio on Sunday nights. ■ *Downtown at Almaden Blvd and Santa Clara St; (408) 286-1000; 233 W Santa Clara St, San Jose, CA 95113; $$$; AE, DC, MC, V; checks OK.*

SANTA CLARA

RESTAURANTS

Calvin's South Philly Diner This nostalgia fest in honor of the City of Brotherly Love is littered with Philly memorabilia: '76ers pennants, photos of Veterans Stadium, and postcards featuring red brick buildings and defective bells. Foodwise, Calvin's authentic cheese steak is the house superstar with thin, curling slices of flank steak piled on a French roll that has plenty of white American cheese and onions. Calvin's ribs come slathered in a zesty barbecue sauce with a hefty, peppery kicker. Side dishes can be dicey; pass on the mediocre green and potato salads and go straight for the crunchy, sweet and tangy coleslaw or crisp russet fries. ■ *Corner of Lincoln and Franklin, (408) 983-1105; 1595 Franklin St, Santa Clara; $; no alcohol; no credit cards; checks OK; lunch, dinner Mon–Sat.*

LODGINGS

Madison Street Inn ★★ Two gigantic pepper trees and a white picket fence studded with roses guard this restored Victorian manse just minutes from downtown. The five guest rooms are small but quaint. The Monroe Room, which over-looks the garden, has a queen-size brass bed and claw-footed tub for two; the Madison Room (often used as a honeymoon suite) has a queen-size four-poster with a lace coverlet. If the smallness of the rooms begins to get to you, you can chill out downstairs in the spacious living room and parlor deco-rated with Oriental rugs and lace curtains, or out by the pool and hot tub. Prepared in a restaurant-size kitchen, the hearty breakfast includes omelets, Belgian waffles, or eggs Benedict, accompanied by home-baked muffins and breads. Also, by prior arrangement, the innkeepers—Ralph and Theresa Wigginton—will whip up masterful California cuisine dinners as well. ■ *Corner of Lewis and Madison; (408) 249-5541; 1390 Madison St, Santa Clara, CA 95050; $; AE, DC, DIS, MC, V; checks OK.*

CAMPBELL

RESTAURANTS

Martha's Restaurant & Cafe ★★ Granted, Martha's Restaurant & Cafe bears all the earmarks of another trendy, cookie-cutter California cuisine restaurant: the location in an upscale mall, and floral arrangements so huge they dwarf the average California bear. But versatile Steve Chan, one of the South Bay's most creative chefs, is anything but a cookie-cutter chef. Chan's voluptuous appetizers include shrimp cakes (deep-fried dollops of shrimp mousse in a spicy roast garlic and hoisin sauce) and five-spiced quail (a whole baby quail spiced with anise, ginger, garlic, coriander, and clove) on a bed of garlicky sautéed spinach. Chan is equally nimble with meat and seafood: check out the salmon fillet in phyllo with shrimp mousse, or the aromatic stir-fry of venison, shiitake mushrooms, red pepper, and cilantro. For dessert, try the crème brulée or the white chocolate and raspberry tart—white chocolate mousse on a crushed-almond crust, topped with fresh raspberries. ■ *The Pruneyard off Bascomb; (408) 377-1193; 2400 The Pruneyard, Campbell; $$; full bar; AE, MC, V; checks OK; lunch Mon–Fri, dinner Mon–Sat.*

LOS GATOS

RESTAURANTS

Pigalle ★★ Named after Paris's red-light district, Pigalle is an intimate, fair-priced restaurant that serves top-notch French country-style cuisine. Chef/owner Steve Lopez's small, tantalizing menu changes seasonally. Lunch offerings range from a grilled pork chop with polenta and applesauce to a chicken pie in a puff pastry with artichokes and mushrooms. For dinner, try the roast duck (half a bird, partially deboned, in a caramelized raspberry sauce garnished with fresh raspberries and served with wild rice and a fan of fresh vegetables) or the tender, braised, boneless rabbit (with a mustardy sherry cream sauce, speckled with whole mustard seeds and served with couscous). Lopez does a particularly fine job with fruit desserts, like poached pears filled with mascarpone and served in a blazing orange fruit reduction sauce with confetti spirals of lemon zest. ■ *Santa Cruz Ave near Main; (408) 395-7924; 27 N Santa*

*Cruz Ave, Los Gatos; $; beer and wine; no credit cards; local
checks only; lunch, dinner every day.*

Cats Restaurant ★ One of the most popular hangouts in the
Los Gatos area, this roadhouse restaurant and bar was once a
pit stop on the stage route that passed through the Santa Cruz
Mountains. Now, instead of miners and loggers, Cats attracts
a thirty-something crowd that comes for the live music on
weekends (jazz Friday, requests Saturday, soft rock Sunday)
and the extraordinary steak and potatoes. The oak-fire barbecue classics include four huge, tender steaks (the best bet),
pork chops, and juicy ribs and chicken served with a worthy
chili sauce and mongo baked potatoes; the ample dinners include salad and garlic bread. The atmosphere is casual and
homey—order your feast from the bar, and you'll be seated
when it's ready. ■ *Call for directions; (408) 354-4020; 17533
Santa Cruz Hwy in Los Gatos; $$; full bar; MC, V; no checks;
dinner Tues–Sun.*

La Hacienda ★ Halfway between Los Gatos and Saratoga in
the foothills of the Santa Cruz Mountains, this peculiar
Japanese-inflected Spanish Revival inn was built in 1901 as a
stage stop and is still a restful stopover for back country trav-
elers (and even a couple of low-key business lunches). Among
the oaks and eucalyptus, La Hacienda emphasizes old fash-
ioned comfort-food. Old standards from the menu may seem
ho-hum (French dip, club sandwiches, steak, prime rib—you
get the idea), but the food is expertly prepared and entrées are
bountifully portioned. Rum cake, flan, and cheesecake are usu-
ally available for dessert. La Hacienda's modern inn next door
rents a few Southwestern-style rooms to weary bodies. ■ *Take
the Saratoga/Los Gatos exit off Hwy 17/880, go 2 miles W on
Hwy 9, (408) 354-6669; 18840 Saratoga-Los Gatos Road, Los
Gatos, CA 95030; $$; full bar; AE, DIS, MC, V; no checks;
lunch Mon–Sat, dinner every day, and champagne brunch Sun.*

SARATOGA

RESTAURANTS

The Plumed Horse ★★★ Mixing the best of classical European and contemporary California cooking, this attractive,
plush eatery has been a South Bay favorite for many years.
Don't miss the escargot in a Provençal sauce with tomato coulis
or the virile game pâté with venison, quail, and pheasant studded with pistachios or green peppercorns. You'll recognize the
California emphasis in the salads (ubiquitous yuppie greens)
and in chef Thomas Crumpton's light but complex reduction
sauces. Crumpton excels at game and seafood: try the grilled
saddle of New Zealand venison in an herby tarragon brandy
sauce and the fresh Monterey Bay salmon in parchment with

olive oil, white wine, and julienne of lettuce, leeks, and carrots. For dessert, opt for the feathery Grand Marnier soufflé, with its pleasantly strong liqueur flavor and no distasteful egginess. The wine cellar has everything from $600 bottles of Romanée-Conti to reasonably priced Santa Cruz Mountain selections. ■ *Saratoga Ave S off Hwy 280; corner of 4th and Big Basin Way, (408) 867-4711; 14555 Big Basin Way; Saratoga; $$$; full bar; AE, DC, MC, V; no checks; dinner Mon–Sat.*

Adriatic Restaurant ★★ Chef/owner Neda Begovic, a native of Dalmatia, is the powerhouse behind this intimate, romantic restaurant specializing in French and Viennese cuisine. She bakes all her own breads and desserts, grows her own herbs, and does all the marketing to ensure that she gets the freshest organic ingredients in season. Be on the lookout for her exotic fruit sauces and unusual root vegetable relishes, such as golden quail stuffed with toothsome wild rice in a delicate kumquat sauce with morel mushrooms. Begovic works equally well with simple dishes like a perfectly grilled California lamb with garlic, pepper, and seasonal herbs or complex creations like the Maine lobster served in a pastry shell with mushrooms and a nantua sauce made with crayfish, Madeira, and cream. For dessert, try a thick slice of real apple strudel loaded with nuts and blond currants. Neda's husband Ed and her daughter Sana provide expert service in the dining room. ■ *Between 4th and 5th streets; (408) 867-3110; 14583 Big Basin Way, Saratoga; $$$; beer and wine; AE, DC, MC, V; no checks; dinner Tues–Sat.*

LODGINGS

Sanborn Park Hostel This opulent log cabin, built in 1908 and later owned by James Tick, the discoverer of uranium, is leagues beyond your run-of-the mill hostel. Set on a pond in a grove of redwoods, the cabin's interior is all glowing light wood, polished like a ship's interior, with a gorgeous staircase, hardwood floors, a big stone fireplace, and comfortable couches. Too bad AYH rules still apply: you'll have to do your own cooking and cleaning, but roughing it here will cost you less than $10. You should expect dormitory sleeping arrangements, though there are two small bedrooms available for couples or families. While you're here, check out the Youth Science Institute and 8 miles of hiking trails in the Sanborn Skyline County Park nearby. Congress Springs winery is also within walking and tasting distance. ■ *Call for directions; (408) 741-9555; 15808 Sanborn Rd, Saratoga, CA 95070; $; no credit cards; checks OK.*

104

Looking for a particular place? Check the index at the back of this book for specific restaurants, hotels, nightclubs, and more.

RESTAURANTS

Chez T.J. ★★★ Right around the corner from Mountain View's chi-chi Castro Street, the South Bay's best French restaurant has a quiet charm that puts its trendier neighbors to shame. Chez T.J.'s four homey dining rooms are decorated with colorful modern artwork, and each table has its own unique blown-glass lamp. The prix fixe menu (equally unique), created by Chef Thomas J. McCombie, features traditional French cuisine, sometimes with a touch of California. There are menus within the menu here, ranging from the menu petit at $45 to the overwhelming seven course menu gastronomique at $57. A recent extravaganza gastronomique featured a lineup of tart goat cheese with rich port and raspberries in delicate puff pastry, juicy prawn potstickers with lime and chile oil, tart-sweet pineapple and mint ice in a sparkling champagne float, succulent duck breast with cranberry sauce and parsnip gratine, a very fresh salad made with organic baby greens from their own garden, an international selection of cheeses, and a luscious dark chocolate cup filled with rich vanilla bean ice cream and vibrant caramel sauce. Each course is a visual work of art, a shame to destroy, but once the exquisite aromas reach you, you'll find your fork has a mind of its own. An extensive wine list allows you to select the perfect accompaniment (prices range from $23 to $550). ■ *Villa St, between Castro St and Shoreline Blvd, (415) 964-7466; 938 Villa St, Mountain View; $$$; wine only; AE, DIS, MC, V; checks OK; dinner Tues–Sat.*

Mountain
View

Restaurants

Jacqueline Cafe & Wine Bar ★ This quaint little restaurant has a lot to recommend it, perhaps too much given its popularity and small size. If you can get there early enough to be seated in the patio off Castro Street, do it—too many bodies get squeezed into the inside room, and the combination of body heat and kitchen heat can turn a romantic candle-lit dinner into a sweaty affair. In fact, the candles just make the place seem hotter. On the plus side, the food is innovative and quite good. Co-owner Jacqueline Martin greets everyone personally with great warmth (is there any other way around here?), setting a high standard for the restaurant's service. Chef Terry Tenopir calls his menu "California freestyle," and uses lots of citrus, wine, and herbs. The seafood and wild game specials are usually good bets, as is the tangy chicken breast piccata with lemon, capers, and dry vermouth, or the New York steak served with sautéed green peppercorns and brandy cream sauce. For dessert, no one can resist the crème brulée with white chocolate and sun-dried cherries or the flawless chocolate regal torte. ■ *Castro between Evelyn and Villa;*

(415) 964-2075; 185 Castro, Mountain View; $$$; beer and
wine; MC, V; no checks; dinner Tues–Sat, lunch Tues–Fri.

PALO ALTO

RESTAURANTS

Osteria ★★★ Osteria was the first nouveau Northern Italian
restaurant on the Peninsula and it's still one of the best. Week-
end evenings find an upscale herd milling around the entrance
wearing everything from business suits to shorts. Inside, the
noisy dining room is comfortable in spite of the din and the
tightly packed tables. Start with the melt-in-your-mouth carpac-
cio and move on to huge, juicy prawns in an ethereal lemon
cream sauce with a fan of steamed vegetables. Homemade
pasta dishes (all 12 of 'em) compete for your attention. Try the
linguine con vongole in a sprightly clam sauce or the angel hair
pasta with fresh tomato-basil sauce. There's also a fine array of
veal dishes and grilled fish specials. A refreshing hazelnut flan,
rich with the flavor of hazelnut butter, brings the meal to a sen-
sational close. ■ *Hamilton and Ramona; (415) 328-5700; 247
Hamilton Street, Palo Alto; $$; beer and wine; AE, MC, V; no
checks; lunch Mon–Fri, dinner Mon–Sat.*

Fuki Sushi ★★ No contest—this is the best Japanese restaurant on the Peninsula and has been for years. Set amid El
Camino Real's neon fast food sprawl of pseudo-Mexican,
pseudo-Italian, and pseudo-German architecture, this little slice
of Kyoto offers food that is anything but pseudo. The breadth
of sushi choices is vast and the fish is unfailingly fresh. Fuki
usually offers six or seven different varieties of tuna, including
the flavorful and very-hard-to-find fatty tuna belly. It serves almost every kind of West Coast fish available but also flys in
fresh fish from Japan, the Philippines, and Latin America. The
chefs here can produce any sushi roll you care to dream up, so
don't feel you have to settle for what's on the menu. What's
more, the tempura is the lightest and crispest around, and the
variety of flavorful teriyakis is stunning: tuna, yellowtail, and
grilled or barbecued eel, as well as the usual standards. Don't
miss the fresh-tasting, moist soft-shell crab appetizer. The service is unfailingly polite and precise. ■ *El Camino Real, just N
of San Antonio Road, (415) 494-9383; 4119 El Camino Real,
Palo Alto; $$; full bar; AE, DIS, MC, V; no checks; lunch
Mon–Fri, dinner every day.*

Il Fornaio Cucina Italiana ★★ Il Fornaio began as a baker's
school in Milan. The initial goal of the Veggetti family was to
collect regional recipes and save the disappearing art of Italian
baking. In the late 1980s, the Veggettis expanded their activi-
ties to include several retail bakeries, wholesale bakeries, and
restaurants in California. The Palo Alto restaurant serves its

fantastic baked goods and good Italian food in a beautiful setting. Breads and bread sticks, served with pungent, extra virgin olive oil, provide simple and unpretentious proof of bread
as art form—flavorful, crisp-crusted breads that pull back when
you bite into them: a culinary experience in their own right.
Dessert tortes, cakes, and cookies offer further proof of the
skills of Il Fornaio's bakers. Try the biscotti assortiti for a variety of delicious baking samples or treat your mouth to the apple and walnut torte with caramel sauce. The antipasti are
generally very good, but the grilled eggplant with goat cheese,
sun-dried tomatoes, sweet onions, and capers offers an exciting combination of contrasting flavors and textures. Pizzas and
calzones, crisp and smoky-flavored from the wood burning
ovens, are universally delightful. ■ *Cowper near University Ave;*
(415) 853-3888; 520 Cowper St, Palo Alto; $$; beer and wine;
MC, V; no checks; breakfast, lunch, dinner every day.

MacArthur Park ★★ You can see that the clientele here has
a Stanford spin: very white and conservative with lots of blue
blazers, dresses with big bows, and pearls. Not your usual ribs
fans, true, but devotees nonetheless. They come for the lean,
tender, oakwood-smoked ribs and first-rate mesquite-grilled
steaks. The rest of the menu seems more appropriate—grilled
meats, fish, and fowl sporting respectable California-cuisine
sauces such as fresh tomato chutney, jalapeño jelly, or orange-
tamari glaze (but the ribs are still the raison d'être). Finish with
a killer slice of mud pie, chocolate and coffee ice cream on a
chocolate cookie crumb crust topped with hot fudge and
chopped nuts. The excellent wine list is rich in California caber-
nets; the single malt Scotch list is even better; and the dessert
wine list is long and interesting enough to keep you there late
into the evening. ■ *University Ave at El Camino, next to the*
Palo Alto Caltrain station; (415) 321-9990; 27 University
Ave, Palo Alto; $$; full bar; AE, DC, MC, V; no checks; lunch
Mon–Fri, dinner every day, brunch Sun.

Hobee's California Restaurants ★ Although there are now 11
Hobee's in California, the menu and decor still cling to its
down-to-earth origins in tofu and alfalfa sprouts. But you
don't have to wear Birkenstocks to feel comfortable here—you
just have to like big breakfasts (lunch and dinner are dependable, but breakfast, served all day, is Hobee's real forte).
Choose from a large array of omelets and scrambles, including the toothsome seven-veggie omelet and the High Hat,
stuffed with ham and potatoes. The Sonoma hash browns—
fried potatoes topped with breast of chicken pieces, tomatoes,
cheese, and pesto—elicits contented sighs from stomachs
everywhere. Hobee's is known for its moist blueberry coffee
cake, served warm with plenty of butter, and its nutty gourmet
granola with sesame seeds and almonds. For the cholesterol-

conscious, there's an oatmeal bar, an eggless tofu scramble, and a selection of smoothies. Lunch and dinner menus offer a salad and homemade soup bar, plus hearty specials like black bean chili, quesadillas, and papaya teriyaki chicken. ■ *El Camino Real near Charleston/Arastradero; (415) 856-6124; 4224 El Camino Real, Palo Alto.* ■ *El Camino Real and Embarcadero; (415) 327-4111; 67 Town & Country Village, Palo Alto; $; beer and wine; V, MC; local checks only; breakfast, lunch every day, dinner Tues–Sat.*

Pearl's Oyster Bar ★ The first thing you see when you walk into Pearl's is a South Pacific–style oyster bar with a colorful mosaic counter depicting the ascent of humanity to the high point in our evolution—the discovery of Pearl's. Well, we could have done worse than oceans of seafood appetizers (including 5 varieties of oysters) and 65 beers and a huge wine list from the bar. If you're not wild about the South Seas or restaurant anthropology and want a wider selection of food, head into the restaurant, where the staff wear eccentric headgear and the atmosphere is Gulf Coast. You can sit outside in the New Orleans–style courtyard or inside one of several surrounding rooms. The chalkboard menu lists a selection of grilled fish and other catch-of-the-day seafood specialties (steamers, perhaps, or irresistible Cajun gumbo thick with succulent fish, crab, crawfish, and steamers). The helpful, friendly waiters will bring out a sample of each kind of oyster and steamer and give you a quick course in bivalve appreciation. ■ *Ramona, between Hamilton and University; (415) 328-2722; 535 Ramona St, Palo Alto; $$; beer and wine; V, MC; no checks; lunch Mon–Fri, dinner Mon–Sat.*

Palo Alto

Restaurants

▲

Vicolo Pizzeria ★ This glorious little yup pizzeria has all the charm of one of those romantic Italian alleyway cafes—rust-colored textured walls and faux marble tables spilling out onto the sidewalk. Vicolo's thin, crisp cornmeal crust is topped with dizzying combinations of 32 fresh toppings—try the garlic mozzarella with whole roasted garlic cloves, provolone, tomato sauce, Parmesan, and oregano. Other good choices include the "Sun-Herb" (mozzarella and fontina cheeses, sun-dried tomatoes, garlic, chile peppers, fresh basil, oregano, chives, and Italian parsley) and the "Southwestern" (mozzarella, French feta, roasted sweet and hot peppers, fresh tomato, and salsa). Vicolo's pizza is available by the slice, half, or whole pie. ■ *Downtown Palo Alto at Cowper; (415) 324-4877; 473 University Ave, Palo Alto; $; beer and wine; no credit cards; checks OK; lunch, dinner every day.*

If you know of a restaurant, hotel, or other establishment that you think deserves "Best Place" consideration, send in the report form at the back of this book. We value reader input.

LODGINGS

The Garden Court Hotel ★★★ If you like elegance, luxury, pampering, and great location—well, some people might not—this is a darn good choice. A flower-laden courtyard, which provides the balcony view for most of the 61 rooms, is surrounded by Italianate architecture, draped with arches, and studded with colorful tile-work and hand-wrought iron fixtures. The European-modern rooms are tinted in pastel shades of green, peach, and purple-blue; all have four-poster beds, white faux marble wood furniture, and thick, cushioned couches. The suites approach decadence—the penthouse, for example, has a fireplace, a whirlpool bath, and a wet bar. All the little details are covered in style, from terrycloth robes to the *Wall Street Journal*. The hotel is in a good shopping and nightlife area, just off University Avenue, and only 25 minutes from San Francisco International Airport. Blessedly, room service uses the kitchen and menu of Il Fornaio Cucina Italiana, located on the ground floor of the hotel (see review). ■ *Cowper St between University and Hamilton; (415) 322-9000; 520 Cowper St, Palo Alto, CA 94301; $$$; AE, DC, MC, V; checks OK.*

PORTOLA VALLEY

RESTAURANTS

Iberia Restaurant ★★★★ Some of the finest Spanish food in Northern California is located in the forested hills above Stanford in one of the state's wealthiest suburbs. Owned by Spaniard Jose Luis Relinque and his wife Jessica, Iberia is gloriously elegant, romantically lit, and unrelentingly formal. Dressed in black tie, with white V-necked sweaters bearing the Iberia Restaurant coat of arms, the all-Spanish waiters offer the distant, deferential service rarely seen on this side of the Atlantic. The menu is elaborate and the food is nothing short of spectacular. After a few tapas (such as the juicy gambas prawns in butter and garlic) and a glass of sherry (from the best sherry list around), the voluminous dinner menu beckons: five kinds of soups and salads, and a vast array of meat dishes, including quail, pheasant, venison, wild boar, and baby goat. Try the tender braised lamb shank, glazed with honey; the veal medallions in a sauce of creamy, sweet, saffron-kissed wine sauce studded with finely chopped almonds, hazelnuts, and macadamia nuts; or the pheasant with port wine and morel mushrooms. Although the chef considers it common, their paella is one of the best in the Bay Area. For dessert, choose (if you can) between the chocolate hazelnut torte and the apricot-walnut chocolate soufflé cake. ■ *¼ mile W of I-280 on Alpine Rd in Portola Valley; (415) 854-1746; 190 Ladera-Alpine Road, Portola Valley; $$$; full bar; AE, DC, MC, V; no checks; foreign currency accepted; lunch, dinner every day, brunch Sun.*

LOS ALTOS

RESTAURANTS

Chef Chu's ★★ Take a culinary tour of mainland China without ever leaving your table: feast on dim sum from Guangzhou, banquet dishes from Shanghai and Beijing, dumplings and stretched noodles from Xian, and spicy favorites from Sichuan and Hunan—all from the kitchen of Lawrence Chu, a chef who's been expanding the culinary horizons of Los Altos for 20 years. Chef Chu does all the standards well, and offers some delicious innovations of his own, like crisp salmon rolls—tender filleted salmon mixed with Chinese herbs, wrapped in sheets of dried tofu, and deep fried. Munch on jumbo prawns with candied pecans in mild mustard sauce. The Peking duck, which must be ordered in advance, is crisp-skinned and flawless, with virtually all the fat melted away. ■ *San Antonio Rd at El Camino; (415) 948-2696; 1067 N San Antonio Rd, Los Altos; $$; full bar; AE, MC, V; no checks; lunch, dinner every day.*

MENLO PARK

RESTAURANTS

Carpaccio ★★★ Carpaccio was started by the same folks responsible for the wildly successful Osteria in San Mateo, but a parting of the ways has left this restaurant to evolve along its own lines. Although attractive presentation and light touch smack of California cuisine, Carpaccio holds tightly to its Northern Italian roots. Chef Martin Gonzalez's mozzarella salad sings with soft, sun-dried tomatoes, fresh basil, and smoked mozzarella in a tart balsamic vinaigrette; the namesake dish comes with onions, capers, lemon, and mustard, with a grating of grana cheese and a drizzle of olive oil. Heavenly. The angel hair pasta sports a lively pomodoro sauce made from sweet, vine-ripened tomatoes and fresh basil. The real treat here is the free-range veal: veal piccata is light and pleasantly lemony, but those in search of the platonic veal ideal should choose the simple, grilled veal chop. Also keep an eye out for the prosciutto-wrapped grilled prawns, served with garlic and shallots in a smooth lemon cream sauce. The kitchen has recently added an oak-burning oven (with bricks imported from the motherland) that makes divine pizza, for which premium toppings are laced together with fresh mozzarella, Gorgonzola, and chèvre on wonderful smoke-flavored crusts. ■ *Crane St, between Oak Grove and Santa Cruz Ave in downtown Menlo Park; (415) 322-1211; 1120 Crane St, Menlo Park; $$; full bar; AE, DC, MC, V; no checks; lunch Mon–Fri, dinner every day.*

Flea St. Cafe ★★★ Flea Street has come a long way since it was accused, years ago, of serving "tasteless organic food." That was then and this is now, and now it's winning raves for feisty California cuisine. Organic ingredients are still the rule (most coming from a nearby farm that sells only to Flea Street), but no one's complaining any more about Suzy Chapman's innovative creations. A recent meal offered a summer-tomato and white-cheddar tart with a marzipan crust (the vine-ripened tomatoes were as sweet as the crust); a salad of delicate organic baby greens served with sweet purple potatoes and Gorgonzola cheese; a smoky breast of chicken with a sauté of apricots and muscat wine and served with savory bread pudding—a tender, rich, sweet, four-star dish. ■ *On the Alameda near Santa Cruz Ave; (415) 854-1226; 3607 Alameda de las Pulgas, Menlo Park; $$; beer and wine; MC, V; checks OK; lunch Tues–Fri, dinner Tues–Sun, brunch Sun.*

Dal Baffo ★ Dal Baffo has pretty good food and one of the best wine lists in the world, but it takes itself more seriously than it deserves to. The atmosphere is unforgivingly staid: soft classical music, padded gilt-edged menus, pretentious waiters in tuxedos with thick "continental" accents—even the busboys have an attitude. But if you like fine wine and are dying for an obscure vintage (and don't mind paying a fairly high price for the privilege), you might just like this place. Hence, the first thing to consider is not the food menu, but the wine list. The cellar, represented by the 4-inch thick volume of 1,000 selections, has won *Wine Spectator's* Grand Award seven years in a row. The traditional, Roman-style food scores with classic appetite-whetters such as the tomatoes with mozzarella, basil, and balsamic vinaigrette and fried calamari. The quality of main courses is spotty. ■ *Downtown Menlo Park at University; (415) 325-1588; 878 Santa Cruz Ave, Menlo Park; $$$; full bar; AE, DC, MC, V; no checks; dinner Mon–Sat; lunch Mon–Fri.*

Siam Garden ★★ Our favorite Thai stop on the mid-Peninsula is Siam Garden. The ingredients are always fresh and of high quality; the use of spices is balanced and invigorating; and, as one would expect from a first-rate Thai restaurant, the service is always impeccable. Siam Garden has been owned and operated by the Tacha family for about five years; the family has taken great care to ensure that the traditional Thai classic dishes are consistently well-prepared. The musuman beef, made of large chunks of tender, hearty beef and potatoes simmered in a dark coconut curry sauce, is a special favorite. Thai barbecue chicken is cut into pieces and marinated on the bone in a sweet, sour, and tangy marinade. Among the potables are Thai beers and the always startlingly good Thai iced tea. ■ *Crane St between Santa Cruz Ave and Oak Grove;*

*(415) 853-1143; 1143 Crane St, Menlo Park; $$; beer and wine;
MC, V; local checks only; lunch Mon–Sat, dinner every day.*

WOODSIDE

RESTAURANTS

The Village Pub ★★★ This pub in the hills of Woodside is
hardly typical of the genre—no bangers and mash here. The
pub part is a broad, carved oak bar that flows with friendly con-
versation and palate-friendly ale, but the food diverges to
hearty California cuisine in a classy, serene modern setting. En-
trées cover a wide range of standards to suit the pickiest of
eaters (seafood, steak, chicken, duck, and pasta) and goes out
on a limb with a few creative specials every night. Try the fra-
grant roast rack of lamb with wild rice and fresh asparagus, or
the juicy grilled double chicken breast with mild corn spoon
bread spiced with Anaheim chile cream. Fish lovers will come
back again and again for the wild striped bass with Japanese
sweet potatoes and honey-rosemary vinaigrette. The capellini
with sun-dried tomatoes and roasted sweet peppers is simple
but first-rate. Allow yourself to be tempted by the dessert
menu. ■ *Woodside Road; (415) 851-1294; 2967 Woodside
Road, Woodside; $$; full bar; AE, DC, MC, V; no checks; lunch
Mon–Fri, dinner every day, brunch Sun.*

▼

Menlo Park

Restaurant

▲

REDWOOD CITY

RESTAURANTS

The Redwood Cafe and Spice Company ★★ We can't think
of a better way to spend a sunny Sunday morning than luxuri-
ating over Swedish oatmeal pancakes on the patio of this pretty
blue Victorian surrounded by a peaceful flower garden. These
rich, nicely textured pancakes, heavy with rolled oats and buttermilk, are topped with real maple syrup and your choice of
fresh lingonberries, homemade applesauce, bananas, eggs, or
ham. You can also try to chose from the 10 varieties of country egg scrambles, including the Alex (green onions, shrimp,
Jack cheese, and sour cream) and Northern Lights (smoked
salmon, spinach, and cream cheese). Good fresh-squeezed
juices too. Lunch, offering a nice variety of salads and sandwiches, is competent, but breakfast and brunch are the real
draws. ■ *Corner of Main and Middlefield; (415) 366-1498;
1020 Main St, Redwood City; $; beer and wine; AE; checks
OK; breakfast, lunch Tues–Fri, brunch Sat–Sun.*

---

*The Best Places series rates establishments on value,
performance measured against the business's goals, uniqueness,
enjoyability, loyalty of clientele, cleanliness, excellence and ambition
of the cooking, and professionalism of the service.*

SAN CARLOS

RESTAURANTS

Kabul Restaurant ★★★ Afghani food is cosmopolitan in the truest sense as it comes from a land that was a key link in the old overland trade route between Europe and Central Asia. Afghanistan has developed a national cuisine whose roots reach from the Mediterranean to Southeast Asia. Kabul owner Bashir Ahmad re-creates these tastes for Northern California with the highest quality ingredients, including well-marbled meats and spices he shops for while on buying trips to Asia and the Middle East. The candle-lit, white-washed stucco interior is richly decorated with Afghani carpets and tapestries, as well as photographs of Afghani people. The management and servers are charming and attentive. A few dishes shouldn't be missed: the fragrant charbroiled lamb chops are marinated for 24 hours in yogurt, olive oil, fresh garlic, and black and white pepper; the splendid sautéed pumpkin topped with yogurt and a tomato-based ground beef sauce yields a suprising and delicious meld of flavors; the savory fried pastry filled with ground beef and chick peas is similar to the Indian samosa but is more pungent and uses lighter pastry and fillings. ■ *San Carlos Plaza, between Holly and Harbor; (415) 594-2840; 135 El Camino Real, San Carlos.* ■ *On W El Camino Real, between Pastoria and Mary; (408) 245-4350; 833 W El Camino Real, Sunnyvale; $$; beer and wine; MC, V; checks OK; lunch Mon–Fri, dinner every day.*

SAN MATEO

RESTAURANTS

231 Ellsworth ★★★ This upscale eatery caters to the refined palates and well-padded wallets of old money Peninsulites from Hillsborough and surrounding surburbs. Trained at L'Esperance in France, owner/chef Ambjorn Lindskog offers a highly evolved form of nouvelle cuisine, using fresh California ingredients in innovative ways. The menu is in constant flux, but the appetizers are irreproachable—a warm shredded cabbage salad in balsamic vinaigrette with chunks of Roquefort and fresh herbs is the only immutable item on the menu and only because customers complain loudly any time Lindskog tries to remove it. A recent Foie Gras 231 came on a bed of baby spinach with raspberries and buttery brioche while delicate, fresh morelles were richly draped in Dijon-crème sauce. The pastas (such as the delicate ravioli stuffed with walnuts and arugula and topped with Gorgonzola cream sauce) are dependably topnotch. But then, so is everything else. Savor every bite of the mild sweetbreads in a carrot–port wine sauce and the roasted salmon marinated in olive oil, garlic, and fresh herbs and topped with fresh chanterelle-cream sauce. Primo desserts include the hot, bittersweet chocolate soufflé cake with lime-caramel sauce and whipped cream (sometimes crème Anglaise and fresh mint) or the chocolate salad—fettuccine-style strips of chocolate topped with two scoops of chocolate and mango sorbet and decorated with edible flowers. The prodigious wine list includes over 200 fine wines from Europe and California. ■ *Ellsworth between 2nd and 3rd; (415) 347-7231; 231 Ellsworth St, San Mateo; $$$; beer and wine; AE, DC, MC, V; no checks; lunch Mon–Fri, dinner Mon–Sat.*

Gandhi Cuisine of India ★★★ Just another Indian place in a 5-mile stretch that already had half a dozen others? That's what locals thought when Gandhi opened in 1989 in the same location where three other restaurants had opened and closed their doors in just 18 months. Gandhi didn't just survive. It prospered. This restaurant does standard dishes well and also offers some exciting innovations, such as a unique curried pumpkin and lamb that blends the spice of curry and the heartiness of lamb with sweet mashed pumpkin. The samosa here is light, crisp and greaseless, while the tender nan and poppadum breads come hot from the oven. The tandoori chicken and lamb, served on a sizzling hot iron tray with barely sautéed onions, are pungent and perfectly cooked. Top off your meal with an Indian beer or a cool yogurt-papaya drink. A friend from India has called Gandhi's the best food he's ever tasted outside South Central Asia. The once-skeptical locals now enthusiastically agree. ■ *Between 24th and 25th on El Camino Real; (415) 345-4366; 2299 S El Camino Real, San Mateo; $$; beer and wine; AE, DC, MC, V; no checks; lunch, dinner every day.*

First Watch ★★ First Watch's dynamite breakfasts range from health-conscious to suicidal, and both varieties are tongue-tinglingly fine. The only problem is that everyone knows it so that mornings are always a crush. Even this isn't much of a problem because the restaurant serves free cups of rich, strong, dark coffee to everyone waiting for a table. Traditionalists will like the vast offering of American standards: bacon and eggs, eggs Benedict, and a delicious array of pancakes and waffles. Worriers will find comfort in the omelets made with a cholestrol-free egg substitute, fruit salads, or the delicious Siesta Key cocktail, a mixture of yogurt, fresh fruit, and granola. Particularly good are the "skillets": sautéed potatoes topped with eggs, mushrooms, cheese, sausage, avocado, and sour cream. Both black and herbal teas are available, along with very good espresso and fresh-squeezed juice. ■ *2nd Avenue at Ellsworth; (415) 342-2356; 201 2nd Ave, San Mateo; $; MC, V; checks OK; breakfast, lunch every day.*

La Bonne Auberge ★★ When mid-Peninsulites don't feel like cooking, this is where they feel like eating. For nearly 20 years, chef Philippe del Perugia has been serving dependably fine French country-style food in this dark candle-lit cottage incongruously set among trashitecture retail stores on San Mateo's busy main drag. Perugia designed and built the kitchen, as well as the wine cellar with its large and excellent selection of French and California wines. He shops for the day's produce before dawn each morning and has hired someone to cultivate his fresh herbs. All of the starters, from the escargot to the house pâtés, are reliable and the French onion soup, with a good half-inch of cheese on top, is the best around. Perugia does a fine job with poultry, including the boneless chicken breast with a sherry cream sauce with pert, toothsome mushrooms. Steaks, like the New York steak with pepper, shallots, and Madeira wine sauce, never fail to satisfy. For dessert, try the feathery Grand Marnier soufflé, the purists' crème brulée, or the homemade pastries. Perugia's very French wife, Huguette, manages the dining room with unflappable finesse.
■ *2 blocks S of Hwy 92 on El Camino Real; (415) 341-2525; 2075 S El Camino Real, San Mateo; $$; beer and wine; MC, V; no checks; dinner Wed–Sun.*

BURLINGAME

RESTAURANTS

Kincaid's Fish and Chop House ★ Great fresh fish, good chops, and an unforgettable bar. What more does one need? Arguably nothing this busy dinner house can't provide. A dozen varieties of fish are prepared according to a daily theme. On Hawaiian day, a treasure trove of fresh fish rarely found on the mainland appeared on our plates: spearfish grilled with vermouth and garlic butter and served with ginger cream sauce; uku baked with macadamia nut butter; walu-escalar baked with coconut and bread crumbs and served with mango aioli; and deep-fried tiger prawns rolled in spices and coconut beer batter and served with zesty tropical marinade. Non–fish fans can dig into pork and lamb chops, but fish seems to be the point here. The awe-inspiring bar, lined floor-to-ceiling with shelves groaning with liquor bottles, is an earthquake disaster waiting to happen, but in the meantime, you can have your choice of 50 single-malt Scotches, 20 American bourbons, 20 North American blends, 25 Cognacs, 25 brandies and liqueurs, and 25 beers. ■ *Bayview Pl at Airport Blvd; (415) 342-9844; 60 Bayview Pl, Burlingame; $$; full bar; AE, DC, MC, V; no checks; lunch Mon–Fri, dinner every day.*

Crown Sterling Suites Hotel ★★★

It's a towering pink and aqua spectacle savoring more of the sunnier Southland than Northern California. In front of the hotel, a cobblestone drive encircles a Spanish-style fountain; just inside, another fountain gurgles in front of the junglelike atrium. Every room has a private bedroom and a separate living room complete with refrigerator, wet bar, coffee-maker, microwave oven, two color televisions, two telephones, and a pull-out sofa bed (ask for a room overlooking San Francisco Bay). Amuse yourself by lounging in the enormous indoor swimming pool or by checking out the action at Bobby McGee's, the best singles bar in town. You know the spot—filled with stunningly beautiful people of questionable depth, flirting over tropical fruit drinks and ogling the contestants in the ladies' swimsuit contest on Tuesdays and the men's amateur body building competition on Thursdays. Extroverts only need apply for the Karaoke Sing-Along on Sunday nights. ■ *Anza Blvd off Hwy 101; (415) 342-4600; 150 Anza Blvd, Burlingame, CA 94010; $$$; AE, DC, DIS, MC, V; checks OK.*

Hyatt Regency San Francisco Airport ★★

OK, it's just a Hyatt. No big thrill there, but inside the modern white hulk is an attractive atrium surrounded by 791 pleasant rooms decorated in soft tones of green, rose, and terra-cotta. Though the art on the walls won't shake up anyone's worldview, the furnishings are a cut above generic upscale hotel decor. Ask for a room away from the freeway, overlooking San Francisco Bay. The central atrium houses three restaurants (including Scalini, a decent Northern Italian spot) and a modular sitting area with a rack of daily newspapers from around the country. There's also a sports bar, health club, and outdoor swimming pool. For those whose lives are all work and no play, there's a substantial business center that provides word processing, photocopies, faxes, and personal computer and media equipment rentals. ■ *Bayshore Hwy at Broadway; (415) 347-1234; 1333 Bayshore Hwy, Burlingame, CA 94010; $$$; AE, DC, DIS, MC, V; checks OK; breakfast, lunch, dinner every day.*

MILLBRAE

RESTAURANTS

Hong Kong Flower Lounge ★★★

Hong Kong, probably the world's most competitive culinary arena, has hundreds of excellent restaurants vying to produce the freshest, subtlest, and most exciting flavors. In 1987, Alice Wong, whose family owns four excellent Flower Lounges in and around Hong Kong, exported the empire to California with a small restaurant on

Millbrae's main drag. Its success prompted her to open another fancier branch on Millbrae Avenue and then another in San Francisco. The food hasn't suffered from the expansion; rather it has remained legendary, thanks largely to chefs, imported from the Hong Kong branches, who continue to produce cuisine according to the strenuous standards of their home city. The red-gold-jade decor is pure Kowloon glitz, but the patronage is mainly middle class and informal—and the service is outstanding. Among the best dishes on the vast menu are the exquisite minced squab in lettuce cups, delicate crystal scallops in shrimp sauce, fried prawns with walnuts, and any fresh fish from the live tank. An excellent Peking duck is served at very moderate prices. ■ *El Camino Real and Park Place; (415) 588-9972; 1671 El Camino Real, Millbrae; $$; full bar; AE, MC, V; no checks; lunch, dinner every day.* ■ *Geary between 17th and 18th avenues; (415) 668-8998; 5322 Geary Blvd, San Francisco; $$; full bar; AE, DC, DIS, MC, V; no checks; lunch, dinner every day.* ■ *Millbrae Ave and El Camino Real; (415) 878-8108; 51 Millbrae Ave, Millbrae; $$; AE, DC, DIS, MC, V; no checks; lunch, dinner every day.*

DALY CITY

RESTAURANTS

Tito Rey of the Islands ★★ Filipino cuisine has the same reputation in Asia that English cooking has in Europe. While it's true that this former Spanish-American colony doesn't offer the range, sophistication, and delicacy of Chinese and Thai cooking, it does have some interesting regional specialities, all of which can be found at Tito Rey of the Islands. Tito Rey is a chain of sorts, with four restaurants in the mother country and one in Daly City. Its cuisine reflects the Philippines' colonial past with a mix of Spanish and Asian-Pacific ingredients and techniques. A light and delicious pomfret fish is stuffed with onions and tomatoes and steamed to perfection in banana leaves, while spicy adobo stew made with chicken and pork braised in vinegar, garlic, laurel leaves, and whole peppers is hearty and satisfying. Tito's lumpia spring rolls (the best we've tasted) are filled with chopped hearts of palm and garbanzos, in addition to the usual beef and pork filling. On weekends, the otherwise quiet Tito Rey goes wild when one side of the restaurant turns into a popular disco, playing American and Filipino music. Join in the fun or watch from a safe distance with a chattering group of Filipino families and elders. ■ *St Francis Square shopping center; (415) 756-2870; #3 St Francis Square, South Gate Ave, Daly City; $$; full bar; AE, MC, V; no checks; lunch Wed–Sun, dinner every day.*

CENTRAL COAST

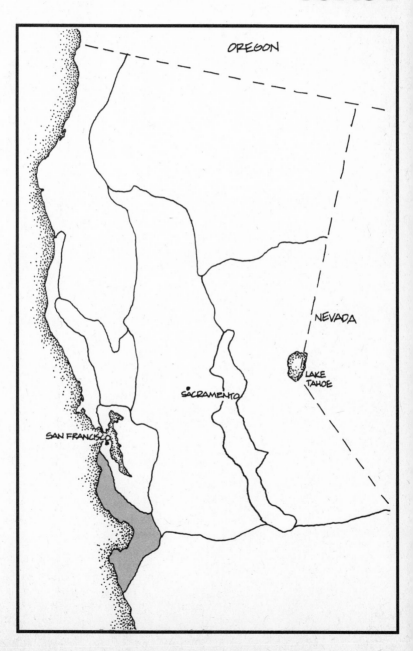

OREGON

NEVADA

LAKE
TAHOE

SACRAMENTO

SAN FRANCISCO

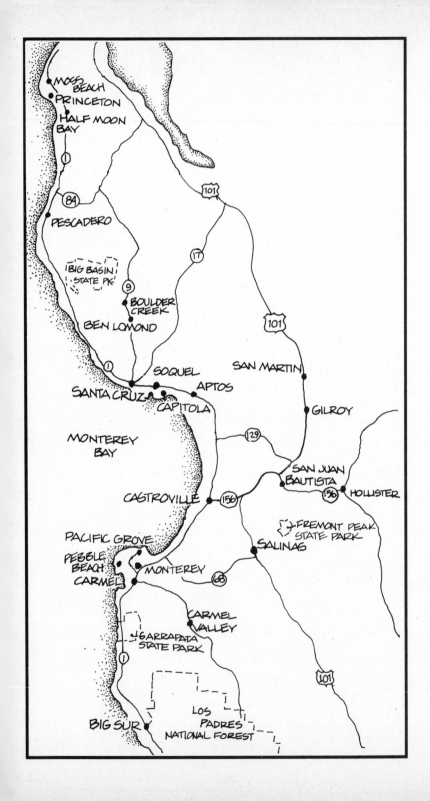

Central Coast

*From Moss Beach south along Highway 1 to
Big Sur with detours inland to Salinas, San Juan
Bautista, Gilroy, and Hollister*

MOSS BEACH

RESTAURANTS

Moss Beach Distillery Used by bootleggers during Prohibition to store their illicit wares, this old stucco distillery on a cliff above Moss Beach has been a local favorite for almost a century. In the '20s, silent film stars and San Francisco politicos frequented the Distillery for drinks—and the bordello next door for other pleasures. Things are considerably tamer these days, though around sunset the Distillery's pleasingly rowdy bar still rings with laughter and the loud voices of well-baked beachgoers knocking back oyster shooters. The food itself is not the best on the coast, but it's competently prepared. The barbecued ribs are decent, but most folks come here for the oysters, drinks, and fine views of the sunset. ■ *W on Cypress Ave off Hwy 1, right on Marine Blvd, which turns into Beach; (415) 728-5595; Beach and Ocean streets, Moss Beach; $$; full bar; AE, DC, MC, V; no checks; dinner every day, brunch Sun.*

LODGINGS

Seal Cove Inn ★★★ Karen (Brown) Herbert quietly searched for the perfect country inn while she authored a guide to California's country inns. Herbert learned what makes a superior inn and doesn't miss a trick. Built in 1990, this large English–style country manor has 10 bedrooms that look out over a colorful, half-acre wildflower garden dotted with birdhouses. All the rooms have fireplaces, fresh flowers, antique furnishings, original watercolors, and grandfather clocks, as well as tastefully hidden away televisions, refrigerators wellstocked with free goodies, and towel warmers in the baths. The upstairs rooms, our favorites, have vaulted ceilings and sliding French-style doors that open onto private decks.

One thing's for sure—you won't starve here. In the morning, you'll find a newspaper and coffee outside your door. Later, Herbert serves a full breakfast (wherever you prefer). In the afternoon, you'll find hors d'oeuvres like cheese and crackers, meatballs, and vegetables with dip in the dining room. Brandy and sherry are always available in the living room next to the fire. At night, there'll be a little plate of truffles or cookies beside your turned-down bed.

There's plenty to do around here during the day. The inn's

extravagant backyard garden opens onto open park land with seaside meadows and a miniforest of cypress trees. On the other side of the park, about a quarter mile away, is the Fitzgerald Marine Reserve, one of the area's best spots for exploring tide pools. ■ *6 miles N of Half Moon Bay on Hwy 1, W on Cypress Ave; (415) 728-7325; 221 Cypress Ave, Moss Beach, CA 94038; $$$; AE, DIS, MC, V; local checks only.*

PRINCETON-BY-THE-SEA

RESTAURANTS

Barbara's Fish Trap ★ To get any closer to the ocean than Barbara's Fish Trap, you'd have to get your feet wet. Situated on stilts above the beach, Barbara's has wonderful indoor and outdoor dining with panoramic views of Half Moon Bay. The decor is classic fish 'n' chips style (complete with checkered plastic tablecloths, fishnets on the walls, and a wooden fisherman by the door) but the food is a cut above. Barbara's offers a selection of deep-fried seafood (calamari, rockfish, scallops, and prawns) and broiled fish like Cajun-spiced snapper. The garlic prawns and steamed mussels are also quite good. The french fries are fat and tasty and you can choose from 52 kinds of beer. ■ *Turn W at the only signal in Princeton; (415) 728-7049; 281 Capistrano Rd, Princeton-by-the Sea $$; beer and wine; no credit cards; no checks; lunch, dinner every day.*

LODGINGS

Pillar Point Inn ★★ This modern-looking, blue-gray wooden inn is the only harbor-side bed and breakfast on the Peninsula coast. Located on a busy fishing harbor with a commercial fleet, half a dozen restaurants, sport-fishing charters, whale-watching vessels, and a fishing pier, Pillar Point Inn is surprisingly quiet. The inn's 11 sunny, modern, country-style rooms have harbor views, private baths, gas fireplaces, feather beds, and concealed televisions with VCRs. The rooms on the first floor have private steam baths as well. Breakfast, served in the common room from 8 to 10am, includes coffee, juice, hot muffins, granola, and a hot dish such as waffles, scrambled eggs, or crêpes. You can have a smaller continental breakfast delivered to your room. Afternoon tea is served by the fire in the living room or outside on the sun deck. ■ *4 miles N of Half Moon Bay on Hwy 1, W on Capistrano Rd; (415) 728-7377; 380 Capistrano Rd, Princeton-by-the-Sea, CA 94018; $$$; AE, MC, V; checks OK.*

HALF MOON BAY

Old Victorian houses and small boutiques line the downtown, while produce stands and you-pick farms ring the perimeter.

There are plenty of **good beaches** nearby: Montera Beach and Saint Francis Beach are arguably the most beautiful. **Surfers** congregate at Surfer's Beach. Venice and Dune beaches are less crowded than some of the others. For the best tidepools, check out Moss Beach (follow the signs to the Fitzgerald Marine Reserve; (415) 728-3584). For **whale watching**, call Huck Finn's Sport Fishing Tours, (415) 726-7133, or Captain John's, (415) 726-2913, both located on the Pillar Point Harbor, about 4 miles north of Half Moon Bay.

Every October, thousands of Bay Area families make their yearly pilgrimage to this picturesque sea coast town in search of the ultimate Halloween pumpkin. The **Great Pumpkin Festival** features pumpkin cuisine and crafts, as well as the Giant Pumpkin weigh-in contest, won recently by a 375-pound monster; (415) 726-5202.

RESTAURANTS

Pasta Moon ★★ This inventive nouveau Italian place follows three time-honored rules of Mediterranean cooking: use only sparklingly fresh ingredients; make everything from scratch; and don't forget the garlic! Despite their fondness for the stinking rose, chefs Kimberly Levin Shenkman and Vince Nannini's wonderfully creative pastas and main entrées are remarkably well-balanced. The fresh linguine, capellini, tagliatelle, lasagne, and fettuccine are always flavorful and perfectly cooked. The linguine alla Fiorentina glistens in a luscious sauce of olive oil, homemade Tuscan sausage, sun-dried tomatoes, pine nuts, and fresh basil. Another linguine comes in a light, sweet sauce with fresh sea scallops, red peppers, garlic, and a hint of anchovies. We especially like the succulent osso bucco, braised

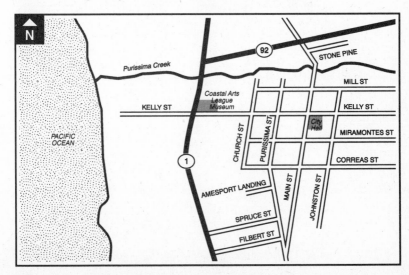

in wine and orange juice with just a hint of bay leaves. The Tuscan fish stew with tomatoes, carrots, onions, garlic, and white wine is wonderfully aromatic. Pasta Moon's appetizers, salads, and desserts are in the same league as the entrées: the achingly fresh mozzarella salad with sweet tomatoes and basil is particularly good, as is the roasted head of garlic served with goat cheese and crostini. The tiramisu, with its layers of Marsala- and espresso-soaked ladyfingers and creamy mascarpone, is perfectly balanced, and the unforgettable mascarpone cheesecake comes in a pool of dark chocolate sauce. ■ *N end of Main St, near Hwy 92; (415) 726-5125; 315 Main St, Half Moon Bay; $$; beer and wine; AE, MC, V; local checks only; lunch, dinner every day.*

San Benito House ★★★ Located in a pastel blue Victorian on Half Moon Bay's Main Street, San Benito House's candle-lit dining room is decorated with garlands of fresh pine branches and vases of colorful, locally grown flowers. The walls are lined with paintings by local turn-of-the-century artists. Chef Carol Mickelsen has trained with such cooking legends as the late Masa in San Francisco, Roger Verge in Provence, and Jacques Pepin in New York. Taking full advantage of Half Moon Bay's prodigious agricultural resources, she uses only the freshest ingredients. An autumn menu includes melt-in-your-mouth homemade ravioli with yams, almonds, and ricotta cheese, served with a fresh mint cream sauce; a midwinter menu offered mesquite-grilled salmon with tomato-almond aioli. Mickelsen's desserts are paradisiacal: fresh blackberry sorbet and Le Montmorency—a rich, flourless chocolate cake with its center scooped out and mixed with fresh apricot, topped with dark chocolate frosting and Chantilly cream.

Avoid the long drive home by staying upstairs in one of Mickelsen's cheerful, hand-stenciled guest rooms. The one above the garden stands out as the best. ■ *Center of town on Main St, (415) 726-3425; 356 Main St, Half Moon Bay; $$; full bar; AE, MC, V; no checks; dinner Thurs–Sun, brunch Sun.*

LODGINGS

Cypress Inn on Miramar Beach ★★★ With Miramar Beach right outside the door, this wonderful modern inn is *the* place to commune with the ocean along the Peninsula coast. From every room, you not only see the ocean, you hear it, smell it, even feel it in the fine mist drifting in with the morning fog. The wood building has beam ceilings, skylights, terra-cotta tiles, colorful folk art, and warm, rustic furniture made of pine, heavy wicker, and leather. Each room has a vaulted ceiling, a soft feather bed, a private balcony (with an occasional cactus), a gas fireplace, and its own bath. The enormous penthouse has a Jacuzzi tub as well. The rooms don't come with televisions, but the obliging innkeepers will put one in your room if you ask.

The Cypress Inn's breakfast is far and above the usual B&B fare—fresh-ground Italian roast coffee, fresh orange juice, croissants, a fruit parfait, and a choice of perhaps smoked salmon and mascarpone omelet, a red bell pepper and goat cheese omelet, or French toast with fresh peaches and cream. In the afternoon, you'll find an elaborate feast of hors d'oeuvres such as prosciutto and melon, freshly baked quiche, fresh fruit pie, and white wine in the common room. The service is flawless. ■ *3 miles N of junction of Hwy 92 and Hwy 1, W on Medio to Mirada; (415) 726-6002; 407 Mirada Rd, Half Moon Bay, CA 94019; $$$; AE, MC, V; checks OK.*

Mill Rose Inn ★★ One of the oldest bed and breakfasts on the Peninsula coast, the Mill Rose Inn fancies itself an old-fashioned English country inn. It's got an extravagant English garden, flower boxes at the windows, plus the requisite lace curtains, antique beds, and nightstands. Its studied Englishness has faltered a bit in recent years with the addition of new-fangled California amenities such as Jacuzzis and wine and cheese in the afternoon, instead of a soothing cuppa. But we won't quibble. Enclosed in a frosted glass gazebo, the Jacuzzi is lots of fun. The six rooms have private entrances and private baths, king- or queen-size feather beds, fireplaces, and views of the garden. They also have telephones, televisions with cable and VCRs, well-stocked refrigerators, fresh flowers, chocolates, and liqueurs. Two rooms, the Bordeaux and Renaissance suites, have sitting rooms as well. In the morning, you'll find a newspaper outside your door and a full breakfast in the dining room. ■ *On Mill St, 1 block W of Main St; (415) 726-9794; 615 Mill St, Half Moon Bay, CA 94019; $$$; AE, DIS, MC, V; local checks only.*

The Zaballa House ★ The oldest building in Half Moon Bay, this pastel blue Victorian is set back from the street and surrounded on three sides by a colorful flower and herb garden. Designed by 19th-century town planner Estanislao Zaballa, the house was originally built for a family of seven. Now carved up into nine guest rooms, the inn can get very cozy indeed, especially when all the rooms are full. The rooms are small and a bit cramped, but each is impeccably decorated with understated wallpaper and country furniture. Some rooms have a fireplace; some have vaulted ceilings; some have garden views; none have telephones or televisions. Wine, hors d'oeuvres, and cookies are served in the late afternoon and evening by the fireplace in the small, wood-paneled living room. Zaballa House offers an all-you-can-eat buffet breakfast. ■ *N end of Main St in Half Moon Bay; (415) 726-9123; 324 Main St, Half Moon Bay, CA 94019; $$; AE, DIS, MC, V; local checks only.*

PESCADERO

RESTAURANTS

Duarte's Tavern ★★ Duarte's (pronounced "doo-arts") is a rustic gem, still owned and operated by the family that built it 98 years ago. Back then it was a place to buy a 10-cent shot of whiskey on the stagecoach ride from San Francisco to Santa Cruz. Set in an Old West–style wooden building across the street from Pescadero's general store, Duarte's is half bar, half restaurant. The bar is dark and loud, filled with locals drinking beer, smoking, and spinning entertaining lies. The unassuming restaurant next door has checkered tablecloths and terrific home-cooked coastal food. Most of the fruits and vegetables come from the Duarte's own farms. Start with the spicy and flavorful cream of artichoke or cream of green chile soup. The salads, made with greens from the backyard, are standard, but fresh. Duarte's offers 10 kinds of fresh fish daily and a competent crab cioppino (you need to call ahead for this). For dessert, try a slice of their wonderful pie—olallieberry, rhubarb, and apricot are our faves. Don't leave town without visiting the oldest church on the Northern California coast and the interesting old graveyard at the north end of town. ■ *Corner of Pescadero and Stage Rd; (415) 879-0464; 202 Stage Rd, Pescadero; $$; full bar; AE, MC, V; local checks only; breakfast, lunch, dinner every day.*

▼

Pescadero

Restaurants

▲

BOULDER CREEK

RESTAURANTS

The White Cockade Public House ★ Named for the white rosette that Bonnie Prince Charlie wore on his cap, The White Cockade earns high marks for authenticity in the pub department. Owners Barbara Stanford and Tom Cramer opened it in 1987 after returning from England and Scotland. Stanford and Cramer have transformed this once rough-and-tumble bar into a homey watering hole where there's always a cozy fire and a friendly game of darts in progress. Check out their vast list of fine imported British ales, lagers, and stouts—there's not a single domestic beer in sight. This is also the place for some of the best genuine pub food—fish and chips, bangers and mash, homemade meat pies—in the Bay area. ■ *S on Hwy 9 about 5 miles from Saratoga; (408) 338-4148; 18025 Hwy 9, Boulder Creek; $; beer and wine; no credit cards; local checks only; dinner every day.*

Books in the Best Places series read as personal guidebooks, but our evaluations are based on numerous reports from local experts. Our inspectors never identify themselves (except over the phone) and never accept free meals or other favors.

RESTAURANTS

Tyrolean Inn ★★ Button up your lederhosen, raise your beer stein, and shout, "Gruss Gott!" That's Austrian slang for "hello" and "good-bye"—sort of a Germanic "aloha." Served amidst fire-lit copper coziness and the unmistakable perfume of smoked pork, the Tyrolean's generous portions of goulash, sausage, and various schnitzels come with sides of red cabbage and potato pancakes. Plaster sculptures of rotund Teutons greet you in the entryway, and real-live Austrians—the Wolf family—serve you once you're inside. They've got a large selection of European beers, plus Gluhwein (hot, spiced wine) or schnapps. ■ *On Hwy 9 in the mountains above Santa Cruz; (408) 336-5188; 9600 Hwy 9, Ben Lomond; $$; full bar; AE, DC, DIS, MC, V; no checks; lunch, dinner Tues–Sun; brunch Sun.*

Ristorante Italiano Squisito (aka Squisi's) ★ An extensive list of Italian wines available for tasting is just one of the reasons to make the drive along Highway 9 to this elegant, intimate restaurant in the tiny mountain enclave of Ben Lomond. Service is knowledgeable but slow, so order some of Squisi's delicious bocconcini before you start tasting the wine. The mushroom tidbits, like the large, baked shiitake mushroom stuffed with fennel-spiced Italian sausage and Parmesan, are always worthwhile. For dinner, try the osso bucco Milano: veal shank braised in butter and garlic, slowly cooked in a sauce of white wine, fresh tomatoes, oregano, and onions, and garnished with Parmesan and gremolada (lemon zest, parsley, garlic, and anchovy). Desserts—all made on the premises—include a Belgian chocolate cup filled with caramel mousse and topped with fresh strawberries and candied walnuts, and a warm bread pudding spiked with cinnamon and brandy zabaglione, topped with toasted almonds, and served warm.

Squisi's serves a Sunday brunch featuring canneloni, grilled chicken and trout, frittatas filled with mushrooms and home-grown herbs or roasted bell peppers and onions, and a complimentary glass of sparkling wine. ■ *Call for directions; (408) 336-2006; 9217 Hwy 9, Ben Lomond; $$$; beer and wine; MC, V; checks OK; dinner Wed–Sun, brunch Sun.*

Ben Lomond

Lodgings

▲

LODGINGS

Chateau des Fleurs ★★ Owners Lee and Laura Jonas are some of the most down-to-earth folks you're likely to meet, yet their bed and breakfast is full of elegant little surprises: huge, supersoft towels in every bath, billowy down comforters, hypnotic ceiling fans, and even a fairy-lit gazebo out front. And everything is scrupulously, almost terrifyingly, clean. The gabled 1879 Victorian was once owned by the Bartlett family and their legendary pear trees still line the drive. The Orchid Room has a small, private deck outfitted with wicker furniture and surrounded by tall, fragrant redwoods. The downstairs gallery is absurdly well-appointed with a wide-screen TV, afternoon wine, books, magazines, guitar, mandolin, and even a trampoline. Mrs. Jonas' lush breakfasts might include velvety little soufflés, hot popovers with three choices of homemade jam, and fresh fruit with mint in fluted glasses. ■ *Just S of Ben Lomond, on Hwy 9 above Santa Cruz; (408) 3368943; 7995 Hwy 9, Ben Lomond, CA 95005; $$; AE, DIS, MC, V; checks OK.*

CENTRAL COAST WINE COUNTRY

It used to be, back before the wine boom of the '70s and '80s, that going wine-tasting was something of an adventure; however, Napa, and to a lesser degree Sonoma, have become major league tourist stops in recent decades, and their wineries have put together elaborate tasting rooms and slick tours for the growing number of visitors. But along California's Central Coast, it's still possible to find wineries on narrow back roads with nothing more than a small sign out front to indicate their presence. Once inside, you're likely to be greeted by the owner/winemaker, and tastings are conducted at a leisurely pace, with plenty of talk about how the wines were made. It's always a good idea to call ahead. You may need detailed directions in order to negotiate the back roads, and tasting hours are often limited and sometimes quite irregular.

    Ridge Vineyards, one of California's original "boutique" wineries, is still among the finest zinfandel and cabernet producers around (17100 Montebello Road, Cupertino, (408) 867-3233). **Sunrise Winery** uses grapes from its 95 year-old vines in order to produce its highly regarded Estate Zinfandel and pinot noir (13100 Montebello Road, Cupertino, (408) 741-1310). Bear Creek Road off Highway 17 is narrow and twisting, and features incredible vistas as you drive the 5 miles to **David Bruce Winery** (21439 Bear Creek Road, Los Gatos, (408) 354-4214). Dr. Bruce makes wines with names like "Old Dog Red," and "Mr. and Mrs. Baggins," but his pinot noir and chardonnay are seriously good. A bit farther down the road, **Byington Winery** makes good cab in a big estate-like building overlooking a redwood forest (28150 Bear Creek Rd, Los Gatos, (408) 354-1111).

    It's easy to get lost on your way to **Roudon-Smith Vineyards,** but their estate-grown chardonnay is worth the risk (2364 Bean Creek Road, Santa Cruz (408) 438-1244). **Hallcrest Vineyards**, secreted away behind a residential neighborhood, is equally easy to miss, but you won't want to miss their riesling (379 Felton Empire Road, Felton, (408) 335-4441). If you want to find out why winemaker Randall Grahm named his

Rhone-style red wine after a "flying cigar," visit **Bonny Doon Vineyard** (10 Pine Flat Road, Santa Cruz, (408) 425-3625). You'll have to make an appointment to try **Santa Cruz Mountain Vineyard's** pinot noir, cabernet sauvignon, merlot, and chardonnay (2300 Jarvis Road, Santa Cruz, (408) 426-6209).

The **Hecker Pass Highway**, aka State Route 152, in Gilroy is home to a number of wineries, some new, some old. **Solis Winery,** offering chardonnay and merlot, is located in the refurbished circa 1917 A. Bertero Winery (3920 Hecker Pass, (408) 847-6306). Just a bit up the road is **Thomas Kruse Winery**, owned by a winemaker with a sense of humor and little tolerance for wine snobbery or hype. Read the back labels and laugh, but try his chardonnay and zin (4390 Hecker Pass, (408) 842-7016). **Fortino Winery** makes hearty, old-style reds, and has a wonderfully kitschy gift shop (4525 Hecker Pass, (408) 842-3305). Back on Route 101 at the intersection of Highway 25 is the not-to-be-missed **Rapazzini Winery** which makes garlic wine, garlic jelly, and believe it or not, garlic ice cream, all of which are better than they sound (4350 Monterey Road, Gilroy, (408) 842-5649).

South of Salinas, wine country continues. Call for an appointment to try **Morgan Winery's** chardonnay (526 Brunken Avenue, Salinas, (408) 422-9855). **Chalone Vineyards**, producers of legendary chardonnays and pinot noirs, is located near the Pinnacles National Monument (Stonewall Canyon Road at Highway 146, Soledad, (408) 678-1717). **Smith and Hook Winery** is far enough up a dirt road so that you're sure you made a wrong turn. But be patient, there's good cab and merlot just ahead (37700 Foothill Road, Soledad, (408) 678-2132). **Jekel Vineyard** makes wonderful riesling and chardonnay a short distance away from homes and shopping centers (40155 Walnut Avenue, Greensfield, (408) 674-5522). Over in the Carmel Valley, **Chateau Julien** makes 60,000 cases of wine a year, and has a pleasant tasting room and patio. Try their Private Reserve Chardonnay and merlot (8940 Carmel Valley Road, (408) 624-2600).

SANTA CRUZ

Santa Cruz is a chimerical place, skittering from diamond-bright beach to swampy slough to moody redwood grove to cafe society to rustic farm in just about the time it takes to say, "Surf's up!" The ubiquitous Father Junipero Serra founded Santa Cruz in 1791 as the site for the Mission of Holy Cross. A half-size replica of the building is now open to the public every day, offering morning Masses and a view of some of the mission's original books and vestments (corner of Emmet and High Streets, (408) 426-5686). The rest of the town seems, at first glance, a devil-may-care, salt-water-taffy seaside resort, embodied by the roller-coaster-ferris-wheel world of the **Santa Cruz Beach Boardwalk** (400 Beach Street) where the roar of the revelers mingles with the plaintive bark of sea lions. But peer a little closer, and Santa Cruz's refreshingly intellectual side emerges: the **University of California** sited on a woodsy modern campus has an unconventional grading system that awards students wordy, thoughtful evaluations instead of soulless alphabetical rankings. Check out the aquarium and marine exhibits at the **Joseph M. Long Marine Laboratory** (100 Shaffer Road, (408) 459-4308) where you can actually handle mollusks and other small sea creatures. The **Santa Cruz Surf Museum**, on W Cliff Drive at Lighthouse Point, caters to sea creatures of the human kind. The tiny museum, filled with photographs and antique surfboards, is open every day but Tuesday; (408) 429-3429. The **Art Museum of Santa Cruz County**, (408) 429-1964, featuring contemporary modern art, was destroyed in the 1989 Loma Prieta earthquake, but plans to reopen its doors on Cooper Street in January of 1993. Architecture fans will want to check out the town's plethora of sumptuous Victorians.

Just a little way up or down the road you'll find fruit orchards, wineries, and little country towns like picket-fenced Corralitos; elegant, equestrian Aptos; and prim and flowery Capitola with its prized begonias. Campers will find numerous

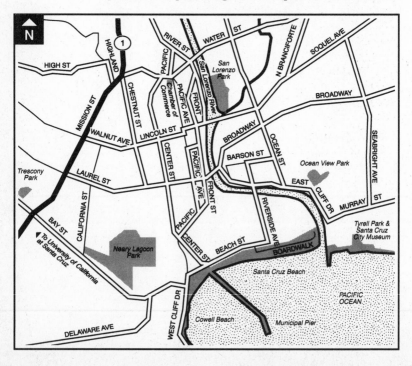

nearby parks, including the well-known **Big Basin Redwoods State Park**, several thousand acres of ancient forest that formed the keystone of the state's park system in 1902. The park offers 147 campsites, 35 tent cabins, and 4 large group camps; (408) 338-6132, or toll free (800)444-7275 for reservations. Finally, consider a train ride through the redwoods courtesy of **Roaring Camp**, located on Graham Hill Road (take Highway 17 to the Mount Herman Road exit, then to Graham Hill). On Wednesdays through Sundays in winter, and daily in summer, the **Roaring Camp and Big Trees Narrow Gauge Railroad**, (408) 335-4484, winds its way through redwood stands on the way to Bear Mountain. And from May to October, the **Santa Cruz, Big Trees and Pacific Railway at Roaring Camp**, (408) 335-4400, loads passengers onto full-size cars for a beautiful 8-mile journey to the Santa Cruz boardwalk.

RESTAURANTS

India Joze Restaurant ★★★ India Joze, a delightful cross-cultural wonder, has been wowing locals for years. The portions are enormous and each dish is lovingly thought out and complete. You'll find steaming, sunset-colored bowls of thick lentil dal, redolent of mustard seed and caraway, and platters of chicken dressed with a ginger-basil-tamarind glaze. The perky Berber burger (half a pound of spiced lamb) comes with yam chips. Even normally understated things like hash browns arrive at your table crowned with artichokes, peppers, and sour cream. The house blend of spiced tea (chai) is intense, dense, and sweet—the closest we've come to grownup cocoa. Odd, wavy art work in salmon-pink and aqua flows across the walls, giving the dining room a pleasant feeling of being undersea. ■ *On Center St at Union St; (408) 427-3554; 1001 Center St, Santa Cruz; $$; beer and wine; MC, V; local checks only; lunch Mon–Fri, dinner every day, brunch Sat–Sun.*

O'mei Restaurant ★★★ We're willing to bet that Madame Chiang Kai-shek's personal chef (who reportedly trained half the Chinese cooks in California) is spinning rapidly in his grave. O'mei, while very skilled at what it does, is, um—experimental. You can, of course, order predictable northern Chinese offerings such as Mongolian beef and mu-shu pork. But if you've got an adventurous palate, don't stick with the old standbys, good as they are. O'mei is a veritable Asian adventure in California-land. These folk push the envelope of Pac-Rim cuisine, offering tasty bizarrities such as black date and sweet potato chicken, lamb shank with Chinese wolf berries, and black sesame ice cream. This kind of originality, pulled off with taste and finesse, is as rare as a phoenix's eggs—which, by the way, are probably the only kind of eggs you won't find here. ■ *On Mission St, near the western edge of Santa Cruz; (408) 425-8458; 2316 Mission St, Santa Cruz; $$; beer and*

▼

Santa Cruz

Restaurants

▲

wine; AE, MC, V; no checks; lunch Mon–Fri, dinner every day.

Casablanca Restaurant ★★ There's nothing very Moroccan about this boardwalk bastion of California cuisine, except, perhaps, the palpable air of romance. Soft music fills the candle-lit dining room and stars wink on the water outside the window. It's the sort of place where you get the urge to hold hands across the table. The food can be a bit too subtle at times, producing spiritless vinaigrettes and cloying gazpacho. But when chef Randy Chowning begins boldly blending the world's culinary resources, his creations delight. Try the meltingly soft, fire-roasted Anaheim chile stuffed with feta cheese, or the fried Brie with jalapeño jelly. Expect to see the unexpected: sole in macadamia nut batter, grilled spearfish with kiwi salsa, or pork with apple-onion chutney. Local wines share a book-length wine list with selections from Italy, Germany, France, and Australia. ■ *On the Santa Cruz waterfront; (408) 426-9063; 101 Main St, Santa Cruz; $$$; full bar; AE, DC, MC, V; dinner every day, brunch Sun.*

Pontiac Grill ★ Most everyone in town agrees that the Pontiac Grill is the best place to take kids. Have a giggle at the streamlined booths (each with its own working mini-jukebox), the jaunty red and black vinyl, the servers' pleated skirts and sweatervests, and the long, long counter. The menu serves up relentless automobile puns: appetizers are called "First Gear"; side orders are "Spare Parts"; drinks are "Heaters and Coolants"; drumettes with barbecue sauce are "Chicken Pistons." Kids love the french fries, onion rings, 14 kinds of burgers, rich milk shakes and malts, and the opportunity to color in the Pontiacs on the place mats. ■ *At the corner of Front and Cathcart streets; (408) 427-2290; 429 Front St, Santa Cruz; $; beer and wine; MC, V; no checks; breakfast Sat–Sun, lunch, dinner every day.*

▼
Santa Cruz

Restaurants

▲

LODGINGS

The Babbling Brook Inn ★★★ The Babbling Brook Inn, Santa Cruz's oldest bed and breakfast, is still one of the best on the coast. Secreted away in a fantastical garden with waterfalls, wishing wells, gazebos, and a babbling brook, the inn offers 12 rooms named after famous artists. The mauve and blue Van Gogh Room has a private deck and beam ceiling. Peach and ivory predominate in the Cézanne Room, with its generous bath and a canopy bed. The blue and white Monet Room has a corner fireplace, canopy bed, private deck, and a view of the waterfall and footbridge. In the morning, innkeeper Helen King lays out a delectable spread of French toast, fruit compote, banana muffins, croissants, breakfast rellenos, freshsqueezed orange juice, yogurt, homeground coffee, and more. She'll even whip up separate dishes for guests with special diets. You can breakfast in the luxurious dining room, on the flowery patio, or in your own private suite. ■ *On Laurel, near Walti St; (408) 427-2437, toll free (800) 866-1131; 1025 Laurel St, Santa Cruz, CA 95060; $$$; AE, DIS, MC, V; checks OK.*

The Darling House: A Bed and Breakfast Inn by the Sea

★★★ There's probably no better view (and no softer carpeting) in all of Santa Cruz than you'll find at the Darling House, a Spanish Revival mansion built as a summer home for a Colorado cattle baron in 1910. From its massive living room, you can see endless miles of gray-blue sea, gulls, boats, and the lights of faraway towns. On chilly days you'll always find a fire crackling in the living room's glorious art deco fireplace. The Pacific Ocean Room, upstairs, is decorated like a sea captain's quarters, with a telescope and huge polished sea shells. Across the hall, the Chinese Room boasts Chinese lanterns and an exotic canopied Chinese wedding bed. Owners Darrell and Karen Darling have worked hard to preserve the house's intricate woodwork and have outfitted every room with museum-quality antiques. (Some mattresses, alas, also feel like antiques.) There's a hot tub in the back yard and you'll find fluffy white robes in every closet. Perpetually smiling Darrell is incredibly attentive. He'll even call to make sure a restaurant's evening menu is to your liking. Karen's breakfasts include fresh fruit, homemade granola made with walnuts from the Darlings' own farm, and fresh-from-the-oven breads and pastries. ■ *On W Cliff Dr, between the pier and the lighthouse; (408) 458-1958; 314 West Cliff Dr, Santa Cruz, CA 95060; $$$; AE, DIS, MC, V; checks OK.*

▼
▲

SOQUEL

RESTAURANTS

Aragona's ★ Tucked away in a nondescript shopping center in one of the few non-touristy parts of town, Aragona's does plain, by-the-book Italian food—no tricks, nothing nouveau, but the food delights. Spaghetti arrives, smelling delightfully of garlic, and glossy (but not sodden) with olive oil; cannelloni is plump and savory. The restaurant prepares veal in seven different ways, as well as seafood, chicken, and eggplant. Pizza can be ordered with thin or thick crust: the thick (Sicilian) style is a glory—colorful and dizzyingly herbacious. ■ *On Main near Porter St; (408) 462-5100; 2591 Main St, Soquel; $$; full bar; AE, MC, V; local checks only; lunch Mon–Fri, dinner every day.*

The facts in this edition were correct at press time, but places close, chefs depart, hours change. It's best to call ahead.

CAPITOLA

RESTAURANTS

Country Court Tea Room ★ If every city in America had a place like this, how mellow, how contented as Persian cats we'd all become. Yes, the Tea Room serves breakfast (muffins, popovers, waffles, granola), brunch (fruit, quiche, champagne), and lunch (soup, salad, homemade ice cream), but as Gertrude Stein might say, what is a tea room for if not for tea? This place shines in the lingering, golden, late afternoon between 3 and 4pm when the weary stagger in, past the topiary and the friendly English bric-a-brac, to cozy up with an invigorating cuppa, complete with delicate little sandwiches and homemade cookies. The house blend of spiced tea is strong and excellent, but you can also have herbal and other black teas. The coffees and wines are for heathens. ■ *On Capitola Ave between Bay Ave and Hwy 1; (408) 462-2498; 911B Capitola Ave; $; beer and wine; no credit cards; local checks only; breakfast, lunch Mon–Fri, dinner Fri, brunch Sat–Sun.*

Shadowbrook Restaurant ★ While locals are forever undecided about the quality of the food at Shadowbrook (a costly array of predictables like scampi, steak, and prime rib), they nevertheless insist that all Santa Cruz visitors dine here at least once in their lives. So don't fight it. Climb aboard the funicular that runs down through the ferny woods, past a waterfall, to the multi-storied, woodsy restaurant bedecked in white lights—a culinary cousin of Disneyland's Swiss Family Tree House. The best place to sit is at the alfresco tables on the brickwork terraces, nestled romantically among rock gardens and rhododendrons. The appetizers, soups, and salads are very ordinary. Red meat is what the Shadowbrook does best. The prime rib (even the petite portion) is huge and flavorful, though a little tough. The Shadowbrook's decent wine list is fairly priced, but the whites are usually overchilled. The Jack Daniels mud pie is stupendous at first bite, but cloying by the third. ■ *On Wharf Rd, near the end of Capitola Rd; (408) 475-1511; 1750 Wharf Rd, Capitola; $$$; full bar; AE, DC, MC, V; local checks only; lunch, dinner every day.*

▼

Capitola

Restaurants

▲

LODGINGS

The Inn at Depot Hill ★★★★ Located in a turn-of-the-century train station, the Inn at Depot Hill is a dream of a place with trompe l'oeil paintings on the walls, and soft, sophisticated lighting that bathes everyone in an angelic glow. The eight rooms, lavishly designed to evoke international ports of call, seem to have sprung directly from the pages of *Architectural Digest*. The terra-cotta-walled Portofino Room, patterned after a coastal Italian villa, sports a stone cherub, ivy, frescoes, and a brick patio. No less charming is the Stratford-upon-Avon, a faux English cottage that has a window seat. The Paris Room with its toile-covered walls dazzles in black and white, while the fussy Côte d'Azur boasts an ornate canopy bed with bronze vines climbing the four-posters. Every room has a TV and VCR (hidden tastefully in the closet), a wall radio, and a marble-appointed bathroom, complete with mini-TV and coffee machine. In the morning, there's a buffet of pastries, cereal, and quiche. In the evening, you'll find sweets and wine in the downstairs parlor. While you're there, browse along the massive wall-length bookcase. If you find a book you like, just take it—it's free. ■ *On Monterey near Park Ave, next to the railroad tracks; (408) 462-3376; 250 Monterey Ave, Capitola-by-the-Sea, CA 95010; $$$; AE, MC, V; checks OK.*

APTOS

LODGINGS

Mangels House ★★★ Set on a neat green lawn in the middle of a redwood forest, this sprawling Italianate Victorian mansion was built as a summer house for Spreckels sugar magnate Claus Mangels in 1886. British-born Jacqueline Fisher and her husband Ron, who bought the place in 1979, have decorated the rooms in a daring, artful, whimsical way that enlivens the house's stately Victorian demeanor. Pastel stenciling dances across the bedroom walls and dramatic modern vases rest on antique marble sinks. We especially like the Nicholaus Room with its huge bed and chocolate-brown walls decorated with masks, shields, and other souvenirs of the Fishers' two years in Africa. Jacqueline's lavish breakfasts, served in the dining room, feature apple-puff pancakes, a spicy chili-cheese fluff, fresh fruit, homemade scones, and yogurt. ■ *570 Aptos Creek Rd, on the road into Nisene Marks State Park ½ mile above Aptos; (408) 6887982; Mail: PO Box 302, Aptos, CA 95001; $$; MC, V; checks OK*

Apple Lane Inn ★ Devotees of the pinafores-and- Pollyanna set will love this place. Other more restrained sorts may gag at relentless Victoriana. Set back from the road in the middle of an orchard, the spotlessly clean Apple Lane Inn is decorated with handmade quilts, high-quality Persian rugs, claw-footed tubs, and too-cute, country-style knickknacks. Guests play croquet and horseshoes and cuddle in a white gazebo. In the parlor, there's a player piano watched over by a roomful of stern-looking Victorian portraits. Hosts Doug and Diana Groom are young and very earnest. They serve a fussy but large breakfast that features sweet, old-fashioned delicacies like Monte Cristo sandwiches, and avail coffee and sherry to guests all day in the library. ■ *On Soquel Dr, just W of Cabrillo College; (408) 475-6868; 6265 Soquel Dr, Aptos, CA 95003; $$; DIS, MC, V; checks OK.*

Bayview Hotel Bed & Breakfast Inn ★ Set on former Spanish land-grant property, Santa Cruz County's oldest hotel combines Old West ambience with up-to-date comfort. The steep staircase, booklined parlor, and bustling cafe-bar downstairs recall Aptos' frontier past. Every period-perfect room has its own bath and a brand-new, four-star mattress resting in an antique frame. The light pastel color scheme and contemporary watercolors impart a delicious sense of coolness and space that so many other Victorian period hotels lack. The house blend of coffee is good and dark. The Duncans plan to add a third level to the 1878 hotel next year. ■ *On Soquel Dr at Trout Gulch Rd; (408) 688-8654; 8041 Soquel Dr, Aptos, CA 95003; $$$; AE, MC, V; checks OK.*

SAN MARTIN

LODGINGS

Country Rose Inn Bed and Breakfast ★★ Set in the midst of open rolling farmland, Rose Hernandez' 1920s Dutch Colonial has four bedrooms, each decorated in a different rose motif. Splurge on the Rambling Rose Suite, the largest and most masculine of the rooms. Decorated in dark wood, the suite has its own private entrance, whirlpool tub, sitting room with a wood-burning stove, and a view through the trees of the surrounding farmland. Summers you might want to stay in the downstairs Victorian Garden Room, with its white wicker furniture, blond hardwood floors, a white, four-poster Victorian double bed, and a breezy view of the garden through lace curtains. After breakfast, the musically inclined can practice on the baby grand piano in the music room. ■ *Masten Ave exit off Hwy 101, go 1 mile; (408) 842-0441; Mail: 455 Fitzgerald Ave E, San Martin, CA 95046; $$$; MC, V; checks OK.*

GILROY

Will Rogers called Gilroy the only town in America where you can marinate a steak just by hanging it out on the line. Then came the **Gilroy Garlic Festival,** held the last weekend in July. Started in 1979, the festival now attracts 150,000 people eager to try oddities like garlic ice cream and garlic chocolate and to enter their garlic-laden home recipes in the Great Garlic Cook-Off. You can also buy a Woolworth's full of "stinking rose" memorabilia. To find out about Gilroy before the age of garlic, check out the **Gilroy Historical Museum** on the corner of 5th and Church streets; (408) 847-2685.

RESTAURANTS

Garlic Aulx Restaurant ★ ★ The entrance to this airy, old hotel ballroom is dominated by a large horseshoe-shaped bar and a handcarved stagecoach. Inside, you'll find elegant tables with pale pink tablecloths, chairs upholstered in green and pink chintz, and efficient, discreet service. If you've come to Gilroy for the garlic, you'll want to try their roasted version of the stinking rose with rosemaried feta cheese, sun-dried tomatoes, and a good crusty bread. The clam chowder is very fresh, with a substantial number of meaty clams in a rich broth. The spinach-avocado-artichoke heart salad comes with a warm, tangy, bacon vinaigrette that wilts the spinach to exactly the right texture. Good central California wine makes up for the limited beer selection. ■ *Monterey St at 6th St, (408) 842-7575; 7397 Monterey Hwy, Gilroy; $$; full bar; AE, MC, V; checks OK; lunch Mon-Fri, dinner every day.*

HOLLISTER

Located in a narrow fault valley, this sleepy little agricultural town sits atop a very active section of the San Andreas Fault. Small earthquakes, most of them imperceptible, are so common here that the US Geological Survey has chosen Hollister as the primary earthquake research site on the West Coast. If you go to **Dunn City Park,** west of Highway 101, you can actually see where the fault has forced apart the curb along Sixth Street. But the ground isn't the only thing shaking around here. In May and June, you can watch some teeth-rattling riding and roping at the **Saddle Horse Show Rodeo** and the **Fiesta Rodeo.** Hikers will want to check out **Pinnacles National Monument,** a glorious 1,600-acre volcanic park.

RESTAURANTS

San Andreas Brewing Company ★ Belly up to the bar for a view of the fermentation tanks and order a plate of nachos, rated on a Richter scale of hotness. The food here, mostly burgers, hot dogs, and fried seafood, is surprisingly good. The seafood (cod, shark, calamari, and prawns) is dipped in a batter made with the pub's own beers. Be sure to try the fries—big chunks of potatoes with a hint of tomato, garlic, and Parmesan. The brewery's dark and thick Survivor Stout has a delicate and nutty flavor and a strong head. For teetotalers the brewery also makes sodas, including cream soda, ginger beer, and a crisp-flavored sarsaparilla guaranteed to catapult you back to your childhood. ■ *San Benito between 7th and Hillcrest; (408) 637-7074; 737 San Benito St; $; beer and wine; no credit cards; checks OK; lunch, dinner Tues–Sun.*

LODGINGS

Ridgemark Golf & Country Club ★ Like most small-town country clubs, the Ridgemark is peopled by balding, middle-aged men in white golf shoes and their large wives. But unlike most clubs, this one's a deal. Ridgemark's remarkably reasonable country club guest cottages are clustered along the golf course. The decor is nothing special—just regular midlevel executive style. Be sure to ask for a room overlooking the green. For ultimate luxury, try the Hospitality Suite ($105)—a huge, high-ceiling room with every imaginable convenience, including a giant bathroom with a separate dressing room and bathtub with Jacuzzi. ▪ *Hwy 25 at Fairview Rd, 3 miles SE of Hollister; (408) 637-8151, toll free (800) 924-1033; 3800 Airline Hwy, Hollister, CA 95023; $$; AE, DC, MC, V; checks OK.*

SAN JUAN BAUTISTA

This sunny, charming, little town is home to one of the most beautifully restored missions in California. Built just two feet away from the main trace of the San Andreas Fault, **Mission San Juan Bautista** was nearly destroyed by the 1906 quake, but locals raised the money to rebuild it. With its glorious chapel and gardens, the mission sits on a broad plaza surrounded by other well-preserved Spanish colonial buildings. Fans of Alfred Hitchcock's *Vertigo* will want to check out the mission's bell tower where Kim Novak's character fell to her

mysterious death. On the first Saturday of the month, from 10am to 4pm, docents dress in period costume and give tours of the mission. San Juan Bautista is also home to the world-famous theater troupe, **El Teatro Campesino;** 705 4th Street, (408) 623-2444. El Teatro Campesino director Luis Valdez left the San Francisco Mime Troupe in the '60s to form a political theater group composed of migrant farm workers. The group puts on plays throughout the year, but is most famous for its Christmas plays, *La Virgen del Tepeyac* and *La Pastorela,* held at the mission.

RESTAURANTS

Felipe's California & Mexican Cuisine ★ One of several Mexican places on San Juan Bautista's main street, this crowded storefront restaurant serves all the standard Mexican dishes—good chicken mole, pork burritos, and light, freshly made tortilla chips—but it specializes in Salvadoran food. Especially delicious are the handmade pupusas (fat corn tortillas stuffed with cheese) and the platanos fritos (fried plantain) served on a bed of rich, nicely textured, refried pinto beans. The Salvadoran dishes are served with an appropriately tangy, pickled cabbage dish called curtido. Felipe's also has several good Mexican beers, as well as espresso and cappuccino. Don't leave without trying the fried ice cream, a house specialty. Vegetarians take note: Felipe's doesn't cook with lard. ▪ *Third St between Mariposa and Polk; (408) 623-2161; 313 Third St, San*

▼

Hollister

Lodgings

▲

Juan Bautista; $; beer and wine; MC, V; no checks; lunch, dinner Wed–Mon.

LODGINGS

Bed and Breakfast San Juan ★ Slivered between the highway and the main street of San Juan Bautista, Todd and Jeanne Cleave's early Gothic Revival house has five theme guest rooms. The quiet and private Nautical Room has a window facing away from the highway and a comfortable queen-size bed. Check out (but don't stay in) the Old West Room with its gigantic claw-footed tub (containing a huge doll floating in a bath of styrofoam peanuts!). Most of the rooms with shared baths have several beds, making this a good B&B for families.

Downstairs, you'll find a teddy bear tea party going on in the dining room. Jeanne collects stuffed toys and Todd has an impressive collection of old and unusual musical instruments, including banjos from the 1890s and 1920s. He'll probably play them for you without too much cajoling. ■ *315 The Alameda at Hwy 156; (408) 623-4101; Mail: PO Box 613, San Juan Bautista, CA 95045-0613; $$; no credit cards; checks OK.*

SALINAS

If John Steinbeck had never written about his hometown of Salinas in *The Grapes of Wrath,* few people would have heard of this dusty, sprawling agricultural town just inland from Monterey Bay. For many years, Salinas' favorite son was treated more like a black sheep (or in this case, a red sheep, since local rednecks branded him a commie). The locals have recently decided that the Steinbeck legacy is distinctly green in color—the color of money. Ergo, you'll find lots of Steinbeck memorabilia around town. **Steinbeck House,** the writer's birthplace, is now a restaurant run by the Salinas Valley Women's Guild; 132 Central Avenue, (408) 424-2735. **The John Steinbeck Library,** 110 W San Luis Street, has a large collection of Steinbeck letters, first editions, and oral histories. In August, there's a **Steinbeck Festival and International Congress,** including films, lectures by Steinbeck critics, tours, and more; (408) 753-6411.

There are also some non-Steinbeck events in town, like the four-day **California Rodeo** and western dance in July; (408) 757-2951. History and architecture buffs will want to check out the well-preserved 1840s **Boronda Adobe,** built of the adobe from the ground it sits on, with wood (not clay) tile shingles; Boronda Road and W Laurel, (408) 757-8085. Call first. The adobe was damaged in the Loma Prieta quake of 1989 and is currently being restored. If you need a place to stay, check into the **Laurel Inn Motel**, a good overnight stop; 801 W Laurel Dr, (408) 449-2474.

CASTROVILLE

Gilroy made history with garlic. Castroville chose the artichoke. The undisputed Artichoke Capitol of the World, Castroville holds its **Artichoke Festival** on the third weekend in September. It's mostly small town stuff: the crowning of the artichoke queen, a 10K run, artichoke cookoffs, and the Firefighter's Pancake Breakfast; (408) 633-2465. A humongous cement version of this thistle-like plant calls itself the **Giant Artichoke Restaurant,** 11261 Merritt Street, (408) 633-3204. It's good for a chuckle and a bowl of artichoke soup.

RESTAURANTS

La Scuola ★★★ We didn't expect to find a buonissimo Italian restaurant on the main street of Castroville—but we did. Housed in a century-plus old schoolhouse, this elegant little place offers classic Italian staples such as veal Parmigiana, lamb saltimbocca, and chicken cacciatore. Our favorite is the chicken Firenze, a tender breast stuffed with prosciutto and fontina, topped with a light mushroom Marsala with a hint of sage. The fettuccine with shrimp is also very good. The homemade fettuccine comes perfectly al dente and the fresh, juicy shrimp explode with flavor. The vegetable side dishes are cooked just enough to bring out their flavor and color, and the buttery, oven-roasted potatoes are delicately crisp on the outside and creamy smooth within. The house wine—from Moresco in Stockton—is very good. ■ *Merritt St (Hwy 183) at Preston Rd; (408) 633-3200; 10700 Merritt St, Castroville; $$; beer and wine; AE, MC, V; no checks; lunch Tues–Fri; dinner Tues–Sun.*

PACIFIC GROVE

Established more than 100 years ago as a retreat for pious Methodists, this beautiful Victorian seacoast village retains its decorous, old-town character, though it's loosened its collar a bit since the early days. At **Pacific Grove Municipal Beach** and **Asilomar Beach** you'll find 4 miles of trails meandering between white sand beaches and rocky, tidepool–dotted coves. You can sit and enjoy the view from **Lovers' Point** on Ocean View Avenue. Pacific Grove happens to be a wintering ground for monarch butterflies (October through December). The best place to see these lovely orange-winged creatures is in the pine and eucalyptus groves on the grounds of the **Butterfly Grove Inn,** 1073 Lighthouse Avenue, near Ridge Road; or **George Washington Park,** just south of the inn.

RESTAURANTS

Melac's ★★★★ This transplanted slice of France, with its open fireplace, delicate white lace curtains, and soldierly rows of wine bottles lining the walls, is a masterly combination of exquisite cuisine and elegant presentation. American chef Janet Melac graduated at the top of her class from Paris' Cordon Bleu cooking school before apprenticing with some of France's pickiest chefs. In three short years, she and her French-born husband Jacques, who oversees the action in the dining room, have turned Melac's into one of the best restaurants on the coast. Melac invigorates her classic French cuisine with unusual local ingredients and light, delicate sauces: roast breast of duck in a white wine and blueberry sauce; rack of lamb, seasoned with rosemary, thyme, sage, and white wine, served with sweet red pepper risotto; or large sea scallops, quickly seared and set around a luscious purée of leeks, white wine, and cream. Appetizers include exquisite pâtés and terrines, smoked salmon, or gravlax. For dessert, you'll find decadent chocolate tortes, pastries, and delicious homemade ice cream and sorbets. The wine list offers a wide variety of excellent (and pricey) French and California wines as well as ports and sherries. ■ *Corner of 19th and Lighthouse; (408) 375-1743; 663 Lighthouse Ave, Pacific Grove; $$$; beer and wine; AE, DC, MC, V; no checks; lunch Tues–Fri, dinner Tues–Sun.*

Central 159 ★★★ Chef David Beckwith's innovative California cuisine shines amidst the crisp, simple decor of this 1920s Hollywood bungalow with its curving white archways and elegant black and white photos. Start your meal with the pumpkin and pesto ravioli with pine nuts and golden raisins, or the lobster quesadilla with leek and cucumber salsa. The corn and red pepper chowder is sweet and delicate. For dinner, try the fire-roasted duck served with wild rice and shiitake stir-fry,

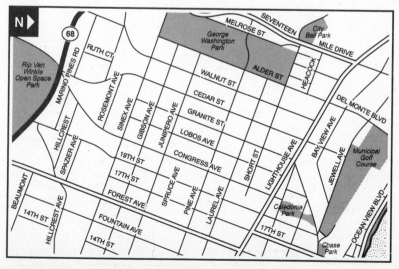

or the salmon served piccata-style with jicama slaw and fries. The prawn fritters are served with a wonderfully piquant tequila-lime cocktail sauce. Decadent, innovative desserts include apple dumplings with vanilla bean sauce. Central 159 has a good California wine list. ■ *On Central near Lighthouse; (408) 372-2235; 159 Central, Pacific Grove; $$; beer and wine; AE, MC, V; local checks only; lunch, dinner every day (closed Mondays in winter).*

Fandango ★★★ Fandango is the perfect name for this kick-up-your-heels restaurant specializing in country Mediterranean cuisine. It's a big, sprawling, colorful place with textured adobe walls and a lively crowd filling five separate dining rooms. Our favorite room is the glass-domed terrace in the back with its stone fireplace and open mesquite grill. Start with a few tapas—spicy sausage, roasted red peppers, or potato and onion frittata. If you're feeling adventurous, follow that with the Veloute Bongo Bongo, an exotic creamy soup with oysters, spinach, and Cognac. The flavorful paella Fandango is cooked and served at your table in a huge skillet. Other wonders include the canneloni Niçoise with spinach, ham, veal, and tomato, and the couscous Algerois, a 130-year-old family recipe featuring lamb, vegetables, semolina, harissa and North African spices. Fandango's wine list is one of the best in the area, featuring an impressive selection of French, California, Spanish, and Italian wines. For dessert, try the profiteroles filled with chocolate ice cream and topped with hot fudge sauce. ■ *One block E of Lighthouse Dr; (408) 372-3456; 223 17th St, Pacific Grove; $$$; full bar; AE, DC, MC, V; no checks; lunch, dinner every day; brunch Sun.*

Taste Cafe & Bistro ★★★ This relatively new restaurant has quickly developed a loyal and enthusiastic word-of-mouth following that's the envy of several more established eateries in town. You'll be hard-pressed to find higher quality food for the same price anywhere else on the coast. Chef/owners Paolo Kautz and Sylvia Medina define their preparation as rustic with French and Southern Italian accents, but that doesn't come close to describing the wonders coming out of their kitchen. The salmon fillet, baked in parchment paper with garlic, herbs, artichokes, and tomatoes on a bed of spinach, is utterly delectable. Be sure to save room for one of Sylvia's wonderful desserts: hearty bread pudding or wine-poached pear in raspberry sauce with crème Anglaise. Regulars elbow up to the wine and espresso bar. ■ *Forest Ave at Prescott; (408) 655-0324; 1199 Forest Ave, Pacific Grove; $$; beer and wine; no credit cards; local checks only; lunch every day, dinner Tues–Sun.*

Allegro Gourmet Pizzeria ★★ With its merry festoons of garlic and red peppers, colorful Italian posters, and trilling Italian music, Allegro Pizzeria is the choice of locals in search of la dolce vita on the cheap. Allegro's pizzas, which come in whole pies or generous slices, have crisp, flavorful crusts, just the right amount of cheese, and well-seasoned sauces. You can choose your own favorite toppings or pick one of Allegro's creative combinations: the quattro stagione (salami, artichoke hearts, mushrooms, anchovies, roasted garlic, and capers); the della mare (shrimp, scallops, garlic, and mozzarella); or the pizza del pastore (goat cheese, roasted garlic, and sun-dried tomatoes). The caesar salad is a local favorite, but we prefer the Cabrese salad: slices of tomato, fresh mozzarella, fresh basil and olive oil, sprinkled with mint and served on a bed of organic romaine lettuce. ■ *Forest off Prescott, in Forest Hill Shopping Center; (408) 373-5656; 1184 E Forest Ave, Pacific Grove; $; beer and wine; AE, MC, V; checks OK; lunch, dinner every day.*

El Cocodrillo Rotisserie and Seafood Grill ★★ Drawing on the sharp, exotic flavors of the Caribbean and Central and South America, Julio Ramirez' exciting, hybrid-Hispanic cuisine manages to cater to the tender sensibilities of norteamericanos without sacrificing authenticity. A portion of the sales goes to funding the Orinoco Crocodile Project in Venezuela. El Cocodrillo purchases all their Brazil nuts from Cultural Survival, a group dedicated to creating sustainable rainforest economies for the native peoples of Central and South America, so you can eat with an environmentally clean conscience among lush tropical plants, posters of Latin America, and dozens of crocodile chotchkas. These fiery, flavorful, fish-focused meals start out with appetizers such as Jamaican curry crab cakes and Salvadoran pupusas (tortillas grilled around two melted cheeses with black beans and salsa). Grilled specialties include red snapper Mardi Gras and spit-roasted Yucatan chicken. El Cocodrillo's interesting selection of inventive desserts includes Paletas Tropicales, those delicious and refreshing frozen fresh-fruit treats so familiar to travelers in Mexico. ■ *Corner of Lighthouse and Congress; (408) 655-3311; 701 Lighthouse Ave, Pacific Grove; $$; beer and wine; MC, V; no checks; dinner Wed–Mon.*

Gernot's Victorian ★★ Located in the beautiful Hart Mansion, Gernot's Victorian has the kind of quiet charm and gracious service that the town's trendier hot spots just can't match (at comparatively modest prices). All of chef Gernot Leitzinger's European country entrées come with soup, salad made with local greens in an herby vinaigrette, and hot country rolls. Our favorite entrées include the Austrian wiener schnitzel (lightly breaded veal with lingonberry compote) and the poached salmon with hollandaise. Adventurous sorts may want to try Gernot's wild boar bourguignon. The lamb Dijon

with bread crumbs, herbs, and garlic is also very popular. The wine list includes California and European selections. ■ *Pacific Grove exit from Hwy 1, left on Lighthouse; (408) 646-1477; 649 Lighthouse Ave, Pacific Grove; $$; beer and wine; AE, MC, V; checks OK; dinner Tues–Sun.*

The Old Bath House ★★ This former (you guessed it) bath house at Lover's Point has a fine view of the rocky coast and a wonderful dark wood interior with a low, carved ceiling. For an appetizer, try the mesquite-grilled prawns and wild boar sausage, or the pasta with grilled scallops. Chef Ken Frost does a fine job with the duck merlot, served with poached apples and a raspberry merlot sauce. The rack of lamb with garlic and fresh rosemary is also very good. Tempting desserts include hot pecan ice cream fritters and the amaretto tiramisu. The service is impeccable and the wine list extensive. ■ *Lover's Point Park; (408) 375-5195; 620 Ocean View Blvd, Pacific Grove; $$$; full bar; AE, DC, DIS, MC, V; no checks; dinner every day.*

Peppers ★★ This Pacific Grove hot spot with strings of red chile peppers dangling from the ceiling is famous for homemade tamales and chile rellenos. We also like the delicately flavored seafood tacos with mahi-mahi, swordfish, or salmon. The prawns Gonzales, with tomatoes, chiles, cilantro, and lime juice are also worth a try. The free chips and salsa are dynamite and they've got a good selection of beers to cool your singed palate. Owners Scott and Linda Gonzalez are always on hand to make sure everything runs smoothly. Consequently, the service is always super friendly. ■ *On Forest right off Lighthouse; (408) 373-6892; 170 Forest Ave, Pacific Grove; $; beer and wine; AE, DIS, MC, V; local checks only; lunch Wed–Mon, dinner Wed–Sun.*

LODGINGS

Centrella Hotel ★★★ The aptly named Centrella (located smack in the center of town) combines the down-home glow of an Old West boarding house with the comfort and attentive service of a modern luxury hotel. This 1886 Victorian is spacious, yet companionable. Downstairs, the front hallway opens onto a roomy parlor overlooking a garden courtyard. The main building offers 20 rooms, all with private baths. The upstairs rooms overlooking the garden are best. Our favorites are the two intimate attic suites with skylights, claw-footed tubs, color TVs, telephones, and fireplaces. Outside, a brick path meanders through an old-fashioned garden of gardenias and camellias, leading to five modern, private cottages.

For breakfast, you'll find crisp waffles hot from the antique waffle iron. In the evening, there'll be sherry and dainty hors d'oeuvres in the parlor. ■ *Central Ave at 17th St; (408) 372-3372, toll free (800) 233-3372; 612 Central Ave, Pacific Grove, CA 93950; $$$; MC, V; checks OK.*

The Martine Inn ★★★ Perched like a vast pink wedding cake on a cliff above Monterey Bay, the Martine Inn is Pacific Grove's most elegant bed and breakfast. Built in 1899 for James and Laura Parke (of Parke-Davis Pharmaceuticals fame), the inn has 18 spacious rooms, all with private baths and gloriously unfussy, high-quality antiques, including interesting beadwork lamps. Most of the rooms have fireplaces; all have views of the water or the garden courtyard with its delightful dragon fountain. Our favorite room is the Parke Room at the very top of the house. Originally the master bedroom, it has a magnificent picture window, a four-poster canopy bed, a large claw-footed tub, and a massive, white brick fireplace. No matter which room you choose, you'll find a silver basket of fruit and a rose waiting for you when you arrive, plus a newspaper by your door in the morning.

The Martine is so large that you'll never feel cramped, even when the house is booked. There are several intimate sitting rooms and three large common areas: the library, the main dining room, and the breakfast parlor. There's also a pool table and Jacuzzi. The Martine serves an elaborate and well-prepared breakfast of eggs, cereal, fruit, and fresh-baked breads, plus wine and hors d'oeuvres in the late afternoon. ■ *On Ocean Blvd, 4 blocks from Cannery Row; (408) 373-3388; 255 Ocean Blvd, Pacific Grove, CA 93950; $$$; MC, V; checks OK.*

The Asilomar Conference Center ★★ Located at the tip of the Monterey Peninsula on a wooded stretch of beach, Asilomar is one of the most beautiful conference centers in California. Donated to the YWCA by Phoebe Apperson Hearst, many of Asilomar's original buildings were designed by famed Bay area architect Julia Morgan. Now owned by the State Division of Beaches and Parks, Asilomar feels a bit like grown-up Girl Scout camp, albeit much more luxurious. Its extensive parklike grounds include an Olympic-size swimming pool, wooded trails, and a fine stretch of beach where you can watch otters and, depending on the season, whales. There are 220 rooms in the whole complex (and breakfast is included). The older rooms designed by Morgan have hardwood floors, but are much smaller and more rustic than the newer suites with their wall-to-wall carpeting, fireplaces, and kitchenettes. The apartment-style Guest Inn Cottage and Forest Lodge Suite can accommodate a large group or family. The better news is, they usually have plenty of room left over for private guests as well—and at surprisingly moderate prices. There is a cafeteria-style restaurant on the premises, but you're better off going into town to eat. ■ *Asilomar Ave at Sinex, ¼ mile N of Sunset; (408) 372-8016; 800 Asilomar Blvd, Pacific Grove, CA 93950; $$; no credit cards; checks OK.*

Gatehouse Inn ★★ When State Senator Benjamin Langford built this ocean-view Victorian in 1884, Pacific Grove was less a town than a pious Methodist meeting ground, swathed in rules and regulations, and separated from wicked, worldly Monterey with a white picket fence to keep the devil out. Ever since the Senator chopped down the gate, the devil and his obedient minions (tourists?) have made themselves at home in Pacific Grove. Langford's domain is now an enticingly eccentric, delightfully uncute bed and breakfast. Decorated in an interesting mix of Victorian and art deco, the inn's eight rooms have queen-size beds and private baths. The Langford Suite is the most luxurious, with an ocean-view sitting room, fireplace, and private bath. The claw-footed tub, just a step away from the bed, commands a stunning view of the coast. You'll find delicious hors d'oeuvres, tea, and sherry every evening. Best of all, you can help yourself to cheese, fruit, juice, and cookies from the kitchen any time of day or night. ■ *Turn right on Central off Forest; (408) 649-1881, toll free (800) 753-1881; 225 Central Ave, Pacific Grove, CA 93950; $$$; AE, MC, V; checks OK.*

The Lighthouse Lodge ★★ The Johnson family lusted after this choice bit of property (less than a block from the ocean and less than five minutes from *anything* in Monterey Bay) for 20 years before they got hold of it. Now that it's theirs, they treat the lodge—and their guests—like pampered, royal pets. The 29 suites, all with beam ceilings, fireplaces, and king-size beds, glow in peacock hues of purple, green, and fuchsia. The deep carpeting, vast bathrooms with marble Jacuzzis, and plushy bathrobes are a bit nouveau riche, but riche all the same. We actually prefer the standard suites to the deluxe ones. All the rooms have kitchens and large-screen TVs with cable. After breakfast in the fireplace lounge, take a morning stroll around the sprawling grounds, cleverly landscaped with native plants and fountains. ■ *Lighthouse Ave at Asilomar; (408) 655-2111; 1249 Lighthouse Ave, Pacific Grove, CA 93950; $$$; AE, DIS, MC, V; checks OK.*

Rosedale Inn ★ While its name may conjure up images of pink petals and white lace, the spanking new Rosedale has decidedly higher-tech sensibilities. The most striking—and, to some, disconcerting—feature is the multiple televisions in every suite. (They even put one in the bathroom so you can watch MacNeil-Lehrer from the bubbling Jacuzzi!) Multiple telephone extensions, clock radios, microwave ovens, and hair dryers give guests even more opportunities to push buttons. Kitchenettes have refrigerators and their own TV. Located across the road from the Asilomar Conference Center, the Rosedale is well-suited for conference-goers, business travelers, and stray videoheads. ■ *Asilomar Blvd at Sinex, across from the Asilomar Conference Center; (408) 655-1000, toll*

MONTEREY

If you're looking for the romantically gritty, working-class fishing village of John Steinbeck's *Cannery Row*, you won't find it here. Overfishing forced most of the canneries to close years ago and Monterey began fishing for tourist dollars instead of sardines. The low-slung factories of Cannery Row and Fisherman's Wharf have been turned into clothing boutiques, knickknack stores, yogurt parlors, and T-shirt marts. Monterey is still a pretty town, of course. Set on a windswept peninsula, it's got more than its fair share of pretty seacoast Victorians and secret gardens full of succulents, herbs, and native plants. To catch the town at its best, come during sunny Indian Summer months (September, October, November), otherwise expect it to be foggy and slightly cool.

The glory of the town is the amazing **Monterey Bay Aquarium**, featuring hundreds of fascinating fish, a seal habitat, and the world's largest indoor, glass-walled aquarium tank. The more adventurous can try their luck at the **Lagoon**, a tide pool dotted stretch of beach where the Carmel River meets the sea. (You may have to do some wave dodging and climbing on sharp rocks, so wear long pants and good sneakers.) From

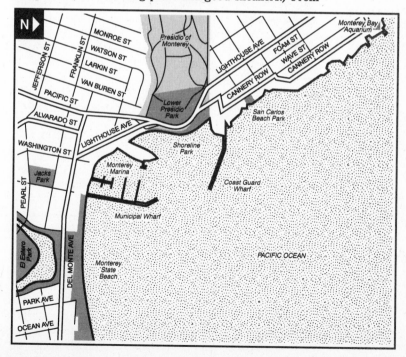

February to May, **whale-watching** trips set sail regularly from Fisherman's Wharf at only $12 for a 3-hour trip; (408) 372-2203.

The **Monterey Jazz Festival**, held the third weekend in September, features jazz greats like Winton Marsalis, Etta James, the Count Basie Orchestra, as well as promising new talent. Make reservations for this popular festival well in advance—by April is recommended. Monterey also hosts a **Blues Festival** in late June, which attracts a respectable but less massive crowd. For tickets or information for either festival, call (408) 373-3366.

RESTAURANTS

Cibo Ristorante Italiano ★★★ Rosa Catalano's old-style Sicilian food looks as bright as a Botticelli painting amid the terra-cotta walls, slick track lighting, and urban-rustic archways of this hot new eatery. This dashing mix of old and new is a cross-generational production: Rosa's son Mario shepherds the sprightly and efficient staff in the dining room, while son Vito manages the kitchen under Rosa's watchful eye. An herby focaccia with a dipping sauce of virgin olive oil and balsamic vinegar starts every dinner here, but there's a large selection of antipasti as well, including the carciofo alla Signora Catalano (artichokes filled with bread crumbs, pancetta, and cheeses) and the scrumptious raviolone (a large pasta pillow filled with veal and pork and finished with browned butter and sage). La famiglia Catalano's imaginative pastas include ditaloni picchi pacchi (an aromatic concoction of short pasta tubes, fresh tomato, basil, garlic, fried eggplant, and ricotta cheese) and the light and tasty perciatelli al crudo (hollow pasta straws, fresh raw tomato, almonds, garlic, olive oil, and basil). The wine list features Italian and California wines. On weekends, a live jazz band heats up the place and diners take to the dance floor. ■ *Corner of Del Monte and Alvarado; (408) 649-8151; 301 Alvarado St, Monterey; $$$; full bar; AE, MC, V; no checks; dinner every day.*

Fresh Cream ★★★ Fresh Cream is one of the most highly rated restaurants on the California coast, with a veritable mountain of rave reviews to its credit. It's easy to see why—from the delightful caviar and onion tartlet that starts each meal to the angelic Grand Marnier soufflé at the end, the food here is exquisitely prepared and presented. If the complimentary tartlet isn't enough to pique your interest, you might try an appetizer of chausson de homard (ravioli filled with lobster in a luxurious shrimp sauce). Chef Jim Nugent's luscious entrées include the perfectly grilled swordfish filet, stuffed with a spicy-sweet mixture of sun-dried tomatoes, garlic, oyster mushrooms, red bell pepper butter, and salsa; roast duck in a black currant sauce; tournedos de boeuf in two bright pools of spicy green peppercorn and tangy red bell pepper sauce; and the pork loin

▼

Monterey

▲

sautéed with a sun-dried cherry glaze set off by a fresh fig chutney. For dessert, try the Grand Marnier soufflé or the sac au chocolat, a dark chocolate sack filled with a creamy espresso milk shake.

So why have we given the purveyor of such marvels three stars and not four? Unfortunately, Fresh Cream mixes its extraordinary classical French cuisine with a generous dollop of French *snobbisme*: the place practically oozes with an arrogance born of an always packed dining room, a waiting list, and one too many rave reviews. Should you be so foolish as to show up without reservations, don't be surprised if you are turned away with a distinct air of contempt. Once inside the sanctum sanctorum, you'll find the service efficient, professional, but annoyingly aloof. ■ *Across from Fisherman's Wharf on the 2nd floor of Heritage Harbor; (408) 375-9798; 99 Pacific St, Monterey; $$$; beer and wine; DC, DIS, MC, V; checks OK; dinner Tues–Sun.*

Spadaro's Ristorante ★★★ This beautifully designed, family-run restaurant in the Spindrift Inn has almost everything you could ask for in a restaurant in Monterey—a grand view of the bay, deliciously creative Italian food, friendly and knowledgeable service, and, best of all, a real sense of local history. Vito Spadaro's father came to Monterey from Sicily to work in the fishing industry in the early 1930s. Beautiful black and white photographs of the family fishing boats still grace the walls of the restaurant and a model of one of the boats is displayed in the middle of the dining room.

Monterey

Restaurants

The star appetizer is the melt-in-your-mouth gnocchi, served in a rich, tomato-basil cream sauce. There's an appealing selection of daily soups and insalate made with organic baby greens from Carmel Valley. Spadaro's large array of inventive pasta and seafood dishes include alla nonna (fettuccine with a sultry combination of Italian sausage, wild mushrooms, and red onions in a homemade vermouth sauce) and the tender calamari ripieni, stuffed with fresh, delicately seasoned crab and baked in a dill cream sauce. Finish off your dinner with espresso and biscotti, a fabulous homemade custard flan with caramel sauce, or the cannoli stuffed with ricotta, chocolate, and cinnamon. ■ *Cannery Row, 1st floor of the Spindrift Inn; (408) 372-7727; 650 Cannery Row, Monterey; $$$; full bar; AE, MC, V; no checks; lunch, dinner every day.*

Bindel's ★★ Located in one of Monterey's historic adobes, plushly elegant Bindel's is the most recent venture of Monterey restaurateur David Bindel, owner of the Old Bath House and the Tinnery. Here in the building which once housed the offices of California's first newspaper, Bindel presents a tasty combination of Spanish, Italian, and Mexican cooking. Dinner begins with fresh-baked Monterey Jack cheese bread, rich artichoke cream soup, Salinas Valley green salad, fresh vegetables, and either rice or potato. Bindel's entrées are hearty affairs: roast leg of lamb stuffed with spinach, feta cheese, and pistachios in a mint pinot noir sauce; a spicy combination of grilled Cajun, lamb, and kobasica sausages served with grilled vegetables and polenta; and roast pork stuffed with Watsonville apples, pine nuts, and sage and topped off with a delightfully sticky honey-brandy sauce. ■ *Hartnell at the junction of Polk and Madison; (408) 373-3737; 500 Hartnell St, Monterey; $$; full bar; AE, MC, V; no checks; lunch Mon–Fri, dinner every day, brunch Sun.*

LODGINGS

Old Monterey Inn ★★★ Nestled among giant oak trees and gardens filled with rhododendrons, begonias, fuchsias, and ferns, this Tudor-style country inn built in 1929 positively gleams with natural wood, skylights, and stained-glass windows. The 10 beautifully decorated guest rooms, each with private bath, are filled with lovely antiques and comfortable beds with plump down comforters and huge, fluffy pillows. Most of the rooms have fireplaces—none, thank heavens—have TVs or telephones. In addition, the spacious and deluxe Ashford Suite has a sitting area (and a separate dressing room), a king-size bed, an antique day bed, and a panoramic garden view. For the utmost privacy, request the lacy Garden Cottage with private patio, skylights, and fireplace sitting room. Another standout— the Library guest room, with its book-lined walls, stone fireplace, and private sun deck.

Breakfast, taken in the dining room or en suite, includes baked apples, artichoke and mushroom strada, French toast, crêpes, cheese rolls, and curiosities such as coconut-lime muffins. You'll also find a delightful afternoon tea and evening hors d'oeuvres. There are plenty of ways to pamper yourself around here—lounge at the picnic tables in the rose garden, simmer in the sauna and spa, stroll around the acre-plus grounds, or wash your car (they supply the rags). ■ *(408) 375-8284; 500 Martin St, Monterey, CA 93940; $$$; no credit cards; checks OK.*

Spindrift Inn ★★★ With its soaring four-story atrium and roof-top garden, the dignified Spindrift makes an elegant refuge amid the hurly-burly tourist world of Cannery Row. Downstairs in this former bordello, plush oriental carpets muffle your footsteps and a tall pair of attractive, if politically questionable, Italian blackamoor statues keep you company in the fireside sitting room. Upstairs, all the rooms have canopy feather beds with down comforters, fireplaces, hardwood floors, telephones, and tiled bathrooms with marble tubs. There's also a nightly turn-down service, cable TV, and terrycloth robes. The corner rooms with their cushioned window seats and breathtaking ocean views are the best in the house. In the morning, there'll be a newspaper, a dewy rose, and a delicious breakfast of fruit, orange juice, croissants, and sweet rolls waiting outside your door on a silver tray. ■ *On Cannery Row; (408) 646-8900, toll free (800) 841-1879 in California, toll free (800) 225-2901 outside California; 652 Cannery Row, Monterey, CA 93940; $$$; AE, DC, DIS, MC, V; checks OK.*

Hyatt Regency ★★ If you crave the immaculate—if predictable—comforts that only an international megachain can provide, then Monterey's Hyatt, squeaky clean and running like clockwork, is the place for you. This 525-room behemoth on the edge of the Del Monte Golf Course is surrounded by sprawling flower gardens, multiple swimming pools, and tennis courts. The Hyatt provides numerous ways to keep fit over your vacation, including hot tubs, massage, a health club, and a par course for joggers. There's also a cafe, restaurant, and conference facilities. The rooms, of course, sport a certain sameness. The quietest and most scenic are those overlooking the golf course.

There are a few surprises here—the peacocks strolling about the grounds and the inexpensive Camp Hyatt child care program featuring movies, arts and crafts classes, nature walks, sports, and picnics. A slightly more advanced form of child care is the hotel's Knuckles Sports Bar, with its giant screen TV and 12 monitors linked up with some 200 satellite stations. Hyatt guests get a break on the green fees at the Del Monte Golf Course. ■ *On the Del Monte Golf Course; (408) 372-1234; One Golf Course Rd, Monterey, CA 93940; $$$; AE, DC, DIS, MC, V; checks OK.*

The Jabberwock ★★ The Jabberwock, as you may or may not remember, is a fearsome creature which sprang, gnashing its jaws and flashing its claws, from the fertile mind of Lewis Carroll. Warm and witty Jim and Barbara Allen set out to pattern their inn after Carroll's bloodthirsty beast. The rooms have Carroll-coined names like The Toves and The Tulgey Woods, and the delicious, whimsical breakfasts (written on a board in backwards mirror-writing) are called "razzleberry flabjous" and "snarkleberry flumptious."

Set well back from the hubbub of nearby Cannery Row, this 1911 former convent has seven guest rooms, three with private baths. All of the baths have showers rather than tubs. The spacious and grand Borogove Room boasts wraparound picture windows with views of the town and the inn's garden. The Mome Rath Room has a bed big enough for any beast. The big, beautifully landscaped garden has a pond, a waterfall, a nifty sundial, and, we wouldn't be surprised, a rabbit—who's very late. ■ *Corner of Hoffman and Laine; (408) 372-4777; 598 Laine, Monterey, CA 93940; $$$; no credit cards; checks OK.*

Hotel Pacific ★★ Like a Modigliani looming angular and bold in a gallery full of Fra Angelicos, the sorta-modern, neo-Hacienda Hotel Pacific tries to look gracefully unobtrusive in the midst of Monterey's authentic old adobes. A sparkling fountain burbles convincingly beside the entrance; inside, you'll find hand-woven rugs, muted southwestern colors, terra-cotta tile, and beamed ceilings soaring above rounded, adobe-style walls. Connected by tiled courtyards, arches, and flowered pathways, 16 asymetrical bungalows hold 105 small suites. All the rooms have private patios or terraces, fireplaces, goosedown featherbeds, three telephones, and two TVs (one in the bathroom). Ask for one of the rooms on the fourth level with their panoramic views of the bay, or a room facing the inner courtyard with its large fountain. Unfortunately, although you can request a certain room, you can't reserve it—one of the many kinks in service that this place has yet to work out. The nonchalant staff seems distracted and is often slow to respond to requests. Were it not for this quibble, the strikingly designed Pacific would rate three stars. ■ *Historic downtown Monterey, (408) 373-5700; toll free (800) 554-5542; 300 Pacific St, Monterey; $$$; AE, DC, MC, V; no checks.*

▼

Monterey

Lodgings

▲

PEBBLE BEACH

LODGINGS

The Inn at Spanish Bay ★★★★ Set on the privately owned, province-of-the-very-rich known as 17-Mile Drive, this sprawling modern inn defines deluxe. Set on a cypress-dotted bluff, the 270 luxuriously appointed rooms and suites all have fireplaces, quilted down comforters, elegant sitting rooms, and gorgeous views of the rocky coast or Del Monte cypress forest. Most have private patios and balconies. Three of the most deluxe suites even come with grand pianos. The bathrooms in all the rooms, with all the mod-cons you could want, are appropriately regal. Hotel guests have access to the world-famous Pebble Beach Golf Links (frequent home of the US Open), as well as eight championship tennis courts, a fitness club, swimming pool, and miles of hiking and equestrian trails. At sunset, a Scottish bagpiper strolls along the golf-course and serenades the guests. Grab a quick bite at the Dunes or relax into a more formal repast at the Bay Club, serving fashionable Northern Italian fare. Follow dinner with an aperitif or a sampling from the selection of single malt whiskeys at Traps Bar and Lounge where Brazilian virtuoso percussionist Helcio Milito and pianist Weber Drummond dazzle audiences every Thursday through Saturday. ■ *On 17-Mile Drive near Pacific Grove side, (408) 647-7500, toll free (800) 654-9300; 2700 17-Mile Dr, Pebble Beach, CA 93953; $$$; AE, DC, MC, V; checks OK.*

CARMEL

Thirty years ago, Carmel evoked images of windswept beaches, silent dark streets, really bad art, and really good food in a relaxed Mediterranean atmosphere. Now the very name has become synonymous with a spectacular fall from grace, and anti-development sorts up and down the coast use the term "Carmelization" with a curl to their lips. The charmingly ragtag bohemian village (which once banned skateboards, high heels, and ice cream cones) and was home to writers and artists like Robinson Jeffers, Mary Austin, Sinclair Lewis, Upton Sinclair, Edward Weston, and Ansel Adams, has long since given way to a cute but conservative coastal tourist village filled with yogurt parlors, T-shirt stores, and chi-chi *House and Garden* marts offering ceramic geese and other essentials.

The best way to discover Carmel is to wander around on foot. Traffic and parking are impossible. Downtown Carmel is a shoppers' Mecca, with shops selling everything from pewter and porcelain to kites to geneological charts. A thick cluster of photography and art galleries is nestled between Lincoln and San Carlos and Fifth and Sixth avenues. Particularly interesting is the **Weston Gallery** on Sixth between Delores and Lincoln (open Wed–Mon, (408) 624-4453), featuring photographs by Ansel Adams, Edward Weston, and others. Just around the corner on Delores is the **Carmel Art Association Gallery** (open every day, (408) 624-6176), featuring paintings and sculpture by local artists.

Carmel

Mission Trails Park (Crespi Avenue at Mountain View), supports 5 miles of winding paths, wildflowers, willows, deer, and redwoods, adjacent to the **Carmel Mission**. Visit the

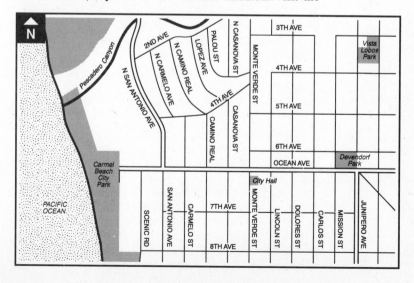

burial place of the ubiquitous Father Junipero Serra, enslaver of Indians and saint-to-be. (He's buried under a slab in the sanctuary). The graceful basilica sports an 11-bell Moorish tower, and the interior features vaulted ceilings, lime plaster walls (made from burnt seashells), and antique oil paintings. The Mission fell into ruin in the 19th century but was restored in the 1930's by Sir Harry Downie. Downie also planted an impressive garden in the cemetery, where lie unmarked the bones of the thousands of Americans who built the mission (3080 Rio Road, just west of Route 1, (408) 624-3600.

Unlike Serra, the poet Robinson Jeffers built his own house with his own two hands. **Tor House**, a rustic granite structure more at home in the British Isles than on the California coastline, is still home to the Jeffers family. Guided tours are available by reservation Fridays and Saturdays (26304 Ocean View Avenue; (408) 624-1813).

Carmel's beaches are still some of the most beautiful on the California coast. **Carmel Beach City Park** downtown is gorgeous but crowded. Instead, take Scenic Road south to **Carmel River State Beach**, a sandy shore surrounded by cypress and eucalyptus. The river's marsh is a bird refuge, sporting pelicans, hawks, sandpipers, kingfishers, willets, and the occasional goose. Middle and Monastery beaches lie beyond.

All these are remarkably scenic, but Mother Nature saved her best efforts for **Point Lobos**, 4 miles south of Carmel. Sea lions, harbor seals, and bold sea otters parade through the coves, and grey whales can be spotted from here during winter and spring. Point Lobos State Reserve is also the only place in the world (besides Pebble Beach), where the gnarled and eerily attractive Monterey cypresses can still be found. This is also a prime site for tide pool aficionados and bird-watchers: there are over 250 species of fauna and 300 species of flora here. Come early, as only 450 people are allowed in the park at one time. Open every day; (408) 624-4909.

RESTAURANTS

Crème Carmel ★★★ In a courtyard behind a liquor store, Crème Carmel is easy to miss. And that's a pity because this small restaurant dotted with eclectic local art offers some of the best, most inventive food in town. Chef Craig Lindy and his wife Cindy turn out wonderful seasonal dishes such as salmon with a fennel purée or a crisp breast of duck. These are served with a leek crêpe stuffed with mashed pototoes and roast duck, and topped with a tamarind-ginger sauce. Appetizers include Maui onion pancakes with Maine lobster in a delicate seafood sauce, or goat cheese tart. For dessert, try the incredible bitterweet chocolate soufflé, spiked with whiskey and Cognac. The wine list includes California and European wines. Reservations required. ■ *San Carlos between Ocean and 7th in*

Carmel; (408) 624-0444; $$$; beer and wine; DC, MC, V; dinner every day.

La Brasserie "Q" Point of Carmel ★★★ Just call it Q Point—everyone else does and if the owners were in their right minds, they would too. Located on the busiest street in town, this long, narrow East–West eatery has a full bar, stone fireplace, and colorful paintings by local artist Yamagata. Start with an appetizer of filet mignon strips and oyster mushrooms sautéed with sweet rice wine and soy sauce, or a romaine and tomato salad with toasted almonds and Gorgonzola vinaigrette. Chef Max Muramatsu's entrées range from oak-grilled veal chops with lemon and green peppercorn butter to seafood pasta with salmon, scallops, clams, and capers. For dessert, try the mouthwatering mango mousse or warm crêpes with fresh apples in a Calvados cream sauce. The wine list offers moderately priced local wines. ■ *Ocean Ave, between Dolores and Lincoln in Carmel; (408) 624-2569;; $$$; full bar; AE, DC, MC, V; no checks; lunch, dinner every day.*

Anton & Michel ★★ This longtime Carmel favorite overlooks the Court of the Fountains with its Louis XV lions and verdigris garden pavilions. Anton & Michel's elegant dining room has pink walls, white wainscoting, and tall, slender pillars topped by elegant curlicue cornices. Despite the interesting decor, the cuisine here isn't very daring. It's the sort that Midwestern business executives think of as traditional French: rack of lamb with Dijon mustard and herbs, or pepper steak flambéed at the table. We particularly like the lamb Wellington, topped with spinach and mushrooms, wrapped in pastry crust, and served with a Madeira wine sauce. Our lunch favorite is the chicken Jerusalem in a white wine and cream sauce, dotted with mushrooms and artichoke hearts. Anton & Michel also offers traditional French desserts like crêpes Suzette, chocolate mousse, and crème caramel. ■ *Mission between Ocean and 7th in Carmel; (408) 624-2406; $$$; full bar; AE, DC, DIS, MC, V; no checks; lunch, dinner every day, brunch Sun.*

Carmel

Restaurants

La Bohême ★★ La Bohême is very small, very cute, and—depending on your luck—very good. The walls of this heartflutteringly romantic restaurant are painted a pale blue and dotted with creampuff clouds. Two of La Bohême's 12 tables are tucked inside a topsy-turvy little house that juts out into the restaurant. Cozy and fun, these are the best seats in the house. La Bohême's prix-fixe menu changes nightly. The restaurant prints up calendars listing the entrées for an entire month, and a lot of Carmel visitors in the know make it a point to pick up this schedule as soon as they hit town. A recent week's offerings included duck with plums, beef with a Dijon and Cognac sauce, veal with sage and wild mushrooms, and scampi conquistador—prawns sautéed with garlic, cilantro, tomato, and wine. The soups, like the salmon bisque, and the salads with Carmel Valley organic greens are universally wonderful. The entrées, alas, are less predictable due to the varying quality of the meat preparation. The lamb can be either splendidly pink and juicy, sweetly redolent of wine, garlic, and rosemary, or dull and overcooked. On the other hand, when everything works, La Bohême's cuisine ranks among the best in Carmel. At worst, you can console yourself with their rich but fluffy chocolate mousse or the crème brulée. ■ *Dolores and 7th in Carmel; (408) 624-7500; $$; beer and wine; MC, V; no checks; dinner every day (closed in mid-December).*

Rafaello ★★ Flickering firelight casts a romantic glow over this ultra-dignified dining room with its gilt-edged mirrors, chandeliers, richly colored oil paintings, and linen-draped tables. We wish that it cast a little warmth as well because the room can be chilly. Bend your heads above big steaming bowls of creamy, rich leek soup and make the best of it. Simple green salads in an accomplished vinaigrette were followed by dinners that were more French than Italian in technique and presentation. A delicious chicken Jerusalem in a delicate cream sauce with plump mushrooms and artichokes, and veal scallopine in a cream and Madeira sauce dotted with truffles came with a side of piquant, sharply seasoned spinach and perfect, buttery mashed potatoes. For dessert, try the torta della nonna, a delicious pâte brisée with vanilla cream filling and lemon zest, or the semi-freddo, a frozen dessert with a texture somewhere between ice cream and mousse, topped with wild black cherries. ■ *Mission between Ocean and 7th in Carmel, (408) 624-1541; $$$; beer and wine; AE, DC, MC, V; local checks only; dinner Wed-Mon.*

Carmel

Restaurants

Rio Grill ★★ This noisy Southwestern-style restaurant (in the middle of Crossroads Shopping Center) is packed to the rooftops from opening to closing. Like so many big nouveau eateries, the Rio Grill really shines on its side dishes. The salads, like the piquant organic greens with curry vinaigrette, are wonderfully fresh. The polenta, seasoned with nutmeg and cayenne, draws raves. The onion rings, which everyone orders, are light and flavorful. Except for the barbecued baby back ribs and the chicken with papaya-fermented black bean salsa, the entrées are less interesting. Don't bother with the sandwiches (the eggplant one sometimes arrives cold and over oiled). The atmosphere is chaotic, but the service isn't. The Rio Grill also has a large selection of wines. ■ *In the Crossroads Shopping Center, Hwy 1 and Rio Rd; (408) 625-5436; 101 Crossroads Blvd, Carmel; $$; full bar; AE, MC, V; no checks; lunch, dinner every day.*

Sans Souci ★★ You'll never have to worry about the food or the service at Sans Souci, a classic French restaurant. The candle-lit dining room has a lovely bay window, fireplace, fresh flowers, and decorative wall sconces. Despite the traditional white linens, silver, china, and crystal, Sans Souci isn't a bit stuffy. American owner John Williams' infectious sense of humor sets the tone of the place and the service is friendly and efficient. The changing menu offers a large selection of appetizers, including escargot in sorrel leaves baked in basil butter, and warm duck salad with sun-dried tomatoes and sherry vinaigrette. There's also a dairyless vegetarian pâté for non–meat eaters. The entrées aren't terribly inventive, but they're well-prepared—try the sole with capers, lemon, and parsley; the milk-fed veal with artichoke hearts and lime butter; or the filet mignon with wild mushrooms and fried onions. ■ *On Lincoln between 5th and 6th in Carmel; (408) 624-6220; $$$; full bar; AE, MC, V; no checks; dinner Thurs–Tues.*

Ciao Mein ★ Mama-san mia! Just when you thought PacRim cuisine couldn't go any further, Ciao Mein's Kenny and Tina Fukumoto invented chicken wasabe pizza. And wonder of wonders—it's actually good. Start with the addictive pizza dough rolls that come with honey mustard dipping sauce. The ginger soy barbecued baby back ribs are mildly sweet and hot. The Thai chicken with basil-mint-chile sauce comes wrapped in a lettuce leaf like a burrito. For dessert, Kenny makes an awesome bread pudding with a warm whiskey sauce and a good hot fudge sundae with homemade fudge sauce. The waiters are fun and friendly and the beer selection is quite international. ■ *In front of the Barnyard Shopping Center; (408) 625-5595; 26344 Carmel Rancho Ln, Carmel; $$; full bar; MC, V; no checks; lunch Mon–Sat, dinner every day.*

Hog's Breath Inn ★ If rowdy crowds, free hors d'oeuvres from 4 to 6pm, and music so loud you can hardly think is your idea of a good time, then join the dinnertime melee at Clint Eastwood's Hog's Breath Inn. You'll always find a crowd of tourists and locals cruising, carousing, and plowing their way through Clint-cuisine. Most of the food is named after Eastwood films, like the succulent Dirty Harry burger on a fresh-baked bun and the aptly named For a Few Dollars More New York steak ($23). Lunchtime is less of a scene. Our favorite sandwich is the Sudden Impact, a broiled Polish sausage with Jack cheese and jalapeño peppers on a French roll. All lunches include soup or salad. Thanks to half a dozen heat lamps and fireplaces, you can eat out on the brick patio no matter what the weather. ■ *San Carlos between 5th and 6th in Carmel; (408) 625-1044; $; full bar; AE, DC, MC, V; no checks; lunch, dinner every day, brunch Sun.*

All the places in this book are recommended; even "no stars" are worth knowing about.

Cypress Inn ★★★ Movie star and animal rights activist Doris Day owns this exquisite Spanish-style inn. Pets, naturally, are more than welcome. In the evening, two-legged guests can crawl into their turned-down beds, while four-legged guests can settle in for the night on a very comfy dog bed. Of course, you don't *have* to bring your dog to enjoy this place. All the rooms are beautifully decorated in soft, warm colors, and floral fabrics, and some have pretty half-canopies above the beds. Some have sitting rooms, wet bars, private verandas, and ocean views. All the rooms have sherry, fresh fruit, and fresh flowers. A fireplace in the peach-colored living room beckons night owls, while an interior brick courtyard brimming with potted plants provides a dreamy spot for breakfast and on. Posters of Doris Day movies add a touch of glamour and fun to the otherwise upscale suburban decor. ■ *Lincoln & 7th Ave, (408) 624-3871; Mail: PO Box Y, Carmel; $$$; AE, MC, V; checks OK.*

Highlands Inn ★★★ This exquisite luxury hotel began as a clutch of honeymoon cabins in 1916, but those rustic days are long gone. Set high above the rocky coastline south of Carmel, with fine views of Yankee point, the Highlands is now a sprawling modern complex of warm, glowing redwood and soaring glass. The neutral, muted earth-tone decor is a tad sterile, but the view from almost any room in the whole complex is so stunning that you probably won't notice. In the main lodge, a skylit promenade leads to a series of glass-walled salons built for watching sunsets. In the fireside lobby, you'll find deep leather settees, a granite fireplace, a grand piano, and elaborate floral displays. Outside, flower-lined walkways connect the cottage-like collections of rooms and suites. The suites and townhouse units come with a full parlor and kitchen and a bath with a massive spa tub. All but 5 of the 142 rooms have fireplaces and private decks.

Pacific Edge, the inn's restaurant, is the one of the best on the Carmel peninsula, serving inspired creations like tender squab in a Middle Eastern mechouia sauce with a heavy hit of cumin and tingle of cayenne. The braised oxtail ravioli in consomme with winter greens is exquisite, as is the radish rémoulade with salmon, caviar, and chive oil. For dessert, try the cocoa-raspberry purse made of chocolate phylo or a macadamia chocolate tart with caramel sauce. ■ *4 miles S of Carmel on Hwy 1, (408) 624-3801, toll free (800) 682-4811 in California, (800) 538-9525 outside California; Mail: PO Box 1700, Carmel CA 93921; $$$; full bar; AE, DC, DIS, MC, V; checks OK; breakfast, lunch, dinner every day, brunch Sun.*

La Playa ★★★ Almost papal in its splendor, this big, imposing luxury hotel spills down a terraced, bougainvillea-and-

jasmine-strewn hillside toward the sea. Winding paths, lit by
gas-light street lamps, connect the main hotel with a network
of private cottages nestled among lush gardens with cast-iron
gazebos and swimming pools festooned with mermaids, La
Playa's mythical mascots. There are 75 rooms in the main hotel, all with hand-carved mermaids on the headboards of the
beds. To do La Playa right, invest in one of the cottages. These
have varying numbers of rooms, full kitchens, fireplaces, and
private patios. Unlike the hotel proper, the cottages have no
nightly turn-down service, but they're cheerier than the hotel,
which is a tad solemn for our taste. The hotel's restaurant,
The Spyglass, has a fine view of the gardens and serves good,
standard dishes. ■ *El Camino Real and 8th; (408) 624-4010;
Mail: PO Box 900, Carmel, CA 93921; $$$; full bar; AE, DC,
MC, V; local checks only; breakfast, lunch, dinner every day;
brunch Sun.*

San Antonio House ★★ Built in the late 1920s, this painted
white, wood shingle home with green trim has four cozy, wood-
paneled rooms, all with fireplaces and antiques. Privacy is
prized here—all rooms have a private bath, refrigerator, and
telephone. In the morning, a breakfast of fruit, coffee cake,
scones, and juice arrives at your door with the morning news-
paper. Two rooms, the Doll House and the Patio Suite, have
separate sitting rooms. Stroll the lovely gardens with their
interesting little nooks and arbors. Carmel Beach is just one
block away. The two-night weekend minimum carries a higher
premium for a Friday-Saturday combination. Children under 12
are not allowed; neither is smoking. ■ *San Antonio between
Ocean and 7th; (408) 624-4334; Mail: PO Box 3683, Carmel,
CA 93921; $$$; MC, V; checks OK.*

Stonehouse Inn ★★ This ivy-covered stone house is one of
those inns where people come back again and again—and have
been since the inn's beginning in 1948. It's a friendly, familial
group of people who actually sit around the fire chatting in the
evenings and schmooze over breakfast. Six beautifully decorated rooms are named after artists or writers. We like the Jack
London Room, with its gabled ceilings, queen-size brass bed,
and ruffled day bed with a sea view. The Sinclair Lewis Room
has a king-size bed, a writing desk, and a fine view of the ocean,
though we quail to think what Lewis—that loather of bour-
geois—would think of the giant teddy bears. Downstairs,
lounge in the wing chairs before a fireplace, and help yourself
to cheese and wine in the late afternoon. At night, port and
cookies are available. Huge bouquets of flowers pretty the
house and antique toy cars line the staircase. Children over 12
are welcome. ■ *8th St between Monte Verde and Casanova;
(408) 624-4569; Mail: PO Box 2517, Carmel, CA 93921;
$$$; MC, V; checks OK.*

Lincoln Green ★ Lincoln Green's four peaked-roof English cottages sport Robin Hood–inspired names like "Maid Marian" and "Friar Tuck." Set back from the street in a quiet residential neighborhood, each cottage is a self-contained house. A complimentary decanter of cream sherry is refilled each night, but don't expect breakfast at this out-of-the-way outpost. There's no innkeeper in residence, so if you need something, you have to call a sister inn downtown. Some people find this annoying. Others enjoy the freedom of not having an innkeeper watching over them. For an extra $10, you can bring your dog. Unfortunately, Lincoln Green has adopted an awkward three-night minimum policy on weekends, a reprehensible scheme that makes it hard on people who actually work. ■ *Carmelo between 15th and 16th; (408) 624-1880; Mail: PO Box 2747, Carmel, CA 93921; $$$; AE, MC, V; checks OK.*

The Green Lantern Inn ★ As far as we're concerned, teddy bears plague the bed and breakfast world. The folks who don't agree with us on this will love the Green Lantern Inn. We even liked it, in spite of the bears. Built as an inn in 1904, the rustic, green-trimmed buildings are nestled among lush gardens just a few blocks above Ocean Beach. We like the Teak Room, with its separate sitting area. On the downside, the inn has an unfortunate policy of closing the living room at 6pm in the winter, squelching any possibility of cozy evenings in front of the fire. On the plus side, the inn is clean, the staff pleasant, the rooms attractive—all for about half to two-thirds the price of very similar bed and breakfasts. ■ *Casanova and 7th; (408) 624-4392; Mail: PO Box 1114, Carmel, CA 93921; $$; AE, MC, V; checks OK.*

▼

Carmel

Lodgings

▲

Carmel River Inn Families favor the cottages and motel units that offer utilitarian but homey accommodations at reasonable prices. Though it's close to the highway, noise isn't a problem because the inn is set back along the Carmel River and surrounded by a natural buffer of trees. The cabins, natch, are the best place to stay. Children (free under 12) and adults alike will like the year-round heated pool, the rustic Sierra-cabin look, and the river nearby. Some of the cottages have kitchens; many have fireplaces and two bedrooms. Coffee-makers are in all the units, and tea is available at the desk. There's a two-night minimum for weekends during high season. ■ *Hwy 1 at the bridge, S of Rio Rd; (408) 624-1575; Mail: PO Box 221609, Carmel, CA 93922; $$; MC, V; no checks.*

CARMEL VALLEY

RESTAURANTS

The Wagon Wheel ★★ This is our favorite breakfast spot in Carmel Valley. The small, nondescript building has a bench outside where you can cool your heels waiting for a table, and a hitching post for your loyal steed. Inside, bridles, lariats, and other Western gear hang from the rafters and walls. There's a picture of co-owner, Katy Curry, bent over picking her horse's hoof. Not that you'll recognize her—it's basically a picture of two rear ends. The place is run by her three daughters now, and is just as homey as it was when Katy held the reins. The Wagon Wheel is known for its eggs Benedict with Canadian bacon or mushrooms. Nicely seasoned cottage fries come with all the egg dishes. The silver-dollar-size buttermilk pancakes (called Katy cakes) can be ordered with fresh fruit in them. ■ *In the Valley Hills Center, off Carmel Valley Rd in Carmel Valley; (408) 624-8878; $; no credit cards; local checks only; breakfast, lunch every day.*

LODGINGS

Stonepine ★★★★ This exquisite Mediterranean villa (former country home of the Crocker banking family) rises in terraced splendor against the oak-covered hills of the Carmel Valley. Surrounded by cypress, imported stone pines, and wisteria trailing from hand-carved Italian stone pillars, the inn has 14 guestrooms between Chateau Noel (named after owner Noel Hentschel), the Paddock House, and the idyllic (and astromically expensive) Briar Rose Cottage, a two-bedroom cottage with a private rose garden, living room with a polished stone fireplace, dining room, kitchen, and bar. The suites in the main house suit most with fireplaces and balconies. All have Jacuzzis, down comforters, soft, natural-fabric linens, and fluffy robes. The lavish gray- and rose-colored living room, with its magnificent medieval fireplace, incorporates interesting contemporary furniture with European antiques and a dash of Asian art. The cost of your room includes a billowing breakfast, afternoon tea with pastries, and a wine reception followed by an elegant four-course dinner prepared by French chef Daniel Barduzzi. During the day, you can float in their jewel-like swimming pool, play tennis, explore the ranch's 330 acres, or horse around at the Stonepine Equestrian Center. ■ *From Hwy 1, 13 miles inland on Carmel Valley Rd, (408) 659-2245; 150 East Carmel Valley Rd, Carmel Valley, CA 93924; $$$; AE, MC, V; checks OK.*

Quail Lodge ★★★ This posh resort hotel catering to golfers and tennis players has a hundred rooms set along winding paths which flank a meticulously kept 18-hole course. Comfort, not ostentatious luxury, is the byword here, and the Quail Lodge does comfort very well. Decorated in restful shades of beige, peach, and green, even the least expensive rooms are spacious and have private balconies or patios. Higher priced rooms have fireplaces, Jacuzzis, and living rooms. There's no air conditioning, just open your patio door; the ocean breeze cools things off right away and you'll fall asleep to the sound of fountains and the frogs croaking in the nearby pond. Service is efficient and friendly, without being overly solicitous. Nice touches: all the rooms have coffee-makers with real coffee (regular or decaf), a wide selection of teas and hot chocolate, full room service available until 10pm (beverage service until midnight). The formal Covey Restaurant offers European cuisine. Hearty, well-prepared, reasonably priced breakfasts and lunches are served at the clubhouse, a pleasant ¼-mile stroll away. Guests are entitled to reduced greens fees at the private club and use of the tennis courts. ■ *Located 3½ miles E of Hwy 1 just off Carmel Valley Road, (408) 624-1581; toll free (800) 682-9303 in California, (800) 538-9516 outside California; 8205 Valley Greens Drive, Carmel, CA 93923; $$$; AE, DC, MC, V; checks OK.*

Robles del Rio Lodge ★★★

Set on an oak-covered ridge 1,000 feet above Carmel Valley, this classic Western lodge constructed of river rock and timber in the 1920s has a wraparound front porch settled with a comfy Adirondack loveseat. The lodge's entrance is dominated by a huge, sunny, stone terrace with a pool and large, tiled hot tub. The rustic rooms in the original lodge are full of history, but a bit cramped. Choose instead the cozy, private cabins with fireplaces and kitchenettes, or the spacious, Laura Ashley–style suites.

The Ridge, the lodge's restaurant, draws customers from as far away as Monterey. French-trained chef David Allen is especially adept with appetizers—like the poached artichoke and prawn cocktail, pumpkin soup, or sautéed wild mushroom feuillete. The crème brulée has a chocolate surprise at the bottom. During the summer, don't miss Robles del Rio's Sunday terrace barbecues. ■ *Take Carmel Valley Rd off Hwy 1 to Esquiline (about 13 miles), follow the signs to Robles del Rio Lodge (about 1 mile); (408) 659-3705, toll free (800) 833-0843 (lodge); (408) 659-0170 (restaurant); 200 Punta Del Monte, Carmel Valley, CA 93924; $$$; full bar; MC, V; local checks only; lunch, dinner Tues–Sun, brunch Sun.*

Los Laureles Lodge and Restaurant ★★

Even if you weren't raised in a barn, some of Los Laureles guest cottages—former stables for Muriel Vanderbilt's thoroughbred race horses—will make you wish that you were. The beautifully refurbished, white clapboard stables are panelled with knotty pine and furnished with attractive country antiques. Los Laureles also has several private (very expensive) cottages, too: Hill House, Vanderbilt House, and the Honeymoon Cottage with a hot tub and a view overlooking a nearby canyon. Shaded by ancient oak trees, the original 1890's lodge house has a wonderful restaurant, dotted with photographs and mementos of early California. The restaurant's seasonal California menu includes roasted venison served with braised red cabbage and poached pears, homemade duck sausage on polenta with tomato chutney, and grilled veal chops with artichoke hearts and chanterelles. Outside, you'll find a large swimming pool and a patio with a terraced garden that's home to big weekend barbecues all summer. A surrey drawn by two handsome Belgian mares might take you for a tour of the 10-acre grounds. ■ *313 W Carmel Valley Road, 10½ miles E of Hwy 1 on Carmel Valley Rd, (408) 659-2233; mail: PO Box 2310, Carmel Valley, CA 93924; $$$; full bar; AE, DC, MC, V; local checks only; dinner every day, brunch Sun; (breakfast, lunch every day Apr–Nov).*

Valley Lodge ★ Set among serenely peaceful gardens, the Valley Lodge offers patio guest rooms and fireplace cottages that sleep up to six people. Though it's really just a very nice version of the standard motel, the Valley Lodge offers plenty of extras. In the morning, you'll find a continental breakfast with pastries and fruit, as well as a newspaper of your choice outside your door. During the day, you can take advantage of the lodge's beautifully landscaped grounds, heated pool, sauna, hot tub, and exercise room. There is a two-day minimum on weekends, but irreproachably hospitable hosts Peter and Sherry Coakley are flexible about this during the off season. Dogs (preferably small) are allowed for a small extra charge. ■ *11 miles E of Hwy 1 on Carmel Valley Rd at Ford Rd; (408) 659-2261, toll free (800) 641-4646; Mail: PO Box 93, Carmel Valley, CA 93924; $$$; AE, MC, V; checks OK.*

BIG SUR

There is something spiritual about the mist-shrouded forests, plunging cliffs, and the cobalt sea of Big Sur which stretches from the Carmel Highlands to San Simeon. As you drive south from Carmel, you'll pass the **Point Sur Lighthouse** and **Bixby Bridge**, the oft-photographed single arch bridge over Bixby Creek. The Lighthouse offers terrific full moon tours once a month, (408) 625-4419. The best tide-pooling is at **Andrew Molera State Park** where you can take a short trail along the east fork of the Big Sur River to a secluded beach and bird sanctuary; (408) 667-2315.

In the town of **Big Sur**, check out the **Coast Gallery**, showcasing local arts and crafts, including watercolors by Henry Miller (on Route 1; (408) 667-2301). Henry Miller aficionados will want to seek out the small **Henry Miller Memorial Library** (just beyond Nepenthe Restaurant on the east side of Highway 1, (408) 667-2574). Seekers of other sorts flock to **Esalen**, the world-famous New Age retreat and home of heavenly massages, (408) 667-3000. Drink in the view at **Nepenthe** (3 miles south of Big Sur State Park; (408) 667-2345) but skip the food.

Just south of town and inland is **Pfeiffer Big Sur State
Park;** (408) 667-2315. With 161,000 acres of madrone and oak
woodlands and misty redwood canyons, Pfeiffer is the most
crowded park, but it's also the best for hiking, with plenty of
camping facilities. Just beyond it on Route 1, take Sycamore Canyon Road to get to the beautiful, but blustery **Pfeiffer Beach**,
with its white and mauve sands and enormous sea caves. The
tiny, but uncrowded **Julia Pfeiffer Burns State Park**, 12
miles south, has a short trail leading to an 80-foot waterfall.

LODGINGS

Ventana Country Inn Resort ★★★★ Set on the brow of a
chaparral-covered hill in the Santa Lucia mountains, this modern, weathered cedar inn is almost too serene and contempla-
tive to be called decadent, and too luxurious to be called
anything else. The 59 spacious rooms, panelled in glowing natural cedar, look out over the plunging forested hillsides, wildflower dotted meadows, and roiling waters of the Big Sur coast.
The rooms in the newly-built Sycamore and Madrone houses
have large private balconies and the best views of the ocean. A
warm, terra-cotta color scheme is found in the Redwood and
Madrone houses. Several rooms have fireplaces, hot tubs, and
wet bars, and the rates climb accordingly ($170 to a whopping
$785). A sumptuous breakfast is included with the room.

Ventana's other big draw is its gorgeous restaurant, a virtual modern cedar cathedral of California cuisine with pink-
draped tables and bentwood and rattan chairs. Look for
delights like marinated oak-grilled quail, redolent of tarragon
and ginger, served with a julienne of jicama, daikon, and
cashews. The guilt-free, naturally raised veal comes in a clear,
dark cabernet sauce laced with shiitake mushrooms and grilled
eggplant. A celestial chocolate torte, too. ■ *2½ miles S of Pfeiffer Big Sur State Park on Hwy 1, (408) 667-2331 or
(800) 628-6500; Mail: Hwy 1, Big Sur; $$$; full bar; AE, MC,
V; checks OK; breakfast, lunch, dinner every day.*

Ripplewood Resort ★ With its 17 spartan cabins clustered
along a rugged section of Highway 1, Ripplewood Resort is a
wonderful place to go with a large group of friends. Try to book
cabins 1–9, which are set on the river far below the highway,
where the air is sweet with redwood. There is a two-day mini-
mum, and during the summer the popular units are booked
four months in advance. Pets are allowed. The Ripplewood
Cafe is clean and pretty, perfectly good for breakfast and lunch.
The muffins and sticky buns are homemade, as are the pies.
Cinnamon French toast is a big favorite here. For lunch, try the
large salad of marinated beans or the grilled Jack cheese sand-
wich slathered with green chile salsa. ■ *Hwy 1, Big Sur;
(408) 667-2242; Big Sur, CA 93920; $$; beer and wine; MC,
V; no checks; breakfast, lunch every day.*

Deetjen's Big Sur Inn During the '30s and '40s, travelers making the long journey up the coast used to drop in and stay the night with Grandpa Deetjen, a Norwegian immigrant. He—no doubt weary of house guests—constructed 19 hand-hewn cottages to accommodate them. Grandpa's idea of comfort was a bit austere, but then he never expected to charge $60–$125 per night. Located in a damp redwood canyon, most cabins are divided into two units, with dark wood interiors, shared baths, minimal lighting, and nonexistent insulation. If you stay in one of the two-story units (some with fireplaces or wood stoves), be sure to stay in the quieter upstairs rooms. No pets are allowed as cats and dogs abound on this property. ■ *Hwy 1; (408) 667-2377; Mail: Big Sur, CA 93920; $$; beer and wine; no credit cards; checks OK; breakfast, dinner every day.*

WINE COUNTRY

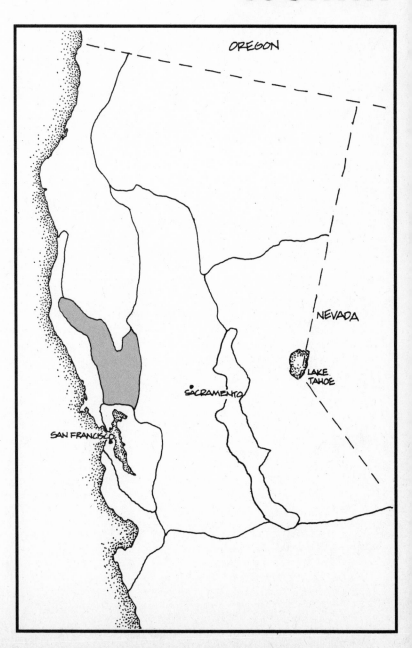

OREGON

NEVADA

LAKE
TAHOE

SACRAMENTO

SAN FRANCISCO

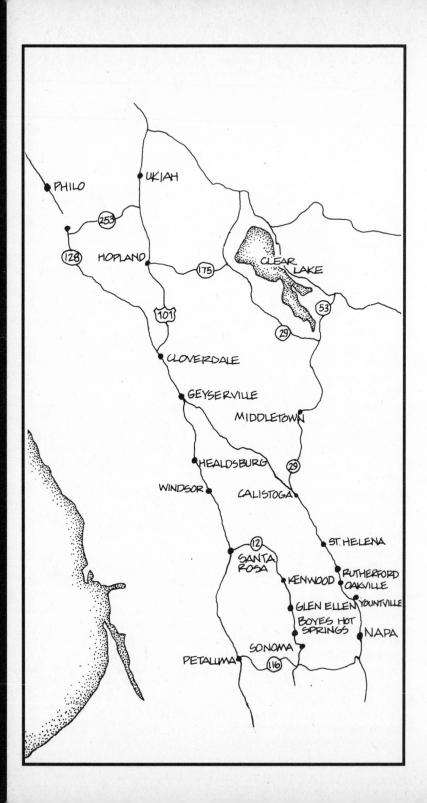

Wine Country

*Two tours. North through Napa Valley to Calistoga.
Then north through Sonoma Valley continuing
on Highway 101 to Ukiah with a side trip to
Anderson Valley on Highway 128 west.*

NAPA WINE COUNTRY

California wine fans have been arguing for years about which
fertile valley produces the best vintages—the more established
(and overdeveloped) Napa Valley or the smaller scale, up-and-
coming Sonoma Valley. We're not about to wade into the
enological fray; suffice it to say that there are enough fine wines
between the two to keep inquisitive tasters on the tips of their
tongues—swirling, spitting, and scouring the thesaurus for as-
yet-untried wine adjectives—for years to come.

Despite the plethora of nouveau chateaus, fake French
barns, and gimcrack stores selling wine bottles full of cabernet-
flavored jelly beans, the Napa Valley is still one of the most
magical spots in Northern California. In early spring, the hills
turn a vibrant green, and bright yellow mustard pokes up
between the vines. Later in the year, after the harvest, the vineyards turn a bright autumnal scarlet. Napa Valley's 125 wineries are clustered along Highway 128 and the Silverado Trail,
two parallel roads running the length of the valley. The valley
is a zoo on weekends—especially in summer and early fall
when the traffic on Highway 128 rivals rush hour in the Bay
area. Because of the demand, most wineries now charge for
tasting (the price usually includes a souvenir wine glass), and
a few require reservations for tours. For the latest info, call
ahead or pick up one of the tasting guides available at most
hotels and tasting rooms.

Wineries Driving north from Napa along Highway 29,
stop at Domaine Chandon, where you can sip a glass of bub-
bly or dine at their first-rate restaurant (1 California Drive,
Yountville; (707) 944-2892). Up the road is the famous Robert
Mondavi Winery (7801 St. Helena Highway, Oakville; (707) 963-
9611), which offers exceptionally informative tours, perfect for
a first-time visitor. Just past the town of Rutherford is Beaulieu
Vineyards ("BeeVee" to friends), famous for its cabernet sauvignon (Highway 29, Rutherford; (707) 963-2411). Across the
highway is Grgich Hills (1829 St. Helena Highway, Rutherford;
(707) 963-2784), operated in part by veteran winemakers Mike
Grgich and Austin Hills, whose cabs and chardonnays (made
for Chateau Montelena in the 1970s) first put California on the

wine map. A right turn on Zinfandel Lane will bring you to Raymond Vineyard and Cellar (849 Zinfandel Lane, St. Helena; (707) 963-8511 or (800) 525-2659), another interesting cabernet and chardonnay maker. Back on the main road, V. Sattui Winery (1111 White Lane, St. Helena; (707) 963-7774) has a large gourmet deli, nice picnic grounds, and the ultimate picnic wine—a fine Johannesburg riesling. Nearby, the venerable Louis M. Martini Winery (254 S St. Helena Highway, St. Helena; (707) 963-2736) has been making merlot since long before the grape became trendy. They make a nice barbera, too.

Farther to the north, Freemark Abbey (3022 North St. Helena Highway, St. Helena; (707) 963-9694) has an elegantly appointed tasting room offering fine cabernets and rieslings. Next door is the intriguingly named Folie à Deux Winery (3070 N St. Helena Highway, St. Helena; (707) 963-1160)—the "shared delusion" of two former mental health professionals—now vintners—who make smashing chardonnay and chenin blanc. Another detour, this time on Dunaweal Lane, leads to three wineries: the well-regarded Stonegate Winery (1183 Dunaweal Lane, Calistoga; (707) 942-6500) with its rich merlots; Sterling Vineyards (1111 Dunaweal Lane, Calistoga; (707) 942-5151), with its tram ride, excellent self-guided tour, and dependable chardonnays and cabernets; and the architecturally imposing Clos Pegase (1060 Dunaweal Lane, Calistoga; (707) 942-4981), where owner Jan Shrem shows off his wine-related art collection, as well as his cabs and chardonnays. Up past Calistoga, on Tubbs Lane, is the beautiful Chateau Montelena (1429 Tubbs Lane, Calistoga; (707) 942-5105).

A less hectic route is the Silverado Trail, winding up the east side of the valley. From south to north, good stops would be at Clos du Val Wine Company (5330 Silverado Trail, Napa; (707) 252-6711) or the nearby Stag's Leap Wine Cellars (5766 Silverado Trail, Napa; (707) 944-2020), both of which helped define Napa Valley cabernets back in the '70s. Steltzner Vineyards (5998 Silverado Trail, Napa; (707) 252-7272) up the road is well known for its cabernet sauvignon. Rutherford Hill (200 Rutherford Hill Road, Rutherford; (707) 963-1871) is a friendly place with fine gewürztraminer and merlot. A short jaunt up Taplin Road takes you to Joseph Phelps Vineyards (200 Taplin Road, St. Helena; (707) 963-2745), with their panoramic view of the valley and excellent riesling. Cuvaison (4550 Silverado Trail, Calistoga; (707) 942-6266) makes full-bodied reds in a lovely Spanish colonial-style building.

NAPA

Roughly half the people in Napa Valley live in this pretty, sprawling, small-town-turned-suburb, whose name has become synonymous with wine. Napa's downtown has plenty of fine looking Victorians (get a walking tour map at the Conference and Visitors Bureau; 1310 Napa Town Center, (707) 226-7459). Most of the galleries in town offer the usual tiresome tourist landscapes, but the **Hess Collection** in the old **Mont La Salle Winery** features provocative modern work by noted artists; 4411 Redwood Road, (707) 255-1144. While you're strolling, amble over to the **Alexis Baking Company** for great espresso and goodies like chocolate caramel cake, pumpkin spice muffins, and pistachio apricot cake; 1517 Third Street, (707) 258-1827. **Napa Valley Roasting Company** is another good coffee choice; 948 Main Street, (707) 224-2233.

RESTAURANTS

Table 29 ★★★ This spare, barnlike restaurant on the outskirts of Napa is a joint venture of well-known Bay area chef Jonathan Waxman and wine merchant Stephen Singer (husband of Chez Panisse's Alice Waters). Table 29 focuses on startlingly fresh local ingredients simply but subtly prepared. Don't look for culinary gymnastics, or even knock-your-socks-off flavor; like a fine claret, the food here calls out to be judged on balance. We recently started off a meal with a luscious baked goat cheese and fried fennel salad, somewhat bland tuna tartare on toastettes topped with a quail egg, and an exquisitely simple salad featuring mixed Forni-Brown organic greens from

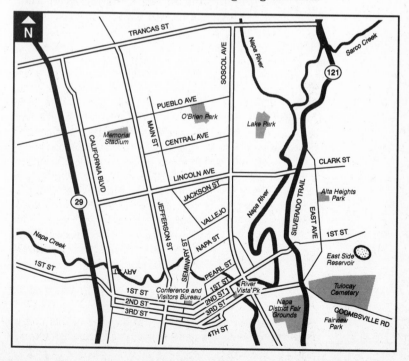

Calistoga. Next came heavenly angel hair pasta in a delicate cream sauce with hauntingly tender scallops and some fine sautéed sandabs in tangy ginger-lime butter served with deliciously crisp shoestring potatoes. Desserts are equally exquisite: the velvety espresso pot du crème has a vibrant coffee flavor; the delicate honey custard with crisp hazelnut cookie is almost angelic in its purity. The wine list offers well-chosen French and Italian wines as well as the best of California. Service is always tip-top. ■ *Just N of Salvador Ave on Hwy 29; (707) 224-3300; 4110 Hwy 29, Napa; $$$; full bar; AE, MC, V; checks OK; lunch, dinner every day.*

La Boucane ★★ Located in a restored Victorian, Napa Valley's sole bastion of classic French cuisine has a small teal and rose dining room that glows with candles and fresh flowers. The wine list, a healthy mix of Bordeaux and Burgundian varietals made by California's top vintners, is perfectly matched to owner/chef Jacques Mokrani's traditional French cuisine: crisp, roasted Sonoma duck in a zesty, bittersweet orange sauce; luminous poached salmon in a delicate, champagne cream sauce; thick, flavorful tournedos forestiere in reduction sauce made from game and beef stock, fresh herbs, and red wine. All entrées come with richly flavored soups such as crawfish bisque or cream of turnip, artfully arranged steamed baby vegetables, and a choice of two simple salads. Despite the restaurant's old-fashioned decor, the atmosphere is delightfully unstuffy and you'll often find Mokrani, a veteran of cruise ship kitchens, chatting with his guests in the dining room. ■ *On 2nd St 1 block E of Jefferson St; (707) 253-1177; 1778 2nd St, Napa; $$$; full bar; MC, V; local checks only; dinner Mon–Sat.*

Petri's Restaurant ★★ Fragrant tea roses line the walkway to this converted farmhouse where almost every table has a view of the gardens through tall, French farmhouse windows. The menu features fine fresh seafood, seafood-pasta combinations, and salads. The cuisine isn't terribly innovative, but the kitchen's got the classics down pat: fresh spinach salad with egg, bacon, and mushrooms in a sweet bacon dressing; shrimp and avocado salad in light thousand island dressing and a side of dark, full-bodied rye. The veal sweetbreads and the sweet-smoked ham on a grilled baguette are both good bets. The pasta with scallops in a garlic-kissed Marsala is another winner. Avoid the bland and unimaginative omelets and canneloni. There's always a good selection of New York–style cheese cakes. In spite of brisk business, the service is efficient and friendly. Reservations are a must for dinner, particularly on the weekends. ■ *Near the entrance to Silverado Country Club; (707) 253-1455; 3342 Vichy Ave, Napa; $$; full bar; AE, MC, V; no checks; lunch Tues–Fri, dinner Tues–Sun, brunch Sun.*

Willett's Brewing Company ★★ Chuck Ankeny's cheerful microbrewery has a large, window-lined dining room that overlooks the Napa River. Most folks, though, hang out on the front patio—a sunny, if noisy, spot that overlooks Riverside Park. The warm, sweet aroma of yeast pervades the restaurant, wafting through the open doors. Willett's turns out several good brews including Willie's Lager, a light ale with a delicate hops character; Tail Waggin' Ale, a caramel amber; and Victory Ale, a darker, roasted malt. The pub grub is equally distinctive. The individual pizzas have thick, chewy crusts topped with homemade sausage, local goat cheese, roasted red peppers, and fresh basil. The Oriental chicken salad combines chunks of white meat, snow peas, and noodles in a tangy, sweet sauce. There's also a selection of Mexican dishes, such as "drunken black beans" in a dark ale with bacon, cilantro, and tortillas. The bockwurst steamed in Willett's beer and served with apple sauerkraut makes a fine sandwich. And don't miss the Victory Ale bread, a heavy dark bread almost sweet enough for dessert. ■ *Downtown Napa, corner of Main and 2nd; (707) 258-2337; 902 Main St, Napa; $$; beer and wine; DC, DIS, MC, V; local checks only; lunch, dinner Mon–Sat.*

La Crêpe Cafe ★ We like to think of La Crêpe's minimasterpieces as compact cuisine—rich coq au vin or zesty ratatouille with crisp vegetables tucked in whole-wheat or white-flour pancakes. For dessert try the French Kiss (chocolate, bananas, almonds, and Grand Marnier) or the Yountville (sliced bananas, fresh strawberries, almonds, raisins, and apple sauce). Noncrêpe partisans will like the Greek salad. ■ *Downtown between Main St and Soscol Ave; (707) 226-5642; 976 Pearl St, Napa; $; beer and wine; no credit cards; checks OK; breakfast, lunch, dinner Tues–Sat, brunch Sun.*

River City ★ This schizoid place is half Reno lizard lounge, half elegant little Wine Country cafe. March right past the ugly mirrored entry and brown vinyl bar to the pastel-colored dining room and patio that overlooks one of the prettiest sections of the Napa River. There's plenty of elbow room on the weathered redwood patio, but the service is better inside. The fish specials here are always dynamite—especially the perfectly grilled salmon in a zingy zinfandel sauce and the seared Ahi tuna. The only seafood to avoid is the fried calamari appetizer, which tastes like batter-dipped pencil erasers. The sirloin steak sandwich will please purists, but we always go for the tenderloin sandwich with grilled garlic on a French roll. The wine list emphasizes Napa Valley cabernets and chardonnays. ■ *Along the Napa River near Silverado Trail and Lincoln Ave; (707) 253-1111; 505 Lincoln Ave, Napa; $$; full bar; AE, DC, DIS, MC, V; local checks only; lunch, dinner every day.*

La Residence ★★★ Set back in the trees along busy Highway 29, Napa Valley's most luxurious bed and breakfast is the multimillion dollar creation of partners David Jackson and Craig Claussen. Twenty guest rooms are scattered throughout two houses separated by a heated swimming pool and an elaborate white gazebo. The main house, an antebellum mansion built by a riverboat captain in 1870, contains nine guest rooms decorated with unusual designer fabrics and the highest quality antiques. Most of the rooms have sitting rooms, fireplaces, and private baths. We particularly like suite 3 in cool moss green with a regal canopy bed and antique settees clustered around the fireplace. Airier accommodations are in the modern, stone French barn across the plaza. Filled with simple English and French pine antiques, these spacious suites have fireplaces, private baths, and French doors that open onto patios or balconies. Service here is friendly, but somewhat distant. A beautifully presented gourmet breakfast is served downstairs in the barn in a dining room dotted with sturdy whitewashed pine tables and chairs, pink and white linen tablecloths, and burgundy flounces above French doors and windows. ■ *N edge of Napa—from Hwy 29, pass Salvador Ave and turn E at Table 29 Restaurant; (707) 253-0337; 4066 St. Helena Hwy N, Napa, CA 94558; $$$, DC, MC, V; local checks only.*

Beazley House ★★ The first thing you notice when you walk into this wood-shingled Colonial Revival mansion is the giant grandfather clock ticking in an entryway that glows with inlaid wood floors and stained glass. But unlike so many stately bed and breakfasts in Napa Valley, Beazley House doesn't seem in the least like a museum. With its velour loungers and floral couches gathered around a tall brick fireplace, the large living room is comfortable rather than grand. The spacious guest rooms upstairs have attractive antique furnishings and private baths. We like the huge Master's Suite with its brass bed, carved armoire, and fireplace, and the petite Sun Room with its small private balcony and huge old-fashioned bath. The most private and luxurious rooms are in the restored carriage house, looking out on the immaculate backyard garden; the upstairs loft rooms with their vaulted ceilings and big arch windows are the best. Pray for a breakfast of Carol's creamy, crustless cheese quiche and rich, cakelike blueberry muffins. Amiable innkeepers and longtime valley residents, Jim and Carol Beazley can tell you everything you need to know about touring the valley. ■ *On 1st St between Jefferson St and Hwy 29; (707) 257-1649; 1910 1st St, Napa, CA 94559; $$$; MC, V; checks OK.*

Silverado Country Club and Resort ★★ Golfers and tennis players love this place, and it's easy to see why. Silverado has two 18-hole golf courses and the largest tennis complex in North America, with 20 superb courts scattered among flowered walkways. If you're not into golf or tennis, however, there's little reason to stay here. The rooms seem to have been designed for people who don't plan to spend much time indoors. Located in a condo-like warren, the standard "bed and bath" rooms start at $130. The one- or two-bedroom suites, overlooking the golf course, are prettier, but equally soulless. They're gleamingly modern with black marble fireplaces, glass-topped tables, and white modern kitchens. A few minutes drive from the main complex are the more secluded Oak Creek East accommodations, street after street of mind-numbingly similar houses and condominiums, owned by country club members, but rented out to guests.

The resort's restaurants are located in a colonnaded Southern Gothic mansion at the heart of the main complex. The Vintage Court is a lovely pink and white dash of unreality serving decent California cuisine—though if that's what you're after, you'd be better off driving to Domaine Chandon. The other restaurant is a luxurious throwback to the days of elegant and quiet club grills. With its exposed wood beams, brickwork, and burnished copper accents, The Royal Oak looks out over oak groves and the golf course. Cuisine here is traditional with a capital T. Starters tend to fresh chilled seafood on silver. The seafood entrees, particularly the fresh Maine lobster, are wonderful, but beef is this place's raison d'être. Well-aged and tender, it's seared over mesquite charcoal and crusted with ground peppercorns. Dinner comes with steamed vegetables with sweet butter and herbs and a giant mushroom cap filled with béarnaise sauce. Dessert and coffee are included with dinner. Try the flaming chocolate fondue with fresh fruits and pound cake. The good dark coffee comes with cinnamon sticks, whipped cream, chocolate morsels, and fresh orange zest. ▪ *Hwy 29 to Monticello Rd, left on Atlas Peak Rd; (707) 257-0200; 1600 Atlas Peak Rd, Napa, CA 94558; $$$; AE, DC, DIS, MC, V; checks OK; breakfast, lunch, dinner every day.*

Inn at Napa Valley/Crown Sterling Suites ★ The charm of this rather stagey inn, which looks more like a miniature golf course than a hotel, is its complete disregard for reality. The guest suites here are arrayed around a small artificial mill pond with a working waterwheel and live nesting swans. There's also a three-story atrium with a carp pond and a tropical jungle's worth of ficus plants. All the rooms are two-room suites. In the morning, sit down to a full breakfast in the atrium; in the evening, return to taste and learn about the featured wine of the month. The hotel has indoor and outdoor pools and Jacuzzis.

The extremely accommodating staff will help you plan your tour of the wine country, make reservations, and generally bend over backward to accommodate special requests. There's an attractive bar (Joe's) and restaurant (Cafe 1991), but you're better off eating elsewhere. Ask for a room away from the freeway and far from the noisy bar where there's live music and dancing on weekends. ■ *On California Blvd at Hwy 29 and 1st St; (707) 253-9540; 1075 California Blvd, Napa, CA 94559; $$$; AE, DIS, DC, MC, V; no checks.*

YOUNTVILLE

RESTAURANTS

Domaine Chandon ★★★ Napa Valley's culinary reputation was born here at this elegant restaurant with its rough-textured walls and wood archways looking out over manicured gardens and vineyards of the Domaine Chandon winery. Rooted in traditional French technique enlivened by California innovation, chef Philippe Jeanty's whimsical flights of culinary fancy are perfectly matched to Domaine Chandon's sparkling wines. An exquisite appetizer of alderwood smoked trout was served on a bed of curly endive and encircled by toothsome yellow potato slices; the savory Japanese eggplant soup arrived not as a customary purée, but as a multicolored mélange streaked with basil and red and yellow peppers. Anything from the grill—such as beef or the divine pancetta-wrapped salmon—packs a salt and peppery punch, followed by a full-flavored unfolding of the meltingly tender meat. The simple but superb roasted chicken arrived sliced and rearranged in the shape of a pear and was served with basil mashed potatoes, a few spears of roasted summer squash, and a tomato-onion coulis. Grand desserts include such jewels as a ground almond shortcake with strawberries and a polenta pudding, saturated with grappa and topped with fresh raspberries and mascarpone. ■ *Just off Hwy 29 at Domaine Chandon Winery; (707) 944-2892; 1 California Dr, Yountville; $$$; wine; AE, MC, V; no checks; lunch every day, dinner Wed–Sun in season (lunch, dinner Wed–Sun in winter).*

Mustards Grill ★★★ Some critics call Mustards feisty American regional cuisine "comfort food," but this is too complacent a word for this sort of vigorous, spicy, vaguely Asian-influenced bistro fare. Part of the Cindy Pawlcyn empire (Fog City Diner, Tra Vigne, etc.), this cramped, always-hopping eatery has a big open kitchen, pale yellow walls, dark wood wainscoting, and a black and white checkerboard floor. Mustards chef Terry Lynch does a fine job with the giant Mongolian pork chop with braised sweet and sour cabbage and the smoked Long Island duck in a pool of curry almond sauce, topped with a savory mélange of spinach, onions, and mango. A side dish of light, crisp, tangled onion rings goes great with the grilled Sonoma rabbit with meaty wild mushrooms in a tarragon red wine sauce. Starters are hit and miss: the grilled pasilla pepper with tamale stuffing and tomatillo salsa is very popular, but we've always found it a bit bland; you're better off with the house-smoked salmon served with soft little pasilla-corn pancakes and dill cream cheese. Mustards' voluminous international wine list includes a vintage chart and quotes from local winemakers recommending various dishes to match their wines. ■ *Just N of Yountville on Hwy 29; (707) 944-2424; 7399 Hwy 29, Napa; $$; full bar; DC, DIS, MC, V; no checks; lunch, dinner every day.*

Ristorante Piatti ★★★ Executive chef Donna Scala's Piatti is a deservedly popular chain of super good, super chic nouvelle Italian restaurants with outlets in cute, touristy towns all over Northern California. And it all started right here in the tiny, but restaurant-ridden village of Yountville. Piatti has a large open kitchen and an L-shaped dining room decorated in soft Mediterranean colors, terra-cotta tile floors, light woods, and plenty o' natural light. Our favorite starters are the melt-in-your-mouth sweetbreads sautéed with mushrooms and the impeccable grilled vegetables with whole roasted garlic. For the main course, try any of the plump, delicately flavored canneloni or a perfectly cooked daily risotto: past favorites have included a creamy risotto packed with artichoke hearts, chicken, and sun-dried tomatoes, or a delicious variation with smoked salmon and fresh asparagus. The grilled items, such as the chicken and rabbit, are also dependably tip-top. Our one miniscule complaint is that Piatti sometimes goes overboard with the seasoning, forsaking balance for knock-your-socks-off flavor. You'll want to choose a wine with a lot of backbone to match this tongue-tingling cuisine. The Italian–Napa Valley wine list gives you plenty of options. A plus at the Yountville branch of Piatti includes Wine Country celeb-gawking at the likes of Robert Mondavi and Danielle Steele. Carbon copies of Piatti can be found in Sonoma and Carmel. ■ *On Washington St, S of Vintage 1870; (707) 944-2070; 6480 Washington St, Yountville; $$; full bar; MC, V; local checks only; lunch, dinner every day.*

California Cafe ★★ Stuck on the corner of a shopping center, this mission-style stone restaurant is a bit of a tourist joint, but it's a great tourist joint. Its airy, peach-colored dining room has large windows with a fine view of rolling vineyards and the Mayacamas Mountains across the highway. Ask for the Caesar salad with grilled chicken on top or the fat little crab cakes served with crunchy jicama coleslaw. Anything with pork loin is a guaranteed winner, from the lusty sandwiches to the pale-pink pork loin medallions roasted with whole peppercorns and served with a lemony-mustard barbecue sauce. The Neiman Schell organic beef cheeseburger comes with french fries, but ask instead for the light, thin-shaved onion rings or the thread-like sweet potato fries. For dessert try the warm fudge cake topped with vanilla gelato and caramel sauce. ■ *At the corner of Hwy 29 and Madison; (707) 944-2330; 7695 Washington St, Yountville; $$; full bar; AE, DIS, MC, V; no checks; lunch, dinner every day, brunch Sun.*

French Laundry ★★ Once a laundromat, this beautiful 1890s stone building is dotted with a few, well-spaced tables draped in peach and yellow linen and decorated with a fragrant bouquet of roses and wildflowers fresh from the garden. There's only one seating each night, so your table will be yours for the entire evening. The prix-fixe, five-course country French dinner proceeds at a civilized, almost languorous pace, but owner/chef Sally Schmitt and her husband Don encourage you to roam around the house between courses, strolling in the formal herb and flower garden where Sally gets many of the ingredients for your dinner. A recent evening found honey sweet, vine-ripened tomatoes with an herb-flecked garlic mayonnaise, a smooth red pepper soup with cumin cream, and succulent chicken supremes infused with citrusy orange and oregano sauce. The simple salad of local greens in a light vinaigrette was less a course than a palate cleanser, preceding a fine, crumbly shortcake piled with blackberries, raspberries, and strawberries. While the quality of the cuisine here is generally very good, it often lacks the complexity of other Wine Country restaurants, and some folks may bridle at the thought of paying $46 for what sometimes seems like fancy home cooking. But the warmth of the your hosts, the leisured atmosphere, and the beautiful surroundings go a long way toward making up for these potential complaints. ■ *Corner of Washington and Creek Sts; (707) 944-2380; 6640 Washington St, Yountville; $$$; beer and wine; no credit cards; checks OK; dinner Wed–Sun.*

Cafe Kinyon ★ Cafe Kinyon's exposed brick and beam interior with formal, white linen tablecloths and fresh flowers provides a restful escape from the rampant consumerism at Vintage 1870—the Wine Country's version of mall hell. You can either snack on fresh-squeezed orange juice, fragrant coffee, and luscious almond scones, or settle in for interesting sandwiches and salads such as the "Last Mango in Paris" chicken sandwich with mango chutney or the salad of grilled chicken with peanut sauce on a bed of mixed greens. Lunchtime's always a crush, but once you wangle a table, service is good and you won't be rushed. The sunny outside patio has a nice view of the vineyards. ■ *Inside Vintage 1870; (707) 944-2788; 6525 Washington St, Yountville; $; beer and wine; no credit cards; checks OK; lunch Mon–Sun.*

Compadres ★ You could, of course, opt for an effete duck taco at a higher-priced joint, but why bother? Because sometimes nothing will do but chips and salsa and fine, stout margaritas. The food here is very fresh and the crowd is young and hip. So don your shorts and flip-flops and wade in for the great tortilla soup filled with chunks of white meat chicken, cilantro, and tortilla strips in a light, flavorful broth. We also like the pollo borracho, a whole chicken baked in tequila with onions, pepper, and garlic, then grilled to crisp finish. The huge array of enchiladas are fresh and spicy. The salads are bright, and the portions are generous. This is also a good place for tots: the energetic, young staff go out of their way to accommodate children and the decor is relatively kid-proof. ■ *At N end of Vintage 1870; (707) 944-2406; 6539 Washington St, Yountville; $$; full bar; AE, MC, V; checks OK; lunch, dinner every day, brunch Sat–Sun.*

LODGINGS

The Magnolia Hotel ★★ This beautiful, ivy-covered brick and fieldstone hotel, built in 1873, did time as a bordello and a 4-H Club before opening in 1971 as Napa Valley's first bed and breakfast. The 12 rooms are classically Victorian. All have private baths; some have fireplaces, private balconies, and patios. The guest rooms are scattered throughout three buildings; the ones in the Garden Court are the most spacious. In the morning, the breakfast menu varies according to the whim of the cook; you might find something as elaborate as French toast with port wine syrup or as simple as good old-fashioned oatmeal with fresh fruit. After a day of wine tasting, recover poolside or soak in the Jacuzzi. ■ *Center of town; (707) 944-2056; 6529 Yount St, Yountville, CA 94599; $$; no credit cards; checks OK.*

OAKVILLE

There's not much in Oakville except the famous **Oakville Grocery** (7856 Highway 29, (707) 944-8802), a gourmet deli disguised as an old-fashioned country grocery store with a fading "Drink Coca-Cola" sign on the slatted wood exterior. Inside you'll find a fine selection of local wines (including a good selection of splits) and picnic supplies from pâté and caviar to sliced turkey sandwiches.

RUTHERFORD

LODGINGS

Auberge du Soleil ★★★ Nestled in an olive grove on a wooded hillside above the Napa Valley, this exclusive resort, inspired by the sunny architecture of southern France, has 11 luxurious *maisons*, with rough-textured adobe-style walls, white French doors and windows, and smashing views of the valley. Set on a winding street on a terraced hillside, each maison is divided into four guest rooms and suites that have private entrances and balconies designed for maximum privacy. The upstairs rooms with their vaulted, exposed beam ceilings are best. The suites start at $445 per night. For a hundred dollars less, the deluxe king rooms have sitting areas around the fireplace and offer plenty of elbow room. Unless you're a tennis fan, avoid the Versailles, Provence, and Normandie maisons which overlook the courts.

The restaurant at Auberge du Soleil has gone through a couple of chef changes in the last year; we're hoping these changes will elevate the cuisine to match the caliber of the resort or at least the decor of the restaurant. The gorgeous, Southwestern-style dining room has rough-textured taupe walls, tree-trunk pillars, pink and white linens, carved wooden chairs, and a kiva-style fireplace. As lovely as the dining room is, we always make a beeline for the sunny balcony with its panoramic view of the valley. Look for classic Wine Country cuisine such as the wild mushroom sauté in an herb garlic phyllo dough nest with black peppercorn sauce, or sautéed Sterling salmon with crisp vegetables and pinot noir sauce, followed by an almond tulip filled with Grand Marnier ice cream, fresh berries, and bittersweet chocolate sauce. Then cross your fingers and hope the chef is on target the night you're there. The elaborate brunch is more consistent. ■ *N of Yountville, turn right on Rutherford Hill Rd off the Silverado Trail; (707) 963-1211; 180 Rutherford Hill Rd, Rutherford, CA 94573; $$$; full bar, AE, DIS, MC, V; checks OK; breakfast, lunch, dinner every day.*

▼

Rutherford

Lodgings

▲

Rancho Caymus Inn ★ There's not a trace of Laura Ashley anywhere in this inn. Like a Spanish villa around a central garden courtyard, the inn has 26 rooms with adobe walls, exposed beams, and folk art rugs and wall hangings from Mexico and Ecuador. All the rooms have private baths with hand-thrown pottery sinks. Ask for a second floor room with a unique adobe beehive fireplace. The east-facing rooms have fine views of the vineyards. The price of a room includes a continental breakfast downstairs in the Garden Grill with its unique hammered copper Spanish chandeliers, peach tablecloths, and big fireplace. Better yet, break your fast on the flowery patio. ■ *1 block E of Hwy 29 at 1140 Rutherford Rd; (707) 963-1777; Mail: PO Box 78, Rutherford, CA 94573; $$$; beer and wine; AE, MC, V; checks OK; lunch every day, brunch Sat, Sun.*

There are probably other small farming towns in California where you can buy a $1,600 owl-skin Japanese lantern, but we can't think of one right off. This former Seventh Day Adventist farming village has come a long way since it found itself the un-official capital of the Napa Valley wine country in the mid-1970s. On its Victorian main street, farming supply stores sit stiffly next to chi-chi women's clothing boutiques and classy gim-crack stores catering to the needs of people who have more money than they know what to do with. You can zip up Spring Mountain Road to see how the fictional other half lives at **Spring Mountain Winery**, the backdrop for the *Falconcrest* TV series about the lives of the rich and famous in Napa Valley (2805 Spring Mountain Road, (707) 963-2504; tasting room currently closed for renovations, call ahead). In town, check out more downhome pleasures at the **Napa Valley Olive Oil Manu-facturing Company**, an authentic Italian deli and general store at the corner of Charter Oak and Allison Avenue; (707) 963-4173. Picnic under the walnut trees in the front yard or take your goodies to **Lyman Park** (on Main Street between Adams and Pine streets) with its beautiful little white gazebo band-stand. More bucolic picnicking can be found at **Bale Grist Mill State Park**, 3 miles north of St. Helena on Highway 29, where you'll find a still-working waterwheel grinding grain into meal and flour.

St. Helena

Restaurants

RESTAURANTS

Terra ★★★ Located in a historic stone hatchery building with high ceilings and arched windows, Terra's subdued dining rooms aren't exactly hushed, but they do have an ineffable sense of quiet intimacy about them. Fervid tête-à-têtes here, however, are more likely to include raves about Terra's fine, Japanese-inflected Wine Country cuisine than whispered sweet nothings. And yet this isn't the sort of food that screams to be noticed. Unlike the offerings in so many Pacific Rim palaces, those of co-owners Lissa Doumani and chef Hiro Sone's cuisine never grandstand. Unusual combinations such as mild duck liver wontons with earthy wild mushroom sauce may sound a little forced, but they don't play that way on the palate. The sashimi of scallop in a hollow of seafood tartare with lemon vinaigrette is exceptionally subtle and wonderful. Oriental del-icacy is not the only thing featured here: the braised lamb chop in a slightly sweet, almost gooey cabernet sauce with fleshy figs and polenta shows the chef's earthier side. For dessert, try the complex, creamy tiramisu with a heavy dusting of bitter co-coa—a perfect textural and flavor complement. Or devour the exquisite pithivier (a buttery, almond-infused pastry) with homemade vanilla bean gelato. ■ *1 block E of Main, between*

Adams and Hunt; (707) 963-8931; 1345 Railroad Ave, St. Helena; $$$; beer and wine; MC, V; checks OK; dinner Wed–Mon.

Tra Vigne Restaurant ★★★ It's become the fashion these days in Napa Valley to trash this once favored (now too famous) Tuscan-inspired temple to Wine-Country Italiana, but if you've never eaten at Tra Vigne, you haven't really "done" the Wine Country. The vast dining room has soaring ceilings, taupe walls covered with big, bright Italian poster art, antique amber beaded lamps hung low above intimate tables, and a partially open kitchen covering one full wall of the restaurant. The food here is exceptionally fresh, and almost everything is made on the premises: not just the soft, anise-flecked bread, but the pasta, cheese, smoked meats, and desserts. Appetizers are chef Michael Chiarello's forte. The menu changes seasonally but you can always find the delicately crisp polenta round topped with meaty wild mushrooms in a rich, gamey balsamic vinaigrette or the house-smoked salmon tartare on crostini with asparagus and dill vinaigrette. Entrées are chancier: the ravioli (stuffed with homemade ricotta, spinach, and red chard in a sage butter sauce) and the risotto del giorno are always dependable. The popular lemon-marinated grilled chicken can be either tangy and succulent or dry and ordinary, depending on luck alone. Desserts are stellar: try the velvety espresso custard with a thin layer of fudgelike chocolate, dusted with powdered sugar and served with a crisp hazelnut cookie. Service is knowledgeable, witty, and hyperefficient. The wine list, though not large, includes a nice array of Italian and Napa Valley wines. ■ *Off Hwy 29, at Charter Oak Ave; (707) 963-4444; 1050 Charter Oak Ave, St. Helena; $$; full bar; DIS, MC, V; no checks; lunch, dinner every day.*

Brava Terrace ★★ Another intriguing new restaurant to add to your Wine Country itinerary, Brava Terrace serves lively French Mediterranean cuisine in an idyllic setting: the beautiful dining room has vaulted ceilings with exposed wood beams, white walls with bright modern art, glowing hardwood floors and furniture, and a big stone fireplace decorated with tiny white lights. Even better are the large, beautifully landscaped terrace patios—the perfect place for a lazy lunch, a late afternoon snack, or dinner on a warm evening in the Wine Country. Owner Fred Halpert, of San Francisco's Portman Hotel and Restaurant 101, is single-handedly breathing life into old classics like a red wine–infused coq au vin or spunky cassoulet, but he also has a challenging menu of daily pastas and risottos (like the creamy pesto and pistachio). First-rate starters include the piquant five-spice duck served with cucumbers and mushrooms and the steamed Prince Edward Island mussels in a lively ginger and zinfandel broth. A warm, rich chocolate cake with a punchy cappuccino ice cream will appease chocoholics; more restrained sorts won't miss a thing sticking to the exquisite housemade sorbets. A full, reasonably priced wine list to boot. ■ *Between St. Helena and Calistoga, next to Freemark Abbey; (707) 963-9300; 3010 St. Helena Hwy, St. Helena; $$$; beer and wine; DC, DIS, MC, V; checks OK; lunch, dinner every day.*

Rissa ★ A lot of persnickety ethnic food aficionados sneer when they notice that Rissa includes Chinese, Japanese, Korean, and Thai food all jumbled together on a single menu. Then they settle in at one of the simple wood tables set with neat little trays of green chiles, red pepper flakes, coarse ground sea salt, and pepper, and begin to eat their words. Owned by the same folks who run Terra, the exquisite Japanese-California cuisine palace up the street, Rissa turns out interesting variations on Oriental favorites such as spicy Thai beef salad, delicately crunchy Japanese gyoza, and Chinese fried rice flecked with fresh mushrooms, snow peas, and bok choy. Start with an exquisite half eggplant seared in hot oil to an almost liquid, velvet texture and served with a sweet miso and red chile sauce. The Thai vegetarian curry comes with satisfyingly huge, firm chunks of sweet potato, fried tofu, onions, red peppers, and peanuts (beware of those little green chiles). United cuisines, indeed. ■ *Corner of Main and Adams; (707) 963-7566; 1420 Main St, St. Helena; $; beer and wine; MC, V; local checks only; lunch, dinner Mon–Sat.*

Spring Street Cafe ★ One of the best, most relaxing lunch places in town, this casual stucco bungalow was once the home of opera singer Walter Martini and his wife Dionisia. The interior is restful and very simple—white walls with prints and hardwood floors—but head for the balcony with its view of the carp pond blooming with lotus or the garden tables shaded by grape arbors and wisteria. Spring Street's soups and salads are always exceptionally fresh and flavorful (a surprisingly spicy bowl of cream of cauliflower soup or a cool, frothy soup of mixed fruit with a strong hit of olallieberry). Heartier appetites can opt for chunky, all-steak chili with cheddar cheese and sour cream, served with a salad and warm corn muffins. Chocoholics should head straight for the dense, chocolate rocky road mousse cake; saner sorts can wax nostalgic over the old-fashioned bread pudding served warm with a vanilla custard sauce. ■ *Hwy 29 to Spring St, turn left; (707) 963-5578; 1245 Spring St, St. Helena; $$; beer and wine; DIS, MC, V; local checks only; lunch, dinner every day, brunch Sat, Sun.*

LODGINGS

Meadowood Resort ★★★★ Summer whites and shirts with collars are de riguer on the croquet lawn. Rising like twin wedding cakes out of a surreal green sea of golf courses and croquet greens, Meadowood's white-trimmed, pearl gray New England–style mansions are resolutely Eastern. Winding landscaped paths and roads connect the central buildings with smaller lodges scattered over 256 acres; each is strategically situated near the golf course, croquet lawn (with a full-time croquet expert on hand), tennis courts, or Olympic-size swimming pool. The accommodations range from one-room suites with fireplaces, private porches, and balconies to more elaborate and larger ones. The suites tucked back in the woods are the most private, but the Lawnview Terrace rooms are the best with their vaulted ceilings, massive stone fireplaces, and French doors opening onto balconies that overlook the croquet green. The vast bathrooms have hair dryers, magnified makeup mirrors, thick bathrobes, and more towels than you could ever hope to use. The floors have radiant heating to keep your toes cozy as you pad to the cavernous shower.

The octagonal-shaped Restaurant at Meadowood has a high pitched ceiling and a fleet of French doors opening onto a balcony overlooking the golf-course. Appetizers, like the sweet bell pepper ravioli with wild mushrooms in a browned sage butter or the Miyagi oysters on the half shell with champagne sauce and caviar, are more exciting than the expensive but merely competent classic entrées: grilled scallops, roasted veal with chutney, herb encrusted rack of lamb. Especially perplexing is the Spanish-born chef's lackluster paella Catalan, which has so many promising ingredients combined to so little effect. European accents seem to be a requirement for the waiters. ■ *E of St. Helena, off Howell Mountain Rd; (707) 963-3646; 900 Meadowood Lane, St. Helena, CA 94574; $$$; full bar, AE, DC, DIS, MC, V; checks OK; breakfast, lunch, dinner every day, brunch Sat, Sun.*

Ambrose Bierce House ★ Literary curmudgeon Ambrose Bierce, author of the *Devil's Dictionary*, lived in this comfortable Victorian in the 1880s before taking off to parts unknown—leaving a wife, a daughter, a mistress, and cynics ever after to mourn his untimely disappearance. Despite its location smack on Highway 29 in the center of town, this gray and burgundy two-story inn is relatively quiet and feminine without being overly frilly. The rooms in back (the violet Lillie Langtry and the gray-blue Eadweard Muybridge) are probably the quietest, but the Lillie Coit Suite, named after Bierce's high society mistress, is more spacious. Perhaps because of its name and history, the inn draws an interesting, eclectic, vaguely intellectual crowd—the sort you wouldn't mind chatting with over breakfast, and usually do. ■ *Just N of the downtown business district; (707) 963-3003; 1515 Main St, St. Helena, CA 94574; $$; no credit cards; checks OK.*

Hotel St. Helena ★ You'll either love this place or you'll hate it; there's no middle ground. Hotel St. Helena looks like an old-fashioned house of ill-repute run by a madam with a penchant for sad-eyed Victorian dolls. There are dolls in the lobby, dolls in display cases in the upstairs hall, and dolls stuffed into baby carriages in the claustrophobic, little red upstairs parlor. A second, larger, pink and white wicker parlor off the south wing is refreshingly free of the little devils, and so, happily, are the 18 guest rooms. The suites overlooking St. Helena's main street are spacious and elegant, but very noisy. The smaller standard rooms in the southern wing are a better choice and have bent willow bedsteads, marble-top dressers, and shared baths. In the morning, a standard buffet breakfast is served in the pink and rose country-style dining room. After breakfast you can visit the hotel's newly added doll store. ▪ *On Main St (Hwy 29), between Spring and Adams streets; (707) 963-4388; 1309 Main St, St. Helena, CA 94574; $$; AE, DC, MC, V; no checks.*

The Ink House Bed and Breakfast ★ This gorgeous Italianate Victorian built in the shape of an ink bottle by Napa settler Theron Ink in 1884 would be a three-star inn but for its no-star location right on a busy, noisy stretch of Highway 29. This three-story yellow and white home has four sumptuously decorated guest rooms upstairs and a lavish museumlike living room and parlor with an old-fashioned pump organ and grand piano downstairs. (You might luck into an impromptu morning concert of Chopin by talented innkeeper Ernie Veniegas.) The most interesting architectural feature of the house is the glass-walled belvedere that sits like a stopper of an inkwell on top of the house and has a sweeping 360-degree view of Napa Valley hills and vineyards. The best room in the house (and the quietest) is the spacious, high-ceilinged French Room with its richly carved mahogany French-style bed with an elegant half canopy. The rooms at the front of the house are for sound sleepers only. Ernie and his partner Jim Annis are incredibly friendly and helpful, and there's nothing skimpy about the continental breakfast. ▪ *1½ miles N of Rutherford at Whitehall Lane; (707) 963-3890; 1575 Hwy 29, St. Helena, CA 94574; $$$; no credit cards; checks OK.*

CALISTOGA

Taking the waters is still the main activity in this little spa town at the northernmost tip of Napa Valley. **Dr. Wilkinson's Hot Springs** has the friendliest staff and best masseuses; 1507 Lincoln Avenue, (707) 942-4102. The more modern **Calistoga Spa Hot Springs** has the best mineral pools: four big pools at various temperatures; 1006 Washington Street,

(707) 942-6269. **Golden Haven Spa** is the most New Age and hedonistic; 1713 Lake Street, (707) 942-6793.

If you weary of still waters, you can drop by the **Old Faithful Geyser** and watch a plume of 350-degree mineral water shoot high in the air every 40 minutes; 1299 Tubbs Lane, (707) 942-6463. Other wacky things to see and do include the **Petrified Forest**, with giant stone redwoods and a truly tacky gift shop (look for the Flintstones-style sign at 4100 Petrified Forest Road, (707) 942-6667). The **Sharpsteen Museum and Sam Brannan Cottage** (1311 Washington Street, (707) 942-5911) brings Calistoga's pioneer past to life with displays of antique clothing, dolls, and quilts, plus a diorama of Calistoga in 1865. At **Robert Louis Stevenson State Park**, you can take a beautiful trail winding through redwood canyons and oak-madrone woodlands to the top of Mount Saint Helena for a fine view of the whole valley; 8 miles north of Calistoga, (707) 942-4575.

RESTAURANTS

All Season's Cafe ★★ Many restaurants in Napa Valley have elaborate wine lists, but none match the All Season's Cafe for completeness. The rear of the restaurant—a retail wine store with a tasting bar—contains hundreds of first-rate selections (both foreign and domestic) at remarkably low prices. If nothing catches your fancy on the restaurant's wine list, ask to see the wine shop's enormous computerized catalog. The menu is structured around wine: appetizers such as crisp, herby bruschetta and creative salads are recommended to accompany sparklers, chardonnay, and sauvingnon blanc; respectable California pizzas and pastas are paired with sauvingnon blanc, zinfandel, and Rhone wines; and entrées such as delicate roast quail with walnut-studded polenta, grilled lamb with fresh sprigs of dill, and fish with fruity sauces are suggested for chardonnay, cabernet, and pinot noir. So much emphasis is placed on wine, in fact, that the food sometimes suffers—great-sounding ingredients often fail to marry, while the consistency of the starches (gnocchi, polenta, potatoes, etc.) can be downright weird. The enthusiastic and opinionated servers, however, can usually steer you safely to the better choices on a particular night's menu. ■ *Center of town, corner of Washington St and Lincoln Ave; (707) 942-9111; 1400 Lincoln Ave, Calistoga; $$; beer and wine; MC, V; checks OK; breakfast Fri–Sun, lunch Thurs–Tues, dinner Thurs–Mon.*

Boskos Ristorante ★ Its dark, hulking interior has sawdust on the floor, a large central bar, and a rowdier crowd than its more refined neighbors. The menu is the same for lunch and dinner: big, fresh salads and heaping plates of fresh homemade pasta in hearty sauces. The spinach salad with turkey, pancetta bacon, toasted pine nuts, crumbled blue cheese, and honey

▼
Calistoga
▲

mustard dressing is a powerhouse of flavor. We particularly like the linguine with lots of tender shrimp, clams, and green onions in a peppery white sauce (Piacere) and the pasta shells with garlic, olive oil, mushrooms, and red chiles (Glorioso). You can also get good gelato, espresso, and homemade cheesecakes like the incredibly rich, almost mousselike chocolate cheesecake. ■ *Corner of Lincoln and Washington; (707) 942-9088; 1403 Lincoln Ave, Calistoga; $; beer and wine; no credit cards; checks OK; lunch, dinner every day.*

LODGINGS

Foothill House ★★ This serene bed and breakfast doesn't look like much from the road but the simple, slate-gray wood farmhouse hides some of the most luxurious yet homey accommodations in the Napa Valley. Our favorite room is the Quail's Roost, a separate cottage on a hill above the main house. Decorated in ivory and pale rose, this splendid hideaway has a vaulted, whitewashed pine ceiling, a big four-poster bed, a comfortable fireplace sitting area, and a gleaming modern kitchen. Its vast modern bathroom has a fireplace, two-person shower, and Jacuzzi that looks out onto a small waterfall. In the main house is the spacious, salmon and jade Evergreen Room has maple antiques and a small private garden patio. The Lupin Room, while beautifully decorated in storm blue florals, is a little dark for our taste. Doris Beckett, a former student of the California Culinary Academy, turns out treats throughout the day: from her scrumptious mushroom breakfast crêpes, to her artichoke heart quiche for afternoon social hour, to the delicious chocolate chip cookies by your bedside at night. ■ *N of the junction of Hwy 128 and Hwy 29; (707) 942-6933; 3037 Foothill Blvd, Calistoga, CA 94515; $$$; AE, MC, V; checks OK.*

Meadowlark Country House and Inn ★★ You're more likely to find innkeeper Kurt Stevens training horses in the corral than fussing around this casual but refined bed and breakfast surrounded by 20 acres of meadows and forest. Located in an 1886 farmhouse, the Meadowlark has four guest rooms: three airy contemporary rooms upstairs and a quiet, English country-style room dotted with hunt prints and elegant florals downstairs. Ask for a room in back that looks out into the forest. Stevens lives next door, so you'll have the house to yourself. There's also a nice swimming pool down near the corral. Service here is helpful, but very hands-off. Stevens will get you settled in, make sure you have everything you need (including breakfast), then leave you to your own devices. ■ *Call for directions; (707) 942-5651; 601 Petrified Forest Rd, Calistoga, CA 94515; $$; MC, V; checks OK.*

Mount View Hotel ★★ From the moment you step into this relaxed and relaxing art deco hotel, the kinks in your neck begin to unwind. Maybe its the influence of 70 years' worth of supermellow spa-goers, or maybe you're just picking up the vibes from the laid-back bunch around the pool and Jacuzzi in the courtyard out back. All of the rooms here are more or less deco: from the black and white and chrome Jean Harlow Suite to the moderately priced (but too minimalist) standard rooms. Suites are definitely the way to go here. The bar downstairs is a bit of a lounge lizard joint, but it's got live jazz and blues on weekends and soothing piano music during the week. The hotel's restaurant, Valeriano's, serves top-flight northern Italian food. ■ *Downtown Calistoga; (707) 942-6877; 1457 Lincoln Ave, Calistoga, CA 94515; $$$; full bar; DIS, MC, V; checks OK; dinner every day.*

Quail Mountain Bed and Breakfast ★ Quail Mountain is a good choice for people who want to escape the bustle of the valley floor but still want to be near the action. A long private drive winds up (and up and up) from Highway 29 through pine and oak woodland to a serene, slate-gray modern house with a gurgling carp pond and a beautiful patio with a trellised grape arbor out front. Decorated with contemporary furnishings, artwork, and a smattering of antiques, the inn's three rooms open onto the outside balcony through sliding glass doors. During the day, you can read in the glass enclosed solarium, swim in the small lap pool out back, warm up in the hot tub, or chill out in the hammock tucked in the trees on the hill above the house. The bad news is that this idyllic place is always booked; you'd be wise to make reservations several months in advance. ■ *Turn W off Hwy 29, just after Dunaweal Lane; (707) 942-0316; 4455 N St. Helena Hwy, Calistoga, CA 94515; $$; MC, V; checks OK.*

SONOMA COUNTY WINERIES

Wine tasting in Sonoma takes a bit more effort than Napa, where most wineries are clustered along main roads. Sonoma's wineries are spread out over a much wider area. You may have to spend some time poking around side roads in order to seek out the best. For the latest information about tours and tasting, call ahead or look at the listing of winery events on the bulletin board in Sonoma's main square.

Starting in the south, the first winery you'll encounter on Highway 121 going towards Sonoma is Cline Cellars (24737 Arnold Drive, (707) 935-4310), one of the original "Rhone Rangers," a group of winemakers creating blends styled after wines of France's Rhone Valley. Not far away is Gloria Ferrer Champagne Caves (23555 Highway 121, (707) 996-7256), owned by Freixenet, the big Spanish producer. If you're lucky, they'll be serving chile-roasted almonds with their sparkling wines. Nearby, Schug Carneros Estate Winery (602 Bonneau Road, (707) 939-9363), is owned by Walter Schug, the former winemaker at Joseph Phelps Winery in Napa.

In the town of Sonoma, look for Buena Vista Winery (18000 Old Winery Road, (707) 938-1266), founded in the 1850s by Count Agoston Haraszthy, the "father" of the California wine industry, and the well-known Sebastiani Vineyards (389 4th Street E, (707) 938-5532), a longtime jug-wine producer that's moving into vintage wines. When you visit Gundlach-Bundschu (2000 Denmark Street, (707) 938-5277) ask for their gewürztraminer. Hacienda Winery (1000 Vineyard Lane, (707) 938-3220) is a friendly place with good wines, including a nice dry chenin blanc. Also on the outskirts of Sonoma is Ravenswood (18701 Gehricke Road, (707) 938-1960), one of the state's best zinfandel and merlot producers.

Sip an excellent sauvignon blanc up the road at Kenwood Vineyards (9592 Sonoma Highway, (707) 833-5891). Its neighbor, Chateau St. Jean (8555 Sonoma Highway, (707) 833-4134) has a big picnic area with lush, rolling lawns and flower gardens, as well as fine chardonnay, fumé blanc, and riesling. Nearby St. Francis Winery and Vineyard (8450 Sonoma Highway, (707) 833-4666) offers buttery chardonnays and merlots. Smothers Brothers Store (9575 Sonoma Highway, (707) 833-1010) is not far to the north—they may still argue about who Mom liked best, but their wines are pretty good.

Ranging farther afield, Santa Rosa's De Loach Vineyards (1791 Olivet Road, (707) 526-9111) makes a white zinfandel that even wine snobs love. Over on Westside Road, which runs north to Healdsburg, are Davis Bynum Winery (8075 Westside Road, (707) 433-5852) which does everything well, but excels at pinot; Hop Kiln (6050 Westside Road, (707) 433-6491) with its bold zinfandel and Russian-style barn-winery; and Mill Creek Vineyards (1401 Westside Road, (707) 433-5098), offering merlot. Just off Highway 101 is Foppiano Vineyards (12707 Old Redwood Highway, (707) 433-7272), a good, solid, working-class winery with an interesting petite sirah. North of Healdsburg, take the Lytton Springs Road exit to Lytton Springs Winery (650 Lytton Springs Road, (707) 433-7721) for bold zinfandel, Robert Stemmler Vineyards (3805 Lambert Bridge Road, (707) 433-6334) for pinot, and A. Rafanelli Winery (4685 W Dry Creek Road, (707) 433-1385) for outstanding zins and cabs. Also check out Dry Creek Vineyard (3770 Lambert Bridge Road, (707) 433-1000), with its grassy picnic grounds, crisp fumé blanc, and zinfandel.

Heading east from the freeway, Alexander Valley Road winds over the Mayacamas Mountains to Calistoga. Along the way, stop at Sausal Winery (7370 Highway 128, (707) 433-2285), where the Demostene family has been producing highly regarded zinfandel since 1974. Johnson's Alexander Valley Wines (8333 Highway 128, (707) 433-2319) is another pleasant, family run operation. Alexander Valley Vineyards (8644 Highway 128, (707) 433-7209) grows and produces a large variety of wines, as does Field Stone Winery (10075 Highway 128, (707) 433-7266), noted for its cabernet and petite sirah.

PETALUMA

The gentrification rocking the rest of the county was slow in coming to Petaluma, perhaps because it's one of the few towns in the Wine Country whose claim to fame has nothing to do with wine. This town made its mark in the chicken business, producing 22 million eggs a year in the 1920s. You can still view the world's only chicken pharmacy and the birthplace of the incubator. The chicken business isn't as big as it once was, but agriculture is still the mainstay of the economy, a fact celebrated in the annual **Butter & Egg Days Parade** in May. Other yearly events include the **Summer Music Festival**'s three weeks of opera and chamber music in August, (707) 763-8920, and the **World Wrist-Wrestling** (known to amateurs as arm-wrestling) **Championship** in October, (707) 778-0210.

▼
Sonoma County Wineries
▲

RESTAURANTS

De Schmire ★ In spite of the white table clothes, artwork, and floor to ceiling wine racks, De Schmire's dining room is informal and almost funky. The open kitchen is separated from the dining room by a big oak table where the waiters linger after hours, drinking wine at the end of the night. The staff is unfazed (even by late evening arrivals) and presents a hearty, country French meal worth lingering over at any hour. De Schmire's chefs use first class ingredients: the chicken perigourdine was served with puréed foie gras and truffles; the delicatedly flavored salmon came topped with caviar. Dinner was preceded by a buttery Swiss chard and beet greens soup. So why one star? Consistency is not these folks' forte. Another visit found tasteless overcooked lamb in a lusterless rosemary-cabernet sauce and rubbery white fish in a soggy pastry. There is an extensive wine list that focuses on Sonoma County wines. Don't leave without checking out the wall-size '60s-flashback mural by Sonoma artist Green Greenwald in the men's room.
■ *At Bodega and Baker; (707) 762-1901; 304 Bodega Ave, Petaluma; $$$; beer and wine; no credit cards; checks OK; dinner every day.*

Fino Cucina Italiana ★ Trapped between its Old World roots and the nuova Italiana raging all around it, Fino Cucina doesn't really know what kind of Italian restaurant it wants to be, so it tries to be them all. Fino offers respectable nouveau dishes like polenta and sun-dried tomatoes as well as old country standards like veal Parmigiana, seafood, and pasta. The chicken breast stuffed with aromatic herbs and the ricotta-filled ravioli topped in a creamy walnut sauce are standouts on an otherwise unspectacular menu. The white linen and candlelight is strictly traditional, as is the campy but entertaining practice of making the caesar salad right at your table. The pleasingly attentive staff (who all seem to have Italian accents) can guide you through the Sonoma and Italian wine list. ■ *At Washington and Petaluma Blvd; (707) 762-5966; 208 Petaluma Blvd N, Petaluma; $$; beer and wine; AE, MC, V; local checks only; dinner Tues–Sun, lunch Tues–Fri.*

Playa Azul ★ With its swimming-pool blue walls and seafood-oriented menu, Playa Azul reminds us of the tacky seaside cantinas of Acapulco. The food selections will be familiar to those who've spent time on Mexico's Pacific Coast—whole fish fried Vera Cruz style in a chunky tomato and onion sauce; lobster or shrimp dripping with garlicky butter. This wouldn't be the best restaurant in town if you were in Puerto Escondido, but you can be damn sure it's the only place in Petaluma where you can get ceviche made from scallops, oysters, shrimp, octopus, or clam. ■ *At Washington and Petaluma Blvd; (707) 763-8768; 228 Petaluma Blvd N, Petaluma; $; beer and wine; no credit cards; no checks; breakfast, lunch, dinner every day.*

LODGINGS

Cavanagh Inn ★ This impressive neo-classic Georgian Revival manor near the center of town is the first stop on the city's self-guided walking tour of Petaluma's Victorians. The inn has seven rooms: four in the main house, three in a cottage. The guest rooms in the ponderously Victorian main house fan out from a circular, redwood-paneled hallway on the second floor. The blue-toned Sterling Rose Room is the most elegant, with a king-size bed, marble-top night tables, and a black-and-white-tiled bathroom complete with a whirlpool tub. The cottage next door is cheaper and cheerier than its imposing neighbor. With its three sunny bedrooms tucked beneath the eaves, the cottage has a game room, a sun porch, and a living room with a fireplace as well as a downstairs kitchen where guests can cook. Service here isn't particularly friendly, but you do get lots of goodies, morning and afternoon. Be sure to bring a sweater; the house is drafty during the cool months. ■ *At Keller and B streets; (707) 765-4657; 10 Keller St, Petaluma, CA 94952; $$; AE, MC, V; checks OK.*

Seventh Street Inn ★ If it weren't for the extraordinary hospitality of innkeepers Mark and Terry Antell, the Seventh Street Inn would be just another gloriously restored Queen

Anne Victorian B&B, decorated with carefully chosen antiques and irreproachable good taste. But the Antell's friendliness and genuine interest in their guests put them in another league altogether. Terry is a fine cook, and Mark, a former Air Force navigator, seems genuinely to enjoy chatting with guests around the fire in the living room. The guest rooms are scattered throughout the main house, in the water tower, and in a newly built carriage house. The roomiest accommodations are in the New England saltbox-style carriage house, which has a fireplace and a full modern bath. Our favorite, however, was the Rapunzelesque water tower suite with its spiral staircase, sleeping loft with skylights, and a large antique tin bathtub in front of the fireplace. You'll always encounter a plate of homemade cookies at night. There's also free juice and soda during the day. ■ *7th and H streets; (707) 769-0480; 525 7th St, Petaluma, CA 94952; $$; AE, MC, V; checks OK.*

Quality Inn Petaluma This meandering collection of neo-New England–style cottages right off the highway is a good choice for families or wine aficionados who'd rather buy wine than an evening with calico and lace. Don't bother with the deluxe rooms: they're $20 more and all you get is two queen beds, whirlpool jets in a standard bathtub, and a remote attachment for the TV. Outside, you'll find a swimming pool (summers only), Jacuzzi, sauna, and sun deck. The inn serves an array of cereals and pastries in the lobby every morning. ■ *Off N McDowell; (707) 664-1155, toll free (800) 221-2222; 5100 Montero Way, Petaluma, CA 94954; $$; AE, MC, V; no checks.*

▼
Petaluma

Lodgings

▲

SONOMA

Sonoma's slide into gentrification has been slower than Napa's, though just as relentless. Designed by Mexican General M.G. Vallejo, Sonoma is set up like a Mexican town, with a spacious parklike plaza in the center. It's quite easy to get around—streets are named in relation to **the Plaza:** First Street E and First Street W. **Mission San Francisco Solano,** the northernmost mission built by the Spanish fathers, is located on the square at the corner of the First Street E and Spain, (707) 938-1519.

RESTAURANTS

L'Esperance ★★ Located at the end of a picturesque alley, this romantic, intimate French restaurant is the sort of place that makes you want to stretch dinner into an evening-long affair. Chef/owner Bob Subai's French-California fare doesn't really qualify as cuisine minceur, but it is refreshingly light. His sauces are vigorous and complex and the flavors in each dish are so perfectly blended that you'll want to linger over each bite, then order another basket of bread to wipe the plate clean.

Soups tend toward delicate cream of vegetables or bolder bowls of peppery red lentils. The warm duck salad on a bed of greens garnished with fresh mushrooms is particularly fine. For dinner, try the tender, briny mussels painted with a vibrant, technicolor-yellow saffron cream sauce or beef fillet bathed in aromatic black pepper and Cognac. Subai's dessert specialty is fresh stawberries marinated in raspberry liqueur in a heart-shaped puff pastry with whipped cream, but his flourless chocolate cake in tart raspberry sauce is equally stellar. ■ *In the Place Des Pyrenees on the E side of the plaza; (707) 996-2757; 464 1st St E, Sonoma; $$$; beer and wine; AE, MC, V; no checks; lunch, dinner Wed–Mon, brunch Sun.*

Pasta Nostra ★★ Any cold and rainy night you'll be immediately warmed by the amiable staff, hearty cuisine, and playful decor. Located in a Victorian-era building, the dining rooms are decorated with murals of angels and frolicking cherubim, and the well-spaced tables provide plenty of privacy. Start with a basket of cheesy garlic bread and a pungent, oddly kimchi-like salad of artichokes, mushrooms, green olives, and tomatoes that comes on a bed of lettuce and is garnished with a blizzard of grated carrot and cabbage and dressed with a pickly vinaigrette. From there, dive headlong into the home-made cheese and red bell pepper ravioli in a lemon cream sauce. Pasta Nostra's soft, spongy, highly alcoholic tiramisu,

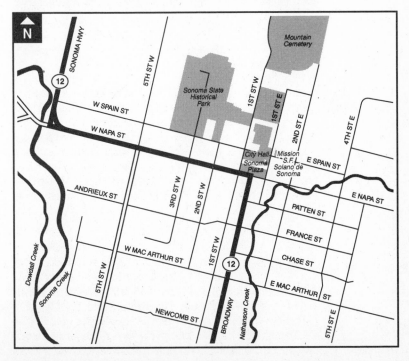

dusted with shaved chocolate, comes with a fan of crisp, refreshing apple slices. ■ *Just off the plaza at E Napa and 1st streets; (707) 938-4166; 139 E Napa St, Sonoma; $$; beer and wine; AE, MC, V; local checks only; lunch Mon–Fri, dinner every day.*

Ristorante Piatti ★★ See Yountville this chapter ■ *On the plaza at 1st St W and Spain; (707) 996-2351; 405 1st St W, Sonoma; $$; full bar; MC, V; no checks; lunch, dinner every day.*

LODGINGS

Sonoma Chalet ★★ Almost everyone in Sonoma County collects antiques, but the owners of this cute but cluttered bed and breakfast are in a league of their own. Every room here overflows with memorabilia from bygone eras—not just furniture, but lamps, cocktail glasses, gnome-shaped doorstops, figurines, quilts, books, and bottles. The rooms in the two-story 1940s chalet have balconies, but we like the three cottages with their little sitting areas, fireplaces, and kitchens. Proprietor Joe Leese's love for the strange and beautiful extends beyond the house to the barnyard where a collection of unusual chickens strut about with their plainer cousins. The chickens provide eggs for breakfast while the rooster's early morning crowing will make sure you're awake in time to eat. ■ *At the end of 5th St W, continue straight on the gravel road; (707) 938-3129; 18935 5th St W, Sonoma, CA 95476; $$; AE, MC, V; checks OK.*

Victorian Garden Inn ★ This 1870s Greek Revival farmhouse with a wraparound verandah has one of the most inviting gardens we've ever seen: lush bowers of roses, azaleas, and camellias encircle wonderful little tables and chairs, while flowering fruit trees bend low over Victorian benches. The inn's four guest rooms, decorated in white wicker and florals, are pretty, if a bit cloying. The blue and white Top of the Tower Room is the most spacious. In the evening, owner Donna Lewis serves drinks in front of the fireplace in the parlor. In the morning, head for the garden for granola, croissants, and fruit fresh from the garden. Extra points for the Eden-like swimming pool in the backyard. ■ *Between 3rd and 4th streets E, 2 blocks from the plaza; (707) 996-5339; 316 E Napa St, Sonoma, CA 95476; $$; AE, MC, V; checks OK.*

Sonoma Hotel Sonoma makes quite a fuss about its place in California history, yet the 140-year-old Sonoma Hotel is the only inn in town where you really get a feel for the Old West town that Sonoma once was. With its long oak bar, the old-fashioned, swinging-door saloon looks like the perfect place for a brawl or a game of poker (although you'll probably not witness either). The Sonoma Hotel is the budget choice in an otherwise pricey area—and sometimes this shows. Decorated with marble-top dressers, antique lampshades, and even a few vintage sewing machines, the guest rooms are uncomfortably small (rooms with private baths are somewhat roomier). Avoid room 25, which is cramped, airless, and noisy. A few basics (like towels and soap) are sometimes missing and the young staff is not alway competent. The rooms can be hot in the summer. In the morning, take croissants and coffee in the lobby downstairs. ∎ *At 1st St W and Spain; (707) 996-2996; 110 Spain St, Sonoma, CA 95476; $$; AE, MC, V; checks OK.*

Trojan Horse Inn The decor here is generic B&B—lots of dried flowers, pastel pictures of cats in gardens, and duck and bunny motifs. Fortunately, proprietors Susan and Brian Scott make up in friendliness and genuine hospitality what they lack in originality for interior decorating. Although this turn-of-the-century home is filled with antiques, it feels quite modern. Of the six rooms, our favorites are the Grape Arbor Room, with its big Jacuzzi tub, and the Bridal Veil Room, with its canopy bed and a wood-burning stove. The Scotts serve wine and hors d'oeuvres in the living room in the afternoon. Out back, you'll find a cement patio and a hot tub surrounded by apple, peach, and bay trees. ∎ *At W Napa and Hwy 12; (707) 996-2430; 19455 Sonoma Hwy 12, Sonoma, CA 95476; $$$; AE, MC, V; checks OK.*

▼

**Boyes
Hot Springs**

Lodgings

▲

BOYES HOT SPRINGS

RESTAURANTS

El Compita ★ Sonoma is so full of elegant inns and restaurants that it's easy to miss the Mexican subculture that is as much part of the Wine Country as Brie, grilled polenta, and cabernet. One of a half dozen Mexican cantinas between Sonoma and Glen Ellen, El Compita is where the folks who actually *pick* the grapes go after a hard day. You should too. Ask for guacamole and the proprietor will grab an avocado, tomato, and lemon from the bin next to the cash register, take them back to the kitchen, and mix up your order on the spot. The result? Fresh and flavorful, with a good spicy kick. Try the chiles rellenos (in a pocket of spongy batter topped with equally fresh salsa) or the succulent enchiladas. They've got a good selection of Mexican cerveza and the bilingual service is muy amigo. ∎ *Midway between Sonoma and Glen Ellen; (707) 935-0951; 17263 Sonoma Hwy 12, Boyes Hot Springs; $; beer only; no credit cards; no checks; lunch, dinner Thurs–Tues.*

LODGINGS

Sonoma Mission Inn and Spa ★★★ With its ethereally serene grounds and elegant pink stucco buildings, the Sonoma Mission Inn feels a bit like a convent—except that novitiates wear white terrycloth bathrobes or running suits instead of nuns' habits. Chic sportif sorts carry tennis rackets and jog about the grounds looking glisteningly fit; less athletic types lounge poolside with umbrella-topped fruit drinks. Indulgence, in body and spirit, is the order of the day. The spa offers everything from aerobics classes and massage to aromatherapy, seaweed wraps, and tarot card readings. You'll also find exercise rooms, saunas, Jacuzzis, yoga, and meditation classes. The best rooms (those overlooking the swimming pool and, in particular, room 232 in a turret) are in the original 65-year-old building; there are 70 more in the new wing.

The inn's two restaurants, the Grille and the Big 3 Cafe, are both basic Californiana. With its French doors and stained glass, the Grille is one of the most expensive restaurants in Sonoma; the food isn't as stratospheric as the prices. The less expensive Big 3 Cafe offers Cal-Mediterranean fare like light pastas, pizzas, and grilled items. ■ *2 miles N of Sonoma at 18140 Sonoma Hwy 12; Boyes Hot Springs, (707) 938-9000, toll free (800) 862-4945 in California, (800) 358-9022 or (800) 358-9027 outside California; Mail: PO Box 1447, Sonoma, CA 95476; $$$; full bar; AE, DC, MC, V; checks OK; breakfast, lunch, dinner every day.*

▼
**Boyes
Hot Springs**

Lodgings

▲

GLEN ELLEN

There are more places and things named after Jack London in Sonoma County than there are women named Maria in Mexico. This cult reaches its apex in Glen Ellen, where the writer built his aptly named **Beauty Ranch,** now an 800-acre state park (London Ranch Road, (707) 938-5216). London's vineyards, piggery, and other ranch buildings are here, as well as a house-turned-museum containing his art collection and mementos. Ten miles of trails lead through oaks, madrones and redwoods. The town of Glen Ellen itself is really little more than an excuse to go wine-tasting and antique-hunting. The **Wine Country Film Festival,** a two-week summer splurge of screenings and parties throughout Napa and Sonoma, is headquartered in Glen Ellen (12000 Henno Road, (707) 996-2536).

LODGINGS

Top o' the World Lodge ★★★ This hilltop haven set at the end of a long wooded drive sits on a ridge between the Napa and Sonoma valleys. Surrounded by 45 acres of woods and meadows, this rustic yet elegant lodge is an architectural hodgepodge of massive fir beams, pine walls and floors, and a huge bedrock outcropping that makes up one wall of the living room. The downstairs common rooms sport cowhide rugs, rough-hewn wood, and hide furnishings. The two guest rooms are simple but spacious. The Winter Creek Room has its own kitchen and a balcony overlooking Hooker Creek. The Cherry Room has a stone patio looking out at the vineyards and a turtle-filled pond. You can take a dip in the pond or paddle about in the inn's inflatable boats. Hosts Judy and Bill Barsky are genuinely friendly. ■ *From Glen Ellen take Trinity Rd to Cavedale; (707) 938-4671; 4614 Cavedale Rd, Glen Ellen, CA 95442; $$$; AE, MC, V; checks OK.*

Beltane Ranch ★★ Surrounded by vineyards at the foot of the Mayacamas Mountains, this 100-year-old yellow clapboard farmhouse was a bunkhouse before it was bed and breakfast—but we doubt the cowhands of old ever had it so good. Each of the four rooms is different, but they all have sitting areas, private baths, separate entrances, marble-top dressers, and claw-footed writing tables. Ask for one of the upstairs rooms that opens onto the wraparound porch with a hammock and porch swing. Blissfully calm and beautiful, this whole place makes you feel you should be wearing a wide-brimmed hat and drinking a mint julep. Should you tire of lolling Southern-belle style, you can knock a few balls around the tennis courts next to the house, pitch horseshoes in the garden, or hike the trails through the vineyards and hills. ■ *2½ miles past the center of town at 11775 Sonoma Hwy 12; Glen Ellen, (707) 996-6501; Mail: PO Box 395, Glen Ellen, 95442; $$$; no credit cards; checks OK.*

Gaige House ★ This Italianate Victorian was a boarding house, school, and home of slaughterhouse magnate A.E. Gaige before its inevitable conversion to a bed and breakfast. Completely remodeled by innkeepers Michol and Steve Salvo, the eight antique-filled guest rooms all have private baths; one has a fireplace. The Gaige Suite has a four-poster canopy bed, a private balcony, and an enormous blue-tiled bathroom with Jacuzzi big enough for you and several very close friends. The downstairs parlors are crammed with old furniture, books, and even a prancing carousel horse. Out back, there's a fine deck overlooking the lawn and swimming pool, and a smaller deck shaded by maples and neighboring a trickling creek. ■ *Glen Ellen exit off Hwy 12, ½ mile to Arnold Dr; (707) 935-0237; 13540 Arnold Dr; Glen Ellen, CA 95442; $$$; AE, DIS, MC, V; checks OK.*

Glenelly Inn ★ A graceful grove of oak trees forms the backdrop for this serene, former railway inn built in 1916. The five guest rooms open onto a verandah with a fine view of the Sonoma Valley and the tree-covered mountains beyond. The Grand Cru is a Victorian delight with a wrought-iron and brass bed and a treadle-base sink. Three larger suites, located in the cottage out back, have small private patios. Here, choose the memento-filled Jack London Suite with its wooden sleigh bed and several Jack London first editions. Rock the afternoon away in the tree swing suspended from a 200-year-old oak or mellow out in the hot tub. ■ *Warm Springs Rd and Arnold Dr; (707) 996-6720; 5131 Warm Springs Rd, Glen Ellen, CA 95442; $$; AE, MC, V; checks OK.*

KENWOOD

RESTAURANTS

Kenwood Restaurant and Bar ★★ Chef Max Schacher's European soul food is the culinary equivalent of an oaky cabernet. The menu changes constantly, but you can't go wrong if you stick to the red meat accompanied by Schacher's rich and complicated sauces, like the exquisitely grilled venison in a Cognac pepper cream sauce, or the roast rack of lamb with herbs and mushrooms. Keep your eye out for the grilled polenta appetizer—crisp triangles in tomato relish, topped with milk-white moons of goat cheese, sun-dried tomatoes, and a garnish of fresh herbs. Everything on the menu contains meat, but the chef will willingly whip up a vegetarian entrée for the noncarnivores in your party. ■ *3 miles past Glen Ellen at 9900 Sonoma Hwy 12; (707) 833-6326; $$, full bar; MC, V; no checks; lunch, dinner Tues–Sun.*

LODGINGS

Kenwood Inn ★★★ Barely a year old, this charming anachronism created by restaurateurs Terry and Roseann Grimm looks like a centuries-old Italian pensione. The four beautifully decorated guest rooms have temptingly fluffy feather beds, fireplaces, and sitting areas. Pleasantly masculine room 3 in Ralph Lauren shades of burgundy and green paisley has a nice private patio, but room 6 sports a sitting room with a stereo, Jacuzzi, and a balcony overlooking the vineyards and courtyard with its swimming pool and fountain. The Grimms serve an ample gourmet breakfast with fresh fruit, polenta with poached eggs, and buttery homemade croissants. ■ *3 miles past Glen Ellen on Hwy 12; (707) 833-1293; 10400 Sonoma Hwy, Kenwood, CA 95452; $$$; AE, MC, V; checks OK.*

SANTA ROSA

Santa Rosa is the closest thing Sonoma County has to a big city, but it's more like a countrified suburb. Happily, it's got more than its share of peculiar, off-beat museums: botantists, gardeners, and other plant fans will want to check out the gardens and greenhouses at the **Luther Burbank Home and Gardens;** (707) 527-0297. Burbank, for those struggling to recall their elementary school history, created 800 new strains of flowers, fruit, and vegetables at the turn of the century.

Pop culture fans will get a kick out of **Snoopy's Gallery**

and Gifts, a Peanuts cartoon museum with memorabilia donated by Santa Rosa resident Charles Schulz (1665 W Steel Lane, (707) 546-3385) and the tacky but fun **Ripley Museum,** filled with information about Robert Ripley of "Ripley's Believe It or Not" fame (492 Sonoma Avenue, (707) 524-5233).

The best event of the year is the **Sonoma County Harvest Fair,** a wine-tasting orgy at the fairgrounds; (707) 545-4203. **Santa Rosa wineries** include **De Loach Vineyards** (1791 Olivet Lane), (707) 526-9111), best known for its chardonnays, and **Martini & Prati** (2191 Laguna Road), (707) 823-2404), known mainly for its dessert wines. If you tire of the wine trail, grab an elegant box lunch at **Tote Cuisine** in the Montgomery Village mall, (707) 578-0898, and head out for the 5,000 acres of wilds at **Annadel State Park;** (707) 539-3911.

RESTAURANTS

John Ash & Co. ★★★★ John Ash makes it seem so easy, you wonder why every other restaurant isn't as wonderful. The service is expert yet informal, the food is fabulous, and the serene, elegant dining room with cream-colored walls, tall French windows, and a crackling fire will make you want to settle in for a good long time. The menu, under the direction of chef Jeff Madura, is a classic California hybrid of French, Italian, and Southwestern cuisines. Each meal begins with a petite canapé, usually a palate-cleansing dish of fire and ice—chilled fresh

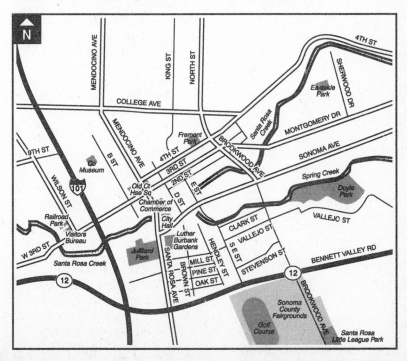

fruit with a spicy ginger and pepper after-bite. A recent visit started out with warm red cabbage and pancetta on a bed of greens and a delicate crêpe filled with a flavorful and distinctive combination of spinach, mushrooms, onions, and Jack cheese. These were followed by roasted wild mushrooms in a pungent fennel butter sauce, a perfectly pink loin of lamb in a nutty walnut-thyme sauce, and an exquisite flower-shaped eggplant tart filled with cheese and tomatoes. (Everything looked as good it tasted: a bouquet of green beans came tied with a Chinese long bean bow; three bright spears of papaya topped a hillock of sour cream-cinnamon pesto.) The large, reasonably priced wine list, showcasing Napa and Sonoma wines, includes a good selection of ports, sherries, and dessert wines. ■ *Hwy 101 at River Rd; (707) 527-7687; 4330 Barnes Rd, Santa Rosa; $$$; full bar; MC, V; checks OK; lunch Tues–Fri, dinner Tues–Sun.*

Fans ★★ Chef Barbara Hom turns out globally eclectic Eurasian cuisine from this hip little downtown eatery. The menu changes every six weeks, but a recent visit found a succulent smoked duck salad with candied ginger and mixed greens, as well as a peppery grilled salmon in a coriander–lemon grass crust. The ravioli with Smithfield ham, chicken, and baby bok choy in a ginger cream sauce is another savory wonder. Not every dish is a success here, of course, but Hom's adventuresome experiments work out more often than not. Desserts are dependably spectacular: blood orange cheesecake in Grand Marnier crème Anglaise; framboise chocolate torte with shaved white chocolate; and passion fruit and harvest riesling mousse in a toasted almond cookie crust topped with a raspberry sauce. Fans' small dining room has high ceilings, contemporary art, and the best looking waiters in town. ■ *Between D and Mendocino streets; (707) 527-9797; 620 5th St, Santa Rosa; $$$; beer and wine; AE, DC, DIS, MC, V; local checks only only; lunch Mon–Fri, dinner Mon–Sat.*

Caffe Portofino ★ Pray that you get here on a good day. The food at Caffe Portofino ranges from wonderful to okay and the service from competent to embarrassing. Locals don't seem to mind the fluctuations, because the handsome oak dining room, located in a narrow, red-brick building, is always jammed. The vast California-Italian menu (over 30 entrées) includes meat, poultry, and seafood, plus an array of pastas. The fettuccine Portofino with bite-size bits of pork tenderloin and tender mushrooms in a garlickly red wine sauce is a dependable winner. We also like the prawns in an olive, tomato, and wine sauce. Their vast wine list focuses on California and Italian wines. The service is from another realm of weird. On a recent visit the waiters seemed to be possessed by the spirits of Abbott and Costello, dropping trays, spilling drinks, clearing plates while we were in the midst of eating, and then proceeding to overcharge, all the while smiling horribly sweet, Debbie Boone smiles. On other visits, they've merely seemed understaffed but coping. ■ *Between Mendocino and B streets; (707) 523-1171; 535 4th St, Santa Rosa; $$$; full bar; AE, MC, V; no checks; lunch, dinner Mon–Sat.*

The China Room ★ Located deep in mini-mall hell, this serene Chinese restaurant is an oasis of good food in a desert of Taco Bells and 7-Elevens. While the outside looks like just another storefront in a mall, the inside is quiet and polished, with peach walls, black lacquered chairs, and George Winston piped through the sound system. The vast menu will please everyone from chop suey Philistines to Sichuan connoisseurs. The seafood here is exceptionally fresh and the vegetables are always bright and perfectly crisp. Check out the peppery hot and sour soup bobbing with fresh mushrooms. Also recommended are the clay pot dishes, brimming with succulent scallops and prawns—and anything with garlic sauce. Avoid the dry, foil-wrapped chicken. ■ *Hwy 12 and Mission; (707) 539-5570; 500 Mission Blvd, Santa Rosa; $; beer and wine; AE, MC, V; local checks only; lunch, dinner every day.*

LODGINGS

Vintners Inn ★★ Set amidst vineyards with its four Provençal-style buildings clustered around a central courtyard, the Vintners Inn combines the charm of a country inn with the conveniences of a modern hotel. The simple and pretty rooms have pine beds, plush carpets, antique armoires and desks, and separate sitting areas. French doors open onto a balcony or patio with a view of the vineyards or the landscaped grounds. Ask for a room with a vineyard view that faces away from Highway 101. The young, courteous staff is very attentive. When you check in, the bell-hop brings an ice bucket to your room; in the evening, he will return to turn down your bed and put a chocolate on your pillow. A complimentary breakfast of fruit, granola, pastries, and waffles is served in the main building's sunny dining room until 11am. There's also a fine deck for sunning, and a Jacuzzi. ■ *Hwy 101 at River Rd; (707) 575-7350, toll free (800) 421-2584; 4350 Barnes Rd, Santa Rosa, CA 95403; $$$; beer and wine; AE, DC, MC, V; checks OK.*

Fountain Grove Inn ★ The Fountain Grove's 85 rooms are elegant to the point of austerity—gray carpets, gray bedspreads, mirrored walls, pen and ink drawings of horses over the beds. Outside, the swimming pool and Jacuzzi are surrounded by a slate sun deck next to the kind of fountain you usually only see in the lobbies of corporate headquarters. It all seems very serious, perhaps because the motel caters more to business travelers than to tourists. But there's no reason that you have to take it as seriously as it takes itself. In the morning, you can grab a quick continental breakfast in the lobby before heading out for a hard day of wine-tasting. Or if you insist on working, there is a place to hook up your modem. ■ *At Mendocino Ave; (707) 578-6101, toll free (800) 222-6101; 101 Fountain Grove Pkwy, Santa Rosa, CA 95403; $$$; full bar; AE, DC, DIS, MC, V; checks OK.*

The Gables Bed and Breakfast ★ This aptly named Gothic Victorian boasts not just 7, but 15 gables. Innkeepers Judy and Michael Ogne have decorated the eight cheerful guest rooms with antiques and old-fashioned furnishings. The spacious Brookside Suite, overlooking a creek, has a Ben Franklin fireplace and a king-size bed. The brand-new Parlor Suite boasts a gorgeous Italian marble fireplace and furniture handmade by Ogne. At the edge of the backyard creek is William and Mary's Cottage, an enchanting little cabin that has a sleeping loft, a wood stove, and a tiny kitchen. The inn has a 3-acre backyard and a roomy wooden deck inhabited by a multitude of identical white cats. ■ *4 miles from Rohnert Park Expressway; (707) 585-7777; 4257 Petaluma Hill Rd, Santa Rosa, CA 95404; $$$; AE, DIS, MC, V; checks OK.*

Melitta Station Inn ★ Set on a sleepy country road close to Annadel State Park, this quixotic little inn surrounded by fragrant pepperwood trees has done time as stagecoach stop, a railroad station, a general store, and a post office. The narrow, brick-red building has six small, sunny guest rooms decorated with antiques, stuffed animals, quilts, and oddball collectibles—especially rabbits. (Owners Diane Crandon and Vic Amstadter collect rabbit sculptures of every description.) The sitting room is a bit too cramped for all the guests to gather at once, but if you get there first, you can spend a very peaceful evening camped in front of its wood stove. In the morning, we like to linger on the balcony under the fragrant boughs of the overhanging pepperwood trees. ■ *⅛ mile off Hwy 12; (707) 538-7712; 5850 Melita Rd, Santa Rosa, CA 95409; $$; MC, V; checks OK.*

WINDSOR

LODGING

Country Meadow Inn This comfortable, brown-shingled house is just a cork pop away from some of Healdsburg's best wineries. Innkeepers Sandy and Barry Weber can tell you which ones are worth checking out and why. Of the five guest rooms here, request the lush and charismatic Woodrose and Mahogany rooms with their tiled fireplaces. The Garden Suite, while showy, isn't really worth the price. Guests gather in the dining room at 9am for a giant country breakfast with oatmeal–black walnut pancakes in an orange butter sauce. Most guests head out to the wineries immediately afterwards; the less ambitious can spend the day loafing around the backyard deck and swimming pool. In the late afternoon, Sandy puts out a plate of cheese and crackers and a bottle of chilled sparkling cider to revive her wine-soaked guests. ■ *2 miles S of Healdsburg Ave exit off Hwy 101; (707) 431-1276, toll free (800) 238-1728; 11360 Old Redwood Hwy, Windsor, CA 95492; $$; DIS, MC, V; checks OK.*

HEALDSBURG

This is one tourist town whose charm seems completely unforced. Boutiques and bakeries surround a parklike plaza where you can sit and read the newspaper while downing pastries from the marvelous **Downtown Bakery and Creamery** (308A Center Street, (707) 431-2719). At night, head for **The Raven** (115 North Street, (707) 433-5448), the wine country's best movie house for new releases and art films.

RESTAURANTS

Tre Scalini ★★★ There are so many northern Italian restaurants in the Wine Country that one can grow to dread the mere thought of sun-dried tomatoes. But chef Fernando Urroz' imaginative creations are enough to revive even the most jaded palate. Start out with a heavenly antipasto of grilled eggplant, smoked shiitake mushrooms, roasted peppers, marinated artichoke hearts, and calamata olives. This and the peppery Cajun bread would be dinner enough for timider (and thinner) souls. Tender ravioli stuffed with sweet butternut squash play

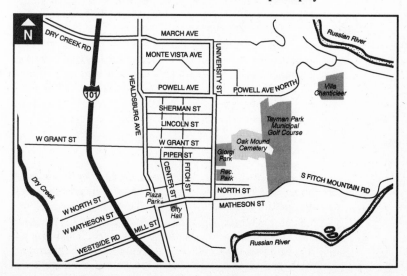

in a sage beurre blanc; squid ink pasta is topped with a pungent and spicy sauce of baby lobster tails, tomatoes, cilantro, rosemary, and wine. The friendly waiters are full of wise recommendations and are utterly invisible when it comes to removing dishes or sweeping up crumbs. Make a reservation for the back dining room with its warm gold walls and arches. ■ *S of the plaza between Mill and Matheson streets; (707) 433-1772; 241 Healdsburg Ave, Healdsburg; $$$; beer and wine; MC, V; checks OK; dinner Wed–Mon, lunch Mon–Fri.*

Samba Java ★★ The verve and bustle at this festive Caribbean-flavored cafe seems more in keeping with an address in the East Village than with placid little Healdsburg. Ten multicolored tables are crammed into a tiny room whose walls are covered with immense Haitian-style paintings. The place is always packed in the evening. The wise make reservations; the less wise try to find a vacant stool at the mosiac counter made of bright tiles and pot shards. The day's offerings may include such disparate items as delicious smoked-beet borscht, Mexican black bean soup with a swirl of chile cream and fried cilantro, a flash-fried red snapper served with a chile-studded hominy, and a juicy braised beef brisket topped with onion gravy and served with wilted mustard greens and mashed potatoes. The knowledgeable—if somewhat chilly—servers can recommend good wines to go with your meal from their ever-changing Sonoma County wine list. But be sure to order a glass of the spicy homemade ginger beer—it's too good to miss. Wonderful homebaked breads and pastries, like warm gingerbread studded with candied ginger, show up on the dessert and breakfast menus. ■ *On the N side of the plaza; (707) 433-5282; 109A Plaza St, Healdsburg; $$; beer and wine; DIS, MC, V; no checks; breakfast, lunch Tues–Sun, dinner Fri–Sat.*

LODGING

Belle de Jour Inn ★★★ In a region where rampant Victoriana is all the rage, Belle de Jour's four romantic hillside cottages have a refreshingly spare, uncluttered feel. In the Terrace Room, you can savor a fine view of the valley from the comfort of a giant Jacuzzi located right in the bedroom. We also like the Caretaker's Suite with its lace-canopied four-poster bed, private deck with a vine-covered trellis, and blue-tiled whirlpool tub. All the rooms have a fireplace or wood stove, and are air-conditioned in summer—a big plus around these parts. Innkeepers Tom and Brenda Hearn will deliver a breakfast basket to your door, or—if you're one of those odd souls who actually enjoy morning conversation—you can can take breakfast with the other guests in the Hearn's attractive kitchen, or out on the deck. ■ *1 mile N of Dry Creek Rd, across from Simi Winery; (707) 431-9777; 16276 Healdsburg Ave, Healdsburg, CA 95448; $$$; MC, V; checks OK.*

Healdsburg Inn on The Plaza ★★★ Originally built as a Wells Fargo Express office in 1900, this surprisingly quiet inn on the plaza has high vaulted ceilings and a lovely old staircase leading from the ground floor art gallery to the nine interesting guest rooms upstairs. The four rooms facing the plaza have beautiful bay windows and are more elaborately decorated than the rest: the spacious Song of the Rose Room, in pale yellow and white, has a claw-footed tub and a shower; Sweet Dreams and Sonnet have fireplaces. The lace-covered Moonbeam Suite has a big, two-room bath with a separate tub room. A full breakfast and afternoon wine and snacks are served in the glass-enclosed solarium. ■ *On the S side of the plaza; (707) 433-6991; 116 Matheson St, Healdsburg, CA 95448; $$$; MC, V; checks OK.*

Haydon House ★★ This pretty blue Queen Anne Victorian behind a white picket fence seems like it should be the home of some sweet, but daft, older relative. In the main house, the cozy downstairs parlor and big front porch provide comfortable common areas, while the six guest rooms are cheerful and romantic. The best room in the main house is the Attic Suite, a sunny two-room garret with a bathtub in the main room and low slanted ceilings that will frustrate tall people but enchant everyone else. Behind the main house is the Victorian Cottage, a modern replica house that looks as if someone put a regular-size Gothic Victorian in the dryer. Innkeepers Tom and Keiu Woodburn live downstairs in the cottage; the upstairs has been turned into two spacious suites with high dormer windows, big whirlpool tubs, and loads of charm. In the morning, you'll find a full breakfast featuring green chile fritattas with basil and cilantro, fresh fruit or baked apples, and plenty of just-baked muffins and croissants. ■ *Haydon and Fitch Sts; (707) 433-5228; 321 Haydon St, Healdsburg, CA 95448; $$$; MC, V; checks OK.*

Madrona Manor ★★ Surrounded by lush green lawns, exotic gardens, and a citrus orchard, Madrona Manor looks a like a cheerier version of the Addams Family's Gothic abode. The inn's 21 rooms are divided between the main house and the carriage house. Several of the rooms in the main house contain the house's original furnishings, which means that they are somewhat shabbier than you might expect in so pricey an establishment. Oddly enough, this doesn't detract from the charm; instead, it lends a homey sense of authenticity. Most of the rooms have fireplaces, some with delicate hand-painted borders. Rooms 203 and 204 are the most ample, with French doors opening onto lovely, if somewhat precarious feeling, balconies. Weekend rates ($80 more than weekday rates) include a four-course, prix-fixe dinner for two in their much-heralded restaurant where waiters stand at attention next to the fireplace mantle, feigning invisibility in the manner of the household staffs of yesteryear. The menu allows you to choose between two prix-fixe options, although the very accommodating waiters may let you mix and match. Despite the fact that most of the vegetables and herbs come from their own garden, the food doesn't quite measure up to the ambience—or to the restaurant's sterling reputation. ■ *Dry Creek and Westside roads at 1001 Westside Rd; (707) 433-4231, toll free (800) 258-4003; Mail: PO Box 818, Healdsburg, CA 95448; $$$; beer, wine, champagne; AE, DC, DIS, MC, V; checks OK; dinner every day, brunch Sun.*

Raford House ★ This Victorian farmhouse has a great front porch—brick red with white railings—sturdy wicker furniture, and a sweeping view of the vineyards. The house itself, though quaint, is nothing spectacular but the setting is quiet and pastoral. There are seven guest rooms; all but two have private baths. The Bridal Suite has a fireplace, plus wonderful French doors that open onto a patio with the same glorious view as the front porch. If you're traveling with another couple, you might try June's Room and the Red Room, an inexpensive pair with an English game table perfect for a four-handed game of cards. ■ *Off River Rd, 10 miles S of downtown Healdsburg; (707) 887-9573; 10630 Wohler Rd, Healdsburg, CA 95448; $$; MC, V; checks OK.*

GEYSERVILLE

RESTAURANTS

Château Souverain ★★★ Château Souverain is one of the best restaurants in the entire Wine Country. But if you're anything like us, your first reaction to this brooding, slate-gray faux château in Alexander Valley is likely to be: "Oh, come off it!" From the ornate stone and wrought iron archway at the end of the drive to the grand, curving white staircase and formal gardens leading up the entrance, the whole place seems calculated to awe. Inside, the formal dining room has soaring cathedral ceilings with spidery chandeliers and tall French windows overlooking vineyards and hills. The cuisine is equally impressive, though it, too, falters from trying too hard. We started with an exquisitely simple ravioli with fennel, prosciutto, and Swiss chard dusted with a fine confetti of flowers, and a fresh, chunky ahi tuna tartare with bits of tomato and onion. The tartare was served with crisp, thin crostini and a garnish of salsa and avocado spears that looked and tasted good but didn't seem to go with anything in particular. The perfectly grilled, free-range (i.e., guilt free) veal chop with merlot sauce and lemon verbena butter on a creamy bed of citrus risotto combined its array of flavors more successfully than did the beef tenderloin in an overkill of three sauces: a cabernet garlic sauce, a roasted red pepper béarnaise, and a rosemary pesto. Patricia Windisch's cuisine has been trembling on the border of four-star for quite a while: with a little more attention to harmony and a little less grandstanding, her prodigious talents could tip the scale. Sometimes, however, this grandstanding pays off in spades: the delicately sweet rose petal ice cream, topped with sugared rose petals and served in a crisp, almost Florentine-like almond tuille with a light rose petal sauce flew to the top of our best-desserts-of-a-lifetime list. The cakey, cocoa-imbued tiramisu was pleasant, but could have done without the intrusive fruit sauce. Château Souverain's wine list offers the best of Sonoma County at remarkably reasonable prices (several less expensive than the entrées), though the restaurant pours only its own wine by the glass. Some people complain that the service here is aloof, but we've always found it unobtrusive and down-to-the-earth, a feat given the surroundings. ■ *West side of Hwy 101 at the Independence Lane exit, south of Geyserville; (707) 433-3141; $$$; beer and wine; AE, MC, V; local checks only.*

LODGINGS

Hope-Merrill House ★★★ Since every mediocre shack built in the late 19th century gets termed Victorian, it's easy to forget the dizzying architectural and design heights reached during this period. This imaginatively restored Eastlake Gothic will remind you: three stories tall, painted brown and cream, the Hope-Merrill House has expansive bay windows and a wraparound front porch with comfortable cane chairs. The landscaping is formal and strictly symmetrical with box hedges and weeping mulberries. Inside, you'll find extravagant hand–silk-screened wallpapers, carved armchairs, and velvet-covered divans which are just as uncomfortable now as they were in their heyday.

The inn has seven rooms. In the Peacock Room, gold, rose, and gray-blue peacocks strut around a ceiling border, a wood-burning fireplace takes up one wall, and French doors open into a bathroom containing an immense marble-top whirlpool tub. For the best views, try the Vineyard View Room or the Bradbury Room, which looks out over the swimming pool and verdant gardens. Both rooms have fireplaces and showers big enough for two. A full gourmet breakfast comes with your room. ■ *1 mile N of the Geyserville exit off Hwy 101, at 21253 Geyserville Ave; (707) 857-3356, toll free (800) 825-4BED; Mail: PO Box 42, Geyserville, CA 95441; $$$; MC, V; checks OK.*

Hope-Bosworth House ★★ Across the street from its showier cousin, the 1904 Hope-Bosworth House provides a cheerful, informal, and less-expensive alternative. There are five bedrooms, only two of which have full baths. The downstairs Sun Porch Room has the dry, woody fragrance of a summer cottage; in the morning it's filled with the twitter of birds in the backyard. Our upstairs favorite is the sunny and spacious Chintz Room with its old-fashioned flowered wallpaper. Guests at the Hope-Bosworth House are treated to the same elaborate breakfasts as their neighbors across the way, and also have access to the Hope-Merrill House pool. ■ *From 101, 1 mile N of the Geyserville exit, at 21238 Geyserville Ave; (707) 857-3356; Mail: PO Box 42, Geyserville, CA 95441; $$; MC, V; checks OK.*

CLOVERDALE

RESTAURANTS

World Famous Hamburger Ranch and Pasta Farm ★ Rave reviews from satisfied customers from all over the world paper the walls of this converted service station. A typical homage: "Killer burgers/ Awesome fries/ We asked the locals/ and they didn't lie." A favorite with truck drivers and travelers for over 50 years, the Hamburger Ranch offers homemade pastas, summer barbecues, great burgers, funky blues music, and charming service. Burgers of 12 different styles include the British Burger (cheeseburger with bacon) and the Latin Lover Cheeseburger (with Jack cheese and chopped jalapeño pepper). The fresh, round-cut fries with the skins on are a nice touch. Another plus is the microbrew selection featuring brews from the nearby Anderson Valley Brewing Company. ■ *On Hwy 101, top of the hill, N end of town; (707) 894-5616; 31995 N Redwood Hwy, Cloverdale; $; beer and wine; no credit cards; local checks only; breakfast, lunch, dinner every day.*

LODGINGS

Vintage Towers Bed and Breakfast Inn ★★ Innkeepers Garrett Hall and Jim Mees have filled this magnificent, tri-towered Queen Anne Victorian mansion with books, art work, and antiques with interesting histories: look for a plaque on the wall explaining who was born in your bed. Listed on the United States Registry of Historic Places, this beautiful mansion has seven upstairs guest rooms. The three corner suites have tower sitting rooms (one round, one square, and one octagonal). Downstairs you'll find a large dining room with a fireplace, music room, library, and conversation parlor. A full breakfast includes Garrett's fresh biscuit pudding and other goodies. ■ *East on 3rd St off Hwy 101, corner of N Main; (707) 894-4535; 302 N Main St, Cloverdale, CA 95425; $$; AE, DIS, MC, V; checks OK.*

Ye Olde' Shelford House ★★ Don't be put off by the "Ye Olde'" label, so often associated with phony antiquation. There's nothing phony about the Shelford House, an 1885 Victorian bed and breakfast set on a knoll overlooking the vineyards of the Russian River valley. Owners Ina and Al Sauder have decorated this beautifully restored home with their own handicrafts: Ina's hand-embroidered bedspreads, pillow covers, and quilts; Al's fine wood accessories that include the gravity-defying wine bottle holder. Although the rooms in the adjoining "carriage house" have more space, we like the rooms in the main house with their smattering of antiques from Ina's native Scotland. There are plenty of extras at the Shelford House: bicycles to borrow, a hot tub, a horse-drawn surrey to take you on a romantic tour of the Wine Country's back roads, and the chance to have a glass of wine in the big swing on the porch. ■ *1 mile E on 1st St off Hwy 101; (707) 894-5956; 29955 River Rd, Cloverdale, CA 95425; $$; DIS, MC, V; checks OK.*

Abrams House Inn ★ The best thing about this beautiful Victorian is the wonderful service. Unseen hands always seem to be depositing some new treat: hot chocolate appears in the sitting room before bedtime; fresh muffins and good, dark coffee materialize first thing in the morning—along with a newspaper. Though you'll be tempted to devour the entire platter of muffins, remember owner Betty Fitzgerald's wondrous breakfast is yet to come: a huge fresh fruit salad and shirred eggs on toast made from an old family recipe (one of the finest bed and breakfast breakfasts we've had anywhere). There are four guest rooms here, ranging from the Spellacy Suite, a lavish private suite with a king-size four-poster bed and a private porch to more modest rooms in the front, with queen-size beds and delicious morning sunshine. Betsy will even let you pick your fill of fresh raspberries in the rose garden out back. ■ *Between 3rd and 4th streets 1 block E of Hwy 101; (707) 894-2412; 314 N Main St, Cloverdale, CA 95425; $$; AE, MC, V; checks OK.*

ANDERSON VALLEY WINE COUNTRY

Anderson Valley—once noted only for sheep, apples, and timber—has become the premiere producer of cool-climate California wine. The trailblazer in this adventure was **Navarro Vineyards**, which opened the first of many tasting rooms on Highway 128, the main thoroughfare. Navarro pioneered production of the region's trademark wine—dry, fruity, spicy Alsatian-style gewürztraminer—and also makes excellent chardonnay, pinot noir, and riesling; 5601 Highway 128, (707) 895-3686. Right next door, **Greenwood Ridge** also offers fine riesling in addition to cabernet, merlot, sauvignon blanc, and zinfandel from other areas; 5501 Highway 128, (707) 895-2002. Up the road a few miles, **Husch Vineyards**—another early (circa 1971) arrival—makes clean and fruity pinot noir and gewürztraminer, plus a host of warmer country wines from its vineyards in Ukiah; 4400 Highway 128, (707) 895-3216. In a beautiful tasting room full of exotic folk art, **Handley Cellars** pours chardonnay, sauvignon blanc, pinot noir, and sparkling wine; 3151 Highway 128, (707) 895-3876. A recent transplant from the San Francisco peninsula is **Obester Winery**, which produces crisp riesling, gewürztraminer, sauvignon blanc, and chardonnay, as well as sturdy, old-fashioned cabernet sauvignon and zinfandel; 9200 Highway 128, (707) 895-3814. Two tiny, off-the-beaten-track places worth calling for an appointment are **Lazy Creek Vineyards**, offering first-rate, reasonably priced gewürztraminer, chardonnay, and pinot noir (4610 Highway 128, (707) 895-3623) and **Pepperwood Springs**, making pinot noir and chardonnay that are richer than the local norm; 1200 Holmes Ranch Road, (707) 895-2920.

The enological future of the valley—whose climate is almost identical to that of the Champagne region of France—appears to reside in sparkling wine. In the early 1980s, **Roderer Estate**, one of France's most prestigious champagne producers, opened up a surprisingly low-key, low-slung facility producing high-quality sparkling wine; 4501 Highway 128, (707) 895-2288. The valley's original sparkling wine house is **Scharffenberger Cellars** which—under the wing of Pommery and Greno, owners of Dom Perignon, Veuve Cliquot, and Möet and Chandon—continues to produce excellent brut, blanc de blancs, brut rose, and cremant; 8501 Highway 128, (707) 895-2957.

In late July, Greenwood Ridge Vineyards is the site of the annual **California Wine Tasting Championships**, where novices and professionals alike can put their palates to the test. Advance registration required, (707) 877-3262.

BOONVILLE

This speck of a town in the heart of Anderson Valley is best known for a regional dialect called Boontling, developed by townsfolk at the beginning of the century. No one really speaks Boontling anymore, though a few old-timers remember the lingo. Like most private languages, a large percentage of the words refer to sex, a fact glossed over in most touristy brochures on the topic. We don't know the Boontling word for beer, but the folks at the **Anderson Valley Brewing Company**, a fine little microbrewery across from the Boonville Hotel, probably do; (707) 895-BEER. While you're in town, grab a copy of the *Anderson Valley Advertiser*, a rollicking, crusading (some say muckraking) small town paper with avid readers from San Francisco to the Oregon border.

Boont Berry Farms, an organic produce market and deli in a small, weathered wood building, turns out terrific lunch and dinner treats; (13981 Hwy 128; (707) 895-3576). There are a few tables out front in a dusty parking area off 128, but get your food to go and head for the picnic grounds at the **Tinman Apple Juice Tasting Room** (left side of the highway) west of town.

LODGINGS

The Boonville Hotel and Restaurant ★★★

In the mid-1980s, the Boonville Hotel was the most famous culinary destination in the Northern California outback. Swells from San Francisco and New York flew by private plane to Anderson Valley's tiny airport just to nosh on the precious culinary creations of former owner Charlotte Rollins. Pressed by debts, she and her partner skipped town in the dead of night, leaving an unpaid staff and a bad taste in the mouths of locals, who had their doubts about the hotel's ritzy clientele in the first place. The Boonville Hotel languished for a few years, until new owners John Schmitt and Jeanne Eliades brought it back to life as a quiet little restaurant and inn.

The decor of the Boonville Hotel is pleasantly austere—we deem it "Shaker Southwestern." The beautiful wood bar downstairs and most of the exquisite furniture in the guest rooms are the work of local craftspeople. Two large suites share a spacious balcony on busy Highway 28. The smaller rooms at the back of the hotel are quieter and less expensive, but here the inn's austerity shades dangerously close to bareness. Medium-size room 3, with its unique iron bedstead, is a nice compromise of price, spaciousness, and quiet.

The restaurant in the Boonville Hotel is still one of the best eateries north of the Napa Valley. A gathering spot for local winemakers, the hotel offers a fresh mix of California, Southwestern, and backwoods regional cuisine: sliced pork tenderloin with cumin, cilantro, and oranges; and chicken breast with roasted tomato-mint salsa. Every one seems turned on to the garlic potatoes. The hot crusty bread makes a terrific sponge for the always terrific soups. Reservations recommended, especially in summer. ■ *In the center of town, on Hwy 28 at Lambert Lane; (707) 895-2210; PO Box 326, Boonville, CA 95415; $$$; beer and wine; no credit cards; checks OK; lunch, dinner Wed–Sun.*

The Toll House Inn ★★

Set high in the oak-covered hills on the twisting road between Boonville and Ukiah, this wonderful old 1912 farmhouse feels far away from everything. There are no telephones or televisions in the rooms, only books and big baskets of magazines. With the exception of the claustrophobic red and black Victorian room at the top of the stairs, the guest rooms have a modern, almost suburban feel, softened by a few nice antiques. Like every other roadside inn in Anderson Valley, the rooms toward the front of the house suffer from truck noise at night. Set on a 360-acre ranch, the Toll House provides plenty of room to roam. The less-adventurous can luxuriate in the hot tub or in the beautiful, landscaped back yard.

Until this year, The Toll House was also one of the best up-and-coming restaurants in Mendocino. Chef Ross Browne (formerly of Zuni Cafe in San Francisco) did fine things with all-organic produce and wild game. Unfortunately, Browne was injured recently, and the Toll House restaurant is closed until mid-1993. ■ *From Hwy 128 in Boonville, take Hwy 253 north; (707) 895-3632; 15301 Hwy 253, Boonville, CA 95415; $$$; DIS, MC, V; checks OK; Call for restaurant information.*

PHILO

There's not much in town, but a little ways out you'll find **Gowan's Oak Tree**, a great roadside fruit and vegetable stand; 6600 Highway 128, (707) 895-3353.

RESTAURANTS

Floodgate Store and Grill ★★ A sign outside advertises "Solid Food," but this terrific little regional American cafe (several miles north of Philo) is so much more than that. For lunch, expect backcountry rarities like cauliflower, cheddar, and chili soup; whole steamed artichokes with roasted pepper mayo; and perfect duck breast salad with apples, pecans, and Gorgonzola. For a recent dinner here we had a simple French onion soup, sans the usual croutons and a pound of Gruyère, but with a rich, sweet broth and plenty of toothsome onions. The smoked (almost hamlike) porkchop with a tangy citrus sauce came perfectly pink with a side of grilled asparagus, deliciously buttery mashed potatoes, and steamed baby carrots that taste like obligatory roughage. Served with a nice lemony pepper sauce and grilled vegetables, the thinly sliced, but still tough venison flank steak is earthy and flavorful. Earl's strawberry shortcake—sweet strawberry compote on buttermilk biscuits, topped with a mound of whipped cream—tastes more like good homecooking than gourmet restaurant fare, but that's no reason not to lap it up.

In summer, the restaurant can be sweltering, so opt for the cooler patio. ■ *N of Philo on Hwy 128; (707) 895-3000; 1810 Hwy 128, Philo; $$; beer and wine; no credit cards; checks OK; lunch, dinner Wed–Sun, brunch Sat–Sun (lunch, dinner Thur–Sun in winter).*

LODGINGS

Philo Pottery Inn ★★ This 1889 redwood farmhouse is pure and authentic country—no frilly ruffles, no overdressed dolls—

just a lavender-filled English garden in the front yard and bright handmade quilts and sturdy frontier furnishings in each room. You can linger in the library downstairs or snooze in the bent willow loungers on the rustic front porch. Evaline's and Donna's rooms are the lightest and most spacious, but light sleepers might try Lynn's Room upstairs. It's smaller and a bit dark but quieter than the rooms that face the road, a major logging route. Owner Sue Chiverton, a transplanted Bostoner, will direct you to all the best biking and hiking trails and will happily arrange private tastings at the valley's many small private wineries. ■ *W end of Philo at 8550 Hwy 128; (707) 895-3069; Mail: PO Box 166, Philo, CA 95466; $$; MC, V; checks OK.*

HOPLAND

RESTAURANTS

Hopland Brewery Brewpub and Beer Garden ★★ California's first brewpub since Prohibition, the Hopland Brewery is a refreshing break from the grape circuit. This quintessential brewpub has tasty pub grub, foot-stomping live music on Saturdays (blues to Cajun), and four fine beers brewed on the premises. The classic beer garden in the back has long tables shaded by trellised hops and a sandbox to keep the kids amused while you chow down on the large, lush burgers on homemade buns or the Red Tail chili with fresh vegetables, sirloin steak, and a generous splash of Red Tail Ale. The chili's usually medium-hot, but once in a while a Texas scorcher escapes the pot. ■ *13351 S Hwy 101 in central Hopland; (707) 744-1015; $; beer and wine; MC, V; no checks; lunch, dinner every day.*

LODGINGS

Thatcher Inn ★★ Built as a stage stop in 1890, this haughty cream-colored combination of Gothic spires and gabled windows still looks like a luxurious frontier saloon-hotel. The lobby is dominated by a long, mirrored, polished wood bar, and the gorgeous, dark, wood-paneled library is filled with interesting old books, velvet settees, and shiny brass reading lamps. A wide, curving wood stairway leads from the lobby to 20 beautifully decorated guest rooms on the second and third stories. The quietest rooms with the best view are on the south side of the hotel overlooking the backyard patio, with its fountain, wrought iron lamp posts, and giant spreading oak trees. Our favorite room is actually on the north side, overlooking the Hopland Brewery's beer garden: the cream and moss green Executive Suite has a claw-footed tub next to the bed and two pretty love seats in the sitting area. A full breakfast comes with your room. The Thatcher Inn Restaurant serves uninspired but acceptable California cuisine. ■ *Downtown*

Hopland; (707) 744-1890; Hwy 101, Hopland, CA 95449; $$$; full bar; AE, MC, V; checks OK; lunch Thurs–Sat, dinner Wed–Sun, brunch Sun.

UKIAH

Located at the upper reaches of the California wine country, Ukiah is still what Napa, Sonoma, and Healdsburg used to be—a sleepy little agricultural town surrounded by vineyards and apple and pear orchards. Peopled by an odd mix of farmers, loggers, and back-to-the-landers, Ukiah is a down-to-earth little burg with few traces of Wine Country gentrification. That doesn't mean there isn't any wine, however. Check out the chardonnay, sauvignon blanc, and sparkling wine at **Jepson Vineyards** (10400 S Highway 101, (707) 468-8936, call for appointment) or the chardonnay at **Domaine St. Gregory**; 4921 East Side Road, (707) 463-1532. Started in 1932, Mendocino County's oldest winery is **Parducci**, specializing in reds; 501 Parducci Road, (707) 468-8936. A short drive north to Redwood Valley brings you to **Frey Vineyards**, an organic wine specialist offering interesting petite sirah and cabernet; 14000 Tomki Rd, Redwood Valley, (707) 485-5177, appointment only. A good selection of local wines and good espresso can be found at **Main Street Wine and Cheese**; 113 S State Street, (707) 462-0417.

Soak away the aches and pains of your long drive (Ukiah is a long drive from almost anywhere) at North America's only warm and naturally carbonated mineral baths: the clothing-optional Orr Hot Springs (13201 Orr Springs Road, (707) 462-6277) and the more old-fashioned Vichy Springs Resort; 2605 Vichy Springs Road, (707) 462-9515. Hikers will want to check out Montgomery Woods, 1,100 acres of undeveloped redwoods on Big River with trails along Montgomery Creek.

The Grace Hudson Museum and the Sun House, with its interior laid out in a Pomo basket pattern, features Grace Hudson's paintings of Pomo Indians and some beautiful Pomo baskets; 431 S Main Street, (707) 462-3370.

RESTAURANTS

North State Cafe ★★ The North State Cafe is an attractive reflection of the cosmopolitan, bohemian spirit expressed in a nearby museum devoted to the works of Ukiah's patron artiste, Grace Hudson. This light and modern eatery is one of California's northernmost outposts of nouvelle cuisine. Stop in and savor the mixed vegetable salad, the terrine of pesto and sun-dried tomatoes, or the penne pasta with olives and artichokes—all worthy representatives of the sophisticated fare found farther south. Chef and co-owner Patrick Duggan's entrées range from delicate pasta dishes to Asian-influenced grilled brochettes or Mediterranean stuffed pork loins. If your tastes tend to the traditional, try the personal pizzas, braised chicken, and New York steak. Check out the World's Largest Redwood Tree Service Station next door—a remnant from the days that preceded both personal pizza and environmentalism. ■ *Perkins St exit from Hwy 101, then north on N State St; (707) 462-3726; 801 N State St, Ukiah; $$; beer and wine; MC, V; local checks only; lunch, dinner Tues–Sat.*

Super Taco ★★ Your happy fellow eaters are, for the most part, local Latinos; English is rarely spoken here. This should tip you off right away to the autentico factor: while every Mexican restaurant in the US claims to offer puro Mexicano food, Super Taco delivers. For immediate proof, check out those tacos—delicious little morsels encased in the same kind of tiny tortillas you'd find at a sidewalk stand south of the border. In addition to such norteno standbys as carne asada and spicy chorizo, Super Taco offers two kinds of pork and three kinds of chicken, as well as lengua, cabeza, and sesos (if you don't know, don't ask). You can also get shrimp quick-fired in garlic butter and smothered in ranchera or diabla (very hot) sauce. This amazing, so-much-more-than-a-mere-taqueria even offers two kinds of octopus cocktail. ■ *In the Pear Tree shopping center, E Perkins St exit from Rte 506; (707) 462-5979; 506 E Perkins, Ukiah; $; beer only; no credit cards; checks OK; lunch, dinner every day.*

Mutt Hut ★ Try thinking of the Mutt Hut as the Der Wienerschnitzel of an alternative universe. It's got 17 imaginative, variations on the traditional dog (kraut dogs, salsa dogs, and bacon cheese dogs), plus a potato cellar full of stuffed, baked spuds—mushroom spuds, taco spuds, beef spuds. Owner Ellie Moore also caters to Ukiah's health-conscious former hippies and small town yups with her big garden-fresh salads, tofu and brown rice dinners, and great fruit smoothies, and wonderful cappuccino. Mutt Hutt has comfortable tables, an airy patio, friendly service, and—most unlike fast food of all—a genuinely devoted clientele. ■ *Talmadge St exit from Hwy 101, then north on S State St; (707) 468-5376; 732 S State St, Ukiah; $; beer and wine; no credit cards; local checks only; breakfast, lunch, dinner Mon–Sat.*

Sunset Grill ★ The Sunset Grill is a civic institution—a meeting place for locals who, depending on their circumstances, might convene in the bar in front or in any of the numerous booths, banquet halls, or dining rooms. All are housed in a '60s-era building without any windows—the better for patrons to focus on food and drink without any annoying distractions such as weather or time of day. Despite its Rotarian decor, the Grill manages comfort and dependability without being boring. Watch for chef Stephen Yundt's specials, such as the locally raised Mendocino leg of lamb roasted with a red currant glaze and juniper berries. For Sunday brunch, try the flawless eggs Benedict served with fresh croissants and free, if standard, champagne. Reservations are advised on weekend evenings. ■ *Perkins St exit from Hwy 101; (707) 463-0740; 228 E Perkins, Ukiah; $$; full bar; MC, V; local checks only; lunch, dinner Wed–Mon, brunch Sun.*

LODGINGS

Orr Hot Springs ★★ This hot spot at the headwaters of the Big River was once a favorite of the Pomo Indians, and, later, with travelers on the Ukiah-Mendocino stage line. Now it's popular with anybody seeking a cure for world-weariness. The tonic, in this case, is the 99 to 110 degree mineral baths filling old porcelain bathtubs, a sheltered redwood hot tub, or the shallow outdoor pool open to the sky. Sweat in the gas-fired sauna, then dive into the large, cool, mineral-water swimming pool. Professional massages are available. This laid-back resort is open to day use, but after taking the waters you're better off spending the night in one of the private cabins and cottages (the largest holds 14 people) or the common room that sleeps 12. There are also 11 small tent sites scattered through the surrounding woods. The main lodge has a big, well-equipped kitchen (BYO food) and some of the cabins have kitchenettes. Orr Hot Springs is a popular place, so be sure to call ahead for reservations. Only a mile down the road is Montgomery Redwoods State Park—the perfect spot for a morning jog or afternoon stroll. ■ *13½ miles out Orr Springs Rd, off N State St; (707) 462-6277; 13201 Orr Springs Rd, Ukiah, CA 95482; $$; V, MC; checks OK.*

The Sanford House ★★ There's something indisputably small town about this tall, yellow Victorian on a tree-lined street just west of Ukiah's Mayberry-like downtown. Peaceful, unhurried, and bucolic, Sanford House boasts only one Gothic turret, but it does have a big front porch dotted with white wicker chairs and an old-fashioned baby buggy. Inside, antiques grace every room and everything is freshly painted and immaculately clean, but it's far too comfortable and unpretentious to be called a showplace. Its three guest rooms are named after turn-of-the-century presidents: the Taft Room with its dark four-poster bed, floral fabrics, and a Princess Di doll in a wedding dress is the most elegant, but we also like the spacious, cream and green Wilson Room with its floral wallpaper, beautiful armoire, and sunny turret sitting area. Dorsey serves her own biscotti (dipped in white and dark chocolate) in the evening with wine in the parlor. ■ *From Hwy 101, take Perkins Rd west; (707) 462-1653; 306 S Pine St, Ukiah, CA 95482; $$; no credit cards; checks OK.*

NORTH COAST

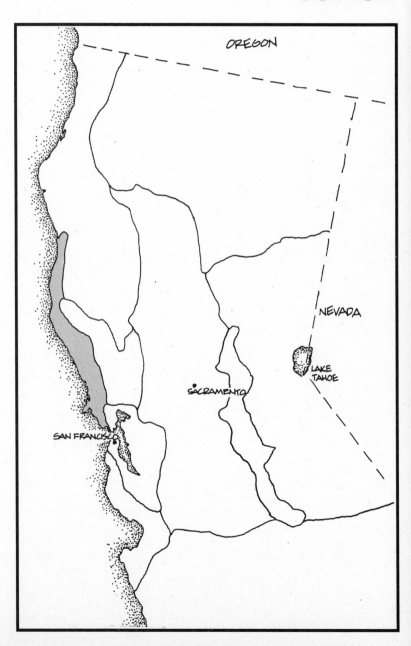

OREGON

NEVADA

LAKE TAHOE

SACRAMENTO

SAN FRANCISCO

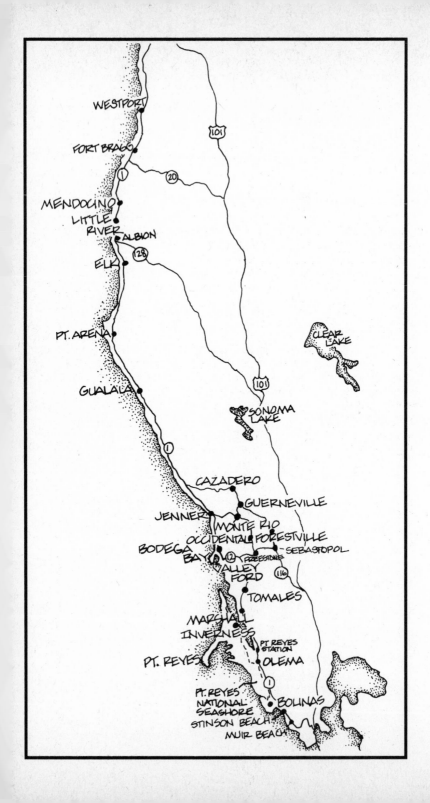

North Coast

*The Pacific Coast north of San Francisco
from Muir Beach to Westport.*

MUIR BEACH

LODGINGS

The Pelican Inn and Restaurant ★★ The stretch of Highway
1 just south of Muir Beach is an Anglophile's fantasyland:
horses graze knee-deep in the meadows, green hills tumble to
the sea, and—wait—is that really an old English pub in the
distance? Built by a homesick expatriate, The Pelican Inn is a
replica of a 16th-century English farmhouse, complete with a
Tudor exterior, beamed ceilings, and cottage gardens. It serves
traditional British fare—heaping portions of prime rib, rack of
lamb, shepherd's pie, and a goodly number of British beers on
tap. It's probably the only place in Marin to get lager and lime,
half and half, and beer shandies. The Pelican Inn's six rooms
with private baths each have leaded windows, heavy brocade
curtains, canopy beds, and English antiques. There's also a
snug (Brit for a common room) for lounging by the fire, reading, or playing the piano. In the morning, you'll find a proper
English breakfast of bangers and eggs, toast and marmalade,
coffee and tea. ■ *Center of town on W side of Hwy 1; (415) 383-
6000; Hwy 1, Muir Beach, CA 94965; $$$; beer and wine;
MC, V; no checks; dinner Tues–Sun, lunch Tues–Sat, lunch
buffet Sun.*

STINSON BEACH

RESTAURANTS

The Parkside ★ A wonderful neighborhood cafe, this place
bustles with locals and visitors chatting or reading the paper
and working their way through large and scrumptious meals.
Customers in a hurry can serve themselves coffee, home-
baked muffins, bread, and coffee cake. Most people prefer to
soak up the scene in front of the fireplace while indulging in
huevos rancheros, waffles, omelets, or blueberry pancakes. If
you're here on a weekend, be sure to try the delicious raisin-
nut bread. On warm days, sit outside next to the flower and veg-
etable garden. In summer, The Parkside operates a take-out
bar that serves burgers, fries, and very good milk shakes.
■ *W on Arenal off Hwy 1; (415) 868-1272; 43 Arenal Ave,
Stinson Beach; $; beer and wine; no credit cards; checks OK;
breakfast, lunch, dinner every day.*

LODGINGS

Casa Del Mar ★★★ Stinson Beach's only bed and breakfast is a 1989 Mediterranean villa nestled at the foot of Mount Tamalpais and surrounded by spectacular terraced gardens. Sunlight pours through the large windows into four simple Mediterranean-style rooms decorated with fresh flowers from the garden and colorful, whimsical works from West Marin artists. Permeated by the sound of the ocean and nearby Eskoot Creek, all the rooms have private balconies with French doors. Innkeeper Rick Klein (who has also done time as a lawyer and a fisherman) constructed his establishment to meld with the surroundings. The decor is refreshingly sparse—just a luscious platform bed, piled high with pillows and a down comforter, and a few comfortable chairs. The rooms with ocean views (Penthouse, Heron, and Shell) are our favorites. Breakfast features an ever-changing array of wonders like black bean, scallion, and ginger root pancakes or three-egg omelets with garden fresh sugar snap peas. During the day, sunbathe in Casa Del Mar's lovely walled garden or stroll down to the beach. ■ *Heading N on Hwy 1, turn right at the fire station to 37 Belvedere Ave; (415) 868-2124; Mail: PO Box 238, Stinson Beach, CA 94970; $$$; MC, V; checks OK.*

▼

BOLINAS

Home to a handful of rich and famous '60s rock stars, writers, and former hippies, Bolinas is one of the most reclusive towns in Northern California: residents regularly take down highway signs pointing the way to their rural enclave. Set on a forested knoll between the ocean and beautiful Bolinas Lagoon, Bolinas has a hopping cultural scene with frequent concerts and performances at the **Bolinas Community Center** (14 Wharf Road, (415) 868-2128), as well as live music (jazz, country, blues, and rock) almost every night at **Smiley's Schooner Saloon** (41 Wharf Road, (415) 868-1311). The **Bolinas Museum** (48 Wharf Road, (415) 868-0330, Fri–Sun) displays local artists along with exhibits of local history. Down the street, the **Bolinas Bakery** (20 Wharf Road, (415) 868-0211, open every day) offers good baked goods, pizza, and beer.

LODGINGS

Thomas' White House Inn ★ Thomas' White House Inn is a lot like the town of Bolinas—charming, offbeat, slightly funky, and surrounded by incredible beauty. From the front lawn, you can see the whole sweep of the Bay area coastline from Marin to Half Moon Bay. Almost every window has an ocean view; the tower has a widow's walk. There's even an aviary in the downstairs bathroom. The two guest rooms are upstairs: the larger has a cathedral ceiling, a lovely window seat with a view of the ocean, and rustic country decor; the smaller room, decorated in white wicker, also has a vaulted ceiling and window seat with a view. Owner Jackie Thomas serves a simple continental breakfast with pastries, juice, coffee, and tea. ■ *Call for directions; (415) 868-0279; Mail: PO Box 132, Bolinas, CA 94924; $$; no credit cards; checks OK.*

OLEMA

LODGINGS

Point Reyes Seashore Lodge ★★ Built in 1988, this three-story cedar inn is the perfect place for those who want the beauty of the country without giving up the creature comforts of the city. Most of the lodge's 21 rooms have fireplaces, telephones, down comforters, and whirlpool baths with views of the garden below. If price is no obstacle, try a two-story suite with a sleeping loft, refrigerator, wet bar, and breakfast delivered right to your room. One note of caution: the lodge is located on Highway 1, right next to a busy restaurant. For peace and quiet, look for a room in the northern wing. The inn serves a continental breakfast in the common room downstairs. ■ *N of junction at Hwy 1 and Sir Francis Drake Blvd; (415) 663-9000; 10021 Hwy 1, Olema, CA 94950; $$$; AE, DIS, MC, V; checks OK.*

Bear Valley Inn ★ Ron and JoAnne Nowell's pleasant (and reasonable) bed and breakfast is an ideal home base for exploring Point Reyes. The emphasis here is on the word "home"—because that's how the Nowells make you feel. Bear Valley Inn is quite small, with three rooms and two baths. As with most older homes with bedrooms close together, you might lack privacy when there's a full house. If concerned, request the Rose Room, slightly set off from the rest of the house. The buckwheat blueberry pancakes and Ron's mountain bike expertise (he owns the store next door) will keep you pedaling Point Reyes all day. ■ *1 block N of light in Olema; (415) 663-1777; 88 Bear Valley Rd, Olema, CA 94950; $$; AE, MC, V; checks OK.*

POINT REYES STATION

Point Reyes Station, affectionately known as "Mootown" for its noontime cow siren, is the social center of West Marin's vast ranching and farming community—and the gateway to **Point Reyes National Seashore**, 71,000 acres of forested coastal mountains, bare rolling hills, and windswept beaches. Stop by the **Bovine Bakery** (111315 Highway 1, (415) 663-9420, open every day) and load up on their "udderly divine" baked goods.

Before heading off into the wilds of Point Reyes, drop by

the **Bear Valley Visitors' Center,** (415) 663-1092), to pick up maps and hiking guides and visit **Kule Loklo,** an authentic reconstruction of a Miwok Indian village. Every July, native American basket-makers, wood- and stone-carvers, singers, and dancers convene here for an annual public celebration.

Point Reyes boasts dozens of beautiful beaches: **Limantour Beach** is excellent for swimming and bird-watching; wildflower fans will want to check out **Kehoe Beach** for its display of spring flowers. **Bear Valley Trail** runs from the visitors' center through a beautiful, foxglove-dotted creek canyon to Arch Rock, a natural arch in the seaside cliffs that you can walk through at low tide. Athletic sorts will want to test their aerobic fitness on the 307 stone steps leading up to the **Point Reyes Lighthouse** where you can see sea lions and grey whales (October to March, (415) 669-1534). Dress warmly.

RESTAURANTS

Station House Cafe ★★★ The Station is West Marin's favorite stop. The large dining room has high ceilings, parchment-colored walls, and a view of the open kitchen. Dinner begins with a basket of hot, light popovers and corn bread. You can count on chef Dennis Bold to work wonders with local produce, seafood, and Niman-Schell organic beef. You can either get homey fare such as chili or polenta with cheese and tomatoes or go for something more elaborate, such as chicken with cranberry chutney, creamed onions, shoestring yams, and green beans. The Niman-Schell calf's liver with onions and homemade catsup resembles nothing you'd find at a roadside diner. In the mornings, the Station House serves a tasty array of pancakes, waffles, and omelets. The specials, like berry-buckwheat pancakes and sausage scrapple, are usually the way to go. All the pastries, like the tart and delicious olallieberry muffins, are baked on the premises. ■ *On Hwy 1; (415) 663-1515; 11180 Main St, Point Reyes Station; $$; full bar; MC, V; no checks; breakfast, lunch, dinner every day.*

Chez Madeleine ★ With its knowledgeable, solicitous staff, this popular French country restaurant makes up in service what it lacks in ambience. Although Madeleine is no longer here, Chuck and Kristi Edwards continue to turn out reliable French classics. The menu changes seasonally, but you're likely to find a savory boeuf bourguignon, smooth cassoulet, and fricassée de lapin, along with pasta, seafood, and vegetarian specials. We always start with Chez Madeleine's chewy, nutty-flavored wild rice crêpes. Light eaters can make a delicious under-$10 meal of onion soup and caesar salad. The reasonably priced wine list is short but well-chosen. ■ *½ mile S of Point Reyes Station on Hwy 1; (415) 663-9177; 10905 Hwy 1, Point Reyes Station; $$; beer and wine; MC, V; checks OK; dinner Tues–Sun.*

▼

Point Reyes Station

▲

Taqueria La Quinta ★ Mexican folk music fills the air and bright colors abound at this cheerful taqueria where nothing on the menu is over $6. The taqueria offers a full selection of tacos, burritos, and tostadas with several different fillings—including a surprisingly tasty tofu variant. Their sopas are excellent, too; try a bowl of exquisite pozole surrounded by small, impeccably fresh piles of cilantro, chopped onion, and cabbage. There are four kinds of homemade salsas; one is only for the fire-resistant. ■ *Corner of 3rd St and Hwy 1; (415) 663-8868; 11285 State Rte 1, Point Reyes Station; $; beer only; no credit cards; checks OK; lunch, dinner Wed–Mon.*

LODGINGS

Thirty-Nine Cypress Remember the days when all your friends (and maybe you?) lived in big, sprawling communal houses that were warm, informal, friendly, and kind of funky? If so, Thirty-Nine Cypress will give you a major case of déjà vu. Thirty-Nine Cypress has an open floor plan, redwood paneling, plenty of glass, and a panoramic view across upper Tomales Bay marshland. The common rooms are stuffed with art work and books, and there's a fireplace to snuggle up to on cool nights. Three small guest rooms have private patios with outdoor showers (only for the hardiest sorts). Indoor showers cost a bit more. At the bottom of the hill on the 3½-acre plot is an outdoor hot tub overlooking the bay. In the morning, you'll enjoy deliciously sweet Cherry Tree cherry juice from Sonoma, a yogurt fruit salad, an egg and sausage casserole, and organic bread freshly baked by a neighbor in his outdoor stone oven. ■ *39 Cypress Rd, N of Point Reyes–Petaluma Rd, W to Cypress; (415) 663-1709; Mail: PO Box 176, Point Reyes Station, CA 94956; $$; MC, V; checks OK.*

INVERNESS

RESTAURANTS

Barnaby's by the Bay ★★ Located on Tomales Bay overlooking the Golden Hinde Marina, Barnaby's serves a wonderful variety of creative and well-prepared American regional dishes ranging from seafood to pasta and home-smoked barbecued meats. For appetizers, try the smoked Norwegian salmon with three nicely arrayed mustards or the tender, juicy Petaluma duck sausage with sweet and sour braised red cabbage and a grainy brown mustard. Chef Ron Ramos' melt-in-your-mouth beef brisket comes with a dense, bready corn pudding, spicy black beans, and coleslaw. We've also had the piquant Dungeness crab stir-fried in the shell with crisp Japanese vegetables and black bean sauce, and the sinfully rich fettuccine with poached salmon, shiitake mushrooms, leeks, and tomato concasse in white wine and olive oil. Service can be a little slow, so grab a table by the window. ■ *Approximately 1 mile W of Inverness at the Golden Hinde Motel; (415) 669-1114; 12938 Sir Francis Drake Blvd, Inverness; $$; beer and wine; MC, V; local checks only; lunch, dinner every day.*

Vladimir's Czech Restaurant ★ With its dark paneling, beer steins on the wall, and crackling wood fire, Vladimir's brings to mind the dark woods and frosty winters of Czechoslovakia. Tasty but heavy dishes like roast duck, pork, and wiener schnitzel come with dense but delicious dumplings. Vladimir's extensive list of European beers is a perfect match for the food. On weekends, the place feels like a tourist trap and the service is lackadaisical. During the week, however, things slow down and, if Vladimir is around to tell his war stories, eating here can be as entertaining as it is filling. ■ *Downtown Inverness; (415) 669-1021; 12785 Sir Francis Drake Blvd, Inverness; $$; full bar; no credit cards; checks OK; lunch Wed–Sun, dinner Tues–Sun.*

LODGINGS

Manka's Inverness Lodge and Restaurant ★★★★ For years Manka's was a mediocre Czech restaurant. Today, Manka's appears to do everything right. New owner Margaret Grade has transformed this former hunting lodge into an oasis of American rustic cuisine and an exquisite small inn. The restaurant is

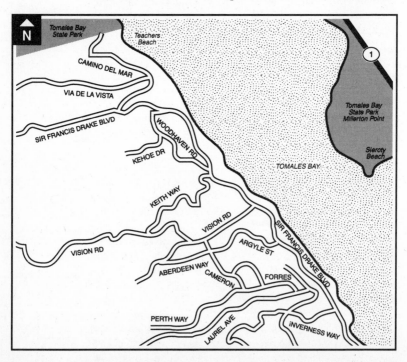

sublimely romantic, especially the intimate Fireplace Room with its roasting venison turning over a crackling fire in the large fireplace. Chefs Heather Staten and John Luther work magic with what Luther labels lodge food: roast suckling pig with winter squash gratin, pork stew with golden raisins and almonds, and poached Tomales Bay oysters with fall vegetables and cream. Save room for the simple but divine desserts such as persimmon pudding, homemade ice cream, and flourless chocolate cake. Service is attentive but discreet.

Upstairs, the Lodge's four rooms are right out of a Hans Christian Andersen fairy tale—small and cozy with tree-limb bedsteads, down comforters, high ceilings, and old-fashioned bathrooms. Rooms 1 and 2 extend out to large private decks overlooking Tomales Bay, perfect for sunrise breakfast. Manka's also has two spacious one-bedroom cabins in the woods with living rooms and kitchenettes. Morning delights (walnut-raspberry or chile pepper scones, applewood-smoked bacon, and a delicious Czech dish called kned licky a pivo—dumplings sautéed with onions and eggs served with rye toast and homemade marmalade) can be delivered to your room. ■ *W on Argyle St; (415) 669-1034; 30 Callendar St, Inverness; Mail: PO Box 1110, Inverness, CA 94937; $$$; beer and wine; MC, V; checks OK; dinner Thurs–Mon, brunch Sun.*

Blackthorne Inn ★★ With four levels, decks galore, a spiral staircase, and a whimsical fire pole for rapid exit from the main deck, the Blackthorne Inn looks like an overgrown treehouse in the forest. The romantic Eagle's Nest perches on the top level, with windows on all sides and a private deck. Walk across a skybridge to your bath—somewhat of a nuisance on cold and rainy nights. The spacious Studio and Hideaway rooms, which share a bath, have sitting areas looking into the woods. Blackthorne Inn serves a healthy buffet breakfast at 9:30am. ■ *¾ mile N of Bear Valley Rd and Sir Francis Drake Blvd, W to 266 Vallejo Ave; (415) 663-8621; Mail: PO Box 712, Inverness, CA 94937; $$$$; AE, MC, V; checks OK.*

Holly Tree Inn ★★ Nestled in a 19-acre valley with a meandering creek and wooded hillsides, the Holly Tree Inn makes an ideal retreat. Innkeepers Tom and Diane Balogh bought this 1938 farmhouse-turned-hunting-lodge-turned-bed-and-breakfast in the late 1970s. Its four cozy guest rooms, each with private bath, are decorated with Laura Ashley prints and country antiques. The large, airy living room has a fireplace and overstuffed chairs—a perfect place for savoring an afternoon glass of wine.

A dollhouse of a cottage is stashed in the woods, with comfortable chairs, a small fireplace, a kitchen, an old-fashioned tub, and a view of the hills. Breakfast goodies are delivered to the cottage the night before. ■ *From Hwy 1, turn W onto Bear*

Valley Rd; proceed for 2½ miles to 3 Silverhills Rd; (415) 663-1554; Mail: PO Box 642, Point Reyes Station, CA 94956; $$$; MC, V; checks OK.

Ten Inverness Way ★★ A curving flagstone stairway winds up through a lush garden to the wisteria-trellised entryway of this three-story, wood-shingled home built in 1904. The fir-paneled living room has a fine stone fireplace, comfortable couches, and a large array of *National Geographic* magazines awaiting your perusal. With their hooked rugs, lace curtains, and lovely quilts, the four upstairs guest rooms are warm and comfortable with good reading lamps, overstuffed chairs, and private baths. We particularly like room 4 with its raised platform bed looking out over Tomales Bay. Separated from the other rooms by a whole floor, room 3—with its sitting room, kitchen, and private garden—is perfect for a couple with a baby.

Innkeepers Mary Davies and Bonnie Fisk-Hayden's banana-buttermilk-buckwheat pancakes, chicken-apple sausages, fresh fruit, and grapefruit-apricot juice will fortify you for a long day of hiking in Point Reyes; when you return, you can soak your sore muscles in the garden hot tub. ■ *Turn left at Inverness Inn Restaurant just past Vladimir's, proceed to 10 Inverness Way; (415) 669-1648; Mail: PO Box 63, Inverness, CA 94937; $$$; MC, V; checks OK.*

Dancing Coyote Beach ★ The Miwok Indians called falling stars "dancing coyotes." It's hard to know what they'd think of this little piece of heaven stashed on the beach in a pine-covered cove. Decorated in pale Southwestern pastels and simple, spare furniture, the four cabins look more Hopi or Navajo than Miwok. All the cabins have sky-lit sleeping lofts, private decks, fireplaces, and fully equipped kitchens. Three of the units rent for $125 per night; the fourth for $95. Avoid Acacia cottage, which gets a fair amount of traffic noise. ■ *Just N of Inverness Grocery and Gas Station at 12794 Sir Francis Drake Blvd; (415) 669-7200; Mail: PO Box 98, Inverness, CA 94937; $$$; no credit cards; checks OK.*

MARSHALL

Tony's Seafood Restaurant The barbecued oysters are the only thing worth getting at Tony's, but they're so good that they alone are worth the drive to this ramshackle building on the east shore of Tomales Bay. Tony's has had 44 years to perfect its oyster technique—shucked right outside the door and barbecued in a piquant tomatoey broth as you watch. The rest of the shellfish is standard and fried. ■ *1 mile S of Marshall on Hwy 1; (415) 663-1107; 18863 State Route 1, Marshall, CA 94940; $; beer and wine; no credit cards; no checks; lunch, dinner Fri–Sun.*

LODGINGS

Tomales Country Inn ★ Genuinely eccentric. Owned for years by the painter Byron Randall, the inn used to be an inexpensive, down-at-the-heels, serve-yourself kind of place: the keys were left outside and you helped yourself in the kitchen. It was renowned for its art (Byron Randall's, natch) and its collection of hand-powered potato mashers. In 1989, KQED exec JoAnne Wallace and NPR reporter John McChesney bought the place, spiffed it up (unfortunately covering the floor with some jarringly ugly industrial strength carpeting), and renamed it the Tomales Country Inn. The inn retains its eccentricity *and* much of Byron Randall's artwork (he still lives in a neighboring cottage); the days of serve-yourself, however, are over. Innkeeper Peter Ruddick caters to his guests' every need. Best of all, thanks no doubt to the NPR connection, you'll often find brainy and interesting fellow guests here—the sort you'll be happy to chat with over breakfast. ■ *From Hwy 1 in central Tomales go W on Dillon Beach Rd, turn left to 25 Valley St; (707) 878-2041; Mail: PO Box 376, Tomales, CA 94971; $$; no credit cards; checks OK.*

US Hotel ★ The owners of this elegant, not-so-old "historic" hotel built it from the bottom up in 1989, using a photograph of the original 19th-century inn that burned down in 1920. And they've done a bang up job—this place is so authentic, so evocative of another time, that you could film a Western movie here and never need a set decorator. With high ceilings and antique furnishings, the US Hotel is a pleasingly crisp and private alternative to the fussy bed and breakfasts that abound along the coast. Service is extremely hands off, even a little cold. A self-serve continental breakfast of coffee and muffins is available in the upstairs sitting room. ■ *Center of town; (707) 878-2742; 26985 Hwy 1, Tomales, CA 94971; $$; AE, MC, V; no checks.*

▼

Valley Ford

Lodgings

▲

VALLEY FORD

LODGINGS

The Inn at Valley Ford ★ The Inn at Valley Ford is an 1860s Victorian farmhouse that's been lovingly restored by its current owner, Sandy Nichols. Decorated in Laura Ashley wallpapers and period antiques, the four guest rooms share two bathrooms. The Somerset Maugham Room is actually a separate cottage in the back. Because the Inn is small, the rooms near the front door can be a bit noisy; if you're a light sleeper, ask for the Sun Room or the cottage. Between 9 and 10am, Sandy serves a full country breakfast with fresh fruit, homemade scones, and eggs seasoned with herbs from her garden.

■ *14395 Hwy 1 in the center of town; (707) 876-3182; Mail: PO Box 439, Valley Ford, CA 94972; $; MC, V; checks OK.*

The Valley Ford Hotel ★ The pleasant and old-fashioned Valley Ford Hotel, built in 1864, is a good choice for travelers who prefer the privacy of a hotel to the close quarters of a bed and breakfast. It's not a spectacular place, but it's clean and quite comfortably furnished with overstuffed chairs and good, hard beds. The Valley Ford Hotel is a family-run operation, and that gives it a special charm. The Duffy family is very obliging. A continental breakfast is served downstairs. With advance notice, Peg Duffy will also cook dinner for you. ■ *14415 Hwy 1 in downtown Valley Ford; (707) 876-3600, toll free (800) 696-6679; Mail: PO Box 329, Valley Ford, CA 94972; $$; AE, DC, MC, V; checks OK.*

BODEGA BAY

Alfred Hitchcock probably wouldn't recognize Bodega Bay nowadays. When he filmed *The Birds* here in 1963, it was a tiny, white clapboard seacoast town. The intervening years have brought an explosion of vacation homes and condo construction on this windblown stretch of coast. (You can, however, still see the famed schoolhouse from *The Birds* in the neighboring town of Bodega, just off Bodega Highway.) Fishing remains big business in Bodega Bay. In April, you can catch the **Fisherman's Festival** and the **Blessing of the Fleet,** when 25,000 partiers flock to the free-wheeling boat parade, kite-flying championships, bathtub races, barbecues, and art shows. In a more pastoral vein, there's the week-long, 50-mile **Sonoma Coast Walk** from Gualala to Bodega Bay in August; (707) 579-8511.

The rocky Sonoma coast has a slew of fine beaches. Tranquil **Doran Park Beach,** just south of Bodega Bay, is the best and safest beach for kids. When the water's rough everywhere else, Doran is still calm enough for swimming, clamming, and crabbing. Bird-watchers will want to stake out the Doran mudflats, home to snowy egrets, brown pelicans, and blue herons. Tidepool fans should visit the north end of **Salmon Creek Beach,** 2 miles north of town, or **Shell Beach,** a small low-tide treasure trove just south of touristy **Goat Beach,** 13 miles north of Bodega. Whale-watchers should drive out to **Bodega Head Park** at the end of Bay Flat Road.

RESTAURANTS

Lucas Wharf Restaurant and Bar ★ Good fresh seafood marries well with the fine views of Bodega Bay and its harbor. The food is very similar to that at the Tides Wharf Restaurant just up the road, though Lucas Wharf has a slightly fancier decor and somewhat lower prices. Light eaters can happily make a meal of Lucas Wharf's wonderful smoked salmon pâté and a bowl of chowder. Others will twirl in a plate of garlic fettuccine with prawns. Ask your waiter for suggestions concerning the catch of the day. A good selection of microbrews. ■ *S end of town; (707) 875-3522; 595 Hwy 1, Bodega Bay; $$; full bar; MC, V; no checks; lunch, dinner every day.*

LODGINGS

Inn at the Tides ★★ Bodega Bay architecture tends toward "nouveau Californian"—wood-shingled boxes with lots of glass—and the Inn at the Tides is no exception. Perched on a hillside overlooking Bodega Bay, all 86 rooms have a fine view of the water, clean-lined, contemporary, spacious interiors, and a bunch of nice extras: terrycloth robes, fancy soaps, cable TV, coffee pots, refrigerators, and fresh flowers. Some of the rooms have fireplaces. You can swim in the indoor-outdoor pool or relax in the sauna and whirlpool baths. The inn's restaurant, the Bayview room, serves expensive, not particularly interesting California cuisine. ■ *N end of town at 800 Hwy 1; (707) 875-2751, toll free (800) 541-7788; Mail: PO Box 640, Bodega Bay, CA 94923; $$$; AE, MC, V; checks OK.*

Bodega Harbor Inn In a town where much looks brand-new, the Bodega Harbor Inn is a homey old-timer—an old-fashioned conglomeration of clapboard buildings with a big lawn overlooking the harbor. The inn rents out a number of houses and cottages, some on the property and some around town. The Hummingbird House, our favorite, sits on the edge of the lawn nearest the water and is divided into two suites; both have two bedrooms, a living room, and nice views. If you stay in the motel, try to get an end room with a view of the water—a real bargain by Bodega Bay standards. ■ *N end of town, turn E to 1345 Bodega Ave; (707) 875-3594; Mail: PO Box 161, Bodega Bay, CA 94923; $; MC, V; California checks only.*

Freestone

Lodgings

FREESTONE

This tiny farming community consists of 10, cute-as-a-button restored Victorian farmhouses. Check out the **Osmosis Enzyme Baths** (209 Bohemian Highway, (707) 823-8231), a spa offering a rare Japanese form of heat therapy. The baths are actually large, wooden boxes filled with hot and fragrant fermenting cedar sawdust. The treatment, including tea first and blanket wrap afterwards, costs about $40.

LODGINGS

Green Apple Inn ★ Rogers and Rosemary Hoffman bought this lovely little Victorian farmhouse on the outskirts of Freestone 12 years ago. From the moment Rogers and his dog Concierge greet you at the door, you know you're in the hands of a man who truly enjoys his role as an innkeeper. Staying at the Green Apple Inn is a bit like staying at the home of a favorite relative—where chatting with the amiable hosts and fellow guests is much of the appeal. The Green Apple Inn has four rooms in the farmhouse and a separate cottage. The nicest is the back room with its claw-footed tub and view of the Hoffmans' goat pasture. ■ *N edge of Freestone; (707) 874-2526; 520 Bohemian Hwy, Freestone, CA 95472; $$; MC, V; checks OK.*

OCCIDENTAL

RESTAURANTS

The Bohemian Cafe ★ Although it's the new kid on the only block in Occidental, the Bohemian Cafe's intimate dining rooms and casually elegant tables set it apart from its older competitors. The Athenian pizza with spinach, artichoke hearts, feta, and olives is particularly fine. We wish the spicy turkey had a bit more pep. At breakfast, flapjack fans should try the incredibly light "cotton cakes" with real maple syrup. The nicely seasoned home-fries go well with the large selection of frittatas, especially the herbacious frittata with its mix of fresh cilantro, basil, parsley, and garlic. The Hangtown fry, an oyster, ham-and-eggs combo with homemade applesauce, is also a favorite. ■ *S end of town; (707) 874-3931; 3688 Bohemian Hwy, Occidental; $$; beer and wine; MC, V; checks OK; breakfast, dinner Tues–Sun, lunch Sat–Sun.*

Howard Station Cafe This cheerful cafe in an old train station bustles on weekend mornings with local families enjoying the Station's homemade corned beef hash, or the eggs with home fries and Italian sausage. Pass on the omelets. For lunch, go for anything between two slices of bread, including the hamburger. The espresso, milk shakes, and beer are all good. ■ *Main St at 2nd; (707) 874-2838; 75 Main St, Occidental; $; beer and wine; no credit cards; no checks; breakfast, lunch every day.*

LODGINGS

The Inn at Occidental ★★ This meticulously renovated 1860s Victorian has wide covered porches, a walled garden, and a comfortable parlor. Its eight airy and spacious rooms, each with private bath, are softened with antiques, down comforters, large European down pillows, and fresh flowers. The Master Suite has a brick fireplace, an antique pine four-poster bed, a shower for two, and a private balcony overlooking the rooftops of Occidental. At press time, Robert H. McDaniel took over as the new innkeeper. Reportedly, he'll cook you anything you want for breakfast; even lunch and dinner in case you never want to venture beyond the garden terrace. ■ *From Main St, turn E to 3657 Church St; (707) 874-1311, or toll free*

(800) 551-2292; Mail: PO Box 857, Occidental, CA 95465;
$$$$; AE, MC, V; checks OK.

SEBASTOPOL

Sebastopol boasts a good bookstore (**Copperfield's,** 138 North Main), a bagel store (**The Grateful Bagel,** 200 South Main Street), and several excellent restaurants. Despite these urbane outposts, this part of Sonoma County is still primarily agricultural—you'll happen on many farm and U-pick stands. To find several stands all in one place, check out the **Farmers' Market** (McKinley Street at Petaluma Avenue, Sundays 11am–2pm, June through October). Berries are best in the pies at **Mom's Apple Pie,** 4½ miles north of Sebastopol on Hwy 116; (707) 823-8330. Local wineries include **Iron Horse Vineyards,** creators of prestige sparkling wines (9786 Ross Station Road, (707) 887-2913) and **Dehlinger Winery,** specializing in chardonnay, pinot noir, and merlot (6300 Guerneville Road, (707) 823-2378). Kids will enjoy interacting with the critters of the **Pet-A-Llama Ranch** (5505 Lone Pine Road, (707) 823-9395).

RESTAURANTS

Truffles ★★★ The decor here is run-of-the-mill postmodern—pleasantly peach-colored walls with black track lighting—but the food is spectacular. The fresh-baked bread that begins each meal is fragrant with orange and coriander, and the pleasingly light appetizers of tempura squash blossoms filled with a creamy mixture of white corn, tomatoes, and goat cheese are miniature masterpieces. Entrées include multicultural wonders like duck canneloni with Indonesian peanut sauce (sounds weird, but it works) and salmon with pepper and tomatillo salsa. The salmon comes with yellow wax beans wrapped in a spicy chapatilike tortilla and some lightly sautéed vegetables. There's always a splendid array of desserts, including crumbly peach shortcake and creamy chocolate mousse torte. The extensive wine list showcases Sonoma County wines. ■ *Center of town; (707) 823-8448; 234 South Main St, Sebastopol; $$$; beer and wine; MC, V; no checks; lunch Mon–Fri, dinner every day.*

Chez Peyo ★★ Don't be put off by the unprepossessing decor—the orange chairs and tacky landscape photographs tell nothing of the fine fish and pastas. Chef Pierre Lagourgue isn't bothered by modern ideas about fat and cholesterol. His dishes are the old-fashioned, artery-clogging kind—slathered with thick, creamy béarnaise sauce or drenched in Swiss cheese. Warning: even the light dinners, like the grilled fish, are sinfully rich. The lemon tart and the Grand Marnier mousse cake are both delectable. ■ *On Gravenstein Hwy, 2 miles S of town; (707) 823-1262; 2295 Gravenstein Hwy S, Sebastopol; $$;*

beer and wine; MC, V; checks OK; lunch Tues–Sat, dinner Tue–Sun, brunch Sun.

LODGINGS

The Gravenstein Inn ★★ Built in 1872, this charming yellow farmhouse in the middle of an apple orchard is completely free of the studied quaintness of so many bed and breakfasts. Hosts Jacque and Don Mielke make you feel like you're right at home—in their very beautiful home. Of the four guest rooms, we especially love the Bavarian Suite, with its fireplace and a private sun porch overlooking the orchard. Downstairs, the parlor has comfortable chairs and a Chickering grand piano; you're welcome to tickle the ivory all evening if you desire. The back porch has wicker furniture, a hammock, and a view of the pond where fish surface to be petted by Jacque. The heated swimming pool is shaded by a giant sycamore. ■ *3½ miles N of Sebastopol, corner of Hicks and Graton roads; (707) 829-0493; 3160 Hicks Rd, Sebastopol, CA 95472; $$; no credit cards; checks OK.*

FORESTVILLE

From Forestville you can launch an all-day canoe trip down the gentle **Russian River**. Set forth from **Burke's Canoe Trips** and someone there will pick you up 10 miles down the river and take you back to your car; (707) 887-1222. The tiny main drag of this town includes **Brother Juniper's Cafe** (6544 Front Street; closed Sun), home of some of the yummiest breads on the planet. You'll also want to check out **Koslowski Farms,** a family farm turned gourmet food business. Their apple butter, jams, and vinegars are sold in foodie boutiques all over Sonoma County; 5566 Gravenstein Highway N, (707) 887-1587.

RESTAURANTS

Russian River Vineyards Restaurant ★★ Sheltered by redwood trees, the back patio of this intimate Greek restaurant has a waterfall and luxuriant native plants. Not Mediterranean perhaps, but definitely delightful. Chefs Bob Engel and Christine Topolos know how to make Greek food the way it's served in Greece: every meal comes with tzatziki, a garlic-laden cucumber-yogurt dip, and a tomato stuffed with aromatic ratatouille. The meze appetizer plate, a bit small for the price, comes with dolmathes, tiropita (cheese pie), marinated eggplant, and feta. Feast on pesto prawns, prawns with tomato, feta, and dill, or swordfish steak with garlic and ginger. The wine list is strictly Russian River Vineyards organic varietals. Have fun—ask them to bring a different glass of wine with each course of your meal. ■ *½ mile past Forestville on Hwy 116; (707) 887-1562; 5700 Gravenstein Hwy, Forestville; $$; wine only; AE, DC, MC, V; local checks only; lunch, dinner every day, brunch Sun.*

The Farmhouse Inn ★ The Farmhouse Inn's guest cottages can fool. What resemble little more than roadside motel cabins are much more luxurious minilodgettes with plushy carpets, fireplaces, saunas, and oversized Jacuzzi tubs. The grounds include a large swimming pool and six acres of hills and redwoods. Guests gather for breakfast in the restored turn-of-the-century farmhouse with its country-style furniture, giant fireplace, and homelike couches. Breakfast includes fruit, cereal, hot dishes like huevos rancheros and eggs Florentine, as well as homemade croissants, scones, and other delights. Huge, $24 prix-fixe dinners are also available. ■ *At Wohler and River roads; (707) 887-3300, toll free (800) 464-6642 in California; 7871 River Rd, Forestville, CA 95436; $$$; MC, V; checks OK.*

MONTE RIO

Local boosters of this blink-and-you'll-miss-it town have put a gigantic banner over the main street announcing that you are indeed in Monte Rio. Earlier this century, Monte Rio and nearby Cazadero were destinations on the old North Pacific coastline railroad that took thousands of vacationers from the Bay area to the Russian River each summer. Now there's not much here besides the flamingo-pink Rio movie theater and a few mediocre restaurants. A few miles away is **Bohemian Grove,** the exclusive all-male resort where rich and powerful politicians and CEOs dress up like women and cavort naked around bonfires before returning home to preach about family values and the joys of the Protestant work ethic.

Monte Rio

Lodgings

LODGINGS

Huckleberry Springs Country Inn ★★★ A stunning mountain resort surrounded by redwoods and decorated with a smattering of Southwestern art, the secluded cabins here have skylights, decks, wood stoves and two-person hammocks stretched between trees. Best is the barrel-shaped cabin, Cherry Barrel. A short walk through the redwoods takes you to the main house with its comfortable sofas, sun-splashed window-seats, and an intriguing collection of games. The swimming pool looks over a ravine—and there's a hot tub tucked among the trees a short distance up the hill.

The real raison d'être of the inn are the solarium's multicourse meals, included in the price of the room. Innkeeper Suzanne Greene's cooking emphasizes local ingredients: organic greens and vegetables from nearby farms, salmon and crab from Bodega Bay, and spring lambs from a local rancher. A recent dinner included tomato-fennel soup, Sonoma greens with a champagne vinaigrette, and a choice of two entrées:

roast pork loin stuffed with cashews and sun-dried cherries in a rosemary sherry sauce; and angel hair pasta with bay shrimp, halibut, scallops, roasted red peppers, and onions in a wine sauce. Cassis whipped cream enlivened a traditional strawberry shortcake. No better way to wake up the next morning than to one of Suzanne's breakfasts. ■ *Take Tyrone off the Bohemian Hwy and follow the signs to 8105 Old Beedle Rd; (707) 865-2683, toll free (800) 822-2683; Mail: PO Box 400, Monte Rio, CA 95462; $$; beer and wine; AE, MC, V; checks OK.*

GUERNEVILLE

Guerneville's longtime residents have seen their town change character every decade. First it was a haven for bikers—the leather, not the Lycra sort—then for hippies. Now it's the hot spot for Bay area gays and others attracted by the calm beauty of the redwoods and the Russian River.

The town itself is a good launching spot for winery visits or outdoor expeditions. Stop by **Korbel Champagne Cellars** (13250 River Road, (707) 887-2294) for a free tasting. **Armstrong Woods State Reserve** is a preternaturally peaceful grove of ancient redwoods with a variety of hiking trails; 17000 Armstrong Woods Road, (707) 869-2015. **Armstrong Woods Pack Station** offers half- and full-day horse rides with gourmet lunches; (707) 579-1520. From May to October, rent canoes and paddle boats at **Johnson's Beach,** just under the main bridge; (707) 869-2045. Johnson's Beach is also home to the **Russian River Jazz Festival,** held every September; (707) 869-3940. For reliably good, uncomplicated meals—including a rich, cheesey lasagna—try **Burdon's**; 15405 River Road, Guerneville, (707) 869-2615. Finally, in the weird-but-fun category, there's **Pee Wee Golf,** a wonderfully psychedelic miniature golf course; (707) 869-2887.

LODGINGS

Applewood ★★★ Set on a forested hillside, this gorgeous, sprawling, 1922 California Mission Revival mansion shines with buff-colored stucco, tile roofs, and dark beams. Filled with high-quality antiques and original artwork, the 10 lovely and secluded guest rooms look out into the feathery branches of the surrounding redwoods. All have private baths, well-hidden TVs, and fresh flowers. Room 1, decorated in soothing forest green and English oak, has French doors opening onto a private patio and garden; room 4 has a Louis Phillipe cherry-wood sleigh bed and a sitting room with huge curved bay windows. Downstairs are two comfortable fireplace sitting rooms and a lovely rose-colored dining room with high-arched ceilings and French doors leading out into the garden. For breakfast, you find eggs Florentine, French toast, or other well-prepared treats elegantly served among crisp linens and fresh cut flowers. We have yet to try Applewood's extravagant five-course dinner ($25–$35 extra), but we've heard it's fabulous. The staff is friendly and helpful, and the atmosphere is far more relaxed than you would expect at such an elegant hotel. Outside is a pool, Jacuzzi, and a small garden. ■ *1 mile S of Guerneville; (707) 869-9093; 13555 Hwy 116, Pocket Canyon, CA 95446; $$$; AE, DIS, MC, V; no checks.*

Santa Nella House ★★ Sitting on the wraparound verandah of this Victorian farmhouse, you can hear the whir of cicadas, the croak of tree frogs, and the burble of the Jacuzzi. Santa Nella's four guest rooms are decorated with antiques, old quilts, and dried flowers. All rooms have fireplaces; some have antique claw-footed tubs. The Blue Room is a large, airy chamber with a view of the redwoods from the queen-size bed and a white brass day bed for afternoon naps. Owners Ed and Joyce Ferrington are like some sort of idealized '50s parents: in the morning, Ed will encourage you to eat ungodly amounts of Joyce's delicious waffles or eggs Benedict; in the evening, Joyce will want to hear all about your day. ■ *1½ miles S of Guerneville; (707) 869-9488; 12130 Hwy 116, Guerneville, CA 95446; $$; MC, V; checks OK.*

Ridenhour Ranch House Inn ★ Sunny rooms and colorful antique quilts give this 1906 ranch the sense of a summerhouse. The Russian River is just across the road and Korbel Champagne Cellars is next door. The inn has seven rooms in the main house. The three upstairs rooms share a bathroom; the downstairs rooms have private baths. Don't bother with the Laurel Suite: the sitting room with its wall of windows is nice, but its dark bedroom is too close to the stairs. Instead, request the bright Spruce Room, whose windows invite a fresh breeze through the madronas and lilacs. Outside is an old-fashioned rose garden and a tree-shaded hot tub. ■ *3 miles E of the main bridge; (707) 887-1033; 12850 River Rd, Guerneville, CA 95446; $$$; MC, V; checks OK.*

The Willows ★ The Willows prides itself on its convivial, hang-loose atmosphere. An immense lawn sweeps down from the back of the lodge to the shores of the Russian River. On warm afternoons, relax in the Jacuzzi, lounge in a lawn chair, or live out your Huck Finn fantasies in one of the lodge's canoes. There's even a nude-sunbathing beach. The cheapest rooms are barely distinguishable from your average motel room. Ask for a river view room (numbers 4–8 and 15)—each is decorated with simple wood furnishings and flowered quilts. Room 4 has a sitting room with a big-screen TV and VCR. All guests receive a continental breakfast and have access to the fully equipped kitchen and outdoor barbecue—even those who pitch a tent on the edge of the lawn. ■ *½ mile E of the main*

bridge at 15905 River Rd; (707) 869-3279; Mail: PO Box 465,
Guerneville, CA 95446; $$; AE, MC, V; no checks.

JENNER

Built along Highway 1 on a bluff rising up from the mouth of
the Russian River, the village of Jenner looks out over a vast
tidal lagoon, rimmed on the west by a sweeping milelong beach
swarming with harbor seals. On weekends, orange-vested vol-
unteers answer questions about the seals and lend out binoc-
ulars. A winding, 12-mile drive north on Highway 1 takes you
to **Fort Ross State Historic Park,** a beautifully preserved fort
built by Russian fur traders in 1813. Beyond is Timber Cove,
one of photographer Ansel Adams' favorite places, and **Salt
Point State Park,** (707) 847-3221. Perfect for day hiking, Salt
Point has 14 miles of trails through coastal woodlands, wild-
flower meadows, and rocky beaches. In May and June, the
forests of the neighboring **Kruse Rhododendron Preserve**
are awash in bright pink and purple blossoms.

LODGINGS

Murphy's Jenner Inn ★ The accommodations at Murphy's
Jenner Inn are scattered throughout a cluster of cottages and
houses along Highway 1. Most houses divide into suites or
smaller rooms, but there are a few free-standing cottages. We
especially enjoy the rooms in the River House, a pretty
Victorian-style home. Set back from the highway, the River
House, with views of the Russian River and harbor seals, is
somewhat more protected from traffic noise than are some of
the other cottages. Breakfast is in the main lodge, warmed by
a sun parlor and wood stove. ■ *1 mile N of Hwy 116, S of town;
(707) 865-2377; Mail: PO Box 69, Jenner, CA 95450; $$;
MC, V; checks OK.*

Timber Cove Inn ★ Set on a rocky promontory high above the
roiling surf of Timber Cove, this pricey, austere inn sits in the
shadow of artist Benny Bufano's huge, missilelike sculpture of
the Virgin Mary. Except for the Ansel Adams prints dotting the
walls, the woody Zen decor is a tad sparse, but most rooms
have fireplaces and indoor (or outdoor) hot tubs. The rooms
in the northern wing face directly out to sea (perfect for whale-
watching), while other less-expensive rooms face the misty
hills or the Japanese sculpture garden with swans and annoyingly noisy geese. The cathedral-like lobby has a massive fireplace and a large cast-iron candelabra sporting years worth of
stalactitelike candle drippings. The restaurant offers decent if
uninspired country-club fare. ■ *4 miles N of Fort Ross on
Hwy 1; (707) 847-3231; Mail: 21780 North Coast Hwy 1, Jen-
ner, CA 95450; $$$$; AE, DC, MC, V; checks OK; breakfast,
lunch, dinner every day.*

RESTAURANTS

The Food Company ★ If the Food Company were located in San Francisco, it would be just another chic little deli. On this relatively undeveloped section of the southern Mendocino coast, however, great coffee and light lunches are tough to find. Take your cold poached salmon or Swedish meatballs out to the bright back deck or pack a gourmet picnic for the beach. They've also got a big selection of modestly priced California wines and good fresh-baked bread. ■ *½ mile N of Gualala, W side of Hwy 1; (707) 884-1800; $$; beer and wine; no credit cards; checks OK; lunch, early dinner every day.*

LODGINGS

St. Orres ★★★★ Back in the early '70s, a group of young architects and builders took their back-to-the-land dreams to Gualala and created this dazzling copper-domed inn on a bluff above the ocean where 11 private cottages jewel the 42-acre grounds. The modestly priced Wildflower Cabin has a sleeping loft and outside shower. The most luxurious, the turreted Pine Haven, is studded with stained glass, two broad decks, and three bedrooms. There are eight small but surprisingly uncramped rooms in the charming inn built of redwood timbers scrounged from old logging mills and dilapidated bridges. Request one of the two view rooms, suffused with the delightful smell of dinner wafting up from below.

Gualala

Lodgings

Architecture and decor aside, the restaurant is the real reason that people keep coming back to St. Orres. Reserve a table for dinner when you make your room reservation: breakfast comes with the room, but dinner doesn't and the restaurant is always booked. Even with reservations, there's usually a short wait—spend it in the exquisite fireside wine bar. The restaurant fills the inn's south tower with its high, domed ceiling and three-story windows. St. Orres' menu focuses on wild game, including venison, quail, pheasant, and boar. Self-taught chef Rosemary Campiformio's dark and fruity sauces are perfectly suited to the flavorful game—a distinctly Northern California rendition of French country cuisine. We particularly like the complex huckleberry sauce served with the rich, roast boar; the steamed mussels; and the sea bass poached in parchment. From soups to sauces, Campiformio has a definite sweet tooth and her creations aren't always seasonally appropriate—one crisp autumn evening we were offered a cold-and-creamy strawberry soup—but the food is so good it's hard to quibble. ■ *2 miles N of Gualala at 36601 Hwy 1; (707) 884-3303; Mail: PO Box 523, Gualala, CA 95445; $$$; beer and wine; MC, V; checks OK; dinner every day (Thurs–Tues in winter).*

The Old Milano Hotel ★★ Nestled in the trees on a cliff above Castle Rock Cove, this lovely 1905 hotel with its old-fashioned white verandah has six bedrooms and a downstairs suite. All but one (the Garden View Room) feature wonderful views of the ocean. Two less spectacular but more private rooms are located elsewhere—one inside an old railroad caboose. Try the restaurant's roasted garlic and Brie appetizer with the rich, oregano-saturated herb bread. Entrées include pork tenderloin with plum chutney, roast rack of lamb, quail, and shellfish. Breakfast can be served in your room, on the garden patio, or by a fire in the parlor. ■ *1 mile N of Gualala on Hwy 1; (707) 884-3256; 38300 Hwy 1, Gualala, CA 95445; $$$; beer and wine; AE, MC, V; checks OK; breakfast every day for guests, dinner (guests and non-guests) Tues–Sun.*

POINT ARENA

RESTAURANTS

The Galley at Arena Cove Once located in the dingy old port building, the Galley has now moved to a big, modern, redwood-sided mini-mall replete with tacky gift shops, a pizzeria, offices, and a fish market. Fortunately, the inexpensive dock-fresh fish it serves is as good as it was when the restaurant was in the picturesque port. The huge, fried seafood platter with scallops, shrimp, rock fish, and clam strips comes with a mound of crisp fries and vegetables. The tartar and cocktail sauces are bland, but the very crisp beer batter is terrific. Grab a seat by the window for the best view, and don't forget to check out the bar—a vast, antique, carved oak creation, imported all the way from the old Tommy's Joynt in San Francisco. ■ *W from Hwy 1 on Iverson Dr to the Arena Cove complex; (707) 882-2189; 790 Port St, Point Arena; $; full bar; DIS, MC, V; checks OK; breakfast, lunch Wed–Mon, dinner every day.*

LODGINGS

Coast Guard House ★ Perched above Arena Cove, this beautiful, romantic Cape Cod cottage was originally built by the Life-Saving Service in 1901. Beacon lamps, anchors, and a sea captain's hat tossed haphazardly on a table evoke Point Arena's seafaring past, but the inn's Arts and Crafts interiors, designed by innkeepers Richey Wasserman and Merita Whatley, remain simple and uncluttered. The rooms have all-cotton linens and fluffed down comforters, as well as a nice selection of organic soap, shampoo, conditioner, and body lotion. The Surfman Cove Room, with windows on three sides, has a beautiful view of the ocean and cove, and a sunken Japanese tub. Merita and Richey serve a lavish but healthful continental breakfast with fruit, their own muesli with toasted almonds and apples, and soft cheeses like Brie or Camembert. ■ *1 mile W of Point*

Arena at 695 Arena Cove; (707) 882-2442; Mail: PO Box 117, Point Arena, CA 95468; $$$; MC, V; checks OK.

ELK

RESTAURANTS

Roadhouse Cafe ★ The Roadhouse Cafe doubles as the town garage. On one side of the building Bob Matson repairs autos; on the other, Sue Matson pulls espressos. Customers sip lattes and flip through copies of the *Ridge Review*, the local literary magazine. The breakfast menu lists all the usual standards (eggs, omelets, pancakes, and French toast), but more fun are the chalkboard specials—like the fluffy omelets with roasted garlic, sautéed red peppers, and goat cheese; or the breakfast burritos stuffed with spicy black beans and scrambled eggs and topped with guacamole and freshly made salsa. Don't leave without trying Sue's light and flaky scones studded with currants and grated orange peel. ■ *Next to the Shell Station on Hwy 1; (707) 877-3285; 6061 S Hwy 1, Elk; $; beer and wine; no credit cards; checks OK; breakfast, lunch Tues–Sun.*

LODGINGS

Greenwood Pier Inn ★★ Visually stunning interiors are what separate this cliff-top wonder from the dozens of other precariously perched inns along Highway 1. Innkeepers and artists Isabel Petty and Here Kendrick have combined Petty's whimsical, avant-garde decor and Kendrick's collages to eye-catching effect in the inn's eight rooms and three cliff-hanging suites. All the rooms have fireplaces or wood stoves, but we like the suites best. A favorite suite is the older, elegantly rustic Cliff House with its wonderful deck, marble fireplace, Jacuzzi, and Oriental carpets. These are very expensive, but the rooms in the main house are moderately priced. The innkeepers deliver a tasty continental breakfast at your door every morning, including blueberry turnovers, rhubarb coffee cake, fruit, and coffee. Three-course dinners are possible, too. ■ *In the center of town at 5928 Hwy 1; (707) 877-9997 or (707) 877-3423; Mail: PO Box 36, Elk, CA 95432; $$$; AE, MC, V; checks OK.*

Harbor House Inn and Restaurant ★★ In 1915, the California timber industry unveiled its house of the future—"The Home of Redwood"—at the Panama–Pacific International Exhibition in San Francisco. The next year, Goodyear Redwood Lumber Company built a larger replica of this palatial home on a bluff above Greenwood Landing. Bought by Helen and Dean Turner in 1985, Harbor House is now a luxurious inn and restaurant. The living room downstairs boasts a huge country fireplace, Persian rugs, and comfortable couches. Upstairs, the Harbor Room, a romantic suite with a fireplace, provides a view of the cliffs and surf. The Lookout Room, smaller and less expensive,

▼

Elk

Lodgings

▲

has a small private balcony that opens onto Cuffey's Cove.

The four-course prix-fixe dinner begins with a small, hot-from-the-oven loaf of bread (rye, Portuguese sweet pepper cheese, or herb) perfect for sopping up the delicious soups like tomato-basil or Indian spice-spinach. The salad might be simple mixed greens with herb vinaigrette or sunsprouts with olives and water chestnuts in toasted sesame-seed dressing. Chef Terry Garner seldom repeats nightly entrées, but she receives raves on Harbor House favorites like blanquette of veal, champagne chicken with grapes, or broiled, marinated ling cod. To take full advantage of this restaurant's spectacular view, make a reservation for just before sunset and request a table near the huge wall of windows. Meals are included with your room, but not restricted to guests at the inn. ■ *5600 S Hwy 1; (707) 877-3203; Mail: PO Box 369, Elk, CA 95432; $$$; beer and wine; no credit cards; checks OK; breakfast, dinner every day.*

Griffin House at Greenwood Cove ★ These art deco cottages are named after the colorful figures who settled this part of the coast in the 1800s—characters like Charlie Li Foo, the one-legged town barber, or Gunderson, a Norwegian ship captain known for his swimming prowess. For fabulous views of the rocky coastline and its spectacular arches, ask for the cliff-top cottages, specifically Matson. No matter which cottage you choose, you'll find a basket of wine and fruit on arrival. Innkeeper Leslie Griffin-Lawson is a charming host, warm and friendly without being the least bit intrusive. Every morning she delivers a breakfast of wild rice waffles or a spicy Mexican soufflé with chiles, cheddar cheese, avocado, and salsa to your cottage door. ■ *Center of town at 5910 S Hwy 1; (707) 877-3422; Mail: PO Box 172, Elk, CA 95432; $$$; MC, V; checks OK.*

ALBION

RESTAURANTS

The Ledford House ★★ A country-French restaurant touting one of the best views on the Mendocino coast. Last year, a wayfaring whale wintered in the waters right below the cliff-top dining room. Owners Lisa and Tony Geer can't guarantee such cetacean spectacles every year, but they do their best to make sure you'll have a stunning repast. Meals resemble those at choice auberges in rural France and feature hearty one-pot bistro dishes (fisherman's stew or the vegetarian meal in a bread bowl). The less provincial might want to start out with the wild mushroom timbale, followed by stuffed leg of lamb, garlic and rosemary roasted chicken, or fumet-poached ling cod with basil vinaigrette. Ask for a window table, set beneath billowed floral curtains. ■ *S of Albion on Hwy 1; (707) 937-0282; 3000 N Hwy 1, Albion; $$; full bar; MC, V; checks OK; dinner Wed–Sun, brunch Sun.*

LODGINGS

Albion River Inn ★★★ After a long period of ups and downs, this inn high above the white water of the Albion River is well on its way to becoming one of the best on the coast. The man behind this transformation is chef David Wells, son of co-owner Peter Wells and a veteran of the Culinary Institute of America and trendy California restaurants. His grilled vegetable terrine with tomato vinaigrette and spinach coulis is a colorful and delicious starter. The specials—like Sterling salmon with jalapeño spoon bread—are usually the best choice, but the seafood in spicy broth from the regular menu is also a winner. In the morning, the inn provides a buffet breakfast of fruit, fried potatoes, muffins, and eggs cooked to order. This spacious inn and restaurant has beautiful whitewater views and warm, sophisticated decor. The 20 cliff's edge cottages, most of them duplexes, include deluxe room 5 with deck, Jacuzzi, and ocean view, but you can also get a smaller room (try numbers 17 and 18) with a view for considerably less. ■ *On the NW side of the Albion bridge at 3790 N Hwy 1; (707) 937-1919, toll free (800) 479-7944; Mail: PO Box 100, Albion, CA 95410; $$$; full bar; MC, V; checks OK; dinner every day.*

LITTLE RIVER

Clinging to the steep wooded hillsides above Van Damme cove, Little River is more like a precious suburb of Mendocino than a town in its own right. At **Van Damme State Park** you'll find 15 miles of hiking trails winding up from the beach through the redwood-covered hills; (707) 937-5804. You can also hike or drive to Van Damme's peculiar **Pygmy Forest,** a scrub forest growing on a limestone deposit 3½ miles up Little River–Airport Road from Highway 1. Van Damme is awash in vibrant pink rhododendrons during the spring.

LODGINGS

Heritage House ★★★★ Immortalized as the ultimate sea coast bed and breakfast in the movie *Same Time, Next Year,* Heritage House has a history well-suited to Hollywood melodrama: its secluded farmhouse was used as a safe house for smugglers of Chinese laborers during the 19th century, for rumrunners during Prohibition, and for the notorious bandit "Baby Face" Nelson during the '30s.

Since 1949, the Dennen family has opened its gracious cottages and 1877 farmhouse to a considerably tamer crowd. Nestled among cypress trees, bountiful flower and vegetable gardens, and broad green lawns, Heritage House sits on a cliff overlooking a rocky cove. The best rooms are the cliff-hanging Carousel suites or, for big spenders, Sea Cliff Vista #3, with its glass-enclosed sun porch, panoramic view of the ocean, deck, and Jacuzzi. All room prices include breakfast and dinner.

The spectacular domed dining room with its pastel-colored fruit-and-flowers fresco painted by local artist Stefan Kehr is the perfect showcase for chef Eric Leonard's exquisite cuisine. (There are several dining rooms, so ask to sit here.) A recent meal delivered delicious appetizers that included lobster-textured rock shrimp in a lemon grass and coconut-scented broth with a swirl of lemon aioli, and Thai beef salad with paper-thin strips of spicy beef latticed over greens and tomatoes with a chile-infused red curry dressing. For the main course, there were tender slices of rosemary- and basil-encrusted rare lamb with a stewy mélange of carrots, turnips, rutabagas, and tender French flageolets from the garden; and a simple pan-seared fillet of petrale sole with a colorful mix of artichoke hearts, pink rock shrimp, and whole chanterelles. Sommelier Joseph Stein (whose wine list is consistently ranked among the top in the country) holds two-day winemaker seminars in a separate dining room furnished with antique English sideboards and chandeliers. ■ *N of Dark Gulch on Hwy 1; (707) 937-5885; 5200 N Hwy 1, Little River, CA 95456; $$$; full bar; MC, V; checks OK; breakfast, dinner every day (closed Dec–Jan).*

▼

Little River

Lodgings

▲

Glendeven ★★★ Jan and Janet deVries' stately 19th-century farmhouse resides among well-tended gardens and heather-covered headlands that extend to the blue Pacific. Graced by Jan's fine carpentry and Janet's interior design, the spacious and inviting rooms are a clean, uncluttered mix of country antiques and contemporary art. For ultimate luxury, try the Stevenscroft Annex; the Pinewood and Bayloft suites are our favorites—each has a sitting parlor, fireplace, and Pacific view. The Barn House Suite (located above Glendeven Gallery, the local fine art showcase) is a two-story, redwood-paneled house perfect for families. After breakfast, walk to the Fern Canyon trails in Van Damme State Park. ■ *N of Van Damme State Park; (707) 937-0083; 8221 N Hwy 1, Little River, CA 95456; $$$; MC, V; checks OK.*

Little River Inn ★★★ This striking resort, with its green and white gingerbread trim and bountiful flower gardens, is perfect for North Coast travelers who can't leave their clubs and racquets at home. Susan McKinney operates the inn and restaurant; her brother Dan Hervilla runs the golf and tennis club. The rooms in the Victorian main house and connecting cottages flaunt majestic vistas of the surf and Van Damme State Park. Ask for a west-facing suite with a deck to take full advantage of the inn's ideal location.

Best known for her addictive bread sticks and large, deftly seasoned dishes like pepper steak spiked with a brandy and peppercorn sauce, chef Judy Griswold plays with innovative additions like the margarita swordfish and hazelnut prawns. The Little River Inn sunset soup is a moiré mélange of beets, tomatoes, jicama, basil, onions, and garlic with a flash of saffron cream. On Wednesdays, Griswold prepares a fixed-price Mexican menu that often includes such delights as tamales with black beans, spicy green rice, chile relleno casserole, and white corn chowder. For breakfast, go for Ole's wonderful Swedish hotcakes. ■ *Across from the Little River Market and Post Office at 7751 N Hwy 1; (707) 937-5942; Mail: N Hwy 1, Little River 95456; $$$; full bar; no credit cards; checks OK; breakfast, dinner every day (restaurant closed Jan).*

MENDOCINO

Mendocino has managed to retain more of its gracious, small-town allure than most coastal getaway spots. Set on heather-covered headlands, this classic New England–style fishing village (complete with white-spired church) is still home to a few fishermen and loggers, but writers, artists, therapists, and other urban transplants now outnumber the natives. (Mendocino County is rumored to have the highest percentage of PhDs of any rural county in the country.) Climbing tea roses and wisteria wind around the town's Victorians, sedate salt-boxes, and converted water towers, while tall mantilla poppies wave in the stiff breeze off the ocean.

There are dozens of galleries in town, offering everything from fine arts and crafts to touristy seascapes. **Gallery Fair** at Kasten and Ukiah streets shows exquisite contemporary paintings, fine jewelry, and hand-crafted furniture; (707) 937-5121. Mendocino's two museums, the **Ford House** (735 Main Street, (707) 937-5397) and the **Kelly House** (45007 Albion Street, (707) 937-5791), offer historical exhibits and programs throughout the year. **The Mendocino Art Center,** housed in the mansion featured in James Dean's *East of Eden*, offers art classes, poetry readings, storytelling, and music; 45200 Little Lake Street, (707) 937-5818. Morning walks begin with cappuccino and pastries from the **Mendocino Bakery** (10483 Lansing Street, (707) 937-0836) or the **Mendocino Cookie Company** (10450 Lansing, (707) 937-4843). For picnic supplies, try the **Cheese Shop** (corner of Little Lake and Lansing, (707) 937-0104), a gourmet cheese and wine shop geared toward urban tastes, or **Tote Fête** (10450 Lansing Street, (707) 937-3383), a high-class take-out place with incredible focaccia (try the Gorgonzola with caramelized onions) and wonderful salads. **The Mendocino Market** (699 Ukiah Street, (707) 937-FISH) has the best pesto and olives in town, plus hot and cold sandwiches to go. In July, the **The Mendocino Music Festival** offers classical music, jazz, and opera in a huge circus tent on the headlands; (707) 937-2044. Great walks abound in Mendocino. Runners will have a fine time dashing around the headlands trails. For fine, ferny day hikes, try **Russian Gulch State Park,** three miles north of town, or **Van Damme State Park** in Little River.

RESTAURANTS

Cafe Beaujolais ★★★★ Cafe Beaujolais started out as the best little breakfast and lunch place in Mendocino. Over the years, owner Margaret Fox and her husband Chris Kump have turned this modest little Victorian into one of the best restaurants in Northern California. Breakfast, presided over by Fox, still draws raves. The moist and fluffy omelets are filled with smoked mozzarella and roasted red peppers; the waffles and pancakes are flecked with pecans and berries. Baked in the wood-fired brick oven, the California pizza with goat cheese and roasted garlic on a thin, crisp, slightly smoky crust is a lunch favorite. Ditto the smoked turkey sandwich with rhubarb-ginger chutney and the Chinese chicken salad drizzled with a sweet yet tart sesame dressing and topped with crisp rice noodles. On nice days, lunch outside on the glassed-in deck near the well-tended garden. Inside, avoid the bustling bench section with its itsy-bitsy tables.

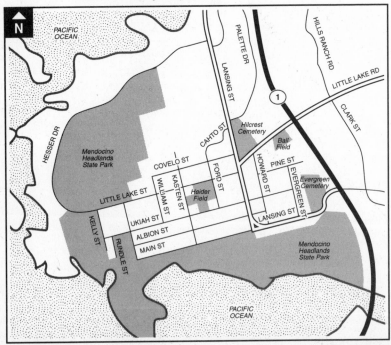

In the evening, Chris Kump's ever-changing dinner menu features delicacies such as braised Barbarie duck, pan-fried bass with fresh grape juice, and a delicate braised osso bucco in a spicy tomato broth. On Mondays, Beaujolais remembers those who frequented the cafe before the word got out by serving a $20 prix-fixe budget dinner. ■ *In Mendocino village; (707) 937-5614; 961 Ukiah, Mendocino; $$$; beer and wine; no credit cards; checks OK; breakfast, lunch, dinner Thurs–Mon.*

MacCallum House Restaurant and Gray Whale Bar/Cafe

★★★ Using fresh, locally grown ingredients, chef Alan Kantor's cuisine strikes a nice balance between traditional favorites like beef tenderloin on a bed of shiitake mushrooms and caramelized onions and nouveau feats like the crisp shrimp cakes with serrano chile crème fraîche. The fresh pastas (Maine lobster risotto with saffron spinach gnocchi, papardelle with rabbit) are always perfectly al dente. Other winners include the salmon with watercress sauce and the seared duck breast with blackberry reduction sauce. The casual bar/cafe and the formal dining room share the same menu and extensive wine list, but make sure you sit in the dining room. The tiny tables in the cramped, noisy, smoky bar are so close together that the waitresses have trouble getting around. ■ *In Mendocino village; (707) 937-5763; 45020 Albion St, Mendocino; $$; full bar; MC, V; checks OK; dinner Fri–Wed (closed Jan–mid-Feb).*

Mendocino

Restaurants

955 Ukiah Street

★★★ "The sleeper restaurant on the coast," say local foodies describing this innovative new eatery in downtown Mendocino. For years, 955 Ukiah Street was one of those cursed locations. Once the studio of noted artist Emmy Lou Packard, this glorious space did time as a movie house, a macrobiotic restaurant, and an alternative lifestyles conference center before Jamie and Peggy Griffith transformed it into a worthy (and much less expensive) rival to its more famous neighbor, Cafe Beaujolais.

The dramatic interior, with its split-level dining room, 20-foot ceilings, rustic wood-trimmed walls, and elegant table settings, sets the mood for the experimental cuisine. All dinners come with soup, salad, and scrumptiously crisp and salty thick bread sticks. Entrées include an exquisite pesto-stuffed red snapper wrapped in phyllo pastry, lean slices of pork loin pinwheeled around salty prosciutto in a mellow port reduction sauce, and a tender fanned duck breast glistening in a ginger-apple mahogany sauce spiked with apple brandy. The upstairs section can get cramped and a little noisy, so try to sit downstairs, where the vaulted ceiling imparts a delicious sense of space. Prompt, friendly service. ■ *Between Howard and Evergreen; (707) 937-1955; 955 Ukiah Street, Mendocino; $$; beer and wine; MC, V; checks OK; dinner Thurs–Sun.*

The Chocolate Moosse Cafe ★★ Chocoholics beware—the folks who run the Chocolate Moosse Cafe are, in the language of 12-step programs, "enablers." Just try to get out of this place without trying the creamy, chocolate-studded Chocolate Moosse Pie or the Moosse Puff, a cream puff filled with vanilla ice cream and topped with hot fudge and whipped cream. Located in a sparse, vanilla Victorian, the Chocolate Moosse also makes a wonderful caesar salad (the best in Mendocino) with a perfect balance of Parmesan and a robust hit of garlic. The richly flavored wild mushroom stew is also terrific. The service used to be a little flaky but seems to be on the mend. Still flaky, happily, is the not-too-sweet deep-dish pecan pie. ■ *Between Main St and Albion, (707) 937-4323; 390 Kasten, Mendocino; $; beer and wine; no credit cards; checks OK; lunch, dinner every day (closed Jan).*

Mendocino Cafe ★★ Despite new carpeting and a recently installed wine bar, the Mendocino Cafe is one of the last vestiges of the Mendocino of the '60s. Nursing mothers, tie-dyed teenagers, and Izod-clad couples queue up for the cafe's eclectic mix of Asian and Mexican specialties. The hands-down winner is the Thai burrito, a steamed flour tortilla filled with brown rice, sautéed vegetables, and chicken, pork, or beef from the kitchen smoker, spiced up with a healthy dash of the cafe's own chile sauce. The hot Thai salad with rock shrimp, the hot and spicy nachos, and the barbecued half chicken are also good bets. Most people sit on the deck. You should too. ■ *In Mendocino village next to the firehouse; (707) 937-2422; 10451 Lansing St, Mendocino; $; beer and wine; MC, V; checks OK; breakfast, lunch, dinner every day.*

LODGINGS

Agate Cove Inn ★★★ Agate Cove cottages provide a degree of seclusion and privacy that the in-town bed and breakfasts just can't match. Furnished with four-poster or canopy-style beds and country furnishings, all but one of the cottages (Diamond) have views of the ocean, fireplaces or wood stoves, and private decks. The parlor in the main house boasts a unique collection of duck decoys clustered around the huge brick fireplace. In the morning, you'll find the *San Francisco Chronicle* on your doorstep, which you can peruse at your leisure over breakfast in the enclosed porch of the main house. Hosts Sallie McConnell and Jake Zahavi serve a full country breakfast, cooked right in front of you on the wood stove in their open kitchen. The French toast is made from thick slices of Jake's coffee-can bread (a first prize winner at the Mendocino County Fair), and the feather-light, fluffy omelets are delightful. ■ *½ mile N of Mendocino at 11201 Lansing St; (707) 937-0551, toll free (800) 527-3111; Mail: PO Box 1150, Mendocino, CA 95460; $$$; AE, DIS, MC, V; checks OK.*

Joshua Grindle Inn ★★★ The most authentic of all of Mendocino's New England–style bed and breakfasts, this masterpiece was built in 1879 by the town's banker, Joshua Grindle. Startlingly white against a backdrop of wind-whipped cypress trees, this two-story beaut has lovely bay windows and a wraparound front porch trimmed with gingerbread arches. There are five Early American rooms in the clapboard house, two in the cottage, and three in an old-fashioned water tower set back in the trees. The spacious water tower rooms have pretty pine furnishings and wood stoves. Chat with hosts Arlene and Jim Moorehead over an evening sherry in the parlor or a luscious breakfast in the dining room. ■ *44800 Little Lake Rd at Hwy 1; (707) 937-4143; Mail: PO Box 647, Mendocino, CA 95460; $$$; DIS, MC, V; checks OK.*

The Mendocino Hotel ★★★ The Mendocino Hotel shines with turn-of-the-century grandeur. The rooms in the original 1878 hotel and the suites in the adjacent Heeser House are decorated with fine-quality antiques, pretty, patterned wallpapers, and old prints and photos. The suites in the Heeser Annex are by far the nicest and most luxurious (Suite 312 has a separate living room and a high four-poster bed). All but three rooms in the refurbished hotel tend toward the small side, so rooms 203, 225A, and 225B are your best bets since each has an extra sitting room and an ocean view or fireplace.

Served in the greenhouselike Garden Room downstairs, breakfast includes pecan pancakes with pear marmalade or a spicy breakfast burrito. For lunch, try the robust Basque lamb chili served in a crisp tortilla shell with crème fraîche or Chinese duck salad on crisp noodles with sweet and sour dressing. The grilled albacore on toasted focaccia is also very good. Fish and chips and hamburgers come with crisp, greaseless angel hair fries.

Dinner, served in the formal, candle-lit dining room with its elegant wainscoting and unique copper samovar, is presided over by chef Colleen Murphy. For starters, we like the raw oysters, baked Brie, and grilled grape leaves stuffed with lamb sausage and goat cheese. The sweet and savory French onion soup comes in an individual crock, topped with a crisp homemade crouton and bubbling over with Gruyère cheese. For a main course, try the grilled sea scallops, lightly seared and served with a beurre blanc spiked with red pepper, or the moist roast chicken breast stuffed with finely chopped prosciutto and creamy mozzarella. The hotel also hosts a series of winemaker dinners one Sunday a month in winter and spring. ■ *Between Lansing and Kasten at 45080 Main St; (707) 937-0511, toll free (800) 548-0513; Mail: PO Box 587, Mendocino, CA 95460; hotel $$$; restaurant $$; full bar; AE, MC, V; checks OK; breakfast, lunch, dinner every day.*

John Dougherty House ★★ This classic saltbox is one of the reasons so many movies supposedly set in New England (*The Russians Are Coming, Summer of '42*) are actually filmed in Mendocino. It's all authentic early Americana throughout: stenciled walls and ceiling, Shaker furniture, and all-cotton linens on the beds. Innkeepers Marion and David Wells assure that each room has its own special charm, but the suites that face Albion Street are the most spacious. ■ *W of Kasten at 571 Ukiah St; (707) 937-5266; Mail: PO Box 817, Mendocino, CA 95460; $$$; no credit cards; checks OK.*

Rachel's Inn ★★ Sandwiched between Van Damme State Park and the breathtaking headlands, Rachel's Inn is perfectly situated for lovers of the outdoors. How anyone could tear themselves away from the sumptuous comfort of the 1860s Victorian, however, is another question. All the rooms have fluffy comforters, fireplaces, and lovely original art. The Parlor room downstairs gets too much highway noise, so opt instead for the Blue Room with its balcony protected by trees. Of course there's always the barn!

Innkeeper Rachel Binah radiates vitality and passion. When she's not busy welcoming her guests, catering a wedding, or preparing one of her grand breakfasts, she's campaigning to protect the Mendocino coastline from offshore oil drilling. And her cooking is as appealing as her politics. ■ *2 miles S of Mendocino on Hwy 1 at 8200 N Hwy 1; (707) 937-0088; Mail: PO Box 134, Mendocino, CA 95460; $$$; no credit cards; checks OK.*

FORT BRAGG

Mendocino's roughneck cousin to the north was built as a fort in the 1850s. It's primarily a logging town, though a recent crop of antique shops downtown hints at gentrification. Fort Bragg's two biggest festivals exemplify the sociological split in town: **Paul Bunyan Days** features a big Labor Day parade, log cutting races, a demolition derby, and a gem and mineral show, while the **Whale Festival** in March boasts whale watching, ranger talks, and beer and chowder tasting; (707) 964-3153. You don't need to wait for the festival to see whales, of course. From October to March, **Todd's Beach** is a good place to catch sight of our cetacean brethren. You can also see logging exhibits all year round at the **Guest House Museum.** This redwood mansion gives you redwood logging as only the timber industry can tell it—learn, for instance, why clear-cutting is good for America's forests, and other arboreal arcana (Wednesday through Thursday, 343 Main Street, (707) 961-2840). Better yet, take a scenic railroad journey through the redwoods to Willits aboard the **Skunk Train,** so called because, in the old days, the mix of diesel and gasoline from the train's engine and stoves meant you could smell it before you saw it (California Western Rail, (707) 964-6371).

Back in town, there are enough galleries to keep you gazing all day. **Tangents Gallery** offers an interesting array of high-quality chotchkas while the art gallery in the back of the store is a nice alternative to the waves-on-rock school of landscape painting common elsewhere; 368 N Main, (707) 964-3884. **The North Coast Artists** gallery is another good choice; 362 N Main, (707) 964-8266. Gallery goers can fortify themselves at **Espresso Express** open at 7am; 103 N Franklin, (707) 964-7006.

RESTAURANTS

The Restaurant ★★ One of the oldest family-run restaurants on the coast, this small unpretentious eatery in a former pharmacy turns out the most consistently good food in all of Fort Bragg. An eclectic menu spans American cooking: Southwestern corn cakes, catfish fillets with black beans, and Denver lamb riblets with sweet and sour glaze. Lunches include favorites like the Philly cheese steak with onion, sweet peppers, and melted Jack cheese and the special flauta topped with guacamole and sour cream. The Restaurant is *the* place for Sunday brunch in town. The comfortable booths are the best places to sit if you want to keep an eye on the entertainment in the kitchen. Jim Larsen's a real showman of a chef who, if he had his druthers, would have a totally open kitchen. As it is, he makes frequent rounds of the dining room, radiating charm and chatting with guests. ■ *1 block N of Laurel on Main St; (707) 964-9800; 418 N Main St, Fort Bragg; $$; beer and wine; MC, V; checks OK; lunch Thurs–Fri, dinner Thurs–Tues, brunch Sun.*

D'Aurelio & Sons ★ D'Aurelio & Sons don't do nouveau pizza—cornbread crusts with ginger-shrimp toppings—they do classic, old-fashioned, New York–Italian pizza, served in a lively atmosphere. You choose what kind of crust you want

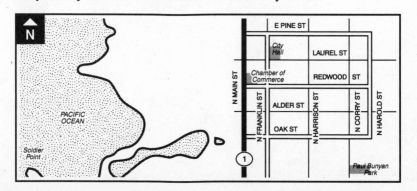

(thick or thin), how much sauce or cheese, and, of course, which traditional toppings (pepperoni, sausage, garlic) to have. The huge antipasto salad, bulging with fresh and marinated vegetables, mozzarella, and feta cheese, works as a dinner salad for a family of four. ■ *1 block E of Main in Franklin Street shopping center; (707) 964-4227; 438 S Franklin St, Fort Bragg; $; beer and wine; no credit cards; checks OK; dinner every day.*

Old Coast Hotel ★ For years, Old Coast Hotel restaurant specialized in Creole cooking—sizzling jambalaya, baked and lightly breaded oysters Bienville, and Mardi Gras shrimp over rice. Over time, owners Bob and Joanna Santos added American classics like pepper steak, house-smoked pork back ribs, and grilled fish. Their newest idea is a create-your-own pasta meal, with a choice of seven kinds of pasta (angel hair, fettuccine, linguine, penne, ravioli, tortellini, and tricolore) and 22 robust sauces (oil and garlic, marinara, fennel and pine nuts, shrimp with black olives, and many, many more). The old Creole standbys are still very good. If you're too sated to find your way home, the hotel's small Victorian rooms upstairs are some of the best values on the coast. ■ *Corner of Oak and Franklin; (707) 964-6443; 101 N Franklin, Fort Bragg; $$; beer and wine; AE, DIS, MC, V; checks OK; dinner Wed–Sun.*

Purple Rose ★ Housed in a low flagstone building on the west side of the highway 3 miles north of Fort Bragg in Cleone, the Purple Rose isn't much to look at—but it serves the best Mexican food on the coast. Although the restaurant is owned by gringos, the Latino sous chefs brighten up the traditional round of burritos, chimichangas, enchiladas, and tostadas with plenty of fresh chiles and cilantro. The spicy, shredded beef (machaca) is our favorite filling. Everything here, from the menudo to the succulent chiles rellenos, comes in satiatingly huge portions. The tomatoey Baja chowder swims with fresh swordfish and clams. The dark and tiny bar, decorated with sombreros and velvet paintings, serves the best margaritas in town. ■ *3 miles N of Fort Bragg; (707) 964-6507; 24300 N Hwy 1; Cleone; $; full bar; no credit cards; checks OK; dinner Wed–Sun.*

Viraporn's Thai Cafe ★ When Viraporn Lobell opened this tiny Thai cafe a few years ago, Asian food aficionados on the North Coast breathed a communal sigh of relief. Born in northern Thailand, Viraporn attended cooking school and apprenticed in restaurants before coming to the United States. After moving to the North Coast with her husband Paul, she worked for a time at Cafe Beaujolais. A master at balancing the five traditional Thai flavors of hot, bitter, tart, sweet, and salty, Viraporn works wonders with refreshing Thai classics like fish cakes, satays, shrimp and beef salad, and a wide range of curries. ■ *1 block off Main St at Chestnut; (707) 964-7931; Chestnut St at Main, Fort Bragg; $; no credit cards; local checks only; lunch, dinner Tues–Sat.*

LODGINGS

Grey Whale Inn ★★ The wide doorways and halls here are the only vestiges of the town hospital this inn used to be. Owners Colette and John Bailey have worked a masterful transformation on this stately four-story building, turning it into one of the most comfortable and distinctive inns on the coast. Decorated with quilts and interesting antiques (like the gimballed surgical lamp in room 11), the 15 very large guest rooms have private baths and wonderful views of the town or the sea. Sunrise has a view of the town, pretty wicker furniture, and a double whirlpool bath; Sunset has a private deck with a sweeping view of the sea. ■ *On Main at Fir; (707) 964-0640, toll free (800) 382-7244; 615 N Main St, Fort Bragg, CA 95437; $$$; DIS, MC, V; checks OK.*

Harbor Lite Lodge ★ Its simple redwood architecture and bird's-eye view of the scenic fishing village of Noyo make this otherwise ordinary motel a pleasant and economical base camp for exploring this section of the California coast. Barbara Hurst has operated the lodge for nearly 20 years. Her spacious, well-maintained rooms offer all the amenities you would expect in a better motel. Nearly all the rooms have ocean views. The suites in the new wing overlooking Noyo Harbor have king-size beds, wood-burning stoves, and refrigerators. ■ *On the N side of Noyo Bridge; (707) 964-0221, toll free (800) 643-2700; 120 N Harbor Dr, Fort Bragg, CA 95437; $; AE, DIS, MC, V; checks OK.*

WESTPORT

LODGINGS

DeHaven Valley Farm ★ This Victorian farmhouse, with its sublime rural setting and access to a sandy beach, comes complete with a barnyard menagerie of horses, geese, sheep, rabbits, chickens, donkeys, and even llamas. The inviting parlor has deep, comfortable couches while the guest rooms are decorated with colorful comforters and rustic antiques. Try to stay in one of the upstairs ocean-view rooms—they're quieter. In the morning you'll awake to fried apples or baked pears, chocolate sour cream coffee cake, potato-artichoke frittata, or cornmeal pancakes. DeHaven Valley Farm also operates a small, prix-fixe restaurant now presided over by chef Ben Kemp. ■ *1½ miles N of Westport at Hwy 1; (707) 961-1660; 39247 Hwy 1, Westport, CA 95488; $$; beer and wine; AE, MC, V; checks OK; dinner Wed–Sun.*

Howard Creek Ranch ★ This magnificent 40-acre ranch appeals to adventurous travelers who don't mind accommodations that are a little rough around the edges. Sally and Charles Griggs have been renting out rooms in their farmhouse and partially renovated railroad barn for 12 years now. Set back from the beach on opposites sides of Howard Creek, the farmhouse and barn are connected by a long, swaying foot bridge. Guest rooms in the farmhouse have separate sitting areas, original antiques, and homemade quilts. The rooms in the barn are more rustic, with curly-grain redwood walls and Early American collectibles. A hot tub, sauna, and swimming pool are perched at the edge of the ranch's ravine. The Griggs serve a full Western breakfast with hotcakes, eggs, and sausage. Massages are available by appointment. ■ *3 miles N of Westport; (707) 964-6725; 40501 N Hwy 1; Mail: PO Box 121, Westport, CA 95488; $; MC, V; checks OK.*

REDWOOD EMPIRE

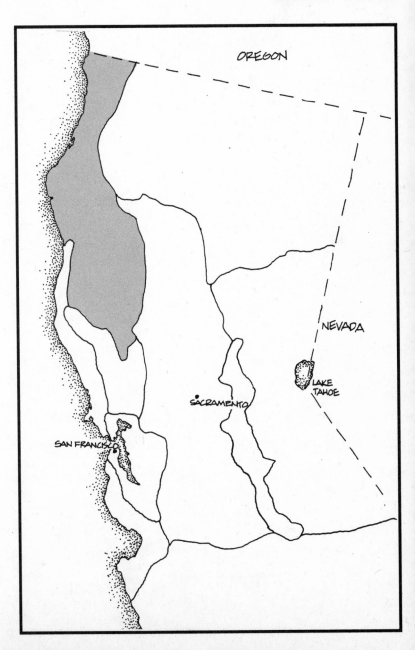

OREGON

NEVADA

LAKE
TAHOE

SACRAMENTO

SAN FRANCISCO

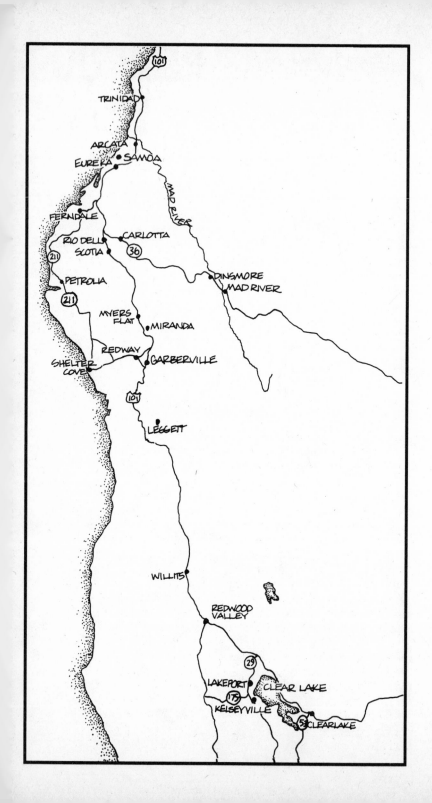

Redwood Empire

*Highway 101 from Redwood Valley to the Oregon border,
with side trips to Shelter Cove, Mad River (on Highway 36),
and Willow Creek (on Highway 299).*

MIDDLETOWN

RESTAURANTS

Las Conchita's Restaurant ★ This dark little cantina has plenty
going for it: hot light tortilla chips, fiery homemade salsa,
speedy service, and a vast menu of well-prepared Mexican
standbys. The spicy chicken enchiladas come in soft, moist,
homemade tortillas, topped with plenty of good, gooey cheese,
and the gigantic "super quesadillas" are fairly smothered in
cheese, guacamole, and sour cream. Owners Paula and Javier
Arroyo have also made sure there's a decent selection of Mexican beers. ■ *On Hwy 29 in Middletown, (707) 987-9454;
21308 Calistoga St, Middletown; $; beer and wine; MC, V;
checks OK; breakfast Fri–Sun, lunch Mon–Thurs, dinner
every day.*

CLEAR LAKE

Despite the recent proliferation of wineries along its southern
shore, there ain't nothing nouveau about Clear Lake. Country
music wafts from the windows of pickup trucks, and the Fourth
of July weekend here is a sunburnt orgy of flag-waving. The
lake itself, one of the state's largest, is abuzz all summer with
the whine of motor-powered watercraft, though that doesn't
seem to bother the flourishing population of bass, carp, crap-
pie, and catfish, or the thousands of fisherfolk who flock here
every year. Boats of all shapes and sizes, as well as jet skis, too-
bies (powered inner-tube boats), and wave-runners can be
rented from **Mike's Watersports** (6235 Old Highway 53, Clearlake, CA 95422; (707) 994-6267), or from **On The Waterfront**
(60 Third Street, Lakeport, CA 95454; (707) 263-6789). Fishing
equipment cannot be rented, so bring your own. For a bird's
eye view of the lake and the small towns and low, dry mountains that surround it, try a glider plane ride, glider plane in-
struction, or skydiving at **Crazy Creek Soaring** (18896 Grange
Road, Middletown, CA 95461; (800) 987-SOAR).

With its old-fashioned downtown, **Lakeport** is the petti-
est town on Clear Lake. The big event here is the **Lake County
Fair** in September, which includes 4-H exhibits, livestock auc-
tions, horse shows, and the Classic Car Show (707) 263-6181.

Library Park, with its white bandstand, offers free jazz, country, and pop concerts in the park every Friday evening during the summer. You can also find such top-of-the-line country music acts as Charlie Daniels or Crystal Gayle at the lake's big resort, Konocti Harbor, all summer, (800) 862-4930.

Clear Lake State Park, just south of Lakeport, has hiking trails, picnic areas, and a beach for swimming. On summer Saturdays rangers conduct one-hour, free, guided nature walks in the morning and host night-time campfires that include talks on various topics including the local Pomo Indians (707) 279-4293.

Wine Touring Clear Lake once had 32 wineries ringing its shores, but Prohibition put an end to all that. The land was converted to walnut and Bartlett pear orchards, and only in the last 20 years have the grapes been coming back. Traveling north from Napa Valley to Middletown, you'll find Guenoc Winery pouring chardonnay and a trendy red blend called Meritage (21000 Butts Canyon Road, (707) 987-2385). Also in Middletown, Horne Winery offers petite sirah and cabernet sauvignon (22000 Highway 29, (707) 987-3503). At Wild Hurst Winery in Lower Lake, try the zinfandel and the sauvignon blanc (11171 Highway 29, (707) 994-6525). Konocti Winery in Kelseyville offers fumé blanc, chardonnay, cabernet sauvignon, and cabernet franc (Highway 29 and Thomas Drive, (707) 279-8861). At Kendall-Jackson in Lakeport, try the Vintner's Reserve Chardonnay and the cabernet sauvignon (600 Matthews Road, (707) 263-5299).

RESTAURANTS

Kathie's Inn ★ Surf and turf's the thing here (the usual array of halibut, breaded scallops and oysters, prawns, and beef), but Kathie's has better than average food and a view of the lake from almost every table. Menu standouts include the prime rib roasted slowly with garlic and onion and the French pepper steak—a grilled fillet with a creamy sauce of pepper and onions. Indulge in the fresh, greaseless cottage fries or the princess potatoes stuffed with cheese, chives, and sour cream. Desserts are nothing special, but there is a wide selection of sweet coffee and cocoa drinks. ■ *About 1 mile off Hwy 53 on Lakeshore Blvd by Redwood Park, (707) 994-9933; 14677 Lakeshore Dr, Clearlake; $$; full bar; MC, V; checks OK; lunch Wed–Fri, dinner every day.*

LODGINGS

Best Western El Grande Inn El Grande Inn is a lot like every other Best Western—clean, modern, predictable—but a few extras pull it above the usual caliber of bland roadside motel. An attractive Spanish-tiled lobby has a four-story atrium with a fountain. There's a small, indoor pool (pleasant to loll around in, but too small for serious lap swimmers), an outdoor Jacuzzi, and an indoor sauna (though the latter was out of order when we were last there). All rooms open onto the atrium and 24 suites overlook the lake. If you tire of watching the sun flashing on the water, the suites have televisions in both the bedroom and the sitting room. ■ *Off Hwy 53, turn left on 40th St, which turns into Lakeshore Dr, (707) 994-2000; 15135 Lakeshore Dr, Clearlake, CA 95422; $$; AE, DC, DIS, MC, V; no checks.*

KELSEYVILLE

RESTAURANTS

Loon's Nest ★★ Wings down, the Loon's Nest wins the award as the best, most romantic restaurant in the entire Clearlake area. Owner/chef Richard Prondinski challenges diners' palates with unusual ingredients in innovative dishes: dark slices of New England red deer in zingy Jamaican pepper sauce and richly flavorful herb and garlic lamb chops, perfectly pink in the center and served with a side of roasted red potatoes. Don't bother with the intriguing-sounding—but dull—alligator bites (they taste like Chicken McNuggets), but do try the rich, savory soups (especially if buttery corn-clam chowder is the soup du jour) and fresh mixed green salads (probably the only radicchio and arugula in the whole county). At meal's end, try the rich flourless chocolate cake in raspberry purée. The service is friendly and unpretentious. If this restaurant were in the Bay Area, it would be just another pleasant yet vaguely ambitious neighborhood dinnerhouse. Where it is, it's a miracle. ■ *Corner of Main St & Hwy 29, far S end of town; (707) 279-1812; 5685 Main St, Kelseyville; $$$; beer and wine; AE, MC, V; checks OK; dinner Tues–Sun.*

Lodgings

Lakewood Restaurant and Bar ★ Located on Soda Bay, this off-the-beaten-track restaurant is easy to miss, especially at night, but since it's one of the few decent restaurants on the lake, it's worth at least a few U turns to find it. Located next to one of Clearlake's ubiquitous trailer parks, the Lakewood offers well-prepared surf and turf, including an immaculate broiled salmon with hollandaise and noisettes of lamb in a creamy truffle sauce. Skip the boring salads and order the rich French onion soup. The look here is very spare, but the dim lighting and tablecloths help to hide the homely furnishings. The bar is livelier than the main dining room, but the latter has a better view of the water. ■ *7 miles from Lakeport on Soda Bay Rd; (707) 279-9450; 6330 Soda Bay Rd, Kelseyville; $$; full bar; MC, V; checks OK; dinner every day.*

LODGINGS

Featherbed Railroad Co. ★ Eight Disneyland-like caboose rooms are laid out like a trailer park at this gimmicky but fun bed and breakfast. The cabooses are burdened with cutesy names, but graced with quilt-topped featherbeds, private baths (some include Jacuzzi), and other amenities that make up for the silliness. While the red and white Casey Jones caboose (with two watchman's seats), and the more feminine Lover and Mint Julep are fun and attractive, the black and maroon Loose Caboose, with its bordello decor and mirror over the bed, is tacky but always booked. Rosebud and Chocolate Mousse have two small bunk beds for the kids ($10 extra per kid). In the morning, you'll find a newspaper on your doorstep; breakfast is served in the main house in front of the fire or on the porch overlooking the lake. A small pool is available for splashing in the summer. ■ *By the lake at 2870 Lakeshore Blvd, (707) 274-8378; Mail: PO Box 4016, Nice, CA 95464; $$; AE, MC, V; checks OK.*

LAKEPORT

RESTAURANTS

Park Place ★★ This cheerful lakeside cafe proffers the best modern Italian food in Lake County. Owners Barbara Morris and Nancy Zabel make their fettuccine anew every day and complement the pasta with simple, fresh sauces: homemade pesto, creamy alfredo, zingy marinara, and quattro formaggi (a blend of four dreamy Italian cheeses). The soups are supernal—to wit, a savory cream of summer squash with a subtle hit of curry, and a chunky Italian vegetable soup redolent of basil, oregano, and garlic fresh from the owners' greenhouse. Unlike many places around Clear Lake, you won't have to contend with other people's smoke as long as you eat inside (smoking is only allowed at outside tables). ■ *On 3rd St across from Library Park near the lake, (707) 263-0444; 50 3rd St, Lakeport; $$; beer and wine; MC, V; checks OK; lunch every day, dinner Mon–Sat.*

LODGINGS

The Forbestown Inn ★★ Inside this wisteria-draped, cream and brown Victorian is a comfortable and engaging accommodation. The four guest rooms are tastefully decorated with fine American oak antiques, needlepoint, and bric-a-brac. The two downstairs rooms are best: the mauve and cream Anna's Rose Room and the more masculine Bartlett Suite in cream and forest green. The upstairs rooms are small and sweet but can get very hot during the summer. Innkeepers Nancy and Jake Dunne live in the cottage out back and are friendly, casual sorts. In the morning, you may find them puttering around the kitchen in their bathrobes preparing your grand breakfast fête: Grand Marnier French toast stuffed with cream cheese and jam or hearty three-or-more-egg omelets (chorizo and veggies is a favorite), served with muffins or Nancy's delicious Lake County walnut pie. In the afternoon, the inkeepers serve wine and snacks on the garden patio by the gorgeous black-bottom swimming pool. ■ *6 blocks off Hwy 29 in downtown Lakeport, 1 block W of Main St; (707) 263-7858; 825 Forbes St, Lakeport, CA 95453; $$; AE, MC, V; checks OK.*

REDWOOD VALLEY

RESTAURANTS

Broiler Steak House ★★ The Broiler is more than a steak house—it's a temple to meat. On a normal weekend night, the number of diners here is equal to half the total population of Redwood Valley. (On Mother's Day, the Broiler turns out more than 1,000 steaks.) Those rash enough to arrive without reservations are consigned to a pleasurable stay in the limbo of a giant cocktail lounge—a good place to catch up on the latest in Western fashions and blender drinks. Eventually an angelic waitress ushers you to the inner sanctum, where the true acolyte will order a juicy dinner steak grilled over an oakwood pit to the most exacting specifications and accompanied by a mammoth potato and a garden-fresh dinner salad the size of your head. ■ *7 miles N of Ukiah, West Rd exit W, right on Uva; (707) 485-7301; 8400 Uva Dr, Redwood Valley; $$; full bar; AE, MC, V; checks OK; dinner every day.*

Mario's Ristorante Italiano ★ Mendocino County has a number of venerable, family-style Italian restaurants; this is one of the best. While you're waiting for your dinner (and you probably will), peruse the list of appetizers: sautéed button mushrooms stuffed with garlic and cheese in a Marsala sauce; Sicilian garlic bread with fresh garlic, mozzarella, and Romano; and eggplant arecante (fried eggplant in a marinara sauce). The pastas come with sauce or classically stuffed with sausage or meatballs. The fare includes such rarities as steak pizzaiola (mushrooms and peppers in wine sauce) and a cheesy, baked veal with eggplant and prosciutto in a red sauce with mushrooms, peppers, and olives. In the unlikely event that you have room left over, there's always spumoni for dessert. Chef/owner Mario Scaturro is a solicitous soul, eager to accommodate his customers' needs, whether they're a large party or a couple with eyes only for each other. ■ *7 miles N of Ukiah on Hwy 101, right on West Rd, left on N State St; (707) 485-7400; 9601 N Hwy 101, Redwood Valley; $$; beer and wine; no credit cards; checks OK; dinner Wed–Sun.*

Looking for a particular place? Check the index at the back of this book for individual restaurants, lodgings, shops, attractions, and more.

WILLITS

RESTAURANTS

Tsunami ★★ No matter where you're coming from, by the time you get to Willits, odds are you'll be ready for what Tsunami has to offer: simple, Japanese-inspired preparations of organic vegetables and seafood caught off the Mendocino coast by proprietor Wesley Wake. Purists may scoff at sushi made with cooked seafood, but they've probably never tried peddling raw fish to the locals. Still, fish this fresh deserves to be raw. At Tsunami, fish and chicken suppers come in four categories: grilled, tempura, Cajun-style, or in a "colache" atop a bed of organic vegetables with a healthy serving of rice. Picky or light eaters can easily content themselves with tempura vegetables, always-satisfying miso soup, or such exotica as Cajun tofu cubes. ■ *On Hwy 101, near corner of Commercial; (707) 459-4750; 50 S Main St, Willits; $; beer and wine; no credit cards; local checks only; lunch and dinner Mon–Sat.*

LODGINGS

The Doll House Bed and Breakfast If this place were any smaller, it would be a doll house in more than name. This turn-of-the-century Queen Anne cottage—originally constructed for the widow of the eponymous Hiram Willits—has only three guest rooms and more than 500 dolls crowding the living room. All the rooms have handmade quilts and fresh flowers. The nicest room is upstairs, with a private sundeck and bed with a view of the town out the gabled windows. Given the limited number of beds and the fact that owner Laura LeClear is often out walking her little dog, advance reservations are recommended. ■ *1 block W of Hwy 101, corner of W Mendocino and School streets; (707) 459-4055; 118 School St, Willits, CA 95490; $$; no credit cards; checks OK.*

LEGGETT

LODGINGS

Bell Glen Bed and Breakfast ★★ Here's a rarity: an inn that caters to travelers of every ilk. For the romantically inclined, there are private, rustic-suburban cottages (with breakfast) along the Eel River. All of the country cottages have modern baths, well-lit easy chairs, and decks with barbecue grills; some have honeymoon tubs for two while one even has a private Jacuzzi built into its deck—plus all have access to a European-style all-night sauna on the banks of the river. Casual travelers will find hostel-type lodgings: dormitories, couples' cabins, and single rooms. Cottage dwellers and hostel patrons get free swimming tubes for the river, as well as access to bicycles, badminton, table tennis, volleyball, basketball, horseshoes, snorkeling, hiking, and campfires.

The candle-lit restaurant is a historic landmark—it was a stage stop in the late 1800s—and retains its venerable charm. Casual dress and fine linen impart a comfortable but elegant atmosphere. Dinner is a limited daily choice of excellent seafood and fowl dishes. The dinner schedule is somewhat erratic, so call ahead. Below the restaurant is a bistro with espressos and an extensive selection of microbrews, wines, and spirits to complement pub food such as spicy lamb sausage and chicken pot-pie. The atmosphere is highly sociable, occasionally with live entertainment. If not, there are always spare instruments available so you can make your own music. ■ *2 miles N of Leggett on Hwy 101; (707) 925-6425 (inn), (707) 925-6469 (hostel); 70400 N Hwy 101, Leggett, CA 95455; $$; full bar; DIS, MC, V; checks OK; dinner Thurs–Sun (Fri–Sun in winter).*

Big Bend Lodge ★★ Too far from the highway to be considered a motel, too homespun and rustic to be called a resort, the Big Bend Lodge has nine one- or two-room cabins—all with fully furnished kitchens—a short walk from a delightful swimming hole at the big bend in the South Fork of the Eel River. In season, this spot is a hangout for salmon and steelhead fisherpeople, and if the water is high enough, rafters can put in here for a float down to Leggett. During the summer, loll by the river, read, chat with friends on a porch swing, or laugh by the nightly campfires. Kids busy themselves by playing basketball, table tennis, or volleyball—or by feeding the chickens. For a proper respite from the hurly-burly world, plan on staying several days; be aware, however, that the supply in nearby grocery stores is limited—you're better off bringing provisions from home. Call ahead for reservations and directions—it's a little tricky to find. ■ *4 miles S of Leggett off Drive Through Tree Rd, watch for sign; (707) 984-6321; Mail: PO Box 111, Leggett, CA 95455; $; no credit cards; checks OK.*

GARBERVILLE

RESTAURANTS

Woodrose Cafe ★ This late-blooming flower child coffee shop is the social center of Garberville—a place to eavesdrop on local gossip from a booth, table, or counter stool. With its plain white walls decorated with posters of herbs and tea, the interior is no great shakes, but out back there's a small outdoor patio perfect for sunning and enjoying the cafe's whole-grain, unprocessed orgo-fare: omelets, tofu burgers and rancheros, granola, vegetarian sesame burgers and organic fruit-yeast shakes. The chunky, vegetable-based soups are served with sourdough garlic bread. Everything is skillfully and tastefully prepared. ■ *Garberville exit off Hwy 101; (707) 923-3191; 911*

*Redwood Dr, Garberville; $; beer and wine; no credit cards;
checks OK; breakfast every day, lunch Mon–Fri.*

LODGINGS

Benbow Inn ★★★★ From its high tea and scones to its beautifully cultivated gardens of primroses, narcissus, tulips, and
roses, this elegant Tudor-style inn built in 1924 is a little slice
of England in the redwoods. A National Historic Landmark, the
inn's main building reeks of old money at play. Its inviting
lobby has a huge fireplace, cherry-wood wainscoting, comfortable sofas, oriental rugs, grandfather clocks, and partially
completed jigsaw puzzles. Rooms vary in size and amenities.
Deluxe accommodations include private patios and Jacuzzis,
fireplaces readied with kindling, and VCRs (a large movie library is available at the desk); the least expensive rooms are
rather small, but are still quite comfortable and have many antiques. All rooms come with a wonderful little basket of
books—mysteries or love stories. Sherry, coffee, and tea are
complimentary.

    The aristocratic dining room has carved wood and marble
sideboards and large paned windows overlooking the river and
gardens. The atmosphere is quiet and sedate; the service attentive. Seafood and poultry—quail with grapes, roasted duck
with lingonberries, salmon with wild rice—abound, though
rack of lamb and steak and kidney pie are offered in keeping
with the cultural context. An extraordinary Sunday brunch
comes with unlimited champagne. On weekends, the lounge
has a pianist and free hors d'oeuvres 5–7pm. In addition to all
this, the inn hosts many special events including a Halloween
masquerade, a Christmas celebration, a New Year's dinner
dance, and—quite naturally—Shakespeare on the Lake during
the summer. ■ *Benbow exit off Hwy 101; (707) 923-2124; 445
Lake Benbow Dr, Garberville, CA 95440; $$$$; full bar; AE,
DC, MC, V; checks OK; breakfast, lunch, dinner every day,
brunch Sun (sometimes closed Jan to mid-Apr).*

REDWAY

RESTAURANTS

The Mateel Cafe/Jazzbó Room ★★ With its delicious,
healthful food and live entertainment, this diverting complex
has become a social and cultural magnet for the region. Dinner is served in the cafe with its high-backed wooden booths
and an eclectic collection of local and thrift-store art. Roast rack
of lamb, linguine chow mein, tournedos of beef, Chinese stir-
fry with scampi, and manicotti are all prepared with fresh herbs
and accompanied by appetizers, soup or salad, and pita bread.
    For lunch, there's counter service in the African-flavored
Jazzbó Room with its rattan and giraffe motif. Try one of the

stone-baked pizzas (with 20 toppings to choose from) or gourmet salads—like the one with Napa cabbage, tomato, spinach, almonds, and chicken, served with a curry dressing. In the evenings, the Jazzbó Room showcases local musicians, comedians, and writers. ■ *Redway exit off Hwy 101, 2 miles NW; (707) 923-2030; 3342 Redwood Dr, Redway; $; beer and wine; no credit cards; checks OK; Cafe: dinner Tues–Sat; Jazzbó Room: lunch and light dinner Mon–Sat.*

Shelter Cove Grotto ★★ It isn't located in Shelter Cove; nor does it resemble a grotto. Built originally as a real estate headquarters, it was later the inland seafood outlet for Shelter Cove Marina. Now under the guidance of ex–Southern Californians Marion Cain and Joan Hannan, the Grotto leans strongly toward LA suave (an anomaly for southern Humboldt County): decorator lights, crisp spotless linen, and an improvisational jazz combo with a pianist from Palm Springs and a drummer who appeared in *Some Like It Hot.*

Chef Bret LaMott's handwritten, seasonal menu changes weekly. One winter holiday-week selection included a beautifully presented rockfish en papillote, salmon in puff pastry, very spicy peppered prawns and linguine, two styles of duck with corn cakes, rack of lamb, and ribeye steak. First-course options included marinated calamari and tortellini in a white wine butter sauce. Dinners come with a choice of salad or homemade soup with freshly baked, still-warm rolls. Soup is usually the best choice—a luscious sweet-and-sour borscht or the delicate cream of fennel. On Sundays from April through December, there's a gin-fizz brunch with truffles and eggs Benedict. Fried oysters, vegetable and prawn tempura, and a "Grotto burger" are available in the bar. ■ *Redwood Dr and Briceland Rd in Redway; (707) 923-4323; $$; full bar; DC, MC, V; checks OK; dinner every day, brunch Sun (Jan-Mar: closed Mon, no brunch).*

SHELTER COVE

RESTAURANTS

Pelican's Landing ★★ This rather exclusive destination—voted one of America's best lunch spots to *fly into* by *Private Pilot* magazine—is located in an A-frame beach house with two-story picture windows and an undiscovered view of the lost coast. The menu's limited offerings are well-prepared: charbroiled, Cajun-style fresh fish, chicken, and oysters, preceded by a creamy clam chowder and a shrimp or green salad with fresh, crusty sourdough bread. Try the blackened salmon, topped off with a slice of pie—either the creamy chocolate mousse or the wonderfully tart wild huckleberry or apricot. Weekends feature live entertainment—usually a funny, talented acoustic guitarist. ■ *Shelter Cove exit off Hwy 1 to Shelter Cove Rd, right onto Upper Pacific Dr, left onto Lower Pacific Dr, right onto Wave Dr in Shelter Cove; (707) 986-7793; $$; beer and wine; no credit cards; no checks; breakfast, lunch, and dinner Thurs–Sun (Thurs–Mon in summer).*

LODGINGS

Shelter Cove Bed and Breakfast ★★ Flocks of quail, foraging rabbits, grazing deer, and migrating pods of whales are regular sights in Shelter Cove—and all four rooms in this 1991 inn take full advantage of the view. Owners Ron and Jacquetta Perchinsky have filled their inn with native American rugs and medicine bags that Jacquetta has collected from reservations around the country. The two largest rooms sport Jacuzzi/whirlpool tubs. The upstairs room has its own dining area that has an incredible 25-foot-high ceiling with a skylight. The other two rooms are fairly small—but not too small for a queen-size bed, bureau, and dining table, where a vegetarian breakfast can be served. Good fishing, surfing, kayaking, and hiking all wait nearby. ■ *Shelter Cove Dr, right on Lower Pacific Dr, right onto Dolphin Dr; (707) 986-7161; 148 Dolphin Dr, Shelter Cove, CA 95489; $$$; no credit cards; checks OK.*

PETROLIA

LODGINGS

Lost Inn ★ Keep one eye on the road and its hairpin turns and another on the lookout for an antique green tractor with a hand-painted sign: "Welcome! You have found the Lost Inn." Watch out for chickens as you walk past the discarded farm machinery, flowers, fruit trees, and outbuildings that line the long drive leading up to Gail and Phil Franklin's home and bed and breakfast. The guest room is a suite with a single and double bed, kitchen, private bath, and private entrance. The Franklins will give you a continental breakfast, then they'll give you privacy. If you aren't hunting for town doings, you'll have a very pleasant stay. Just remember to bring a compass. ■ *On Old Mattole Rd in Petrolia; (707) 629-3394; Mail: PO Box 161, Petrolia, CA 95558; $; no credit cards; checks OK.*

MIRANDA

LODGINGS

Miranda Gardens Resort ★ Haunted by the ghosts of family vacations past (and future), this redwood-shaded motel and cottage complex offers a plethora of amusements for the mildy athletic: a heated swimming pool, table tennis, tetherball, croquet, shuffleboard, and volleyball. There's even a communal fire ring for those who want to exercise their vocal chords at nighttime sing alongs. Skip the motel rooms and book one of the eight newly renovated cabins with their refurbished antiques, brass headboards, new carpets, and acoustic tiled ceilings. The redwood paneling has been painstakingly sanded and refinished to a warm luster—a harmonious counterpoint to the old-growth redwoods just outside the windows.

Most of the cabins have fireplaces and decks with barbecue grills overlooking the adjacent state park. All contain fully equipped kitchens and a few offer whirlpools. Considering the multitude of activities available on the grounds, you might not want to go anywhere—except, perhaps, the nearby forest, tennis courts, and the Eel River. ■ *Old Redway Hwy (Ave of the Giants); (707) 943-3011; Mail: PO Box 186, Miranda, CA 95553; $$; AE, MC, V; no checks.*

MYERS FLAT

LODGINGS

Myers Inn ★ Situated just outside a state park in Myers Flat—a small cardboard-cutout saloon town, complete with fierce patriotism—Myers Inn is an imposing two stories worth of early Californiana. A spacious lobby with a player piano, Victrola, and sofas arranged around a restored Rumford fireplace greet you on the way to the front desk. The hotel's 10 rooms have recently been renovated with an eye toward upscale country charm—comfortable, clean, and pleasant. Since 360-degree verandahs encircle both floors, every room has a balcony with a view of the town, mountains, and forest. The hotel is close to the highway, but the nearby Eel River and all-encompassing redwoods seem to absorb most of the noise. Trouble is, the adorable inn has no restaurant (just a continental breakfast in the morning). Bring sustenance for the evening since the nearest decent restaurant is miles away. ■ *Ave of the Giants; (707) 943-3259; Mail: PO Box 173, Myers Flat, CA 95554; $; MC, V; no checks.*

Lodgings

SCOTIA

LODGINGS

Scotia Inn ★★ It's hard to miss the Scotia Inn when you're driving into town. Three stories worth of redwood-Victorian charisma, it's the pride of the area. Originally a dormitory for mill workers, the inn's one renovated floor has eight spacious rooms and three suites—all buffed up with antiques, balloon drapery, and bathrooms with claw-footed tubs and showers. The bridal suite, with a beautiful crocheted half-canopy over its king-size bed, has a separate room with a hot tub.

The redwood dining room, lit by brass chandeliers, serves exquisite dinners featuring locally grown vegetables, berries, and fowl. Traditional choices like steak, prime rib, and seafood are offered alongside inventive entrées such as chile and roasted eggplant pasta with tahini, garlic, and tomato sauce. Sunday is ethnic night with Greek-style mustard lamb or Thai-roasted pork loin. The cafe began serving home-style lunches in the spring of 1992, after the big earthquake torched most of the other lunch places in town. ■ *Scotia exit from Hwy 101 to Main and Mill streets; (707) 764-5683; Mail: PO Box 248, Scotia, CA 95565; inn, $$; restaurant, $$$; full bar; MC, V; local checks only; dinner Wed–Sun, lunch Mon–Fri.*

RIO DELL

RESTAURANTS

Riverside Coffee Shop ★ Stark vinyl booths, a large U-shaped counter, decoupage plaques, linoleum floor—nothing indicates that the food here is anything other than standard coffee shop fare. Fact is, chef/owner Marlena Dyer serves some mighty fine—that is to say, down-home, Southern-style, and unpretentious—food. Everything is made from scratch, be it the biscuits, the soups, or the pies. The sandwiches and burgers are decent enough, but it's the Cajun specialties—straight from Marlena's Louisiana grandmother's recipe box—that keep folks coming back: honey-sweetened hush puppies and deep-fried zucchini with ranch sauce. After that, it's a carnival of flavors with Marlena's blackened catfish, spicy but well-balanced jambalaya, or pork chops. All come with fluffy white rice and Louisiana red beans. The fruit pies, made with local apples and blackberries, are sure bets. ■ *Rio Dell exit off Hwy 101; (707) 764-3877; 116 Wildwood Ave, Rio Dell; $; alcohol license pending; no credit cards; no checks; breakfast, lunch, and dinner every day.*

CARLOTTA

RESTAURANTS

Pepperwood Falls Country Inn ★ The carpenter, collector, and cook who run this '40s veteran's hall restaurant have big plans for the future—they're adding four guest rooms, enlarging the performance stage, and building a new deck out back. What they've got right now is a fun little restaurant with lustrous redwood and knotty-pine woodwork and a cornucopia of antique dolls, stuffed animals, magic mirrors, specialty clocks, and ancient (pre-Classic) Coke machines. The cook (the owner's brother) is a master of Mexican cuisine, evidenced by the spicy relish assortment, homemade salsa, and sopa seca, (a delectable vermicelli soup). Wednesday, Friday, and Saturday are south-of-the-border days when the menu features sophisticated (very un-Tex-Mex) specialties like the Milanesa de Puerco (a breaded pork cutlet sautéed with tomatillos, avocado, and chiles). Thursdays offer "country cooking"—old-fashioned chicken, ham, and meat loaf; Mondays there's homemade pizza; and Sundays it's up to the cook. Regardless of the day of the week, the quality is impeccable and quantity ample. Expect lots of rollicking personal attention from the staff. ■ *3½ miles W of Bridgeville on S side of Hwy 36; (707) 777-3676; 21170 Hwy 36, Carlotta; $$; beer and wine; no credit cards; checks OK; lunch, dinner Wed–Mon, breakfast Sun.*

DINSMORE

RESTAURANTS

The Weekender Cafe ★ All the proceeds of this homey, volunteer-run cafe go to support the local fire department. Neighbors donate the homemade rolls, muffins, breads, pies, cakes, cookies, soups, relishes, salads, and the fresh flowers on every table. Ingredients originate largely in local gardens, pastures, and chicken coops and are prepared in a family-size kitchen behind the five-stool counter. (We're talking still-warm, sun-ripened tomatoes and sweet, fresh-picked carrots and celery.) For breakfast there are the traditional egg, meat, and potato platters, waffles, pancakes, fresh-baked Danish, and homemade biscuits and gravy. This is the kind of place where the coffee's self-serve and if the vinyl chairs are too hard, you can always take a nap on the couch in front of the fire. ■ *1½ miles E of Dinsmore, between Bridgeville and Mad River; (707) 574-6521; Bridgeville; $; no alcohol; no credit cards; checks OK; breakfast, lunch every day.*

MAD RIVER

LODGINGS

Flying AA Ranch ★★ At 3,000 feet into the South Fork Mountains near the spectacular Trinity Alps stands a 500-acre working cattle ranch with guest lodgings. The drive in is beautiful, but the aerial view flying into their private airstrip is even better. Elegance is a foreign concept here; big and basic are beautiful. The modern motel units offer nothing more than minimal support for existence outdoors. (Four family units—one prefab building and three mobile homes—and 12 tent houses are available in addition to the standard-occupancy rooms.) But that's really all you'll need them for, since the expansive environs variously encourage horseback riding, hiking, biking, fishing, hunting, trap shooting, and backpacking into the Yolla Bolly Wilderness—to say nothing of tennis courts, a heated pool, table tennis, volleyball, badminton, horseshoes, dancing, and billiards. In addition to these activities, the Flying AA offers encounters with real cowboys—

dressed working-Western, smelling rather ranchy, and mincing no discouraging words.

For indoor sustenance, a large main building encloses a restaurant and banquet room, fireside lounge, and bar. The latter has chess setups, a gift shop, a dance hall, and a recreation area with table games, a jukebox, and occasional live music. A split-level outdoor deck offers breathtaking views of South Fork Mountain—the longest mountain in the continental United States. Appetites are Texas-size at the end of a ranch day; we're talking slabs of beef up to two pounds! Dinners include soup or salad, baked potato or fries, vegetables, and homemade bread. Lunches feature traditional barbecue fare, and dessert treats include just-cranked homemade ice cream and fresh-baked fruit and walnut pies. For breakfast, there's charbroiled steak with eggs, hashbrowns, toast or homemade biscuits, and country gravy. ■ *Turn SE off Hwy 36 between Mad River and Forest Glen, continue 5 miles on Lower Mad River/Ruth Lake Rd; (707) 574-6227 or 574-6417; Ruth Lake, Star Rte Box 700, Bridgeville, CA 95526; $; full bar; AE, DC, DIS, MC, V; checks OK; breakfast, lunch, dinner every day (closed Nov–Mar).*

Journey's End Resort ★ Fancy isn't fashionable at the edge of civilization. The rooms at this four-unit motel are basic, clean, and warm—but not far removed from nature. Firm beds are piled with cozy quilts; the wall heater fires up with some coaxing; hot water will happen if you don't give up. Entertainment is left to the imagination rather than the networks.

The food at the restaurant is the gastronomical equivalent of insulated underwear, intended to ensure survival among the elements. No frozen, packaged, or pretend nourishment here—and no fat- and cholesterol-free sissy fare, either. These are John Wayne rations prepared by wilderness wives and mothers. The house specialty is pizza made from scratch, but most dinners are range-fed—ribeye, sirloin, porterhouse—with homemade fries, sautéed mushrooms, and grilled onions. For lunch, you'll find burgers no smaller than a quarter pound, and no fewer than a dozen hot dogs. The breakfast is designed for the long haul. ■ *NE end of Ruth Lake; (707) 574-6441; Mail: Star Rte Box 200, Mad River, CA 95552; $$; seasonal full bar (beer and wine Oct–Dec); AE, DIS, MC, V; checks OK; breakfast, lunch, dinner every day.*

KING SALMON

RESTAURANTS

Gill's by the Bay ★★ Nauticalness virtually overflows from this coffee shop–styled seafood house, from its steamy interior to its patio, where the smell of the salt air goes perfectly with the fresh seafood chowder. The service can be a bit slow at the grill. So ogle the postcard-like rocky vista, complete with pelicans and other waterfowl, or watch the boats bob in the marina. Try a burger or thin-sliced roast beef, turkey, or grilled-chicken sandwich. Particularly good are the pounded and breaded calamari and the deep-fried oysters. For breakfast, consider the formidable Hangtown Fry—fresh oysters, sautéed onions, mushrooms, and bacon in an open-faced omelet.

The **Whaler's Inn** in nearby Field's Landing (6690 Field's Landing Drive, (707) 443-6026) is owned and operated by the same family. A more expensive dinner-only restaurant, it too maintains a maritime attitude; scallops and oysters figure most prominently. ■ *King Salmon Ave exit off Hwy 101, follow W 1½ miles; (707) 442-2554; 77 Halibut Ave, King Salmon; $; beer and wine; MC, V; local checks only; breakfast, lunch every day.*

FERNDALE

Strolling through Ferndale—the entire town is a historic landmark—is like a walk on Main Street USA 90 years ago. Victoriana, art galleries, and gift shops galore. Be sure to stop at **Golden Gate Mercantile** for penny candy, red long johns, handsome pottery, and hats of every description. The owner of **Ferndale Books** leaves an assortment of reading material in front of the store each night for browsers—her customers pay on the honor system! The **Ferndale Museum,** located just off Main Street, has an interesting collection of memorabilia from the village, and **The Ferndale Repertory Theatre** offers local productions on a fairly regular basis. The best event in town is the wild and zany **Cross-Country Kinetic Sculpture Race** in late May. Over 100 people-powered vehicles race 40 miles over land and sea from Arcata to the finish line on Ferndale's Main Street.

LODGINGS

The Gingerbread Mansion ★★★ The awe-inspiring grande dame of Ferndale, this Queen Anne inn is a lavish blowout for Victoriana buffs. Gables, turrets, English gardens, and gingerbread galore have made it one of the most photographed buildings in Northern California—so if this peach and yellow place seems a tad self-conscious, it's understandable. It's been through several reincarnations since 1899: a private residence, a hospital, a rest home, an apartment building, and even an American Legion hall before being converted by Ken Torbert into a B&B in 1983. And world-class it is.

In the morning, guests are greeted by a tray of tea or coffee outside their rooms. An excellent continental breakfast follows in the formal dining room overlooking the garden.

Afternoon tea is served in one of four exquisitely furnished parlors, with ample books, board games, and a 1,000-piece puzzle depicting the mansion itself.

All nine guest rooms have queen-size beds and private baths as noteworthy as the rooms themselves. The Fountain Suite has twin claw-footed tubs for his-and-hers bubble baths, a grand view of Ferndale and the garden, and a fainting couch. The corner Rose Suite has a wonderful view and a vast, mirrored bathroom (as big as the bedroom) with a bidet, stained-glass windows, and hanging plants. Bicycles, raincoats, and boots are available for guests who might explore further than their rooms. ■ *Ferndale exit off Hwy 101, 5 miles to Ferndale on Main St, left on Brown St, one block to 400 Berding St; (707) 786-4000; Mail: PO Box 40, Ferndale, CA 95536; $$$; MC, V; checks OK.*

The Shaw House Inn ★★★ This Carpenter Gothic beauty—built in 1854 by Seth Louis Shaw—is modeled on Hawthorne's House of the Seven Gables. Meticulously restored by owners Norma and Ken Bessingpas, the oldest house in Ferndale is filled with books, photographs, baskets, antiques, and all manner of memorabilia; the couple also added a gazebo and fish pond to the inn's well-tended acre. About those seven gables—there's a guest room nestled under each one. The Shaw Room, under the central gable, features the original bed where Shaw and his bride spent their honeymoon.

Norma's breakfasts include cheddar French toast with maple syrup specked with dried apricots and currants and oven-baked Dutch babies. Tea, coffee, and freshly baked cookies are served in the fire-lit library, where classical musicians gather to practice. Conveniently located on Main Street among the welter of art galleries, gift shops, and preserved Victoriana, the Shaw House masters the delicate art of the successful B&B—creating an exquisite atmosphere without being overly precious. ■ *Ferndale exit off Hwy 101, 5 miles to town at 703 Main St; (707) 786-9958; Mail: PO Box 1125, Ferndale, CA 95536; $$$; AE, MC, V; checks OK.*

EUREKA

With a population of 25,000, Eureka is the largest city in Humboldt County. The heart of the city is Old Town, where commercial and residential Victorian buildings abound near the waterfront of Humboldt Bay. The gabled and turreted **Carson Mansion,** built in 1885 for lumber baron William Carson, is now a private men's club (talk about Victorian!). Also in Old Town, the **Clarke Memorial Museum** houses more than 1,200 examples of Hupa, Yurok, Karok, and Wiyot basketry as well as dance regalia and stonework. In addition to the native

American artifacts, the museum has other permanent collections and changing displays. The nearby **Humboldt Cultural Center** is a beautifully restored commercial structure. It doubles as a gallery with changing exhibits and an intimate hall for concerts on Friday nights.

For a relaxing perspective on Old Town, try a cruise on the **Madaket**, the oldest passenger vessel on the Pacific coast. Watch for the egrets in the cypress trees. Yet another perspective of the waterfront is gained from the **Woodley Island Marina.** There's room for 350 vessels to put down anchor here.

RESTAURANTS

Lazio's Seafood Restaurant ★ For more than four decades, if you came to Humboldt County and wanted seafood, you went to Lazio's. In recent years, at least half a dozen other terrific seafood places have begun to compete for Lazio's clientele, but most folks agree that Lazio's is still the best. The reason is simple: the food is fresh and superbly prepared. If salmon is in season, order it: poached, broiled, or en brochette. Also trustworthy is the baked sole stuffed with shrimp and green onions and topped with Newburg sauce. The Humboldt Bay shore plate—deep-fried halibut, prawns, scallops, salmon, cod, and oysters—is quite popular; blackened ling cod is liberally spiced and very moist. Portions are large and there's a long list of specials, depending on the day's catch. The one thing you

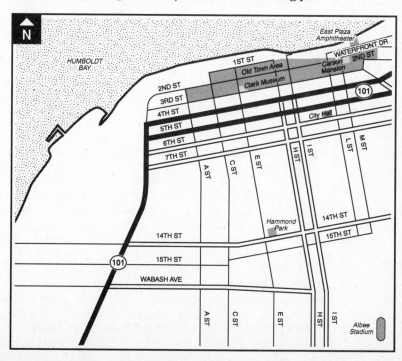

won't get at Lazio's anymore is an ocean view: the restaurant has moved from its bay view perch to an attractive, high-ceilinged, multilevel place in the heart of Old Town. ■ *2nd St between D and E streets; (707) 443-9717; 327 2nd St, Eureka; $$; full bar; MC, V; checks OK; lunch, dinner every day, brunch Sun.*

Tomo Japanese Restaurant ★ Chef Fukiko Marshall prepares some of the best Japanese food on the northern coast. If you're inexperienced with Japanese cuisine or unsure about what to order, don't worry—the staff will bring you a sample plate. One of the most popular selections is a family-style dinner for four—after miso soup and a small salad, it includes chicken katsu, tempura, teriyaki, and sushi. The latter, prepared at a traditional sushi bar in the back, couldn't be fresher. The tempura shrimp and vegetables come in a batter so light it almost evaporates in your mouth. At lunchtime, there's a delicious yakisoba—buckwheat noodles sautéed with fresh vegetables and chicken or tofu. ■ *4th St just N of V St; (707) 444-3318; 2120 4th St, Eureka ; $$; beer and wine; MC, V; checks OK; lunch Mon, Wed, Thurs, Fri, dinner Wed–Mon.*

Tomaso's Tomato Pies For family-style Italian dining in Eureka, Tomaso's is the place—capable of satisfying huge and tiny appetites alike. The house specialties are chicken cannelloni and a square pizza with a whole wheat crust. Our hands-down favorites—the calzone and the spinach pie—are both made fresh to order, take half an hour to cook, and will make garlic lovers (and their opposites) swoon. For a proper finish, try one of the espresso options or a treat called Cremosa (Torani Italian syrup, milk, soda water, and whipped cream, infused with a fruity flavoring). ■ *E St between 3rd and 2nd streets; (707) 445-0100; 216 E St, Eureka; $; beer and wine; AE, MC, V; local checks only; lunch Mon–Sat, dinner every day.*

LODGINGS

Carter House Country Inn, Hotel Carter, and Hotel Carter Restaurant ★★★★ Innkeepers, historic preservationists, and restaurateurs Mark and Christi Carter spare absolutely nothing in this award-winning trio of luxury establishments that takes up an entire block of downtown Eureka. They started several years ago with the Carter House Country Inn, built from the original blueprint for an 1884 San Francisco mansion destroyed in the 1906 earthquake. With bay windows and white-washed walls, the inn's light and airy main floor has three parlors, where hors d'oeuvres and wine are served in the early evening. (Freshly baked cookies, tea, and brandy are brought out later on.) Flowers and bathrobes are found upstairs in the seven guest rooms, several of which have private baths, fireplaces, or Jacuzzis. We particularly like the suite with a sitting room and a double-headed shower. While the breakfast special might be anything from eggs Florentine to smoked salmon, the pièce de résistance is Christi's apple-almond tart.

When the Carters began turning away more people than they could take in, they decided to add a bona fide hotel to their empire. Mark, a former builder, decided to build a replica of a historic 19th-century Eureka hotel called the Old Town Cairo Hotel. The result—the Hotel Carter—has 20 rooms furnished primarily in pine; beds are fitted with down comforters and many of the bathrooms have whirlpool jets. (The most opulent rooms, with fireplaces and Jacuzzis, are on the second and third floors.) Ask for rooms 201 or 202, which have all these amenities plus particularly good views of the bay.

As for the Hotel Carter Restaurant, it's one of the best dinner spots on the northern coast. The fresh seafood, grilled rack of lamb, and pork tenderloin with chutney and homemade applesauce are all spectacular. A recent dinner found grilled squash cakes flecked with onion and red peppers, topped with crème fraîche and served on a bed of baby greens. The richly flavored squash and black bean soup came swirled in a pinwheel design and decorated with edible flowers from the inn's garden. Top off dinner with a scoop of homemade cappuccino ice cream. The wine list features West Coast wines. ■ *3rd and L streets; hotel and restaurant: (707) 444-8062, 301 L St; inn: (707) 445-1390, 1033 3rd St; both Eureka, CA 95501; $$$; beer and wine; AE, DC, MC, V; checks OK; dinner Thurs–Sun.*

An Elegant Victorian Mansion ★★★ This place is a kick. From the moment when "Jeeves"—owner Doug Vieyra in his Wodehouse mode—opens the front door, you know you're in good, if somewhat whimsical, hands. The house itself is a jewel—a National Historic Landmark lovingly maintained by the amazing Doug and his wife Lily. Built in 1888, it's a paradise for anybody with a passion for—well, almost anything. Doug and Lily are maniacal collectors—and their guests are beneficiaries of this pleasant personality disorder. The Vieyras have an incredible array of 1915–1940 movies, along with a collection of popular music from the same era. Then there's Doug's obsession with antique autos: he's frequently seen motoring (with guests on board) in his 1928 Model A Ford.

Upstairs are four guest rooms, each with furnishings reflecting a different period, place, or personage. The light-filled Lillie Langtry Room, named for the famed 19th-century chanteuse who once sang at the local Ingomar Theatre, has a lovely oak four-poster. The Governor's room, done in country French, has a great view of Eureka and a small side room that makes a good separate space for children. All the rooms, which share three bathrooms, have terrycloth bathrobes—perfect for curling up in after a visit to the Veiyras' state-of-the-art sauna.

Doug and Lily are incredibly attentive hosts—they'll lend you bicycles, pore over road maps with you, and make your dinner reservations. Lily, trained as a French chef, prepares a morning fête. ■ *14th and C streets; (707) 442-5594; 1406 C St, Eureka, CA 95501; $$; MC, V; checks OK.*

The Eureka Inn ★★★ Behind the inn's Old World exterior, guests discover such modern details as a Jacuzzi, a cedar-paneled sauna, and an outdoor swimming pool. Request a room that faces the landscaped courtyard and plan to spend some time in the lobby, which—with its deep leather settees, writing tables, and fireplace—could almost pass for a Hearst creation. The Palm Lounge is a popular meeting place for drinks, piano music, and—best of all—complimentary caviar. The Rathskeller has domestic and imported beers, and there's a lovely cafe called The Bristol Rose that serves lunch and breakfast (*not* included in the price of a room).

The heavyweight culinary arena, however, is the Rib Room. In a region where dress is almost always casual, this grandiose spot is a notable exception. Tuxedoed waiters, wood paneling, a roaring fire, wall tapestries, and pewter plates all contribute to the impression that time has stood still here for decades, if not centuries. The service here is a bit of a dog and pony show—many different people perform many different functions, but it's fun to watch them prepare the meats and salads at your table. While the menu is far from adventurous, the meals are beautifully prepared. Gorge as thou might in the Tudor tradition, your appetite will reappear when the dessert cart approacheth or the waiter ignites the bananas Foster. The wine list is suitably large. In December, the staff transforms the place into a Christmas fantasyland. One year, a 22-foot-tall tree was decorated with live orchids; another, it was encircled by model trains. Afternoon tea is served in the lobby, with live classical music every afternoon and evening. ■ *7th and F streets; (707) 442-6441, toll free (800) 862-4906 outside California; 518 7th St, Eureka, CA 95501; inn, $$$; restaurant, $$; full bar; AE, DC, DIS, MC, V; checks OK; dinner every day.*

SAMOA

RESTAURANTS

Samoa Cookhouse Visiting the Eureka area without a stop at the Samoa Cookhouse is like visiting the US without having a slice of apple pie. One of the last surviving cookhouses in the West—in operation for over 100 years—the Samoa is a Humboldt County institution. Guests are served logging camp–style at long tables covered with checkered tablecloths. (One room is a logging museum.) Few decisions are required—just sit down, and food will come until you say uncle. Breakfast usually consists of sausage, biscuits, scrambled eggs, potatoes, and French toast or pancakes. Lunch and dinner include at least two entrées such as ham, fried chicken, pork chops, roast beef, barbecued chicken, or fish. Mashed potatoes are a staple. The food isn't great, but there's plenty of it. The delicious bread is baked on the premises. Just when you think you're about to burst, along comes fresh-baked pie. ■ *Hwy 101 to Samoa Bridge, left on Samoa Rd, first left on Cookhouse Lane, Samoa; (707) 442-1659; $; no alcohol; AE, DC, DIS, MC, V; checks OK; breakfast, lunch, dinner every day.*

ARCATA

The jewel of this wonderful, far-north college town is **Arcata Plaza,** a marvelous place to people-watch, stroll, and window shop. Be sure to check out the exquisitely restored **Jacoby's Storehouse** and the works of local artists at **Plaza Design.** The plaza is home to several annual festivities, including the Fourth of July, the North Country Fair in September, crafts fairs, and the start of the oddly famous **Kinetic Sculpture Race** in May (see Ferndale). A **Farmers Market** takes place here on Saturdays, June through October.

Arcata was recently awarded a $100,000 Ford Foundation grant recognizing the city's innovative sewage system; the city built several ponds and marshes as natural filters for treated sewage water. The result is the best place for miles around to bird-watch. Some 200 bird species call the **Arcata Marsh and Wildlife Sanctuary** home. Visitors jog or stroll past egrets, waterfowl, and marsh wrens. Guided walking tours are given on Saturday mornings. **Humboldt State University** is situated in

▼

Arcata

▲

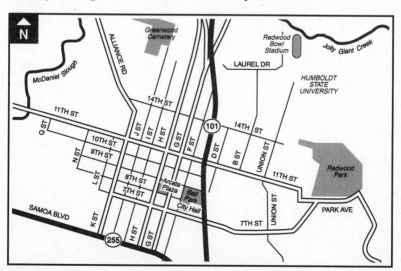

Arcata as well, and has a full calendar of exhibits, concerts, and lectures available to the public. And, for those in need of a public radio fix, fear not: tune in to 90.5FM, KHSU.

Arcata is nestled at the base of a beautiful portion of **Redwood Park** and the **Arcata Community Forest.** The **Community Forest,** the first one ever owned by a city in California, has 10 miles of trails through 600 acres of second growth redwoods. There is a lovely picnic area within the park, where children can slide down an enormous redwood stump.

Lamphere-Christensen Dune Preserve allows visitors to observe the fragile sand dune flora. To warm up after, head for the **Finnish Country Hot Tubs and Saunas;** (707) 822-2228.

RESTAURANTS

Abruzzi ★★ Named for a region on the Italian Adriatic, Abruzzi is located on the bottom floor of the 140-year-old Jacoby Storehouse in historic Arcata Plaza. If you have any trouble finding the place, follow your nose: the smell of garlic and fresh bread will soon steer you to Chris Smith and Bill Chino's friendly spot. Baskets blossoming with fresh bread sticks, focaccia, and baguettes arrive warm at each table. We particularly like the pasta carbonara and linguine pescara—prawns, calamari, and clams in a light Sicilian tomato sauce. The spinach calzone, filled with fresh spinach, ricotta, and garlic in marinara, is also very good. Chocolate paradiso—a fudgelike cake in a pool of champagne mousseline—stands out on the dessert tray. The staff is enthusiastic and energetic, and portions are ample and beautifully presented.

Smith and Chino also own the **Plaza Grill** on the third floor of the same building—a great place to go for a drink or a light, grilled-seafood supper and live music. ■ *H St between 7th and 8th streets on Arcata Plaza; (707) 826-2345; 780 7th St, Arcata; $$; full bar; AE, DC, DIS, MC, V; checks OK; dinner every day, lunch Mon–Fri.*

Folie Douce ★★ To say that Folie Douce just serves pizza is like saying that Tiffany's just sells jewelry. Designer pizza is more like it. Try the Thai chicken pizza—marinated bits of breast in fontina and mozzarella, topped with bean sprouts and mushrooms—cooked in a wood-fired oven. Other iconoclastic offerings include spicy shrimp, clam-and-cheddar, and lamb pizzas. Pizza isn't the only thing going here: garlic-roasted leg of lamb or monk's chicken—a full boneless breast sautéed in butter, flambéed in brandy, and simmered with white wine, mustard, and cream—are both superb. Brightly painted walls boost the festive but unhurried atmosphere. Locals love the place, so reservations—even for early birds—are strongly advised. ■ *G St between 15th and 16th streets; (707) 822-1042; 1551 G St, Arcata; $$; beer and wine; no credit cards; checks OK; dinner Tues–Sat.*

Los Bagels ★★ In 1987, bagel companies all over America sent their products to NBC's *Today Show* to vie for the title of Best Bagel. The verdict: The best bagel outside of New York City was made by Los Bagels in Arcata. Locals concluded that the 3,000-mile trip must've tired their bagel out. This is, understandably, one of Arcata's most popular hangouts—the kind of place where, people muse their way through morning papers while munching one of the planet's more perfect snacks. That's as far as traditions go here, though. You can order a jalapeño bagel with guacamole as easily as you can a classic pumpernickel with cream cheese and lox or with cream cheese, walnuts, and raisins. There are plenty of other things to order for here or to go including empanadas, corn-rye bread, and fresh-baked challah. Second location in Eureka's Old Town. ■ *I St between 10th and 11th streets; (707) 822-3150; 1061 I Street, Arcata; $; no alcohol; no credit cards; local checks only; breakfast, lunch Sun–Mon; In Old Town, 321 3rd St between D and E streets, Eureka; (707) 442-8525.*

Ottavio's International Cuisine ★ Kahish and Ottavio Sabia are miracle workers. They've taken a boxlike room in a nondescript building in a small shopping center and—with little more than a few screens and planters—created a sublimely congenial space where eating is an aesthetic as well as gustatory pleasure. The fare might best be described as international eclectic—the culinary heritage tends toward Italian, but also encompasses Asia, Africa, France, Hungary, and Greece. The spanakopita, a blend of spinach, cheeses, and herbs, has a light and golden phyllo pastry. Also popular are gnocchi and gallina con limone—butterflied breast of chicken delicately browned in olive oil and simmered in lemon, wine, and garlic with mushrooms and artichoke hearts. There's a terrific dessert tray and live music (usually some variety of folk) Friday through Sunday; service is excellent and accommodating. It's equally acceptable to linger here or eat and run. ■ *7th and F streets in Uniontown Plaza; (707) 822-4021; 686 F St, Arcata; $$; beer and wine; MC, V over $25; checks OK; lunch Tues–Fri; dinner every day.*

Arcata

Lodgings

LODGINGS

Hotel Arcata ★ Managed by Big Lagoon Rancheria—a local collective of native American tribes—this recently renovated 1915 hotel has two major drawing cards: location and old-fashioned charm. Located at the northeastern corner of Arcata Plaza, the hotel is within walking distance of great restaurants, bookstores, gift shops, and a city square that conjures up images of New England or the American South. The lobby is graced by unpretentious sofas and historic photographs of Union (Arcata's original name). Truth to tell, the lights in the hall are a bit dim and gloomy, but the rooms—singles, doubles, mini- and executive suites, all with private baths—are comfortably furnished. The suites—quite spacious with a splendid view of the plaza—make an ideal base camp for several days of exploration in the redwoods. A night's stay includes continental breakfast. The hotel restaurant isn't very interesting. ■ *9th St between G and H streets on Arcata Plaza; (707) 826-0217, toll free (800) 344-1221; 708 9th St, Arcata, CA 95521; $$; DC, MC, V; checks OK.*

The Lady Anne ★ Located just a few blocks away from Arcata Plaza in a quiet residential neighborhood, this exquisite example of Queen Anne architecture has been painstakingly restored by innkeepers Sam Pennisi and Sharon Ferrett. There are five large and airy guest rooms. The most romantic room in the house is the Lady Sarah Angela with its four-poster bed, fireplace, and great view of the bay. Families often request the Cinnamon Bear Room, with its queen-size and trundle beds. The Lady Anne's three parlors are filled with games and musical instruments; clement afternoons are best spent on the verandah. Longtime Arcata residents Sam and Sharon suggest plenty of places to prowl around town. Beg for Belgian waffles for breakfast. ■ *Corner of 14th and I streets; (707) 822-2797; 902 14th St, Arcata, CA 95521; $$; MC, V; checks OK.*

TRINIDAD

Although Trinidad, with a population of 400, is one of the smallest incorporated cities in California, the view of the ocean here is quite big. Fish in Trinidad's sheltered cove. Commercial fishing boats moor in the harbor, and salmon, cod, and crab charters are available. Or try casting from Trinidad's pier. The folks at **Katy's Smokehouse** will smoke your catch for you.

Six miles north of Trinidad, along scenic Patrick's Point Drive, is **Patrick's Point State Park,** a hiker's paradise. Beachcombers adore its **Agate Beach,** where the semiprecious stones surface among beautiful pieces of driftwood. Watch out for sea lions, harbor seals, and gray whale from **Wedding Rock, Ceremonial Rock,** and **Lookout Rock.**

Patrick's Point was once a seasonal fishing village for Yuroks. In 1990, descendants of these original settlers reconstructed an authentic Yurok village including dwellings, a sweat house, dance pit, and preparation areas. Some ceremonial dances are open to the public.

RESTAURANTS

Larrupin' Cafe ★★★ Larrupin' is well-loved for lots of reasons: its fireplace, its lovely artwork, its rustic building set off with huge vases of flowers. But its reputation rests primarily on its food, especially its awesome pork ribs and sweet, mildly hot barbecue sauce. The locally caught red fish in a spicy marinade is excellent, as is boneless chicken breast stuffed with cream cheese and artichoke hearts and wrapped in phyllo pastry. The oysters, mussels and barbecued crab are incredibly fresh, plucked from Humboldt Bay the same afternoon. Every meal comes with a colorful, fresh, deliciously dressed salad and appetizer board including gravlax, paté, dark pumpernickel, apple slices, and the house mustard sauce. Order the delicious twice-baked potato, stuffed with local cheese, sour cream, and scallions. Pecan pie and chocolate cake with caramel layers are scrumptious, as is the edible logo that comes with the bill—a small chocolate fish. You can opt for patio seating in summer; reservations are a must at any time of year. ■ *Patrick's Point Dr, N of Trinidad; (707) 677-0230; 1658 Patrick's Point Dr, Trinidad; $$; beer and wine; no credit cards; checks OK; dinner Wed–Sun in summer (Thurs–Sun in winter).*

Seascape Restaurant ★ This is where the fishermen dine and where glass-enclosed patios afford views of the working pier. One taste of the deliciously fresh seafood will explain the longevity of this 40-year-old restaurant. Order the Trinidad Bay platter: scallops, prawns, oysters, cod, sole, salmon, and halibut—grilled, fried, poached, charbroiled, oven-broiled, or sautéed, as you wish. Another good choice is one of the Louies—crab or shrimp. After your meal, take a stroll down the pier to watch the fisherfolk and sea otters. ■ *Hwy 101 to Trinidad, left on Main, left on Trinity, right on Edwards to the Trinidad Pier; (707) 677-3762; Trinidad Pier, Trinidad; $$; beer and wine; DC, MC, V; checks OK; breakfast, lunch, dinner every day.*

LODGINGS

The Lost Whale Bed and Breakfast Inn ★★★ The Lost Whale B&B isn't just a place to stay overnight—it's a destination in itself. The traditional Cape Cod–style building, built in 1989, sits alone on a cliff overlooking the sea. A private stairway leads down to a blissfully empty rocky beach. Innkeepers Suzanne Lakin and Lee Miller manage the considerable trick of indulging their customers' needs for space while also providing for travelers with children. Large sleeping lofts in some rooms enable kids to bunk upstairs and parents down. Two of the four suites boast private balconies and spectacular views of the rugged coast. The balcony in the Beluga Whale Room opens to a southern exposure. Two rooms without ocean view are airy and nicely furnished.

The living room is an ideal vantage point for whale watching or basking in the hot tub while listening for the distant bark of sea lions. Kids can explore the enclosed grounds—equipped with a menagerie of goats and rabbits and a playhouse with its own loft—while parents sunbathe, relax in the living room, or linger over breakfast. The inn even provides full-fledged babysitting with advance notice. Suzanne and Lee take great pride in their huge breakfasts and provide plenty of snacks throughout the day and evening. It also has private access to a secluded beach via a wooded trail, and right next door is Patrick's Point State Park—nirvana for an agate- and driftwood-hunter. ■ *Seawood Dr exit off Hwy 101 N of Trinidad, 1.8 miles N on Patrick's Point Dr; (707) 677-3427; 3452 Patrick's Point Dr, Trinidad, CA 95570; $$$; MC, V; checks OK.*

Trinidad Bed and Breakfast ★ Perched on a bluff overlooking a fishing harbor and the stunning coast, this Cape Cod–style inn is the dream house of innkeepers Carol and Paul Kirk, a couple of Southern California transplants who fell in love with the area while visiting Arcata in 1985. The Kirks cater to their guests' desires for privacy: two suites are completely self-contained, with private entrances, ample sitting rooms, and breakfast delivered to the door. The Mauve Suite has a large brick fireplace and wraparound windows, the better to showcase the surrounding seascape; unfortunately, the room's occupants are equally on view. The much more private Blue Bay View Suite upstairs has an equally spectacular view, complete with a telescope for whale watching. The hearty breakfasts feature fresh and baked fruit and homemade delicacies such as fresh breads with lemon-honey and molasses butters, muffins (pear-ginger, cranberry-orange, fruited bran), jams, and local cheeses. ■ *Hwy 101 to Trinidad, left on Main, left on Trinity to 360 Edwards St; (707) 677-0840; Mail: PO Box 849, Trinidad, CA 95570; $$$$; MC, V; checks OK.*

ORICK

RESTAURANTS

Rolf's Park Cafe ★ The decidely Teutonic Rolf Rheinschmidt, former executive chef at The Black Forest in Santa Rosa, the Jack Tar Hotel in San Francisco, and aboard the *SS Roosevelt*, decided he wanted to move to a small town; soon afterward (never one for halfway measures) he opened a restaurant and motel outside Orick—population 450. Hence, travel among the lonely redwoods is now abetted by fantastic bratwurst, weiner schnitzel, Hungarian goulash, and crêpes Suzette. The menu here is staggering, actually. Hors d'oeuvres, salad, vegetables, farm-style potatoes, bread, dessert, and port wine are all included with your marinated rack of spring lamb or any of Rheinschmidt's more esoteric offerings. Rheinschmidt also runs **The Silver Lining** at the Eureka/Arcata Airport in McKinleyville. ■ *About 2 miles N of Orick on Hwy 101; (707) 488-3841; $; beer and wine; MC, V; local checks only; breakfast, lunch, dinner every day in summer (call ahead in winter).*

NORTH MOUNTAINS

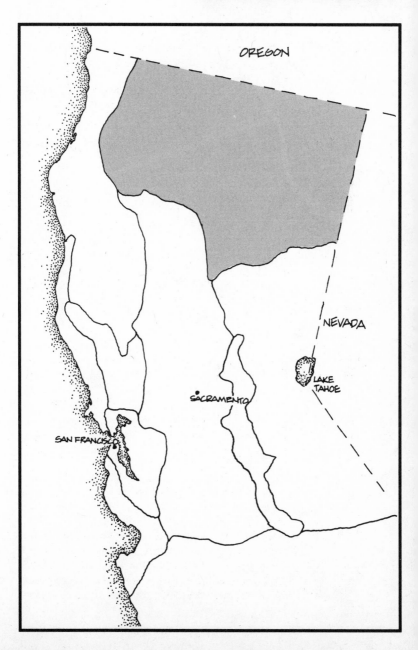

OREGON

NEVADA

LAKE TAHOE

SACRAMENTO

SAN FRANCISCO

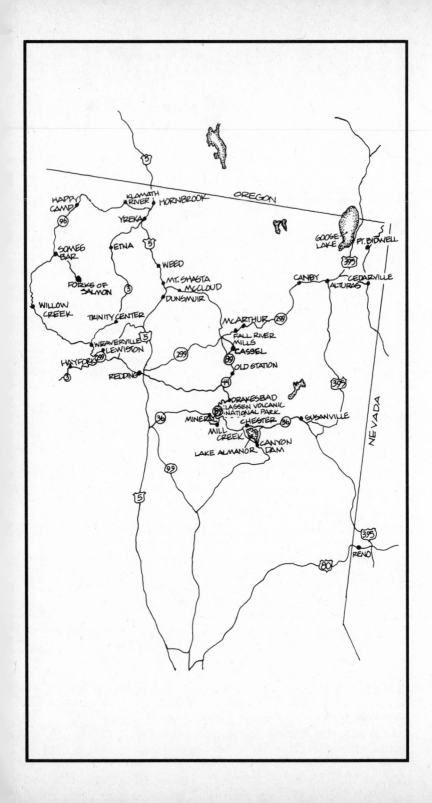

North Mountains

Clockwise from Redding. West on 299 to Willow Creek with diversion to Trinity Lake. North on 96 to I-5 at Hornbrook. South on I-5 to Dunsmuir then east to Alturas. Loop south to Susanville and return via Lake Almanor.

REDDING

Redding is the gateway to California's northern mountains. It's not so much what's here as what's near (prime fishing, hiking, skiing, mountain biking, and boating). **Shasta Lake,** just 20 minutes north of town, requires a boat to fully appreciate its 370 miles of shoreline. It's great for fishing, waterskiing, or just lounging on a houseboat. (For information about rentals, call (800) 874-7562.) **Whiskeytown Lake,** west of Redding, has good beaches, wind-surfing, and sailboating; (916) 225-5356.

In Redding itself, the 6-mile **Sacramento River Trail** meanders along the Sacramento River and over an old stress-ribbon concrete bridge, the only one in the country. **The Redding Museum of Art and History** has local history exhibits and a fine collection of native American baskets; 56 Quartz Hill Road, (916) 225-4155. **The Carter House Natural Science Museum** right next door is a funky, spirited place with wild animals and lots of hands-on activities for kids. Entertainment of a different kind can be found at Andy's Cow Patty Palace where Andy Berwind, chef and standup comic, is a shameless exhibitionist.

RESTAURANTS

Nello's Place ★★ Exuberant Italian wall murals and bright Campari umbrellas hanging from the ceiling add a playful touch to this traditional, romantically dim Italian dinner house. Like the California and Italian wine list, the menu here is vast and wide-ranging. Among the appetizers, be on the lookout for the golden, deep-fried artichoke hearts or the simple but good steamed clams in garlic, butter, and white wine. For dinner, go with the thick, meaty lasagne or the sinfully rich chicken Rossini, a deep-fried boneless chicken breast stuffed with prosciutto, mozzarella, and provolone set in a brandied stock reduction sauce. There's also a whole selection of rich red meat specialties that include veal and truffles or the bistecca pizzalola (a New York steak with caramelized red onions, garlic, mushrooms, and a dash of marinara). Nello's romantic ambience extends from the supertraditional desserts such as crêpes Suzette and cherries to the red carnation, given to every signorina at the end of dinner. For romance on the cheap, try the early bird dinner special (5 to 6:30pm), a four-course Italian dinner for just over 10 bucks. ■ *E side of Bechelli Lane near Hartnell; (916) 223-1636; 3055 Bechelli Lane, Redding; $$; full bar; AE, MC, V; checks OK; dinner Tues–Sat.*

River City Bar and Grill ★★ A wonderful find in the shadow of Mount Shasta, River City Bar and Grill is a dull shingled building with a giant Roberts Motel sign looming overhead—enchantment begins inside with the Cajun popcorn (fresh rock shrimp dredged in cornmeal, pan-fried, and served with rémoulade) and a Louisiana sausage plate (house-made sausages served with mustard cream and Creole sauce). For lunch we found a meaty jambalaya, a filé-heavy seafood gumbo, and a rich Cajun stew with toothsome duck, whole red beans and spicy sausage—all served with a fine freshly baked sourdough cornbread. Dinners are slightly more elaborate with shellfish étouffée and blackened prime rib. ■ *4 blocks S of the downtown mall on Market between Lincoln and Hill streets; (916) 243-9003; 2151 Market St, Redding; $$; full bar; AE, MC, V; checks OK; lunch Tues–Fri, dinner Tues–Sat.*

Cheesecakes Unlimited & Cafe ★ Cory Gabrielson and Nicholas Parker started Cheesecakes Unlimited as a small wholesale cheesecake business. Recently they expanded by opening a small cafe that offers light entrées such as croissant sandwiches and salads. Everything here is good and fresh, but the

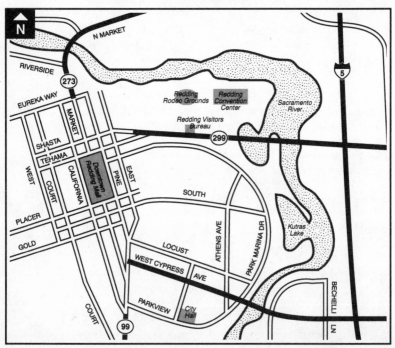

salads are the best bet: the chicken and walnut comes with fresh greens, tomato, cucumber, and red onion in a Dijon mustard vinaigrette; the ham salad arrives with mixed vegetables, pecans, and orange and grapefruit slices in a citrus vinaigrette. Of course the New York–style cheesecakes (lemon, lime, raspberry, Dutch chocolate almond, or perhaps mocha Bailey's) are the kind you want to take home. ■ *On Market St just N of the downtown mall; (916) 244-6670; 1334 Market St, Redding; $; no alcohol; MC, V; checks OK; breakfast, lunch Mon–Sat.*

Jack's Grill ★ A 1930s tavern in cream and brown, Jack's Grill is a beloved institution in Redding—so beloved that few even grumble over the typical two-hour weekend wait for a table in the smoky dining room. Be forewarned: Jack's is a carnivores-only club, specializing in huge juicy steaks, tender brochettes, and fat steak sandwiches. All dinners include garlic bread, green salad, and potato. Jack starts serving dinner at 5pm, and hungry folk get there early. ■ *On California St south of the downtown mall, between Sacramento and Placer streets; (916) 241-9705; 1743 California St, Redding; $$; full bar; MC, V; local checks only; dinner Mon–Sat.*

Le Chamois ★ An unexpected delight along the ugly commercial strip stretching north from downtown Redding, Le Chamois is really two restaurants: a sunny cafe filled with plants, antique bottles, and farm curios, and a slightly more formal, wood-paneled dining room next door. Breakfast (served only from 7 to 10am) features delicious sourdough pancakes and homemade granola, along with the usual array of breakfast egg dishes. For lunch, try the Shasta sandwich (turkey, avocado, and lappi cheese) and the hot Ortega (roast beef with sautéed chiles, onion, bell peppers, and mushrooms). Apple cinnamon crêpes and huevos rancheros clash on the elaborate Sunday brunch menu. ■ *N of town on Hwy 273 in the N Market Square mini-mall; (916) 241-7720; 630 N Market St, Redding; $; beer and wine; AE, MC, V; checks OK; breakfast, lunch Mon–Sat, brunch Sun; call about dinner.*

Maxwell's ★ Kelly Brown started this casual but serene eatery in an old brick building over a decade ago. Done in cool blue and white, the dining room is dotted with the work of local artists, inclucing photographs by Kelly's husband Bruce. Lunchtime pastas include a rich linguine cacciucco that is swimming with shrimp, scallops, crab, clams, and sole or the rigatoni with fresh pesto. Maxwell's delicious spinach salad comes piled high with shrimp, mushrooms, pimento, bacon, and hearts of palm in a tart vinaigrette. Dinner entrées include tender sea scallops in an orange beurre blanc and hot Hunan chicken redolent of garlic, ginger, and anise. The service is somewhat indifferent, alas, and the portions a bit scant. ■ *On Market St between Shasta and Tehama; (916) 246-4373;*

1344 Market St, Redding; $$; full bar; AE, MC, V; checks OK; lunch, dinner Tues–Sat.

Buz's Crab Every day, the bounty of the North Coast is hauled over the hills into California's parched interior to Buz's seafood market. With Naugahyde booths, Formica tables, and molded plastic chairs, the standard fish 'n' chips would be no surprise; however, Buz's seafood baskets include stuffed prawns, oysters, scallops, clam strips, calamari, catfish, Cajun halibut, and crisp no-grease potato rounds. December to May get the fabulous crab (just plucked from the boiling crab pots on the patio) and a slab of Buz's fresh-baked sourdough bread. ■ *East Street N of West Cypress Ave and Pine St; (916) 243-2120; 2159 East St, Redding; $; beer and wine; MC, V; local checks only; lunch, dinner every day.*

LODGINGS

Tiffany House Bed & Breakfast Inn ★★ Perched on a hill above town, Arthur and Roberta Dube's beautifully refurbished Cape Cod–style home offers three elegant guest rooms and a fine view of Mount Lassen. Our favorite room is the black and mauve rose print Victorian Room with its interesting cupola windows and claw-footed tub, but the sunrise is lovely from the smaller French Country Room. Downstairs in the white-wicker music parlor, you'll find an organ with old-time sheet music like "Jazz Baby" and "Baby Face." Another antique-filled parlor supports a fireplace and game table. The gazebo sits pretty in summer. The Dubes have recently added a beautiful little guest cottage out back with lavender and white decor and a pretty scrolled headboard. ■ *E on Benton Dr from N Market St, up the hill on Barbara Rd; (916) 244-3225; 1510 Barbara Rd, Redding, CA 96003; $$; AE, MC, V; checks OK.*

LEWISTON

RESTAURANTS

Lewiston Hotel Built in 1862 as a stage stop, the Lewiston Hotel bills itself as one of California's oldest continuously operating restaurants. It's got a lot going for it: the walls are appropriately decorated with guns, animal furs, photos, and a large collection of highway and city street signs; and the menu shows promise with a first-rate chicken breast in creamy mushroom sauce, scampi that comes in a tasty, rich broth, and a pleasant salad with a mix of sprouts, beets, broccoli, and kidney and garbanzo beans. So what's wrong? The management has an irritating policy of steering hungry patrons first to the bar, even when there are tables to spare. Avoid the restrooms. ■ *Deadwood Rd, one block from bridge in Lewiston; (916) 778-3823; $$; full bar; MC, V; local checks only; dinner Thurs–Mon.*

Old Lewiston Inn ★ Innkeepers Connor and Mary Nixon ran a travel lodge in the Amazon for 13 years before trading up to a bed and breakfast in the wilds of Trinity County. Their inn has seven rooms—three small rooms in the 1875 Baker House and four rooms in the adjoining inn, most with private baths. The Baker House, where the Nixons live, has a lively, typically frontier history of love triangles, murder, and gambling. Skip the thrill of sleeping in Herbert Hoover's room and ask for a room in the adjoining inn—they have less history, but more elbow room, plus private entrances and decks overlooking the Trinity River. No smoking inside. ■ *Deadwood Rd, ½ block from bridge in Lewiston; (916) 778-3385; Mail: PO Box 688, Lewiston, CA 96052; $; MC, V; checks OK.*

WEAVERVILLE

With only 4,000 residents, Weaverville is the biggest town in Trinity County, an area the size of Rhode Island and Delaware combined that includes the stunning Trinity Alps. Many houses in the town's historic downtown have peculiar outdoor spiral staircases—remnants of the days when the different stories were owned by different people. Check out the Chinese Temple built by Chinese miners in 1874. Now called the **Joss House,** the temple is a state park with a museum; (916) 623-5284.

Weaverville

Restaurants

RESTAURANTS

La Grange Cafe ★ Locals dig into Weaverville's best food at La Grange, named for an old mine near town. Exceptionally fresh salads are tossed with a fine Italian dressing and chunks of blue cheese. The marinated steak comes charbroiled, sliced, and served with black bean chili; the chicken, dressed with a light fruit and wine salsa, comes with wheat pilaf and fresh fruit. No one frowns at the prices (or the wine list), but outdoor diners do wrinkle their noses at the dusty parking lot and the intrusion of highway noise into an an otherwise two-star meal. ■ *On Hwy 299 (Main St); (916) 623-5325; 315 N Main St, Weaverville; $$; beer and wine; MC, V; checks OK; breakfast, lunch, dinner Mon–Sat.*

The Mustard Seed ★ Located on the second floor of an old two-story house, this snug, cheerful breakfast spot has lots of windows and a sunny outside deck. In the morning, dig into a bowl of hearty seven-grain cereal with milk or cream. Owner Barbara Killingsworth creates substantial quiches, veggie omelets, and colorful, crisp house salads. Espresso tastes best on the patio. ■ *On Main St 1 block W of Oregon St; (916) 623-2922; 252 Main St, Weaverville; $; no alcohol; no credit cards; checks OK; breakfast, lunch every day.*

Granny's House ★ Built in 1897 from wood milled by owner H.W. Goetze Sr. at his nearby sawmill, this attractive Queen Anne home housed Goetze's son and his bride Clara until she died in 1986 at the age of 102. Blaine and Patricia Menning now run Granny's House as a year-round B&B. A big plus here is the sumptuous feast they serve for breakfast: French toast, strawberry waffles, or eggs Benedict, along with sausage and fruit. Patricia is understandably proud of her lemon curd recipe. ■ *At 313 on Taylor St near Court St in Weaverville; (916) 623-2756; Mail: PO Box 31, Weaverville, CA 96093; $$; AE, MC, V; checks OK.*

Weaverville Hotel Originally known as the Empire, which burned to the ground several times during the town's early days, the Weaverville Hotel has been in continuous operation since 1861 (minus the fiery interruptions). The hotel's eight second-floor rooms are a bit 1940s—on the primitive side, but a good alternative for the budget-conscious traveler who likes historic surroundings and a continental breakfast. All rooms have private baths; most have TVs. Check in at the sporting goods store on the ground floor. ■ *Center of town at 201 Main St; (916) 623-3121; Mail: PO Box 537, Weaverville, CA 96093; $, MC, V; checks OK.*

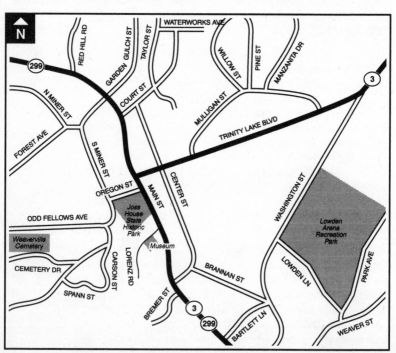

HAYFORK

The frontier town of Hayfork sits astride the south fork of the wild and scenic Trinity River. Hayfork is the home of the **Trinity County Fair,** an old-fashioned country fair featuring a rodeo and livestock show, destruction derby, and logging competitions such as double-handed bucking and ax throwing. A huge natural stone bridge carved by the rushing waters of Carrier Gulch Creek has a sorry history: in the 19th century, a group of native Americans were massacred by settlers under the immense roof of the bridge, where—as local legend has it—God couldn't see.

RESTAURANTS

Alice's Restaurant ★ You may not be able to get anything you want at Alice's Restaurant, but you can get a lot of good quality food for very little money. A large New York charbroiled steak dinner, including soup, salad, homemade bread, and dessert, is less than $15. Other good bets are the delicately seasoned chicken sauté with fresh mushrooms and vegetables, and the tender pan-fried abalone steak. The wine list is limited but well-chosen. For breakfast, try the flapjack sandwich: two large plate-sized flapjacks with sausage, bacon, and an egg cooked any way you like it. The service, provided by Alice Ackerly and her whole clan, is cheerful and welcoming. The electronic organ and wooden toy trains make playful diversions.
■ *SW end of town, corner of Hwy 3 and Hyampom Rd; (916) 628-4212; $; beer and wine; no credit cards; checks OK; breakfast, lunch every day, dinner Mon–Sat.*

TRINITY CENTER

Some say **Coffee Creek** (8 miles north of Trinity Center) got its name because a miners' pack train spilled coffee into it. We suspect it's because spring runoff colors the water coffee brown. Whatever the case, the burg of the same name that sprang up on its banks dates back to the Gold Rush days of the 1850s. There aren't many places to dine around here, but locals consider the **Forest Deli** on Highway 3 at Coffee Creek Road adequate; (916) 266-3575.

LODGINGS

Carrville Inn Bed and Breakfast ★★ It's a beauty. Ray and Barbara Vasconcellos spent six years restoring this spacious two-story landmark before opening it as a bed and breakfast inn during the late 1980s. The original structure dates back to 1854 when James E. Carr arrived with his wife Sarah. It later served as a stage stop. Today, there are five nonsmoking guest rooms elegantly furnished with antiques and local memorabilia. Three rooms open onto the verandah. The Rose Room bridal suite features rose-patterned wallpaper, a four-poster bed, Civil War–era settee, and claw-footed tub. Downstairs, guests share a sitting room with a fireplace and a game room decorated with Old West photos. Wine and hors d'oeuvres are served there in the afternoon. In the morning, Barbara often whips up buttermilk pancakes, along with fruit, juice, and eggs done a variety of ways. ■ *3536 Carrville Loop Rd, ¼ mile W of Hwy 3; (916) 266-3511; Mail: Star Route 2, Box 3536, Trinity Center, CA 96091; $$$; no credit cards; checks OK; open Apr to Oct.*

Ripple Creek Cabins ★ Set among tall pines and cedars where Ripple Creek enters the Trinity River, all seven of Charley and Linda Dunlap's well-furnished cabins have well-stocked kitchens (even corkscrews and garlic presses!) and private baths. Most of the cabins accommodate two to six people. There's also a four-bedroom house that could be used for a family reunion or retreat. The smell of propane is a bit disconcerting, but otherwise this is a good spot, complete with a volleyball/badminton area, table tennis, bicycles, and a swimming hole. For a $10 fee, you can bring Fido along. Smoking is permitted. ■ *On Eagle Creek Loop off Hwy 3; (916) 266-3505 or 266-3608; Mail: Route 2, Box 3899, Trinity Center, CA 96091; $; no credit cards; checks OK.*

HAWKINS BAR

LODGINGS

Madrone Lane Bed and Breakfast ★★ Retired art professors Roger and Jane Cinnamond have opened two gorgeous rooms in their modern, Trinity Village home. One's a studio above the garage; the other's a three-room suite with Jacuzzi inside the main house. Both access the swimming pool and sauna. The Cinnamonds supply color TVs with VCRs and a large film library, but with such striking Trinity scenery, who needs electronics? If you want to try your hand at painting or sketching, you'll get pointers from a couple of experts. Cooking facilities are limited, so you'll have to settle for a toaster oven and a refrigerator stocked with baked goods, fruits, cheese, beer, and wine. The Cinnamonds don't accept credit cards, but they have been known to barter. ■ *In Trinity Village, 1 mile above the Trinity River across from Hawkins Bar (call for directions); (916) 629-3642; Mail: HCR No. 34, Burnt Ranch, CA 95527; $$; no credit cards; checks OK.*

WILLOW CREEK

RESTAURANTS

Cinnabar Sam's ★ When crossing between the coast and Redding, try to save your appetite for this veritable mini-museum of Western memorabilia: antique gas pumps, old-time photographs, movie posters from the golden days—the salad bar is even in a claw-footed tub. The delicious food fits the decor. Do-it-yourself fajitas are popular at lunch and dinner, as are the huge, juicy hamburgers, sirloin steak, barbecued ribs, and London broil teriyaki. Despite our better judgment, our favorite day-starter is the messy Claimjumper: ham, scrambled eggs, hashbrowns, onions, bell peppers, sausage, and cheese. On sweltering days, head for the Cinnabar patio for one of Sam's cooling mixed fresh-fruit drinks. ■ *Hwy 299 at the E end of town, corner of Willow Way; (916) 629-3437; 19 Willow Way, Willow Creek; $; beer and wine; MC, V; checks OK; breakfast, lunch, dinner every day (lunch, dinner every day, brunch Sun in winter).*

SOMES BAR

RESTAURANTS

Young's Ranch Resort ★ This is the best of several fishing lodges a short stroll from the torrential lower Klamath River. The complex includes a main lodge, 11 housekeeping cabins, an RV park, and a tent camping area. We won't rave about the lodgings (most come to fish or raft)—the star stands primarily for its food. Bob and Judy Young put on quite a spread morning and night. Your dinner entrée may be particularly fine barbecued steak (grilled over madrone and oak and then sliced thin), a tangy lemon chicken, or perhaps a platter of finger-licking ribs served buffet style with baked potatoes, fresh vegetables, and salad. You don't have to spend the night to enjoy this feast, but you do need to make a reservation. ■ *7 miles N of Somes Bar on Hwy 96; (916) 469-3322, toll free (800) 552-6284; Hwy 96, Somes Bar, CA 95568; $; wine; AE, DIS, MC, V; checks OK.*

LODGINGS

Somes Bar Lodge The driveway leading to Somes Bar Lodge, a steep dirt road filled with potholes, demands your utmost attention and determination. Even in first gear, the excursion is an adventure. Once there, you'll find a two-story, high-ceilinged fishing lodge with four guest rooms looking out over the Klamath River. The price ($50 a day per person) includes all meals. Most folks come for several days, but one-nighters are welcome. Owners Brad and Vicki Throgmorton serve a set menu for each meal—mostly roast beef, lamb, duck, and roast pork. There's a hot tub to soak in after a long day of casting. ■ *N end of town on Hwy 96; (916) 469-3399; Mail: General Delivery, Somes Bar, CA 95568; $; beer and wine; no credit cards; checks OK.*

FORKS OF SALMON

LODGINGS

Otter Bar Lodge ★★★ This four-bedroom, ranch-style lodge, with its own pond and acres of mowed green grass, features oak floors, French doors, and lots of glass—all designed to bring the outdoors indoors. Two living rooms, two kitchens, a sauna, and a hot tub are available to guests. The cedar-roofed, whitewashed rooms have private decks, antiques, down comforters, and good books. We particularly like the romantic Tower room, an upstairs room with windows all around looking out into the fir trees. There's a separate cabin for families with small children.

The lodge doubles as a world-class kayaking school and offers some of the most beautiful mountain-biking trails in the state. In the fall, Orvis sponsors its famed fly-fishing clinics here and a three-day guided horsepack trip into the Trinity Alps. The food is terrific: no ranch-style meat and potatoes here. Instead look for paella, Thai fish, snapper Vera Cruz, and other healthful, sophisticated delights. Scones, homemade granola, veggie omelets, and berry-flecked pancakes for breakfast. Enjoy. You're here for a week. ■ *15 miles W of Somes Bar on Salmon River Rd; (916) 462-4772; Mail: Box 210, Forks of Salmon, CA 96031; $$$; no credit cards; checks OK; open late Apr-Oct.*

HAPPY CAMP

Happy Camp used to be a lot more, well, happy. Nowadays, the camp is dependent on the uncertain fortunes of lumbering, fishing, and tourism; some locals jokingly suggest a different adjective might be in order.

RESTAURANTS

Indian Creek Cafe ★ This small cafe in one of the most sparsely populated corners of California has one of the state's largest menus. You can get breakfast sandwiches, deli sandwiches, chicken baskets, barbecued turkey, chicken strips, or submarine sandwiches. Then there's a separate Mexican menu—and at night, a dinner menu with steaks, Italian chicken, shrimp, and the like. Owners Ray and Beth Lohn work horrendous hours and put out daily specials, like sautéed shiitake mushrooms or bread pudding with bourbon sauce. It's basic country fare that occasionally tries to be different—how about a chef's salad with chow mein noodles, sprouts, and green onions sandwiched between lettuce and small slices of turkey? ■ *Indian Creek Rd near 2nd Ave; (916) 493-5180; 106 Indian Creek Rd, Happy Camp; $; beer and wine; AE, DIS, MC, V; local checks only; breakfast, lunch, dinner every day.*

KLAMATH RIVER

LODGINGS

Beaver Creek Lodge ★ One of the better lodges on the Klamath, Beaver Creek Lodge has knotty pine cabins and well-groomed grounds. Unlike most lodges in the area, it is right on the river. Four cabins ($54) sleep up to three. A larger unit can accommodate five. All cabins have kitchens, and groceries are available in the town of Klamath River, 2 miles away. The golf course is 5 miles away. Pets are welcome if on a leash. ■ *On Hwy 96, 2 miles E of Klamath River; (916) 465-2331; 16606 Hwy 96, Klamath River, CA 96050; $; no credit cards; checks OK.*

HORNBROOK

RESTAURANTS

Country Kitchen ★ Who'd expect to find a treasure in this town of 600 near the Oregon border? It looks like zilch on the outside, but you know something's up when you see copies of *National Geographic* and *Reader's Digest* on each table. The tiny cafe, which seats about 20, doubles as a community center and library. Help yourself to a book while waiting for breakfast, try your hand at the community jigsaw puzzle, or read the bulletin board. Your hosts Betty and Bob Philps fill you in on the weather, latest real estate transactions, and good fishing spots. Patrons pour their own coffee, pick out their flatware, and order off a basic menu on the wall. The fried potatoes and bran muffins are notable. ■ *1 mile E of Henley-Hornbrook I-5 exit; (916) 475-3355; Old Hornbrook Hwy, Hornbrook; $; beer and wine; no credit cards; checks OK; breakfast, lunch, dinner Mon–Sat.*

Yreka

Restaurants

YREKA

Once a boom town, Yreka today mines its gold from tourists who come to visit the town's **Historic District.** Get a map in the Old Yreka Drug store; 117 West Miner Street, (916) 842-1649; toll free (800) 669-7352. In the summer, take a scenic round-trip train ride to the historic town of Montague on the **The Yreka Western Railroad.** In **Montague,** get a snack at the Opera House Restaurant, built in 1904, and poke around in the historical museum in the 1887 railroad depot; (916) 842-4146.

RESTAURANTS

The Old Boston Shaft ★ Swiss chef-owners Max and Erich Schuler specialize in hearty sauced beef and veal dishes. The veal Zingara, with tomato, julienne of ham, and mushrooms, is pretty good, as is the grenadine of beef béarnaise. The veal à la Swiss comes with tomato, Swiss cheese, asparagus, and hollandaise. Even the ground round comes dressed up with shallots and bordelaise. You get plenty for the money: a three- to four-course meal comes in around $40 for two. The wine list is basic but inexpensive. Service is efficient. ■ *W of I-5 at Fort Jones–Hwy 3 exit; (916) 842-5768; 1801 Fort Jones Rd, Yreka; $$; full bar; MC, V; local checks only; lunch Mon–Fri, dinner Mon–Sat.*

ETNA

RESTAURANTS

Sengthong's ★ Born in Vietnam, Sengthong Phelps lived for a time in Laos and Thailand before making her way to this remote corner of Siskiyou County. Now she and her husband Don run a small Asian restaurant blending the cuisines of the three countries she left behind. You can see the Laotian influence in the sticky-rice balls, accompanied by a salsalike dip. The spring rolls are a tacolike creation with noodles, vegetables, and a spicy sauce in a lettuce wrapping. The Thai hot-spiced beef and seafood stew aren't bad at all. ■ *Center of town; (916) 467-5668; 434 Main St, Etna; $$; beer and wine; no credit cards; checks OK; dinner Wed–Sun.*

WEED

RESTAURANTS

Serge's Restaurant ★★ The best restaurant in Shasta County sits at the end of a winding, pasture-flanked country road in a small unpretentious wood building just inside Stewart Mineral Springs resort. Serge's dining room is very plain, but the outside terraces, dotted with small candle-lit tables overlooking a rushing stream, are spectacular. The small ambitious menu offers classic French dishes, beautifully prepared by French-born chef/owner Serge Margot. Try the tender steak au poivre or the chicken Normande (a succulent chicken breast served in a delicate cream sauce with mushrooms and apple brandy). The bouchée des fruits de mer comes in a flawlessly flaky little pastry basket. The staff is friendly, if less sophisticated than the chef. ■ *Call for directions; (916) 938-1251; 4617 Stewart Springs Rd, Weed; $$; beer and wine; MC, V; checks OK; dinner Thur–Sat, brunch Sun (closed in winter).*

LODGINGS

Lake Shastina Golf Resort ★ With an 18-hole championship course and a 9-hole Scottish links course, Golf Shastina would be a more accurate name for this sprawling resort in the shadow of Mount Shasta. Half of the resort's comfy condominiums overlook the 18-hole golf course, the other have a breathtaking view of Mount Shasta. The condominiums are beginning to show their wear, but the view of the mountain never gets old. Dinner in the resort's unfailingly ordinary restaurant is served all week during summer and on weekends during the rest of the year. For the actively inclined, there's a swimming pool, tennis courts, and—of course—golf. ■ *7 miles N of Weed via Hwy 97 and Big Springs Rd; (916) 938-3201; 5925 Country Club Dr, Weed, CA 96094; $$; full bar; AE, MC, V; local checks only.*

Stewart Mineral Springs ★ Nestled in a forested canyon at the end of a twisting country road, Stewart Mineral Springs is what Californians used to called "mellow." People come here to take the waters and commune with nature. Stewart Mineral Springs bathhouse, located across the creek over a picturesque footbridge, is all scrubbed wood, scented air, and serenity. A detoxifying mineral bath, sauna, and a plunge in the creek will only set you back $15. Overnight accommodations are clean but spartan. You can bed down dirt cheap in spiritually enriching tepees (bring your own bedding) or in utilitarian little cabins with kitchens. There's also a five-bedroom A-frame for groups. If you're planning to cook in your cabin, make sure to do all your shopping before you get here. Stewart Springs is remote enough that nipping out for a quart of milk isn't an option. Fortunately, Serge's very good French restaurant is nearby. ■ *Call for directions; (916) 938-2222, toll free (800) 322-9223; 4617 Stewart Springs Rd, Weed, CA 96094; $; MC, V; checks OK; open Mar–Dec.*

MOUNT SHASTA

RESTAURANTS

Cafe Bellissimo ★★★ Don't be alarmed if the plate of greens served before your entrée at Cafe Bellissimo looks like someone's leaf collection for Botany 101. That's just the approach at this small restaurant where the emphasis is on unusual—and sometimes unrecognizable—ingredients. The cooks thrive on coming up with new things to put in salads, stir-fries, pastas, and wraps (crisp flour tortillas stuffed with cheese, veggies, spicy black beans, and other good stuff). It's a little Cajun, a hint of Indonesian, and a dose of Mediterranean with the common denominators being fresh ingredients and imaginative combinations (grilled snapper with pineapple mango salsa, for instance). The smooth, super-rich white chocolate cheesecake on an Oreo cookie crust is one of the best on the ever-changing menu of overindulgent delights. Like the menu items, the atmosphere is an unusual blend—sort of New Age meets Southwest with a twist of earthiness. Unfortunately, the hours seem to change as often as the menu, so call ahead.

■ *½ mile E of I-5 from the Central Mount Shasta exit, turn left just after the railraod crossing onto W Lake St; (916) 926-4461; 204A W Lake St, Mount Shasta; $$; beer and wine; MC, V; checks OK; dinner every day.*

Michael's Restaurant ★★ Michael and Lynn Kobseff have been running this estimable little eatery since 1980, which makes them old-timers on the Mount Shasta restaurant scene. The crisp and greaseless fried zucchini appetizers and the french fries are terrific, as is the teriyaki turkey sandwich. The Italian dinners, such as the combination ravioli and linguine, are huge and dependable. Skip the wine and order a Sierra Nevada Pale Ale. ■ *Central Mount Shasta I-5 exit; (916) 926-5288; 313 N Mount Shasta Blvd, Mount Shasta; $$; beer and wine; AE, DIS, MC, V; no checks; lunch, dinner Tues–Sat.*

Wendie's Italian Restaurant Breakfast is big and cheap (and so's the decor): homemade sweet linguica and giant muffins baked fresh every morning at the pizza place next door. The Italian-American full dinners offer a main entrée that might be roast beef or chicken accompanied by soup, antipasto, salad, vegetables, homemade pasta, dessert, and coffee. The real reason to stop at Wendie's, however, is the homemade pie. Wendie's always has a half-dozen winners, from tart, delectable berry pies to American classics such as chocolate and coconut cream. ■ *S Mount Shasta Blvd I-5 exit; (916) 926-4047; 610 S Mount Shasta Blvd, Mount Shasta; $; beer and wine; no credit cards; local checks only; breakfast, lunch, dinner every day.*

LODGINGS

Mount Shasta Ranch Bed and Breakfast ★★ Large is the operative word here: large rooms, large baths, large views, large breakfasts. All hip roofs and gabled windows, this bed and breakfast has a main house, a carriage house, and a two-bedroom cottage. The bedrooms in the 70-year-old main house are huge, with vast private baths sporting original 1920s fixtures. The colorful, unstudied country decor boasts braided rag rugs, gauzy curtains, and gaily colored quilts. There are books in the rooms, as well as TVs. Rooms in the carriage house are smaller and share baths, but they've got great views of Mount Shasta and the rugged Siskiyous. Come morning, suit yourself with cream cheese–filled waffles and fresh fruit toppings, crêpes bursting with local blackberries and dusted with powdered sugar, plump sausages, fresh fruit salad, and good strong coffee. After breakfast, curl up with a book in front of the main lodge's gargantuan stone fireplace or work off those waffles by hiking, swimming, or playing Ping-Pong. ■ *S of the fish hatchery; (916) 926-3870; 1008 W A Barr Rd, Mount Shasta, CA 96067; $; AE, MC, V; checks OK.*

Tree House Motor Inn ★ Just about everything in this unusual Best Western motor inn is made of carved redwood: the doors, the paneling, the rustic headboards, and even the redwood-beam ceilings in the the upstairs rooms. Some rooms in the east wing have beautiful views of Mount Shasta. The Tree House has a workout room with LifeCycles and a huge indoor swimming pool that's deserted most of the time. ■ *Central Mount Shasta I-5 exit, right on Lake St, right on Morgan Way to 111 Morgan Way; (916) 926-3101, toll free (800) 528-1234; Mail: PO Box 236, Mount Shasta, CA 96067; $; AE, DIS, MC, V; no checks.*

DUNSMUIR

RESTAURANTS

Hitching Post Cafe OK, so the orange vinyl seats are rump-sprung and the tables are Formica. There are fresh flowers on every table (courtesy of a neighbor with a big garden), steaming homemade soup, half a dozen pies in the fridge, and a waitress who's worked here 30 years. It's basic food: burgers, chicken-fried steak, biscuits and gravy, and broasted chicken—but it's a darn sight better than fast food. *And* in case you ride up on old Tumbleweed, they'll pack a lunch for you. ■ *Central Dunsmuir I-5 exit; (916) 235-9926; 4917 Dunsmuir Ave, Dunsmuir; $; full bar; MC, V; local checks only; breakfast, lunch, dinner every day.*

LODGINGS

The Caboose Motel A must for railroad buffs, a maybe for everyone else, the Caboose Motel is a quiet and comfortable theme motel made out of refurbished railroad cabooses and boxcars from Southern Pacific, Santa Fe, and Great Northern. Most have double or queen beds. Some have four narrow but comfortable bunks. Small bay windows or rooftop cupolas relieve the sometimes claustrophobic linearity of the rooms. Room 20, a boxcar decorated in country antiques, has a claw-footed tub and a small private patio. The Caboose Motel also has a pool and Jacuzzi, plus a great view of nearby Castle Crags. Don't let the fascinating railroad memorabilia sidetrack you into thinking the restaurant's any good. ■ *1 mile S of Dunsmuir in the Railroad Park Resort; (916) 235-4440; 100 Railroad Park Rd, Dunsmuir, CA 96025; Rooms $; restaurant $$; full bar; AE, DIS, MC, V; checks OK; dinner every day (Thurs–Sun in winter).*

Looking for a particular place? Check the index at the back of the book for specific restaurants, hotels, B&Bs, sights, and more.

LODGINGS

Hogin House ★★★ Many innkeepers try, but few have captured the relaxed comfort and charm of a country B&B as well as Angie and Rich Toreson have in this delightfully cluttered hideaway. Located just outside downtown McCloud, Hogin House is a small two-story Victorian, built in 1904 for the town doctor. The four bedrooms are decorated with antique toys, colorful quilts, calico fabrics, and country-style wallpaper. You can curl up in front of the fire in the sitting room or spend a leisurely morning in the airy sun room. You can choose to have breakfast in the dining room, on the porch, or on the lush lawn that sweeps down toward the center of town. Warm, late mornings beg for the latter. ■ *S of Lawndale and W Colombero Dr at 424 Lawndale Ct; (916) 964-2882 or 964-3125; Mail: PO Box 550, McCloud, CA 96057; $; MC, V; checks OK.*

McCloud Guest House ★★ Built in 1907 for McCloud timber baron J.H. Queal, this stately two-story mansion became the McCloud River Lumber Company's guest house after Queal's death in 1921. Herbert Hoover, Jean Harlow, and various Hearsts dallied here in the '20s and '30s, but then the house fell into disrepair. Reopened in 1984, it has been restored as a country inn and restaurant. Downstairs in the lobby and dining room, there's dark wood paneling and delicately wrought cabinetry, beveled glass, antique wallpapers, and a massive stone fireplace. Upstairs, there's a game room (open to guests only) with original lamps and a magnificent, carved antique billiards table. The inn's spacious rooms all have four-poster beds and more antiques. The rooms in the front are the nicest—light and airy with white wicker chairs and large, original claw-footed tubs with views of Mount Shasta. The mountain is also visible from the broad, wraparound verandah downstairs—a pleasant spot for an aperitif. The only drawbacks are the awful canned music in the common areas (movie soundtracks) and the central air conditioning, which means you can't open the windows. The restaurant tends toward charbroiled beef, well-prepared chicken, veal, and pork dishes made with rich wine sauces. An unexceptional, continental breakfast is served every morning. ■ *W of downtown McCloud at 606 W Colombero Dr; (916) 964-3160; Mail: PO Box 1510, McCloud, CA 96057; $$; beer and wine; MC, V; checks OK; dinner Wed–Mon (call ahead for winter hours).*

Stoney Brook Inn Built in 1922, the former Old Park Hotel has been through several owners and renovations since the late '60s. Its latest incarnation is as a New Age–style bed and breakfast, aimed at Mount Shasta's more spiritual seekers. Mellow out in the inn's clothing-optional hot tub and sauna or find inner peace in the backyard meditation dome. There's also a massage room and the inn's owners are both certified body-workers. The building is attractive, though uninterestingly furnished and only haphazardly cleaned (serious dust bunnies!). Five of the suites have kitchens, nine rooms have small private baths, and four rooms share a large, coed bathroom. Breakfast is a do-it-yourself affair in the cramped kitchen. No smoking. ■ *½ mile from Hwy 89 exit at 309 W Colombero Dr; (916) 964-2300, toll free (800) 369-6118; Mail: PO Box 1860, Mc-Cloud, CA 96057; $; MC, V; checks OK.*

CASSEL

LODGINGS

Clearwater House ★★★ This fine, turn-of-the-century farm-house is the only fishing lodge in all of California officially approved by Orvis—that old money purveyor of gentlemanly fishing and sports equipment. Created by former wilderness and fishing guide Dick Galland, this seven-room inn is decorated in the style of an English angling lodge with fish and game prints on the walls, oriental rugs on the hardwood floors, and fine cherry-wood tables for family-style meals. You can pick up points on fly-fishing in Galland's weekend fishing classes or in his weeklong program "Mastering the Art of Fly-Fishing." Meals (included in the $100 tab) aren't elaborate, but they're the best for miles around: traditional breakfasts, picnic lunches, and well-prepared country-style dinners such as barbecued ribs, roast pork loin, and various pastas. ■ *Intersection of Hat Creek and Cassel/Fall River Rd; (415) 381-1173; Mail: 274 Star Route, Cassel, CA 96028; $$; beer and wine; MC, V; checks OK; open April–mid-Nov.*

FALL RIVER MILLS

LODGINGS

Lava Creek Lodge ★ Lava Creek Lodge glories in a panoramic view of the southern Cascades from Mount Lassen to Mount Shasta. Set well back from the main road at the end of a country lane, the main lodge has eight modest guest rooms, most with views of the lake. We prefer the small but comfortable cabins (two with private baths) in the woods nearby. The price of lodging includes three country-style meals served in the lodge's knotty pine dining room. Located in the best of trout fishing country, the lodge also offers boat rentals and guide services. ■ *On Eastman Lake at the end of Island Rd; (916) 336-6288; Mail: Glenburn Star Route, Fall River Mills, CA 96028; $$; full bar; no credit cards; checks OK; breakfast, lunch, dinner every day (May–mid-Nov).*

Rick's Lodge Famed among fly-fishermen, Rick's Lodge sits smack in the middle of the prime trout fishing territory. An average of 3,000 fish per mile school in the Fall River. The lodge devotes itself to mining this ichthyological lucky strike: boat and motor rentals, guide services, and fly-fishing classes—as well as fishing gear. Accommodations are exceptionally spartan considering you pay dearly for the catch: a row of unattractively furnished rooms (fly-tying tables take priority) so small you can't open the door without bumping into the bed. The bar is far more appealing, with its pool table and country music on the jukebox. The adjoining restaurant, with a full herd of deer heads on the walls, offers generally well-prepared beef, chicken, and seafood dishes. The vegetables are predictably overcooked. Don't bother with the sticky and sweet homemade pies. ■ *On McArthur Rd, N of Fall River Mills, S of Dana; (916) 336-5300 April–Nov, (916) 336-6618 off-season; Mail: Glenburn Star Route, Fall River Mills, CA 96028; $$; full bar; AE, MC, V; checks OK; breakfast, lunch, dinner every day.*

McARTHUR

RESTAURANTS

C's Steak House ★ Walking into C's is like stepping into Edward Hopper's *Nighthawks*: the big windows, the long lunch counter, the eerily bright lighting. The friendliness of the three C's (Connie Sellars, Christie Spooner, and Cindy Grove) takes the edge off the vaguely alienating decor. C's menu harks back to the hardy 1940s, when men were men and everyone (men, women, and babes in arms) ate beef—lots of it. Modern carnivores will enjoy steaks of all sizes, from a petite 6-ounce top sirloin to a mammoth 20-ounce T-bone. In the morning, try the Farmers Special: three eggs, the pork of your choice, and all the potatoes or pancakes you can eat. ■ *In the middle of town on Hwy 299 in McArthur; (916) 336-6544; $$; beer and wine; MC, V; checks OK; breakfast, lunch, dinner every day.*

CANBY

RESTAURANTS

Canby Hotel & Trading Company ★ "Best Burgers in Modoc County" reads the fading plywood sign in the parking lot outside the Canby Hotel. Well, we tested them all and the sign is right. The Modoc Burger, a double cheeseburger piled with veggies, is outstanding and addictive. Locals also swear by the Army bean soup. If you're driving south to Nevada, purchase a "Reno insurance policy" before you leave by adding a dollar bill to the hundreds hanging from the ceiling. Then buy yourself a cup of coffee with it on the way back home. ■ *On Hwy*

299 in the middle of town; (916) 233-4841; Hwy 299, Canby; $; full bar; no credit cards; local checks only; breakfast, lunch, dinner every day.

ALTURAS

RESTAURANTS

Nipa's California Cuisine ★★ No seared tuna in loquat sauce here. Nipa's version of California cuisine is dynamite Thai food, beautifully presented, spicy, and delicious—the finest food of any kind in all of Modoc county. The Tom Yum Kung soup is packed with prawns and mushrooms. The red curry with prawns, chicken, or beef cooked in coconut milk is spicy and succulent. The phad Thai—pan-fried noodles with prawns, chicken, egg, bean sprouts, green onions, and garnished with ground peanuts—is satisfyingly sweet. Owners and chefs Ukrit Bhavindhu and Nipa Sakdikul have done a nice job of transforming what used to be an old drive-in burger joint into an attractive, contemporary cafe with silk flowers, linen tablecloths, and glass-topped tables. ■ *On Main St 1 block S of hwys 299 and 395; (916) 233-2520; 1001 N Main St, Alturas; $; beer and wine; MC, V; local checks only; lunch, dinner every day.*

Knob Hill Mercantile ★ Southern Cal refugees created the King Hill Mercantile on a bare hillside 25 miles from Alturas. Way out here the mercantile triples as a market, hardware store, and deli. Sit at a window table, view the Warner Mountains, and take your pick of 20 deli sandwiches. ■ *W from Alturas 9 miles on CR 54, then left on CR 71 for another 16 miles; (916) 233-9739; Alturas; $; beer and wine; no credit cards; checks OK; breakfast, lunch Tues–Sun, dinner Tues–Sat (closed Dec–Mar).*

Niles Hotel High Grade Room ★ The Niles Hotel High Grade Room is where locals go for a fancy night on the town. The decor is frontier *fin de siècle*: stained-glass windows, heavy oak furniture, rusty antiques, red linens, candlelight, and very formal service. It's a bit much, but so is everything else in this place, except the prices. The menu reflects the agricultural strength of the region: beef. Choose from a variety of cuts—prime rib to filet—all well-prepared. The lone poultry offering, Cornish game hen, is cooked on a spit and comes to your table crisp on the outside, and succulent and tender on the inside. Each entrée comes with sourdough bread, soup du jour, garden salad, a goofy and pretentious champagne sorbet, plus a potato or rice pilaf. Try the creamy Kahlua parfait for dessert. ■ *1 mile S of hwys 299 and 395, E side of Main St; (916) 233-3261; 304 S Main St, Alturas; $$; full bar; MC, V; checks OK; dinner every day.*

LODGINGS

Dorris House ★★ There is no such thing as a room without a view at Dorris House, a turn-of-the-century, two-story ranch house named after Alturas's founding brothers in 1870. Set on a sage-covered plain at the edge of Dorris Lake below the towering Warner Mountains, the property is a favorite stop for migratory birds. Hosts Karol and Mary Woodward have decorated their inn's four rooms with family antiques. Everything is spotlessly clean. Longtime residents of Alturas, the Woodwards know all the choice spots for hiking, bird-watching and picnicking. Breakfast, served in the Woodwards' homey kitchen, is simple but very good: moist zucchini nut bread and sweet bran muffins, a gorgeously arranged fruit platter, and strong coffee. ■ *3 miles E of Hwy 395 on CR 56, 1 mile S on CR 57; (916) 233-3786; Mail: PO Box 1655, Alturas, CA 96101; $; no credit cards; checks OK.*

California Pines Lodge ★ California Pines' developers have been hawking half-acre parcels of Modoc County on late night, non-network TV for 20 years now. Despite the developers' best efforts, however, the resort doesn't look like a suburb yet—the log and cedar shingle vacation homes dotting the landscape are still pretty sparse. The lodge sits at the center of this 33,000-acre real estate empire. The smallish rooms are pleasant and clean, with attractive knotty pine woodwork. All have good views of the spectacular high desert scenery. Because of the surrounding development, there's plenty to do at California Pines, especially for kids. There's a swimming pool, an activity room, a 256-acre lake with paddle boats, three fishing ponds, an airfield, and the completely uninteresting Cookhouse Restaurant. ■ *9 miles SW of Alturas off Centerville Rd; (916) 233-4672; Mail: HC04 Box No. 45001, Alturas, CA 96101; $; MC, V; checks OK.*

FORT BIDWELL

LODGINGS

Fort Bidwell Hotel and Restaurant ★★ Popular with hikers and hunters, the relaxed and informal Fort Bidwell Hotel is the only thing happening in this former 1860 military outpost. Although the sagging building may have seen better days, it can't have seen better innkeepers. Eva and Charles Massie are friendly and endlessly thoughtful. The seven guest rooms upstairs are clean and cozy. The restaurant is a sensitive mix of homeyness and professionalism: Eva does the cooking; Charles does the waiting. A recent meal started with a rich beef barley soup and a lightly dressed mixed green salad. The entrées are a bit uneven: the fettuccine alfredo came nicely al dente in a rich sour cream sauce, but the blackened chicken was a tad too dry. The apple and pumpkin pies were good. Morning brought a big plate of delicious flapjacks with hot syrup, homemade lumberjack bread, and tart preserves. ■ *On Surprise Valley Rd in the middle of Fort Bidwell; (916) 279-6199; Mail: PO Box 100, Fort Bidwell, CA 96112; $; beer and wine; MC, V; checks OK; breakfast, lunch, dinner Thurs–Sun (every day for hotel guests).*

CEDARVILLE

RESTAURANTS

Country Hearth Restaurant & Bakery ★ The Country Hearth should be called "The Country Heart" for all the love owner Janet Irene puts into her honest, satisfying meals served in a homey pinewood dining room with checked curtains and a wood-burning stove. The terrific hamburgers are perfectly cooked, served on toasted, fresh-baked rolls, and garnished with crisp lettuce and a sweet, generous slice of tomato. All the breads, rolls, pastries, and desserts are made on the premises by Janet and sold from the bakery case near the front door. ■ *Just S of Hwy 299 on Main St; (916) 279-2280; 551 Main St, Cedarville; $; beer and wine; no credit cards; checks OK; breakfast, lunch, dinner every day.*

SUSANVILLE

RESTAURANTS

St. Francis Cafe ★ The cafe in the 70-year-old St. Francis Hotel has been owned and operated by the Goni family since 1946. Homemade soups and salads are served Basque-style in tureens and large bowls. The specialty of the house is prime rib, indisputably the best (and the largest) in the area—and everybody knows it. If you're not at the door by 6pm on Friday or Saturday, you may be out of luck. There's also a 10-ounce New York steak sandwich that we dare you to finish. Strict vegetarians are outta luck. The adjacent hotel bar, the Round Up Room, serves Picon Punch, the tasty Basque drink that makes everyone very friendly. ■ *Corner of Union and Main streets; (916) 257-4820; 830 Main St, Susanville; $$; full bar; MC, V; no checks; lunch Mon–Sat, dinner every day.*

Grand Cafe The art deco light fixtures in this time warp of a restaurant are the real McCoy. Owned by the Sargent family since 1921, this faded pink stucco building has green and black tiles, dark, wooden booths, and a long Formica counter. There's even a nickel jukebox (don't try it) in each booth and a small lamp with pull chain. At the counter, wooden chairs on ornate iron bases have clips to hold diners' hats. The mounted deer on the walls were shot by a Sargent in the '30s—back when a tuna sandwich was 35 cents. It's not a whole lot more now. Coffee is only 50 cents. For breakfast, try the sweet buckwheat hotcakes. For lunch it should be soup and a chocolate malt. ■ *On Main near Gay St; (916) 257-4713; 730 Main St, Susanville; $; full bar; no credit cards; checks OK; breakfast, lunch Mon–Sat.*

LODGINGS

The Roseberry House Susanville's only bed and breakfast inn may remind you of your great aunt's home in the 1950s—flowery, full of lace, ornate knickknacks, family photos, and dark wood antiques. Bill and Maxine Ashmore's 90-year-old, two-story house has four big guest rooms with private baths. John William's Room has a massive four-poster bed and matching dresser with miniature carved lion heads, plus a bathtub and reading chairs. There's plenty going on within walking distance of the inn—movies, tennis courts, even a golf course. This is probably a good thing, because Mrs. Ashmore teaches piano to young students during the day.

Mrs. Ashmore sets a thermos of coffee (with powdered creamer, alas) at your door at 7am, and serves a breakfast of fresh fruit and yogurt, warm homemade biscuits and apple pastries, a thin ham slice, poached eggs, and golden hashbrowns in the formal dining room at 8:30am on the dot. ■ *2 blocks E of Main St; (916) 257-5675; 609 North St, Susanville, CA 96130; $; AE, MC, V; checks OK.*

CHESTER

RESTAURANTS

Chester Saloon and Italian Restaurant ★ This simple saloon dishes up Chester's best pasta. Owner/chef Olga Gallo's specialty is full Italian dinners. The veal and eggplant Parmigiana are quite good, and the desserts are sublime. Don't miss the rich chocolate rum cake, with its savory, light rum sauce, or the dainty, waffled pizzelle cookies, dusted with powdered sugar and just a hint of anise. Service is attentive and friendly, and the jukebox in the bar offers an eclectic menu of rock and country. Live music on weekends. ■ *Corner of Main and Stone streets in Olde Towne; (916) 258-2887; 159 Main St, Chester; $$; full bar; MC, V; checks OK; dinner every day.*

LODGINGS

The Bidwell House ★★★ Set back from the highway amid tall aspens and reaching cottonwoods, the beautifully restored Bidwell House looks out over mountain meadows and the broad expanse of Lake Almanor. The former home of Chico pioneer John Bidwell opened as a bed and breakfast in 1991. The Aspen Room features a fishing motif, with an antique creel, fish-shaped bottles, and pillows appliqued with trout designs.

Other rooms sport cows, calico cats and rabbits, and hunting motifs. A small cottage is available for family rentals.

Downstairs, the pretty, enclosed porch/sitting room has wicker furniture, antique doll buggies and tricycles, and a Gibson Girl sketchbook. Breakfast in the airy dining room is light but delicious: frothy cranberry frappé, tasty fresh muffins, rich and heavy Scotch potted eggs. ■ *E end of Chester at 1 Main St; (916) 258-3338; Mail: PO Box 1790, Chester, CA 96020; $$; MC, V; checks OK.*

The Cinnamon Teal ★★★ From the carved pineapple finials on the four-poster beds to the vintage floral wallpapers and colorful quilts, no touch has been spared to make the Cinnamon Teal bed and breakfast feel as homey as a visit to Grandma's—if Grandma had excellent taste in fabrics. Lush, plumped-up feather beds are the crowning glory of each of the four guest rooms. Two of the rooms have private baths; one suite, separate from the main house, has a living room, wood stove, and cable TV. The sitting room in the 1930s-vintage main house is spacious and inviting. The grounds, covering a full acre, stretch out over a lush lawn, through an apple and pear orchard, to the banks of the north fork of the Feather River. ■ *Near Main St at 227 Feather River Dr; (916) 258-3993; Mail: PO Box 1517, Chester, CA 96020; $$; no credit cards; checks OK.*

LAKE ALMANOR

RESTAURANTS

BJ's Bar-B-Que & Deli ★ An unassuming roadside eatery where the BBQ basics—beef, pork, and chicken—reign. The ribs are thick, tender, and meaty, with a tangy sweet sauce. The baked beans and Jerry's special barbecued pork sandwich are pretty good as well. Get plenty of napkins and sit in the sunny, enclosed porch area to the left of the front door. Don't bother with the soggy corn on the cob or the too-sweet pies. ■ *On Hwy A-13, S of town; (916) 596-4210; 3881 Hwy A-13, Hamilton Branch, Lake Almanor; $; beer and wine; no credit cards; checks OK; lunch, dinner Tues–Sun.*

Wilson's Camp Prattville ★ Certainly the funkiest place at Lake Almanor, Camp Prattville has been around since 1928 when it was founded by Frank and Nettie Wilson. Now run by their son Kenneth and his wife Carol, the restaurant's chef, it offers three meals a day in a small, natural-wood dining room, crowded with knickknacks and warmed by a wood stove. The menu is prodigious, with breakfasts served until 4pm. Sandwiches and fries are the way to go here, but save room for the dessert (a superb bread pudding with an applejack hard sauce). The homemade pies have delicate and flaky crusts and the fillings are supreme. During warm weather, lunch at the picnic tables on the deck overlooking the lake. ■ *On Lake Almanor at 2913 Almanor Dr W; (916) 259-2464; $; beer and wine; MC, V; checks OK; breakfast, lunch, dinner every day (April–mid-Oct).*

LODGINGS

Dorado Inn What sets the Dorado Inn apart from the other resorts along the commercialized east shore of Lake Almanor are the spectacular views of Mount Lassen across the lake from the deck outside your cottage. The prosaically furnished one- and two-bedroom cottages come with fully equipped kitchens, electric heat, and wood stoves; all are located near the water's edge. Boating, fishing, and swimming are the resort's chief amenities. ■ *On Hwy 147 on the E shore of Lake Almanor; (916) 284-7790; 4379 Hwy 147, Lake Almanor, CA 96137; $$; no credit cards; checks OK.*

MILL CREEK

RESTAURANTS

Black Forest Lodge ★ This predominantly German restaurant serves some of the best food in the area. Owner/chef Hilde Schleicher's homemade soups are a meal in themselves: the beef barley soup, sprinkled with nutmeg, comes in a giant bowl with a big hunk of sourdough bread. If you're still hungry after that, there are fat wursts, hunchen (honey-dipped chicken), sauerbraten, and wiener schnitzel. Vegetables tend to be overcooked, but traditional pork, veal, and beef dishes are well-prepared. The trout—fresh from the restaurant's trout pond—is outstanding. For dessert, try one of Hilde's flaky and traditionally sweet strudels. ■ *10 miles W of Chester on Hwy 36/89; (916) 258-2941; $$; full bar; Mail: Route 5, Box 5000, Mill Creek, CA 96061; MC, V; checks OK; breakfast, lunch, dinner every day (Fri–Sun in winter).*

LODGINGS

Mill Creek Resort ★★ Nothing much happens here. The Mill Creek Resort makes you feel like you've stepped back in time to a quieter, gentler, infinitely more affordable era (somewhere around 1925). A picture-postcard country general store and coffee shop serves as the resort's center. Housekeeping cabins, available on a daily or weekly basis, are clean, homey, and furnished in vintage '30s and '40s furniture. Seclusion is one of the main charms of the place, but it's also close to both downhill and cross-country skiing and Lassen Volcanic National Park. Children and pets are welcome. ■ *3 miles S of Hwy 36 on Hwy 173; (916) 595-4449; Mail: Mill Creek, CA 96061; $; no credit cards; checks OK.*

Fire Mountain Lodge ★ A classic, old-fashioned high country lodge, Fire Mountain boasts three massive stone fireplaces, wagonwheel chandeliers, and a truckload of lumberjack and hunting memorabilia. Utilitarian cabins are tucked behind the main lodge. The lodge's game room has vintage pinball machines, video games, a pool table, and a honky-tonk piano. At press time, the restaurant was closed for renovations. ▪ *On Hwy 36/89 between Mineral and Hwy 32; (916) 258-2938; Mail: Mill Creek, CA 96061; $; no credit cards; checks OK.*

St. Bernard Lodge ★ The meadow behind the lodge and the trout pond look like they've seen better days, and the carny-prize dogs in the window are a tacky replacement for the real stuffed St. Bernards that once stood there. (The last owner defiantly stuffed his pets, after a neighbor shot them.) Nonetheless, the atmosphere is casual and friendly, and the seven rooms upstairs are comfortably and attractively furnished. Handsome landscapes and Wyeth prints soften the hall walls and the shared bathrooms have deep claw-footed tubs. No children in hotel rooms.

The restaurant and the antique bar with painted glass windows are open to guests and nonguests alike. The large, fluffy pancakes and savory honey ham are standouts on the breakfast menu. Steak and fresh sweet corn are good bets for dinner. The salads and desserts are only passable. ▪ *10 miles W of Chester on Hwy 36/89; (916) 258-3382; Mail: Route 5, Box 5500, Mill Creek, CA 96061; $$; full bar; MC, V; checks OK; breakfast, lunch, dinner Thur–Mon (Fri–Mon in winter).*

MINERAL

LODGINGS

Lassen Mineral Lodge ★ Popular with skiers, hunters, and fishermen, the lodge offers comfortable motel-style accommodations (available by the week) on the doorstep of Lassen Volcanic National Park. Set back in the pines and away from the highway, traffic noise isn't a problem here, but the main lodge bustles. If privacy and quiet are what you're after, try for one of the cabins. There's also a general store, gift shop, old-fashioned saloon, and restaurant, all connected to the main lodge by a wraparound verandah. Check out the interesting bottle window in the saloon. ▪ *9 miles S of the south entrance to Lassen Volcanic National Park on Hwy 36; (916) 595-4422; Mail: PO Box 160, Mineral, CA 96063; $; full bar; MC, V; checks OK.*

*The facts in this book were correct at press time,
but places close, chefs depart, hours change.
It's best to call ahead.*

DRAKESBAD

LODGINGS

Drakesbad Guest Ranch ★★★★ A glorious spa hidden in a high mountain valley inside Lassen Volcanic National Park, Drakesbad is probably the worst-kept secret in California. This mountain retreat is so popular that it has a three-year waiting list. Fortunately, plans made that far in advance often change. May or June are good times to call to take advantage of cancellations. There's no electricity at Drakesbad; kerosene lamps cast a warm yellow glow over the rustic accommodations. The tables, chairs, and bedsteads are made of smooth-sanded logs and branches. There are nice rooms upstairs in the main lodge, but we prefer the quieter cabins at the edge of the meadow— a good place to watch wildlife.

Breakfast, lunch, and dinner (included in the price of lodging) are exceptionally good for national park food—fresh wild-greens salads with simple, light dressings, gently steamed vegetables, and savory wild rice. Breakfasts are huge: fresh fruit, hot and cold cereals, buttermilk pancakes, and excellent sausage.

During the day, explore the wonders of Lassen. At night, park rangers tell stories around the campfire. The star attraction, though, is the thermal swimming pool, fed by a natural hot spring and open 24 hours a day. The pool is best at night when the steam swirls up around you and rises into the star-studded sky. ■ *Call for directions. In summer, call the long distance operator and ask for "916-Drakesbad Ring 2." In winter, call (916) 529-1512; Mail: California Guest Services, 2150 North Main St, Suite 5, Red Bluff, CA 96080; $$; beer and wine; MC, V; checks OK; open Jun–Oct.*

OLD STATION

LODGINGS

Mount Lassen Inn ★ Shaded by cottonwoods, the Mount Lassen Inn is a large, white frame house with a wraparound verandah and a gently creaking porch swing. The inn's four airy guest rooms have been tastefully renovated by host Gene Nixon, with special attention paid to coordinated floral fabric prints, lush comforters, and other comfortable country inn details. You'll wake up in the morning to breakfast delicacies like heart-shaped French toast and smoked almond omelet— served in your room, if you'd like. Family-style dinners are available by reservation only. ■ *In Old Station at the junction of hwys 44 and 89; (916) 335-7006; Mail: PO Box 86, Old Station, CA 96071; $$; MC, V; checks OK.*

SIERRA

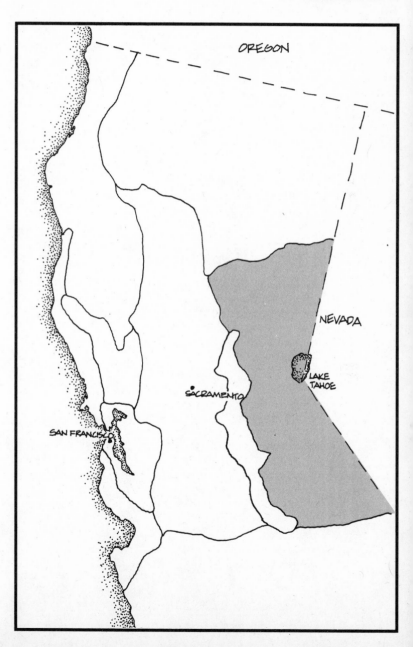

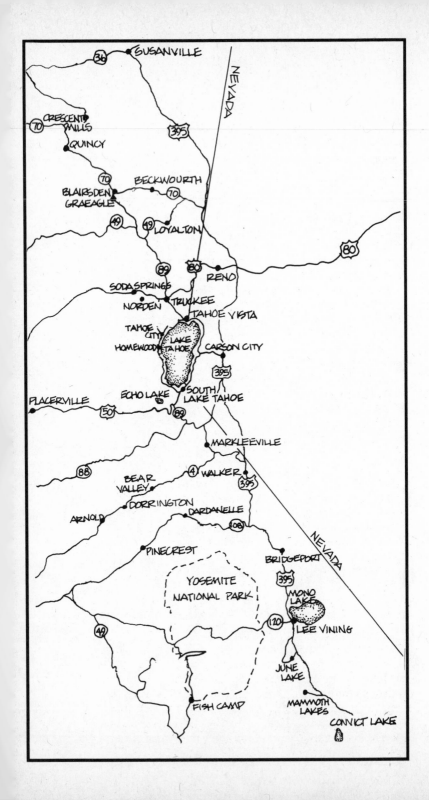

Sierra

A north-to-south sweep of the Sierra beginning south of Susanville at Crescent Mills and continuing on to Mammoth and Convict lakes.

CRESCENT MILLS

LODGINGS

Crescent Hotel ★ In continuous operation since 1927, the Crescent Hotel suffered a bit of deterioration in the '50s and '60s. But since 1974, owners Jack and Barbara Tucker have taken the place back up to a better standard. Pretty much the heart of the tiny town of Crescent Mills, the hotel looks from the outside like a quaint roadside inn from another era. Inside, there's a gaily packed gift shop, an old-fashioned saloon, and an antique-furnished, dark-wood dining room. Upstairs, the place becomes a light and airy bed and breakfast with seven sun-splashed rooms. The best rooms, which overlook a garden, are toward the rear of the hotel (specifically numbers 8 and 67). ■ *On Hwy 89 in the middle of Crescent Mills; (916) 284-9905; Mail: PO Box 10, Crescent Mills, CA 95934; $; full bar; MC, V; checks OK; dinner Wed–Sun, brunch Sun.*

QUINCY

RESTAURANTS

Larry's Northwoods Inn ★ Larry and Susan Vogelesang's inn has quickly established a reputation for good family dining. There's a bakery on the premises and a selection of full-flavored soups (chicken noodle is a superb rendition of Mom's); the rest of the menu, however, is more of a hit-or-miss affair. Among the hits: the seafood is prepared with intelligent care, the steaks are tender and juicy, and the onion rings succulent. Among the misses: overcooked vegetables and the vacuous (though fresh) bread. ■ *On E Main St; (916) 283-3770; 2004 E Main St, East Quincy; $$; beer and wine; MC, V; local checks only; lunch Mon–Fri, dinner every day.*

Moon's Choose among four dining areas in this roomy, ramshackle rustic wooden building—from a formal dining room to a junglelike open-air patio. Moon's has been one of Quincy's favorite dining spots since the mid-'70s. Pizza and pasta are the house specialties. The air is warm with yeasty smells and vintage jazz. Moon's is timid on the garlic and some pasta dishes verge on bland—though the thick lasagne, heavily laden with sausage, is delicious. Be sure to request the Thai ranch dressing on your salads. Where else will you find Mom's Apple Pizza Pie? ■ *On Lawrence St at Plymouth; (916) 283-0765; 497 Lawrence St, Quincy; $; beer and wine; MC, V; checks OK; dinner Tues–Sun.*

LODGINGS

The Feather Bed ★ From its fish-scale shingles and colon-naded porch (in faded pink and white) to the dark-stained woodwork of the lobby and dining room—where full breakfasts are served each morning—the Victorian building suggests old-fashioned, low-key hospitality. There are seven cozy and at-tractively furnished (in turn-of-the-century country styles) rooms in the main building and two private cottages under the maple tree out back. Borrow a bike from Chuck and Diana Goubert for an afternoon pedal. ■ *1 block off Hwy 70 at Court and 542 Jackson St; (916) 283-0102; Mail: PO Box 3200, Quincy, CA 95971; $$; AE, DC, MC, V; checks OK.*

Ranchito Motel ★ More than just another roadside motel, the Ranchito conceals unusual amenities behind its generic neo-Spanish colonial facade. Behind the front row of motel units lies a small babbling brook in a miniforest of tall pines with picnic tables in a pleasant open garden. The newer back units are rather ordinary, but the older front units—arrayed along a ram-bling hacienda-style verandah branded with horseshoe and spur tracks—stand boldly with old wooden doors and impres-sive ceiling barn beams. Ask for the rooms farthest from the road and closest to the brook. ■ *At 2020 E Main St in East Quincy, (916) 283-2265; Mail: PO Box 3518, Quincy, CA 95971; $; AE, DC, DIS, MC, V; checks OK.*

BLAIRSDEN

RESTAURANTS

Gray Eagle Lodge ★ Gray Eagle Lodge shows off some spec-tacular scenery at the east edge of Lakes Basin Recreation Area. Ironically, there isn't a lake right nearby but a lovely stream, waterfall, and beautiful high Sierra trails. Although you can stay here, you'll be happier if you just eat. The popular restaurant in the main lodge—rebuilt after being destroyed by snow in 1983—is a rather showy concoction of enormous an-gulated beams. The entrées change but might include chicken breasts in a nice light mustard sauce; tender baby back ribs dressed in a tasty, moderately sharp barbecue sauce; and Long Island duckling, slow roasted and finished in a light orange glaze. Where the Gray Eagle shines on the main course it dulls elsewhere: a disappointing tomato paste-y Creole soup, boring tossed salads, unappetizing desserts (gooey brownies), and gut-poor coffee. On the flip side, the wine list is the best in the Lakes Basin. ■ *5 miles up Gold Lake Rd, ½ mile S of Graeagle;*

(916) 836-2511, toll free (800) 635-8778; $$; full bar; MC, V; local checks only; breakfast, dinner every day May–Oct (closed winters).

LODGINGS

Feather River Inn ★★ Back in the '20s and '30s, when train-trip vacations were all the rage, the Feather River Inn was one of *the* places to go in the high Sierra. Now operated as a conference center by the University of the Pacific in Stockton, the palatially rustic 1914 lodge and beautifully landscaped grounds retain their gentility. Conference groups (from 15 to 148 people) take precedence, but the center does take other guests on a space available basis. The attractive chalets, simply furnished, look out over the surrounding mountains. The broad verandah, its roof supported by enormous tree-trunk columns and rafters, looks out over the lovely grounds interrupted only by a swimming pool, volleyball and tennis courts, and gymnasium. There's also a nine-hole golf course. Conference attendees receive buffet-style breakfast, lunch, and dinner. No food is available to nonconference guests, however. ■ *2 miles N of Graeagle and ½ mile N of Blairsden on Hwy 70; (916) 836-2623; Mail: PO Box 67, Blairsden, CA 96103; $$; MC, V; checks OK.*

Gold Lake Lodge ★ Located at 6,620 feet, Gold Lake Lodge is in the heart of the Lakes Basin Recreation Area within hiking distance of spectacular high Sierra scenery, wildflower-filled meadows, and numerous small and large lakes excellent for water play. Clean, unprepossessing cabins line the edge of a pretty meadow. Standard cabins include a bathroom; in the more rustic ones you have to skip across the lawn to the communal facilities. Included in the price is breakfast and dinner in the main lodge (open to nonguests, too) with its nickel-plated Franklin stove, picnic tables, and wagonwheel chandeliers. The food fits right into the decor (nightly specials ranging from lasagne to pot roast to fried chicken). The sun tea is the perfect antidote to a hot summer day. ■ *N on Hwy 89 toward Graeagle, left on Gold Lake Rd for 7 miles; (916) 836-2350, summer; (916) 836-2751, winter; Mail: PO Box 25, Blairsden, CA 96103; $$; beer and wine; MC, V; checks OK; breakfast, dinner Tues–Sun; June–Oct.*

Iron Door ★ Johnsville, an 1876 mining town, supports one business. This is it. This restaurant has occupied the former century-old general store and post office since 1961. Now owned by the Cerrito family, the Iron Door retains the same look and menu it has since its inception some 30 years ago. The bar and interior dining room (preferred seating is in the pleasant porch) are adorned with antique farm implements, lanterns, floral wreaths, and Gibson Girl-style hangings. The bill of fare is heavy on steaks, Australian lobster, and fowl. Soups are thick and hearty, tossed iceberg represents the salad offerings, vegetables are overcooked. The tender Cornish game hen is infused with a light apple flavor, and mustard fans will knife into the excellent pepper steak. The Johnsville special desert—vanilla ice cream with crème de menthe and Ovaltine sprinkled on top—is both prettier and tastier than it sounds. ■ *In Johnsville within Plumas Eureka State Park between Graeagle and Blairsden; (916) 836-2376; $$; full bar; MC, V; checks OK; dinner Tues–Sun; Apr–Oct.*

GRAEAGLE

RESTAURANTS

Olsen's Cabin Restaurant ★ Within its attractive chalet-style exterior, Olsen's offers the homiest atmosphere and best dining experience in the Graeagle-Blairsden-Portola area. The dining room is awash in pastel pinks and greens, ruffled yellow floral tablecloths, calico print napkins, and hummingbrid feeders just outside the windows. The service is gracious and attentive. The farm-raised trout is quite good; the steak and the pork medallions (roasted in garlic butter and white wine and topped with sherry and peppercorns) are succulent and tender. Vegetables might be overcooked, but the seasoned wild rice adds a nice dimension and the twice-baked ruffled potatoes are superb. Don't miss Olsen's "Famous Cabin Coffee," laced with Bailey's and Kahlua and decorated with chocolate shavings. ■ *¼ mile N of Graeagle on CR A-14; (916) 836-2801; $$; full bar; MC, V; checks OK; dinner Mon–Sat; (weekends only Jan–Apr).*

LOYALTON

LODGINGS

Clover Valley Mill House ★ The square two-story cream-colored house with white columns looks faded behind its pale picket fence. Proprietor Leslie Hernandez has restored and decorated the interior with exquisite care. She searched for local antiques, gathered family treasures (her grandparents lived in historic Bodie, now a state park near Mono Lake), and added thoughtful details such as white linen duvet covers and crystal perfume bottles. The Sugar Pine Room has a four-poster queen bed, a sitting room with a day bed, and a private bath with two sinks. Jump into a game of volleyball, croquet, or horseshoes on the spacious yard. Breakfast is presented outside on the deck under the weeping birch and tall willows. Although trains are infrequent, the tracks are nearby, and the lumber mill's faint drone is constant. You can bring your horse (it will have its own corral) but not your children. ■ *S of Hwy 49 on*

Railroad Ave and S First St; (916) 993-4819; Mail: PO Box 928, Loyalton, CA 96118; $$; MC, V; checks OK.

BECKWOURTH

RESTAURANTS

Beckwith Tavern ★ If you're in the mood for an exceptional beef dinner in the company of cowboys, gallop over to the Beckwith Tavern. It was built of logs by Blackie Turner in the 1930s in the town then named after pioneer James Beckwith. Decades later, someone discovered Beckwith often signed his name Beckwourth (which he thought worthier), so the town changed its name. On weekends the place fills up fast with people who travel for miles to slice into the meltingly tender prime rib which might be gone after the first hour. There were times when cowboys went wild here, but cattle rancher and owner Francis Carmichael put his boot down. It's a family place now. The long bar has been branded by local ranchers. Tunes on the old jukebox—from Bob Wills to Fats Waller—are still three for a quarter. The rib steak hangs over the plate's edge. ■ *5 miles E of Portola; (916) 832-5084; Hwy 70, Beckwourth; $$; full bar; MC,V; checks OK; dinner Thurs–Tues.*

ALTA

RESTAURANTS

Belarde's Alta Restaurant ★ Just when you feel miles from anywhere, stop in to Belarde's—where Tim Belarde is simmering a delicious pot of soup and baking pies. Within minutes of your arrival, his wife Vicki befriends you by the stone fireplace as if you were just another one of the locals. Booths and tables seem to overlap because there's likely to be someone who will start a conversation with you—even if you're an outta-towner. The entrées are generous, usually deep- or pan-fried, but regulars especially return for those soups and Tim's deep-dish cherry pie (sometimes made the meal in itself). You'll find yourself walking out with a smile, a full tummy, and barely a dent in your wallet. ■ *Downtown Alta off I-80 at 33945 Alta Bonnie Nook; (916) 389-2828; $; beer and wine; MC, V; checks OK; breakfast, lunch, dinner Wed–Sun.*

DUTCH FLAT

RESTAURANTS

Monte Vista Inn ★ Monte Vista Inn, a roadhouse for 60 years, caters to many locals and to travelers lucky enough to find it. Built of indigenous logs and stone, the inn is a comfortable place. There's a wood stove in the bar and large sofas near the petrified wood fireplace in the lounge. Kerosene lamps light the wooden dining tables and old farm implements hang on the walls. Co-owner John Wardwell tends the bar while Dave Talso and Larry Kelly cook up generous portions of tender pork chops with homemade apple sauce and sautéed scampi with fresh mushrooms and garlic. Fresh baked pies (ooh, that blackberry pie tangy with lemon) sit neatly on the counter along the dining room wall. Folk music in the lounge on Friday and Saturday nights brings everything (and everyone) together. ■ *On I-80 at Dutch Flat exit (7 miles E of Colfax); (916) 389-2333; $$; full bar; MC, V; local checks only; dinner every day, brunch Sun.*

DONNER SUMMIT

A whirl of white in wintertime, Donner was named after the ill-fated Donner party, an 1846 wagon train that tried to cross the pass too late in the year, got caught in a snowstorm, and resorted to cannibalism for the survival of only a few. **The Emmigrant Trail Museum** in Donner Memorial State Park tells their grim story. It still snows here in winter, making Donner a major ski destination; however, in the summer you'll be able to spy the long blue fingers of a lake dotted with sailboats and flagged with forested slopes and granite palisades. **Donner Lake**, great for fishing and boating, has a public beach to the east end and a boat ramp to the west. **Donner Memorial State Park** has campsites, picnic tables and hiking trails; toll free (800) 444-7275 or (916) 587-3841.

SKIING

Located on old US 40 (I-80's predecessor) near the summit, **Sugar Bowl** remains in another time—say the 1940s. Although a few things change every year (snowmaking one year, child care the next), much stays the same. You park at the Highway 40 parking garage and ride a four-passenger gondola up to the ski area's base. Some 1,500 feet of vertical powder lace Sugar Bowl's two peaks (Mount Lincoln and Mount Disney) with close to 50 runs. With an elevation of 6,800 feet at the base and 8,383 feet at the summit, Sugar Bowl often has superior ski conditions when other areas are praying for snow; (916) 426-3651. Overnighters can stay in the 1939 **Sugar Bowl Lodge**. The 28 rooms are small, so better to rent one of the 54 rustic homes (nothing condo about these) in the nearby woods, many of which belong to longtime San Franciscans. The lodge is not open to the public in summer.

Nearby is the **Donner Ski Ranch**, a friendly, pocketsize area especially appealing to telemark skiers; 3½ miles off I-80 at the Soda Springs exit, Norden; (916)426-3635. Over the hill is **Boreal Ski Area,** a diminutive ski area with a big Central

Valley fan club. Boreal has dependable snow conditions and extensive snowmaking, night skiing until 9pm, and a very convenient just-off-the-interstate location, Truckee; (916) 426-3666. Boreal also operates one of the first ski areas developed in California—**Soda Springs**.

Amidst all the downhill activity, Donner Summit harbors one of the premiere cross-country ski areas in the country. **Royal Gorge,** one of the world's largest skinny-ski resorts, boasts of over 9,172 acres of skiable terrain, 317 kilometers of groomed tracks, 80 trails, and an average of 650-plus inches of snow a season. It also operates several trailside cafes (including 10 warming huts), a day lodge, a wilderness lodge (see review), and an extensive lesson program; Soda Springs, (916) 426-3871.

Loch Leven Lodge Those who want to get away from Tahoe hordes but desire easy access to restaurants and shops choose the Loch Leven Lodge. It's quiet, albeit simple, and each of the eight units faces Donner Lake. Beyond the 5,000-square-foot redwood deck is an Astroturf putting green (putters and balls provided), picnic tables, lawn chairs, a barbecue, and a spa. The rooms in the lower level offer the best view of the lake (but offer the least privacy). Travel with the gang and reserve the two-level townhouse with a fireplace, fully equipped kitchen, upstairs bedroom, and adjoining bunkroom. ■ *1½ miles from I-80 at 13855 Donner Pass Rd; (916) 587-3773; Mail: PO Box 162, Truckee, CA 96160; $$; no credit cards; checks OK.*

SODA SPRINGS

LODGINGS

Royal Gorge's Rainbow Lodge ■ Wilderness Lodge ★★ The 1922 Rainbow Lodge was built at a bend in the Yuba River of hand-hewn pine timbers and local granite. The owner of Royal Gorge bought this charming retreat six years ago. The pine-paneled room choices are quite simple: private bath, shower, and sink, or sink only. Rooms 12 and 23 look out over the river (no televisions or telephones). Oversized chairs and sofas in the lounge invite guests to read or play Monopoly by the fire. All meals are served in The Engadine Cafe where the stone walls are softened by floral drapes. Breakfast (included with a night's stay) begins with homebaked muffins, perhaps a delectable frittata with Italian sauce, sweet red peppers, and cheddar cheese, and a steaming cup of French roast. Lunch might be Swiss fondue or roast beef sandwich on grilled sourdough bread with cheddar cheese, tomatoes, and roasted green chiles. The chef prepares five seafood specials nightly along with the regular menu. Mondays are locals' night, when everything is under $10. Wednesdays are all-you-can-eat pasta—what better way to carbo load for the next day's ski?

Royal Gorge also hosts cross-country skiers in its **Wilderness Lodge**, an inviting building where the former dormlike accommodations have been converted to private rooms with bunks. Wilderness Lodge guests arrive via skis or horse-drawn sleigh. In the European tradition, meals at Royal Gorge are an event. The highly trained chefs cook in the French country manner, three times a day. Ah, wilderness! ■ *½ mile W of I-80 at the Rainbow Road exit; (916) 426-3661 or (916) 426-3871; Mail: PO Box 1100, Soda Springs, CA 95728; $; full bar; MC, V; no checks; breakfast, lunch, dinner every day.*

NORDEN

LODGINGS

Clair Tappaan Lodge This is no place for wimps, but it is great for those who want to meet new people, share in a healthy experience, and limit expenses. Built by Sierra Club volunteers in 1934, Clair Tapaan Lodge (formerly members only) is a massive, rustic three-story lodge near the Donner Summit. Guests carry their own bedding and luggage 100 yards uphill from the road to dorm-style rooms with 2 to 20 bunks and community baths. Wood-burning stoves and pine-paneled walls warm up the bare floors and simple furnishings in the living room and library. Guests get a hot breakfast and bag their own lunches to take skiing or hiking (tracks, slopes, and trails are close at foot). Dinner, after a full day of skiing, is always a hearty and simple highlight (perhaps pasta primavera with salad, homemade bread, and ice cream). The meals are included in a night's stay but so are caretaking chores such as dishwashing or mopping the floors (guests take turns). The two-bunk cubicles offer some privacy but the walls are thin. Snowshoes, ski equipment, and lessons are available in winter. ■ *2½ miles from Soda Springs/Norden exit at 19940 Donner Pass Rd; (916) 426-3632; Mail: PO Box 36, Norden, CA 95724; $; no credit cards; checks OK.*

TRUCKEE

Truckee began in 1863 as a railroad–lumber town with construction of the First Transcontinental Railroad over Donner Summit. Its transformation from a dirty, run-down one-horse town to a hip place began in 1971 with the opening of OB's Pub & Restaurant. **Sierra Mountaineer**, in the stone building that was once a livery and garage on Bridge Street, is a great resource for hiking and cross-country skiing guide books, maps, and supplies (Bridge and Jibbom, Truckee, (916) 587-2025). The eastbound and westbound **Amtrak** passenger trains make a whistle stop at the yellow depot daily.

In summer months, the attractions are the **Truckee-Tahoe Air Show** in June, the **Fourth of July** parade, and the **Truckee Championship Rodeo** in August. The Truckee River Regional Park, ½ mile south of town on Highway 267, has softball diamonds, picnic tables, tennis courts, and an outdoor amphitheater with music programs (many free) throughout the summer. During winter, skiers take advantage of Truckee's proximity to many alpine and nordic ski areas and return here to eat or sleep. For information on ski areas in Truckee, see the Donner Summit section in this chapter.

RESTAURANTS

Cottonwood ★★ Cottonwood stands at the base of California's oldest ski jump. Inside, a window seat in the spacious dining room overlooks the bright lights of Truckee. Begin the evening by sharing a whole leaf caesar salad slathered with garlic and meant to be eaten with your fingers. The seasonal menu often displays a Southwest twist (pork loin marinated in tequila and cilantro and grilled with a nectarine-lime salsa; or chicken grilled with Roma tomatoes, basil, sun-dried tomatoes, Gorgonzola, and Asiago—then tossed with linguine).Don't pass up the cranberry-apple crisp à la mode for dessert. A jazz combo plays in the bar every Saturday night; dine under patio umbrellas in summer. ■ *Above Truckee off Hwy 267 at Hilltop Lodge; (916) 587-5711; 10142 Rue Hilltop, Truckee; $$; full bar; MC, V; checks OK; dinner Tues–Sun.*

Zina's! ★★ When Zina Krakowsky opened her restaurant in the CB White House, a collective "ahhh" could be heard throughout Donner Summit. At long last, locals didn't have to travel to Sacramento or San Francisco to find a decent coffee house. Temptation begins at the counter often laden with still warm pastries (raspberry-graham muffins, coffee-hazelnut scones, and cinnamon swirls, for example) and dark French roast coffee or an espresso. Sunlight filters through lace curtains and healthy plants onto the porch–dining area conducive to reading the house *New York Times* or *Wall Street Journal*.

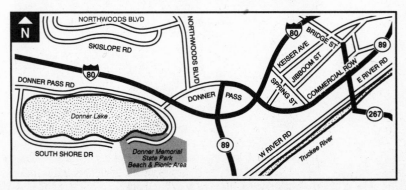

The lunch menu changes daily, always displaying beautiful fresh vegetables and fruits as main staples and garnish. Recently, the choices included a pasta pie (layers of spinach, pesto, angel hair pasta, marinara, sweet onions, eggplant, artichoke hearts, mushrooms, and Parmesan and mozzarella cheeses), a steamy curried lentil, ham, and broccoli soup served with fresh baked bread, and a smoked turkey sandwich with apple-raisin chutney and cream cheese. Desserts like Zina's Dark Chocolate Delirium, luscious cheesecakes, and deep-dish fruit pie are presented in pools of crème Anglaise and puréed berries. ■ *1 block W of Commercial Row; (916) 587-3494; 10292 Donner Pass Rd, Truckee; $$; beer and wine; AE, MC, V; local checks only; breakfast, lunch every day, dinner Fri–Sat.*

Squeeze In ★ Yes, you'll need to squeeze into the narrow space covered with old hats, photos, and hippie art. A Truckee tradition since 1974, the Squeeze is known for its omelets—57 of them—all named for local characters. They're generous and come with a choice of tomato, cheese, or mushroom sauce (order it on the side). Homemade soups, the Davo (a flour tortilla filled with refried beans, potatoes, vegetables, salsa, green chiles, avocado, and Swiss cheese), or 22 triple-decker sandwiches are a mouthful at lunch. A few tables have checkerboard tops (pieces available) and the back patio is a best in the morning. Occasionally, the wait line spills onto the sidewalk, so go early. Great restroom graffiti. ■ *On Commercial Row in downtown Truckee; (916) 587-9814; 10060 Donner Pass Rd, Truckee; $$; beer and wine; no credit cards, checks OK; breakfast, lunch every day.*

Donner Lake Kitchen This kitchen, located behind the Donner Pines Market, may be the only restaurant rolling flapjacks with sautéed fresh fruit and nuts or frying up huge platefuls of huevos rancheros within miles. Sally and Ray Edwards have maintained the quality and atmosphere that locals grew to love when they knew it as The Impasse. The pine-paneled walls with old Tahoe photos and green-checked curtains add a cheery tempo. For lunch, it's hard to beat the quesadilla grande or number 20 (a hot flour tortilla filled with refried beans, cheese, onions, tomatoes, avocados, mushrooms, olives, sour cream, and salsa). There can be a long wait on weekends, so bring along a newspaper. ■ *1½ miles from Donner Lake on Donner Pass Rd; (916) 587-3119; 13710 Donner Pass Rd, Truckee; $; no alcohol; no credit cards; local checks only; breakfast, lunch every day.*

El Toro Bravo A big mint green building houses the most dependable Mexican restaurant in town. Not only for the food (try the fajitas—a steaming flour tortilla wrapped with lime-marinated sautéed chicken, refried beans with melted cheese, guacamole, and fresh salsa—or the tacolada—a burrito look-alike topped with enchilada sauce and cheese—but also because El Toro is open when other restaurants might close (off season, snowstorms, whatever). When it's warm outside, you'll want to sit under the trees and umbrellas with a chilled margarita, possibly serenaded by live mariachis. ■ *W end of downtown Truckee on Donner Pass Rd, (916) 587-3557; 10186 Donner Pass Rd, Truckee; $; full bar; AE, MC, V; local checks only; lunch, dinner every day.*

LODGINGS

The Truckee Hotel Built when Truckee was founded in 1863, The Truckee Hotel has escaped devastating fires and overzealous developers for nearly 130 years. New owners Karen and Jeff Winter painted and wallpapered their 37 guest rooms, added linens, curtains, and blinds, and retained the antique dressers and glass chandeliers. At press time, a new lobby, breakfast room, and gift shop were under construction. The multiple configurations of rooms and suites can comfortably accommodate one to five people. Rooms facing north and in the back of the hotel, away from the railroad track and main street, are quietest (we suggest rooms 205 and 215, which have private baths and televisions). A continental breakfast includes hot cereal, warm breakfast breads, and fresh fruit and is available from 7:30 to 10am. The Passage restaurant offers special theme meals with guest chefs every week. ■ *At Donner Pass Rd and 10007 Bridge St; (916) 587-4444 or toll free (800) 659-6921; Mail: PO Box 884, Truckee, CA 96160; $$; full bar; AE, MC, V; checks OK; lunch, dinner every day, brunch Sun.*

LAKE TAHOE

Lake Tahoe is North America's largest alpine lake (the highest freshwater lake of its size in the world): 22 miles long, 12 miles wide, and 72 miles around with an average depth of 989 feet. Homes and businesses along the west shore are reminiscent of Lake Tahoe some 50 years ago, when residents were here only in summer. A lovely **bike path** follows the lake's shore for 10 miles from **Sugar Pine State Park** on the west end. The monthlong **Lake Tahoe Summer Music Festival** presents classical music at outdoor venues around the north shore; (916) 583-3101. The east shore's Sand Harbor in **Lake Tahoe State Park** is one of the area's most beautiful beaches. The **Shakespeare at Sand Harbor** and **Sand Harbor Music Festival** performances have Lake Tahoe as a backdrop on clear August nights; for more information on area festivals call (916) 583-9048.

  Emerald Bay (on Tahoe's west shore) is Lake Tahoe's

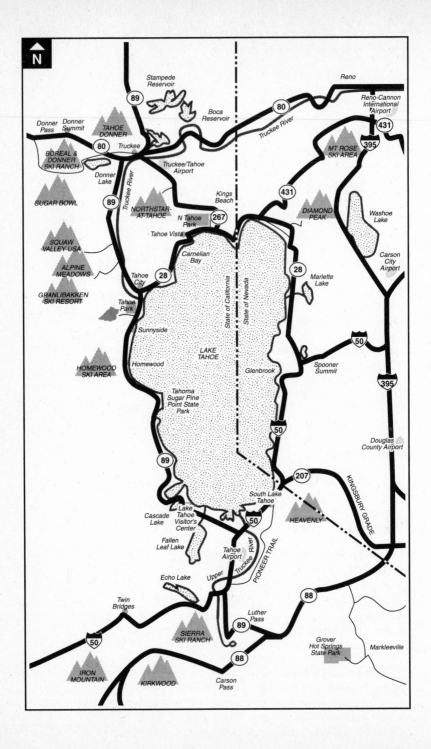

most photographed vista, usually from the highway or Viking-sholm Castle by the lake's edge.

SKIING

A short 6-mile hop south from Truckee on State Route 267 (or 6 miles from Kings Beach, Lake Tahoe), **Northstar at Tahoe** has carved a niche for itself as one of the country's best-rated family ski resorts. Could be, in part, Northstar's outstanding Minors' Camp (ages 2 through 6). Or perhaps it's because of STARKIDS (ages 5 through 12), with its own set of innovative teaching techniques aimed at that age grouping. Another plus is everything is right there—the skiing, accommodations, dining facilities. Northstar has a hefty number of ego runs on its 2,200 feet of vertical, as well as plenty of challenges on the backside. The area's lodging (which includes rooms in the base lodge, several clusters of condominiums, and some rental homes) is serviced every few minutes by Northstar's free shuttle buses; Northstar Drive and Highway 267; Truckee, (916) 562-1010, toll free (800) 533-6787. Northstar's **Basque Club Restaurant** offers traditional, five-course Basque meals; (916) 562-2460. Best way to arrive here is by horsedrawn sleigh.

For years **Squaw Valley/USA,** 8 miles from Truckee and Interstate 80, has been considered by many Northern Californians as the best skiing experience in the region (Squaw's terrain covers six peaks and climbs 2,850 feet). Highway 89, Lake Tahoe; (916) 583-6955. Today, it is on the brink of developing into a full-blown destination ski resort. Ever since Squaw's founder, Alex Cushing, snagged the 1960 Winter Olympic Games for his little known ski area, countless master plans and developers have come and gone. Recently, thanks to a flurry of construction, the trip out of the Valley for quality accommodations is no longer necessary. One **central reservation** number services all Valley properties, as well as numerous other hotels, motels, bed and breakfast inns, and condos in the North Lake Tahoe area; toll free (800) 545-4350.

At elevation 8,200 feet, Squaw's **High Camp Bath and Tennis Club** includes six outdoor tennis courts (two heated for winter use) and a swimming lagoon and spa complex. The adjacent outdoor **Olympic Ice Pavilion** allows would-be Olympians the chance to skate on the highest artificial ice rink in the world. It's accessible by Squaw's cable car and open for skating daily year round from 10am to 9pm.

Not to be missed is the pocket-size **Backstage Bistro** run by Graham Rock touting primarily Greek cuisine. In the back of the Opera House, the 12-table restaurant serves up new inventions every evening. The slow-paced, relaxed ambience is a much-welcome respite from Squaw Valley's usual bustle; (916) 581-0454. Each summer Rock brings his entire staff from his Backstage Bistro in Squaw Valley to **Chambers Landing Restaurant**, 7 miles south of Tahoe City. It joins a small seasonal list of superb restaurants at the lake's shore. Besides the restaurant, he also operates the bar in the historic Chambers boathouse (built in 1875) that rests on a pier stretching into the lake. Begin your evening here drinking in the glorious view. Stroll along the piers or beach until dinnertime when you can sit outdoors on the patio, or inside beyond the open glass doors under a skylit ceiling. Reservations are essential in July and August; (916) 525-7262.

Squaw lodgings Tucked quietly away in the forest at the bottom of Snow King (formerly Red Dog), the nine-story, 405-room **Resort at Squaw Creek** brings a new dimension of amenities to the area—from valets and a sports concierge to room service with gourmet eats and a children's activity program. Understated, yes, but with spectacular touches such as a rock-framed waterfall above the ice rink. The resort's Squaw Creek lift (exactly 59 steps from the lodge) gets guests up Snow King and over to the rest of Squaw Valley's slopes; (916) 583-6300, toll free (800) 3-CREEK-3.

The Squaw Valley/USA gondola soars right over the **Squaw Valley Lodge**. In fact, the lodge is so close to the ski area you can slide right in the back door. In the past decade, the lodge has grown to 154 condos housed in separate buildings. The condos sport Southwestern touches and the usual wear and tear of a temporary clientele. Extras are just about the max skiers can fit into a day: outdoor and indoor hot tubs; health spa with aerobics classes, a workout room, and a masseuse; (916) 583-5500, toll free (800) 922-9970.

Across the street from Squaw Valley's gondola, the two-story **Squaw Valley Inn**, purchased by multimillionaire Gordon Getty in the mid-'80s, has been transformed into a manse from the heart of the English countryside. The lobby and the guest rooms are all brass, oak, and green plaid, with fox-and-hounds paintings on the walls. Surprisingly, such an alien atmosphere in the heart of ski country works. The Inn also has a lap swimming pool, hot tubs, bar and grill, and Benton's Restaurant; (916) 583-1576, toll free (800) 323-ROOM.

A short walk from the gondola, the **Olympic Village Inn** began life as dormitories for the 1960 Olympic athletes. What the rooms lack in space they make up for in charm—with Bavarian furnishings and exquisite decor right down to the sink fixtures. Also on the premises: four hot tubs and a heated pool; (916) 581-6000, toll free (800) 845-5243.

Over the ridge from behemoth Squaw Valley/USA is the smaller, equally challenging **Alpine Meadows**; (2600 Alpine Meadows Rd; toll free (800) 441-4423). Alpine has distinguished itself over the years for its friendly, bend-over-backwards attitude, its no-kidding-around ski school, the humongous annual

Corporate Ski Challenge (a week's worth of racing among 750-plus corporations), and its usually successful attempt to remain open until at least the end of May. Closest lodging to Alpine is River Ranch Lodge (see review).

There are few ski settings as spectacular as the one provided by **Heavenly Valley**. From its 10,100-foot Monument Peak you can savor a sweeping view of cobalt blue Lake Tahoe in one direction and the barren landscape of Nevada in the other. The mountain, with 25 lifts and 3,600 vertical feet, straddles the state lines of California and Nevada. Heavenly has overcome its temperate weather by implementing one of the most extensive snowmaking operations in the world. Those in the know head for the Nevada side (fewer people, a straight shot from top to bottom, wide open bowls), either by driving to its base at Nevada Route 207 or by taking a series of lifts up the California side from its base on Ski Run Blvd, off I-50; South Lake Tahoe; (916) 541-1330.

TAHOE CITY

RESTAURANTS
See also Lake Tahoe introduction.

Christy Hill ★★★★ The setting entices: white walls, blue-gray carpet, and rose tablecloths reflect alpenglow sunsets over

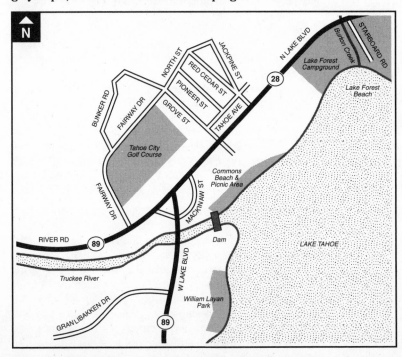

Lake Tahoe. And so does the food. Chefs Matt and Debbie Adams established a devoted following soon after they opened their first restaurant in Squaw Valley. Since moving Christy Hill to Lake Tahoe six years ago, they're now able to accommodate *all* their devotees. Matt's preparations are from the freshest ingredients around. One day he may serve Malpeque Bay oysters in salsa fresca, or, perhaps, fresh Maine lobster (flown in from the other coast). Another day his menu may include the imaginative broiled Australian lamb loin with apple, ginger, and mint chutney, or fresh Eastern scallops sautéed with julienne vegetables and fresh sorrel in a champagne butter cream sauce. Christy Hill's experienced servers know their menu and extensive wine list; rely on them to make reliable suggestions. Dessert is a wonderful excuse to extend your evening. Try the fresh fruit cobbler (peach or raspberry in the summer) or a crème brulée en croûte. Romantics time dessert with the setting sun. ■ *Behind the Village Store in Tahoe City; (916) 583-8551; 115 Grove St, Tahoe City; $$$; beer and wine; MC, V; checks OK; dinner Tues–Sun.*

Wolfdale's ★★★★ Soft sculptures and original modern art paintings accentuate the soothing atmosphere at Wolfdale's. They set the mood for chef/owner Douglas Dale's distinctly innovative food influenced from the Far East and true West. Everything served—breads, sausages, smoked and cured fish and poultry, and desserts—is made in-house. The menu selections are thoughtfully prepared and merit contemplation. A perfect meal begins with a cured salmon salad and a seafood spring roll with Vietnamese dip; it then continues with steamed sea bass with shu mai and Sichuan dip or grilled venison with poached pear and kabocha pumpkin. Many regulars who love the ambience at Wolfdale's dine in the bar. The wine list emphasizes California selections. There is outdoor seating in the summertime with a filtered view of Lake Tahoe. The dining room is nonsmoking and reservations are vital during high season. ■ *1 mile from Hwy 89 on Hwy 28; (916) 583-5700; 640 N Lake Blvd, Tahoe City; $$$; full bar; MC, V; no checks; dinner every day in summer, Wed–Mon off-seasons and winter.*

Fire Sign Cafe ★★ In a converted Old Tahoe home, Fire Sign Cafe's country miscellanea and reproduction antique furnishings seem to fit. Locals come for a familiar face, French roast coffee, fresh-squeezed orange juice, eggs (dill and artichoke omelet with home-fries stirred with onions, green peppers, mushrooms, and Monterey Jack cheese), and homemade raspberry cobbler. Owner/chef Bob Young smokes his own salmon for his omelets and variation on eggs Benedict. Popular lunch items are the garden burger, chicken burrito, and grilled turkey sandwich with ortega chiles and cheese. The best summertime seat in the house is on the deck under the pines; Lake Tahoe's shore is hidden from view but it's only a short walk across the street to a small public park. Expect long waits on Sundays. ■ *2 miles S of the Tahoe City Y on Hwy 89; (916) 583-0871; 1785 W Lake Blvd, Tahoe City; $$; beer and wine; MC, V; local checks only; breakfast, lunch every day.*

Za's ★★ The name comes from the second syllable in pizzas. Za's is hidden behind Pete 'n' Peter's bar. Out of this unlikely spot with half a name come delicious pastas, pizza, and calzone. With only a dozen tables, Za's is cozy: forest green carpets, cafe curtains, natural-wood walls. The herbed bread is baked fresh and the crusty brown loaves, stacked under hanging braids of garlic, is filling—especially when soaked in olive oil from the spicy antipasto at your table. Start with the whole leaf caesar salad or the polenta with wild mushrooms in a Marsala sauce. The vegetable calzone (a golden brown pillow filled with fresh vegetables and mozzarella) rests in a pool of light marinara sauce. Chianti comes—properly—in tumblers. Skip the dessert, but not a shot of the espresso drinks. This is some kinda place. ■ *Across from the fire station behind Pete 'n' Peter's downtown, (916) 583-1812; 395 N Lake Blvd, Tahoe City; $; beer and wine; no credit cards; checks OK; dinner Wed–Mon.*

Cafe Cobblestone ★ Decorated in country French prints and pine paneling on Tahoe City's main drag, Cafe Cobblestone is a local favorite for breakfast. The outdoor patio is especially popular on the frequent sun-drenched days. Homemade scones with yummy Devonshire cream and lemon curd go well with a cappuccino or foamy caffè latte in a barrel-shaped mug, while the eggs Benedict and Florentine are breakfast specialties. The list of international beers is bigger than their burger. Save room for banana cream or chocolate cream pie. ■ *Next to the Clocktower in the Cobblestone Center; (916) 583-2111; 475 N Lake Blvd, Tahoe City; $$; beer and wine; MC, V; no checks; breakfast, lunch every day (dinners on occasion, call ahead).*

Cafe O'Lake ★ Although very new, this cafe is already a hit. Longtime Tahoans (including world champion alpine skier Tamara McKinney) started with a long customer list of friends for whom good coffee in good company at a pleasant cafe is life itself. The menu is simple with limited homemade pastries, soup (spinach mushroom), deli-style salads (curried turkey), sandwiches, and desserts. Espresso drinks are served in big bowls—Euro-style. Louis Armstrong sings "A Kiss to Build a Dream On." You are encouraged to hang out, read the local and San Francisco papers, or gather at the stammisch (the local's table) with its view of Lake Tahoe through the French doors. ■ *Near the Big Tree on the lake side in downtown Tahoe City; (916) 5815104; 550 N Lake Blvd, Tahoe City; $; no alcohol; AE, MC, V; checks OK; breakfast, lunch every day.*

LODGINGS
See also Lake Tahoe introduction.

Sunnyside Restaurant & Lodge ★★★ All 23 rooms in this beautifully restored lodge have a view of Lake Tahoe. In summer, locals and visitors meet for lunch, dinner, or a drink on the huge redwood deck and gaze for hours upon one of the world's natural jewels. Request a lakefront room (numbers 32–39) or suite (numbers 30–31). They are bright and airy: high ceilings, country pine furnishings, and large baskets with dried flowers. All have decks, but number 39 is the only lakefront room with a fireplace. A breakfast buffet is served every morning. Downstairs, the indoor and outdoor bars offer uninterrupted views of the lake and marina as does the Chris Craft dining room which serves dinner daily. The seafood specials and prime rib are excellent. ■ *2 miles S of the Tahoe City Y on Hwy 89; (916) 583-7200, toll free (800) 822-2SKI in California; Mail: PO Box 5969, Tahoe City, CA 96145; $$$; full bar; AE, MC, V; checks OK; dinner every day (lunch, Sun brunch every day in summer).*

The Cottage Inn ★★ What was once a six-cottage motor court (circa 1939) is now one of the more appealing stays in Tahoe City. Carol and Phil Brubaker painted, carpeted, and furnished each knotty pine cabin with European pine furniture and thick colorful quilts. Two of the new 15 cottages have small wood-burning stoves generating ample heat for the limited space. Three one-bedroom studios (numbers 12, 14, and 15) are very quiet and face Lake Tahoe. You can order breakfast in your room or at family-style tables in the main house. Sofas around the stone fireplace invite with a good book or the morning paper. Other amenities include a semiprivate beach nearby, a Scandinavian sauna, an old-fashioned cookie jar in the kitchen, and popcorn by the fire (they get lots of snow here). There are no telephones or televisions in the rooms; smoking is not allowed. ■ *2 miles S of the Tahoe City Y on Hwy 89 at 1690 West Lake Blvd; (916) 581-4073; Mail: PO Box 66, Tahoe City, CA 96145; $$; MC, V; checks OK.*

River Ranch Lodge ★ Many of the rooms in this historic lodge have private balconies that overlook the Truckee River as it winds its way from Lake Tahoe to Truckee, then east to Pyramid Lake in Nevada. Good thing, since the sound of a rushing river drowns out traffic sounds. Unfortunately, the recent dry winters have lowered the river to a trickle during late summer. The prettiest rooms are the noisiest, so opt instead for numbers 9 and 10, which are furthest from the road. The River Ranch circular cocktail lounge cantilevers over the river and has been a locals' haven for years. Diners eat in the lounge by a window or near the stone fireplace. ■ *On Hwy 89 at the entrance to Alpine Meadows Rd; (916) 583-4264, toll free (800) 535-*

9900 in California; Mail: PO Box 197, Tahoe City, CA 96145; $$; full bar; AE, MC, V; checks OK; lunch, dinner every day (summer only).

TAHOE VISTA

RESTAURANTS

The Boulevard Cafe & Trattoria ★★★ Organic produce and herbs plus Napa Valley extra virgin olive oil are staples in chef Daniel Paolillo's kitchen. You'll find the Napa olive oil in a dipping dish accompanied by an anchoiate (a roasted eggplant-garlic-anchovy spread) and chef Paolillo's chewy bread; you'll see it again drizzled over fresh mozzarella and organic yellow tomatoes with fresh basil. The menu features a tender boneless roast quail with a wild mushroom and herb stuffing, a hearty ragout of venison with whole-wheat pappardelle noodles, or cheese ravioli with a porcini mushroom sauce. Delve into Daniel's own chocolate ice cream spiked with sun-dried cherries. Owner Steve Marks opens the small patio for dinner on balmy eves. The service is informed and casual, so relax and enjoy. ■ 1½ miles W of Hwy 267 on Hwy 28; (916) 546-7213; 6731 N Lake Blvd, Tahoe Vista; $$; beer and wine; MC, V; no checks; dinner every day.

LODGINGS

Franciscan Lakeside Lodge ★ The Franciscan is the local best in the motel genre. Guests have access to a private beach and pier, mooring buoys, a heated swimming pool, volleyball nets, a croquet set, horseshoe pits, a children's play area, and nearby golf course, tennis courts, and ski areas. The 57 units are studios or have one or two bedrooms. The newly redecorated lakeside rooms are more cheerful than those with brown carpets and standard motel furnishings on the mountain side, but the lakefront cabins are rented first, so plan in advance for those. Telephone booths around the property take the place of those in rooms. Manager Duke Eberle and his parents are friendly and helpful, as is their efficient staff. ■ 1 mile W of Hwy 267 on Hwy 28 at 6944 N Lake Blvd; (916) 546-7234, toll free (800) 564-6754 in California; Mail: PO Box 280, Tahoe Vista, CA 96148; $$; AE, DIS, MC, V; checks OK.

▼

Kings Beach

Restaurants

▲

KINGS BEACH

RESTAURANTS

Log Cabin Caffe ★ Originally a summer home, this log cabin has a backyard picnic area where you can delight in ice cream sundaes and sodas from 11am to 11pm all summer long. The restaurant is crowded on weekends, so locals go early and get their cappuccinos to go—or they wait for a winter weekday when they can sit quietly by the wood stove with the newspaper. This is *the* place from morning to noon. Croissants and muffins are baked fresh. Order the fluffy Belgian waffles topped with fresh fruit or nuts. Add to that fresh-squeezed orange juice and an espresso drink. Midday it's hearty fresh vegetable soup, tofu burger, and sliced turkey breast sandwich with cranberries and cream cheese. ■ *⅓ mile E of Hwy 267 on Hwy 28; (916) 546-7109; 8692 N Lake Blvd, Kings Beach; $$; no alcohol; MC, V; no checks; breakfast, lunch every day.*

Peluso's Bring the kids and settle into the old wooden booths for a meal of East Coast pizza. Order the plain Parmesan cheese pizza with thin crust, homemade tomato sauce, and Parmesan cheese. Add fresh garlic and pepperoncinis and you have a spicy ahealthy apizza. Or try baby clams and bacon, or sautéed escarole and fresh garlic. Other outstanding entrées include manicotti and lasagna made with Peluso's homemade egg noodles and marinara sauce. The Kings Beach movie theater is next door, so this is a convenient preshow dinner stop. ■ *Next to the Kings Beach Theatre on Hwy 28; (916) 546-7022; 8703 N Lake Blvd, Kings Beach; $; beer and wine; AE, DC, MC, V; no checks; dinner every day (lunch summers only).*

HOMEWOOD

RESTAURANTS
See also Lake Tahoe introduction.

Swiss Lakewood ★★★ Helga and Albert Marty's consistently superb French continental restaurant is the oldest operating restaurant at Lake Tahoe (since 1920). The dining room has a feel of tradition with its knotty pine walls covered with clocks, old photographs, and Swiss cow bells. Albert Marty's offerings are distinguished by an abundance of perfectly executed sauces: the salmon ravioli appetizer is touched with a light fresh basil, sun-dried tomato sauce; roasted duck comes married with a Swedish lingonberry sauce; and the chocolate soufflé with Grand Marnier sauce creates a lovely finale. You can sample this chef's simpler fare at a fraction of the price in the summertime—when Helga serves lunch (grilled veal bratwurst or smoked trout on Belgian endive and fresh berries with Grand Marnier sauce) on the patio among her potted flowers. The Martys rent six cabins on the property by the night or week. ■ *6 miles S of Tahoe City next to Homewood ski area; 5055 W Lake Blvd; (916) 525-5211; Mail: PO Box 205, Homewood, CA 96141; $$$; full bar; AE, MC, V; no checks; lunch Tues–Sun (mid-Jun–mid-Sept), dinner Tues–Sun.*

LODGINGS

Rockwood Lodge ★★★ If you've always wanted to know someone who lives in the historic mansions around the lake,

Rockwood Lodge is, at least, your chance to pretend. Innkeepers Lou Reinkens and Connie Stevens restored this native stone and timber house and subsequently opened it as an exquisite inn. The plush cream carpet caresses your feet (no shoes in the house) and sets the mood for your stay. All four rooms in this bed and breakfast are furnished with European and American antiques, feather beds and down comforters covered in Laura Ashley fabrics, and terrycloth bathrobes in the bedroom closet. The bathrooms have brass fixtures, hand-painted tiles, and double showers. The largest room, Rubicon Bay, has a four-poster bed, private bath, and lake view ($200). Guests are encouraged to play backgammon or sip cordials in the sitting room. Connie or Lou serves breakfast at 9am. Besides shoes, you're asked to leave behind your pets, children, and smokes. ■ *On Hwy 89 next to Homewood ski area at 5295 W Lake Blvd; (916) 525-5273, toll free (800) LETAHOE; Mail: PO Box 226, Homewood, CA 96141; $$$; no credit cards; checks OK.*

SOUTH LAKE TAHOE

RESTAURANTS
See also Lake Tahoe introduction.

Evan's American Gourmet Cafe ★★★ Owner Candice Williams graciously welcomes every diner. The softly lit dining room with 11 cloth-covered tables is decorated in pastels and vases of fresh alstromerias. Young chef and co-owner Evan Williams creates his menu pulling flavors from Italian, Caribbean, Oriental, and American Southwest cuisine using select fresh produce and herbs. His signature corn galettes come with caviar in fresh herb cream sauce. An excellent entrée is the boneless rack of lamb with glazed onions, muscat raisins, fresh basil, and a port wine–lamb stock sauce. Candice will tempt you with lavish desserts: frozen white chocolate mousse torte, homemade white chocolate macadamia nut ice cream, or a most decadent cheesecake. Two hundred wines make up the award-winning wine list. Sweet kitchen fragrances filter into the room. ■ *1 mile N of the Y on Hwy 89 at 15th St; (916) 542-1990; 536 Emerald Bay Rd, South Lake Tahoe; $$$; beer and wine; MC, V; no checks; dinner Mon–Sat (closed Nov).*

Spatz ★★★ Like an eagle's nest on the tallest pine, Spatz has a grand mountaintop view of Lake Tahoe. German-born and European-trained, Michael and Rita Janke like to introduce their loyal clientele to inventive meals that awaken the senses. Take, for instance, the grilled mahi-mahi topped with salsa, resting in a black bean sauce and served with a Brie-and-melon quesadilla. Or marinated pork tenderloin with peach onion confit. Or grilled lamb with Dijon and rolled in rosemary and bread crumbs. Rita may suggest starting with the house-cured ceviche with tequila or the Spanish shrimp sautéed in olive oil with chile peppers and fresh garlic. For dinner, try the fillet of veal with pepper Brie and shiitake mushrooms in puff pastry. Presentation is distinctive (they're real artists here) and the flavors are an event in themselves. Lunch is served on the spacious deck in summer. Otherwise, find a window seat and drink in the view. ■ *On the road to Ski Incline ski area; (702) 831-8999; 341 Ski Way, Incline Village; $$; full bar; MC, V; local checks only; lunch Mon–Fri, dinner every day.*

Samurai ★★ There are only two Japanese restaurants in South Lake Tahoe—and this is the best one. Samurai has an enticing sushi bar as well as traditional Japanese dishes such as tempura and teriyaki. The menu features seafood yosenabe (fresh vegetables, tofu, noodles, mushrooms, bamboo shoots, and seafood in a soy sauce and lemon broth) and tonkatsu (breaded, deep-fried pork cutlets with a special sauce and pickled cucumber). Owner Geoffrey Goto has decorated his restaurant in uncluttered Japanese style and has added a robata (a table around a volcanic rock fireplace) and very private tatami room for parties of 12. ■ *1½ miles E of the Y in South Lake Tahoe; (916) 542-0300; 2588 Hwy 50, South Lake Tahoe; $$; beer and wine; AE, MC, V; no checks; lunch Mon–Fri, dinner every day.*

Scoozi's on Ski Run ★★ Don't be distracted by the casino lights. This is a popular spot for South Lake Tahoe epicureans. You'll love it from the start for the homemade bread tasting of rosemary and garlic and dipped in extra virgin olive oil. White textured walls, tables covered with red and green tablecloths, and an earthy fragrance in the air all evoke definite Italian coast appeal. Continue to the meal where you'll find delicately browned calzones with lightly cooked fresh vegetables, artichoke hearts, ricotta cheese, and a savory marinara sauce. Another savory dish is herb pasta tossed with roasted red peppers, mushrooms, garlic, fresh herbs, and chunks of house-smoked salmon. Butter and oil are basic ingredients here. Desserts are simple and tempting, and the wines are fairly priced. ■ *6 blocks up toward Heavenly Valley from Hwy 50; (916) 542-0100; 1142 Ski Run Blvd, South Lake Tahoe; $$; beer and wine; AE, MC, V; no checks; dinner every day.*

The Beacon ★ On a summer afternoon, there are few better spots to contemplate the good life. A frosty Rum Runner (a blend of light and dark rums and seven juices) in hand, a bucket of steamed New Zealand clams on the table, and Lake Tahoe sparkling at your feet may be too much bliss. Although the service here can be a bit slow, the food is good. Lunch fare includes Cobb salad, hamburger, teriyaki chicken sandwich, and homemade soup. Dinner specialties are seafood (salmon drizzled with a strawberry hollandaise sauce, for example) or a tasty New York steak sautéed in a green peppercorn sauce. An extensive wine list is all California. There's often live entertainment in the summer (jazz, reggae, country, or oldies rock). ■ *2½ miles N of the Y on Hwy 89 at Camp Richardson; (916) 541-0630; 1900 Jamieson Beach Rd, South Lake Tahoe; $$; full bar; AE, MC, V; no checks; lunch, dinner every day (closed Nov).*

The Red Hut America's ubiquitous coffee shop: L-shaped Formica counter, booths, antique cash register, and bubble gum machine. The coffee is better here than in most small town cafes and so are the pecan waffles and omelets (asparagus and cheese or hot Italian sausage). The quarter-pound burgers are big and cheap and all of the food comes very hot and very fast. Regulars remember when hungry patrons often had to wait outside for a table. Since then, the owners have added a waiting room but "the wait" is immortalized on their T-shirts. ■ *¼ mile S of Al Tahoe Blvd; (916) 541-9024; 2723 Hwy 50, South Lake Tahoe; $; no alcohol; no credit cards; no checks; breakfast, lunch every day.*

LODGINGS
See also Lake Tahoe introduction.

Christiania Inn ★★ This charming European-style inn, located above South Lake Tahoe's busy streets, is a few hundred yards from Heavenly Valley's ski lifts (but it's especially appealing spring through fall). Rooms 1 and 2 each have a queen-size bed and dining nook where you can have a complimentary continental breakfast or afternoon Cognac. The suites have various combinations of wood-burning fireplaces, overhead mirrors, dry saunas, or whirlpools. The inn's noteworthy restaurant offers spendy dinners of veal medallions grilled with sautéed escargot in a brown pesto cream, or grilled mustard quail paired with a beef tournedo topped with a brown shallot Cognac butter. Guests with lighter appetites may order from the appetizer menu in the lounge. ■ *Off Ski Run Blvd at the base of Heavenly Valley at 3819 Saddle Rd; (916) 544-7337, toll free (800) 4CALSKI; Mail: PO Box 18298, South Lake Tahoe, CA 96151; $$$; full bar; MC, V; local checks only; dinner every day.*

Lakeland Village ★★ Although many of the nondescript brown buildings of Lakeland Village are on busy Highway 50, the resort has over 1,000 feet of beach and 19 acres with two tennis courts and two swimming pools beyond sight and sound of the traffic. All 206 units are individually owned, so the interior decorations differ but meet high standards set by the resort's management company. The most desirable townhouses front the lake, but they are difficult to get to in high season. Studio rooms in the main lodge and one-bedroom suites are the least expensive. All the units have fireplaces, fully equipped kitchens, and daily maid service. The resort staff is professional and friendly. ■ *Between Ski Run Blvd and Fairway Ave at 3535 Hwy 50; (916) 544-1685, toll free (800) 822-5969; Mail: PO Box 1356, South Lake Tahoe, CA 96156; $$$; AE, MC, V; checks OK.*

Richardson's Resort at Camp Richardson Richardson's, a same-time-next-year kind of resort for many families, seems worlds away from the high-rise casinos and bustle of South Lake Tahoe. Still, it is within reach of almost anything you need. New owners leased this Forest Service property in 1985, restored the 60-year-old log lodge, and upgraded the motel and cabins. The lodge—a five-minute walk from the water—has 29 sparsely furnished rooms with private baths and a six-foot-high stone fireplace in the lobby. Near the lake is the Beach Inn, a seven-room motel, and 35 cabins which are named for cars. The best cabins are usually reserved far in advance (and only some are open in the winter), but you usually can find a room at the lodge any time of year. In the summer months, an ice cream parlor, general store, camping facilities, hiking and biking trails, volleyball nets, horseshoe pits, and equipment rentals (for almost anything that floats or rolls) are available for guests. This isolated place is a great place to take the kids (but not your dog). ■ *2½ miles N of the Y in South Lake Tahoe on Hwy 89 at Jamieson Beach Rd; (916) 541-1801, toll free (800) 544-1801 in California and Nevada; Mail: PO Box 9028, South Lake Tahoe, CA 96158; $$; AE, MC, V; no checks.*

ECHO LAKE

Sierra Ski Ranch is one of the last true mom-and-pop ski resorts in the Sierra. It is predominantly an intermediate mountain, but advanced skiers venture here for some of the best in-the-trees skiing near Tahoe. Just off US 50 near Echo Summit, the ski ranch bears the marks of its founding parents (Vern and Bobbie Sprock)—from its friendly personnel to the homemade goodies in its three cafeterias; (916) 659-7519.

HOPE VALLEY

RESTAURANTS

Hope Valley Store and Cafe ★ We rolled into this inconspicuous place on the east fork of the Carson River looking for a small late afternoon snack. There were six homemade pies sitting on the shelf above the wooden cafe counter. We thought we'd split a piece, so we started out with a slice of tart blackberry pie in a perfect buttery crust. We proceeded to work our way down the line: peach, apricot, apple, pecan, chocolate cream. This place serves the best pie we have ever had in any restaurant, bar none. The breakfast menu offers well-prepared classics. For dinner, look for good fried chicken, steak, and dynamite pastas like thick, gooey lasagne and meaty spaghetti made by co-owner Cindy Homer. This is home-style cooking at its homiest. ■ *4 miles W of Woodfords on Hwy 88, (916) 694-2292; 14655 Hwy 88, Hope Valley; $; beer and wine; MC, V; no checks; breakfast, lunch, dinner every day.*

LODGINGS

Sorenson's ★★ It's almost impossible to arrive at Sorenson's at the wrong time of year. This friendly cluster of cabins, nestled among the meadows and aspen groves of alpine Hope Valley, offers fine cross-country skiing in winter, prime hiking in late spring and summer, and a terrific display of fall colors when the aspens turn vibrant shades of yellow, gold, and even red. Good trout fishing too. The accommodations range from inexpensive, rustic-but-still-comfy cabins to grander new chalets. Norway House, an elaborate carved replica of a 13th-century Norwegian house with a big open loft bedroom, kitchen, and living room, is a good choice for larger groups. The country decor—quilts and vintage furniture—is attractive and unfussy. We especially like the cozy, creekside Waterfir cabin with its brass bed, wood stove, natural stone hearth, and tall, wooden bathtub. Three of the smallest, least expensive cabins include breakfast in the cost of the room—a great deal! The regular dinner fare of steak, pork chops, and pastas is a cut above most mountain resort food. The breakfast, featuring quiche, waffles, and fresh fruit, is even better. ■ *⁹⁄₁₀ mile E of the junction of Hwys 89 and 88, (916) 694-2203, toll free (800) 423-9949; 14255 Highway 88, Hope Valley, CA 96120; $$$; beer and wine; MC, V; checks OK; breakfast, lunch, dinner every day.*

MARKLEEVILLE

Renown among bicyclists all over United States, this tiny mountain town is home to the **Markleeville Death Ride**, a grueling 128 mile bike trek over five mountain passes (15,000 feet of climbing) in mid-July (Alpine Chamber of Commerce, (916) 694-2475). And where do those weary bikers (and run-of-the-mill hikers) go to rest their weary limbs at the end of a long day? **Grover Hot Springs State Park**, of course (4 miles west of Markleeville at the end of Hot Springs Road). You can soak in their mineral pools (which look too much like YMCA pools for our taste) or strike out across the meadow for the hot and cold running water in the creek ((916) 694-2248). Back into town, pop into the redneck **Cutthroat Bar** inside downtown's Alpine Hotel and Cafe with its collection of brassieres hanging from the ceiling. Don't risk your tastebuds by eating here, but a whiskey at the bar wouldn't be out of order.

RESTAURANTS

Bruno's Cafe and Deli ★ This terrific little deli was just starting out when we dropped by in autumn, but we knew something was up when a burly friend of owner Bruno Huff brought a giant tin of olive oil in on his shoulders saying, "Your shipment arrived from Italy." Never has Markleeville been privy to deliciously sweet cantaloupe generously wrapped in lean slices of prosciutto, followed by a terrific pasta salad whipped up each morning by Bruno's wife Theresa. Deli sandwiches are first rate, piled high with turkey, pastrami, provolone, and red onions. Word must have gotten out about this place because Bruno's now open for breakfast and lunch every day and dinner on weekends, serving barbecue in addition to his hearty deli creations. ■ *Next to Markleeville General Store, (916) 694-2747; 14811 Hwy 89, Markleeville; $; beer and wine; no credit cards; local checks OK; breakfast, lunch every day; dinner Fri–Sat.*

KIRKWOOD

Kirkwood Ski and Summer Resort, just a few miles from Carson Pass, 35 miles south of the Tahoe glitz, is one of the most pristine downhill skiing sites in the state. Far from the madding crowd at a base elevation of 7,800 feet in a rugged wilderness, Kirkwood is distinguished by its usual dry snow conditions and its attention to families (from Mighty Mountain Ski School for kids 4 to 12 to economical on-site condo ski packages). **Cross-country skiers** can glide over 80 kilometers of tracks at Kirkwood's cross-country operation; (209)258-6000.

ARNOLD

LODGINGS

Lodge at Manuel Mill ★★★ This 43-acre site is totally remote—a log lodge on San Antonio Creek in the Stanislaus National Forest. It operated as a lumber mill (with its own short-line rail system and a steam-powered engine) for almost 100 years until just after World War II. In 1989, it opened as a Western frontier–style lodge with a massive stone fireplace, a mallard print couch, and splashes of native American influence. It has five rooms furnished in comfortable, understated elegance, each with a private bath. Most rooms and the expansive deck overlook the 3½-acre stocked pond. There is a rowboat for the explorers, and plenty of open space for wanderers. We almost expect to see hunters coming in with their shotguns on one shoulder, their kill on the other. ■ *Follow Dunbar Rd N from downtown Arnold for 2 miles; (209) 795-2622 or (209) 795-3935; Mail: PO Box 998, Arnold, CA 95223; $$$; no credit cards; checks OK.*

DORRINGTON

LODGINGS

The Dorrington Hotel ★★ A few miles from the magnificent Calaveras Big Trees State Park sits the 1862 Dorrington Hotel which once served as a depot for stockmen and—because of its 5,000-foot elevation—an appealing winter retreat. The hotel, surrounded by some of the largest pines and sequoias in California, is only 6 miles from the Stanislaus River. It's all quite country, complete with lace curtains, period wallpaper, handmade decorative pillows, dolls and wreaths, and shared bathrooms. The Dorrington has an overall homey feeling. Complimentary sherry and fruit greet you in the rooms, and a continental breakfast with delicious coffee and a newspaper is unobtrusively left outside your door come morning. ■ *Hwy 4 Dorrington at 3431 Hwy 4; (209) 795-5800; Mail: PO Box 4307, Dorrington, CA 95223; $$; MC, V; checks OK.*

BEAR VALLEY

Tucked away in the central Sierra 7,000 feet above sea level is the small town of Bear Valley. Amid an untrampeled wilderness near the summit of State Route 4, Bear Valley is one of the undiscovered gems of downhill-skiing in Northern California. With 82 runs in 1,900 vertical feet, the area has two triple chairs and seven double chairs. The longest run here is a 3-mile ski. Bear has the distinction of having a midmountain day lodge (parking is midmountain, as well); (209) 753-2301, toll free (800) 695-3737. Four miles from the alpine ski area is its cross-country ski operation (and ice-skating on a real pond). The network of 35 trails makes for plenty of excellent gliding in the winter and mountain biking in the summer (over 100 miles of summer trails); Bear Valley Cross Country Area, (209) 753-2834.

LODGINGS

Bear Valley Lodge and Restaurant ★★ Bear Valley Lodge, the center of this small mountain community, is a full-service, year-round resort catering to sporting enthusiasts. There are cross-country and downhill skiing facilities available nearby and plenty of mountains and space for most summer activities. The high elevation keeps the summer heat at bay (a welcome relief if touring Gold Country). There are 53 rooms, 3 suites,

2 restaurants and bars, a heated swimming pool, and 2 outdoor hot tubs. For the tired and weary, the lodge offers a host of rejuvenating treatments at the spa. There are also condos and homes for rent with a two-night minimum stay.

Bear Valley Lodge Restaurant offers a pleasing balance between the white tablecloths and candlelight and the casual dress of the patrons—a nice touch of unpretentiousness. Good food, fresh mountain air, a good night's sleep, and a continental breakfast in the morning sun. ■ *Bear Valley Road, Bear Valley; (209) 753-BEAR, toll free (800) 794-3866; Mail: PO Box 5440, Bear Valley, CA 95223; $$; full bar; MC, V; checks OK.*

Lake Alpine Lodge This quaint alpine resort, nestled beside a lake, makes you feel as if you have the entire world to yourself. Eight rustic, but fully equipped cabins come with outdoor barbeques, kitchens (in some). All the cabins have showers and a deck with views of the lake. The lodge itself offers boat rentals and a decent little cafe serving breakfast, lunch, and dinner in the summer. There is also a small saloon and convenience market that sells bait and tackle, ■ *Hwy 4 at Ebbets Pass/Lake Alpine; (209) 753-6358; Mail: PO Box 5051 Bear Valley, CA 95223 (May–Oct), PO Box 579, Big Sur, CA 93920 (Nov–Apr); $$; MC, V; local checks only; Mid-May–mid-Oct.*

PINECREST

Dodge Ridge has a decades-long reputation as a friendly ski area that's low on frills and high on family convenience. It's also the closest ski area to the Bay area, just above Sonora and Columbia off State Route 108. Best thing about Dodge is that you can barbecue your own marinated chicken or shrimp out on the deck of the Waystation cafeteria; (209) 965-3474.

RESTAURANTS

Steam Donkey Restaurant ★★ Not a stubborn animal, but a steam-powered logging machine dragged timber from the woods to the railroad. It doesn't take as much, however, to get Sonorans to make the 32-mile trek up to Dodge Ridge for Steam Donkey's barbecue. The ribs, steaks, and chicken rate high, and the lounge is lively on weekends. Try not to think about spotted owls among all the logging memorabilia; in stead, sit at an outside table and chow down on some finger-lickin' ribs. ■ *Off Pinecrest Ave and Hwy 108 in Pinecrest; (209) 965-3117; $; full bar; MC, V; checks OK; lunch, dinner every day.*

For excursions farther north; consult Northwest Best Places, *the guidebook for the best restaurants, lodgings, and touring in Oregon, Washington, and British Columbia.*

RESTAURANTS

Bridgeport Inn ★★ Bridgeport is cattle country and no place in the eastern Sierra cooks cow better than this attractive 1887-vintage hotel. Everyone within 50 miles knows this, so you'll probably have to wait a bit, even if you have reservations. Cool your heels in the inn's virile Western bar, or if that's too rowdy, seek shelter in the elegant parlor with Victorian furniture, a player piano, and a pot-bellied stove. Don't hesitate to order Terry Nolan's terrific spinach salad, made tableside. This place is renowned for prime rib and rack of lamb, but we've always been impressed with their straight-ahead, super-high–quality steaks, especially the thick and flavorful fillet. They've got a surprisingly extensive and sophisticated California wine list, heavy on rich and heady reds. In the morning, good eggs Benedict, Belgian waffles, and sometimes scrambled eggs with chorizo appear on the menu. Skip lunch. ■ *Center of town; (619) 932-7380; 85 Main St, Bridgeport; $$$; full bar; MC, V; no checks; breakfast, lunch, dinner every day in summer (closed Wed in winter).*

LODGINGS

The Cain House: A Country Inn ★★ James Stuart Cain made his fortunes in the rough-and-tumble boomtown of Bodie (known in its day as the wickedest town in the West), but later generations (perhaps weary of the lack of sanitation and proliferation of whorehouses) moved over the hill to the comparatively genteel cowtown of Bridgeport. Set in one of the prettiest valleys in the eastern Sierra, Bridgeport is ringed by forested, granite peaks in the west and round, sage- and piñon-covered dessert hills in the east. This modest turn-of-the-century house, owned by the obliging Marachel Myers, has beautifully decorated guest rooms with private baths, queen-size beds with quilts and down comforters, and televisions tucked discreetly inside armoires. In the morning, expect good dark coffee (a rare treat on this side of the Sierra) and a full breakfast, including homemade muffins. ■ *North end of town at 11 Main St, (619) 932-7040; Mail: PO Box 454, Bridgeport, CA 93517; $$; AE, MC, V; checks OK.*

▼

Yosemite

▲

YOSEMITE

One of the earth's most spectacular valleys hosts somewhere around 3½ million visitors each year. **Yosemite National Park** is not the place to head during high summer when hoping to get away from *them* all; walking below the sheer granite cliffs of Yosemite Valley's El Capitan, Half Dome, and Sentinel Rock, or taking in an inspiring vista in the Sierra high country means negotiating one's way around crowds more typical of Disney World than a national park. The adventurous are advised to trek here in spring (when the wildflowers are plentiful and people are few) or bring a tent and camp in the Tuolumne Meadows area, where the crowds are not nearly as intense and where there is easy access to the Grand Canyon of the Tuolumne River trail. Off-season explorers should call ahead to check on road conditions.

Yosemite accommodations range from $12 per night for a campsite to $200 per night for a room at the Ahwahnee (see review). Reservations (made no more than eight weeks in advance) are required for most Yosemite campsites—only a few are set aside for first-come, first-serve; toll free (800) 365-CAMP. The valley campsites, near the Merced River, offer easy access to the park's most sought after attractions but not much in the way of privacy. Moderate-priced motel rooms are available at the valley's bare-bones Yosemite Lodge (a quick walk from Lower Yosemite Falls). Spartan cabins (some are just woodframes with canvas covers, others are heated in winter) offer inexpensive alternatives to camping that are great for families. There are also 69 tent cabins at Tuolumne Meadows Lodge; (209) 252-4848.

Backpackers require a wilderness permit; (209) 372-0310. The 3½-mile hike to May Lake is understandably popular, and the 6-mile hike to the Glen Aulin High Sierra backpacker's camp offers a spectacular spot for pitching a tent. Five clusters of canvas cabins (four to six occupants) are for rent in the High Sierra region. Price runs about $140 for two and includes breakfast, dinner, and a shower. The cabins are booked through an annual lottery each fall; (209) 454-2002. Easier to reserve are vacation home rentals, call Yosemite West Condominiums; (209) 454-2033.

Badger Pass, with its predominantly intermediate ski runs, 23 miles from Yosemite Valley's lodges and restaurants via State Route 41, keeps its runs well-manicured and offers a couple of unique activities: daily snow-cat rides around the perimeter of the area for nonskiers, snowshoe walks led by a ranger-naturalist, and ice skating in the shadow of Half Dome. Badger is also the headquarters for the **Yosemite Cross-Country Ski School,** which offers rentals and a variety of lessons and excursions over the 90 miles of groomed cross-country trails (there's a total of 350 miles of skiable cross-country trails and roads throughout the park). For information about Badger Pass, call (209) 372-1330; for the Cross-Country Ski School, call (209) 372-1244; for ski package reservations, call (209) 454-2000; and for 24-hour snow conditions, call (209) 372-1000.

LODGINGS

Ahwahnee Hotel ★★★ Flush against the soaring cliffs of Yosemite sits the majestic Ahwahnee, temporary home to Winston Churchill, John Kennedy, Greta Garbo, and Queen Elizabeth. Built in 1927 and constructed from native granite and redwood-hued concrete, the multitiered six-story building blends comfortably into its surroundings. The lobby, dressed in a native American motif, is oversized in all dimensions: thick-beamed high ceilings, fireplaces worthy of a medieval castle, and chandeliers seemingly designed for an opera hall. For some the contrast between the hotel's rustic mountain venue and its upscale personality—overeager bellhops and a dress code that requires men to wear a sportcoat and tie at dinner—might be a bit much. But the rooms are spacious enough with a king-size bed, a large bathroom, and (in some rooms) a view of Half Dome. For a real splurge, request one of the hotel's suites. Cottages are also available.

The Ahwahnee dining room is more noteworthy for its ambience than its food. The dining room is a behemoth room with stone columns and big beamed ceilings. Starched white table cloths, candles, and a piano player give the gigantic room a warm, intimate feel. The food is the best in the region, to be sure, but don't expect a fantastic meal; its prices are those of San Francisco's finer establishments but the quality of the food is not. Stick to the simpler preparations such as the grilled salmon. Those in the know apply for the Bracebridge Dinner—a three-hour feast held each Christmas that 60,000 people want to participate in but only 1,750 can. ■ *In Yosemite Valley; (209) 252-4848 (hotel), (209) 372-1489 (restaurant); Mail: 5410 E Home Ave, Fresno, CA 93727; $$$; full bar; DC, DIS, MC, V; checks OK; lunch, dinner every day.*

Wawona Hotel ★ A bit of the Old South tucked into a corner of Yosemite. A pair of century-old large white buildings, adorned by white pillars and a verandah, look out on an expansive manicured lawn, giving the Wawona the look of adjoining antebellum Victorian mansions. The Wawona has been remodeled but maintains its cozy feel. The rooms are small; and about half don't have their own bathrooms. The Wawona's biggest drawback—at least for first-time Yosemite visitors—is its long distance from most of the park's glories. The giant sequoias in the nearby Mariposa Grove are inviting, but they don't compare to the cliffs and vistas elsewhere in Yosemite. Includes a nine-hole golf course, a tennis court, and a swimming pool. The piano player and good cheer of happy hour in the Victorian lobby is a real treat. For all its pretensions, the Wawona's restaurant is upscale institutional food that fills up but doesn't quite please. Don't miss the Saturday evening lawn barbecues in summer; otherwise, drive to Fish Camp for dinner. ■ *SW corner of Yosemite National Park, 27 miles from Yosemite Valley; (209) 375-6556; Mail: 5410 E Home Ave, Fresno, CA 93727; $$; full bar; DC, DIS, MC, V; checks OK; breakfast, lunch Mon–Sat, dinner; brunch Sun.*

FISH CAMP

RESTAURANTS

Narrow Gauge Inn ★★ Ask a native to name the Mariposa Grove area's best restaurant and you'll learn the wonders of the Narrow Gauge, nestled in the thick of the Sierra National Forest (elevation 4,800 feet): great food, down-home service, views of Mount Raymond, and country ambience. Its specialties include a scrumptious stuffed pork tenderloin baked with fruit and nut stuffing and topped with an apricot brandy glaze, and a charbroiled New York Steak Broadway stuffed with crab, shrimp, and scallops and topped with bordelaise. All dinners include homemade soup or salad, fresh vegetables, and a rice or potato dish. Dinner by oil-burning lamp and a crackling fire make for a romantic evening. Reservations essential.

The Narrow Gauge Inn has 26 rooms and 1 three-bedroom cabin. When making a reservation, ask for one of the rooms recently remodeled in rustic European knotwood accents. Most rooms have their own balcony; the four creekside rooms have particularly splendid views. ■ *4 miles S of the south gate of Yosemite on Hwy 41, (209) 683-7720; Mail: 48571 Hwy 41, Fish Camp, CA 93623; $$; full bar; AE, DC, MC, V; local checks only; breakfast, dinner every day, brunch Sun (closed mid-Oct–mid-Apr).*

LODGINGS

Tenya Lodge ★ What this 242-room hotel lacks in charm, it makes up for in location. Built by the Marriott Corporation in 1990, the decor is exactly what you'd expect from a major hotel chain—except for the Mariposa Grove a few miles away. The lobby—stone floors, high ceiling, huge fireplace, and a native American motif—are a welcome antidote to the assault of the building's exterior. Rooms ($129–$210) are tastefully decorated in a Southwestern motif. There's an outdoor/indoor pool, a small fitness center (with steam room, sauna, and whirlpool), a deli for picnic lunches, and an events desk for mountain bike rentals and arranging Yosemite tours. An inspiring locale for a conference. ■ *2 miles S of the SW entrance to Yosemite at 1122 Hwy 41, (209)683-6555 or toll free (800)635-5807; Mail: PO Box 159, Fish Camp, CA 93623; $$$; full bar; AE, DC, MC, V; checks OK; breakfast, lunch, dinner every day.*

MONO LAKE

Set at the foot of the craggy Sierra Nevada and ringed with a fairyland of fragile limestone tufa spires, this hauntingly beautiful desert salt lake has been one of California's hottest environmental battlegrounds for over 20 years. Mono Lake has dropped more than 40 feet since the Los Angeles Department of Water and Power began diverting water from one of the lake's main tributaries, Lee Vining Creek, to the lawns of the southland's sprawling suburbs. The diversions have endangered the lake's population of rare fairy brine shrimp and the millions of birds that depend on them for survival. Lower water levels have created land bridges to the lake's two islands, opening previously protected nesting grounds to marauding coyotes and other predators. Even the lake's landmark tufa formations, growing like white castles around the lake's edge, are disappearing as the water that feeds them recedes. Environmentalists have won several recent court battles against the LDWP. For now, at least, the lake has stopped shrinking. The new **Mono Basin National Forest Scenic Area Visitors Center** educates visitors with a theater, bookstore, and art gallery; (619) 647-6595. The **Mono Lake Committee at the Visitors Center** in Lee Vining uses nature walks and canoe tours to present environmental, legal, and political issues that endanger this fragile jewel; (619) 647-6572.

June Lake

Restaurants

LEE VINING

RESTAURANTS

Mono Inn ★ Travelers have stopped at the Mono Inn, which has filtered views of mystical Mono Lake, since 1922. Barbara and Harry Williams have been serving up American home cooking here since 1984. There's a stone fireplace in the dining room decorated with an odd assortment of historic Inn photos, china plates, and copper pots hanging from the rough-sawn beams. Barbara makes the Sierra's best chicken-fried steak with spicy gravy. Her marinated, charbroiled swordfish steak is perfection. Trouble is, you fill up fast on the hot rolls, homemade soup, and salad, which come with dinner . . . and a big wedge of Harry's lemon cream pie, which should. ■ *4 miles N of Lee Vining on Hwy 395; (619) 647-6581; Hwy 395, Lee Vining, CA 93541; $$; full bar; DC, MC, V; local checks only; dinner Wed–Mon (Fri–Sun in winter).*

JUNE LAKE

RESTAURANTS

Carson Peak Inn ★★ The weatherbeaten sign out front belies the polished performance inside. The barn-red building (5 miles from the highway) has had multiple former lives as an American Legion headquarters, dance hall, and pizza parlor. Complete dinners come in regular and hearty portions (and they're serious about the hearty stuff). Melt-in-your-mouth filet mignon is smothered with sautéed mushrooms. Many regulars come in just for the Australian lobster tail (a rarity in these parts— pricey too). Most of the fish, chicken, and pork are served broiled, deep-fried, pan-fried, or barbecued. Dessert is an ice cream sundae or sherbet. The few wines are inexpensive. ■ *5 miles from the S entrance to the June Lake Loop on Hwy 395, (619) 648-7575; Hwy 158, June Lake; $$; beer and wine; MC, V; checks OK; dinner every day.*

MAMMOTH LAKES

At the base of 11,053-foot Mammoth Mountain spreads the town of Mammoth Lakes—a mishmash of inns, motels, and restaurants servicing, mostly, **Mammoth Mountain** ski area. Southern California skiers have been flocking to Mammoth Mountain for decades; every Northern California downhill aficionado should make the long winter trek at least once. The mountain that Dave McCoy and his family built (starting in 1955) is impressive from every angle: 3,500 acres of skiable terrain and 150 runs serviced by 2 gondolas, 5 quads, 7 triple chairs, and 14 double chairs. The list goes on: three day lodges, two mountain restaurants, and a day care operation that even takes infants in diapers. Its 3,100 feet of vertical are an equal mix of bowls above the treeline, steep chutes, and numerous intermediate runs through the forest. And its season stretches at least through June—and sometimes into July—an ideal time for Northern Californians to head for the area, as most Sierra passes are open by May; (619) 934-2571.

Mammoth Lakes has plenty to offer after the snow melts. For spectacular hiking, head to **Devil's Postpile National Monument** and the **Minaret** range. Mammoth Mountain ski area becomes a mountain bike park in the summer. Afterward, you can soak your body in **Hot Creek** natural hot springs, 10 miles from town. Traditional summer events are the **Mammoth Mountain Motocross**, US championship bicycle competitions, and the **Jazz Jubilee** in July; (619) 934-8006, toll free (800) 367-6572.

A half-hour drive to the north is **June Mountain,** bought by McCoy in 1986, and offering skiers a less frantic, milder ski experience. About one-fifth the size of Mammoth, June too offers bowl skiing, steep chutes, and forested trails, with the added attraction of a spectacular Sierra view from its two peaks: 10,050-foot Rainbow Summit and 10,135-foot June Mountain Summit; (619) 648-7733.

Anything Goes ★★ Like steamed milk and espresso, Mary Pipersky and Susan Beck are perfectly paired to make anything go. Their six-year-old catering/cafe/bakery business has become a local hit. While fragrant scones and coffee cake emerge from the oven, fresh roasted beans are ground for the house coffee and espresso drinks. Steamed eggs and scalloped potatoes with ricotta and Gruyère cheese are breakfast specialties. Mary bakes bread daily (spinach, tomato, or rosemary, perhaps). Susan blends the mayonnaise, and makes daily "pizzettes" and pasta salads (cheese ravioli with roasted vegetables, smoked chicken, feta, and kalamata olives with a sundried tomato–tarragon sauce). Dinner might be Thai curried lobster—lobster meat and julienne vegetables tossed in a green curry sauce over orange-basil basmati rice. Take breakfast or lunch on the patio whenever possible. ■ *½ mile off Main St on Old Mammoth Rd; (619) 934-2424; 645 Old Mammoth Rd, Mammoth Lakes; $; beer and wine; no credit cards; checks OK; breakfast, lunch Thurs–Tues, dinner Thurs–Mon (closed for three weeks, spring and fall).*

Mammoth Lakes

Lodgings

Natalie's ★★ Like many good restaurants in Mammoth Lakes, Natalie's is located in a shopping mall. Fresh flowers brighten each of the 12 tables, and young owner Randall Sussex is adept at making guests feel like old friends. Appetizers include warm smoked salmon with baked Brie and a crisp, garlicky caesar salad. About eight entrées fill the menu and include a mixed grill with chicken breast, rack of lamp chop, sausage, and veal medallion served with a three-mustard sauce. The family cheesecake recipe (red raspberry, pumpkin, or lemon, for example) and flourless chocolate cake are divine. The wine list is limited but reasonably priced. No waiting area, so reservations are important. ■ *¾ mile off Main St on Old Mammoth Rd; (619) 934-3902; Sherwin Plaza III, Mammoth Lakes; $$; beer and wine; MC, V; local checks only; dinner Tues–Sun (may be closed off season).*

The Mogul ★ For years, The Mogul was a cook-your-own steak place. Now your waiter or waitress expertly charbroils fresh fish, shrimp, or steak for you under your watchful eye. Owner Dan Haydon has contributed the Haydon family recipes such as the baked beans dish (mother's) and Cinnamon Charlotte (grandma's), which is made with a cupcake and vanilla ice cream topped with cinnamon sauce. He has added on to the multiroom restaurant many times over the past 20 years and has brightened it up with shades of rose and green. ■ *One block S of Main St off Old Mammoth Rd; (619) 934-3039; 1528 Tavern Rd, Mammoth Lakes; $$; full bar; AE, MC, V; local checks only; dinner every day.*

Tamarack Lodge Resort ★★ Built in 1924 by the movie star Foy family of Los Angeles, the Tamarack Lodge sits at 8,600 feet on the edge of Twin Lakes, 2½ miles above Mammoth Lakes. Dave and Carol Watson have improved the resort's 11 rooms and 26 cabins with pine furnishings and soft-hued fabrics. Some have private baths; others share a community bath. We like the lake views in rooms 2, 7, and 10. The cabins range from studios to three bedrooms and sleep up to nine people. Lakefront cabins are Fisherman's, Lakeside, and numbers 8 or 36. Guests can read books or play games in comfy sofas and chairs near the fireplace in the lobby. The restaurant is pricey but the dinner of salmon with ginger or the wild berry duckling is expertly cooked. ■ *2½ miles above Mammoth Lakes on Lake Mary Rd; (619) 934-2442, toll free (800) 237-6879; Mail: PO Box 69, Mammoth Lakes, CA 93546; $$; beer and wine; AE, MC, V; checks OK; breakfast, dinner every day.*

Mammoth Mountain Inn ★ In the winter, the Inn (built in the '50s) at the base of Mammoth Mountain is a home base for alpine skiers. In summer, it's a perfect launch for mountain bikers, fly-fishers, hikers, or horseback riders. The 214 rooms in the hotel, although a bit worn with thinnish walls, are nicely furnished; request a junior suite with a view in the part that has been refurbished. The hotel's Mountainside Grill and Dry Creek Lounge are open year around, and an additional restaurant and bar are open during the busy seasons. You will probably want to go to Mammoth Lakes for more restaurant and entertainment choices, however. ■ *At Mammoth Mountain ski area, 4 miles from downtown Mammoth Lakes; (619) 934-2581, toll free (800) 228-4947; Mail: PO Box 353, Mammoth Lakes, CA 93546; $$$; full bar; AE, MC, V; checks OK; breakfast, lunch, dinner every day.*

Wildasinn House ★ Pronounced "wille-dess-in," this B&B was named after Charles Wildasinn, the first Mammoth Lakes hotelier in the 1880s. Over time it became run-down and had the reputation of being a party house. A few years ago, Roxanne and Tony Romo changed that by brightening the bedrooms with curtains and quilts and furnishing the living room with family antiques and paintings by Roxanne's grandfather. Five snug bedrooms have queen, double, or twin beds and private wash basins but share two baths. The Attic Hideaway is just that—most private and farthest from les toilettes. Roxanne sets out continental breakfast each morning; coffee, tea, and wine are available all day. A whirlpool spa on a wooden deck soothes après-ski muscles. ■ *Just off Main St at 26 Lupin St; (619) 934-3851; Mail: PO Box 8026, Mammoth Lakes, CA 93546; $$; no credit cards; checks OK.*

Mammoth Lakes

Lodgings

RESTAURANTS

The Restaurant at Convict Lake ★★★ The fishermen who come to Convict Lake to catch German brown and rainbow trout have kept this restaurant a secret for many years. Some of their prize catches hang on the rough-sawn Douglas fir boards at the bar. Word is slowly slipping out. It would be tough to find a more perfect setting for a restaurant than on Convict Lake. The dining room's open beam ceiling and bare wood floors are softened by overstuffed chairs and sofas and a wood-burning stove. Bar patrons make a meal of appetizers or move to the more elegant dining room where booths encircle a free-standing fireplace with a glistening copper chimney. The chef specials might include a Chilean sea bass with mango-pineapple-cilantro relish or lamb loin in a hazelnut and rosemary sauce. Popular dishes from the regular menu are beef Wellington and duck breast sautéed with caramelized shallots, apple purée, and juniper berries. The chef's meringue with kiwi fruit and whipped cream is a nice finishing touch. ■ *3½ S of Mammoth Lakes, take exit off Hwy 395 to Convict Lake; (619) 934-3803; Convict Lake; $$$; full bar; AE, DIS, MC, V; checks OK; dinner every day.*

▼

Convict Lake

Restaurants

▲

GOLD
COUNTRY

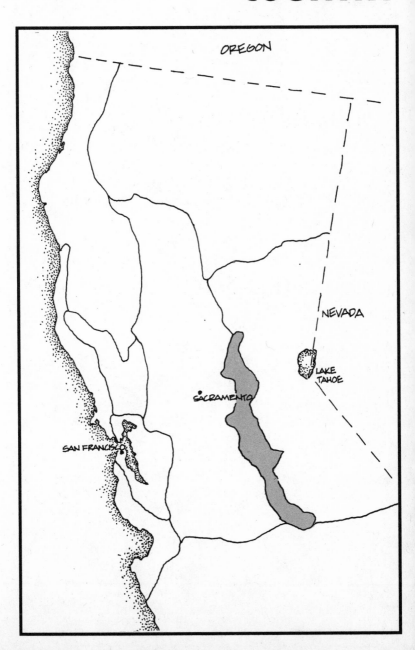

OREGON

NEVADA

LAKE
TAHOE

SACRAMENTO

SAN FRANCISCO

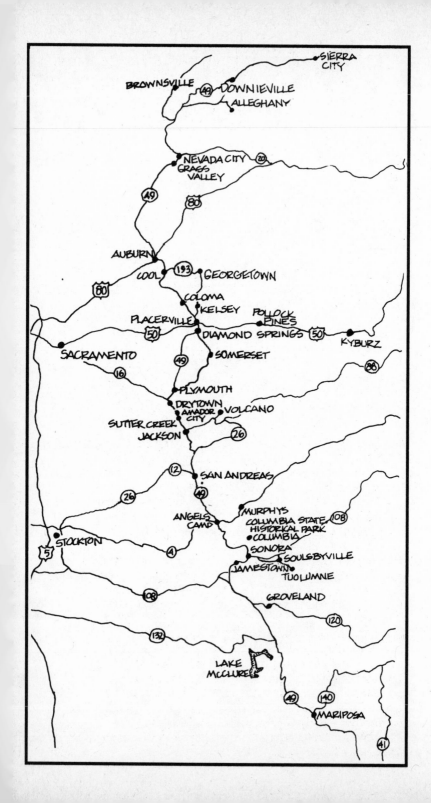

Gold Country

A southward exploration down Highway 49 from Sierra City to Oakhurst with occasional diversions into the gold hills.

SIERRA CITY

RESTAURANTS

Sierra Buttes Inn ★ Deep into Gold Country, time slows down; at this quaint 1872 inn, you'll want ample time to enjoy the Stanley family's generosity. A log anteroom serves as the bar where a collection of old photos, liquor bottles, and mounted game animals reflect the heritage of this remote hamlet. Some nights the cook might prepare an extra, such as a crunchy cheese bread, and add it to your plate of teriyaki chicken. The entrées include a choice of rice or potatoes, a loaf of freshly baked bread (still hot), and fruit. With Nat King Cole and Patty Page crooning from the jukebox in the bar, this is the place to catch up on the local news and fishing reports. There are also 11 rooms for rent, 6 with private baths—but, really, you're here for the food. ■ *Corner of Hwy 49 and Hayes Rd in Sierra City; (916) 862-1300; $; full bar; MC, V; checks OK; breakfast Sat–Sun, dinner every day (hours vary off season).*

LODGINGS

High Country Inn ★★★ A grove of aspens along the North Fork of the Yuba River flutters in a light summer breeze at this Sierra Buttes lodge. A spectacular view of the buttes and the High Country's trout pond is central to the back deck, the inviting living room with sofas and ottomans clustered around the fireplace, and the Golden Pond Room (aka the Duck-and-Dog Room, due to its hunting motif). The very large Howard Creek Room fits two double beds—popular with families. One suite with a cathedral ceiling encompasses the entire second floor, west-facing windows frame the buttes, and a Franklin stove sits atop a raised corner hearth. The bathroom area is almost a suite of its own with a dressing room closeting cozy flannel nightshirts and terrycloth robes. Thanks to owner Marlene Cartwright's culinary talents, breakfast is a healthy and wholesome three-course event. Dozens of nearby hiking and cross-country ski trails wind through the Tahoe National Forest to over 30 mountain lakes (great trout fishing). The Cartwrights can inform and equip you for almost any mountain activity (cross-country skiing, mountain biking, horseback riding, or snowmobiling). ■ *E of Sierra City at Bassetts, Hwy 49 and Gold Lake Rd; (916) 862-1530; Mail: HCR 2 Box 7, Sierra City, CA 96125; $$; MC, V; checks OK.*

Packer Lake Lodge ★★★ What separates Packer Lake Lodge from its neighbors in the Lakes Basin is its unparalleled combination of superb food and scenery (elevation 6,218 feet). The tall pines, gently rippling waters, and profusion of wildflowers provide an atmosphere of serene seclusion. Accommodations are in rustic log cabins—simply and attractively furnished (calico quilts, tree-branch handles on bureau drawers)—each with its own rowboat. The cabins closest to the shore are simple, one-room deals; larger ones with kitchens and baths are available nearby (ask for one of the two log cabins). The lodge with a big stone fireplace contains a small store in one corner, a bar in another, a reading and games nook in the third, and a restaurant in the fourth. Chef Kevin McMahon of Santa Cruz mans the kitchen. All meals are open to nonguests and include dishes such as thick, rich homemade soups (black bean, cream of mushroom); tender, creamy beef stroganoff; and succulent baby back spare ribs. ■ *Sardine Lake Rd turnoff from Gold Lake Rd, N of Bassetts; (916) 862-1221 (May–Oct), (415) 921-5943 (Oct–April); Mail: PO Box 237, Sierra City, CA 96125; $$; full bar; MC, V; checks OK; breakfast, lunch, dinner Wed–Mon (mid May–Oct).*

Busch & Heringlake Country Inn ★★ Former investment banker Carlo Giuffre banished the memory of spreadsheets in 1986, when he bought this one-time Wells Fargo Express outpost. Today, Busch & Heringlake Country Inn is a sophisticated surprise in the otherwise rough beauty of Sierra County (population 3,000)—a Gold Country version of the European-style pensione. Downstairs, there's a sturdy wood-burning furnace, the A.C. Busch safe, 10-foot-high steel-and-wood French doors, and an open-format dining room where there's a gold mine of Italian fare in Carlo's Ristorante (from an osso bucco to an exceptional pizza, dough rises well at 3,265 feet). Winter travelers—Highway 49 to Tahoe is always open, no matter how often snowstorms may snarl traffic on I-80—should consider stopping here for some untracked cross-country skiing opportunities in the nearby Sierra Buttes and Gold Lake area. Also nearby is the Downieville Downhill—an exceptional downhill mountain bike ride. ■ *On Hwy 49 in downtown Sierra City; (916) 862-1501; PO Box 68, Sierra City, CA 96125; $$; MC, V; checks OK; dinner Tues–Sun (Weds–Sun in winter).*

Salmon Lake Lodge ★ You can't drive to this 1920s resort; you drive to the north shore of Salmon Lake, telephone the lodge, and get ferried across the lake—or you can hike around the lake's splendid western rim. The tent cabins—canvas roof and rough wood walls—contain built-in double beds and bunks and electric stoves; you bring your own sleeping bags, dishes, cooking gear, ice chest, and groceries (refrigerators, showers, and a washing machine are available). We prefer the ridge-top cabins which come with fully equipped kitchens (though you'll still need your sleeping bag). Request the small hill cabin with a loft and a beautiful high mountain view. The lake is great for swimming and boating (rowboats, sailboats, canoes, and kayaks provided). Guests paddle over to a lake island for a once-a-week barbecue. ■ *End of Salmon Lake Rd off Gold Lake Rd, 3 miles S of Gold Lake; (916) 842-3108; Mail: PO Box 121, Sierra City, CA 96125; $$; no credit cards; checks OK.*

Sardine Lake Resort With the towering craggy peaks of Sierra Buttes mirrored in the waters of the lake, each of the six tiny cabins at Sardine Lake Resort enjoys a big view. Fishing and boating (for an extra fee) are popular in Upper and Lower Sardine Lake (no sardines—the lakes were named after a salty miner's mule). Nearby Sand Pond is a choice swimming hole. The lodge, with its porch dining area and small cocktail porch jutting out into the lake, contains a beer and wine bar and a reasonably good restaurant open only on an erratic seasonal schedule. The cabins rent by the week in summer, though the owners also do 2-day rentals at the beginning and end of the season. The place fills quickly, so make reservations well ahead of time. ■ *End of Sardine Lake Rd at Lower Sardine Lake, off Gold Lake Rd, 2 miles N of Bassetts; (916) 862-1196 summer, (916) 645-8882 winter; $$; no credit cards; checks OK.*

▼

▲

DOWNIEVILLE

This little mountain town at the junction of the Yuba and Downie rivers looks much the way it did in the 1850s, with venerable buildings lining boardwalks along the crooked Main Street and trim homes cut into canyon walls above. Downieville's population hovers around 300 now; during its heyday, 5,000 prospectors panned the streams and worked the mines. The lusty gold camp had the dubious distinction of being the only place to lynch a woman.

An old Chinese store houses the **Sierra County Museum** (open daily in summer, weekends spring and fall). The **Sierra County Courthouse** displays gold from the rich Ruby Mine; next door stands the only original gallows in the Gold Country. Pick up a copy of the *Mountain Messenger*, published weekly since 1853, to read when you join locals for coffee and a snack at the **Downieville Bakery** in the old stone Craycroft Building (on Highway 49, beside the bridge). Or assemble a picnic at the 49er Store to enjoy while dipping your gold pan into the stream. A small park downstream contains mining relics. **Sierra County Historical Park,** just north of Sierra City, features the restored Kentucky Mine and a 10-stamp mill. It's worth a stop. Open Wednesday–Sunday in summer and autumn weekends, (916) 862-1310.

RESTAURANTS

Cirino's at the Forks ★★ When you enter Cirino's, you know you're in a time-honored building because you can feel the floor sloping toward the bank of windows and the view of the Downie River below. Decorated with wagonwheel lights, knotty pine paneling, and redwood lattice, this dining room is a cross between the Old West and the Old World. Cirino's is known for its family-style Italian dishes, including veal piccata with a tangy caper sauce; fettuccine alfredo garnished with freshly ground Parmesan; and garlicky shrimp linguine. Each dinner comes with a thick Boston clam chowder or salad, spaghetti with marinara sauce, garlic bread, and a baked potato. Summertime barbecues on the ivy-laced flagstone terrace are fun occasions. Cirino's in Nevada City is a local institution. ■ *On Main St, ½ block N of Hwy 49 in Downieville; (916) 289-3479, toll free (800) 540-2099; $; full bar; AE, MC, V; checks OK; lunch, dinner every day (hours vary in winter).*

Downieville Diner ★ In 1991, the Funk family converted this narrow former butcher shop into an attractive dining room by whitewashing the paneled ceiling and decorating the exposed wood walls with antique kitchen utensils, old snowshoes, skis, pack frames, and locally made floral wreaths and pine needle baskets. A 20th-century sliding glass door leads down to a patio that sits alongside the Downie River—a choice breakfast nook. Try the tart sourdough French toast served with a miniature jug of warmed syrup. Best are the cow patties and Kay Funk's saucer-size sweet cinnamon rolls draped with a thick vanilla-walnut icing. At lunch the burger grilled with mushrooms and avocado is a fistful. The classical music that plays in the background and a variety of wines—as well as a fresh-air wine bar in the summertime—give this little cafe the feel of a European bistro. ■ *1 block N of Hwy 49 at 1 Main St in Downieville; (916) 289-3616; $; beer and wine; MC, V; checks OK; breakfast, lunch, dinner every day (breakfast, lunch only in winter).*

LODGINGS

Sierra Shangri-La ★★ Sierra Shangri-La sits, for its 50th year, on the site of the long-gone mining camp of Crow City, beside the Yuba River, at the base of Jim Crow Canyon. There are three brass-bed rooms in the magnificent lodge, but it's the riverside cottages (roomy decks, patios, kitchens, barbecues, and wood stoves—the canyon cools down in the late afternoon) that are booked solid each summer. La Vista Cabin, at the elbow of the river, is the hands-down fave. Bring your own charcoal, food, and bathing suit and you're set. Some of the most sparkling swimming holes on the Yuba are right outside the cottage doors. Closed January through February. By the way, no one smokes in Shangri-La. ■ *2 miles E of Downieville on*

ALLEGHANY

LODGINGS

Kenton Mine Lodge ★ Pack up the pickup or Cherokee instead of the BMW and prepare to go where few have ever ventured—miles from nowhere, miles from Alleghany (rumored to be where DEA agents disappear without a trace). The Kenton Mine Lodge, open year round except when the roads are impassable, includes remnants of the Gold Rush–era Kenton Mine. This old work camp still housed miners until 1970 when the nearby Oriental Mine closed down (the last in the state to fold). The buildings deep in the Kanaka Creek Canyon are almost as tough as the dry landscape while the boarding house and cabins are a study in simplicity. Some rates include breakfast and family-style dinner in the old cook house. The accommodations may be spartan, but the location teems with fascinating hiking trails to the top of Lafayette Ridge, rivers to pan for gold or fish for trout, old mines to discover, and a creekside barbecue to fire in the evening. Because of the potential dangers of abandoned mine sites in the area, the Lodge does not encourage guests to bring children under 10. ■ *Call for directions; (916) 287-3212; Mail: PO Box 942, Alleghany, CA 95910; $$; MC, V; checks OK.*

▼

Brownsville

───────────

Restaurants

▲

BROWNSVILLE

RESTAURANTS

Lottie Brennan's Bakery & Eating Establishment ★★ Lottie Brennan's, the hub of Brownsville, was once the very proper Knoxdale Institute for Girls. When there was no longer a need for finishing schools in the California foothills, the building did time as a grocery store, card room, flea market, and meeting hall. Today it's a cheery restaurant serving exemplary food which we hope will keep it an eatery for a long time. Lunch consists of a few salads such as a spicy Thai sea scallop salad with a cooling ginger-orange vinaigrette, enticing variations on standard sandwiches, and entrées such as chicken valentine served cold with aspic and grill marinated vegetables. Friday dinner entrées include standards such as ribeye steak and Lottie's garlic-grilled prawns plus seasonal specialties such as Austrian peasant casserole (pork and sirloin simmered with herbs and wine with winter vegetables and butter dumplings). On Saturday night, consider smoked leg of lamb marinated with garlic, shallots, tarragon, and port or roast duckling with wild mushrooms and a port-tarragon sauce. The stellar array of desserts is always changing (hope for the Swedish princess cake with

───────────

355

marzipan). ■ *On La Porte Rd in downtown Brownsville; (916) 675-1003; 9049 La Porte Rd, Brownsville; $; beer and wine; no credit cards; checks OK; lunch Wed–Sat, dinner Fri–Sat, brunch Sun.*

LODGINGS

Mountain Seasons Inn ★ This delightful mountain cottage surrounded with open-air sun porch and herb gardens is a colorful olfactory retreat—part decorative dried herb and flower shop, part bed and breakfast with three quiet guest rooms (one with twin beds, two with queens). Breakfast continues the country theme with a basket of goodies that can be savored on the porch or in the garden. ■ *On La Porte Rd next to Lottie Brennan's; 9067 La Porte Rd; (916) 675-2180; Mail: PO Box 59, Brownsville, CA 95919; $; no credit cards; checks OK.*

NEVADA CITY

Established in 1849 when miners found gold in Deer Creek, Nevada City occupies one of the Sierra foothills' most appealing sites. When the sugar maples blaze in autumn, Nevada City resembles a New England village.

Nevada County Historical Society Museum, in the gingerbread-trimmed building at 214 Commercial Street, formerly Firehouse No. 1, houses Gold Rush memorabilia including the bones of the infamous Donner Party, (916) 265-5468. **Malakoff Diggins State Historic Park** contains a 3-mile loop trail showing the devastating results of hydraulic mining. Within the 3,000-acre park stands **North Bloomfield**, a former mining town turned into a museum. Rangers lead tours on weekends (every day in the summer) and rent out campsites and replicas of miners' cabins, (916) 265-2740.

RESTAURANTS

Peter Selaya's ★★★ Peter Selaya's is the Gold Country's answer to big city cuisine. This restaurant has a decidely international air, one which extends to the lengthy list of special entrées and creative desserts. Appetizers include smoked salmon carpaccio and blue walnut mushrooms (large caps stuffed with blue cheese and roasted walnuts). For pasta, select the market ravioli (which one day might envelop pine nuts and three cheeses and another day fresh mozzarella, porcini, and sun dried tomatoes). For dinner, look forward to anything from scallops Rockefeller or fresh salmon to tournedos béarnaise. Lunch hours are satisfying at Peter Selaya's Gourmet Food To Go just around the corner, (916) 265-0558. Everything in this deli outlet is vitally fresh. ■ *Downtown on Broad St; (916) 265-5697; 320 Broad St, Nevada City; $$; beer and wine; AE, MC, V; checks OK; lunch Mon–Fri (to go), dinner Tues–Sun.*

Cirino's ★★ See Downieville. ■ *Downtown on Broad St; (916) 265-2246; 309 Broad St, Nevada City; $$; full bar; AE, MC, V; local checks only; lunch, dinner every day.*

Country Rose Cafe ★★ It's only appropriate that Nevada City's Country Rose cooks up country French fare. Even the brick building, tall and stately, has a contemporary but quaint Old World ambience. A good regular selection is the half-sandwich (such as salmon cucumber with herb spread on a baguette). More substantial appetites will call for the ratatouille, beef stroganoff, or salmon quiche. Seasonal fresh fish and seafood are emphasized at dinner, though rack of lamb, tournedos, and poultry are usually offered as well. On sunny days (in abundance here) ask to be seated out on the pretty walled-in patio. ■ *Corner of Commercial and N Pine streets; (916) 265-6248; 300 Commercial St, Nevada City; $$; beer and wine; AE, MC, V; local checks only; lunch Mon–Sat, dinner every day.*

Cowboy Pizza ★ Cowboy Wally (owner Wally Hagaman) stirs up cowpoke kitsch from the Gene Autry *Singing Cowboy* poster to the official emblem of Manure Movers of America to . . . Etch-a-Sketch? You can smell the garlic from the Gilroy pizza before you even walk in the door of this wacky place, but bite into the Greek vegetarian (artichoke hearts, feta, black olives, fresh tomatoes, garlic, and oregano) and you'll be bucking for more. Wash down your breath with an all-natural microbrew and a Chinese fortune cookie at the end of the meal. Tip: Locals know to order in advance, otherwise it takes a bit of time to lasso one of these untamed pies cooked in an old stone-floor oven. ■ *On Spring St near the Miners Foundry*

▼

Nevada City

Restaurants

▲

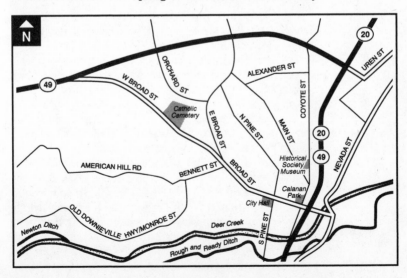

Cultural Center; (916) 265-2334; 315 Spring St, Nevada City; $; beer and wine; no credit cards; checks OK; dinner Wed–Sun.

Posh Nosh ★ Nothing too posh about this great breakfast nosh—a dozen omelets, steak and eggs, crêpes, waffles, and a few rarities like apple sausage. Not strictly a morning spot, you can grab a ham sandwich (made with thinly sliced glazed ham) from the deli at noon or night. Posh Nosh spiffs up a little at dinnertime by adding charbroiled or grilled fresh fish, an apple-brandy chicken, or maybe a fisherman's pasta. Choose your own dining atmosphere: streetside tables and tall booths, the wine cellar, or the small garden patio out back. ■ *Downtown on Broad St; (916) 265-6064; 318 Broad St, Nevada City; $; beer and wine; AE, MC, V; checks OK.*

LODGINGS

Downey House ★★★ Impeccably restored, the Downey House wears a very traditional cloak of respectability; once inside, however, the inn exudes a more contemporary personality. Each room (in different soothing pastel hues) is a study in California (some say, Southwestern) style: built-in beds, comfortable reading chairs, and an aquarium. Before bedtime, expect some candies from Hooper's in Oakland. Guests make themselves at home in the upstairs sun room which opens to an expansive view of Nevada City or the downstairs garden room with phone, brownie-stocked cookie jar, and soft drinks in the cooler. Breakfast (quiche to chiles rellenos, cinnamon rolls to fresh fruit) is served buffet style. You park your car in a little red barn. ■ *Just beyond the historic district at Bennett and W Broad streets; (916) 265-2815, toll free (800) 258-2815; 517 W Broad St, Nevada City, CA 95959; $$; MC, V; checks OK.*

Grandmere's Inn ★★★ Generally considered the grande dame of Nevada City's hostelries, Grandmere's Inn is indeed a showplace. This three-story Colonial Revival mansion is also a bit of a history lesson. Once owned by Aaron and Ellen Clark Sargeant, Susan B. Anthony often stayed here. Aaron was a major catalyst behind the Transcontinental Railroad; Ellen, a suffragette, helped champion women's rights. (It's no coincidence that Aaron authored the legislation that ultimately allowed women to vote.) Moving on, the house itself offers few clues to its illustrious past. She's a beauty—dignified and correct—set amid terraced and time-honored gardens like a small city park. Best is the downstairs suite of blond hardwood floors, a sitting area, an antique gas fireplace, and a private porch; knotty pine paneling encloses the suite's striking bathroom. Families do best when they reserve Gertie's Room, with its private garden entrance, kitchen, and a tub-and-shower bath. The meatless morning breakfast consists of a 9am feast of hot dishes, baked goods, and fresh fruits. ■ *Corner of Bennett and Broad streets; (916) 265-4660; 449 Broad St, Nevada City, CA 95959; $$$; MC, V; checks OK.*

The Red Castle Inn ★★★ A towering four-story brick manse painted barn-red and trimmed with lacy white icicle trim, the Red Castle Inn is a Gothic Revival–style architectural gem. It's a delightful, eclectic treasure with surface formalities and genuine friendliness. All rooms have either a private porch or a garden terrace. The oft-photographed Garden Room on the mansion's entry level is furnished in American Empire (canopied bed, French doors, and two mannequin arms reaching out for your towels in the bathroom). Equally embracing is the Rose Room with its four-poster bed and Jesse Wilcox Smith illustrations. The child-size quarters are upstairs on the former nursery floor (with tissue dispensers fashioned from fishing tackle baskets). Climbing still higher, the stairs narrow and steepen on the way to the three-room Garret Suite, where the private verandah supports the finest view of Nevada City. Breakfast is a complete feast, entirely homemade (with the occasional exception of French bread), and constantly changing. Mary Louise Weaver, a warm and friendly hostess, genuinely loves this house—and all its quirky effects. Learn more about it at an afternoon tea. ■ *Some tricky turns, so call for precise directions; (916) 265-5135; 109 Prospect St, Nevada City, CA 95959; $$$; MC, V; checks OK.*

Flume's End Bed and Breakfast Inn ★★ Flume's End B&B is a surprise on many levels; and this eclectic building—first a quartz mill, later a brothel—does indeed have many levels. Inside or out in the terraced gardens, visitors to Flume's End are never far from the namesake Gold Rush–era flume—or from the refreshing and restorative sound of rushing water. (Gold panners, bring your pans and prepare to get wet! Locals say Gold Run Creek, which flows by an old mine, is particularly generous with flecks of gold.) Decks, large and small, are everywhere; this 3-acre wooded lot also features a large creekside patio. There are many whimsical touches here—such as the large pastel butterflies that dangle from the ceiling of the Garden Room located over the flume. Our favorite room is the Creekside Room as it appears the creek runs right under it (Californians will like all those negative ions). The attic has been converted into a minisuite where morning sun streams in the window and a steamy morning bath soothes. The Cottage, popular with honeymooners and complete with kitchenette and wood stove, is perched above the creek near the small parking area. ■ *Turn S onto Pine from Broad St, continue over the one-lane bridge; (916) 265-9665; 317 S Pine St, Nevada City, CA 95959; $$$; AE, MC, V; checks OK.*

Kendall House ★★ Nevada City's newest inn is a light, sunny place graced by Southern hospitality. On the outskirts of town in a very large garden setting, The Kendall House is quiet and serene, a gentle escape for city dwellers. The Garden Room downstairs (with its elevated bedchamber), is inviting and private, hidden away near the pool. Or wake up to the morning sun in the country French guest room. We prefer the barn, once home to the Cicogni family's cow. Now it's all yours—tiled kitchen, breakfast nook, and wood-burning stove in the living room. Just outside is a private deck with built-in seating that looks down to the large swimming pool surrounded in the spring by a flowering of crab apple, plum, and apple trees. Ted Kendall, an avid jogger, often shares his knowledge of the best local running trails. Jan Kendall's Arkansas breakfast makes a fine morning send-off. ■ *On Spring St just S of W Broad St; (916) 265-0405; 534 Spring St, Nevada City, CA 95959; $$$; MC, V; checks OK.*

Parsonage Bed & Breakfast Inn ★★ Once home to the minister of the Nevada City Methodist Church, The Parsonage is quiet and unassuming—and an essential stop for true California history buffs. Owned and operated by a great-granddaughter of California pioneer (and Mark Twain's editor) Ezra Dane, The Parsonage is something of a living museum. Deborah Dane maintains the home with family antiques and other pieces from the family's international travels (a Turkish pillow chair here, Chinese rice paper and silk peacock screens there). The master bedroom is furnished with Deborah's great-grandparents' impressive bedroom set; the two rooms in the back are a bit less imposing. ■ *On Broad St just past the historic district; (916) 265-9478; 427 Broad St, Nevada City, CA 95959; $$; MC, V; checks OK.*

Piety Hill Inn ★ When mining for gold, this is the place to park the whole family. Piety Hill Inn is a motor court–style motel from the early 1900s. Families like this place because all 10 cottages come with a modern bath and kitchen (or kitchenette). The quieter units, generally a bit pricier, are those farthest from Sacramento Street. Between 8:30am and 9:30am, the innkeeper delivers a breakfast basket—filled perhaps with grilled potatoes and salsa, homemade sweet breads and muffins, and fresh fruits and juices—to every guest's door. Visitors are free to linger in the lodge-style living room, soak in the gazebo-sheltered spa, or barbecue on the outdoor grills. There are horseshoe pits and volleyball nets, not to mention an outdoor dance floor and amenities appropriate for wedding parties. ■ *1½ blocks SW from Hwy 49, Sacramento St exit; (916) 265-2245, toll free (800) 443-2245; 523 Sacramento St, Nevada City, CA 95959; $$$; MC, V; checks OK.*

▼
Nevada City

Lodgings

▲

Once known for rich quartz mines, Gold Rush entertainers like Lola Montez and Lotta Crabtree, and Cornish pasties (meat and potato turnovers), Grass Valley is growing and changing. Its historic and slightly scruffy downtown is a delight to explore. **North Star Mining Museum,** at the south end of Mill Street and once the powerhouse for the North Star Mine, shows how the quartz mines operated. The huge Pelton waterwheel is impressive. Open May–October, (916) 273-4255. **Empire Mine State Historic Park**—the oldest, largest, and richest gold mine in state history—has tunnels that once extended 367 miles and descended 11,000 feet. A museum occupies a former stable. Open daily, (916) 273-8522.

For a detour, take Highway 20 to tiny **Rough and Ready,** which once seceded from the Union rather than pay a mining tax. Head north on Pleasant Valley Road to reach the state's **longest covered bridge** (built in 1862) in Bridgeport. It's a good spot for a picnic or fishing.

RESTAURANTS

Main Street Cafe & Bar ★★ Quite contemporary yet casual and colorful, the Main Street Cafe is one of the area's newer restaurants. Appreciated for its American standards as well as more innovative entrées, Main Street offers lunch specials such as warm Thai peanut salad, Greek pasta salad, and various pastas, in addition to burgers and sandwiches. Also special here is the extensive selection of coffee drinks, from espresso to hot nut (hazelnut, espresso, steamed milk, and whipped cream). Cafe specials might include New Zealand rack of lamb, halibut

▼

Grass Valley

Restaurants

▲

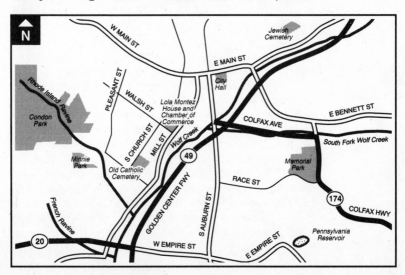

with dill mustard sauce, or orange-walnut pork tenderloin. The grilled teriyaki chicken or chicken with lime and cilantro is consistently good. Among unusual appetizers: wild boar sausage and tempura veggies. Good wine list. ▪ *Across from the Holbrooke Hotel on Main; (916) 477-6000; 213 W Main St, Grass Valley; $$; full bar; AE, MC, V; checks OK; lunch Mon–Sat, dinner daily.*

Tofanelli's ★★ This is Grass Valley's esteemed people's eatery, something of a cultural and culinary meeting place for just plain folks as well as the local alternative crowd. Tofanelli's cooks up earthy food for earthy people. Tofanelli's is famous for its design-your-own-omelet deal. To customize the basic egg model, patrons can add almost anything—from corned beef or bacon to feta cheese or sour cream, from Spanish sauce or salsa to fresh tomato. Predictably good lunches include veggie and tofu burgers; artichoke, Asiago, cheddar, and mushroom quiche; Caribbean tomato or borscht soups; and tofu sauté. Customers arrive early to fill up on midday favorites like the Santa Fe chicken burger; vegetarian moussaka; or tortellini with Gorgonzola and toasted walnuts. Dinner selections range from vegetarian lasagne and fajitas to fresh catfish and garlic grilled snapper. Only the truly decisive can pick from the dozen or so coffee and espresso drinks (made with regular coffee or unleaded) and the chocolate-dipped strawberries or the moist hummingbird cake. ▪ *On W Main next to the Holbrooke Hotel; (916) 273)9927; 302 W Main St, Grass Valley; $; beer and wine; MC, V; checks OK; breakfast, lunch Mon–Fri, dinner Mon–Sat.*

Peppers ★ Almost invisible from the street—one of those niggling negative side effects of historical preservation ordinances—Peppers, once found, is a surprise. The soft, cool, and uncluttered dining area hints at Peppers' fresh approach to Southwest and Mexican fare. One-time home to the town's Union newspaper—note the historic photos on the old brick walls—the building has been transported, somehow, to Mexico or New Mexico. The interesting enchiladas here, with an unusual mole sauce, come with cheese only or beef, chicken, or pork. Also available: homemade tamales, chiles rellenos, burritos, tacos, and tostadas, even a chimichanga, all served with beans (light-tasting, not too salty), rice, and salad. For dessert, try the traditional Mexican flan or—quite untraditional—the fresh fruit chimichanga with vanilla ice cream. ▪ *Downtown on Mill near Neal St; (916) 272-7780; 151 Mill St, Grass Valley; $; beer and wine; MC, V; local checks only; lunch Mon–Sat, dinner daily.*

Gold Star Cafe The homemade breakfasts served at the hole-in-the-wall Gold Star Cafe are especially delightful—breakfast crêpes, olallieberry buttermilk pancakes, Greek baked eggs (with feta, garlic, and black olives on a bed of spinach), mushroom-pesto-Jack cheese omelet, and homemade sausage. You can even get genuine maple syrup. Despite the abundant menu choices, specials are prominent, and might include fresh crab and artichoke baked eggs (served with home-fries and fresh muffins), croissant French toast, or a mushroom-cheese omelet topped with scallions. Some lunch choices are less successful than others (such as the pesto pizza on a roll), but unusual fare like the tofu tempeh sauté is consistently good. ■ *Downtown and across the street from the Holbrooke Hotel; (916) 477-1523; 207 W Main St, Grass Valley; $; beer and wine; no credit cards; checks OK; breakfast, lunch Wed–Sun.*

Mrs. Dubblebee's Pasties William Brooks, the founder of this restaurant, patented the Billy Brooks Pie Machine that is used to make pasties worldwide. No wonder the original Cornish miners favored Mrs. Dubblebee's pasties. Their descendants still think that these tasty meat and vegetable pasties are the best around. The traditional butter-crust beef pie—the Cornish pasty—is the one true progeny here of the British legacy; the spinach pasty (with mushrooms and three cheeses) is manager Neal Gullate's own recipe. Pick up some pasties (and a few squares of Scottish shortbread) and pack a picnic to nearby Empire Mine State Park, where the actuality of miners' hard lives will become quite real. ■ *Next to Veterans' Memorial Building on S Auburn St; (916) 272-7700; 251-C S Auburn St, Grass Valley; $; no alcohol; no credit cards; checks OK; lunch, early dinner every day (closes by 6pm).*

▼

Grass Valley

Lodgings

▲

LODGINGS

The Holbrooke Hotel ★★★ Mark Twain slept here. So did Lola Montez, Lotta Crabtree, and the notorious gentleman bandit Black Bart. Other heavyweight visitors to this historic Gold Rush hostelry include champion boxers and political prizefighters of presidential caliber. But don't be intimidated; despite its rugged Gold Rush grandeur, the brick 140-year-old Holbrooke Hotel is relaxed and accommodating. Many rooms have private balconies; all offer antiques, cable TVs tucked away in armoires, contemporary bathrooms (roomy enough for claw-footed tubs), and a continental breakfast in the library. The Holbrooke's Golden Gate Saloon is the best bar on Main Street, so light sleepers should request a suite away from the downstairs bar.

The venerable Holbrooke Hotel Restaurant is excellent. Dinner entrées, which change seasonally, might include wild mushroom chicken, blackened prime rib, and prawns Pernod. Salads, pastas, and sandwiches are the lunch fare. Don't miss the outrageous onion rings or the hazelnut chocolate cake (at any meal). ■ *W Main St between S Church and Mill streets; (916) 273-1353, toll free (800) 933-7077, fax*

(916) 273-0434; 212 W Main St, Grass Valley, CA 95945; $$; full bar; AE, MC, V; checks OK; lunch Mon–Fri, dinner Mon–Sat, champagne brunch Sun.

Murphy's Inn ★★★ Once the personal estate of North Star and Idaho mines owner Edward Coleman, Murphy's Inn has become an after-the-Gold Rush legend. A decade ago, Marc and Rose Murphy established the inn's tradition of quiet, countrified elegance. New proprietors Tom and Sue Myers have taken this task to heart. A topiary garden surrounds the elegant Victorian with bubbling fountains, a fish pond, and a giant 2,000-year-old sequoia. The spacious deck with spa is the perfect antidote after a long day of gold digging. The main house has remained true to its 19th-century origins with its downstairs sitting parlors and a bold brass-fronted fireplace with wood-and-tile trim; the kitchens, however—there's an abbreviated one in Sara's Suite—are quite contemporary. The floral motif in the Victorian mood are tastefully understated in all eight rooms. Breakfast would be a feast in any century. ■ *One block from Main at Neal and School streets; (916) 273-6873; 318 Neal St, Grass Valley, CA 95945; $$$; AE, MC, V; checks OK.*

Swan-Levine House ★★ The Swan-Levine House, a small-town hospital until 1968, is as notable for its bold, bright artistic decor as its naturally eclectic architecture. Not surprising, as both the owners are artists. (The carriage house is a print-making studio that can be used by guests for a small fee.) The library downstairs sets the tone for the house: jukebox in one corner, chess table and stuffed chairs elsewhere, fabric sculpture and artful oddities almost everywhere. The most popular guest rooms are the three on the second floor: the Suite, the Surgery (this Victorian once served as Grass Valley's hospital) throbbing with splashes of red and heart artwork, and the Bunk Room (great for kids). At press time, renovations were underway, and new rooms may become available. A morning meal is a joy in the bright blue commercial-size kitchen—a very social place. ■ *2½ blocks from Main St on S Church; (916) 272-1873; 328 S Church St, Grass Valley, CA 95945; $$; AE, MC, V; checks OK.*

Golden Ore Bed & Breakfast Inn ★ This lovingly renovated country Victorian has many thoroughly modern charms. Rooms upstairs have skylights, for one thing, plus direct access to a pleasant two-tiered deck. Downstairs, the large Parlor Room fronts the street and features elegant antiques and a private bathroom with a showered claw-footed tub. Mistress Mary's Room, also right off the wood stove–heated living room, has a wonderful gardenside bay window and a small bathroom with shower. The tiny but tasteful Butler's Room in the back has a semiprivate bath with both tub and shower. Innkeepers Margaret and John Westwell greet you in the morning with a splendid repast. ■ *On S Auburn St between Empire St and Hwys 49 and 174; (916) 272-6872; 448 S Auburn St, Grass Valley, CA 95945; $$; MC, V; checks OK.*

AUBURN

The Gold Country's largest town sprawls across a bluff overlooking the American River. A gigantic stone statue of Claude Chana, 1848 discoverer of gold in Auburn Ravine, marks historic Old Town. **Lawyer's Row** on Commercial Street now houses antique shops. Also of interest are the whimsical firehouse, the former Wells Fargo office, and a post office that opened in 1849. Step into the **Shanghai Bar,** if only to see the memorabilia.

In **Auburn State Recreation Area** the north and middle forks of the American River are destinations for gold panners, swimmers, picnickers, and rafters. Great camping and hiking trails, too; (916) 885-4527.

RESTAURANTS

Butterworth's ★★ Butterworth's almost shares the same landmark status in Auburn as the adjacent copper-domed Placer County Courthouse. This place gained fame in the 1970s for Sunday brunches and specialties like prime rib and Yorkshire pudding served in an elegant Victorian ambience. The Butterworths are gone but the turn-of-the-century character and brunches remain. Chef Dennis Parsons presides over the kitchen and continues to employ locally grown meats and produce in all his preparations. Sunday brunches include unusual crêpes and omelets plus eggs Benedict, eggs Sausalito, and vol au vent (two puff pastry shells filled with poached salmon and topped with a poached egg and Maltese sauce). Stack your plate with Dutch pancakes and homemade apple sausage. Butterworth's fans still come for prime rib on Friday and Saturday nights, but chef Parsons has proved that there is more to life than a good piece of meat. ■ *On Lincoln Way behind the county courthouse. (916) 885-0249; 1522 Lincoln Way, Auburn; $$; beer and wine; AE, MC, V; local checks only; lunch Mon–Fri, dinner every day, brunch Sun.*

Auburn

Restaurants

The Headquarter House ★★ Here's a restaurant that unofficially doubles as the clubhouse for the golf course and putting greens nearby. Perhaps that explains why a deli outlet has opened near the pro shop. Beef eaters herd into this place (once part of a working Angus cattle ranch) for the Winner's Circle club—a lunch favorite of avocado, turkey, ham, and an abundance of roast beef on The Headquarter's own mission bread. Later in the day, the patrons move on to the slow-baked prime rib or a meltingly fine tenderloin. It's rare to find a restaurant that prepares steak so well and can still cook up a canneloni, stuff it with Italian sausage, chicken, broccoli, cheese, and marinara sauce, and call it a feast. ■ *E of Auburn via I-80 then Bell, right on Musso Rd; (916) 878-1906; 14500 Musso Rd, Auburn; $$; full bar; AE, DC, MC, V; no checks; lunch Wed–Sat, dinner Wed–Sun, brunch Sun.*

LODGINGS

Victorian Hill House ★★ This stately 1864 Victorian is a charming step into the past, poised just above Auburn's Old Town historic district. Tucked in amid tall trees and flower gardens—not to mention the above-ground pool, gazebo with hot tub, outdoor picnic tables, and covered patio—Victorian Hill House offers four unique rooms with colors and atmospheres cued from antique appointments. (The front hallway displays a Louis XVI writing desk and chair while a likeness of Louis himself is on porcelain display above the dining room fireplace.) Two of the finest rooms are Grandma's Golden Gingerbread (with a full view of Old Town and the county courthouse) and the Blue Willow. Guests pass time in the parlor or on the patio. Outdoor showers, by the hot tub, rain on sunny days. ■ *From I-80, take Maple St exit, right on Park to 195 Park St in Auburn; (916) 885-5879; Mail: PO Box 9097, Auburn, CA 95604; $$; MC, V; checks OK.*

Lincoln House Bed and Breakfast ★ The front entryway footbridge leads over a pond filled with koi (Japanese carp). Guests can read by the brick fireplace in the living room, swim in the outdoor pool, or browse through the inn's localized library. In the inn's own history department, there's a 1934 gas stove (accompanied by a wood-fired trash burner) and a display of antique cooking implements on the kitchen wall. Breakfast is served on pink Depression-era glassware. Children are welcome here; one of the three rooms, the pretty and pink Mary Todd Room with a four-poster mahogany bed, includes a fanciful dormer with a single brass bed. ■ *On Lincoln Way between I-80 and Hwy 49; (916) 885-8880; 191 Lincoln Way. Auburn, CA 95603; $$; AE, MC, V; checks OK.*

COOL

RESTAURANTS

The Nugget Jens Hoppe established this restaurant in 1978 because he believed people would enjoy his German recipes. He was right. The Nugget has become a favorite on the Georgetown Divide. It has a casual, coffee-shop atmosphere and a menu that includes non-Teutonic offerings such as Luau chicken (mein Gott!). Hoppe knows Germany much better than Hawaii, so for lunch we suggest the bockwurst, rundstueck warm (pork roast on a French roll with homemade gravy), or a strammer Max (grilled German schwarzbrot,

Black Forest ham topped with two eggs). This isn't the fanciest place around, but the service is good and the food is substantial—very substantial. It's just about the only place to eat along Highway 49 between Coloma and Auburn. ■ *Intersection of Hwy 49 and Hwy 193 in Cool; (916) 823-1294; $$; beer and wine; no credit cards; local checks only; breakfast, lunch every day, dinner Tues–Sun.*

GEORGETOWN

LODGINGS

American River Inn ★★ This is the hotel that gold built. In the nearby community of Growlersburg, the gold nuggets were so big they growled as they rolled around in the miners' gold pans. One nugget taken from the Woodside Gold Mine, a portion of which runs under the 1850s American River Hotel, weighed 126 ounces. Innkeepers Will and Maria Collin have done an exemplary job of maintaining the lush furnishings and the 25 rooms throughout the three buildings. The hands-down best room is number 18, which takes up a generous portion of the Queen Anne House's second floor. If that's taken, request a gardenside room in the main house. There is little to do in Georgetown, but the hotel does have a pool and can provide bicycles if you choose to take a ride out of town. For those flying into Sacramento, take advantage of the hotel's free airport limo. ■ *At corner of Main and Orleans streets; (916) 333-4499, toll free (800) 245-6566; Mail: PO Box 43, Georgetown, CA 95634; $$; AE, DIS, MC, V; checks OK.*

Coloma

Lodgings

COLOMA

As every California schoolchild knows, the Gold Rush began here when James Marshall found traces of the precious metal at John Sutter's sawmill in January 1848. Most of the tiny town of Coloma is included within the limits of the **Marshall Gold Discovery State Historic Park**, (916) 622-3470. Stop first at the museum for a guide to the handful of original buildings still standing.

LODGINGS

Coloma Country Inn ★★★ Every weekend adventure-seekers and innkeepers Alan and Cindi Ehrgott transform this intimate 1852 inn into one of Gold Country's wildest adventures. What the Ehrgotts really sell is thrills. Sign up for a whitewater raft trip down the South Fork of the American (Class III), which runs through the park. Or hop into a hot-air balloon in the early morning. If you dare, innkeeper-cum-pilot Alan Ehrgott will take you whitewater ballooning, swinging the balloon's carriage within inches of the river, then soaring to 2,000 feet above the valley. Back on earth, the five-guest-room inn, set in the heart of the lovely Marshall Gold Discovery State Park, is a tranquil retreat. Every day ends in a most civilized manner with iced tea and homemade cookies in the garden gazebo. After tea, feed the ducks, take a canoe ride around the pond, and stroll through the gold discovery exhibits in the park. Sleep soundly in the periwinkle and sage Cottage Room, dream of tomorrow's challenge, and lap up the sun come morning. Of course, you never have to leave the grounds if you don't want to. ■ *In Marshall State Historic Gold Discovery Park at 345 High St; (916) 622-6919; Mail: PO Box 502, Coloma, CA 95613; $$; no credit cards; checks OK.*

The Vineyard House ★ Built in 1878 by wealthy winemakers Robert and Louisa Chalmers, this tall Victorian Gothic home offers seven guest rooms furnished in antiques and fin de siècle prints and artifacts. Whereas the prettiest (with wraparound windows and a sitting area) is Mrs. Chalmers' Room, room 5 is notorious for being haunted. Just behind the inn are the stone ruins of the old winery. Over the years this has been a favored place for weddings, honeymoons, or just romantic escapes for the weekend. The Vineyard Restaurant (chicken and dumplings to prime rib) thrives on the first floor. Downstairs, the wine cellar is now part saloon, part gift shop, part jail cell. A word of caution: the inn has been through numerous owners lately and we've found that the quality fluctuates with each. Hopefully the new owners will be here long enough to reestablish its reputation for quality service and consistency. ■ *S of Hwy 49, just S of old Coloma Theater at 530 Cold Springs Rd; (916) 622-2217; Mail: PO Box 176, Coloma, CA 95613; $$; MC, V; checks OK; breakfast, lunch, dinner Tues–Sun (hours vary in winter, call ahead).*

KELSEY

LODGINGS

Mountainside Bed and Breakfast ★★ Kelsey is practically a ghost town. Only the pines whisper about the boom times when Kelsey was alive with miners prospecting for gold in Kelsey Creek and Spanish Flat. Built in 1929, well after the Gold Rush, the Mountainside B&B sits on 80 forested acres. If you are looking for the perfect place to finish your novel, this is it. Owners Mary Ellen and Paul Mello offer three quiet rooms (ask for the one with the cathedral windows and sunken tub) and—for budget travelers—an eight-bunk dormitory with its own bath, deck, and entrance. A huge deck (hot tub, too) has a sweeping 180-degree westward view. Inside, a baby grand dignifies the parlor. There isn't much to do in this neck of the woods, which is exactly why people covet this place.

■ *1½ mile N of Kelsey post office on Hwy 193, turn right on Spanish Flat Rd, go 1 mile; (916) 626-0983, toll free (800) 237-0832; 5821 Spanish Flat Rd, Kelsey, CA 95643; $$; no credit cards; checks OK.*

SIERRA WINE COUNTRY

Mother Lode wineries have roots that extend deep into history, when those who came seeking gold turned to slaking the thirsts of others. The old **D'Agostini Winery**, east of Plymouth in Shenandoah Valley, was started in 1856; its cellars now serve as a wine museum for Sobon Estate. A century later, winemakers rediscovered the region, and today wineries from El Dorado south to Tuolumne counties produce everything from the special rich, spicy zinfandels to full-bodied chardonnays and fruity rieslings. Between Placerville and Murphys lie several first-rate cellars; most offer tours and tasting and are small family-owned cellars, with picnic sites. Spring and autumn are particularly pleasant in the Gold Country; Amador County's Shenandoah Valley wineries offer musical concerts in summer.

A north to south sampling: **Boeger Winery** (Placerville, (916) 622-8094), tasting room in early 19th-century winery; tables with shade. **Sierra Vista Winery** (Placerville, (916) 622-7221), picnic areas with great views of Crystal Range. **Madrona Vineyards** (Camino, (916) 644-5948), wood-sided winery at 3,000-feet elevation. **Granite Springs Winery** (Somerset, (916) 621-1933), barn-style building; separate tasting room; picnic area by pond. **Amador Foothill Winery** (Shenandoah Valley, (209) 245-6307), state-of-the-art building; tasting counter in winery. **Charles Spinetta** (Shenandoah Valley, (209) 245-3638), good nature gallery in beautiful tasting room; picnic site overlooking pond. **Montevina Wines** (Shenandoah Valley, (209) 245-6942), impressive tasting room; arbor-covered patio. **Shenandoah Vineyards** (Shenandoah Valley, (209) 245-4455), tasting room in old cellar; adjoining art gallery; grand views. **Story Vineyard** (Shenandoah Valley, (209) 245-6208), tiny winery; tasting room with dramatic setting overlooking Consumnes River. **Black Sheep Vintners** (Murphys, (209) 728-2157), small downtown tasting room. **Stevenot Winery** (Murphys, (209) 728-3436), picturesque winery and setting. **Chatom Vineyards** (Douglas Flat, (209) 736-6500), attractive building; patio for picnics.

▼

Placerville

▲

PLACERVILLE

One of the first camps settled by miners who branched out from Coloma, Placerville was dubbed Dry Diggins because of the lack of water. Its name was changed to Hangtown in 1849 after a series of grisly lynchings; it became Placerville in 1854 to satisfy local pride. The brick and stone City Hall was built in 1860 as a firehouse; a museum occupies the **Fountain-Tallman Soda Works** building (open Tues–Fri), (916) 626-0773. **The Cary House**, where Mark Twain once lodged, has been meticulously restored on its original site. A dangling dummy marks the location of the infamous "hanging tree."

Gold Bug Mine, a mile north of downtown in Bedford Park, offers tours of a city-owned gold mine that takes visitors into the shaft. Picnic sites and hiking trails, (916) 642-5232. **El Dorado County Museum,** adjacent to the county fairgrounds (on Placerville Drive), includes nostalgic period furniture, an original Studebaker wheelbarrow, Sierra mailman Snowshoe Thompson's skis, and a stagecoach. Open Wed–Sun, (916) 621-5865.

Apple Hill encompasses many of the apple ranches, Christmas tree farms, and wineries that lie around Camino, east of Placerville. Autumn is the time to buy fruit, pies, apple butter and gifts. Thanks to its out-of-the-way location, **Georgetown** is a pleasant discovery. After a blaze burned the 1852 tent city, the mountain town was rebuilt with much wider streets. A former boarding house is now the American River Inn. Down the street are the I.O.O.F. Hall and Georgetown Hotel. In spring, spectacular displays of wild Scotch broom cover the hillsides.

RESTAURANTS

Smith Flat House ★★ Until last year, this longtime Placerville favorite (formerly The Carriage Room) called a shopping mall its home. Today, the determined owners have made Placerville's preferred restaurant an even better spot. They moved it to the Smith Flat House, a former wagon-train stop just east of town. The authentic inn recalls the heady days when gold fever swelled the population of Placerville to five times the size of the fledgling southern California city called Pueblo de Los Angeles. Turn your attention to the nightly specials, which travel confidently from Italian to French to Pacific Rim cuisine. The menu favorites are the deep-fried prawns (dipped in a beer batter) and the chicken breast sautéed in butter, wine, and mushrooms and mixed with tomato, onions, mild chile peppers, and Jack cheese. The slow service allows time to peruse the vintage photographs throughout the restaurant or sip a cocktail in the basement bar carved out of rock like an old gold mine. ■ *1 mile E of Placerville on Hwy 50, N on Point View Rd, then left on Smith Flat Rd; (916) 621-0667; 2021 Smith Flat Rd, Placerville; $$; full bar; DC, MC, V; no checks; dinner Mon–Sat, lunches Mon–Sat, barbecue luncheon Sat.*

Lil' Mama D. Carlo's ★★ This excellent little Italian find has hop-scotched around Main Street several times in the past few years; lately it finds itself in a large building across from the county court house. The linguine with light clam sauce is a standing favorite as is the chicken carcciofini and chicken Parmigiana. The pasta entrées (under $10) are smothered in flavor-packed rich sauces such as the carcciofini (a light cream-based sauce with artichoke hearts, white pepper, fresh tomatoes, and garlic). The veal piccata with capers and pine nuts is sublime. Finish up with a slice of the sinful chocolate cheesecake. The service is excellent. ■ *On Main St across from the court house; (916) 626-1612; 482 Main St, Placerville; $; beer and wine; no credit cards; local checks only; lunch Mon–Fri, dinner Mon–Sat.*

Zachary Jacques ★★ Owners Christian and Jennifer Masse have put together an excellent French menu that belies the Western motif of the restaurant's decor. The specialties of the house are classic French: medallions de boeuf elder (filet mignon with port wine and bearnaise sauces), valrèas (rack of lamb with Dijon mustard, garlic, and red wine sauce), and a fish almond stew in a saffron and garlic broth (a fine example of the Southern France emphasis here). Service is good, but make reservations because the restaurant is fairly small. A new wine list supports over 100 labels, mostly French. ■ *3 miles E of Diamond Springs on Pleasant Valley Rd; (916) 626-8045; 1821 Pleasant Valley Rd, Placerville; $$$; beer and wine; AE, MC, V; local checks only; dinner Tues–Sun, brunch Sun.*

Dignity Dragon ★ There is dignity in this shopping mall restaurant and it comes in the form of surprisingly good Mandarin, Sichuan, and Hunan food. There are more than 100 spicy entrées on the menu, ranging from the most obvious Chinese almond chicken and sizzling rice shrimp to more exotic hot and spicy thin-sliced pork Chang-sha and squid with Sichuan sauce. Every dish is carefully presented (each comes with chow fun, soyed rice noodles), and the eager waitpeople will gladly describe any unfamiliar dish. Reservations suggested on weekends. ■ *In shopping center across from Raley's supermarket off Ray Lawyer Dr; (916) 622-4293; 2851 Ray Lawyer Dr, Placerville; $; beer and wine; MC, V; local checks only; lunch, dinner Tues–Sun.*

Tortilla Flats Hungry and in a hurry? Head for Tortilla Flats, a friendly and casual Mexican restaurant across from the town hall. The traditional Mexican food—tacos, burritos—is good, but it is the crack service that makes Tortilla Flats shine. Most of the time, your order will be ready within minutes. That's all. ■ *2 blocks E of Bedford St at 564 Main St; (916) 626-0101; Placerville; $; full bar; AE, DC, MC, V; local checks only; lunch, dinner every day.*

LODGINGS

Chichester House ★★ This gracious Victorian home was built in 1892 by lumber baron D.W. Chichester. It was not only the finest house in Placerville at the time, it was the first to have indoor plumbing. Today the refurbished home still has the look and feel of the late 1800s. All three guest rooms have Victorian-era bedsteads, stained glass, and fireplace trimmed with carved wood and marble. A polished Pullman basin adds a touch of elegance to the Yellow Rose Room, our favorite. There are no televisions in the rooms, but the grand old house offers something even better—a library. Located on busy Spring Street, the Chichester House is better suited for travelers than vacationers looking for peace and quiet. Children are welcome. ■ *One block N of Hwy 50 on Hwy 49 (Spring St); (916)626-1882, toll free (800) 831-4008; 800 Spring St, Placerville, CA 95667; $$; MC, V; checks OK.*

Combellack Blair House ★★ The Combellack Blair House is a spectacular sight, painted in five shades of pink, trimmed with gingerbread, and guarded by a white picket fence. White wicker furniture is poised on the large front verandah and a love swing hangs on the back porch. Just off the porch there's a gazebo, rose garden, and a little waterfall in a rock garden. The Queen Anne Victorian theme carries inside to the sweeping spiral staircase, rich wood moldings, and floral-designed carpets. Like the Chichester House, however, this house fronts a relatively busy street and isn't necessarily a retreat. But given there are only two guest rooms here, you won't be tripping over many other people. No children. ■ *Off Hwy 50, take Bedford exit S, turn left onto Main St, right on Cedar Ravine; (916) 622-3764; 3059 Cedar Ravine Rd, Placerville, CA 95667; $$; MC, V; checks OK.*

Milton's Cary House Hotel ★ Originally built in 1857 and refurbished in the late 1980s by owner Doug Milton, the Cary House is one of the less-touted Victorian inns in Placerville—which makes it all the better. The four-story brick building headquartered the Wells Fargo stage lines during the Gold Rush days. Local lore tells of the days when $90 million worth of bullion was literally dumped on the hotel's porch to be transported to the mint in San Francisco. Years later, the same porch was used by newspaper editor Horace Greeley during an impassioned presidential campaign speech to miners. Many of the original mahogany beams and banisters have been preserved from those days, but there are few antiques or other artifacts left in the hotel to reflect the boom times. Many of the 20 rooms have kitchenettes; all have TVs and private baths; only four (1b, 1d, 3b, 3d) overlook the street. ■ *Main St, (916) 622-4271; 300 Main St, Placerville, CA 95667; $$; DC, MC, V; checks OK.*

River Rock Inn ★ Perched on the north bank of the beautiful South Fork of the American River, this inn is a river hound's dream. The River Rock Inn (built originally as a private residence) lacks the architectural splendor of the other Gold Country inns but the view of the river's edge from its sprawling deck and the soothing river sounds more than compensate. All but one of the inn's four rooms open onto the deck, with its roomy hot tub. Just upstream is the Chili Bar, a common starting point for whitewater rafting. You can watch the rafters hit the first of the waves, or you can strap on a life jacket and do some whitewater rock and rollin' yourself. ■ *Take Hwy 193 N from Placerville, turn left after crossing the S Fork of the American River Bridge at Chili Bar, follow road until it ends; (916) 622-7640; Mail: PO Box 827, Placerville, CA 95667; $$; no credit cards; checks OK.*

POLLOCK PINES

RESTAURANTS

The Haven ★★★ This may be the best-kept secret in the mountains. The menu is large and the food is consistently delicious. The Haven is famous among locals for its scallops and superb stir-fry (a delicious mess of chicken, beef, shrimp, broccoli, water chestnuts, and other tenderly cooked veggies). The steaks are thick and the salads mountainous—nobody walks away from this restaurant hungry. The decor—polished wood and stained glass—makes the small restaurant seem larger. During the summer months, dine outside on the deck under the towering pines and ubiquitous fuchsia blossoms. At breakfast, try the hot, hot cinnamon rolls with cider sauce. In winter, be sure to check weather conditions as the restaurant is at 4,000 feet, well above the snow line. ■ *½ mile W of Safeway in Pollock Pines; (916) 644-3448; 6396 Pony Express Trail, Pollock Pines; $$; beer and wine; MC, V; local checks only; dinner, lunch every day; breakfast Sat–Sun.*

Weird Harold's ★★ Tucked under a grove of towering ponderosa pine trees, this chalet-style restaurant offers outstanding prime rib and fine mountain trout with a creamy rice stuffing. Lobster, crab, and scallops are also usually available. Owner Harold Stebner is more than holding his own against the competition, in part by ensuring excellent service. The waiters and waitresses make you feel at home and are quick to fill up your champagne glass. In winter, call for weather conditions. ■ *In Pollock Pines on Pony Express Trail; (916) 644-5272; 5631 Pony Express Trail, Pollock Pines; $$; full bar; AE, MC, V; checks OK; dinner every day.*

Pollock Pines

Restaurants

▲

If you've found a place around town that you think is a Best Place, send in the report form at the back of the book. If you're unhappy with one of the places, please let us know why. We depend on reader input.

KYBURZ

LODGINGS

Strawberry Lodge ★★ Wedged between the giant conifers and granite headwalls of Tahoe's southwestern rim, Strawberry Lodge is the headquarters for a virtual cornucopia of year-round outdoor sports. You can downhill and cross-country ski, rock climb, bike, hike, swim, fish, ride horses, or just sit back and enjoy the solace of a High Country evening. About the only thing you can't do is pick strawberries. Strawberry Lodge (the name mystifies even the owners) has 43 rooms, and during the summer heat and winter snows they run to capacity. The rooms aren't lavish (the quieter rooms are nearer to the river) but neither is the price. The lodge offers live music on weekends during the summer, usually soft dance music. There is an equestrian center across the street and challenging Sierra Ski Ranch is just 15 minutes up the road. Families or small groups might prefer the River House, a two-bedroom cabin at the edge of the South Fork of the American River. ■ *On Hwy 50 about 40 miles E of Placerville; (916) 659-7200; Mail: Strawberry Lodge, Hwy 80, Kyburz, CA 95720; $$; full bar; AE, MC, V; no checks; breakfast, lunch, dinner every day.*

SOMERSET

LODGINGS

Fitzpatrick Winery and Lodge ★★ Winemaker Brian Fitzpatrick realized his dream out here in the wilderness: lodge, vineyard, and winery. The lodge is an impressive, country-style log structure. It sits atop a hill with a commanding 360-degree view of the countryside. One of the five rooms is French Basque, another Irish; each is filled with the appropriate photos and paintings. A third room, the Old Fairplay Room, displays artifacts from the old gold mining town of Fairplay during the boom times. Theme dinners are featured every other Saturday night. These can range from Algerian fare to an Alice in Curryland culinary adventure. Often these are cooked by guest chefs who visit from San Francisco and other locales. ■ *Off Mt. Aukum Rd, 6 mi SE of Somerset; 7740 Fairplay Rd, Somerset, CA 95648; (209) 245-3248; $$; MC, V; checks OK.*

PLYMOUTH

LODGINGS

Indian Creek Bed and Breakfast ★ Part of its popularity is simply a matter of location; Indian Creek provides the most convenient access to Amador County's Shenandoah Valley wineries. But it's not all location: Jay Cusker and Geof Denny run a nice lodge on their ten wooded acres outside of Plymouth. You can meditate by the frog pond or visit with their dogs and sheep. Indian Creek isn't much from the outside (painted with overgrown foliage—a bad trompe l'oeil), but the interior is much more successful. Guests congregate in the lodge's living room, a beautiful log-framed room with a cathedral ceiling. The nicest room is the Joan Elaine with its own fireplace. Large country breakfasts. ■ *3 miles N of Plymouth on Hwy 49; (209) 245-4648, toll free (800) 24-CREEK; 21950 Hwy 49, Plymouth, CA 95669; $$; DIS, MC, V; checks OK.*

AMADOR CITY

RESTAURANTS

Ballads Fine Dining ★★ When chef/owner David Funston opened Ballads, his first restaurant, he had the unenviable chore of taking over the site of Au Relais (once regarded as one of the best restaurants in the region). Those who miss Au Relais will be relieved to know that they have lost little in the trade. Funston, who has cooked professionally since age 15, consistently offers the most adventurous and delicious food in these foothills. This California cooking might even begin to compete with reputable restaurants in the Bay area. Preparations are dictated by seasonal availability and by chef's whim: an excellent moist roast and grilled duck with a sauce of plums, pine nuts, and scallions; and salmon with mango. The blackberry fox is a gorgeous concoction of caramel meringue, fresh blackberry sorbet, and a raspberry coulis. Brunch is a mother lode of hazelnut Belgian waffles and poached eggs with Dungeness crab. If there is any drawback to the restaurant, it's the relatively spartan decor—but the service is friendly and Funston often wanders out of the kitchen to mingle with his guests. ■ *Downtown Amador City; (209) 267-5403; 14220 Hwy 49, Amador City; $$; beer and wine; AE, MC, V; local checks only; dinner Thurs–Tues, brunch Sun.*

Rollie's Express Bar-B-Q If you have the urge for barbecue, Rollie's offers the best in the area. (Well, the only in the area that we could find, but it's pretty darned good.) This is slow-cooked barbecue in Texas tradition. It isn't going to blow off the roof of your mouth, but it's tangy enough to satisfy. Choose from ribs, chicken, beef, and ham. The weekday lunch special is always a hefty serving (almost enough to call it all-you-can-eat). Washed down with one of Rollie's delightfully icy mugs of beer, these ribs make a fine dinner. ■ *Downtown Amador City; (209) 267-0966; 14235 Hwy 49, Amador City; $; beer and wine; no credit cards; no checks; lunch, dinner Tues–Sun.*

All the places in this book, even the "no stars," are recommended.

LODGINGS

Imperial Hotel ★★ Bruce Sherrill and Dale Martin run a classy operation which strikes a marvelous balance between elegance and whimsy. One of the best examples of their playful talent is on display in the Oasis Bar: with a confidence born of supremely good taste, Sherrill and Martin have lightened it up with a trompe l'oeil fantasy of a Saharan oasis complete with palm trees, belly dancers, and painted camels. Several of the upstairs rooms feature more of the marvelous works of local artist John Johannsen (room 5 is a particularly good choice). Room 1 is huge and airy with high ceilings, two giant windows, and French doors to the balcony overlooking the street. You have to put up with some traffic noise, but the old brick hotel is located on a slow curve, so no one's going terribly fast. Enjoy a surprisingly large continental breakfast downstairs or in your room. The Imperial also features a first-rate restaurant. Chef Tracy Boehm changes her small but well-designed menu on a weekly basis. ■ *Downtown Amador City at 14202 Hwy 49; (209) 267-9172; Mail: PO Box 195, Amador City, CA 95601; $$; full bar; AE, MC, V; checks OK; dinner every day, brunch Sun.*

▼

Amador City

Lodgings

▲

SUTTER CREEK

The self-proclaimed "nicest little town in the Mother Lode" consists of photogenic buildings from the 1800s. Don't overlook the native American and Mexican folk art at the **Cobweb Collection** (83 Main Street, (209)267-0690), contemporary and traditional American handicrafts at **Fine Eye Gallery** (71 Main Street, (209)267-0571) and the local prints, watercolors, and stone carvings at **Sutter Creek Gallery** (35 Main Street, (209)267-0228). Among the landmark buildings are the Knight's Foundry (the country's only water-powered foundry) and the Downs Mansion (former home of the foreman at Leland Stanford's mine).

Detour to **Amador City** and **Drytown** (originally named for lack of water, not saloons), both which lie a few miles north of Sutter Creek. **Volcano,** a hamlet to the east (truely the nicest little town in the Mother Lode), sports a cannon that was ready for action during Civil War days. An outdoor amphitheater, hidden behind stone facades, is the site of summer theatricals. You'll find an enormous limestone outcropping used by the Miwok Indians to grind their food and a fine Indian artifacts museum at nearby **Indian Grinding Rock State Historic Park,** (209) 296-7488.

RESTAURANTS

Pelargonium ★ The South African herb pelargonium is not used here by chef Kent Wilson, but lots of rosemary and garlic is seared into the thick, tender slab of lamb served with a spicy plum sauce. One recent daily special, salmon prepared with a cucumber sauce, was overcooked and rather bland, so stick with the tried-and-true menu items which feature local seasonal produce and health-conscious preparation (using cholesterol-free or low-saturated fats). The decor, with its dark flowered wall paper, pink tablecloths, and silver serving pieces, resembles a formal hotel dining room. ■ *Downtown Sutter Creek; (209) 267-5008; 51 Hanford St, Sutter Creek; $$; beer and wine; no credit cards; checks OK; dinner Mon–Sat.*

Ruby Tuesday Cafe The Ruby Tuesday Cafe, in a pretty courtyard just off Main Street, has the feeling of a funky college town coffeehouse, replete with eclectic table decorations, scarf-draped windows, and an assortment of scraggly ferns and ivy. The menu, designed to feed those with more on their minds than dinner, offers soups and salad and baked goods with mixed results. If you're in Sutter Creek on a Monday night, the weekly acoustic jam session at Ruby's is the place to be. Ruby's wouldn't be much of a find in Berkeley, but in Sutter Creek people dig it. ■ *In the Eureka St Courtyard ½ block E of Main St; (209) 267-0556; 15 Eureka St, Sutter Creek; $$; full bar; AE, MC, V; checks OK; breakfast Sun, lunch Wed–Sat, dinner Thurs–Sat.*

LODGINGS

Sutter Creek Inn ★★ Jane Way's inn, one of the first in the state, is still one of the best. The amazing thing about this complex is how intimate and relaxed it feels despite its size. With 19 rooms, you'd expect this place to feel overrun on a busy weekend, but it doesn't. Part of the secret is the layout: while there are four rooms in the main 1859 house, over a dozen others are found in remodeled outbuildings scattered around the grounds, behind hedges, under grape arbors, and up stairwells. It all has the feeling of a secret garden. The rooms themselves are all quite distinctive; part of what pulls guests back here again and again is the fun of discovering them all (four feature Way's fabled swinging beds). Back inside the house, the living room is an inviting place to relax. Browse through Way's library and her eclectic selection of magazines; tickle tunes on the piano; or play some board games. You can also make an appointment for handwriting analysis or a massage. Breakfast, served at several large tables in the kitchen, is freshly prepared and abundant—and the company is usually as good as the food. ■ *Between Keyes and Hayden at 75 Main St; (209) 267-5606; Mail: PO Box 385, Sutter Creek, CA 95685; $$; no credit cards; checks OK.*

The Gold Quartz Inn ★ If you enjoy the ambience of a B&B but are reluctant to give up the comfort and privacy of a hotel, the Gold Quartz Inn is a good compromise. Both the strengths and weaknesses of this 24-room Queen Anne replica stem from its age—3 years. On the plus side, the newness delivers all the amenities you'd expect in a hotel: king-size beds, king-size bathrooms (some with Jacuzzis), cable TV, telephones, and even hair dryers. On the other hand, you'll have to make some aesthetic sacrifices to pay for these luxuries. The inn is plunked on the outskirts of town (aka suburbia), and the furnishings remind you of the "Country Living" collection at Macy's. That said, the emphasis here is on privacy: separate room entrances, a seating arrangement in the parlor which discourages mingling, and individual breakfast tables. The idea is, you're here to be with your partner. Or perhaps you are here for the food, as it is good and plentiful. You are encouraged to make frequents raids on the buffet, stocked with a seemingly endless progression of goodies from the kitchen. ■ *Bryson and Hwy 49 just S of Sutter Creek; (209) 267-9155, toll free (800) 752-8738; 15 Bryson Dr, Sutter Creek, CA 95685; $$; AE, MC, V; checks OK.*

VOLCANO

LODGINGS

St. George Hotel In its heyday in the 1860s, the burgeoning village of Volcano offered a tired miner his choice of 17 hotels; miners with money chose the St. George. Its 1862 elegance has faded considerably in the last century, but this three-story hotel wrapped with balconies entwined with trumpetvine and wisteria is still a gold mine for an evening in Volcano, arguably the most truly picturesque town in the Gold Country. The rooms themselves aren't luxury anymore, as they lack both heating and air conditioning and share four baths. Ask for a balcony room in the front. Rooms in the back have a lovely view of the garden but heat up quickly in the early morning sun. Avoid the rooms with baths in the modern annex (1961); they are dingy and dark. On Saturday nights, Sara Gillick, a fourth generation Volcanean and the St. George's cook for over 40 years, whips up slabs of prime rib fit for a prospector-sized appetite. Room rates ($100) include breakfast and dinner for two. ■ *Corner of Main and St. George streets; (209) 296-4458; Mail: PO Box 9, Volcano, CA 95689; $$; full bar; MC, V; checks OK; dinner Wed–Sun.*

JACKSON

The Amador County seat hides most of its rowdy past behind modern facades, but old-timers know Jackson (once called "little Reno") as the last place in California to outlaw prostitution. The Mother Lode's deepest mines, the Kennedy and Argonaut, have been closed for decades, but their headframes and some huge tailing wheels still remain. Follow Jackson Gate Road northeast of town to **Kennedy Tailing Wheels Park.** Only two wheels remain standing, but you get a good idea of how they carried waste from the mines to a settling pond over the hills. Operators take wannabe gold panners to **Roaring Camp Mining Company** on the Mokelumne River to try their luck or to enjoy a cookout, (209) 296-4100.

RESTAURANTS

Michael's Restaurant ★★ Amador County native Michael Golsie has worked wonders since he came to manage the National Hotel's basement restaurant. The menu shows staples of steak and scampi, but Golsie's specials exhibit a willingness to experiment that is rare in these parts. His filet mignon, for example, is stuffed with oysters and glazed with a heavenly sauce of shiitake mushrooms, heavy cream, and chardonnay. We recently had freshly prepared ravioli, stuffed with turkey and mushrooms and served on a bed of watercress and radicchio; though tasty, it swam in a bit too much oil. But with another dish, we found ourselves sopping up the tart lemon-caper sauce of our huge helping of poached salmon with pleasure. ■ *In the basement of the National Hotel; (209) 223-3448; 2 Water St, Jackson; $$; full bar; AE, MC, V; local checks only; dinner Fri–Sun, brunch Sun.*

Mel and Faye's Diner Mel and Faye have been churning out good eats at their highway-side diner since 1956—and the place is still a local favorite thanks to the cheap prices and the generous-size burgers. Mel chops the onions himself for his special Moo-Burger, a gloppy double cheeseburger smothered in onions and a mayonnaise-y special sauce. The shakes are thick enough to properly clog your straw, but skip the pies. ■ *Hwy 49 at Main St; (209) 223-0853; 205 Hwy 49, Jackson; $; beer and wine; no credit cards; local checks only; breakfast, lunch, dinner every day.*

LODGINGS

Court Street Inn ★ Janet and Lee Hammond's pretty 1870 Victorian with its tin ceilings, redwood staircase, and marble fireplace has earned a well-deserved spot on the National Register of Historic Places. The real attraction in this B&B, a two-minute stroll from Main Street, is the extensive collection of wonderful, whimsical treasures Janet and Lee have gathered for over 20 years: grocery store scales, cash registers, dental chairs, and shoeshine stands—not to mention the vintage furnishings with which each flounced-and-frilled room is furnished. If you can put up with a bit of excess, you'll enjoy it (those with more clean-lined tastes should go elsewhere). The Peiser Room, the largest in the house, has an adjoining sitting room just perfect for a lazy read of the morning paper. Bring a bathing suit and an appetite: Court Street has a hot tub and the breakfasts are enormous, although you'll probably still be full from the hors d'ouevres of stuffed mushrooms, crab dip, and Brie from the night before. ■ *Court just off Church; (209) 223-0416; 215 Court St, Jackson, CA 95642; $$; MC, V; checks OK.*

National Hotel In continuous operation since 1862, the National Hotel has built up quite a guest list over the years: Will Rogers, John Wayne, Leland Stanford, and every California governor in the last century (except Wilson, tsk, tsk). You may want to think twice before you add your name to the registry, however. True, this hotel does capture the feeling of the Old West like no other around: on a weekend afternoon, when Dennis Yancey is playing ragtime tunes on the grand piano, the poker games are smoking up the card room, and you register with the bartender through a wooden cage at the back of the saloon, it doesn't take much imagination to conjure up the previous century. But once you get upstairs, be prepared for spartan accommodations. The furnishings may well be the original ones (and they're starting to get ratty), the hot and cold water surges in the shower, and the tiled and painted walls are chipping. Still, it's a far sight more interesting than the Best Western units down the road. ■ *Corner of Main and Water; (209) 223-0500; 2 Water St, Jackson, CA 95642; $; AE, MC, V; checks OK.*

SAN ANDREAS

LODGINGS

Robin's Nest ★ There isn't much to see in this rather nondescript foothill whistle-stop; the Nest commands a view over the high school football field and is by far the best-looking building in town. But if you just need a pleasant place to overnight, the accommodations within this nine-room Queen Anne Victorian are quite cozy. The five upstairs rooms, carved into the sloping rooflines of the very large converted attic, are all bright and airy. Downstairs, the spacious Snyder Suite features a seven-foot tub and brass shower. The separate Carriage Room is best for longer stays. New innkeepers George and Carolee Jones' bountiful breakfasts usually include eggs Benedict or souffle, fruit, coffee cake (perhaps raspberry), and, in season, a delicious strawberry soup. ■ *Facing Hwy 49 between Russells Rd and Church Hill Rd at 247 St. Charles St; (209) 754-1076; Mail: PO Box 1408, San Andreas, CA 95249; $$; MC, V; checks OK.*

Star system: (no star) worth knowing about if nearby ★ A good place ★★ Excellent, some outstanding qualities ★★★ Distinguished, many wonderful features ★★★★ The very best in the region.

LODGINGS

Utica Mansion Inn ★★ Utica Mansion owners Cheri and Tad Folendorf put seven years of love and hard work into this beautiful 1882 Victorian before opening it to guests in 1988. In 1991, they turned the place over to innkeepers and restaurateurs René and Catherine Masvidal. Romantic and elegant (yet sweetly laid back), the Utica Mansion has three upstairs guest rooms that open onto a shared verandah with a view of the park across the street. Decorated in rich Victorian burgundies and mauves, all the rooms have period antiques—including the original light fixtures (tough to read by). Our favorite room is the Anna Suite with its wonderful little divan and a mannequin dressed in period costume. Both Anna and Excelsior suites have English tiled fireplaces with wood-burning stoves. All the rooms have private baths (showers, no tubs). The Masvidals, both trained chefs, turn out a whopping 12-course breakfast, heralding such surprises as a hot fruit course (strawberries Martinique, for example) or fanciful eggs in saffron-tomato sauce. When you arrive, a basket of fruit and split of champagne greet you in your room. ■ *1 block W of Hwy 49 at 1090 Utica Lane off Main St; (209) 736-4209; Mail: PO Box 1, Angels Camp, CA 95222; $$; beer and wine; MC, V; checks OK.*

Cooper House Bed and Breakfast ★ This 1911 restored Craftsman-style bungalow was originally built for Dr. George P. Cooper, Angels Camp's long-ago physician, to serve as both his home and office. The B&B nestles in a quaint garden setting well away from the main highway. Original artwork by local artists embellishes the walls throughout the house and gives some local flavor. The names of the three suites (the Zinfandel, the Cabernet, and the Chardonnay) are indicative of the influence the winemaking community has on this town; buy a bottle of your favorite to sip in the grapevine-covered gazebo. A commanding greenstone and quartz fireplace in the living room beckons on cold nights. ■ *E on Raspberry Lane off Main St, very sharp left to 1184 Church St; (209) 736-2145; Mail: PO Box 1388, Angels Camp, CA 95222; $$; MC, V; checks OK.*

Murphys

MURPHYS

Gingerbread Victorians peek from behind white picket fences while tall locust trees border Murphys' main streets. The **Murphys Hotel,** opened in 1856, has an illustrious guest register, including U.S. Grant, Horatio Alger, and Charles Bolton (Black Bart). The large stands of giant redwoods east of Murphys in **Calaveras Big Trees State Park** makes a cool summer retreat with camping, swimming, hiking, and fishing along the Stanislaus River, (209) 795-2334.

The **caves** around Murphy were explored early in the 1800s by avid prospectors. Mercer Caverns, (209) 728-2101, has the usual stalactites and stalagmites in a series of descending chambers; you reach Moaning Cavern, (209) 736-2708, by descending staircases or rappelling from the surface; California Caverns, (209) 736-2708, was reportedly the West's first commercially developed cave.

RESTAURANTS

Murphys Hotel and Motor Lodge ★★ For a step back in time, back to the days when women wore petticoats and men wore spurs, the Murphys Hotel is part of a frontier land that's not just a tourist destination, but a center of real social activity. People come from all over for a drink or a night. The original 1856 hotel is now a registered landmark kept cool by its limestone foundation and warmed by the dry heat of a wood stove come winter. In the dining room, there is an oil-burning hurricane lamp and old-style restaurant china at each table. The service is perfectly paced and the waitresses quite knowledgeable on the local wines, all available by the glass. Chef Marc Kirby succeeds in everything from his delicately seasoned clam chowder to the ahi tuna grilled in a simple lemon butter sauce, and the prawn and pasta dish in a fresh Provençal tomato sauce tweaked with herbs and wine.

The main building has 9 guest rooms reflecting the turn-of-the-century era (without phones or television), while the newer building has 20 more modern rooms. If it's character, charm, and adventure (or a piano in your room) you want, this is the ticket. ■ *You can't miss it—457 Main St; (209) 728-3444; Mail: PO Box 329, Murphys, CA 95247; $; full bar; AE, MC, V; checks OK; breakfast, lunch, dinner every day.*

LODGINGS

Dunbar House: 1880 ★★★ Century-old gardens adorn this lovely Italianate home in the heart of the Gold Country. The lush grounds surprise with simple touches such as a hammock and a gazebo with a swing. Personal touches abound (plenty of games, reading material, and music available), and fresh flowers embellish the rooms. All four rooms are enhanced with down pillows and comforters, touched with lace, equipped with wood stoves, and fully furnished with heirloom antiques. The Cedar Room seems made for lounging, be it on the sun porch or the private Jacuzzi spa. Fresh juices, coffee, homemade pastries, and a fabulous concoction of crab and cheese on an English muffin wake you up in the morning. A fine bed and breakfast inn, indeed—especially if you're fond of Italian operas. ■ *Just off Main St at 271 Jones St; (209) 728-2897; Mail: PO Box 1375, Murphys, CA 95247; $$$; MC, V; checks OK.*

RESTAURANTS

Columbia House Restaurant ★ Locals will tell you this Americana restaurant has had its ups and downs over the years, but they've continued to frequent the place for its basic breakfasts, knowing that if it's bad one time, it may be good the next. This does not bode well for the one-time traveler to this area, but word is, the former saloon is on an upswing, with new owners wooing the locals back with a thriving lunch trade of soup and bread to go and hearty, simple fare any time of day. Any miner would feel right at home: bacon and egg or biscuits and gravy breakfasts, and chili, meat loaf, steaks, chicken, and the like for lunch. Swill them down with locally made sarsaparilla. ■ *Corner of State and Main streets in Columbia; (209) 532-5134; $; beer and wine; MC, V; local checks only; breakfast, lunch every day in summer (call ahead off season).*

El Sombrero Restaurant Mexican gold seekers were among the first gold miners scrambling these hills. Today, Beatrice DeLeon and her daughter Lori Eszlinger have set their stakes in the restaurant business. They've turned their century-old house fronted by a garden and surrounded by a white picket fence into a local fave. The food is familiar, Americanized Mexican with a slightly New Mexican flair. Don your sombrero, grab a cerveza, and head for a table on the porch. ■ *On State St; (209) 5339123; 11256 State St, Columbia; $; beer and wine; MC, V; local checks only; lunch, dinner Thurs–Tues (winter hours vary).*

Columbia

Lodgings

LODGINGS

City Hotel ★★★ City folk who originally frequented this opulent hotel in 1856 came to see the gem of the southern mines. Predictably, the building's gone through several incarnations since then—including gold assay shop and dance hall—but when the town turned into a state historic park in the 1940s, city folk began returning to the once-again opulent City Hotel. In the '70s, nearby Columbia College obtained grant money to renovate the structure and turn it into a training facility for their hotel program so that zealous students learn the hospitality business alongside seasoned professionals. The lobby is fitted with period settees and marble-top tables. Six of the ten high-ceilinged rooms open off a parlor, also the setting for a simple continental breakfast. Rooms 1 and 2 have balconies overhanging Main Street. All boast half-baths, with showers down the hall, but the hotel provides comfy robes, slippers, and wicker baskets of toiletries to ease the trip.

The restaurant is one of those rarities—a culinary palace right in the heart of a state park. Inside, it's nicely turned out with red velvet drapes, oil paintings, and antique furniture topped with crisp linen and flowers. The serving staff—this might be Hotel Hospitality 101, but these are A students—dresses in period costumes. You can order from a prix-fixe menu or à la carte. California vintages feature prominently on the wine list. Reservations are essential on weekends and advised anytime. Until your name is called, do some time in the hotel's What Cheer saloon. ■ *Main St between Jackson and State streets; (209) 532-1479; City Hotel, Columbia; Mail: PO Box 1870, Columbia, CA 95310; $$; full bar; AE, MC, V; checks OK; dinner Tues–Sun, brunch Sat–Sun.*

Fallon Hotel ★★ Another addition to the town's limited room count, this 1850s hostelry has been beautifully restored to a more elegant 1890s splendor with embossed wallpapers, antique oak furnishings, ornate porcelain basins, and pull-chain toilets. It's a far cry from the building's early days as a courthouse, a bakery, and ultimately a miners' rooming house with sagging beds and sparse, uncomfortable furnishings. The adjoining Fallon Theatre (still in use) was added shortly afterwards. Like the City Hotel, some staff are trainees from Columbia College. The 13 bedrooms are quite small; be sure to request one of the five larger balcony rooms. Robes, slippers, and baskets brimming with soap, shampoo, and towels make the walk to the showers practically painless. Continental breakfast, served in the ice cream parlor, is included in the room rate. ■ *Washington St off Broadway; (209) 532-1470; Mail: PO Box 1870, Columbia, CA 95310; $$; AE, MC, V; checks OK.*

JAMESTOWN

"Jimtown" has been preoccupied with gold since the first dust was taken out of Woods Creek in 1848; a marker commemorates the discovery of a 75-pound nugget. For a fee, you can pan at troughs on Main Street or go prospecting with a guide. Free **Jamestown Mine** tours take place on Wednesdays; call (209) 984-4641 for reservations. The Emporium and Jamestown Mercantile Too are loaded with antiques. Sierra Railway's vintage cars and steam locomotives are on display at **Railtown 1897 State Historic Park**. These old-timers have starred in many movies, TV shows (remember "Bonanza" and "Little House on the Prairie"?), and commercials. Tour the roundhouse daily or ride the rails on weekends in the summer, (209) 984-3953.

RESTAURANTS

Michelangelo ★★ Faux marble, black and white tile, and Michelangelo prints contrast pleasantly with the tin ceiling and walls of the vintage Main Street building that houses this modern Italian restaurant. This is not your usual trattoria. Busy René Parent (she also oversees The Smoke Cafe across the street) has assembled a creative menu that might include grilled eggplant and smoked mozzarella antipasti; linguine with prawns in garlic butter sauce; or chicken with pancetta, capers, mustard, and Parmesan cheese. Of course, nothing should restrain you from devouring a chicken sausage, apple, and Gorgonzola pizza. ■ *Downtown at 18228 Main St in Jamestown; (209) 984-4830; $; full bar; DIS, MC, V; no checks; dinner Wed–Mon.*

Smoke Cafe ★★ When René Parent is not at Michelango, she's here. Maybe the cactus and coyote theme is passé elsewhere; it prevails, however, in one of Jimtown's liveliest cafes named after a 1920s baseball pitcher from the Cleveland Indians who smoked fast balls and was the first owner of this slot-machine saloon. With the same creative chef and owners as Michelangelo across the street, it's not surprising Mexican dishes here are infused with a bit of Southwestern playfulness. Black bean burritos, flautas, and fajitas are favorites, but so are the spicy corn chowder and powerful garlic soup made with a beef base and sprinkled with croutons and Jack cheese. Ask bartender Greg Humphrey to make you his award-winning "After Burner" (a concoction of Kahlua, cinnamon, schnapps, and Absolut Peppar). You can smoke or not smoke at the Smoke; we prefer the streetside porches. ■ *Downtown at 18191 Main St in Jamestown; (209) 984-3733; $; full bar; no credit cards; checks OK; dinner Tue–Sun (hours vary, call ahead).*

Kamm's ★ Nearly 150 years ago, Chinese miners were among the area's most industrious. Not surprising, then, to find remnants of this culture in an old Gold Rush–era building. This is one of the few (and one of the better) Gold Country Chinese

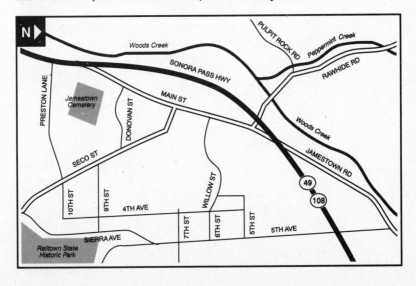

restaurants, and Jimtown locals vie with tourists for a large selection of mild Cantonese dishes or spicier Hunan and Mongolian fare. ■ *Downtown on Main St; (209) 984-3105; 18208 Main St, Jamestown; $; beer and wine; MC, V; local checks only; lunch Mon–Fri, dinner Mon–Sat.*

LODGINGS

Jamestown Hotel ★★ Built at the turn of the century and converted to a hospital in the 1920s, this two-story brick charmer with its wood verandah-style balcony was redone as a country inn 10 years ago. Upstairs, eight handsome guest rooms commemorate Gold Rush personalities. The Lotta Crabtree suite is romantically furnished with plenty of wicker, floral fabrics, and a pink tub. It's hinted that the masculine-looking Black Bart suite, with its black tub and black iron bed, is haunted. The cozy, country French dining room begs for distinctive food, but though the presentation of individual dishes is good and the ingredients fresh, the entrées themselves depend heavily on who owns the hotel and who's cooking the food, as there have been a number of owners over the years. Incidentally, smokers get the best tables in the handsome saloon with its elegant back bar. ■ *Downtown on Main St; (209) 984-3902; Mail: PO Box 539, Jamestown, CA 95327; $$; full bar; AE, DIS, MC, V; checks OK; lunch, dinner every day, brunch Sun.*

National Hotel ★★ A healthy rivalry between the vintage National and Jamestown hotels has been going on for years. Both have their fans. The 11 restored rooms in this 1859 hotel blend 19th-century atmosphere (handmade quilts, brass beds) with 20th-century comforts. Five have private showers; all have antique washstands. A generous continental breakfast (with morning paper) is served in the dining room or the garden courtyard. While the National's menu is a little more limited and the dining room plainer than at the Jamestown, the quality of the food is better (the trout is fresh from the stream). The saloon, with its 19th-century redwood bar is the best place to catch up on local gossip. No connection to the hotel of the same name in Jackson. ■ *Downtown on Main St; (209) 984-3446; Mail: PO Box 502, Jamestown, CA 95327; $; full bar; MC, V; checks OK; lunch, dinner every day, brunch Sun.*

Sonora Country Inn ★ Clint Eastwood rested his famous self here; if that's not enough of a draw, this attractive modern motel is close to all area attractions and far enough off the highway to ensure quiet. The 59 rooms and 2 suites are modest but clean and roomy. Singles have king-size beds, doubles have two queens. All rooms offer phones and cable TV. On request, you can get a free continental breakfast in your room. Cast off the summer heat in the cool pool. ■ *1½ miles W of Sonora off hwys 108 and 49; (209) 984-0315, toll free (800) 847-2211;*

18755 Charbroullian Lane, Jamestown, CA 95327; $; AE, DC, DIS, MC, V; no checks.

TUOLUMNE

LODGINGS

Oak Hill Ranch ★★ Jane and Sanford Grover's architect son Don designed this elegant Victorian replica to house a quarter-century's worth of collected treasures, such as the stained-glass window, heirloom furniture, elaborate fireplace mantels, and even the grand staircase. The Grovers dress in costume from that long-ago era to serve a lavish breakfast in the dining room. Of the five bedrooms, our choice is the Queen Anne–era Eastlake Room, furnished with appropriate antiques. At 3,000 feet, the house affords a wondrous view of woods and mountains. ■ *Off Apple Colony Rd at 18550 Connally Lane; (209) 928-4717; Mail: PO Box 307, Tuolumne, CA 95379; $$; no credit cards; checks OK.*

SONORA

Highway 49 traffic crawls along narrow Washington Street past shops, restaurants, and hotels in the heart of bustling Sonora. To look at the city's tumultuous past, park and walk up to the **Tuolumne County Museum** in the century-old jail on Bradford Street, (209) 532-1317, or wander through the history room of the St. James Episcopal Church.

Sonora

Detour Route 108 heads west into the Sierra over Sonora Pass. Along its route several alpine communities have sprung up. Side roads turn off to Gold Rush survivors

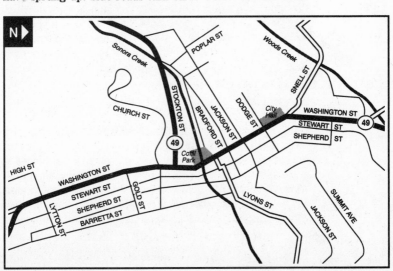

like Tuolumne and Soulsbyville, a trim little town with tin-roofed homes.

RESTAURANTS

Good Heavens: A Food Concern ★★ According to local lore, this historic building once housed a coffin-maker downstairs and a bordello upstairs. Today it's the setting for a delightful boutique cafe noted for its homemade soups, breads, crêpes, pastas, salads, and creative sandwiches. Each meal starts with fresh herb and cheese biscuits and some unusual homemade jams (tart orange marmalade with walnuts; rich raspberry-chocolate). Salads and homemade soups are the order of the day, embellished with creative assemblages such as the crêpe St. Thomas, a sauté of mushrooms, spinach, and turkey sausage, drizzled with béchamel sauce. Jason MacKenzie, presiding over the dining room with its floral linens and old-fashioned paintings, waxes poetic over the desserts—and rightfully so. *Gourmet* magazine requested the recipe for Don's butter cake—and the chef proudly turned them down. ■ *Downtown on N Washington St; (209) 532-3663; 49 N Washington St, Sonora; $; no credit cards; local checks only; lunch Mon–Sat.*

Hemingway's ★ Here's a clean, well-lighted place with a little bit of everything: ranch-style exterior, European-bistro interior, California contemporary cuisine, and Papa Hemingway memorabilia. Soups and salads are usually imaginative and entrées excellent, if eclectic. Salmon and filet mignon come wrapped in pastry puffs topped with a Thai pepper glaze, and New Zealand lamb is soaked in a sweet vinegar marinade before hitting the grill. On most weekends and holidays, musical theater accompanies your meal. ■ *Downtown on Stewart St; (209) 532-4900; 362 S Stewart St, Sonora; $$; wine and beer; AE, MC, V; local checks only; lunch, dinner Tues–Sat (call for summer hours).*

Ristorante LaTorre ★ The influence of San Francisco's North Beach Italians is felt east of the big city in Sonora. This cozy rosewood-and-brass-with-a-view establishment is, hands down, the Mother Lode's best *looking* Italian restaurant—and the food's not bad either. The canneloni, fettuccine alfredo, and other fresh, homemade dishes keep this a favorite dinner house with locals. Steak and grilled chicken are other good possibilities. ■ *On N Washington St in downtown Sonora; (209) 533-9181; 39 N Washington St, Sonora; $$; full bar; AE, DIS, MC, V; checks OK; lunch Mon–Fri, dinner every day (hours vary, call ahead).*

LODGINGS

Serenity ★★★ It's hard to find this idyllic inn—and that's part of its appeal. Tucked away at the end of a country road on six wooded acres near the Stanislaus National Forest and Phoenix Lake, the inn has quite a history for such a new house. Thanks to an arsonist, the house has been rebuilt. The good news is that if there were any flaws in the original plans, Fred and Charlotte Hoover have corrected them. Virtually flawless, the antique-filled house combines the gracious atmosphere of the past with the latest in modern conveniences. Attention to detail is the thing here. Board games, cards, and books fill a sunlit upstairs sitting area, while a wraparound verandah downstairs encourages nothing more strenuous than sunning or waiting for visiting deer. Charlotte's four-course gourmet breakfasts appear out of the cavernous kitchen with treats like gingerbread, mushroom-crust quiche, and cobbler. All four generous rooms have full baths and handsome, color-coordinated furnishings in floral themes. It would be hard to pick a favorite. ■ *6 miles E of Sonora off Phoenix Lake Rd; (209) 533-1441, toll free (800) 426-1441; 15305 Bear Cub Dr, Sonora, CA 95370; $$; AE, MC, V; checks OK.*

Barretta Gardens Inn ★★ Expansive gardens of native flowering shrubs (and wonderful sunset views) surround this small country inn on a hillside southeast of downtown Sonora. The appealing wraparound porch is perfect for curling up with a good book in spring or autumn. Winter conversation takes place on comfy sofas around the fireplace in the comfortable living room. Most impressive of the five bedrooms is the pretty Periwinkle Room with its queen-size bed and ornate floor-to-ceiling mirror. The innkeepers greet guests with an afternoon beverage and send them off after a full breakfast in the dining room on the porch. ■ *¼ mile N of Hwy 108 on Barretta St; (209) 532-6039; 700 S Barretta St, Sonora, CA 95370; $$; AE, MC, V; checks OK.*

Sonora

Lodgings

Ryan House B&B ★★ Dennis and Susan Ryan came to Sonora in 1855 from Cork, Ireland, to escape the potato famine. Here they built this house, which stayed in their family until the early 1980s. To this day, the small house retains an authentic feel, with square nails, handmade windows (with the original glass), and other architectural oddities of the 19th century. The only drawback is its small size, but the four guest rooms do have unexpectedly high ceilings, cheerful wallpaper, antique furnishings, handmade quilts, and private baths. Guy and Nancy Hoffman are converting the attic into a suite with a parlor. Guests gather around the library's wood-burning stove or breakfast in the rose garden near the croquet court. ■ *On Shepherd St near downtown; (209) 533-3445; 153 S Shepherd St, Sonora, CA 95370; $$; AE, DIS, MC, V; checks OK.*

Lulu Belle's Bed and Breakfast ★ Roses bloom at Lulu Belle's all summer. No wonder guests spend most of their time breathing deeply from lawn chairs on the expansive grounds. The musically inclined can retire to the music room where impromptu concerts often take place when guests test their lips on a flute, tickle ivories on the piano or organ, or strum a folk song on the guitar. Two of the guest rooms are inside the main house, three in a quiet carriage house. One suite has a TV; another has a private entrance. Furnishings throughout are in keeping with the casual atmosphere. ■ *On Gold St near downtown; (209) 533-3455; 85 Gold St, Sonora, CA 95370; $$; AE, DIS, MC, V; checks OK.*

SOULSBYVILLE

LODGINGS

Willow Springs Country Inn ★ Built by Ben Soulsby, who settled the area in 1851, the ranch house makes a good overnight stop for backroad explorers. Bedrooms all have private baths; there's a cottage too. A full breakfast (maybe with an "apricot flaky") is included; guests are also welcome to use the kitchen or barbecue to fix other meals. Sink into the hot tub to relax muscles tired from a spirited game of tennis, shuffleboard, or horseshoes at the park next door, or perhaps a vicious game of croquet in the yard. ■ *Off Soulsbyville Rd from Hwy 108, take first left turn onto King's Court; (209) 533-2030; 20599 King's Court, Soulsbyville, CA 95372; $$; no credit cards; checks OK.*

COLUMBIA STATE HISTORIC PARK

This living museum of the past, with its sizable collection of renovated buildings and mining artifacts, is an ideal first stop for Gold Country explorers. Not a dull building tour, but a traffic-free town where you can eat, drink (sarsaparilla for kids), ride a stagecoach, or get a haircut. The park headquarters has a stroller's map; (209)532-0150.

GROVELAND

LODGINGS

Berkshire Inn ★★ By the time you reach this Tudor-style B&B, you've climbed out of the foothills into the mountains. Your fellow guests at this quiet retreat may be boaters, golfers, or hikers bound for nearby Pine Mountain Lake recreation area or on to Yosemite. All of the six rooms and four suites have private entrances (some have decks) and access to the large gazebo to look over the countryside. Added benefits: complimentary wine and continental breakfast. ■ *2 miles E of Groveland at 19950 Hwy 120; (209) 962-6744; Mail: PO Box 207, Groveland, CA 95321; $; no credit cards; checks OK.*

Groveland Hotel ★ The original adobe structure is one of the Gold Country's oldest (circa 1849). The second building was put up some 65 years later as a rooming house. The property has been completely renovated to add an up-to-date conference center with restaurant, saloon, and health spa. Though they cater to execs with their eyes on the future, the owners have attempted to keep some of the charm of yesteryear. The 17 guest rooms aren't large, but the down comforters and private baths make them comfortable while European antiques render them appealing. ▪ *At 18767 Main St; (209) 962-4000; Mail: PO Box 289, Groveland, CA 95321; $$; beer and wine; AE, DC, MC, V; checks OK; lunch, dinner every day.*

Hotel Charlotte ★ Charlotte DeFerreri, an ambitious Italian immigrant, built this hotel in 1918, and soon afterward annexed a small store next door for her dining room. Here she served the men working on the Hetch Hetchy Water Project, a dam used to collect water for San Francisco's depleted supply after the 1906 fire. Today the roadside hotel serves gold-snoopers. Each of the 11 rooms is dressed up with an iron bedstead, lace curtains, and floral wallpaper; only six have private baths. Obviously, DeFerreri doesn't run the place any more, but perhaps it's in her memory that the current owners keep a number of Italian dishes on the menu alongside prime rib, pork chops, and chicken. ▪ *On Hwy 120 in Groveland at 19736 Main St; (209) 962-6455; Mail: PO Box 787, Groveland, CA 95321; $; beer and wine; AE, MC, V; checks OK; dinner Wed–Mon (every day in summer).*

MARIPOSA

The bell of the town clock in the two-story Mariposa County Courthouse has been marking time since 1866. Another hillside landmark is St. Joseph's Catholic Church, built in 1863; behind it lies the entrance to the Mariposa Mine, discovered by Kit Carson in 1849 and later purchased by John C. Fremont, who owned most of the land around these parts.

California Mining and Mineral Museum, the state's new geology center, is 2 miles south of town (5007 Fairgrounds Road). One wing holds 20,000 glittering gems and minerals; artifacts and photos in another tell the mining story. A model stamp mill whirls into action by a simple push of the button, and a mine shaft tour shows the inner workings. Open Wed–Mon in summer, Wed–Sun otherwise; (209) 742-7625.

A side trip off Highway 49 leads to **Hornitos,** "little ovens," a name which probably referred to the shape of the tombs on boot hill. This lawless burg, once a favorite haunt of bandito Joaquin Murieta, is nearly a ghost town. Weathered old buildings (saloons, fandango halls, and gambling dens) stand around the plaza; some carry bullet holes from bygone battles. Here too are the small jail and D. Ghirardelli & Co. store.

RESTAURANTS

Charles Street Dinner House ★★ The name's much more formal than the restaurant. Here the Old West reigns over both decor and food. Waitresses are dressed in period costume, looking like they might have stepped out of the historic photos on the wall. Although the offerings—steaks, chops, chicken, fresh seafood—are fairly pedestrian, the dishes are skillfully prepared and well presented. All dinners come with soup and salad; nightly specials might include broiled chicken breast, scampi, or prime rib. Complete wine list. Locals like it too, so reservations are advised for weekends. ■ *Hwy 140 and 7th St; (209) 966-2366; 5043 Charles St, Mariposa; $$; beer and wine; DIS, MC, V; local checks only; dinner Wed–Sun.*

LODGINGS

Mariposa Hotel Inn ★★ It's only fitting that this downtown hotel has once again become an inn since it first served stagecoach passengers in the early 1900s. Nicely restored in an Early American style complete with lace curtains, it has six rooms and baths. Guests enjoy coffee on the rear garden verandah overlooking the pines and the town's rooftops. ■ *At 5029 Hwy 140 (Charles St); (209) 966-4676; Mail: PO Box 745, Mariposa, CA 95338; $$; AE, MC, V; checks OK.*

▼

Mariposa

▲

Meadow Creek Ranch ★★ A stage stop in the 1850s, this old ranch house has been completely refurbished and enlarged by Bob and Carol Shockley to include a dining room with large windows overlooking a meadow. The three inside rooms share a bathroom, but the cozy cottage in back (a former chicken coop) is self-contained. Guests can wander around the water wheel and arbor and enjoy early morning coffee on the side patio. A hearty breakfast is served family style. ■ *About 11½ miles S on Hwy 49 at Triangle Rd and Hwy 49; (209) 966-3843; 2669 Triangle Rd, Mariposa, CA 95338; $$; AE, MC, V; checks OK.*

Oak Meadows Too ★★ Here's a slice of New England in Gold Country: a contemporary saltbox-style house filled with brass beds, quilts, and Early American furniture and six rooms. A wood-burning stove draws guests to the parlor in cool weather. A generous breakfast is served in a common room. ■ *Eastern edge of town on Hwy 140; (209) 742-6161; 5263 Hwy 140, Mariposa, CA 95338; $; MC, V; checks OK.*

Wondering about our standards? We rate establishments on value, performance measured against the place's goals, uniqueness, enjoyability, loyalty of clientele, cleanliness, excellence and ambition of the cooking, and professionalism of the service.

LODGINGS

Erna's Elderberry House ▪ Château du Sureau ★★★★

Vienna-born Erna Kubin-Clanin selected this Oakhurst hillside 8 years ago as the site for an establishment modeled on a country restaurant in Provence. Ever since she opened the Mediterranean-style dining room, her innovative cuisine has brought the elite of the culinary world to her doorstep. And ever since she built an opulent Provençal-style chateau on her 7½-acre estate, those in search of good food can also stay the night at Château du Sureau. Massive chandeliers and 19th-century paintings adorn the walls of the Elderberry House. Cathedral windows unveil grand Sierra views, but diners usually devote their attention to their food. Erna uses fresh, locally grown ingredients to create her culinary masterpieces. She and the sous chef get innovative with delicate sauces that never overwhelm the food. The six-course, prix-fixe dinners change every day; one recent sampling revealed a salmon appetizer in Madeira gelée in a pool of tarragon mayonnaise, followed by a delicate consommé, a dramatic array of salads, and a combination of pork, duck sausage, and veal schnitzel. Afterwards may come a fruit compote, or perhaps a sacher torte. Order a bottle of wine from an extensive list or by the glass to match the vintage to the course.

▼

Oakhurst

Lodgings

▲

The Château is a place like no other—and priced like no other—in the Gold Country, but romantics feel it's worth the $250–$350 a night splurge. All nine rooms in **Château du Sureau** are replete with antiques, Provençal fabrics, tapestries, and oil paintings. Snuggle under the goose down comforter in your canopied bed, pour a glass of wine, watch the fire, and listen to music you've selected for your stereo. The Thyme Room is equipped for the handicapped; Mint has a private entrance. A European-style breakfast is served in the cozy dining room or alfresco on the patio. Elsewhere on the grounds lie a fountain, a swimming pool, and an outdoor chess court with 3-foot tall pieces. There's even a small chapel where wedding bells sometimes ring. ▪ *Off Hwy 41 at 48688 Victoria Lane; (209) 683-6860 or (209) 683-6800; Mail: PO Box 577, Oakhurst, CA 93644; $$$; full bar; MC, V; checks OK; lunch Wed–Fri, dinner Wed–Mon, brunch Sun.*

Yosemite Gateway Inn ★

Set in a grove of oak trees, this Best Western motel is a good buy for families. Some of the 119 rooms have kitchens; most have cable TV and phones. Let the kids swim in the indoor or outdoor pools while you work out at the fitness center or do a load of wash in the laundry room. The Viewpoint Restaurant, (209) 683-5200, serves better food than what you'll usually find attached to a motel. Homebaked cinnamon rolls, tiny, warm loaves of honey wheat bread, and a large salad bar are some of the things that lift it a notch above commonplace. ■ *1 mile north of the intersection of Hwy 49 and Hwy 41; (209) 683-2378; 40530 Hwy 41, Oakhurst, CA 93644; $; AE, DC, DIS, MC, V; no checks.*

CENTRAL VALLEY

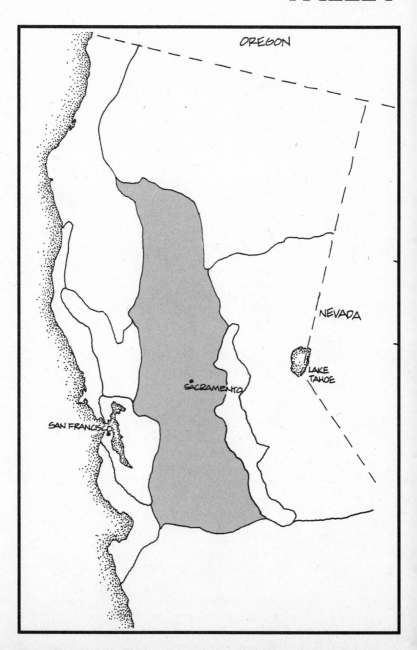

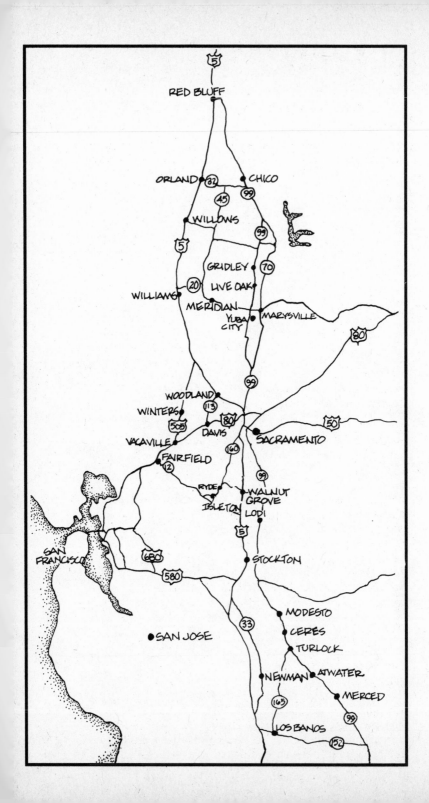

Central Valley

North from Los Banos along two major routes, I-5 and Hwy 99, with short side trips on I-80 to Davis and Vacaville.

LOS BANOS

Located between four major highways—Interstate 5 and highways 152, 33, and 165—Los Banos calls itself the "Crossroads of California." And, all PR aside, they're right. It's hard to drive through this sparsely populated part of the state without stopping for something—food, gas, a night's rest, or to use *los banos* (the bathrooms). Doughnut fans will want to stop in early at **Los Banos Donut Shop** (1024 Pacheco Boulevard at J Street, (209)826-0120). It's open from 2:30am to 1:30pm, but locals usually snap up all the goodies by noon. Nostalgia buffs will want to check out the soda fountain at **Los Banos Drugs** (601 J Street at 6th, (209) 826-5834) for an old-fashioned cherry phosphate, a real milk shake, or a tuna sandwich at the counter. If you've never seen a tule elk, visit the herd at **San Luis National Wildlife Refuge,** 8 miles north of Los Banos off Highway 165; (209) 826-0463. Boaters frolic at nearby **San Luis Reservoir** and **O'Neill Forebay** about 12 miles west.

RESTAURANTS

España's Mexican Restaurant ★★ Located on 19th-century cattle baron Henry Miller's Canal Farm Ranch, España's offers a full range of traditional Mexican specialties like grande burritos, enchiladas, tacos, and flautas, plus a small selection of steak, chicken, and seafood for philistines. Supplement the tame salsa with hefty nachos. Try the albondigas (Mexican meatball soup) or the delicate crab enchiladas, and don't forget to order up a pitcher of margaritas. If you're just passing through town, note that España's makes most of its entrées to go. ■ *Pacheco Blvd off Hwy 165; (209) 826-4041; 1460 E Pacheco Blvd, Los Banos; $; full bar; AE, DIS, MC, V; local checks only; lunch, dinner every day.*

Carlo's Restaurant ★ Though the menu at Carlo and Inez Colzani's old-fashioned dinner house is dominated by the usual surf-and-turf fare, their Italian specialties are noteworthy: the homemade manicotti stuffed with beef, the canneloni stuffed with veal, and the clam linguine—homemade noodles in white clam sauce, surrounded by a necklace of fresh clams. The fish here is fresh and very good. The catfish, boned at the table and topped with a delicate wine sauce, is a real treat. Carlo's is well-known for its extensive (and expensive) wine cellar, as well as for the big eucalyptus tree growing in the dining room.

■ *Pacheco Blvd (Hwy 152) at 4th St; (209) 826-2331; 400 Pacheco Blvd, Los Banos; $$; full bar; AE, MC, V; no checks; lunch, dinner every day.*

Wool Growers Restaurant ★ This old-time Basque restaurant, run by the Iturbide brothers, is a Los Banos institution. Don't expect anything fancy, just heaps of simple, hearty food. Meals always start with a steaming bowl of spicy vegetable soup served with a side of beans (which you can mix in with your soup if you like), a tossed green salad, and a lamb stew appetizer. *Then* comes the real dinner—steak, chicken, lamb chops, or prime rib with a side of fries or chicken-sautéed rice. Red wine (not the boutique variety) comes with your dinner. Finish up (if you can) with a vanilla ice cream cup or some Monterey Jack cheese. ■ *H St, between 6th and 7th, (209) 826-4593; 609 H St, Los Banos; $; full bar; no credit cards; no checks; lunch, dinner Tues–Sun.*

NEWMAN

RESTAURANTS

Marty's Inn A favorite on the west side of Stanislaus County, this rustic, wood-paneled steak house has a mellow, lodgelike atmosphere. Proprietors Leonard and Amelia Silvey serve a relish tray with fresh vegetables and a sour cream herb dip before every meal. Opt for steak or the steak sandwich—a generous slab of beef on a French roll. Marty's popular bar is well-stocked and the drinks are made to near-perfection. It offers a huge selection of icy margaritas—an excellent way to cool down at the end of a hot Big (aka Central) Valley day. ■ *Hwy 33, just S of Newman; (209) 862-1323; 29030 Hwy 33, Newman; $$; full bar; MC, V; checks OK; lunch Thurs–Fri, dinner Tues–Sun.*

MERCED

Thanks to its vigorous tree-planting efforts over the last 10 years, this agricultural burg has been named "Tree City USA" eight years in a row by the National Arbor Association. **Applegate Park,** a 23-acre greenbelt (between M and R streets) boasts over 60 varieties of trees, plus an immaculate rose garden and white gazebo. Kids like the park's free zoo (open daily) and amusement rides in the summer. For fresh produce gathered from local fields, check out the **farmers market** on Main Street between N and K streets or the innumerable fruit stands ringing the city. The best burgers in town can be had at **Sammy's** (corner of Main and I Street, (209) 722-4571); *muy athentico* tacos (and carnitas with lime) are available at the blue and silver **Taco El 2 Hermanos** van parked at the K-Mart store at the corner of J and 16th streets.

The Mansion House ★★ Despite its grand, white columns, brick facade, and broad verandah, Merced's best restaurant is a soothing, refreshingly unpretentious place. On weekends, soft, soulful, live jazz or acoustic guitar floats through the pink, white, and black dining rooms out onto the garden patio. Dinner begins with buttery mushroom soup and a light lettuce, spinach, and watercress salad in a creamy basil Italian dressing. The flavorful, fanned duck breast in a brandy-laced, apricot-orange sauce has just enough tang, but the breast of chicken might be a tad dry if not for the sprightly five-peppercorn sauce. The Mansion House is also a brunch favorite, highlighted by owner Heather Vann's spicy Oklahoma corn bread with whole corn kernels. Try the delicate sour cream and cream cheese blintzes or the cinnamon-dusted French toast with warm maple syrup. ■ *Canal and 20th; (209) 383-2744; 455 W 20th St, Merced; $$; full bar; AE, MC, V; local checks only; brunch Sun, lunch Mon–Fri, dinner Mon–Sat.*

Branding Iron Restaurant ★ This paean to the American Beef Council has delighted Mercedites for almost half a century, thanks in part to chef Bob Freitas, who's presided over the kitchen for the last 27 years. New owners Kara and Greg Parle have added to the Branding Iron's Old West ambience by decorating the rough-hewn redwood walls with registered brands from all over California. A thick cut of tender prime rib, seasoned with coarse ground pepper, garlic, whole rosemary, and whole thyme, doesn't need a drop of the creamy horseradish provided to give it flavor. The meal starts with a zippy and refreshing gazpacho, what passes for salad in beef country, and bubbling hot cheese bread. A small après-dinner sherbet comes with your meal. Those who haven't been satiated by the Iron's he-man portions can examine the well-stocked dessert tray. ■ *On 16th St beside Santa Fe Railway Depot; (209) 772-1822; 640 W 16th St, Merced; $$; full bar; AE, MC, V; local checks only; lunch Mon–Fri, dinner Mon–Sun.*

▼

Merced

Lodgings

▲

LODGINGS

Travelodge ★ Your best bet here is Russian hosts Anatol and Igor Shliapnikoff's Travelodge. Go for one of the minisuites with their attractive cherry-wood furnishings, brass lamps, and love-seat sofabeds. The bathrooms have large showers, sinks with makeup light mirrors, and a coffee-maker. All rooms have TVs with cable and HBO. There's even a pool—a must for those many sweltering days. ■ *E Childs exit off Hwy 99, just past highway patrol; (209) 723-3121; 2000 E Childs Ave, Merced, CA 95340; $; AE, MC, V; checks OK.*

ATWATER

RESTAURANTS

Out To Lunch ★★ Word got out a long time ago about the thick, luscious sandwiches on homemade bread that emerge from this little cottage with its wide verandah. Almost anything on the warm, moist, sweetly spiced zucchini bread is a good bet: try the fresh and crunchy cream cheese and veggie sandwich with cucumber, bell pepper, shredded carrot, avocado, and sprouts, or the zingy English muffin with sautéed mushrooms, Jack cheese, and smoky, crumbled bacon. There's no alcohol here, but there's no corkage fee either, so bring a cold bottle of gewürz and enjoy. ■ *Corner of Winton Way and Drakely, between Santa Fe and Hwy 99; (209) 357-1170; 1301 Winton Way, Atwater; $$; no alcohol; no credit cards; local checks only; lunch Mon–Fri, dinner Thurs.*

TURLOCK

RESTAURANTS

El Jardin ★★ If you ignore the Wells Fargo Bank sign across the street, you could mistake this for a cozy cantina on the plaza in Guadalajara. Located in a cottage with a porch across the front, El Jardin has a fragrant and colorful garden with several outdoor tables—*the* place to sit when the weather is right. This place is authentic—from the homemade salsa and tortillas to south-of-the-border prices. House specials are a Milanesa breaded beef fillet with green salsa, and a succulent pollo la parilla (grilled chicken breast). Para los ninos, the menu offers an enchilada, taco, burrito, or tostada with rice and beans that beats Happy Meal fast-food prices. Breakfast includes huevos rancheros, steak, chorizo scrambled eggs, and other Mexican favorites. Service is friendly and efficient. ■ *1 block W of Golden State Blvd, 1 block N of Main; (209) 632-0932; 409 E Olive, Turlock; $; beer and wine; MC, V; local checks only; breakfast, lunch, dinner every day.*

Trax Bar and Grill ★★ It's been full steam ahead since valley restaurant mogul Dan Costa (founder of the popular Velvet Creamery and Mallard's chains) took over this one-time railroad station. Dining rooms are located in the main station and two rail cars. Lined with booths, the rail cars are crowded and stuffy, so dine instead in the station with its original tile floors, leaded glass, and brass fixtures. A model train, complete with sound effects, runs around the wall above the hand-carved bar—the longest, and busiest, in town. Chef John Moody's soups are homemade, and the moderately priced dinners come with a choice of caesar or spinach salad. You can sample a little bit of everything on the wonderful grill of garlic-basted chicken, beef fillet, and salmon. The desserts, like the apple-caramel cheesecake, are so tempting that you'll want to sample them all—though the Chocolate Suicide may be your last. ■ *Main St between Golden State Blvd and Broadway; (209) 668-8729; 10 E Main St, Turlock; $$; full bar; AE, MC, V; local checks only; lunch Mon–Fri, dinner Mon–Sat.*

CERES

RESTAURANTS

Max's Fifth Street Cafe ★★★ Diners from all around Stanislaus County mob this chic little storefront cafe. Chef/owner Randall Hoff makes everything on the menu in-house, including the bread. He has a special knack for soups and appetizers, like the richly flavored buffalo sausage appetizer with sliced apples and a savory whiskey barbecue sauce. Minestrone and New England clam chowder are always on the seasonal menu, but keep your eye out for his special soups like stracciatella (Roman egg soup with spinach), cream of pistachio, or a cool strawberry soup. Hoff's six-cheese lasagne is the best around. For dessert, the caramel-cranberry walnut tart with a Belgian chocolate glaze is a singularly sinful concoction. You can also get wines by the glass from some of California's best small wineries—and good espressos, too. ■ *In the shadow of Hwy 99 at the Central Ceres exit; (209) 538-1438; 3052 5th St, Ceres; $$; beer and wine; MC, V; checks OK; lunch Mon–Fri, dinner Mon–Sat.*

La Morenita ★ The restaurant that brought fajitas to the Modesto area still serves the best—chicken or beef, with fresh tomato and peppers seasoned just right in a sizzling cast-iron skillet and ready to roll up in a fresh-baked tortilla. The menu's more traditional items, like sopes and flautas, are outstanding, but the menu also features less familiar south-of-the-border specials such as chicken mole, Mexican chicken salad, breaded shrimp with guacamole, or a Milanesa beef filet with green salsa and guacamole. Serapes, sombreros, and friendly waitresses in embroidered peasant dresses add authenticity. Chilled beer mugs and at least two kinds of salsa for dipping chips are the frosting on the enchilada. ¡Ole! ■ *From Hwy 99 take Hatch Rd exit; (209) 537-7900; 1410 E Hatch Rd, Ceres; $; beer and wine; MC, V; local checks only; lunch, dinner every day.*

MODESTO

RESTAURANTS

Benni's ★★ Benni's was once an old Foster's Freeze—and it still looks it, what with the chrome tables and Naugahyde benches lining one side of the restaurant; on the other side, an old enameled metal stove keeps a plastic-enclosed patio area warm on all but the chilliest evenings. Chef Chris Bonora specializes in old country Italian food, like mostaccioli—fat pasta rounds in a fresh tomato-onion sauce with tender braised lamb. This is satisfying fare: homemade pastas in savory tomato, pesto, or cream sauces, garden fresh minestrone, and chubby sausage and mozzarella sandwiches. Bonora makes his own desserts, including poppyseed cake with a mascarpone center, ginger-mascarpone cheesecake, and bread pudding. ■ *1½ miles E of Hwy 99, corner of Santa Ana Ave (Hwy 132); (209) 571-3657; 1105 Yosemite Blvd, Modesto; $$; beer and wine; MC, V; local checks only; lunch Tues–Fri, dinner Tues–Sat.*

Farmer's Catfish House ★★ A down-home dish of catfish is somewhat trendy in these frugal days, but Tom Watkins has been serving it at his little country crossroads diner since 1981. The catfish special is a pair of large and meaty fish breaded with corn meal and fried up light and tender (deboned if you wish). The dirty rice with chicken and pork chunks and Cajun seasonings comes from Watkins' Mississippi grandmother's recipe file. Daring diners can feast on a picante stew of Mississippi farm-grown alligator. Tables are set with tin plates, and the friendly waitresses dish up crisp hush puppies, french fries, and coleslaw as soon as diners are seated. Watkins' peach, boysenberry, and apple cobblers are legendary. The small wine list includes a reasonably priced selection of California's most honored boutique vintners. ■ *From Hwy 99 take the Standiford off-ramp (Standiford becomes Beckwith west of the freeway), go 2 miles W; (209) 526-0969; 4937 Beckwith Rd, Modesto; $$; beer and wine; AE, MC, V; checks OK; dinner Tues–Sun.*

Hazel's ★★ This old house, converted 30 years ago to a restaurant, is wonderfully romantic—candle-lit in the evening and with nice views of the rose garden from window seats during the day. New owner Jeff Morey, a graduate of the California Culinary Academy, maintains Hazel Saylor's time-tested menu; dishes as simple as liver and onions with sautéed mushrooms and as deluxe as the rich lobster Macedonia. Hazel's canneloni, prepared from the original recipe, is still a lunchtime favorite. It takes a hearty appetite to savor all seven courses. There's an excellent wine list, reasonably priced, with many by-the-glass selections. A hometown favorite where reservations on Fridays and Saturdays are almost always a must. ■ *On 12th St, between E and F streets; (209) 578-3463; 513 12th St, Modesto; $$$; full bar; AE, DC, MC, V; checks OK; lunch Tues–Fri, dinner Tues–Sat.*

Opus 13 ★ Classical music filters through the soothing dining room decorated with musical instruments. Homemade soups, fresh-baked breads, and desserts have long been Opus 13's stock in trade, but its recently expanded repertoire includes "hot rock" cooking—teriyaki chicken, beef in a lemon-garlic marinade, or prawns with mint and tomato chutney grilled at the table on a hot granite stone. Dramatic and fun. For breakfast, try the ebelskiber—a fluffy but rich Danish concoction made with buttermilk and sour cream that looks like a spherical pancake. ■ *McHenry Ave, just N of J St and the center of town; (209) 576-7508; 421 McHenry Ave, Modesto; $; beer and wine; AE, DC, MC, V; local checks only; breakfast, lunch, every day.*

STOCKTON

The birthplace of Caterpillar tractor inventor Benjamin Holt, Stockton used to be a blue-collar town and the home to a multicultural mix of European, Mexican, and Asian immigrants who worked in the fields, stockyards, and at the docks. Thanks to the **Deep Water Channel** dredged during the 1930s, this inland city is also an international seaport. Stockton has been growing by leaps and bounds over the last 10 years. Despite suburbanization, agriculture is still king. From April to October, **fruit stands** dot the roadsides. You can also get fresh produce at Stockton's two **farmers markets**: the market at El Dorado and San Joaquin streets operates year round from 7am to noon; the other operates from May to December on Sundays and Thursdays from 9am to 1pm in the parking lot at the Mall at Weberstown at March Lane and Pacific Avenue.

Museums The Haggin Museum is devoted primarily to 19th-century French and American art and a 4,000-year-old Egyptian mummy; 1201 N Pershing, (209) 462-4116. Kids explore a cityscape, a minihospital, and a police car at the **The Children's Museum;** 420 Webster at the Waterfront, (209) 952-0924.

RESTAURANTS

Bagatelle Restaurant ★★ California-French cuisine, fine presentation, and charming south-of-France decor make Bagatelle the best restaurant in Stockton. The food here is clearly

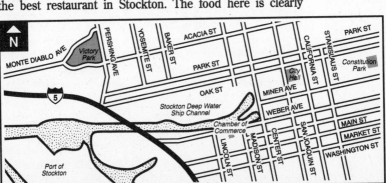

prepared with care; consider the nicely seasoned Alaskan halibut in a light white wine sauce and the seafood fettuccine, perfectly al dente, with chunks of grilled fish and scallops. Dine in one of two pleasant dining rooms—one with salmon-pink walls and a delicate hand-painted floral border, the other with wood paneling, hand-sponged walls with grape leaf stenciling, and a wall-length wine rack. There's a wonderfully intimate wine bar in the front of the restaurant. ■ *Pacific Ave and Benjamin Holt Dr in Lincoln Center; (209) 473-3227; 295 Lincoln Center, Stockton; $$$; beer and wine; AE, DIS, MC, V; local checks only; lunch Tues–Fri, dinner Tues–Sun.*

The Breadfruit Tree ★★ At this Caribbean cafe on the Paradise Point Marina, the daily menu depends on the whims of the cooks. Such good vibrations might produce chicken or fish roti, goat curry, shrimp palau with rice and vegetables, or Bajan chicken—a Barbados specialty with fresh thyme, marjoram, and hot peppers. Desserts include bread pudding, chocolate fudge rum cake, and pecan upside-down cake—all served with ice cream. Don't leave without trying the swonk—a spiced iced tea concoction handed down from co-owner Louis Bynoe's father. During the summer, a reggae band plays for the Breadfruit Tree's outdoor barbecues every other Saturday. ■ *From I-5 take 8 Mile Rd W 4 miles to Paradise Pt Marina; (209) 952-1000; 8095 Rio Blanco Rd, Stockton; $; beer and wine; no credit cards; local checks only; breakfast, lunch, dinner Wed–Mon.*

Nena's Restaurant ★ Owner Maria Elena Reves (called Nena) came to California as a farmworker from Mexico. Not content with picking tomatoes the rest of her life, she and her husband Jesus saved their money and opened Nena's Cafe, a tiny place on Stockton's south side. Extremely popular with Stockton's large Latino population, Nena's was an instant hit. People queued up outside for the weekend specials—menudo and pozole. Now in a larger central Stockton location, Nena's is still drawing crowds. They come for the saucy stews (machaca, chile verde, and chicana) and the birria (shredded beef, goat, or lamb simmered for hours in a thin, spicy barbecue sauce and wrapped in steamed corn tortillas). Even the margaritas are about as authentic as you can get. ■ *Corner of Waterloo Rd and Solari; (209) 547-0217; 1064 E Waterloo Rd, Stockton; $; beer and wine; AE, DIS, MC, V; local checks only; breakfast, lunch, dinner every day.*

Primavera Ristorante ★ Anna and Franceso Piccione's formal Italian restaurant is very traditional—linen tablecloths, candlelight, and waiters spouting Italian accents. Anna makes most of the pasta herself, including the gnocchi, tagliatelle, and fettuccine. Particularly good is the seafood tagliatelle with morsels of salmon; scallops in a white cream sauce; and the spinach fettuccine with a piquant tomato sauce. ■ *In Lincoln Center at Benjamin Holt Dr and Pacific Ave; (209) 477-6128; 856 W Benjamin Holt Dr, Stockton; $$; beer and wine; AE, MC, V; no checks; lunch, dinner Tues–Sun.*

Yen Ching ★ In spite of the neat Chinese wall carvings and bright red partitions, no one comes here for the decor. They come instead for the authentic Shandong steamed bread, dumplings, noodles, and various meat dishes perfected by former owner Kin Fo Ju (a native of China's Shandong province) and now carried on by his sons Billy, Jack, and Tom. They come also for the hot spiced string beans, eggplant with garlic sauce, the house chicken (crunchy bites of batter-fried chicken in a sweet and spicy sauce with vegetables) and the hot braised fish à la Yen Ching (a whole fish sautéed with green onions in a ginger sauce). ■ *Lincoln Center at Pacific Ave and Benjamin Holt Dr; (209) 957-0913; 6511 Pacific Ave, Stockton; $; beer and wine; MC, V; no checks; lunch, dinner Tues–Sun.*

Yoneda's Japanese Restaurant ★ Kunio Yoneda takes great pride in his culinary ancestry. Born into a family of chefs, he attended the Tsugi Cooking School in Osaka. His own restaurant sits in a modern shopping center on the outskirts of town. The dining room retains a touch of old Japan (Japanese swords, silk wall hangings, and colorful paper lanterns dangling behind the sushi counter). Yoneda has a wide selection of sparklingly fresh sushi (including salmon, mackerel, squid, yellowtail, and tuna). There is also the traditional sukiyaki, tempura, sashimi, and teriyaki and a good selection of vegetarian dinners. ■ *Calaveras Square shopping center on March and West lanes; (209) 477-1667; 1101 E March Lane, Stockton; $; beer and wine; AE, MC, V; no checks; lunch Tues–Fri, dinner Tues–Sun.*

Catfish Cafe This floating restaurant at the edge of Stockton's Deep Water Channel is a favorite with delta boaters who arrive at the restaurant's private dock in droves. Ships from all over the world sail in and out of the Port of Stockton and are visible from the outside patio; inside, a chic, warehouse interior is bright and modern, with large windows facing the channel and a high, steel-beam ceiling. The specialty (surprise!) is catfish—fried in beer batter or blackened (the better choice). The service is often slow, however, so go with some time on your hands. ■ *Take Pershing Ave exit from I-5 N or Oak St exit from I-5 S; (209) 466-2622; 1560 W Fremont, Stockton; $$; full bar; AE, MC, V; no checks; lunch, dinner every day.*

LODGINGS

The Old Victorian Inn ★★ Not much has changed inside this Queen Anne Victorian since it was built in 1890. Much of the original furniture still remains, mixed in with the other antiques amassed by owner Rex Buethe. The inn has a number of very fine collector pieces—copper bathtubs, turn-of-the-century chandeliers, and marble-topped tables. The first floor, with its tall ceilings and dusty-pink carpeting, has a large drawing room and two dining rooms. The most impressive room is the third-floor Grand Gable Suite, which has its own sitting room, two bedrooms, a private bath, and French doors that open out onto a balcony overlooking the patio. Families should request the two-bedroom carriage house. Protected from street noise, the suites are generally quieter than the standard rooms. ■ *Corner of Acacia and Madison (take Pershing Ave or Oak St exit off I-5); (209) 462-1613; 207 W Acacia St, Stockton, CA 95203; $$$; V; checks OK (closed mid-Dec–Jan).*

Stockton Hilton ★ Tucked away in a quiet corner of Stockton, this spacious Hilton looks out over a series of man-made canals that gurgle pleasantly night and day. The five-story hotel is nothing special though the rooms are spacious. The executive rooms on the south side of the hotel have small balconies. Guests can relax in the pool or Jacuzzi, or rev up in the athletic club across the street. ■ *E of I-5 off March Lane exit, (209) 957-9090, toll free (800) 444-9094 in California; 2323 Grand Canal Blvd, Stockton, CA 95207; $$$; full bar; AE, DC, MC, V; checks OK; breakfast, lunch, dinner every day.*

LODI

RESTAURANTS

Paprika Restaurant ★★ Walking into Paprika is like taking a short trip to Eastern Europe (via a mini-mall). Carl and Elizabeth Lehner and their son Carl Jr. have managed to impart old country Hungarian charm to their small place. Carl Sr., debonair as ever in his black or maroon tuxedo, dispenses advice about the food (and perhaps a few words about politics). Be sure to order some of the langos (soft sticks of bread, redolent of garlic). The very-Hungarian cuisine here ranges from chicken paprika (with homemade noodles) to stuffed cabbage rolls. Try the Hungarian gulyas (a saucy concoction of beef and homemade noodles). ■ *At English-Oak Plaza on the corner of Harney Lane and Hutchins St; (209) 368-2925; 523 W Harney Lane, Lodi; $$; beer and wine; AE, MC, V; local checks only; dinner Wed–Sun.*

LODGINGS

Wine & Roses Country Inn ★★★ If the Wine & Roses Country Inn had existed in the 1960s, Creedence Clearwater Revival would never have sung "Stuck in Lodi Again." This ivy-covered 1902 farmhouse is surrounded by five acres of cherry trees, rose gardens, and towering deodora pines, and

innkeeper Kris Cromwell has seen to it that flowers and lace abound upstairs and down. The inn's 10 guest rooms (named after songs) have queen-size beds, turn-of-the-century decor, handmade comforters, and fresh flowers. "White Lace and Promises" is a two-room honeymoon suite with a terrace and French doors. In a rose-toned sitting room downstairs, camel-back couches and wingback chairs cluster around the wide fireplace that always has a fire burning in the winter. Kris's daughter-in-law Sherri, a graduate of the Culinary Academy of San Francisco, delights in putting fresh edible flowers in your morning meal. Oh, let's get stuck in Lodi one more night..
■ *E of I-5 or W of Hwy 99; Turner Rd exit; (209) 334-6988; 2505 W Turner Rd, Lodi, CA 95242; $$; full bar; AE, MC, V; checks OK; breakfast every day, lunch Tues–Fri, dinner Wed–Sat.*

SACRAMENTO RIVER DELTA

Flat as a flour tortilla, the Sacramento River Delta is made up of thousands of miles of rivers, canals, and sloughs, snaking through tule grass and farmland. Kept at bay by massive lev-ees, most of the rivers are slightly higher than the surround-ing farmland—all diked and drained former wetlands. The delta contains half the fresh water runoff in California, though by the time it meanders through the valley's agribusiness,its freshness is somewhat debatable. The delta is dotted with quaint, old-fashioned little island towns connected by draw-bridges and ferries. The best (and priciest) Sunday brunch in the delta is at the **Grand Island Mansion,** a Gatsby-esque wonder with 58 rooms, including a private bowling alley and cinema. (West end of Grand Island, 3 miles west of Highway 160 at 13415 Grand Island Road, (916) 775-1705). To experi-ence the real delta, rent a houseboat and meander for a few days. Houseboats can be rented at **Herman and Helen's Ma-rina,** off 8 Mile Road north of Stockton, (209) 951-4634, **Par-adise Point Marina,** 8095 N Rio Blanco Road, (209)952-1000, or **King Island Resort,** 11530 W 8 Mile Road, (209) 956-5209.

RYDE

LODGINGS

The Grand Island Inn ★★ Built as a speakeasy during Prohi-bition, this four-story, pink stucco inn on the banks of the Sacra-mento River harks back to the days when roadsters filled with flappers bounced down the delta's dusty roads in search of il-licit liquor and jazz. The inn's 24 pink and gray rooms come with or without private baths. The 209–210 suite (only $80) has a small separate sitting room and wonderful views of pear or-chards and the Sacramento River. The Master Suite at the front of the hotel overlooks the river and flower garden. ■ *3 miles S of Walnut Grove at 14340 Hwy 160; (916) 776-1318; Mail: PO Box 43, Ryde, CA 95680; $$; full bar;' MC, V; no checks; dinner Fri–Sat, brunch Sun April–Oct.*

WALNUT GROVE

RESTAURANTS

Giusti's Egisto Giusti opened this restaurant in 1910 after immigrating from Lucca, Italy. Today you'll find his grandson Mark Morias continuing the family tradition of good food served in an old-fashioned, laid-back atmosphere. Except for the the 1,500 baseball caps hanging from the ceiling, Guisti's looks like it's been frozen in suspended animation for the last 50 years. You're in luck if you arrive on a Thursday—Italian food night. Mark's wife Linda makes a wonderfully rich, Italian sausage lasagne and a linguine with clam sauce topped with fresh steamed cockles or New Zealand clams. ■ *4 miles W of I-5; (916) 776-1808; 14743 Walnut Grove, Walnut Grove; $; full bar; no credit cards; checks OK; lunch, dinner Tues–Sun, brunch Sun.*

▼
Ryde

Lodgings

▲

ISLETON

RESTAURANTS

Moore's Riverboat ★ This 1931 riverboat is a popular watering hole for river rats and delta residents. The bar looks out over the Mokelumne River, but the real eye-catchers are the hundreds of women's panties hanging above the bar, contributed by fun-loving (or merely inebriated) female clientele. Moore's Riverboat is just as popular for eating as it is for drinking and lingerie watching. Check out the crawdads, served cold in the shell with a fiery chile sauce, the steamed clams with butter and garlic, or the chicken breast covered with sautéed mushrooms, onions, and bell peppers, and topped with Jack cheese. ■ *Off Hwy 12, cross the Mokelumne River Bridge, take 1st right, continue 3½ miles with the levee on the left; (916) 777-6545; 106 W Brannan Island Rd, Isleton; $$; full bar; MC, V; no checks; breakfast Sat–Sun, lunch Fri–Sun, dinner Tues–Sun.*

SACRAMENTO

To the eternal chagrin of residents (and to the self-satisfied glee of everyone else), Sacramento has long been regarded as the déclassé stepsister of San Francisco. Located 90 miles northeast of the Bay area, Sacramento's primary claim to fame is its dual status as the seat of state government and the epicenter of California's biggest industry: agriculture. Neither of

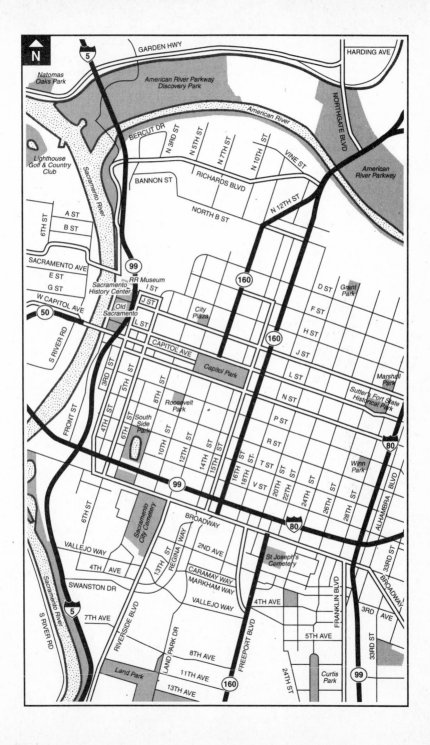

these, alas, has ever been a landmark of culture. But as the city and the state's population have grown, so has Sacramento's appeal. Century-old houses have been refurbished and the once derelict K Street shopping district has been transformed into an attractive, thriving pedestrian mall (complete with light rail). Its streets are so heavily lined with trees that from above it looks like a forest. On the ground, this foliage forms a virtual canopy over the streets, overarching to meet in the middle to form a lush, protective canopy against the summer heat. Architecturally, Sacramento boasts some of the state's most spectacular Victorian homes, as well as many sprawling Craftsman bungalow homes that make this river city feel more Deep South than California.

Stroll down **Capitol Avenue** between 16th and 28th streets and you'll see some of the area's most lavish mansions, as well as a lively coffeehouse scene punctuated by several excellent bookstores and restaurants. Nearby you'll find the recently restored Capitol Building and Capitol Park, which, in winter, when the camellias burst into bloom, is pure pleasure.

Old Sacramento, the historic district along the waterfront, is a tacky tourist trap; avoid it. There are, however, two worthy attractions: the **Sacramento History Museum** (101 I Street, (916) 264-7057), which mounts a continuous series of well-curated ethnic exhibits, and the **Railroad Museum** (111 I Street, (916) 445-7387), the largest of its type in North America.

Coffee and dessert fans should make a beeline for **New Helvetia Roasters and Bakers** (1215 19th Street, (916) 441-1106). This renovated firehouse turns out a wide array of goodies well worth blowing a diet for. You might also want to check out **Weatherstone Coffee & Trading Co** (812 21st Street, (916) 443-6340), Sacramento's original bohemian coffeehouse.

Music The **Sacramento Community Convention Center** (1421 K Street, (916) 264-7777) is a regular venue for the local symphony, as well as big-name jazz, classical, and dance troupes. **Sam's** (1630 J Street, (916) 441-4113) is one of the premier blues venues in Northern California; Also, the **Crest Theatre** (1013 K Street, (916) 442-7378), a refurbished art deco palace, features top-name rock, folk, reggae, and World Beat stars as well as classic movies.

Art The **Crocker Museum** (216 O Street, (916) 264-5423), besides being the most elaborate, ostentatious Victorian structure in the region, is also home to Sacramento's largest collection of historic Western art, as well as ongoing exhibitions of contemporary California art stars. The **Center for Contemporary Art** (1116 15th Street, (916) 448-6269), a recent addition, specializes in cutting-edge artists of international repute, as well as West Coast heavyweights that you won't see anyplace else. As for galleries, the ones worth seeking out are: **Judith Weintraub Gallery** (1723 J Street, (916) 442-3360),

Michael Himovitz (1020 10th Street, (916) 448-8723), Solomon Dubnick (2131 Northrop Avenue, (916) 920-4547), and Jennifer Pauls (1825 Q Street, (916) 448-4039).

Theater No West Coast city of comparable size has a more thriving theater scene than Sacramento. Of late it has been likened to Seattle, and for good reason, as it has a dozen professional performing arts organizations, the best of which are: the **Sacramento Theater Company** (1419 H Street, (916) 446-7501), **The Show Below** (2130 L Street, (916) 446-2787), **B Street Theater** (2711 B Street, (916) 443-5300), and the **California Stage Company** (2509 R Street, (916) 451-5822).

Parks With its **Vietnam Veterans' Memorial**, its cactus and rose gardens, and its profusion of camellias (not to mention the Capitol itself), **Capitol Park** is clearly the centerpiece of downtown Sacramento, followed closely by **McKinley Park**, which features an even more elaborate rose garden as well as tennis courts, a swimming pool, and lots of open space. **William Land Park** is where you'll find the city's zoo.

Recreation For cyclists and joggers, nothing beats the **Bike Trail.** It's more than 22.5 miles of pothole-free, unbroken pavement which run along the American River from Discovery Park to Folsom. Every summer the **State Fair at Cal Expo** offers one of the greatest assemblages of lowbrow entertainment in Northern California.

RESTAURANTS

Biba ★★★★ Biba is a study in understated neo-deco design—the sort of place where you'd expect precious, trendy foods to dominate the menu. Fortunately, they don't. Bologna-born chef/owner Biba Caggiano is a traditionalist to the core, and what comes out of her kitchen is exactly what she learned at her mother's elbow—no-frills cooking based on the finest ingredients available and a painstaking attention to detail: grilled shrimp wrapped in basil and Parma ham, a melt-in-your-mouth nutmeg and ricotta tortelloni, angel hair pasta with sun-dried tomatoes, a phenomenal shrimp-studded linguine, a salad of roasted red peppers and grilled eggplant, duck cooked in port and Italian cherries, rosemary-infused lamb chops. For dessert, try the rich strawberry zabaglione (which you have to ask for, since it isn't listed on the menu). Another thing we've come to admire about Biba is her uncanny ability to transform seemingly mundane side dishes—such as carrots, snap peas, mashed potatoes, and white beans—into star attractions. If that weren't enough (and for Biba it isn't), service is superb, the kitchen is consistent, and the list of wines (both domestic and foreign) is long and well-chosen. ■ *Corner of 28th St and Capitol Ave; (916) 455-2422; 2801 Capitol Ave, Sacramento; $$$; full bar; AE, MC, V; no checks; lunch Mon–Fri; dinner Mon–Sat.*

Capitol Grill ★★★ Few legislative hangouts cater so overtly to the political instincts as Capitol Grill. On brick walls, posters of past campaigns conjure all kinds of memories: of Ike's avuncular countenance, Jerry Brown's smartass smirk, and Richard Nixon's sinister leer, to name but a few. Beneath these relics, customers—most of them lawyerly types in pinstripes and suspenders—dine comfortably in full view of a street corner overrun by expensive foreign cars. The good news is that now, unlike before, Capitol Grill is a terrific place to eat. Last year, owner Randy Paragary took in chefs Doyle Bailey and Kurt Spataro as partners, and the result has been a complete transformation. Bland bar fare has given way to an internationally tinged menu of high California standards, distinguished by freshness, flavor, and a refreshing absence of hype. What's more, prices are fair, and the service is educated and efficient. The house-smoked salmon appetizer alone makes Capitol Grill worth visiting. Grilled salmon, large-portioned and fork-tender, arrives atop a light tomato-basil sauce, while yellowfin tuna comes grilled to perfection with only salt, butter, and lemon, delicious in its own juices. Pan-fried sea scallops with angel hair pasta is a case study in culinary synergy: the sweetness of the fish, the sourness of lemon, the tang of Italian parsley, and the unifying pull of garlic produce what may well be Capitol's signature dish. Desserts are equally spectacular. The wine list here is far too thin for a restaurant of this quality, but that's a small gripe. Capitol Grill in its current incarnation ranks among Sacramento's best restaurants—and its two new chefs are destined for glory. ■ *Corner of 28th and N streets, (916) 736-0744; 2730 N St, Sacramento; $$; full bar; AE, DC, MC, V; checks OK; lunch, dinner every day.*

Greta's Cafe ★★★ Greta Garverick has done the impossible: she's proven that healthful, organic-leaning food needn't taste like the toothsome horsefeed we loathed back in the '60s. No sandwich and salad joint we can think of offers better food for better value. The food is fresh, delicious, sophisticated, and large-portioned, and the prices are embarrassingly low. Which is why, at peak hours, Greta's is jam-packed and loud—thanks also to its uncarpeted warehouse-style floors and ceiling, which amplify conversation to the point of din. No matter. Sandwiches filled with premium-grade meat on fresh-baked breads, and well-crafted salads keep the room filled at all hours. ■ *Corner of 19th St and Capitol Ave; (916) 442-7382; 1831 Capitol Ave, Sacramento; $; no alcohol; no credit cards; checks OK; lunch every day, dinner Tues–Sun.*

Alex Restaurant ★★ Stationed in a long, rectangular storefront done up loft-style (with exposed bricks, ceiling fans, and painted air ducts), this brand-new, low-key establishment offers the best seafood in the valley. Granted, such superlatives may not mean much in a fish-poor, inland city such as this; but the truth of the matter is that Alex, on the strength of its cooking, would be a star anywhere. Whom to thank? Jacques Rousseau, former chef of the much-vaunted (now defunct) Koyas, whose Gallic roots are felt in a bouillabaisse-like cioppino that's rich in shellfish, calamari, clams, and whitefish; in garlicky cream-sauced pastas; and in a variety of fresh, grilled fish offerings with sauces that never challenge the essential flavor of what's beneath. As for Alex's raw bar, the oysters, clams, and crab dispensed are as fresh as one could hope for. Breakfasts get the same meticulous treatment, particularly seafood omelets and lox. Alex's service was a little shaky to start, but given the owner's track record throughout the Bay area, we don't expect this problem to last. ■ *Between 18th and 19th streets; (916) 446-1430; 1806 Capitol Ave, Sacramento; $$; liquor license pending; AE, MC, V; no checks; breakfast every day, lunch Mon–Sat, dinner Thurs–Sat, brunch Sun.*

Cafe Marika ★★ At Cafe Marika the simple home cooking relies heavily on a formula that Hungarians perfected long ago: namely, paprika, paprika, and more paprika. This uncomplicated approach has bred a certain perfection and dexterity in Marika's Czechoslovakian-born owners, Eva and Louie Chruma. Chef Louie, for example, stirs, smiles, loads plates, and greets customers by name—all without breaking a sweat. Eva, his slender, statuesque wife, who functions as waitress and hostess, moves about looking more like a bohemian poet than the proprietress of a Hungarian diner. Incongruities aside, Cafe Marika is the best lunch bargain in midtown. The chicken Budapest is fork tender and ever satisfying. Marika's spectacular stuffed cabbage rolls, not available at lunch, are filled with pork tenderloin and rice and cooked to delectable effect in sauerkraut and paprika juice. Amazingly, these creations compare favorably to real old-country food by those in the know. ■ *Between 20th and 21st streets; (916) 442-0405; 2011 J St, Sacramento; $; beer and wine; no credit cards; local checks only; lunch Mon–Fri, dinner Thurs–Sat.*

Maharani India Restaurant ★★ On the tawdry stretch of Broadway where cruising teenagers reenact scenes from *American Graffiti,* Maharani stands out like an oasis. Under the watchful eye of owner Darsham Gidha, Maharani creates fresh, authentic, Northern Indian cuisine—meats cooked in a real tandoor oven over mesquite; 10 clean, well-defined curries; and 6 different Indian breads. Service borders on angelic. Wonderful tandoori chicken, slathered in a heavily spiced yogurt marinade and grilled, sizzles on an iron platter garnished with green peppers and onions. Saag paneer (a puréed, curried spinach concoction studded with chunks of firm, handmade cheese) scores equally high in flavor. Lastly, there is the wholly unique Maharani special chicken: cubes of dark meat

Sacramento

Restaurants

suspended in a light, creamed curry sauce enlivened with fenugreek. Golden Eagle beer, a sweet Indian brew, cures the heat of curry. ■ *At 18th St; (916) 441-2172; 1728 Broadway, Sacramento; $; beer and wine; AE, MC, V; no checks; lunch buffet Mon–Fri, dinner every day.*

Pennisi's Cafe ★★ Anyone seeking the attention of lobbyists in California need only check in at Pennisi's, a light-filled, Mediterranean-style restaurant at the base of the K Street mall. There, beneath slow-moving fans, you'll find lobbyists, lawyers, and legislators dining on Chicago pastrami sandwiches, meat-stuffed tortellinis (smothered in puréed artichoke hearts, peppers, and garlic-cream sauce), and unadorned but perfectly grilled chunks of fresh sea bass. Chef Clyde Sadler fuses Greek and northern Italian sensibilities, applying a light, masterful touch to fresh ingredients. For breakfast, eggs Florentine, prosciutto omelets (with rosemary-infused home-fries) and French toast (bathed in sweet batter and rolled in cornflakes) are smash hits. Also to Sadler's and owner Bill Morris' credit, Pennisi's stocks a small but expertly chosen selection of California wines, several of which are available by the glass. ■ *At 11th St; (916) 446-6988; 1030 J St, Sacramento; $$; beer and wine; AE, MC, V; no checks; breakfast, lunch Mon–Fri.*

Kagetsu Japanese Restaurant ★ Don't be put off by Kagetsu's down-at-the-heels appearance. This is a good restaurant in deep disguise—a strictly proletarian joint where globe-trotting Japanese businessmen wouldn't be caught dead. Hence, there's no raw bar with an encyclopedic stock of fish. Instead, Katsu Inanaga limits his sashimi offering to tuna (consistently fresh), but mostly serves standard Japanese coffeehouse items: teriyaki, sukiyaki, tempura, and noodles, all of which are delivered with friendly dispatch and aplomb. The sweetly sauced sesame chicken is habit-forming. ■ *Between 16th and 17th streets; (916) 446-0993; 1628 Broadway, Sacramento; $; beer and wine; MC, V; local checks only; lunch Tues–Fri; dinner Tues–Sat.*

Sal's Tacos ★ With its big booths, wrought-iron fixtures, Mexican textiles, plastic plants, and authentic food, Sal's is the kind of taqueria Californians dream of when they're out of state. It's a local shrine disguised as a Mexican soul food kitchen where farm laborers, state workers, cops, retirees, artists, and families gather to pay homage. Be sure to take advantage of what may well be the world's best salsa bar. Here devotees dredge up 10 or so sauces made from tomatoes, chiles, and onions roasted over an open flame. Slathered over entrées, these fiendishly simple concoctions produce a boggling array of taste sensations. Chicken fajitas—a Texas-size portion—spell love at first bite. For smaller appetites, Sal's has feather-light chile rellenos in a fresh tomato-oregano sauce, and cheese enchiladas. There's a full complement of Mexican and American beers, and on the tape deck, a rousing selection of norteños, rancheros, and oldies. ■ *Across the I St Bridge; (916) 454-9404; 400 C St, Sacramento; $; beer only; no credit cards; checks OK; lunch, dinner every day.*

Tower International Cafe ★ When Jim Seyman transformed the long-defunct Tower Drugstore into a restaurant, he scored a great coup: a restaurant stationed next to the Tower Theater, one of the capital's most cherished landmarks. The result is a North African–style cafe whose wraparound windows offer a grand view of Broadway's human parade. The interior is filled with an eclectic collection of art objects from Africa, Asia, and Mexico that somehow manage to work together. Unfortunately, the same can't be said of everything on chef Glenn Weddell's pan-national menu. Fortunately, among the culinary clunkers (pastas and omelets) there are some truly outstanding dishes that keep us coming back: the Brazilian chicken salad studded with large chunks of white meat and fresh papaya; the big, juicy burgers; the pungent Nicaraguan black bean soup, and the French toast served at brunch. Service in this noisy place roams from razor-sharp to neglectful. ■ *Between 15th St and Land Park Dr; (916) 441-0222; 1518 Broadway, Sacramento; $; beer and wine; AE, MC, V; no checks; breakfast, lunch, dinner every day, brunch Sat, Sun.*

Pescados Mexican Restaurant A stone's throw from the highway, this brightly painted, LA-inspired taco bar is a culinary descendent of the clapboard huts that dispense fresh seafood on the beaches of Mexico—despite certain aesthetic deviations. (The menu is grease-penciled onto a surfboard suspended from the ceiling; the walls are painted in screaming pastels with palms fashioned out of corrugated tin; and the young chefs who prepare Vincent Burke's recipes look like career slackers.) The food shouts "Baja!" Beef, shrimp, and chicken wallow in a delicious marinade before being grilled and wrapped in warm tortillas (for tacos), rolled in burritos, or sprinkled atop tostadas. Ironically, the only real disappointment comes from the restaurant's namesake—fish, but for these low prices (and *such* a selection of good alternatives), we'll forgive. ■ *P St exit off I-80, corner of 28th St; (916) 452-7237; 2801 P St, Sacramento; $; beer only; no credit cards; no checks; lunch, dinner every day.*

Tango Bistro and Bar *[unrated]* Tango is a hip, fashionably decorated eatery that has traditionally served elegant (and sometimes ambitious) food at reasonable prices. At press time, a change of ownership left us hanging, however, and we've yet to dine here since the switch. The menu reportedly offers the same addictive appetizers (calamari fried in a cayenne-tinged tempura batter with a red pepper dipping sauce, and a masa pancake stuffed with smoked chicken and cheese and served

over red salsa cruda) and savory entrées (oven-roasted chicken
—an enormous split breast with garlic, parsley, rosemary, and
basil stuffed under the skin—Gorgonzola ravioli, and steamed
shellfish) as before. At lunch, Tango has served lean, delectable burgers on garlic bread with Gorgonzola; a splendiferous
grilled chicken breast glazed with chipotle-honey sauce; and
fresh seafood tacos with orange jicama salad. Hopefully, the
service will not be quite as starchly formal as in the past. ■ *In
midtown, between Capitol and N Sts; (916) 444-9236; 1315
21st St, Sacramento; $$; full bar; AE, MC, V; checks OK;
lunch, dinner Mon–Sat; brunch Sat–Sun.*

LODGINGS

Hyatt Regency Sacramento ★★★ This is the only hotel in
Sacramento that really and truly feels big-city. From the vaulted
marble entryway to the 15th-floor nightclub, and from the
sumptuous, light-filled atrium lounge to the 500 beautifully ap-
pointed rooms, this amenity-rich lodging is a model of urban-
ity and efficiency. To wit: check-in clerks, porters, valets, taxis,
room service, and trade-show support personnel display a de-
gree of dispatch that is rarely seen in sleepy towns such as this.
Another reason for the Hyatt's popularity—and perhaps the
best one of all—is that most rooms command an arresting view
of palm-lined Capitol Park. The higher-priced suites on a "spe-
cial access" floor include shoe-shine machines and compli-
mentary breakfasts and predinner snacks served in a
members-only lounge. If cost is no object and you need to im-
press, there's the $795-a-night Grand Terrace, with a balcony
overlooking the park, a Jacuzzi, baby grand piano, and sump-
tuous living room. With or without these extravagances, the
Hyatt at its most basic level probably offers more diversions
than even the most hedonistic guests will ever use. ■ *Corner
of 12th and L streets; (916) 443-1234, toll free (800) 233-
1234; 1209 L St, Sacramento, CA 95814; $$$; full bar; AE,
DC, MC, V; checks OK.*

Aunt Abigail's Bed & Breakfast ★★ This 1912 Colonial Revival mansion operated by Ken and Susanne Ventura is a prime
example of home-building and hospitality from an era when
both were art forms. Look at the white-pillared entryway, the
high-ceiling living room (with chintz sofas and ornate glass-
work), the banquet-style dining room, its backyard garden
(with hot tub), and the handsome, antique-appointed bedrooms.
There's the dark, masculine Uncle Albert Room (shower only;
all the other rooms also have tubs); the light, airy Aunt Rose
Room overlooking the mansions of verdant G Street; the
Solarium, with French windows, private deck, and garden view;
and the aptly titled Loft, a third-story space that sits—literally—
in the trees. Breakfasts typically feature frittatas, streusel, rasp-
berry-stuffed French toast, or cheese strata. Aunt Abigail's

Sacramento

Restaurants

is smack in the center of midtown's Boulevard Park district, a neighborhood that features some of Sacramento's most opulent Victorian homes and fine restaurants. ■ *Between 21st and 22nd streets; (916) 441-5007, toll free (800) 858-1568; 2120 G St, Sacramento, CA 95816; $$$; DC, DIS, MC, V; checks OK.*

Sterling Hotel ★★ From the outside, this sprawling turn-of-the-century Victorian resembles any number of downtown mansions. Inside, it's a sleek, mannered luxury hotel aimed at the upper echelon of corporate travelers. And in that spirit, Sterling's interior is awash in Asian-influenced, neo-deco flourishes—calming pink hallways, artwork with a decidedly Zen twist—that are all the rage among decorators. The 12 guest rooms are big, spotless, and airy, and each one has a marble bathroom equipped with a Jacuzzi. You'll find replicas of antique furniture and big, CEO-style desks, along with lots of brass fixtures—presumably to remind guests of their status. Please note: Sterling House is not a B&B, meaning that for breakfast you must either order room service or walk downstairs to Chanterelle, an unaffiliated basement restaurant whose undeservingly high reputation rests largely and precariously on a brand of continental cuisine that is fast becoming extinct. On the plus side, Sterling House is located within walking distance of the Capitol. Also, its adjoining conference room is a refreshing, low-key alternative for executives who want respite from sterile motel meeting rooms. ■ *Corner 13th and H streets; (916) 448-1300, toll free (800) 365-7660; 1300 H St, Sacramento, CA 95814; $$$; AE, DC, MC, V; checks OK.*

▼

Davis

▲

Best Western Ponderosa Motor Inn ★ This modest motel is just what you think it is—namely, a good night's rest in clean, comfortable surroundings with few inflationary frills. This particular 98-room outlet, however, is a cut above the usual roadside attraction. It sports an attractive Southwestern theme played out in pink stucco exterior walls, tastefully furnished rooms, a flower-lined courtyard with pool, free continental breakfasts, nonsmoking rooms, off-street parking, free local calls, and two small conference rooms. Most importantly, it's situated within walking distance of all the things that Sacramento visitors deem important. ■ *Corner of H and 11th streets; (916) 441-1314, toll free (800) 528-1234; 1100 H St, Sacramento, CA 95814; $$; AE, DC, MC, V; no personal checks.*

DAVIS

Davis is known mostly for its **University of California** campus. This flat little former farming town, however, is also a pioneer in finding new, more ecological sustainable ways of living on the planet, such as **Village Homes,** its world-famous energy-efficient community. Davis also launched the nation's first functioning co-housing community, **Muir Commons**—a communal approach to building affordable housing. And to encourage people to get out of their cars, Davis has hundreds of miles of bike trails. The great minds of Davis get their world-shaking ideas sipping espresso at **Cafe Tutti** (241 F Street, (916) 758-0704) and **Cafe Roma** (231 E Street, (916) 756-1615); they spend their spare hours pawing through the works of other great minds at **Bogey's Books** (223 E Street, (916) 757-6127) and **Avid Reader** (617 2nd Street, (916) 758-4040). **The Palms** features nationally known blues, country, jazz, and folk acts that will save you a trip to Austin; (916) 756-9901.

RESTAURANTS

Soga's Restaurant ★★★ If you didn't know about this exquisite slip of a restaurant, you might pass it right by (look for the British telephone booth out front). Word of mouth alone has transformed this classy, 16-table eatery into a reservations-only affair. Firelight dances on the wine glasses in the wood-paneled dining room while the aroma of fresh coffee and baking Parmesan wafts from the kitchen. Matt Soga prepares a superb, double-thick pork chop, marinated for 48 hours and then roasted to perfection. The pan-roasted duck breast, served with braised cabbage and port wine sauce, is also tasty. Innovative appetizers include smoked salmon and cornmeal pancakes smeared with cream cheese, onions, and chives, or plump crab and shrimp dumplings, steamed and served with red pepper sauce. Desserts are simple but heart-warming: warm apple crisp, strawberry shortcake, and lemon-mint sorbet on a cookie shell with raspberry purée. ■ *On D St, between*

2nd and 3rd; (916) 757-1733; 222 D St, Davis; $$; beer and wine; AE, MC, V; local checks only; lunch, dinner Tues–Sat.

Dos Coyotes Border Cafe ★★ This far-flung outpost of Southwestern cuisine is the hottest new place in town. (Owners Bobby and Tamre Davidson are already thinking of opening a second location to keep the weekend overflow at bay.) The crowds come for terrifically fresh, consistently interesting food—fresh homemade salsas (help yourself at the salsa bar), shrimp tacos, and ranchero burritos stuffed with marinated steak, chicken, or black beans and rice. We also like the more unconventional offerings such as the Brie and papaya chile quesadilla and the mahi-mahi taco. The Santa Fe cookies are available to finish off any twinges of hunger; we doubt you'll have any. ■ *In the Marketplace shopping center; (916) 753-0922; 1411 W Covell Blvd, #107, Davis; $; beer and wine; AE; local checks only; lunch, dinner every day.*

The Symposium ★★ Ancient Greeks cavort across the mural-covered walls of this lively Greek restaurant and nightspot; one taste of The Symposium's deliciously different Greek pizza may make you want to do a bit of cavorting yourself. Niko's Special pizza, built on a thick yet slightly crunchy crust and packed with salami, ham, pepperoni, feta cheese, olives, mozzarella, and mushrooms, is a local legend. If you're not a pizza fan, the tender souvlaki is ample consolation. Nick and Contilo Pandeleon, true to their roots, create both Greek-American and pure Greek dishes, authentic from the first dolma to the last baklava. This place is usually mobbed, but grab a table in the cozy, wood-paneled alcove if you can. ■ *At E 8th and E St near Albertson's; (916) 756-3850; 1620 E 8th St, Davis; $$; full bar; AE, MC, V; no checks; dinner Mon–Sat.*

Davis

Restaurants

Crêpe Bistro ★★ Tucked into a row of small shops, this tiny, brightly lit cafe is a favorite hangout of the university crowd—and we do mean crowd. There's usually a long line going out the door. True to the name, the specialty here is crêpes—all bursting with with succulent meats, oozing with cheeses, or teeming with tender vegetables. Try the crêpe boeuf bourguignon, filled with tender chunks of beef marinated in wine and herbs; or the crêpe avocado, stuffed with cheese, tomato, mushrooms, avocado, and topped with sour cream. The Bach family puts a high priority on fresh ingredients; they get most of their herbs from their own backyard. For dessert, Papa Bach's lemon cake is a tart treat. ■ *On E St, between 2nd and 3rd; (916) 753-2575; 234 E St, Davis; $; beer and wine; no credit cards; local checks only; breakfast, lunch Mon–Fri, dinner every day.*

Blue Mango ★ Everything seems to be done for a higher purpose at this worker-owned vegetarian co-op; bumper stickers plaster the kitchen, and the menu is a paean to the virtues of vegetarianism. Once you get beyond the rhetoric and get your hands on a Mango Classic (tempeh) burger, it's all much easier to swallow. This food is good—and good for you. East Indian curries are a Sunday-night favorite; on other nights, the stir-fried vegetables spiced with a Sichuan sauce and served over tender udon noodles with two egg rolls is soul-satisfying fare. At breakfast, savor a pesto-laden omelet and a bowl of caffé latte—sit outside if you can. ■ *Next to Salvation Army store on G St; (916) 756-2616; 330 G St, Davis; $; beer and wine; no credit cards; checks OK; breakfast Sat–Sun, lunch Tues–Fri, dinner Tues–Sun.*

Orange Hut Restaurant ★ The Hsieh family holds weekly meetings to fine-tune the details of this wonderful little Chinese cafe, and it shows in the details: white linens, elegant wall hangings, and close attention to the quality of the food. Their homemade chicken broth (the basis of many of their dishes) is simmered with pork and baby shrimp for extra kick, and fullbodied flavors and natural ingredients take the place of MSG in all of their dishes. Mu-shu pork is a house specialty, while Hunan and Sichuan dishes heat the palates of those who crave more fire. ■ *3rd St between A St and University Ave; (916) 758-8888; 226 3rd St, Davis; $; beer and wine; MC, V; local checks only; lunch, dinner Mon–Sat.*

LODGINGS

Davis Bed & Breakfast Inn ★★ This fantasy grandma's house run by Pat Loomis has 18 bedrooms—some in the charming 1919 building and some in a newer section in back. The Balcony Room, with its giant—you guessed it—balcony, has plenty of room for private lounging. All the rooms have private baths, hardwood floors, color TVs (some with cable), and down comforters. You'll probably spend an inordinate amount of time sunk in the deep-cushioned rattan furniture on the spacious front porch. In the morning, meet around the beautiful wood dining table crafted by the Loomises' son. In the evening, you can snuggle in the vine-covered gazebo in the backyard. A favorite with university visitors, this B&B is across the street from UC Davis's football field. ■ *On A St across from UC Davis; (916) 753-9611; 422 A St, Davis, CA 95616; $; AE, DIS, MC, V; checks OK.*

Aggie Inn ★ What sets the Aggie apart from all the other nicely decorated, reasonably priced lodgings in town is a host of little extras and a prime location right next to UC Davis. Decorated in pale terra-cottas and soft blues, all of the 20 rooms include a small refrigerator, microwave, hair dryer, and cable TV. Continental breakfast with croissants is served each morning in the conference room. Best of all, the Aggie has a hot tub and wood-slatted sauna room. ■ *Corner of 1st and B streets; (916) 756-0352; 245 1st St, Davis, CA 95616; $; AE, DC, DIS, MC, V; checks OK.*

VACAVILLE

Located at the foot of the gloriously parched Vaca mountains, Vacaville used to be known as the home of the Nut Tree, a roadside fruit stand and gift shop on growth hormones, and the California Medical Correctional Facility, a prison for the criminally insane. It's now home to thousands of traffic-crazed commuters and—still—**The Nut Tree.** With its Las Vegas–sized neon sign, the Nut Tree's cavernous gift shop offers thousands of dried fruit confections, as well as housewares. Across the freeway, a vast mall of factory outlet stores (93 and still counting) has opened; (707) 447-5755. Far away from all this hype is the **Pure Grain Bakery** (610 Eubanks Court, off Vaca Valley Parkway, (707) 451-0991).

RESTAURANTS

Merchant and Main Bar and Grill ★ Almost everything here is soothing and predictable; nothing is subtle—except for the steak sandwich, a juicy, two-inch-thick slab of charbroiled steak on a toasted French roll. The rich, buttery, grilled crab salad sandwich, crunchy with red and green onion and celery delivers a surprising kick of cayenne; Oriental chicken salad is a nice mélange of chicken, red onion, and toasted sliced almonds on a bed of mixed greens with crisp rice noodles and too-sweet sesame dressing. House-made desserts are the highpoint of the meal, an agonizing choice between rich, triple-layer chocolate cake infused with the essence of raspberry and a cakey chocolate bread pudding studded with chocolate chips and topped with warm rum sauce. Service fluctuates wildly between efficiency and dead slow. ■ *Merchant/Alma offramp, 1 block east of Mason; (707) 446-0368; 349 Merchant, Vacaville; $$; full bar; AE, DC, DIS, MC, V; local checks only; lunch Mon–Sat, dinner every day, brunch Sun.*

Fairfield

Restaurants

FAIRFIELD

RESTAURANTS

Erlenbusch and Sons Erlenbusch and Sons isn't so much a restaurant as a sausage factory extraordinaire with a small lunch counter where you can get a sausage on a French roll for only $1.50. We're not just talking hot links here, but chicken curry, Sichuan beef, and Creole jambalaya sausages. Erlenbusch is a third-generation sausage maker whose grandfather learned the art of sausage making in his native country of Germany. Sausage fans can grab a sausage sampler 10-pack on their way out the door. ■ *Travis Blvd exit off I-80 to Oliver Rd; (707) 426-9097; 1363 Oliver Rd, Fairfield; $; beer and wine; no credit cards; local checks only; lunch Mon–Sat.*

WINTERS

RESTAURANTS

The Buckhorn ★ You know you're in serious meat-eating country. The high walls of The Buckhorn are ringed with a small herd of mounted deer, a moose, goat, and fish, all gazing down with glassy eyes on diners below. Dinner starts with a basket of hot sourdough bread and a mound of whipped butter, and moves on—perhaps—to a tender rack of lamb (a somewhat modest portion) fresh from farms in nearby Dixon. Another entrée is the prime rib roasted with a special blend of spices, herbs, and vegetables. If you don't like red meat, you probably shouldn't be here. ■ *Corner of Railroad and Main; (916) 795-4503; 210 Railroad Ave, Winters; $$; full bar; DIS, MC, V; checks OK; dinner every day.*

WOODLAND

RESTAURANTS

Morrison's Upstairs ★ Located in the attic of a turn-of-the-century apartment building, Morrison's Upstairs combines old-fashioned elegance with a predinner aerobic workout—three flights of stairs. (A serviceable elevator is also an option for the less athletic.) The prawns in beer batter are large and plump and deep-fried to a golden brown. Another local favorite is the fettuccine with prawns served in a Parmesan cream sauce. The steaks have an excellent reputation, but we have sometimes found ours to be a tad tough. Reservations recommended. ■ *Corner of 1st and Bush; (916) 666-6176; 428½ 1st St, Woodland; $$; full bar; AE, MC, V; checks OK; lunch Mon–Fri, dinner every day.*

WILLIAMS

RESTAURANTS

Granzella's, Inc ★ From the outside, Granzella's looks like a feed store. Inside, however, is a fine Italian deli packed with tasty Italian specialties, including a big selection of fine wines and beers, olive oils, and their own exquisite olives (there's even an olive-tasting bar). The deli's sandwiches are piled high with fresh deli meats like turkey, roast beef, and imported prosciutto, as well as fine imported cheeses. In the restaurant, pasta and pizza share the menu with all-American standards but pizzas are the best bet. Try the linguica pizza, with its rich, tangy marinara sauce and crunchy crust. The ice cream parlor offers real ice cream milk shakes and banana splits. ■ *On 6th St just off I-5; (916) 473-5496; 451 6th St, Williams; $; beer and wine; AE, DIS, MC, V; local checks only; breakfast, lunch, dinner every day.*

Louis Cairo's ★ A popular local dinner house, Louis Cairo's offers the warm atmosphere of a traditional Italian cafe, a great variety of entrées, and a good wine list. The simple dining room has red checked tablecloths and red napkins. The walls are covered with nature photographs by owner Fred Leonard. Louis Cairo's is famous for its garlic bread—dipped in fresh garlic butter and broiled. You can get a wonderful open-faced steak sandwich with a charbroiled, 9-ounce top sirloin on the same bread. ■ *Downtown; (916) 473-5927; 558 7th St, Williams; $; full bar; MC, V; local checks only; lunch, dinner every day.*

MERIDIAN

RESTAURANTS

El Rio Club ★★ Once safely ensconced amidst the happy clutter of the dining room (beyond the bar haunted with moose, deer, and antelope heads), begin with an appetizer of excellent roasted garlic bulbs with cheese croutons, or goat cheese in a spicy tomato vinaigrette. A recent visit found a mouth-wateringly tender chicken baked with prunes, olives, and capers, and loin lamb chops with rosemary, pecans, and croutons. All entrées come with well-prepared fresh veggies, pasta, and salad. ■ *Just E of the Meridian Bridge; (916) 696-0900; 1198 3rd St, Meridian; $$; full bar; no credit cards; local checks only; lunch, dinner Tues–Sun.*

YUBA CITY

RESTAURANTS

Al's Cafe American ★★★ You might not come to Yuba City for nouvelle cuisine, but you'd certainly return for it. Al's, an outpost of foodie culture, is hidden away in a colorless minimall. Al's Cafe American is really two restaurants—the main cafe, plus the Blue Parrot Coffee House Bistro, a late-night coffee and dessert stop. Go to the main cafe and prepare yourself for a wildly eclectic meal, ranging from red beans and rice to Cape Cod clam chowder and salad with African lemon dressing. We're particularly fond of the grilled pasilla chile (stuffed with feta and Jack cheese and with a side of rice and beans) and the open-faced grilled chicken sandwich on sourdough. Cajun classics share the dinner menu with California pastas and grilled meats like garlic ribeye steak. The jambalaya in a rich tomato broth is a perennial favorite, as is the shrimp rémoulade (extra-large grilled shrimp in a spicy cream sauce with vegetables and rice). Al's has an adequate selection of beers, plus an impressive wine list featuring California wines. For dessert, try the chocolate mousse cake or the cheesecake. Al's can be a bit pricey, but you can always opt for $4 recession specials. Service at Al's is generally superb, though the crush at high noon stretches the small staff's ability to cope. ■ *1 block N of Hwy 20 in Civic Center Plaza (between Starr Dr and Stabler Lane); (916) 674-3213; 1538 Poole Blvd, Suite W, Yuba City; $$; beer and wine; AE, MC, V; checks OK; lunch Mon–Fri, dinner every day.*

Ruthy's Restaurant and Bakery ★★ Now *this* is breakfast. French toast made with Ruthy's own cinnamon raisin bread, Ruthy's terrific whole wheat and buttermilk pancakes, and interesting egg dishes such as the scampi omelet with Monterey Jack cheese and prawns sautéed in garlic herb butter. If you're in a hurry, drop by the bakery for some of Ruthy's fresh-baked cinnamon rolls and bagels. For lunch, head straight for the salad bar. For dinner, you'll find interesting appetizers such as little chicken quesadillas, bruschetta, and alderwood-smoked salmon mousse with garlic toast. ■ *S of Franklin Ave in the Hillcrest Plaza mini-mall on Clark Ave; (916) 674-2611; 229 Clark Ave, Yuba City; $$; beer and wine; MC, V; checks OK; breakfast, lunch every day, dinner Thurs–Sat.*

Lucio's ★ A great escape from the concrete jungle of Yuba City's fast food strip, this former greenhouse in a working nursery has a two-tiered dining room with dark floral tablecloths, white deck chairs, hanging plants, and wind chimes. Owner Lucio Cueva's menu emphasizes Mexican and Southwestern cuisine and California pastas. Tasty south-of-the-border specials include quesadillas with hot smoked sausage, ham, and mushrooms; homemade chicken tamales; shrimp empanadas; and chicken and cheese sopaipillas. The wonderfully soft buttermilk flour tortillas are made on the premises; no lard is used in cooking. ■ *Just W of Hwy 99, S of the junction with Hwy 20; (916) 671-2050; 890 Onstott Rd, Yuba City; $; full bar; AE, MC, V; local checks only; lunch, dinner Tues–Sat, brunch Sun.*

LODGINGS

Harkey House ★★ The spacious, paisley-themed Harkey Suite has a pellet-burning stove and small sitting room–library. Equally lovely, with a more feminine sensibility, is the soft gray and green Empress Room with an electric fireplace. In the morning, a continental breakfast of muffins, juice, and coffee is served in the solarium-style breakfast room. The swimming pool and spa are available any time, and so is a basketball court, chess table, and antique Chickering piano. ■ *In old downtown, across from the courthouse; (916) 674-1942; 212 C St, Yuba City, CA 95991; $$; DIS, MC, V; checks OK.*

Moore Mansion Inn ★★ This lovely old mansion, built for Omega gold mine owner Charles Moore in the early 1920s, has a spacious, elegant living room with overstuffed sofas and leaded-glass bookshelves on either side of the fireplace. French doors at both ends of the room open onto the library and the lace-curtained dining room with its crystal chandelier. The five elegant guest rooms, all with private baths, radiate off a central hall downstairs. Best is the Feather River—a large, light-filled room with a step-up white pine bed with Battenburg lace linens and fresh white walls with hand-painted ivy accents. Innkeepers Jay and Peggy Harden offer a substantial, healthy breakfast featuring blueberry-streusel muffins, fluffy omelets, and strawberry waffles. ■ *3 stoplights E of Hwy 99 on the corner of Bridge and Cooper; (916) 674-8559; 560 Cooper Ave, Yuba City, CA 95991; $$; MC, V; checks OK.*

MARYSVILLE

RESTAURANTS

Silver Dollar Saloon ★★ Hey pardner, the Silver Dollar is a lively relic of Marysville's frontier past with a massive wooden cowboy in the entryway. You can watch 'em cook your order on the open-pit grill or you can cook it yourself. (The latter is reserved for those unclear on the concept of dining out.) The Silver Dollar's menu is strictly meats: terrific grilled steaks and steak sandwiches, grilled chicken, hot ham or pastrami sandwiches, and delectable half-racks of barbecued ribs. Place your order, pour yourself a cup of java, and grab a table. Upstairs, a former brothel, with a still-functioning warning buzzer once used to warn the girls that the law was on its way, is now used for private parties. It's a veritable museum packed with Western memorabilia. Friday or Saturday nights, the place is packed with cowpokes of both genders in search of live music. ■ *On 1st St between C and D streets in Old Town Marysville; (916) 743-0507; 330 1st St, Marysville; $; full bar; AE, MC, V; checks OK; lunch, dinner every day.*

Marysville

Restaurants

Dragon Inn Restaurant ★ Given the large Chinese presence in Marysville, it's only natural that the town boasts a very good Chinese restaurant. The Dragon Inn specializes in Cantonese and Sichuan cuisines and offers an ample array of specials, like moo goo gai pan (chicken in savory sauce with crisp and colorful vegetables). Lunch specials come with soup, pork-fried rice, and a large eggroll with lemon sauce. Soups range from hot and sour or won ton to winter melon or seaweed. Chef's specialties include kung pao chicken (with vegetables in spicy Mandarin sauce with peanuts), lobster gai kew (lobster and chicken in a light wine sauce), and pressed almond duck. ■ *On G St between 10th (Hwy 20) and 11th streets;*

(916) 742-6923; 1016 G St, Marysville; $; full bar; MC, V; local checks only; lunch Mon–Fri, dinner every day.

LIVE OAK

RESTAURANTS

Pasquini's ★ This roadhouse restaurant has become a regional institution—a favorite detour of locals from Yuba City to Gridley as well as in-the-know interstate travelers. Warm, welcoming, and sometimes raucous, Pasquini's is a working man's fine dinner house. The burgundy-colored dining room is dimly lit and intimate, with wooden tables and chairs and two well-padded booths (grab these if you can). On weekends, there's a separate dining room upstairs for smokers. The dinner menu at Pasquini's is as thick as a magazine. (The wine list, with a respectable collection of California vintages plus Italian Chianti, is a brochure by comparison.) Choose a steak smothered in mushrooms or crusted with cracked pepper, prime rib (weekends only), or seafood. The food here is dependable, if not spectacular. ■ *On Hwy 99, about 5 miles S of the Live Oak stoplight; (916) 695-3384; 6241 Live Oak Blvd, Live Oak; $$; full bar; MC, V; checks OK; dinner Wed–Mon.*

GRIDLEY

LODGINGS

McCracken's Inn ★★ Despite its status as kiwi fruit capital of the world, Gridley is not generally considered a tourist mecca —except by bird-watchers. Every winter, waterfowl fans and photographers flock to Gridley's Gray Lodge Wildlife Area to get a glimpse of the million or more migrating birds (including the largest population of snow geese anywhere along the Pacific Flyway). Many wise birders light at McCracken's Inn, a rambling 1912 California bungalow, whose owner, Diane Mc-Cracken, has worked at the refuge for 20 years. The inn has five guest rooms. One, the A.A. Tolley Room, has a canopied king-size bed, matching daybed, and a private bathroom with an antique barbershop sidebar and sink. There's a small sitting room upstairs and entertainment center with TV and VCR. Diane serves a generous breakfast. Later in the day, enjoy tea or coffee on the old-fashioned front porch. ■ *From Hwy 99, take the Gray Lodge turnoff, continue 1 mile; (916) 846-2108; 1835 Sycamore Lane, Gridley, CA 95948; $; AE, DIS, MC, V; checks OK.*

Books in the Best Places series read as personal guidebooks, but our evaluations are based on numerous reports from locals and traveling inspectors. Our inspectors never identify themselves (except over the phone) and never take free meals or other favors.

RESTAURANTS

Femino's Blue Gum Restaurant ★ When I-5 was built years ago, diverting traffic away from old Highway 99, most folks figured it would spell the end of Femino's Blue Gum, an estimable local eatery named for the impressive groves of eucalyptus surrounding the restaurant. The Blue Gum survived. Sure, the paint outside is starting to peel and the family-style interior hasn't changed in decades, but the food is good, and the service is still friendly in that unpretentious country western way. Italian chef and owner Nunzio Femino uses local veal and pork in all his dishes, and no processed meats. For dinner, chomp down on the mesquite-broiled steaks, barbecue ribs, or the pollo de funghi (chicken with mushrooms, baked in white wine). On weekends, you'll find live country western and rock music. ■ *On Blue Gum Rd (old Hwy 99W) about 5 miles N of Willows proper; (916) 934-3435; $$; full bar; AE, MC, V; local checks only; lunch Tues–Fri, dinner Tues– Sun, brunch Sun.*

ORLAND

LODGINGS

The Inn at Shallow Creek Farm ★★ What a surprise to find such an elegant and absolutely peaceful refuge so close to I-5. Mary and Kurt Glaeseman are the proprietors of this gray and white, ivy-covered farmhouse surrounded by citrus trees at the end of long tree-lined drive. Our favorite room is the upstairs Heritage Room with its striking morning glory wallpaper and wonderful antiques. The Brookdale Room across the way has twin beds and a huge picture window overlooking the wild verdant tangle along the creek. For absolute privacy, though, plan to stay in the Cottage—four rooms complete with fully equipped kitchen, sun porch, and wood-burning stove. Mary serves a breakfast of home-baked breads, juice, and coffee. On a winter's afternoon, you can sink into one of the well-worn, brown leather sofas in front of the fire and sample some Mandarin oranges—a local delicacy. ■ *2½ miles W of I-5 from the Chico-Orland exit, turn right on Rd DD and go ½ mile, (916) 865-4093; County Rd DD, Rt 3, Box 3176, Orland, CA 95963; $; no credit cards; checks OK.*

▼

Chico

▲

CHICO

This pretty little college town gained a national reputation when *Playboy* magazine named **Chico State** the number one party school in the nation. Suitably horrified, local gentry put an end to that by doing away with Chico's biggest celebration, Pioneer Days—a weeklong beer bust rivaling spring break in Palm Beach. There are still plenty of places to play. **Bid-well Park**'s 2,400 acres provide a fine place for a picnic, a glorious stroll among the trees, or even a swim on a hot day. In summer, the city dams two sections of the lower **Chico Creek** to create swimming holes. Those in search of more vigorous exercise might try the **Chico Wildflower Century,** a 100-mile cycling marathon in April. To really find out what's going on around town, settle in at **Caffe Sienna** (128 Broadway, (916) 345-7745) for pastries and espresso and thumb through the *Chico News and Review,* Chico's fine little alternative press newspaper.

RESTAURANTS

Zephyrs 3rd Street Grill ★★★ Zephyrs is easy to miss, even in a tiny town like Chico. And that's a shame. This fine little contemporary cafe serves California cuisine at its small-town best—fresh, wholesome, and interesting without being pretentious. The seasonally changing dinner menu might include mesquite-grilled ahi salad or homemade spinach fettuccine. For lunch try the Thai-style chicken stir-fry and very rich lasagne Bolognese with several cheeses, tomato, and béchamel sauce. The soups are dependable winners: try the gazpacho or the chicken Florentine (a creamy chicken soup with mushrooms and spinach). The vegetables and greens, harvested from the local farmers market, are always very fresh. Zephyrs'

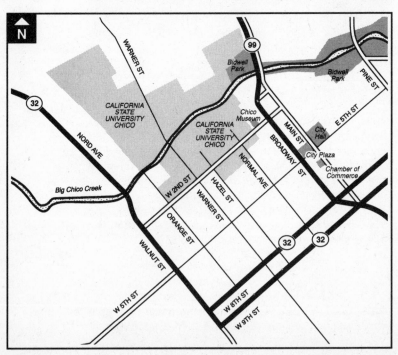

vast array of seductive sweets includes rich chocolate ganache torte, lemon custard cheesecake, and homemade shortbread layered with Chantilly cream and fresh berries. Zephyrs' impressive wine list includes some of California's finest vintages. ■ *Corner of 3rd and Wall streets; (916) 895-1328; 192 E 3rd St, Chico; $$; beer and wine; MC, V; checks OK; lunch Mon–Fri, dinner Wed–Sat.*

Cory's Sweet Treats & Gallery ★★

Calling Cory's a sandwich shop is like calling King Kong a primate. This cheerful little cafe with its walls dotted with local art serves high songs of praise to the 7th Earl of Sandwich—lumberjack-size portions of home cooked roast beef, baked ham, and pastrami, along with vegetarian alternatives. All the sandwich meats are cooked on the premises and shoveled between thick slices of homemade bread. For dessert, try the lemon bars, the Black Forest cake, or the unusual oatmeal cake—an oatmeal spice cake with caramel frosting. ■ *Downtown between Broadway and Salem; (916) 345-2955; 230 W 3rd St, Chico; $; no alcohol; no credit cards; checks OK; breakfast, lunch Tues–Sat.*

Kramore Inn ★★

It doesn't take long to figure out that crêpes are the Kramore's speciality. You'll find 20 different kinds—everything from shrimp and broccoli to the "cluck, oink & moo" (eggs, ham, and cheese). There are plenty of vegetarian crêpes as well, and—to keep our consciences as well as our bodies clean—the Kramore serves organic and pesticide-free vegetables whenever possible. Dinners come with a tasty little opener plate of banana bread and marinated bean salad. For dessert, head directly for the deliciously decadent chocolate mousse crêpe. ■ *Corner of W 19th St and Park Ave; (916) 343-3701; 1903 Park Ave, Chico; $; beer and wine; MC, V; local checks only; lunch Tues–Fri, dinner Tues–Sun, brunch Sat–Sun.*

Chico

Restaurants

Sierra Nevada Taproom & Restaurant ★★

Well-known for its award-winning ales and lagers, Sierra Nevada Brewery has recently opened a brew pub that's fast developing a following among brewery fans who come to worship (and sip) at the source. The interior is all polished copper and mahogany, but the outside patio is most pleasant. Their fish 'n' chips (in beer batter, natch) and sandwiches are very good. The curry chicken sandwich, a frequent special, is a local favorite. Be sure to order a plateful of the beer-batter fried onion rings or Cajun vegetables. Free brewery tours are scheduled Tuesday through Friday at 2:30pm, and every half-hour on Saturday, noon to 3pm. ■ *Just W of Hwy 99 via 20th St exit; (916) 345-2739; 1075 E 20th St, Chico; $; beer and wine; MC, V; local checks only; lunch, dinner Tues–Sat, brunch Sun.*

The Albatross ★

This Hawaiian-theme dinner house in a one-time private home has several small, casual dining rooms and a wonderfully landscaped garden patio. Despite the flowered shirts of the waiters and the tropical and marine artwork on the wall, you won't find any pounded taro root on the menu here— or even papaya salsa. What you will find is well-prepared mahimahi, fresh salmon in champagne butter, broiled blacktip shark with tarragon, plus steak and prime rib. All entrées come with steaming hot sourdough and squaw bread, plus salad. For dessert, try the Island Pie—a macadamia nut ice cream pie with cookie crumb crust, fudge, whipped cream, and almonds. ■ *North of Chico proper on The Esplanade; (916) 345-6037; 3312 The Esplanade, Chico; $$; full bar; AE, MC, V; local checks only; dinner every day.*

Gashouse Pizza ★ College towns sprout pizza parlors like forests sprout mushrooms, and Chico is no exception. The best of the local bumper crop is the Gashouse. The name—worry not—refers to the gas station decor (rusty metal motor oil signs and antique tire ads) rather than the digestive consequences of eating here. The choice of sauces is extensive (pesto is our favorite), and you have your choice of heavenly homemade whole wheat or white crusts. There are now three branches of the Gashouse; if you want it to go call the Longfellow Avenue branch at (916) 345-1315. ■ *Corner of W 15th St at Park Ave, (916) 345-6602; 1444 Park Ave; Chico; $; beer and wine; no credit cards; local checks only; lunch Mon–Fri; dinner every day.* ■ *Between Cohasset and East avenues; (916) 345-3621; 2359 The Esplanade; lunch Mon–Fri, dinner every day.*

Redwood Forest Restaurant ★ Although redwoods might not be native to this part of the state, Redwood Forest Restaurant certainly is. It's the quintessential Chico cafe, offering vegetarian lasagne and excellent enchiladas plus specials such as chicken potpies and cashew chicken salad croissants. The carrot cake here is a perennial favorite, especially good in winter with a cup of herb tea or good dark coffee from Malvina's, a local coffee store. ■ *Downtown between Broadway and Main; (916) 343-4315; 121 W 3rd St, Chico; $; beer and wine; MC, V; local checks only; lunch Mon–Sat, dinner Thurs–Fri.*

Sicilian Cafe ★ Settle in beneath the vineyard mural, order some fine Italian wine, and prepare yourself for a simple but well-prepared Italian meal featuring homemade pasta and luminous calamari. The calamari is prepared in several different ways: fried, sautéed with herbs, or stuffed with baby clams and baked. The pasta comes with a choice of three sauces—plain tomato or with sausage or meatballs. For dessert, try the homemade cannoli or ricotta cheesecake. ■ *Between W 9th St and W 11th St, (916) 345-2233; 1020 Main St, Chico; $$; beer and wine; no credit cards; checks OK; dinner Tues–Sat.*

The Palms of Chico Organic Farm and Lodge ★★ Located in the middle of an arboretum on an organic wheat farm, this stately turn-of-the-century country home was built by Henry Butters, founder of the Sacramento Northern Electric Railroad. A good choice for people who like the scale and serenity of bed and breakfasts but who dislike being fussed over, The Palms offers clean and artful accommodations with hands-off hospitality. Co-owner Winder Baker's minimalist approach to home furnishings lets the house's fine interior woodwork and impressive natural light shine. You get your own coffee from the kitchen in the morning. ■ *On Dayton Rd just SW of Chico; (916) 343-6868; 1525 Dayton Rd, Chico, CA 95928; $$; no credit cards; checks OK.*

The O'Flaherty House ★ Barbi Easter really did have a great-great-aunt by the name of O'Flaherty. The rest of her story about this Victorian's shady past and her dirty aunt Mary is apocryphal. Guests have a choice of a separate cottage or four guest rooms, named after Dirty Mary and three of her imaginary girls. All brightly colored, with brass beds and a mix of antiques and contemporary furnishings, the upstairs rooms share two baths. Out back, past the garden, is the Carriage House, a perfect retreat for honeymooners or traveling families. In honor of Dirty Mary, you can also have breakfast in bed. ■ *Corner of Arcadian and W 5th Ave; (916) 893-5494; 1462 Arcadian Ave, Chico, CA 95926; $; AE, MC, V; checks OK.*

RED BLUFF

LODGINGS

Buttons and Bows Bed and Breakfast ★★ This impressive 1880s Victorian on a tree-lined street is just blocks from downtown and minutes from I-5. It has three fresh and airy guest rooms tastefully decorated with antiques and interesting memorabilia. All three share one bath, but the Peach and Blue rooms have sinks. The Rose Room has a private balcony, perfect for sitting and sipping sherry (available anytime) on a summer's evening. You can browse through an interesting old stamp collection or play the old pump organ in the prim parlor. In winter, the Fisher wood stove in the spacious dining room keeps the downstairs nice and toasty. The hot tub on the back deck is available year round (but you appreciate the air conditioning more in summer). ■ *W on Antelope Blvd, left 1 block past Main St; (916) 527-6405; 427 Washington St, Red Bluff, CA 96080; $; no credit cards; checks OK.*

The Faulkner House ★★ No use looking for the *Absalom, Absalom* room and the *As I Lay Dying* suite in this happily themeless 1890 Queen Anne Victorian. It was named after a local doctor who practiced here in the '30s—not the writer. The Faulkner House features a traditional red velvet parlor, a casual living room, and a spacious, soothing blue dining room. Of the four upstairs rooms, the two smallest are often preferred: the octagonal Tower Room, a light-filled corner room in tan florals, and the Wicker Room with its dark green wallpaper with mauve roses, antique lace-edged bedspread, and tree-shaded window views. Owners Mary and Harvey Klinger greet you with a chilled glass of mineral water when you arrive—a lifesaver during Red Bluff's sweltering summers. When things cool down in the evening, you'll find a decanter of sherry in the upstairs hall. ■ *W on Union, left on Jefferson; (916) 529-0520; 1029 Jefferson St, Red Bluff, CA 96080; $$; AE, MC, V; checks OK.*

Index

Northern California Best Places
REPORT FORM

Based on my personal experience, I wish to nominate/confirm/disapprove for listing the following restaurant or place of lodging:

_____

_____

_____

_____

_____

(Please include address and telephone number of establishment, if convenient.)

REPORT:

(Please describe food, service, style, comfort, value, date of visit, and other aspects of your visit; continue on overleaf if necessary.)

_____

_____

_____

_____

_____

_____

_____

I am not concerned, directly or indirectly, with the management or ownership of this establishment.

Signed _____

Address _____

_____

_____

Phone Number _____

Date _____

Send to: *Northern California Best Places*
1931 Second Avenue
Seattle, WA 98101

Northern California Best Places
REPORT FORM

Based on my personal experience, I wish to nominate/confirm/disapprove for listing the following restaurant or place of lodging:

_____

_____

_____

_____

_____

(Please include address and telephone number of establishment, if convenient.)

REPORT:

(Please describe food, service, style, comfort, value, date of visit, and other aspects of your visit; continue on overleaf if necessary.)

_____

_____

_____

_____

_____

_____

_____

I am not concerned, directly or indirectly, with the management or ownership of this establishment.

Signed _____

Address _____

_____

Phone Number _____

Date _____

Send to: *Northern California Best Places*
1931 Second Avenue
Seattle, WA 98101

Northern California Best Places
REPORT FORM

Based on my personal experience, I wish to nominate/confirm/disapprove for listing the following restaurant or place of lodging:

_____

_____

_____

_____

_____

(Please include address and telephone number of establishment, if convenient.)

REPORT:
(Please describe food, service, style, comfort, value, date of visit, and other aspects of your visit; continue on overleaf if necessary.)

_____

_____

_____

_____

_____

_____

_____

I am not concerned, directly or indirectly, with the management or ownership of this establishment.

Signed _____

Address _____

_____

Phone Number _____

Date _____

Send to: *Northern California Best Places*
1931 Second Avenue
Seattle, WA 98101

Did you enjoy this book?

Sasquatch Books publishes books and regional guides. Our books are available at bookstores and other retail outlets throughout the region. Here is a partial list of our current cookbooks, gardening titles, and guidebooks:

GUIDEBOOKS

Back Roads of Washington
74 Trips on Washington's Scenic Byways
Earl Thollander

Northwest Cheap Sleeps
Mountain Motels, Island Cabins, Ski Bunks, Beach Cottages, and Hundreds of Penny-pinching Travel Ideas for the Adventurous Road-tripper
Stephanie Irving

Northwest Best Places
Restaurants, Lodgings, and Touring in Oregon, Washington, and British Columbia
David Brewster and Stephanie Irving

Portland Best Places
A Discriminating Guide to Portland's Restaurants, Lodgings, Shopping, Nightlife, Arts, Sights, Outings, and Annual Events
Kim Carlson and Stephanie Irving

Seattle Best Places
The Most Discriminating Guide to Seattle's Restaurants, Shops, Hotels, Nightlife, Sights, Outings, and Annual Events
David Brewster and Stephanie Irving

Seattle Cheap Eats
300 Terrific Bargain Eateries
Kathryn Robinson and Stephanie Irving

Seattle Survival Guide
The Essential Handbook for City Living (Absolutely everything You Need to Know to Make Your Way Through the Urban Maze)
Theresa Morrow

West Coast Work Boats
An Illustrated Guide to Work Vessels from Bristol Bay to San Diego
Archie Satterfield, illustrations by Walt Crowley

FIELD GUIDES

Adopt-A-Stream Foundation
Field Guide to the Pacific Salmon

Great Bear Foundation
Field Guide to the Grizzly Bear

The Audubon Society
Field Guide to the Bald Eagle

International Society of Cryptozoology
Field Guide to the Sasquatch

American Cetacean Society
Field Guide to the Orca

The Oceanic Society
Field Guide to the Gray Whale

FOOD AND COOKING

Breakfast in Bed
The Best B&B Recipes from Northern California, Oregon, Washington, and British Columbia
Carol Frieberg

Eight Items or Less Cookbook
Fine Food in a Hurry
Ann Lovejoy

The Good Food Guide to Washington and Oregon
Discover the Finest, Freshest Foods Grown and Harvested in the Northwest
Edited by Lane Morgan

Pike Place Market Cookbook
Recipes, Anecdotes, and Personalities from Seattle's Renowned Public Market
Braiden Rex-Johnson

Vintage Pellegrini
The Collected Wisdom of an American Buongustaio
Angelo Pellegrini, edited by Schuyler Ingle

Sasquatch books are available at most bookstores. To receive a Sasquatch Books catalog, or to inquire about ordering our books by phone or mail, please contact us at the address below.

SASQUATCH BOOKS
1931 Second Avenue • Seattle, WA 98101 • (206) 441-5555